Introduction to
Homeland Security
Fourth Edition

Introduction to Homeland Security

Principles of All-Hazards Risk Management

Fourth Edition

Jane A. Bullock

George D. Haddow

Damon P. Coppola

AMSTERDAM • BOSTON • HEIDELBERG • LONDON
NEW YORK • OXFORD • PARIS • SAN DIEGO
SAN FRANCISCO • SINGAPORE • SYDNEY • TOKYO
Butterworth-Heinemann is an imprint of Elsevier

Acquiring Editor: Pam Chester
Development Editor: Greg Chalson
Project Manager: Paul Gottehrer
Designer: Eric DeCicco

Butterworth-Heinemann is an imprint of Elsevier
225 Wyman Street, Waltham, MA 02451, USA

Notices
Knowledge and best practice in this field are constantly changing. As new research and experience broaden our understanding, changes in research methods or professional practices, may become necessary. Practitioners and researchers must always rely on their own experience and knowledge in evaluating and using any information or methods described herein. In using such information or methods they should be mindful of their own safety and the safety of others, including parties for whom they have a professional responsibility.

To the fullest extent of the law, neither the Publisher nor the authors, contributors, or editors, assume any liability for any injury and/or damage to persons or property as a matter of product liability, negligence or otherwise, or from any use or operation of any methods, products, instructions, or ideas contained in the material herein.

Library of Congress Cataloging-in-Publication Data
Application submitted

British Library Cataloguing-in-Publication Data
A catalogue record for this book is available from the British Library.

ISBN: 978-0-12-415802-3

For information on all BH publications
visit our website at www.elsevierdirect.com/security

Printed in the United States of America

13 14 15 16 17   10 9 8 7 6 5 4 3

Working together to grow
libraries in developing countries
www.elsevier.com | www.bookaid.org | www.sabre.org

ELSEVIER   BOOK AID International   Sabre Foundation

Dedication

This book is dedicated to Dr. Wayne Blanchard. Dr. Wayne provided the vision, leadership, and support to higher education institutions across the United States to establish programs in emergency management and homeland security. Because of his efforts, emergency management moved from being an ad hoc discipline to an education-driven profession. In doing so, he fostered a diverse, highly trained cadre of emergency managers to better serve the people in USA. On a personal note, Wayne had a great sense of humor, was an innovator in dealing with the bureaucracy, and was a constant source of friendship and support to all of us who worked with him over the years.

Contents

Acknowledgments

The authors of this book would like to express their appreciation for the continued support and encouragement we have received from Dr. Jack Harrald, Dr. Joseph Barbera, and Dr. Greg Shaw. In addition to contributing a large dose of practical advice and humor, these three individuals provide outstanding leadership to institutions and governments in designing and implementing homeland security projects.

We would like to acknowledge the many individuals whose research, analysis, and opinions helped to shape the content of this volume.

We would also like to thank Pam Chester, Greg Chalson, and Paul Gottehrer at Elsevier for their assistance in making the fourth edition of this text possible, and for their patience and faith in us. Our gratitude also extends to Barbara Johnson, Ryan Miller, Ehren Ngo, Bridger McGaw, Don Goff, Jack Suwanlert, Sarp Yeletaysi, Erdem Ergin, Lissa Westerman, Terry Downes, Steve Carter, and David Gilmore.

Finally, we recognize the thousands of professionals and volunteers who, through their daily pursuits, are giving form and substance to creating a more secure and safe homeland.

Introduction

It has been 10 years since the events of September 11 precipitated a dramatic series of actions in response to those events. The National Commission on Terrorist Attacks upon the United States (informally known as the 9/11 Commission) was formed and issued a report calling for sweeping changes in the U.S. approach for dealing with terrorism. The Department of Homeland Security (DHS) was established, the most comprehensive reorganization of the federal government ever undertaken. Congress continued to pass new laws to address all aspects of national security, including the Patriot Act, which provides the Attorney General of the United States with significant new authority relative to civil liberties to fight the war on terrorism.

The United States and its allies became embroiled in two significant wars in Iraq and Afghanistan to try to find and dismantle Osama bin Laden's operations and other terrorist organizations.

Significant progress has been made as demonstrated by the disruption of a potential threat in New York's Times Square, the failed attempt to detonate explosives on Flight 253 on December 25, 2009, and the publication of the first-ever Quadrennial Homeland Security Review (QHSR) by the DHS in February 2010. Perhaps the most significant action has been the capture and killing of Osama bin Laden in 2011 as well as other key leaders in his organization.

With the U.S. government being increasingly focused on terrorism, natural hazards have continued to impact thousands of our communities, reminding us that the likelihood of a natural disaster far exceeds a terrorist event. The aftermath of Hurricane Katrina brought sweeping legislative changes to the Federal Emergency Management Agency (FEMA), within DHS, and served to remind officials of the exacting toll natural disasters can take on public safety and our social and economic security. The devastating wildfires, floods, weather, and drought problems that impacted the Nation in 2011 continued this trend, although the response from FEMA/DHS and other partners was much improved. Striking the right balance, between the various hazards, looking for commonalities among the hazards in mitigation, preparedness, response, and recovery, and adopting a more all-hazards approach to homeland security remain priorities for the officials responsible for public safety.

At the same time, concerns continue to be raised on the impacts of illegal and legal immigration on the economic and social stability of our communities, especially along the border areas that consume the activities of the Immigration and Customs Enforcement (ICE). The Coast Guard (CG) is vigilant in maintaining territorial waters and safety and security at our ports that are of the highest priority to ensure homeland commerce can continue.

New emerging and evolving threats require greater attention to cybersecurity, preventing cybercrime, and protecting our critical infrastructure. The complexities and speed with which the cyber environment changes require a diligence and a level of cooperation and coordination between the government and the private sector not evidenced before. As more of our daily lives are dependent on the continual operation of computers and computer systems, for example, transportation, energy, and banking systems, preventing an attack on these systems becomes a critical priority for homeland security officials.

Vicksburg, MS, May 12, 2001 – The lower floor of the historic Yazoo Mississippi Valley Railroad Station, which is located in Vicksburg, Mississippi, is submerged by the rising Mississippi River. FEMA is working with local, state, and other federal agencies to assist residents affected by the floods. (Photo by Howard Greenblatt/FEMA)

Galveston Island, TX, September 20, 2008 – The U.S. Coast Guard patrol boat USCGC Manowar continues missions in the intercoastal waterway after Hurricane Ike. (Photo by Jocelyn Augustino/FEMA)

This Fourth Edition reflects the evolving environment of homeland security and includes structural changes to allow focus on more urgent threats such as cybersecurity and new public policy initiatives while still providing the hazards context and the historic and organizational framework of homeland security operations.

The first chapter is intended to introduce the concept of homeland security and how that concept has changed in the 10 years since the events of September 11, where there is finally a recognition that there needs to be a balance between the terrorism threat and natural and other hazards fueled by the trauma of the failed response to Hurricane Katrina.

The second chapter provides a historical perspective on the terrorist events that preceded September 11 and how the government's mechanisms to respond to emergencies have evolved, including descriptions of the statutory actions that were taken in reaction to September 11 and in support of preventing future attacks.

The book continues with complete descriptions and fact sheets on the types of hazards and risks that make up the potential homeland security vulnerabilities from future terrorist events, natural hazards, or human-made hazards. This section is followed by an overview presentation of the organization of DHS so that subsequent chapters and discussions will have a structural context.

In the revised format, we have developed chapters that describe the programs and actions being undertaken by government agencies, organizations, and the private sector to reduce or minimize the threat. We have focused chapters on the areas of intelligence and counterterrorism, border security and immigration, transportation safety and security, and cybersecurity and critical infrastructure protection.

A significant section is devoted to all-hazards response and recovery as these responsibilities are now recognized as a primary focus for DHS. In this chapter, we describe the current state of the art in first responder applications and discuss the changes that are under way within the national response and recovery system network. This is followed with a chapter focused on mitigation, prevention, and preparedness.

Recognizing the critical role that communications now play in our everyday lives and the use of social media in emergencies are now highlighted in a separate chapter, as are advancements in science and technology that support the homeland security enterprise mission.

We have included more case studies to demonstrate practical application to the materials being presented. In addition, we have included full texts of critical guidance documents, directives, and legislation for use and reference. Wherever possible, budget and resource charts show past allocations and future projections through 2011.

The volume concludes with a chapter that examines potential future and still unresolved issues that are relative to the disciplines of homeland security, with more of focus on public safety and emergency management that must be addressed as we meet the challenges of establishing a secure homeland.

Homeland security is a still-evolving discipline, changing to adapt to new threats and challenges. This book was written at a particular point in time, and changes to programs, activities, and even organizations occur regularly. For that reason we have included online references wherever possible so the reader will have access to websites that can provide up-to-date information on program or organization changes, new initiatives, or simply more detail on specific issues.

The authors' goal in writing this book was to provide a source of history, practical information, programs, references, and best practices so that any academic, homeland security official, emergency manager, public safety official, community leader, or individual could understand the foundations of homeland security and be motivated to engage in actions to help make their communities safer and more secure. The homeland security function clearly is an evolving discipline that will continue to change in reaction to the steps we take to reduce the impacts of known hazards and as new threats are identified.

In the end, achieving homeland security will not be accomplished by the federal government but by each individual, each organization, each business, and each community working together to make a difference.

1

Homeland Security: The Concept, the Organization

What You Will Learn

- What was the history behind the establishment of homeland security
- How events have altered the concept of homeland security
- What is the homeland security enterprise (HSE)
- How the concept of a homeland security enterprise has changed priorities
- How other agencies and entities besides DHS contribute to the homeland security enterprise

Introduction

In the immediate aftermath of the September 11, 2001 attacks, as search-and-rescue teams were still sifting through the debris and wreckage for survivors in New York, Pennsylvania, and Virginia, the federal government was analyzing what had just happened and what it could quickly do to begin the process of ensuring such attacks could not be repeated. It was recognized that nothing too substantial could take place without longer-term study and congressional review, but the circumstances mandated that real changes begin without delay.

The idea of homeland security was primarily the result of the White House, the federal government, and the U.S. Congress's reactions to September 11 events. However, the movement to establish such broad-sweeping measures was initiated long before those attacks took place. Domestic and international terrorists have been striking Americans, American facilities, and American interests, both within and outside the nation's borders, for decades — though only fleeting interest was garnered in the aftermath of these events. Support for counterterrorism programs and legislation was, therefore, rather weak, and measures that did pass rarely warranted front-page status. Furthermore, the institutional cultures that characterized many of the agencies affected by this emerging threat served as a resilient barrier to the fulfillment of goals. Only the spectacular nature of the September 11 terrorist attacks was sufficient to boost the issue of terrorism to primary standing on all three social agendas: the public, the political, and the media.

Out of the tragic events of September 11, an enormous opportunity for improving the social and economic sustainability of our communities from all threats, but primarily terrorism, was envisioned and identified as homeland security. Public safety officials and emergency managers championed the concept of an all-hazards approach, and despite some unique characteristics, they felt terrorism could be incorporated into that approach as well (Figure 1–1).

However, in the immediate aftermath of 9/11, the single issue of preventing a future terrorist attack was foremost in the minds of federal officials and legislators. On September 20, 2001, just 9 days after the attacks, President George W. Bush announced that an Office of Homeland Security would be established within the White House by executive order. Directing this office would be Pennsylvania Governor Tom Ridge. Ridge was given no real staff to manage, and the funding he would have at his disposal was minimal. The actual order, cataloged as Executive Order 13228, was given on October 8, 2001. In addition to creating the Office of Homeland Security, this order created the Homeland Security Council, "to develop and coordinate the implementation of a comprehensive national strategy to secure the United States from terrorist threats or attacks."

Four days later, on September 24, 2001, President Bush announced that he would be seeking passage of an act entitled "Uniting and Strengthening America by Providing Appropriate Tools Required to Intercept and Obstruct Terrorism," which would become better known as the PATRIOT Act of 2001. This act, which introduced a large number of controversial legislative changes in order to significantly increase the surveillance and investigative powers of law enforcement agencies in the United States (as it states) to "... deter and punish terrorist acts in the United States and around the world," was signed into law by the president on October 26 after very little deliberation in Congress.

FIGURE 1–1 New York City, New York, October 13, 2001 — New York firefighters at the site of the World Trade Center. (Photo by Andrea Booher/FEMA News Photo)

On October 29, 2001, President Bush issued the first of many homeland security presidential directives (HSPDs), which were specifically designed to "record and communicate presidential decisions about the homeland security policies of the United States" (HSPD-1, 2001). The sidebar titled "Homeland Security Presidential Directives" lists the HSPDs and their stated purposes.

The legislation to establish a Department of Homeland Security (DHS) was first introduced in the U.S. House of Representatives by Texas Representative Richard K. Armey on June 24, 2002. Similar legislation was introduced into the Senate soon after. After differences between the two bills were quickly ironed out, the Homeland Security Act of 2002 (Public Law 107–296) was passed by both houses and signed into law by President Bush on November 25, 2002.

Select Homeland Security Presidential Directives

Homeland Security Presidential Directives are issued by the President on matters pertaining to Homeland Security.

- **HSPD-1**: Organization and Operation of the Homeland Security Council. Ensures coordination of all homeland security-related activities among executive departments and agencies and promote the effective development and implementation of all homeland security policies.
- **HSPD-2**: Combating Terrorism Through Immigration Policies. Provides for the creation of a task force which will work aggressively to prevent aliens who engage in or support terrorist activity from entering the United States and to detain, prosecute, or deport any such aliens who are within the United States.
- **HSPD-3**: Homeland Security Advisory System. Establishes a comprehensive and effective means to disseminate information regarding the risk of terrorist acts to Federal, State, and local authorities and to the American people.
- **HSPD-4**: National Strategy to Combat Weapons of Mass Destruction. Applies new technologies, increases emphasis on intelligence collection and analysis, strengthens alliance relationships, and establishes new partnerships with former adversaries to counter this threat in all of its dimensions.
- **HSPD-5**: Management of Domestic Incidents. Enhances the ability of the United States to manage domestic incidents by establishing a single, comprehensive national incident management system.
- **HSPD-6**: Integration and Use of Screening Information. Provides for the establishment of the Terrorist Threat Integration Center.
- **HSPD-7**: Critical Infrastructure Identification, Prioritization, and Protection. Establishes a national policy for federal departments and agencies to identify and prioritize United States critical infrastructure and key resources and to protect them from terrorist attacks.
- **Presidential Policy Directive/PPD-8**: National Preparedness. Aimed at strengthening the security and resilience of the United States through systematic preparation for the threats that pose the greatest risk to the security of the nation, including acts of terrorism, cyberattacks, pandemics, and catastrophic natural disasters.

- **HSPD-8 Annex 1**: National Planning. Rescinded by PPD-8: National Preparedness, except for paragraph 44. Individual plans developed under HSPD-8 and Annex 1 remain in effect until rescinded or otherwise replaced.
- **HSPD-9**: Defense of United States Agriculture and Food. Establishes a national policy to defend the agriculture and food system against terrorist attacks, major disasters, and other emergencies.
- **HSPD-10**: Biodefense for the 21st Century. Provides a comprehensive framework for our nation's biodefense.
- **HSPD-11**: Comprehensive Terrorist-Related Screening Procedures. Implements a coordinated and comprehensive approach to terrorist-related screening that supports homeland security, at home and abroad. This directive builds upon HSPD-6.
- **HSPD-12**: Policy for a Common Identification Standard for Federal Employees and Contractors. Establishes a mandatory, government-wide standard for secure and reliable forms of identification issued by the federal government to its employees and contractors (including contractor employees).
- **HSPD-13**: Maritime Security Policy. Establishes policy guidelines to enhance national and homeland security by protecting U.S. maritime interests.
- **HSPD-14**: Domestic Nuclear Detection.
- **HSPD-15**: U.S. Strategy and Policy in the War on Terror.
- **HSPD-16**: Aviation Strategy. Details a strategic vision for aviation security while recognizing ongoing efforts, and directs the production of a national strategy for aviation security and supporting plans.
- **HSPD-17**: Nuclear Materials Information Program.
- **HSPD-18**: Medical Countermeasures Against Weapons of Mass Destruction. Establishes policy guidelines to draw upon the considerable potential of the scientific community in the public and private sectors to address medical countermeasure requirements relating to CBRN threats.
- **HSPD-19**: Combating Terrorist Use of Explosives in the United States. Establishes a national policy, and calls for the development of a national strategy and implementation plan, on the prevention and detection of, protection against, and response to terrorist use of explosives in the United States.
- **HSPD-20**: National Continuity Policy. Establishes a comprehensive national policy on the continuity of federal government structures and operations and a single national continuity coordinator responsible for coordinating the development and implementation of federal continuity policies.
- **HSPD-20 Annex A**: Continuity Planning. Assigns executive departments and agencies to a category commensurate with their COOP/COG/ECG responsibilities during an emergency.
- **HSPD-21**: Public Health and Medical Preparedness. Establishes a national strategy that will enable a level of public health and medical preparedness sufficient to address a range of possible disasters.
- **HSPD-22**: Cyber Security and Monitoring.
- **HSPD-23**: National Cyber Security Initiative.
- **HSPD-24**: Biometrics for Identification and Screening to Enhance National Security. Establishes a framework to ensure that federal executive departments use mutually compatible

methods and procedures regarding biometric information of individuals, while respecting their information privacy and other legal rights.

- **HSPD-25**: Arctic Region Policy. Establishes the policy of the United States with respect to the Arctic region and directs related implementation actions.

Creating DHS would provide the United States with a huge law enforcement capability that would deter, prepare, and prevent any future September 11 type events. Agencies such as Federal Emergency Management Agency (FEMA) became part of DHS because it was responsible for the consequences to our communities of natural and technological disasters, and had played a major role in providing federal assistance to recover from the previous terrorist events on U.S. soil: the 1993 World Trade Center bombing and the Murrah Federal Building bombing.

Prior to 9/11, the majority of FEMA's efforts and funding were focused on the mitigation of, preparedness for, response to, and recovery from natural disasters. Much of this changed with the establishment of DHS. Many, if not all, of the grant programs established within the new DHS focused on terrorism. FEMA programs and funding were diverted or reduced to support terrorism. The all-hazards concept was not embraced in the early years of DHS. State and local governments, who were more concerned about their flooding or hurricane threat, had to focus on terrorism. Just like in the 1980s when FEMA insisted that to be eligible for FEMA grants, State and local governments had to engage in nuclear attack planning, DHS insisted that terrorism planning was the top priority for recipients of funding.

The decision of the 1980s to focus on nuclear attack planning led to the botched response to Hurricane Andrew, under the first Bush administration. The decision by the leadership of DHS to focus on terrorism, at the expense of other threats, and to diminish the role of FEMA, led directly to the horrible events and aftermath of Hurricane Katrina (Figure 1–2).

Hurricane Katrina, which struck on August 29, 2005, and resulted in the death of over 1,800 people (and the destruction of billions of dollars in housing stock and other infrastructure), exposed significant problems with the United States' emergency management framework. Clearly, the terrorism focus had been maintained at the expense of preparedness and response capacity for other hazards, namely the natural disasters that have proven to be much more likely to occur. FEMA, and likewise DHS, were highly criticized by the public and by Congress in the months following the 2005 hurricane season. In response, Congress passed the Post-Katrina Emergency Management Reform Act (H.R. 5441, Public Law 109–295), signed into law by the president on October 4, 2006.

This law established several new leadership positions within the Department of Homeland Security, moved additional functions into (several were simply returned) FEMA, created and reallocated functions to other components within DHS, and amended the Homeland Security Act in ways that directly and indirectly affected the organization and functions of various entities within DHS. The changes were required to have gone into effect by March 31, 2007. Transfers that were mandated by the Post-Katrina Emergency Management Reform Act included (with the exception of certain offices as listed in the Act):

- United States Fire Administration (USFA)
- Office of Grants and Training (G&T)
- Chemical Stockpile Emergency Preparedness Division (CSEP)

FIGURE 1–2 New Orleans, LA, September 8, 2005 — Neighborhoods and roadways throughout the area remain flooded as a result of Hurricane Katrina. (Photo by Jocelyn Augustino/FEMA News Photo)

- Radiological Emergency Preparedness Program (REPP)
- Office of National Capital Region Coordination (NCRC)

In passing this Act, Congress reminded DHS that the natural disaster threats to the United States were every bit as real as the terrorist threats and required changes to the organization and operations of DHS to provide a more balanced approach to the concepts of homeland security in addressing the threats impacting the United States.

The Obama Administration is building on the past efforts of the Bush Administration to understand and implement a more balanced, universal approach to homeland security. This balanced approach is reflected in the first ever Quadrennial Homeland Security Review (QHSR) published by the Obama Administration and DHS in February 2010. In the years since the events of September 11 and the establishment of DHS, knowledge and recognition of the real scope of threats and hazards to the United States has greatly increased.

When we look at how fast ideas, goods, and people move around the world and through the Internet, we recognize that this flow of materials is critical to the economic stability and the advancement of the U.S. interests. However, this globalization of information and commerce creates new security challenges that are borderless and unconventional. As evidenced by the U.S. and Europe economic recession and the Arab Spring both of 2011, entire economies and groups organized through social media, and the criminal networks and terrorist organizations now have the ability to impact the world with far-reaching effects, including those that are potentially disruptive and destructive to our way of life.

As noted in the sidebar below, homeland security is certainly becoming tied to the impacts of globalization.

Threats, Hazards, and Long-Term Global Challenges and Trends

Threats and Hazards	Global Challenges and Trends
• High-consequence weapons of mass destruction	• Economic and financial instability
• Al-Qaeda and global violent extremism	• Dependence on fossil fuels and the threats of global
• High-consequence and/or wide scale cyberattacks, intrusions, disruptions, and exploitations	climate change
	• Nations unwilling to abide by international norms
• Pandemics, major accidents, and natural hazards	• Sophisticated and broadly available technology
• Illicit trafficking and related transnational crime	• Other drivers of illicit, dangerous, or uncontrolled
• Smaller scale terrorism	movement of people and goods

Source: Quadrennial Homeland Security Review Report: A Strategic Framework for Secure Homeland, DHS, February 2010, http://www.dhs.gov/xlibrary/assets/qhsr_report.pdf.

▪ ▪ Critical Thinking ▪

Can you identify the reasons why FEMA should not have been incorporated into the new DHS?

A New Concept of Homeland Security

Reflecting the increasingly complex issues surrounding homeland security, the recently completed QHSR has revised the definition of homeland security to incorporate a more global and comprehensive approach. The Department now identifies with the "homeland security enterprise (HSE)."

DHS Secretary Janet Napolitano, in her letter in the QHSR, describes the HSE as, "the Federal, State, local, tribal, territorial, nongovernmental, and private-sector entities, as well as individuals, families, and communities who share a common national interest in the safety and security of America and the American population. DHS is one among many components of this national enterprise. In some areas, like securing our borders or managing our immigration system, the Department possesses unique capabilities and, hence, responsibilities. In other areas, such as critical infrastructure protection or emergency management, the Department's role is largely one of leadership and stewardship on behalf of those who have the capabilities to get the job done. In still other areas, such as counterterrorism, defense, and diplomacy, other Federal departments and agencies have critical roles and responsibilities, including the Departments of Justice, Defense, and State, the Federal Bureau of Investigation, and the National Counterterrorism Center. Homeland security will only be optimized when we fully leverage the distributed and decentralized nature of the entire enterprise in the pursuit of our common goals."

The Executive Summary of the QHSR elaborates on the definition of homeland security as "the intersection of evolving threats and hazards with traditional governmental and civic responsibilities for civil defense, emergency response, law enforcement, customs, border control, and immigration. In combining these responsibilities under one overarching concept, homeland security breaks down longstanding stovepipes of activity that have been and could still be exploited by those seeking to harm America. Homeland security also creates a greater emphasis on the need for joint actions and efforts across previously discrete elements of government and society" (DHS, 2010).

By creating this broader definition of homeland security, DHS is stressing the diversity of organizations and individuals who have responsibility for, and interest in, the safety and security of the United States — from the President, as Commander in Chief, to the Secretary of DHS, Secretaries of other federal departments and agencies (D&A's), to Governors, Mayors, City Council Chairs, business leaders, nongovernmental leaders, educators, first responders, Neighborhood Watch captains, and down to each and every citizen. Under this definition, with the diversity of stakeholders, no single person or entity is wholly responsible for achieving homeland security; it is a shared responsibility.

DHS has defined the following three concepts as the foundation for a comprehensive approach to homeland security:

1. *Security*: Protect the United States and its people, vital interests, and way of life.
2. *Resilience*: Foster individual, community, and system robustness, adaptability, and capacity for rapid recovery.
3. *Customs and exchange*: Expedite and enforce lawful trade, travel, and immigration.

The QHSR says the following about security: "Homeland security relies on our shared efforts to prevent and deter attacks by identifying and interdicting threats, denying hostile actors the ability to operate within our borders, and protecting the Nation's critical infrastructure and key resources. Initiatives that strengthen our protections, increase our vigilance, and reduce our vulnerabilities remain important components of our security. This is not to say, however, that security is a static undertaking. We know that the global systems that carry people, goods, and data around the globe also facilitate the movement of *dangerous* people, goods, and data, and that within these systems of transportation and transaction, there are key nodes — for example, points of origin and transfer, or border crossings — that represent opportunities for interdiction. Thus, we must work to confront threats at every point along their supply chain — supply chains that often begin abroad. To ensure our homeland security then, we must engage our international allies, and employ the full breadth of our national capacity — from the Federal Government, to State, local, tribal, and territorial police, other law enforcement entities, the Intelligence Community, and the private sector — and appropriately enlist the abilities of millions of American citizens" (Figure 1–3) (DHS, 2010).

On resilience, the QHSR has the following explanation of resilience "to foster individual, community, and system robustness, adaptability, and capacity for rapid recovery. Our country and the world are underpinned by interdependent networks along which the essential elements of economic prosperity — people, goods and resources, money, and information — all flow. While these networks reflect progress and increased efficiency, they are also sources of vulnerability. The consequences of events are no longer confined to a single point; a disruption in one place can ripple through the system and have immediate, catastrophic, and multiplying consequences across the country and around the world" (Figure 1–4) (DHS, 2010).

The third concept in the foundation of the HSE as discussed in the QSHR is Customs and Exchange. Under this concept DHS seeks to "expedite and enforce lawful trade, travel, and immigration. The partners and stakeholders of the HSE are responsible for facilitating and expediting the lawful movement of people and goods into and out of the United States. This responsibility intersects with and is deeply linked to the enterprise's security function. We need a smarter, more holistic approach that embeds security and resilience directly into global movement systems. Strengthening our economy and promoting lawful trade, travel, and immigration must include security and resilience, just as security and resilience must include promoting a strong and competitive U.S. economy, welcoming lawful immigrants, and protecting civil liberties and the rule of law. We view security along with customs and exchange as mutually

FIGURE 1–3 A Customs and Border Patrol (CBP) officer directs a truck with a seaport container to an inspection area at a port. (DHS photo by James R. Tourtellotte. http://www.cbp.gov/xp/cgov/newsroom/multimedia/photo_gallery/afc/field_ops/inspectors_seaports/cs_photo26.xml)

FIGURE 1–4 Greensburg, KS, May 16, 2007 — The center of town 12 days after it was hit by an F5 tornado with 200 mph winds. Debris removal is moving at a record pace, but reconstruction will likely take years. (Photo by Greg Henshall/FEMA News Photo)

reinforcing and inextricably intertwined through actions such as screening, authenticating, and maintaining awareness of the flow of people, goods, and information around the world and across our borders" (Figure 1–5) (DHS, 2010).

To support these concepts, DHS has identified the five core missions and goals.

Five Core Missions and Goals Identified by DHS

Mission 1: Preventing Terrorism and Enhancing Security
- **Goal 1.1**: Prevent Terrorist Attacks
- **Goal 1.2**: Prevent the Unauthorized Acquisition or Use of Chemical, Biological, Radiological, and Nuclear Materials and Capabilities
- **Goal 1.3**: Manage Risks to Critical Infrastructure, Key Leadership, and Events

Mission 2: Securing and Managing Our Borders
- **Goal 2.1**: Effectively Control U.S. Air, Land, and Sea Borders
- **Goal 2.2**: Safeguard Lawful Trade and Travel
- **Goal 2.3**: Disrupt and Dismantle Transnational Criminal Organizations

Mission 3: Enforcing and Administering Our Immigration Laws
- **Goal 3.1**: Strengthen and Effectively Administer the Immigration System
- **Goal 3.2**: Prevent Unlawful Immigration

Mission 4: Safeguarding and Securing Cyberspace
- **Goal 4.1**: Create a Safe, Secure, and Resilient Cyber Environment
- **Goal 4.2**: Promote Cybersecurity Knowledge and Innovation

Mission 5: Ensuring Resilience to Disasters
- **Goal 5.1**: Mitigate Hazards
- **Goal 5.2**: Enhance Preparedness
- **Goal 5.3**: Ensure Effective Emergency Response
- **Goal 5.4**: Rapidly Recover

Public safety officials, including police, fire, public health, emergency managers, and border security, will continue to be in the forefront of mitigation, preparedness, response, and recovery from the potential threat of terrorism, natural hazards, as well as other man-made hazards. However, the new concept of a HSE broadens the spectrum of responsibility to include risk managers, computer analysts, public policy officials, health and environmental practitioners, economic development leaders, educators, the media, businesses, and other elected officials responsible for the safety of their communities. Each and every individual is now responsible for helping to achieve the HSE.

FIGURE 1–5 A Border Patrol agent uses a computer word translator to assist in determining the needs of this illegal immigrant. (DHS photo by James Tourtellotte. http://www.cbp.gov/xp/cgov/newsroom/multimedia/photo_gallery/afc/bp/32.xml)

Not everyone is enamored with the new HSE. Several individuals and organizations have questioned whether it is just another example of the DHS trying to rebrand an organization that is not well understood by the public. The main public/DHS interface is either being subjected to TSA security at airports or reading about immigration raids and border patrol problems. In the following Another Voice article, the TransBorder Project, part of the Center for International Policy in Washington, DC, is critical of the new enterprise.

ANOTHER VOICE: AMERICA'S FAILING "HOMELAND SECURITY ENTERPRISE" BY TOM BARRY, BORDER LINES BLOG, FEBRUARY 2010.

They don't know what it is, so they call it an "enterprise."

In the tradition of the Defense Department's quadrennial review, Janet Napolitano, secretary of the Department of Homeland Security, released the department's first *Homeland Security Quadrennial Review* on Feb. 1. As part of an attempt to address the department's deep-seated identity problem and to distinguish it from its DOD big brother, DHS now refers to itself as a "Homeland Security Enterprise."

George W. Bush will be remembered as the president who created this unwieldy new federal bureaucracy as part of his "Global War on Terror." But Democratic Party security hardliners like Sen. Joe Lieberman of Connecticut were some of the original proponents of a homeland security department, and the new Democratic Party administration of Barack Obama has unconditionally embraced the department as a core government institution.

(Continued)

Rather than using the review (mandated by Congress in 2007 in the midst of rising criticism of DHS) as an opportunity to reexamine the wisdom of creating this amalgam of 22 separate agencies organized around the homeland security theme, the Obama administration is allowing the department to consolidate and expand. Last year the administration moved ahead with plans to construct a $3.4 billion building to house this sprawling admixture of disparate agencies. The newly released *Quadrennial Review* now outlines plans for "maturing and strengthening the homeland security enterprise," and the department's budget will rise 2% in 2011.

Faced with persistent criticism about management, oversight, and its lack of a unifying mission, DHS is putting a new spin on its diffuse identity. In the *Quadrennial Review*, DHS states: "Homeland security is a distributed and diverse national enterprise."

According to DHS, the term enterprise "refers to the collective efforts and shared responsibilities of Federal, State, local, tribal, territorial, nongovernmental, and private-sector partners — as well as individuals, families, and communities — to maintain critical homeland security capabilities. It recognizes the diverse risks, needs, and priorities of these different stakeholders, and connotes a broad-based community with a common interest in the public safety and well-being of America and American society."

Politics and a rush to create a new font of security-related funding were largely responsible for the ill-considered creation of DHS; and the continuing search for meaning and definition at DHS, as illustrated by this new DHS report, underscores the department's fundamental and continuing dysfunction.

It's worth recalling that, as part of his aggressive but badly focused response to the Sept. 11 attacks, President Bush created at first not a department but rather a new White House office — the Office of Homeland Security. However, the homeland security office, headed by Pennsylvania governor Tom Ridge, was short-lived. Congressional Democrats, led by Senator Lieberman, insisted that the country needed more than an executive office to monitor domestic security.

According to Lieberman, the country needed a full-fledged homeland security department to organize domestically against terrorism. Lieberman, a leading Senate hawk and foreign policy neoconservative, also began beating the drums of war. He campaigned for the launching of wars against Iraq and Iran in the aftermath of Sept. 11, as well as for boosting the Pentagon's budget and its domestic response capabilities.

President Bush — although increasingly won over by the neoconservative foreign policy agenda promoted by Lieberman and others — initially rejected the senator's demand for the creation of a homeland security department, arguing that bureaucratic expansion was a typically big-government Democratic response. But nine months after Sept. 11, President Bush reversed course, tacitly accepting the proposals of congressional Democrats led by Lieberman to establish a new department.

In announcing his plan to establish the department on June 6, 2002, President Bush declared that the government should "be reorganized to meet the new threats of the 21st century" and that the new department would involve "the most extensive reorganization of the federal government since the 1940s."

Although the Homeland Security Act of 2002 was largely his proposal, it did not bear Lieberman's name but was sold to Congress as the president's initiative. But having succeeded in his mission to expand the nation's security apparatus, Lieberman didn't begrudge the president and the Republicans for having adopted his proposal. Instead he began pushing hard for the other parts of his security agenda.

In a speech to the Progressive Policy Institute (an affiliate of the center-right Democratic Leadership Council) on June 26, 2002, Lieberman not only reiterated his vision for a domestic defense department but also proposed adopting a new vision of the Pentagon's role in the domestic response to terrorism. With respect to the need for a homeland security department, Lieberman proclaimed:

"Our challenge and our responsibility after September 11th is to meet the deadly fervor of our terrorist enemies by adapting, responding, and reforming to protect our people from future attacks."

"For the U.S. Congress today, that means taking the disconnected pieces of a disorganized federal bureaucracy and reordering them into a unified, focused domestic defense department. While we create the new department, we must also develop a coherent and comprehensive homeland security strategy that can and will safeguard the American people — and that the new department can implement as soon as it is up and running."

But the core of Lieberman's speech concerned not this new "domestic defense department" but the Defense Department itself. As Lieberman told his fellow Democrats:

"Today I want to talk to you about what should be one of the core components of such a larger strategy: maximizing the use of our military resources here at home. Our Department of Defense has more tools, training, technology, and talent to help combat the terrorist threat at home than any other federal agency. Our military has proven capable of brilliance beyond our borders. Now, we must tap its expertise and its resources within our country — by better integrating the Defense Department into our homeland security plans."

Lieberman went on to sketch out his proposal for the Pentagon's own role in domestic defense, with the homeland security department as its new junior partner. He set forth his vision of a well-funded security sector at home, including expanded domestic use of the National Guard by the Pentagon, funding for a new array of security technologies, and stepped-up intelligence operations.

This post-Sept. 11 rush to create a new security department and at the same time beef-up the Pentagon's and intelligence community's role in counterterrorism at home rose in part from a new bipartisan fervor to protect the homeland and strike out against Islamist terrorists.

But the birthing of DHS cannot be explained without also considering how military contractors and their politician partners had begun rallying around proposals calling for Congress and the White House to unleash vast sums of federal revenues in new homeland security-related contracts, issued either by the new department or by the Pentagon and the intelligence agencies.

DHS's Missing Mission

From its conception the Department of Homeland Security was a hodge-podge without a clear mission or clear authority. It brought together 22 agencies and more than a hundred bureaus and subagencies. The decision as to which agencies to include was based more on political bargaining than on any clarity about the department's mission or what would it take to create a cohesive department.

The one entity that had already had a mission somewhat aligned with the notion of homeland security was the National Guard, but it was reported that White House officials couldn't figure out how to extract the Guard from DOD. It was also likely that both the Democratic Party architects of homeland security and White House officials saw from the beginning that DHS in counterterrorism matters would always be subservient to DOD, the intelligence agencies, and to a certain extent the FBI.

Organizational and mission problems plagued DHS from the start, as excellently reported by the *Washington Post* in its Dec. 22, 2005 investigative article, "Department's Mission Undermined from the Start." Reporters Susan B. Glasser and Michael Grunwald concluded:

(*Continued*)

■■ Critical Thinking ■

What do you think were the reasons for DHS establishing the HSE?
Based on your current knowledge of homeland security, describe the responsibilities a Mayor, a nongovernmental organization leader, or a citizen would have for achieving homeland security.

The Department of Homeland Security

On November 25, 2002, President Bush signed into law the Homeland Security Act of 2002 (HS Act) (Public Law 107–296), and announced that former Pennsylvania Governor Tom Ridge would become secretary of a new DHS to be created through this legislation. This act, which authorized the greatest federal government reorganization since President Harry Truman joined the various branches of the armed forces under the Department of Defense, was charged with a threefold mission of protecting the United States from further terrorist attacks, reducing the nation's vulnerability to terrorism, and minimizing the damage from potential terrorist attacks and natural disasters.

The sweeping reorganization into the new department, which officially opened its doors on January 24, 2003, joined more than 179,000 federal employees from 22 existing federal agencies under a single, cabinet-level organization. The legislation, which was not restricted to the newly created department, also transformed several other federal agencies that at first glance may have appeared only remotely affiliated with the homeland security mission. To the affected government employees, millions of concerned American citizens, the entire world media, and even the terrorists themselves, it was clear that the U.S. government was entering a new era.

The creation of the DHS was the culmination of an evolutionary legislative process that began largely in response to criticism that increased interagency cooperation between federal intelligence organizations could have prevented the September 11 terrorist attacks. Based on the findings of several pre-September 11 commissions, it appeared that the country needed a centralized federal government agency whose primary reason for existence would be to coordinate the security of the "homeland" (a term that predated the attacks). The White House and Congress were both well aware that any homeland security czar position they conceived would require both an adequate staff and a large budget to succeed. Thus, in early 2002 deliberations began to create a new cabinet-level department that would fuse many of the security-related agencies dispersed throughout the federal government.

For several months during the second half of 2002, Congress jockeyed between differing versions of the homeland security bill in an effort to establish legislation that was passable yet effective. Lawmakers were particularly mired on the issue of the rights of the 179,000 affected employees — an issue that prolonged the legislative process considerably. Furthermore, efforts to incorporate many of the intelligence-gathering and investigative law enforcement agencies, namely, the National Security Agency (NSA), the Federal Bureau of Investigation (FBI), and the Central Intelligence Agency (CIA), into the legislation failed.

Despite these delays and setbacks, after the 2002 midterm elections, the Republican seats that were gained in both the House and Senate gave the president the leverage he needed to pass the bill without further deliberation (House of Representatives, 299–121 on November 13, 2002; Senate, 90–9 on November 19, 2002). While the passage of this act represented a significant milestone, the implementation phase to come presented a tremendous challenge.

▪ ▪ Critical Thinking ▪

Do you think that the CIA should have been moved into DHS? If so, why, or if not, why not?
The Department of Transportation's Office of Lifeline Safety was not moved into DHS. What would the reasons be to keep it in Transportation and not move it to DHS?

Department of Homeland Security Establishment Timeline

September 11, 2001 — Terrorist attacks occur in Washington, DC; New York; and Pennsylvania.
September 20, 2001 — In an address to Congress, President Bush announces the creation of the Office of Homeland Security (OHS) and the appointment of Tom Ridge as director.
October 8, 2001 — President Bush swears in Tom Ridge as assistant to the president for homeland security and issues an executive order creating the OHS.
October 9, 2001 — President Bush swears in General Wayne Downing as Director of the Office of Combating Terrorism (OCT) and issues an executive order creating the OCT.
October 16, 2001 — President Bush issues an executive order establishing the president's Critical Infrastructure Protection Board to coordinate and have cognizance of federal efforts and programs that relate to protection of information systems.

October 26, 2001 — President Bush signs the USA PATRIOT Act.

October 29, 2001 — President Bush chairs the first meeting of the Homeland Security Council (HSC) and issues Homeland Security Presidential Directive No. 1 (HSPD-1), establishing the organization and operation of the HSC, and HSPD-2, establishing the Foreign Terrorist Tracking Task Force and increasing immigration vigilance.

November 8, 2001 — President Bush announces that the Corporation for National and Community Service (CNCS) will support homeland security, "mobilizing more than 20,000 Senior Corps and AmeriCorps participants."

November 8, 2001 — President Bush creates the Presidential Task Force on Citizen Preparedness in the War against Terrorism to "help prepare Americans in their homes, neighborhoods, schools, workplaces, places of worship and public places from the potential consequences of terrorist attacks."

November 15, 2001 — FEMA announces the Individual and Family Grant program for disaster assistance.

January 30, 2002 — President Bush issues an executive order establishing the U.S.A. Freedom Corps, encouraging all Americans to serve their country for the equivalent of at least 2 years (4,000 hours) over their lifetimes.

February 4, 2002 — President Bush submits the president's budget for FY 2003 to Congress, directing $37.7 billion to homeland security (up from $19.5 billion in FY 2002).

March 12, 2002 — President Bush establishes the Homeland Security Advisory System (HSPD-3).

March 19, 2002 — President Bush issues an executive order establishing the President's Homeland Security Advisory Council.

September 17, 2002 — President Bush declares the National Strategy to Combat Weapons of Mass Destruction (HSPD-4).

November 25, 2002 — President Bush signs the Homeland Security Act of 2002 (HR 5005) as Public Law 107–296. Tom Ridge is announced as secretary, Navy Secretary Gordon England is nominated as Deputy Secretary of the DHS, and Drug Enforcement Agency (DEA) Administrator Asa Hutchinson is nominated as the undersecretary of border and transportation security.

January 24, 2003 — Sixty days after it was signed, the Homeland Security Act becomes effective.

February 28, 2003 — President Bush calls for the creation of the National Incident Management System (NIMS) through HSPD-5.

March 1, 2003 — Most affected federal agencies are incorporated into the DHS.

June 1, 2003 — All remaining affected federal agencies are incorporated into the DHS.

Source: Compiled from Multiple Sources, by Damon Coppola, January 2003.

The Department of Homeland Security is a massive agency, juggling numerous responsibilities between a staggeringly wide range of program areas, employing approximately 180,000 people, and managing a massive multi-billion-dollar budget and an ambitious list of tasks and goals. The department leverages resources within federal, state, and local governments, coordinating the ongoing transition of multiple agencies and programs into a single, integrated agency focused on protecting the American people and their homeland. In total, more than 87,000 different governmental jurisdictions at the federal, state, and local levels have homeland security responsibilities.

At the federal level, the DHS organizational composition remains in a state of flux. Scattered readjustments have occurred throughout its first years of existence, with multiple offices being passed between the department's components. Though it seemed by the end of DHS Secretary Tom Ridge's years of service that the basic organizational makeup had been established, incoming DHS Secretary Chertoff proposed several fundamental changes to the department's organization, which were implemented under Secretary Chertoff's Reorganization Plan. Again, the department was reorganized following the 2005 hurricane season according to the requirements of the Post-Katrina Emergency Management Reform Act (PKEMRA) of 2006.

The Obama Administration has retained the fundamental organizational structure as mandated by PKEMRA at the agency and subcomponent level, adding one new subcomponent, an Office of Intergovernmental Affairs. At the subcomponent level some minor changes were made. There was hope within the emergency management community that President Obama might move FEMA out of DHS and return it to its former status as an independent Agency. That did not happen nor does it look like it will ever happen unless there is another catastrophic failure as experienced in Hurricane Katrina.

■ ■ Critical Thinking ■

Should President Obama have taken FEMA out of DHS and made it an independent agency? Discuss the pros and cons of your opinion.

Other Federal Departments Responsible for the Homeland Security Enterprise

Appendix A of the QHSR details the roles and responsibilities of the other Federal agencies in the HSE. They are summarized below:

- The Attorney General has lead responsibility for criminal investigations of terrorist acts or terrorist threats by individuals or groups inside the United States, or directed at U.S. citizens or institutions abroad, as well as for related intelligence collection activities within the United States. The Attorney General leads the Department of Justice, which also includes the Federal Bureau of Investigation, Drug Enforcement Administration, and Bureau of Alcohol, Tobacco, Firearms, and Explosives, each of which has key homeland security responsibilities.
- The Secretary of State has the responsibility to coordinate activities with foreign governments and international organizations related to the prevention, preparation, response, and recovery from a domestic incident, and for the protection of U.S. citizens and U.S. interests overseas. The Department of State also adjudicates and screens visa applications abroad.
- The Secretary of Defense leads the Department of Defense (DOD), whose military services, defense agencies, and geographic and functional commands defend the United States from direct attack; deter potential adversaries; foster regional stability; secure and assure access to sea, air, space, and cyberspace; and build the security capacity of key partners. DOD also provides a wide range of support to civil authorities at the direction of the Secretary of Defense or the President when the capabilities of State and local authorities to respond effectively to an event are overwhelmed.

- The Secretary of Health and Human Services leads the coordination of all functions relevant to Public Health Emergency Preparedness and Disaster Medical Response. Additionally, the Department of Health and Human Services (HHS) incorporates steady-state and incident-specific activities as described in the National Health Security Strategy.

- The Secretary of the Treasury works to safeguard the U.S. financial system, combat financial crimes, and cut off financial support to terrorists, WMD proliferators, drug traffickers, and other national security threats.

- The Secretary of Agriculture provides leadership on food, agriculture, natural resources, rural development, and related issues based on sound public policy, the best available science, and efficient management. The U.S. Department of Agriculture (USDA) is the sector-specific agency for the Food and Agriculture Sector, a responsibility shared with the Food and Drug Administration with respect to food safety and defense.

- The Director of National Intelligence serves as the head of the Intelligence Community (IC), acts as the principal advisor to the President and National Security Council for intelligence matters relating to national security, and oversees and directs implementation of the National Intelligence Program. The IC, composed of 16 elements across the U.S. government, functions consistent with law, executive order, regulations, and policy to support the national security-related missions of the U.S. government. It provides a range of analytic products that assess threats to the homeland and inform planning, capability development, and operational activities of HSE partners and stakeholders. In addition to IC elements with specific homeland security missions, the Office of the Director of National Intelligence maintains a number of mission and support centers that provide unique capabilities for homeland security partners, including the National Counterterrorism Center (NCTC), National Counterproliferation Center, and National Counterintelligence Executive. NCTC serves as the primary U.S. government organization for analyzing and integrating all intelligence pertaining to terrorism and counterterrorism, and conducts strategic operational planning for integrated counterterrorism activities.

- The Secretary of Commerce, supportive of national economic security interests and responsive to Public Law and Executive direction, is responsible for promulgating Federal information technology and cybersecurity standards; regulating export of security technologies; representing U.S. industry on international trade policy and commercial data flow matters; security and privacy policies that apply to the Internet's domain name system; protecting intellectual property; conducting cybersecurity research and development; and assuring timely availability of industrial products, materials, and services to meet homeland security requirements.

- The Secretary of Education oversees discretionary grants and technical assistance to help schools plan for and respond to emergencies that disrupt teaching and learning. The Department of Education is a supporting Federal agency in the response and management of emergencies under the *National Response Framework*.

- The Secretary of Energy maintains stewardship of vital national security capabilities, from nuclear weapons to leading edge research and development programs. The Department of Energy (DOE) is the designated federal agency to provide a unifying structure for the integration of federal critical infrastructure and key resources' protection efforts specifically for the Energy Sector. It is also responsible for maintaining continuous and reliable energy supplies for the United States through preventive measures and restoration and recovery actions.

- The Administrator of the Environmental Protection Agency (EPA) is charged with protecting human health and the environment.

- The Secretary of Housing and Urban Development coordinates Federal support to State, tribal, regional, and local governments, nongovernmental organizations (NGOs), and the private sector to enable community recovery from the long-term consequences of extraordinary disasters.
- The Secretary of the Interior develops policies and procedures for all types of hazards and emergencies that impact Federal lands, facilities, infrastructure, and resources; tribal lands; and insular areas. DOI, together with the Department of Agriculture, also operates the National Interagency Fire Center.
- The Secretary of Transportation collaborates with DHS on all matters relating to transportation security and transportation infrastructure protection and in regulating the transportation of hazardous materials by all modes (including pipelines). The Secretary of Transportation is responsible for operating the national airspace system.
- Other federal agencies are also part of the HSE and contribute to the homeland security mission in a variety of ways. This includes agencies with responsibilities for regulating elements of the nation's critical infrastructure to assure public health, safety, and the common defense, developing and implementing pertinent public policy, supporting efforts to protect the homeland (DHS, 2010).

■ ■ Critical Thinking ■

After DHS which federal entity has the most critical role in the HSE and what are the factors that support your choice? In addition, the QHSR defines the roles of State and local governments and the private sector, which are summarized in the following sidebars

■ ■ ■

Roles and Responsibilities of State and Local Governments in the Homeland Security Enterprise

- **State and Territorial Governments** coordinate the activities of cities, counties, and intrastate regions. States administer Federal homeland security grants to local and tribal (in certain grant programs) governments, allocating key resources to bolster their prevention and preparedness capabilities. State agencies conduct law enforcement and security activities, protect the Governor and other executive leadership, and administer State programs that address the range of homeland security threats, hazards, and challenges. States government officials lead statewide disaster and mitigation planning. During response, States coordinate resources and capabilities throughout the State and are responsible for requesting and obtaining resources and capabilities from surrounding States. States often mobilize these substantive resources and capabilities to supplement the local efforts before, during, and after incidents.
- **Tribal Leaders** are responsible for the public safety and welfare of their membership. They can serve as both key decision makers and trusted sources of public information during incidents.
- **Tribal Governments**, which have a special status under Federal laws and treaties, ensure the provision of essential services to members within their communities, and are responsible for developing emergency response and mitigation plans. Tribal governments may coordinate

resources and capabilities with neighboring jurisdictions, and establish mutual aid agreements with other tribal governments, local jurisdictions, and State governments. Depending on location, land base, and resources, tribal governments provide law enforcement, fire, and emergency services as well as public safety to their members.

- **Local Governments** provide front-line leadership for local law enforcement, fire, public safety, environmental response, public health, and emergency medical services for all manner of hazards and emergencies. Through the Urban Areas Security Initiative (UASI) program, cities (along with counties in many cases) address multijurisdictional planning and operations, equipment support and purchasing, and training and exercises in support of high-threat, high-density urban areas. UASI grants assist local governments in building and sustaining homeland security capabilities. Local governments coordinate resources and capabilities during disasters with neighboring jurisdictions, NGOs, the State, and the private sector.
- **County Governments** provide front-line leadership for local law enforcement, fire, public safety, environmental response, public health, and emergency medical services for all manner of hazards and emergencies. In many cases, county government officials participate in UASIs with other urban jurisdictions to assist local governments in building and sustaining capabilities to prevent, protect against, respond to, and recover from threats or acts of terrorism. County governments coordinate resources and capabilities during disasters with neighboring jurisdictions, NGOs, the State, and the private sector.

Source: Quadrennial Homeland Security Review Report: A Strategic Framework for Secure Homeland, DHS, February 2010, http://www.dhs.gov/xlibrary/assets/qhsr_report.pdf.

ROLE OF PRIVATE SECTOR IN HOMELAND SECURITY ENTERPRISE

- **Critical Infrastructure and Key Resource (CIKR) Owners and Operators** develop protective programs and measures to ensure that systems and assets, whether physical or virtual, are secure from and resilient to cascading, disruptive impacts. Protection includes actions to mitigate the overall risk to CIKR assets, systems, networks, functions, or their interconnecting links, including actions to deter the threat, mitigate vulnerabilities, or minimize the consequences associated with a terrorist attack or other incident. CIKR owners and operators also prepare business continuity plans and ensure their own ability to sustain essential services and functions.
- **Major and Multinational Corporations** operate in all sectors of trade and commerce that foster the American way of life and support the operation, security, and resilience of global movement systems. They take action to support risk management planning and investments in security as a necessary component of prudent business planning and operations. They contribute to developing the ideas, science, and technology that underlie innovation in homeland security. During times of disaster, they provide response resources (donated or compensated)—including specialized teams, essential service providers, equipment, and advanced technologies—through

public–private emergency plans/partnerships or mutual aid and assistance agreements, or in response to requests from government and nongovernmental-volunteer initiatives.

- **Small Businesses** contribute to all aspects of homeland security and employ more than half of all private-sector workers. They support response efforts by developing contingency plans and working with local planners to ensure that their plans are consistent with pertinent response procedures. When small businesses can survive and quickly recover from disasters, the nation and economy are more secure and more resilient. They perform research and development, catalyze new thinking, and serve as engines of innovation for development of new solutions to key challenges in homeland security.

Source: Quadrennial Homeland Security Review Report: A Strategic Framework for Secure Homeland, DHS, February 2010, http://www.dhs.gov/xlibrary/assets/qhsr_report.pdf.

DHS has determined that in order to "mature and strengthen" the HSE and the agency itself, it must focus its effort in several strategic areas growing out of each mission area as described earlier in this chapter. These are:

- Enhanced shared awareness of risks and threats
- Build capable communities
- Foster unity of effort
- Foster innovative approaches and solutions through leading edge science and technology

The future existence of the DHS seems very safe under the Obama administration. They have yet to be tested in a major event. While they have performed well during recent natural disasters such as the Joplin, Missouri tornadoes, they have not faced a significant event such as a major earthquake or hurricane. In addition, the United States has been spared any major terrorist events on U.S. soil.

Conclusion

The QHSR report establishes a vision for the future of the HSE. It reflects lessons learned from the past that homeland security is not just about terrorism. While building protections, securing our borders, or preventing terrorism, measures are all critical to homeland security, it encompasses so much more. To be successful, the HSE needs to acknowledge and focus on threats other than terrorism, both natural and manmade, that have had devastating impacts on the United States in the past decade. It must recognize and build protective mechanisms for new and evolving threats such as cybercrime. Fundamentally, the HSE is about protecting the American way of life and ensuring our resilience in a challenging world.

As the DHS matures and critical funding continues, we should have better-trained and better-equipped first responders; a stronger, less vulnerable national infrastructure; more rational immigration and border policies; an enhanced delivery system for public health and new technologies; and mechanisms to improve and safeguard our information, communications, and cybernetworks.

In embracing the new concept of a HSE, DHS is one among many components. It is a department with unique expertise such as securing our borders or managing our immigration system. In many other areas, such as emergency management, the Department's role is largely one of leadership among the governmental family to get the job done. In counterterrorism, defense, and diplomacy, other Federal departments and agencies have critical roles and responsibilities, including the Departments of Justice, Defense, and State, the Federal Bureau of Investigation, and the National Counterterrorism Center.

As the QHSR states, "The effectiveness of the evolving concept of homeland security will only be accomplished when we leverage the capabilities of our partners at all levels of government, within the private sector, and among our citizens to achieve the goals of the homeland security enterprise."

Key Terms

Critical Infrastructure: Critical infrastructure includes any system or asset that, if disabled or disrupted in any significant way, would result in catastrophic loss of life or catastrophic economic loss. Some examples of critical infrastructure include the following:
Public water systems
Primary roadways, bridges, and highways
Key data storage and processing facilities, stock exchanges, or major banking centers
Chemical facilities located in close proximity to large population centers
Major power generation facilities
Hydroelectric facilities and dams
Nuclear power plants

Executive Order: A declaration issued by the president or by a governor that has the force of law. Executive orders are usually based on existing statutory authority and require no action by Congress or the state legislature to become effective.

Federal Response Plan: The FRP was developed to establish a standard process and structure for the systematic, coordinated, and effective delivery of federal assistance to address the consequences of any major disaster or emergency declared under the Robert T. Stafford Disaster Relief and Emergency Assistance Act, as amended. This plan was later replaced by the National Response Plan.

Homeland Security Enterprise: A new concept defined as "the Federal, State, local, tribal, territorial, nongovernmental, and private-sector entities, as well as individuals, families, and communities who share a common national interest in the safety and security of America and the American population."

National Incident Management System: This is a system mandated by Homeland Security Presidential Directive (HSPD) 5 that provides a consistent nationwide approach for governments, the private sector, and nongovernmental organizations to work effectively and efficiently together to prepare for, respond to, and recover from domestic incidents, regardless of cause, size, or complexity.

Presidential Directive: A form of executive order issued by the president that establishes an action or change in the structure or function of the government (generally within the Executive Office). Under President Bush, directives have been termed *Homeland Security Presidential Directives* (HSPDs) and *National Security Presidential Directives* (NSPDs). Under President Clinton, they were termed *Presidential Decision Directives* (PDDs) and *Presidential Review Directives* (PRDs).

Quadrennial Homeland Security Review (QHSR): A comprehensive report published by DHS in February 2010 that establishes the future direction of the DHS and the discipline of homeland security.

Statutory Authority: The legally granted authority, bestowed on the named recipient by a legislature, that provides a government agency, board, or commission the power to perform the various functions, expenditures, and actions as described in the law.

Review Questions

1. What is the Quadrennial Homeland Security Review?
2. What legislation required DHS to undertake the QHSR?
3. What changes to the definition of *homeland security* were manifested in the QHSR?
4. How has the PKEMRA influenced the QHSR and DHS?
5. Discuss the role of federal agencies other than DHS in the HSE.
6. Discuss the role of state and local governments in the HSE.
7. Do you think the new concept of a HSE is valid? Explain the pros and cons of your position.

Further Readings

Barry, T., Border Lines Blog. http://www.borderlinesblog.blogspot.com/2010/02/Americas-failing-homelandsecurity.html.

Baldwin, T.E., 2002. Historical Chronology of FEMA Consequence Management, Preparedness and Response to Terrorism. Argonne National Laboratory, Argonne, IL.

Clarke, R., 2010. Cyber War: The Next Threat to National Security and What to Do about It. New York, New York.

Communications Sector Coordinating Council. 2007. Communications Sector Specific Infrastructure Protection Plan. Communications Sector Coordinating Council. http://www.dhs.gov/xlibrary/assets/nipp-ssp-communications.pdf.

Department of Homeland Security. 2007. Department Subcomponents and Agencies. www.dhs.gov/xabout/structure.

Department of Homeland Security. 2002. National Strategy for Homeland Security. http://www.dhs.gov/xlibrary/assets/nat_strat_hls.pdf.

Department of Homeland Security. 2003. National Strategy for the Protection of Physical Infrastructure and Key Assets. http://www.dhs.gov/xlibrary/assets/Physical_Strategy.pdf.

Department of Homeland Security. 2006. DHS Releases Cyber Storm Public Exercise Report. http://www.dhs.gov/xnews/releases/pr_1158341221370.shtm.

Department of Homeland Security. 2009a. National Infrastructure Protection Plan. http://www.dhs.gov/files/programs/editorial/gc_1204738275985.shtm.

Department of Homeland Security. 2009b. NIPP: Sector Specific Plans. http://www.dhs.gov/files/programs/gc_1179866197607.shtm

Department of Homeland Security. 2010. Quadrennial Homeland Security Review Report: A Strategic Framework for a Secure Homeland. http://www.dhs.gov/xlibrary/assets/qhsr_report.pdf.

Department of Homeland Security. 2011. Implementing the Recommendations of the 9/11 Commission. A Progress Report. dhs.gov/xlibrary/assets/progress_report.pdf.

Historic Overview of the Terrorist Threat

What You Will Learn

- The evolution of the federal government in responding to emergencies, disasters, and terrorist threats before September 11
- Measures taken to address the terrorism hazard within the United States following the September 11 terrorist attacks
- Significant statutory measures taken before and after September 11
- The actions taken by DHS to address the recommendations in the 9/11 Commission report

Introduction

Harry Truman once said, "The only thing new is the history we don't know." For many Americans, the rush of activities by the government to pass new laws, reorganize government institutions, and allocate vast sums of money in the aftermath of the September 11, 2001, terrorist attacks may have seemed unprecedented. The reality is that similar actions in terms of both type and scope have happened in the past, and these historical experiences can provide insight into the prospect of the ultimate success or failure of the actions that have been taken since the September 11 attacks occurred.

The purpose of this chapter is to provide a historic perspective of the evolution of the programs, policies, and organizations established to address the problem of terrorism, nuclear threats, and other emergencies in the United States. It will examine the chronology of events and actions leading up to and beyond September 11, 2001. This perspective will help frame the issues to be discussed in subsequent chapters of this book, which will detail the legislative, organizational, and operational underpinnings of America's homeland security structure.

This chapter provides summaries of terrorist events aimed at the U.S. government outside its shores including the Khobar Towers bombing and the attack of the USS Cole. Information is provided for the two terrorist incidents prior to September 11: the 1993 World Trade Center (WTC) bombing and the 1995 Oklahoma City bombing of the Murrah Federal Office Building. There is an extensive section of the tragic events of September 11 including updated statistics and timelines.

New material will include information on the 9/11 Commission and the July 2011 Department of Homeland Security (DHS) Report on Implementing the Recommendations of the 9/11 Commission.

Before It Was Called Homeland Security: From the 1800s to the Creation of FEMA

The U.S. government has a long history of responding to all types of threats and emergencies before terrorism became an emerging threat in the 1990s. A brief history of the evolution of government's role is outlined below, primarily focusing on the evolution of government response to these threats. It is important to note that each major change was event driven, just as the attacks of September 11 drove the adoption of homeland security.

In 1803, a congressional act was passed to provide financial assistance to a New Hampshire town devastated by fire. This is the first example of the federal government becoming involved in a local disaster.

During the 1930s, the Reconstruction Finance Corporation and the Bureau of Public Roads both were granted the authority to make disaster loans available for repair and reconstruction of certain public facilities after disasters. The Tennessee Valley Authority (TVA) was created during this era to produce hydroelectric power and, as a secondary purpose, to reduce flooding in the region.

The next notable period of evolution occurred during the 1950s. The Cold War era presented the potential for nuclear war and nuclear fallout as the principal disaster risk. Civil defense programs proliferated across communities during this time. Individuals and communities alike were encouraged to and did build bomb shelters to protect themselves and their families from a nuclear attack by the Soviet Union.

Federal support for these activities was vested in the Federal Civil Defense Administration (FCDA), an organization with few staff and limited financial resources whose main role was to provide technical assistance. A companion office to the FCDA, the Office of Defense Mobilization, was established in the Department of Defense (DOD). The primary functions of this office were to allow for the quick mobilization of materials and the production and stockpiling of critical materials in the event of war. In 1958, these two offices were merged into the Office of Civil and Defense Mobilization.

As the 1960s began, three major natural disasters occurred. In a sparsely populated area of Montana in 1960, the Hebgen Lake earthquake struck, measuring 7.3 on the Richter scale, calling attention to the fact that the nation's earthquake risk extended far beyond California's borders. Later that year Hurricane Donna hit the west coast of Florida and in 1961 Hurricane Carla blew across Texas. The incoming Kennedy administration decided to change the federal approach to disasters. In 1961, it created the Office of Emergency Preparedness inside the White House to deal with these large-scale events. It distinguished these activities from the civil defense responsibilities, which remained in the Office of Civil Defense within DOD.

During the remainder of the 1960s, the United States was struck by a series of major natural disasters. In 1964, in Prince William Sound, Alaska, an earthquake, measuring 9.2 on the Richter scale, killed 123 people and generated a tsunami that affected beaches as far south as the Pacific Coast of California. Hurricane Betsy struck in 1965 and Hurricane Camille in 1969, together killing and injuring hundreds and causing hundreds of millions of dollars in damage along the Gulf Coast. The response to these events, as with previous disasters, was the passage of ad hoc legislation for funds. However, the financial losses resulting from Hurricane Betsy brought about the passage of the National Flood Insurance Act of 1968, which in turn created the National Flood Insurance Program (NFIP) that allowed the government to provide low-cost flood insurance to individuals.

During the 1970s, responsibility for dealing with different threats was allotted to more than five separate federal departments and agencies, including the Department of Commerce (weather, warning, and fire protection), the General Services Administration (continuity of government, stockpiling, federal preparedness), the Treasury Department (import investigation), the Nuclear Regulatory Commission (power plants), and the Department of Housing and Urban Development (HUD) (flood insurance and disaster relief).

With the passage of the Disaster Relief Act of 1974, prompted by the previously mentioned hurricanes and the San Fernando earthquake of 1971, the Department of HUD possessed the most significant authority for natural disaster response and recovery through the NFIP, which it administered under the Federal Insurance Administration (FIA) and the Federal Disaster Assistance Administration (FDAA). On the military side, there existed the Defense Civil Preparedness Agency (nuclear attack) and the U.S. Army Corps of Engineers (flood control).

In the 1970s, a partial release of radioactive materials occurred at the Three Mile Island nuclear power plant in Pennsylvania, requiring the evacuation of thousands of residents. This accident brought national media attention to the lack of adequate off-site preparedness around commercial nuclear power plants and the role of the federal government in responding to such an event.

On June 19, 1978, President Carter transmitted to Congress the Reorganization Plan Number 3 (3 CFR 1978, 5 U.S. Code 903). The intent of this plan was to consolidate emergency preparedness, mitigation, and response activities into a single federal emergency management organization. The president stated that the plan would provide for the establishment of the Federal Emergency Management Agency (FEMA) and that the FEMA director would report directly to the president.

Reorganization Plan Number 3 transferred the following agencies or functions to FEMA: National Fire Prevention Control Administration (Department of Commerce), Federal Insurance Administration (HUD), Federal Broadcast System (Executive Office of the President), Defense Civil Preparedness Agency (DOD), Federal Disaster Assistance Administration (HUD), and the Federal Preparedness Agency (GSA).

After congressional review and concurrence, the FEMA was officially established by Executive Order 12127 of March 31, 1979 (44 FR 19367, 3 CFR, Compilation, p. 376). A second executive order, Executive Order 12148, mandated reassignment of agencies, programs, and personnel into this new entity.

The early and middle 1980s saw a renewed interest and concern for threats from the Soviet Union, causing the federal efforts to once again focus on civil defense and nuclear attack planning. There were no significant natural disasters, and a robust program for commercial nuclear power preparedness was begun as part of the new Nuclear Regulatory Commission (NRC) licensing process so that threat was believed to have dissipated.

As Congress debated and finally passed major reform of federal disaster policy as part of the Stewart McKinney-Robert Stafford Act, FEMA, the agency responsible for responding to any threat, natural or man-made, was having severe problems with leadership and organization, and its ability to support a national threat response remained in doubt. It was in conflict with its partners at the state and local levels over agency spending and priorities for nuclear attack planning when they wanted to plan for natural hazards. In 1989, two devastating natural disasters, Hurricane Hugo and the Loma Prieta earthquake, called into question the continued existence of FEMA. In 1992, Hurricane Andrew struck Florida and Louisiana and Hurricane Iniki struck Hawaii within months of each other (Figure 2–1). FEMA wasn't ready, and neither were FEMA's partners at the state level. The agency's failure to respond was witnessed by Americans all across the country as major news organizations followed the crisis. It was not just FEMA that failed during Hurricane Andrew; it was the whole federal emergency management process and system. Investigations by the General Accounting Office (GAO) and other governmental and nongovernmental watchdog groups called for major reforms. None of this was lost on the incoming Clinton administration. President Clinton appointed James Lee Witt to be director of FEMA with a mandate to make the Agency ready to respond to any threat or disaster facing the country. Witt was a seasoned Arkansas State Director of Emergency Management, ex-local elected official, who had been through numerous natural and man-made disasters.

FIGURE 2–1 Hurricane Andrew, Florida, August 24, 1992 — Many houses, businesses, and personal effects suffered extensive damage from one of the most destructive hurricanes ever recorded in America. One million people were evacuated, and 54 died in this hurricane. (Source: FEMA News Photo)

The threat of a major natural disaster or even multiple disasters was the U.S. government's concern as the U.S. started the 1990s. Other threats from man-made incidents such as the Valdez oil spill or a nuclear attack seemed remote. There was an increasing awareness of an ever growing terrorist threat throughout the world, but it hadn't really impacted the U.S. mainland or its property. U.S. intelligence agencies were monitoring an increase in terrorist attacks all over. Within the United States, there were many incidents of bombings, but they were perpetrated by homegrown citizens and rarely for ideological reasons. This was to change with the first terrorist attack on U.S. soil on the WTC in 1993.

■ ■ Critical Thinking ■

In light of the events that have transpired, how would you apportion the amount of Federal effort and funding between natural hazards and man-made hazards and terrorism?

World Trade Center Bombing

The bombing of the WTC presented a new threat on U.S. soil, that is, the first large-scale terrorist attack. Prior to this, bombings that occurred at post offices, medical facilities, etc. were considered to be criminal acts by individuals. This bombing changed that. On February 23, 1993, a massive explosion occurred in the basement parking lot of the WTC in New York City. Six adults and one unborn child were killed and more than 1,000 people sustained injuries. The explosive device, which weighed more than 1,000 pounds, caused extensive damage to seven of the building's floors, six of which were below grade. A blast crater that resulted from the explosion measured 130 ft in width by 150 ft in length. More than 50,000 people were evacuated, 25,000 of whom were in the twin towers of the Trade Center. The entire evacuation process required approximately 11 h to complete (Fusco, 1993).

New York Fire Department Responds to World Trade Center Bombing

At the time, the response to the bombing was described as being the largest incident that the City of New York Fire Department (FDNY) had ever managed in its 128-year history. In terms of the number of fire units that responded, the event was described as being "the equivalent of a 16-alarm fire" (Fusco, 1993). The following list provides a summary of relevant data from the bombing event:

- Deaths: 6
- Injuries: 1,042
- Firefighter injuries: 85 (one requiring hospitalization)
- Police officers injured: 35
- EMS workers injured: 1
- Firefighter, police, and EMS deaths: 0
- Number of people evacuated from WTC complex: approximately 50,000
- FDNY engine companies responding: 84
- FDNY truck companies responding: 60
- FDNY special units responding: 26
- FDNY personnel responding: 28 battalion chiefs, 9 deputy chiefs
- Percentage of FDNY on duty staff responding: 45% (Fusco, 1993)

This incident resulted in increased efforts to address the terrorist threat. Shootings in California and the botched raid in Waco, Texas, added to public concern over terrorism and crime in general. Through the work of the Joint Terrorism Task Force, four suspects were arrested and convicted of the WTC bombing. In response to these incidents, the Congress passed and President Clinton signed the Violent Crime Control and Law Enforcement Act of 1994. This was the most comprehensive crime legislation in U.S. history. Among the provisions of this Act was an expanded application of the death penalty to "acts of terrorism or the use of weapons of mass destruction." It included a 10-year ban on assault weapons, which was later allowed to expire, programs to fight violence against women, and significant increases in funding for the Immigration and Naturalization Service (INS), Border Patrol, Drug Enforcement Agency (DEA), and the Federal Bureau of Investigation (FBI).

Murrah Federal Building Bombing

The bombing of the Murrah Federal Building represented the next incident of domestic terrorism. On April 19, 1995, a massive truck bomb exploded outside of the Alfred P. Murrah Federal Building in downtown Oklahoma City. All told, 168 people died, including 19 children attending a daycare program

FIGURE 2–2 Oklahoma City, Oklahoma, April 26, 1995 — Search-and-rescue crews work to save those trapped beneath the debris after the Oklahoma City bombing. (Source: FEMA News Photo)

in the building. A total of 674 people were injured. The Murrah building was destroyed, 25 additional buildings in the downtown area were severely damaged or destroyed, and another 300 buildings were damaged by the blast. The ensuing rescue and recovery effort during the next 16 days involved, among many other resources, the dispatch of 11 FEMA urban search-and-rescue teams (see sidebar, "FEMA Urban Search …") from across the country to assist local and state officials' search first for survivors and, ultimately, for victims' bodies (Figure 2–2) (City of Oklahoma City Document Management, 1996).

■ ■ ■ ▬▬▬▬▬▬▬▬▬▬▬▬▬▬▬▬▬▬▬▬▬▬▬▬▬▬▬▬▬▬▬▬▬▬▬▬

FEMA Urban Search and Rescue at Murrah Building Bombing in Oklahoma City, 1995

At 9:02 on the morning of April 19, 1995, a bomb exploded from inside a Ryder truck under the Alfred P. Murrah Federal Building in Oklahoma City. The blast caused a partial collapse of all nine floors of the 20-year-old building, and 168 people died.

Rescuers from the Oklahoma City Fire Department entered the building unsure of whether the building would continue to support its own weight. Most of the steel support system had been blown out.

Within five hours of the blast the first FEMA urban search-and-rescue task force was deployed. By 6 PM the task force was in the building, searching for victims. One of the first assignments was to search the second floor nursery for victims.

Teams with search-and-rescue dogs began the search in the nursery. The dogs are trained to bark when they find live victims. No dogs barked that night.

Eleven of FEMA's 27 USAR [U.S. Army Reserve] task forces worked in the building, with representation from virtually every task force in the country. The FEMA teams coordinated with local fire departments, police departments, and military and federal agencies during the search-and-rescue effort.

The rescue effort involved extensive stabilization of the fragmented building, rescuing of people trapped within tight spaces, rescues from high angles, and breaking through concrete and hazardous materials analysis and removal.

An innovative plan was developed to help rescuers deal with the psychological and emotional trauma of such a grisly scene. The plan allowed workers to be briefed in advance and prepared for what they were to experience; extensive debriefing sessions were also included.

Source: FEMA, www.fema.gov

At this time, Congress was debating the Nunn-Lugar Domenici legislation that was aimed at better preparing this nation and its responsible organizations for a terrorist attack. The Nunn-Lugar-Domenici legislation provided the primary authority and focus for domestic federal preparedness activities for terrorism. Several agencies — including the FEMA, Department of Justice (DOJ), Department of Health and Human Resources (DHHS), DOD, and the National Guard — were involved in the terrorism issue, and all were jockeying for the leadership position. Several attempts at coordination among these various agencies were launched, but in general, each agency pursued its own agenda. The single factor that provided the greatest distinction between these agencies related to the levels of funding they received, with DOD and DOJ controlling the majority of what was allocated. State and local governments generally found themselves confused by the federal government's approach, and likewise felt unprepared as a result. Although many of these state and local agencies appealed to the federal government to recognize local vulnerabilities and to establish stronger systems to accommodate anticipated needs, the majority rarely considered the possibility of an attack at all. The Oklahoma City bombing tested this thesis and set the stage for interagency disagreements over which agency would be in charge of terrorism.

The Nunn-Lugar legislation of 1995 (Defense against Weapons of Mass Destruction Act of 1996) left open the question as to who would be the lead agency in terrorism. Many fault FEMA leadership for not quickly claiming that role and the late 1990s were marked by several different agencies and departments assuming various roles in terrorism planning. The question of who should respond first to a terrorism incident — fire or police department, emergency management, or emergency medical personnel — the FBI, DOJ, or FEMA — was closely examined, but no clear answers emerged. The state directors looked to FEMA to claim the leadership role. In an uncharacteristic way, the leadership of FEMA vacillated on this issue. Terrorism was certainly part of the all-hazards approach to emergency management championed by FEMA, but the resources and technologies needed to address specific issues, such as weapons of mass destruction and the consequences of a chemical/biological attack, seemed well beyond the reach of the current disaster structure.

■ ■ Critical Thinking ■

Was there an obvious federal agency to be named as lead? If so, which one and what is the rationale for naming that Agency?

Khobar Towers Bombing, Saudi Arabia

On June 25, 1996, a truck bomb was detonated at the U.S. forces command in the Khobar Towers building in Riyadh. The force of the bomb damaged or destroyed six high-rise buildings within the compound. The blast was felt 20 miles away. Some security measures that had been previously erected including Jersey barriers and the marble construction of the building minimized damages. The quick actions of an Air Force sentry, noticing the suspicious actions of the terrorists and alerting security, minimized the deaths and injuries. In anonymous communications to the United States prior to the attack, there were indications that some level of attack would occur as an impetus to get the U.S. troops out of the country. In the aftermath of the attack, the U.S. military and different members of the intelligence-gathering community were criticized for the lack of preparation for such an event. Most people viewed this as an intelligence failure.

The Three Commissions

In 1998, President Clinton and House Speaker Newt Gingrich petitioned Congress to form a 14-member panel called the United States Commission on National Security/21st Century (USCNS/21), also known as the Hart-Rudman Commission, to make strategic recommendations on how the U.S. government could ensure the nation's security in the coming years. The independent panel, created by Congress, was tasked with conducting a comprehensive review of American security with the goal of designing a national security strategy.

The commission's report, titled "Road Map for National Security: Imperative for Change," dated January 31, 2001, recommended the creation of a new independent National Homeland Security Agency (NHSA) with responsibility for planning, coordinating, and integrating various U.S. government activities involved in homeland security. This agency would be built on the FEMA, with the Coast Guard, the Customs Service, and the U.S. Border Patrol (now part of U.S. Customs and Border Protection [CBP] within the DHS) transferred into it. NHSA would assume responsibility for the safety of the American people as well as oversee the protection of critical infrastructure, including information technology. Obviously, the commission's recommendations were not heeded before 2001, but many of its findings would later be integrated into the justification and legislation behind the creation of the DHS.

Two other commissions were established to study the terrorist threat during these years: the Gilmore Commission and the Bremer Commission, as discussed next.

The Gilmore Commission, also known as the Advisory Panel to Assess Domestic Response Capabilities for Terrorism Involving Weapons of Mass Destruction, produced a series of annual reports beginning in 1999 (with the final report released in 2003). Each of these reports presented a growing base of knowledge concerning the weapons of mass destruction (WMD) risk faced by the United States, and a recommended course of action required to counter that risk.

The Bremer Commission, also known as the National Commission on Terrorism, addressed the issue of the international terrorist threat. The commission was mandated by Congress to evaluate the nation's laws, policies, and practices for preventing terrorism and for punishing those responsible for terrorist events. Its members drafted a report titled "Countering the Changing Threat of International Terrorism." This report, issued in 2000, arrived at the following conclusions:

- International terrorism poses an increasingly dangerous and difficult threat to America.
- Countering the growing danger of the terrorist threat requires significantly stepping up the U.S. efforts.
- Priority one is to prevent terrorist attacks. U.S. intelligence and law enforcement communities must use the full scope of their authority to collect intelligence regarding terrorist plans and methods.
- U.S. policies must firmly target all states that support terrorists.

- Private sources of financial and logistical support for terrorists must be subjected to the full force and sweep of U.S. and international laws.
- A terrorist attack involving a biological agent, deadly chemicals, or nuclear or radiological material, even if it succeeds only partially, could profoundly affect the entire nation. The government must do more to prepare for such an event.
- The president and Congress should reform the system for reviewing and funding departmental counterterrorism programs to ensure that the activities and programs of various agencies are part of a comprehensive plan.

Each of these conclusions and recommendations would take on new meaning in the aftermath of the September 11 attacks, and would guide many of the changes incorporated into the Homeland Security Act of 2002. However, in the absence of a greater recognition of a terrorist threat within the borders of the United States, no major programs were initiated to combat the growing risk.

■ ■ Critical Thinking ■

President Clinton and Congress were concerned enough about terrorism in the late 1990s that they chose to form and fund the three terrorism commissions. Do you feel that the U.S. public was adequately concerned or aware of the threat of terrorism during this time, and leading up to the September 11 terrorist attacks? Do you believe that the U.S. government was adequately concerned during this same time period? Explain your answer.

Presidential Decision Directives 62 and 63

As these commissions were conducting their research, President Clinton was addressing other recognized and immediate needs through the passage of several presidential decision directives (PDDs). Terrorist attacks continued to occur throughout the world, aimed at U.S. government, military, and private interests. In 1996, terrorists carried out a suicide bombing at U.S. military barracks (Khobar Towers) in Saudi Arabia, and in 1998, simultaneous bombings were carried out at the U.S. diplomatic missions in Kenya and Tanzania.

In May 1998, President Clinton issued PDD-62, "Combating Terrorism," which called for the establishment of the Office of the National Coordinator for Security, Infrastructure Protection and Counterterrorism. The directive's primary goal was to create a new and more systematic approach to fighting the terrorist threat. PDD-62 reinforced the mission of many U.S. agencies involved in a wide array of counterterrorism activities. The new national coordinator was tasked with overseeing a broad variety of relevant policies and programs including counterterrorism, critical infrastructure protection, WMD preparedness, and consequence management.

Soon after this directive, President Clinton issued PDD-63, "Protecting America's Critical Infrastructure." This directive tasked all of the departments of the federal government with assessing the vulnerabilities of their cyber and physical infrastructures and with working to reduce their exposure to new and existing threats.

Attorney General's Five-Year Interagency Counterterrorism and Technology Crime Plan

In December 1998, as mandated by Congress, the DOJ, through the FBI, began a coordinated project with other agencies to develop the Attorney General's Five-Year Interagency Counterterrorism and Technology

Crime Plan. The FBI emerged as the federal government's principal agency for responding to and investigating terrorism. Congress had intended the plan to serve as a baseline for the coordination of a national strategy and operational capabilities to combat terrorism. This plan represented a substantial interagency effort, including goals, objectives, performance indicators, and recommended specific agency actions to help resolve interagency problems. It clearly did not, however, tear down the walls that prevented interagency sharing of information, as evidenced by the failures that resulted in the success of the 9/11 terrorists.

General Accounting Office Findings on Terrorism

The DOJ asserted that the Attorney General's Five-Year Interagency Counterterrorism and Technology Crime Plan, considered together with related PDDs as described earlier, represented a comprehensive national strategy to address the terrorist threat. However, after a thorough review, the GAO, Congress's investigative arm, concluded that additional work remained that would build on the progress that the plan represented. The GAO contended that a comprehensive national security strategy was lacking.

The GAO report "Combating Terrorism: Comments on Counterterrorism Leadership and National Strategy" (GAO-01-55T), released March 27, 2001, stated that the DOJ plan did not have measurable outcomes and suggested, for example, that it should include goals that improve state and local response capabilities. The report argued that without a clearly defined national strategy, the nation would continue to miss opportunities to focus and shape counterterrorism programs to meet the impending threat. It also made the criticism that the DOJ plan lacked a coherent framework to develop and evaluate budget requirements for combating terrorism since there was no single focal point. The report claimed that no single entity was acting as the federal government's top official accountable to both the president and the Congress for the terrorism hazard and that fragmentation existed in both coordination of domestic preparedness programs and efforts to develop a national strategy.

The GAO released another report in early September 2001 titled "Combating Terrorism: Selected Challenges and Related Recommendations" (GAO-01-822), which it finalized in the last days before the terrorist attacks occurred in Washington and New York. The report stated that the federal government was ill equipped and unprepared to counter a major terrorist attack, claiming also that — from sharing intelligence to coordinating a response — the government had failed to put in place an effective critical infrastructure system. It further stated that

> *Federal efforts to develop a national strategy to combat terrorism … have progressed, but key challenges remain. The initial step toward developing a national strategy is to conduct a national threat and risk assessment … at the national level (agencies) have not completed assessments of the most likely weapon-of-mass destruction agents and other terrorist threats. …*

To prevent terrorist attacks, the GAO recommended:

- A national strategy to combat terrorism and computer-based attacks
- Better protection for the nation's infrastructure
- A single focal point to oversee coordination of federal programs

- Completion of a threat assessment on likely WMD and other weapons that might be used by terrorists
- Revision of the Attorney General's Five-Year Interagency Counterterrorism and Technology Crime Plan to better serve as a national strategy
- Coordination of research and development to combat terrorism

In a later report regarding Homeland Security, "Key Elements to Unify Efforts Are Underway But Uncertainty Remains" (GAO-02-610), the GAO called for more of the same in terms of needing central leadership and an overarching strategy that identifies goals and objectives, priorities, measurable outcomes, and state and local government roles in combating terrorism since the efforts of more than 40 federal entities and numerous state and local governments were still fragmented. It also called for the term *homeland security* to be defined properly since to date it had not.

USS Cole Bombing, Yemen

On October 12, 2000, while refueling in the port of Aden in Yemen, the U.S. Navy destroyer the USS Cole sustained a suicide bomb attack. The terrorist organization Al-Qaeda claimed responsibility for the attack that took the lives of 17 Navy sailors with an additional 39 injured. However, evidence of Al-Qaeda involvement was inconclusive. The 9/11 Commission report does indicate that in December 2000, the Central Intelligence Agency (CIA) had made a preliminary conclusion that Al-Qaeda may have supported the attack. Intelligence agencies produced videos showing Al-Qaeda members and Osama Bin Laden celebrating the bombing of the USS Cole. Further intelligence indicated Bin Laden expressing disappointment that the United States did not retaliate for the attack. There was thought to be complicity by the government of the Sudan, and a U.S. judge determined that Sudan was liable for the attack. At the time, then President Clinton declared it an "act of terrorism." However, some people have questioned whether an attack against a military installation meets the legal definition of "terrorism" as opposed to an act of war. Both the Clinton and, later, the Bush administrations have been criticized for not responding with military force on this attack before the September 11 attack. The Navy, however, was quick to act. They opened an Anti-Terrorism and Force Protection Warfare Center and aggressively implemented stronger Random Anti-Terrorism Measures (RAM) to their security posture. The attack on the USS Cole added to an already heightened terrorism profile within the federal government, especially within the intelligence community.

September 11 Attacks on the World Trade Center and the Pentagon

The concept of homeland security was born on September 11, 2001. On that day, terrorists hijacked four planes and crashed them into the twin towers of the WTC in New York City, the Pentagon in Washington, D.C., and a field in Pennsylvania (see sidebar "September 11, 2001, Terrorist Attacks Timeline"). These actions resulted in the collapse of both twin towers, the collapse of a section of the Pentagon, and the crash of a domestic airliner that resulted in unprecedented deaths and injuries:

- Total deaths for all 9/11 attacks: 2,974 (not counting the 19 terrorists)
- Total injured for all 9/11 attacks: 2,337
- Total deaths in the World Trade Center towers: 2,603

- Total injured at World Trade Center: 2,261
- Total firefighter deaths at World Trade Center: 343
- Total police deaths at World Trade Center: 75
- Total deaths at Pentagon: 125
- Total injured at Pentagon: 76
- Total deaths, American Flight 77, Pentagon: 59
- Total deaths, United Airlines Flight 93, Pennsylvania: 40
- Total deaths, American Airlines Flight 11, WTC North Tower: 88
- Total deaths, United Airlines Flight 175, WTC South Tower: 59 (From: www.september11news .com/911Art.htm and http://en.wikipedia.org/wiki/September_11,_2001_Terrorist_Attack)

September 11, 2001, Terrorist Attacks Timeline for the Day of the Attacks

7:58 AM: American Airlines Flight 11, a fully fueled Boeing 767 carrying 81 passengers and 11 crew members, departs from Boston Logan airport, bound for Los Angeles, California.

8:00 AM: United Airlines Flight 175, another fully fueled Boeing 767, carrying 56 passengers and 9 crew members, departs from Boston's Logan airport, bound for Los Angeles, California.

8:10 AM: American Airlines Flight 77, a Boeing 757 with 58 passengers and 6 crew members, departs from Washington's Dulles airport for Los Angeles, California.

8:40 AM: The Federal Aviation Administration (FAA) notifies North American Aerospace Defense Command (NORAD) about the suspected hijacking of American Airlines Flight 11.

8:42 AM: United Airlines Flight 93, a Boeing 757, takes off with 37 passengers and 7 crew members from Newark airport bound for San Francisco, following a 40-minute delay caused by congested runways. Its flight path initially takes it close to the World Trade Center.

8:43 AM: The FAA notifies NORAD about the suspected hijacking of United Airlines Flight 175.

8:46:26 AM: American Airlines Flight 11 crashes with a speed of roughly 490 miles per hour into the north side of the north tower of the World Trade Center, between floors 94 and 98. (Many accounts have given times that range between 8:45 AM and 8:50 AM). The building's structural type, pioneered in the late 1960s to maximize rentable floor space and featuring lightweight tubular design with no masonry elements in the facade, allows the jetliner to literally enter the tower, mostly intact. It plows to the building core, severing all three gypsum-encased stairwells and dragging combustibles with it. A massive shock wave travels down to the ground and up again. The combustibles, as well as the remnants of the aircraft, are ignited by the burning fuel. Because the building lacks a traditional full-cage frame and depends almost entirely on the strength of a narrow structural core running up the center, the fire at the center of the impact zone is in a position to compromise the integrity of all internal columns. People below the severed stairwells in the north tower start to evacuate. Officials in the south tower tell people shortly afterward by megaphone and office announcements that they are safe and can return to their offices. Some don't hear it; some ignore it and evacuate anyway; others congregate in common areas such as the 78th-floor sky lobby to discuss their options.

9:02:54 AM: United Airlines Flight 175 crashes with a speed of about 590 miles per hour into the south side of the south tower, banked between floors 78 and 84 in full view of media cameras. Parts of the plane leave the building at its east and north sides, falling to the ground six blocks away. A passenger on the plane, Peter Hanson, had called his father earlier from the plane reporting that hijackers were stabbing flight attendants in order to force the crew to open the cockpit doors.

8:46 AM to 10:29 AM: At least 20 people, primarily in the north tower, trapped by fire and smoke in the upper floors, jump to their deaths. There is some evidence that large central portions of the floor near the impact zone in the north tower collapsed soon after the plane hit, perhaps convincing some people that total collapse was imminent. One person at street level, firefighter Daniel Thomas Suhr, is hit by a jumper and dies. No form of airborne evacuation is attempted because the smoke is too dense for a successful landing on the roof of either tower, or New York City lacks helicopters specialized for horizontal rescue.

9:04 AM (approximately): The FAA's air route traffic control center in Boston stops all departures from airports in its jurisdiction (New England and eastern New York State).

9:06 AM: The FAA bans takeoffs of all flights bound to or through the airspace of New York center from airports in that center and the three adjacent centers — Boston, Cleveland, and Washington. This is referred to as a first-tier ground stop and covers the Northeast from North Carolina north and as far west as eastern Michigan.

9:08 AM: The FAA bans all takeoffs nationwide for flights going to or through New York center airspace.

9:24 AM: President George W. Bush is interrupted with the news of the second crash as he participates in a class filled with Florida schoolchildren. He waits out the lesson and then rushes into another classroom commandeered by the Secret Service. Within minutes he makes a short statement, calling the developments "a national tragedy," and is hurried aboard Air Force One.

9:24 AM: The FAA notifies NORAD's Northeast Air Defense Sector about the suspected hijacking of American Airlines Flight 77. The FAA and NORAD establish an open line to discuss American Airlines Flight 77 and United Airlines Flight 93.

9:26 AM: The FAA bans takeoffs of all civilian aircraft regardless of destination — a national ground stop.

9:37 AM: American Airlines Flight 77 crashes into the western side of the Pentagon and starts a violent fire. The section of the Pentagon hit consists mainly of newly renovated, unoccupied offices. Passenger Barbara K. Olson had called her husband, Solicitor General Theodore Olson, at the Justice Department twice from the plane to tell him about the hijacking and to report that the passengers and pilots were held in the back of the plane. As bright flames and dark smoke envelop the west side of America's military nerve center, all doubts about the terrorist nature of the attacks are gone.

9:45 AM: United States airspace is shut down. No civilian aircraft are allowed to lift off, and all aircraft in flight are ordered to land at the nearest airport as soon as practical. All air traffic headed for the United States is redirected to Canada. Later, the FAA announces that civilian flights are suspended until at least noon, September 12. The groundings last until September 14, but there are exemptions for Saudi families who fear retribution if they stay in the United States. Military and medical flights continue. This is the fourth time all commercial flights in the United States have been stopped, and the first time a suspension was unplanned. All previous suspensions were military related (Sky Shield I–III) and took place from 1960 to 1962.

9:45 AM: The White House and the Capitol are closed.

9:50 AM (approximately): The Associated Press reports that American Airlines Flight 11 was apparently hijacked after departure from Boston's Logan Airport. Within an hour, this report is confirmed for both Flight 11 and United Airlines Flight 175.

9:57 AM: President Bush is moved from Florida.

9:59:04 AM: The south tower of the World Trade Center collapses. A vast TV and radio audience reacts primarily with horrified astonishment. It is later widely reported that the collapse was not directly caused by the jetliner's impact but that the intense sustained heat of the fuel fire was mostly or wholly responsible for the loss of structural integrity. Later, a growing number of structural engineers assert that the fire alone would not have caused the collapse. Both towers made use of external load-bearing mini columns, and on one face of each building approximately 40 of these were severed by the jetliners. Had they been intact to efficiently distribute the increasing gravity load as the bunched core columns and joist trusses weakened in the fires, the towers might have stood far longer or perhaps indefinitely. Concrete in the towers' facades might have prevented most of the debris and fuel from reaching the building core. Investigations that may radically change skyscraper design (or result in a radical retreat to full-cage construction with high concrete-to-steel ratios as in pre-1960s skyscrapers) are ongoing.

10:03 AM: United Airlines Flight 93 crashes southeast of Pittsburgh in Somerset County, Pennsylvania. Other reports say 10:06 or 10:10. According to seismographic data readings, the time of impact was 10:06:05. The first reports from the police indicate that none on board survived. Later reports indicate that passengers speaking on cell phones had learned about the World Trade Center and Pentagon crashes and at least three were planning on resisting the hijackers. It is likely that the resistance led to the plane crashing before it reached its intended target. Reports stated that an eyewitness saw a white plane resembling a fighter jet circling the site minutes after the crash. These reports have limited credibility, although fighter jets had been scrambled to defend the Washington, DC, region earlier. These jets, however, stayed within the immediate DC area.

10:10 AM: Part of the Pentagon collapses.

10:13 AM: Thousands are involved in an evacuation of the United Nations complex in New York.

10:15 AM (approximately): The Democratic Front for the Liberation of Palestine is reported to have taken responsibility for the crashes, but this is denied by a senior officer of the group soon after.

10:28:31 AM: The north tower of the World Trade Center collapses from the top down, as if being peeled apart. Probably as a result of the destruction of the gypsum-encased stairwells on the impact floors (most skyscraper stairwells are encased in reinforced concrete), no one above the impact zone in the north tower survives. The fact that the north tower stood much longer than the south one is later attributed to three facts: The region of impact was higher (which meant that the gravity load on the most damaged area was lighter), the speed of the airplane was lower, and the fireproofing in the affected floors had been partially upgraded. Also, the hottest part of the fire in the south tower burned in a corner of the structure, perhaps leading to a more concentrated failure of columns or joist trusses or both. The Marriott Hotel, located at the base of the two towers, is also destroyed.

10:35 AM (approximately): Police are reportedly alerted about a bomb in a car outside the State Department in Washington, DC. Later reports claim that nothing happened at the State Department.

10:39 AM: Another hijacked jumbo jet is claimed to be headed for Washington, DC. F-15s are scrambled and patrol the airspace above Washington, DC, while other fighter jets sweep the airspace above New York City. They have orders, first issued by Vice President Cheney and later confirmed by President Bush, to shoot down any potentially dangerous planes that do not comply with orders given to them via radio.

10:45 AM: CNN reports that a mass evacuation of Washington, DC, and New York has been initiated. The UN headquarters are already empty. A few minutes later, New York's mayor orders an evacuation of lower Manhattan.

10:50 AM: Five stories of part of the Pentagon collapse as a result of the fire.

10:53 AM: New York's primary elections are canceled.

11:15 AM (approximately): Reports surfaced that the F-15s over Washington had shot something down. There was no later confirmation of these reports.

11:16 AM: American Airlines confirms the loss of its two airplanes.

11:17 AM: United Airlines confirms the loss of Flight 93 and states that it is "deeply concerned" about Flight 175.

11:53 AM: United Airlines confirms the loss of its two airplanes.

11:55 AM: The border between the United States and Mexico is on highest alert, but has not been closed.

12:00 PM (approximately): President Bush arrives at Barksdale Air Force Base in Louisiana. He was on a trip in Sarasota, Florida, to speak about education but is now presumed to be returning to the capital. He makes a brief and informal initial statement to the effect that terrorism on U.S. soil will not be tolerated, stating that "freedom itself has been attacked and freedom will be protected."

12:02 PM: The Taliban government of Afghanistan denounces the attacks.

12:04 PM: Los Angeles International Airport, the intended destination of Flight 11, Flight 77, and Flight 175 is shut down.

12:15 PM: San Francisco International Airport, the intended destination of United Airlines Flight 93, is shut down.

12:15 PM (approximately): The airspace over the 48 contiguous United States is clear of all commercial and private flights.

1:00 PM (approximately): At the Pentagon, fire crews are still fighting fires. The early response to the attack had been coordinated from the National Military Command Center, but that location had to be evacuated when it began to fill with smoke.

1:04 PM: President Bush puts the U.S. military on high alert worldwide. He speaks from Barksdale Air Force Base and leaves for the Strategic Air Command bunker in Nebraska.

1:27 PM: Mayor Anthony A. Williams of Washington, DC, declares a state of emergency; the DC National Guard arrives on site.

2:30 PM: Senator John McCain characterizes the attack as an "act of war."

2:49 PM: At a press conference in New York, Mayor Rudy Giuliani is asked to estimate the number of casualties at the World Trade Center. He replies, "More than any of us can bear."

4:00 PM: National news outlets report that high officials in the federal intelligence community are stating that Osama bin Laden is the primary suspect in the attacks.

4:25 PM: The New York Stock Exchange, NASDAQ, and the American Stock Exchange report that they will remain closed on Wednesday, September 12.

5:20 PM: Salomon Brothers 7, commonly referred to as "7 World Trade Center," a 47-storey building that had sustained what was originally thought to be light damage in the fall of the twin towers and was earlier reported on fire, collapses. Structural engineers are puzzled, and the investigation continues. The building was not designed by the same team responsible for the twin towers. The building contained New York's special emergency center, which may well have been intended for such a disaster as September 11.

6:00 PM: Explosions and tracer fire are reported in Kabul, the capital of Afghanistan, by CNN and the BBC. The Northern Alliance, involved in a civil war with the Taliban government, is later reported to have attacked Kabul's airport with helicopter gunships.

6:00 PM: Iraq announces that the attacks are the fruit of "U.S. crimes against humanity" in an official announcement on state television.

6:54 PM: President Bush finally arrives at the White House. Executive authority through much of the day had rested with Vice President Cheney.

7:00 PM: Frantic efforts to locate survivors in the rubble that had been the twin towers continue. Fleets of ambulances have been lined up to transport the injured to nearby hospitals. They stand empty. "Ground Zero" is the exclusive domain of the FDNY and NYPD, despite volunteer steel and construction workers who stand ready to move large quantities of debris quickly. Relatives and friends displaying enlarged photographs of the missing printed on home computer printers are flooding downtown. The New York Armory, at Lexington Avenue and 26th Street, and Union Square Park, at 14th Street, become centers of vigil.

7:30 PM: The U.S. government denies any responsibility for reported explosions in Kabul.

8:30 PM: President Bush addresses the nation from the White House. Among his remarks: "Terrorist attacks can shake the foundations of our biggest buildings, but they cannot touch the foundation of America. These acts shatter steel, but they cannot dent the steel of American resolve."

9:00 PM: President Bush meets with his full National Security Council, followed roughly half an hour later by a meeting with a smaller group of key advisers. Bush and his advisers have evidence that Osama bin Laden is behind the attacks.

11:00 PM: There are reports of survivors buried in the rubble in New York making cell phone calls. These rumors were later proved to be wrong (www.wikipedia.com).

Note: All times in New York time (EDT). This is four hours before GMT. Tuesday, September 11, 2001

The response to these attacks by fire, police, and emergency medical teams was immediate, and their combined efforts saved hundreds if not thousands of lives, especially at the WTC. The following facts provide additional insight into the situation faced by the responders that day:

- Year the World Trade Center was built: 1970
- Number of companies housed in the World Trade Center: 430
- Number working in World Trade Center on average working day before September 11: 50,000
- Average number of daily visitors: 140,000
- Maximum heat of fires, in degrees Fahrenheit, at World Trade Center site: 2,300
- Number of days underground fires at World Trade Center continued to burn: 69
- Number of days that workers dug up debris at Ground Zero, searching for body parts: 230

- Number of body parts collected: 19,500
- Number of bodies discovered intact: 291
- Number of victims identified by New York medical examiner: 1,102
- Number of death certificates issued without a body at request of victims' families: 1,616
- Number of people still classified as missing from the World Trade Center that day: 105
- Number of people who survived the collapse of the towers: 16 (http://observer.guardian
.co.uk/waronterrorism/story/0,1373,776451,00.html and www.snopes.com/rumors/survivor.htm)

The addition of another stairway in each tower, the widening of existing stairways, and regular evacuation drills — actions implemented in the aftermath of the 1993 WTC bombing — are all credited with facilitating the evacuation of thousands of office workers in the towers before they collapsed. Federal, state, and nongovernmental groups (e.g., Red Cross, Salvation Army) also responded quickly, establishing relief centers and dispensing critical services to victims and first responders. The following list illustrates the relief efforts that ensued:

- Cases opened: 55,494
- Mental health contacts made: 240,417
- Health services contacts made: 133,035
- Service delivery sites opened: 101
- Shelters opened: 60
- Shelter population: 3,554
- Meals/snacks served: 14,113,185
- Response vehicles assigned: 292
- Disaster workers assigned: 57,434 (www.redcrossalbq.org/04a_911statistics.html)

In addition to the stunning loss of life and the physical destruction caused by the attacks, two other losses are significant for their size and impact. First, 343 New York City firefighters and 75 New York City police officers were lost in the WTC when the towers collapsed, setting a record for the highest number lost in a single disaster event in the United States. Their untimely deaths brought extraordinary attention to America's courageous and professional firefighters, police officers, and emergency medical technicians. They became the heroes of September 11, and this increased attention has resulted in increased funding for government programs that provide equipment and training for first responders. It has also resulted in a reexamination of protocols and procedures in light of the new terrorist threat.

The second significant aspect of the September 11 attacks is the magnitude and the scope of the losses resulting from the attacks. The total economic impact on New York City alone is estimated to be between $82.8 and $94.8 billion. This estimate includes $21.8 billion in lost buildings, infrastructure, and tenant assets; $8.7 billion in the future earnings of those who died; and $52.3 to $64.3 billion gross city product (Curci, 2004). The economic impact of the attacks was felt throughout the United States and the world, causing jobs to be lost and businesses to fail in communities hundreds and thousands of miles from Ground Zero:

- Value of U.S. economy: $11 trillion
- Estimated cost of attacks to United States based solely on property losses and insurance costs: $21 billion

- Amount of office space lost, in square feet: 13.5 million
- Estimated number of jobs lost in lower Manhattan area following September 11: 100,000
- Estimated number of jobs lost in the United States as a result of the attacks, by the end of 2002: 1.8 million
- Number of jobs lost in U.S. travel industry in the final 5 months of 2001: 237,000
- Amount allocated by Congress for emergency assistance to airline industry in September 2001: $15 billion (http://observer.guardian.co.uk/waronterrorism/story/0,1373,776451,00.html)

The federal government costs were extraordinary, and spending by FEMA on these events easily exceeded its spending on past natural disasters and disasters that have happened since (see also Table 2–1):

- Direct emergency assistance from FEMA: $297 million
- Aid to individuals and families: $255 million
- Direct housing: 8,957 applications processed; 5,287 applications approved (59%)
- Mortgage and rental assistance: 11,818 applications processed; 6,187 applications approved (52%)

Table 2–1 Top Ten Natural Disasters (Ranked by FEMA Relief Costs)

Event	Year	FEMA Funding
Hurricane Katrina (AL, LA, MS)	2005	$7.2 billion[a]
Northridge Earthquake (CA)	1994	$6.961 billion
Hurricane Georges (AL, FL, LA, MS, PR, VI)	1998	$2.251 billion
Hurricane Ivan (AL, FL, GA, LA, MS, NC, NJ, NY, PA, TN, WVA)	2004	$1.947 billion[b]
Hurricane Andrew (FL, LA)	1992	$1.813 billion
Hurricane Charley (FL, SC)	2004	$1.559 billion[b]
Hurricane Frances (FL, GA, NC, NY, OH, PA, SC)	2004	$1.425 billion[b]
Hurricane Jeanne (DE, FL, PR, VI, VA)	2004	$1.407 billion[b]
Tropical Storm Allison (FL, LA, MS, PA, TX)	2001	$1.387 billion
Hurricane Hugo (NC, SC, PR, VI)	1989	$1.307 billion

[a]Amount obligated from the President's Disaster Relief Fund for FEMA's assistance programs, hazard mitigation grants, federal mission assignments, contractual services, and administrative costs as of March 31, 2006. Figures do not include funding provided by other participating federal agencies, such as the disaster loan programs of the Small Business Administration and the Agriculture Department's Farm Service Agency.
Note: Funding amounts are stated in nominal dollars, unadjusted for inflation.
[b]Amount obligated from the President's Disaster Relief Fund for FEMA's assistance programs, hazard mitigation grants, federal mission assignments, contractual services, and administrative costs as of May 31, 2005. Figures do not include funding provided by other participating federal agencies, such as the disaster loan programs of the Small Business Administration and the Agriculture Department's Farm Service Agency.
Note: Funding amounts are stated in nominal dollars, unadjusted for inflation.
Source: Federal Emergency Management Agency (FEMA), "Top Ten Natural Disasters: Ranked by FEMA Relief Costs," http://www.fema.gov/hazard/topten.shtm.
Last Modified: Wednesday, August 11, 2010, 14:38:40 EDT.

- Individual and family grant program: 43,660 applications processed; 6,139 applications approved (14%)
- Disaster unemployment: 6,657 claims processed; 3,210 claims approved (48%)
- Crisis counseling: $166 million
- Aid to government and nonprofits: $4.49 billion
- Debris removal: $437 million
- Overtime for New York Police Department (NYPD): $295.4 million
- Overtime for the New York Fire Department: $105.6 million (Federal Emergency Management Agency, 2003)

The insurance losses resulting from the September 11 events were also extraordinary, especially when considered in light of the relatively small amount of physical property that was directly affected by the events themselves. Despite the fact that many natural hazards affect hundreds, if not thousands and even tens of thousands, of square miles of inhabited and developed land, thereby affecting thousands of structures and infrastructure components, these terrorist attacks that were isolated to one neighborhood in New York City and one building in Arlington, Virginia, exceeded all but two events worldwide in terms of their insurance-related disaster losses (Tables 2–2 and 2–3). This comprehensive terrorist attack

Table 2–2 The Ten Most Costly World Insurance Losses, 1970–2010[a] ($ millions)

Rate	Date	Country	Event	Insured Loss in 2010 ($)[b]
1	Aug. 25, 2005	U.S., Gulf of Mexico, Bahamas, North Atlantic	Hurricane Katrina: floods, dams burst, damage to oil rigs	72,302
2	Aug. 23, 1992	U.S., Bahamas	Hurricane Andrew: floods	24,870
3	Sep. 11, 2001	U.S.	Terror attacks on WTC, Pentagon, and other buildings	23,131
4	Jan. 17, 1994	U.S.	Northridge earthquake (M 6.6)	20,601
5	Sep. 6, 2008	U.S., Caribbean, Gulf of Mexico, etc.	Hurricane Ike: floods, offshore damage	20,483
6	Sep. 2, 2004	U.S., Caribbean, Barbados, etc.	Hurricane Ivan: damage to oil rigs	14,876
7	Oct. 19, 2005	U.S., Mexico, Jamaica, Haiti, etc.	Hurricane Wilma: floods	14,028
8	Sep. 20, 2005	U.S., Gulf of Mexico, Cuba	Hurricane Rita: floods, damage to oil rigs	11,266
9	Aug. 11, 2004	U.S., Cuba, Jamaica, etc.	Hurricane Charley: floods	9,295
10	Sep. 27, 1991	Japan	Typhoon Mireille/No. 19	9,041

[a]Property and business interruption losses, excluding life and liability losses. Includes flood losses in the United States insured via the National Flood Insurance Program.
[b]Adjusted to 2010 dollars by Swiss Re.
Source: Swiss Re, *sigma*, No. 1/2011. International Insurance Institute, International Insurance Factbook, "World Rankings," 2007. http://www.iii.org/international/rankings/
Note: Loss data shown here may differ from figures shown elsewhere for the same event due to differences in the date of publication, the geographical area covered, and other criteria used by organizations collecting the data.

Table 2–3 The Ten Most Costly Catastrophes, United States[a] ($ millions)

Rank	Date	Peril	Insured Loss	
			Dollars When Occurred	**In 2009 ($)[b]**
1	Aug. 2005	Hurricane Katrina	41,100	45,115
2	Sep. 2001	Fire, explosion: World Trade Center, Pentagon terrorist attacks	18,779	22,739
3	Aug. 1992	Hurricane Andrew	15,500	22,231
4	Jan. 1994	Northridge, CA earthquake	12,500	17,179
5	Sep. 2008	Hurricane Ike	12,500	12,648
6	Oct. 2005	Hurricane Wilma	10,300	11,306
7	Aug. 2004	Hurricane Charley	7,475	8,479
8	Sep. 2004	Hurricane Ivan	7,110	8,065
9	Sep. 1989	Hurricane Hugo	4,195	6,624
10	Sep. 2005	Hurricane Rita	5,627	6,177

[a]Property coverage only. Does not include flood damage covered by the federally administered National Flood Insurance Program.
[b]Adjusted for inflation through 2009 by ISO using the GDP implicit price deflator.
Source: ISO's Property Claim Services (PCS) unit. Insurance Services Office, Inc., Insurance Information Institute, http://www.iii.org/media/facts/statsbyissue/catastrophes/

illustrates the far-reaching indirect, intangible consequences of terrorism, and their potential for damaging a nation's economy:

- Amount of federal aid New York received within 2 months of the September 11 events: $9.5 billion
- Amount collected by the 11 September Fund: $501 million
- Percentage of fund used for cash assistance and services such as grief counseling for families of victims and survivors: 89
- Quantity, in pounds, of food and supplies supplied by 11 September Fund at Ground Zero: 4.3 million
- Number of hot meals served to rescue workers by 11 September Fund: 343,000
- Number of displaced workers receiving job referrals: 5,000
- Amount of compensation sought by the families of civilian casualties of U.S. bombing in Afghanistan from the U.S. government: $10,000
- Amount of compensation sought for reckless misconduct and negligence from American Airlines by husband of September 11 victim: $50 million (http://observer.guardian.co.uk/waronterrorism/story/0,1373,776451,00.html)

The Creation of the Department of Homeland Security: 2001–2004

In the immediate aftermath of the September 11 attacks, as search-and-rescue teams were still sifting through the debris and wreckage for survivors in New York, Pennsylvania, and Virginia, the federal government was analyzing what had just happened and what it could quickly do to begin the process of ensuring such attacks could not be repeated. It was recognized that nothing too substantial could take place without longer term study and congressional review, but the circumstances mandated that real changes begin without delay.

On September 20, 2001, just 9 days after the attacks, President George W. Bush announced that an Office of Homeland Security would be established within the White House by executive order. Directing this office would be Pennsylvania Governor Tom Ridge. Ridge was given no real staff to manage, and the funding he would have at his disposal was minimal. The actual order, cataloged as Executive Order 13228, was given on October 8, 2001. In addition to creating the Office of Homeland Security, this order created the Homeland Security Council, "to develop and coordinate the implementation of a comprehensive national strategy to secure the United States from terrorist threats or attacks."

Four days later, on September 24, 2001, President Bush announced that he would be seeking passage of an act titled "Uniting and Strengthening America by Providing Appropriate Tools Required to Intercept and Obstruct Terrorism," which would become better known as the PATRIOT Act of 2001. This act, which introduced a large number of controversial legislative changes in order to significantly increase the surveillance and investigative powers of law enforcement agencies in the United States (as it states) to "... deter and punish terrorist acts in the United States and around the world," was signed into law by the president on October 26 after very little deliberation in Congress.

On October 29, 2001, President Bush issued the first of many homeland security presidential directives (HSPDs), which were specifically designed to "record and communicate presidential decisions about the homeland security policies of the United States" (HSPD-1, 2001). On March 21, 2002, President Bush signed Executive Order 13260 establishing the President's Homeland Security Advisory Council (PHSAC) and Senior Advisory Committees for Homeland Security.

In the flurry of legislation and presidential directives that were enacted immediately after September 11, the PATRIOT Act was clearly the most controversial. The PATRIOT Act of 2001 (Public Law 107–56) was signed into law by President Bush on October 26, 2001. This legislation was introduced in the U.S. House of Representatives by Representative F. James Sensenbrenner, Jr. (R-WI) on October 23, 2001, "to deter and punish terrorist acts in the United States and around the world, to enhance law enforcement investigatory tools, and for other purposes" (www.congress.gov, 2003).

Under normal circumstances, legislation, especially that which has broad-sweeping reach and which brings into question constitutional rights, requires years and even decades of deliberation before it is finally passed — if that day ever comes. Considering the PATRIOT Act was passed less than a month after the event that inspired it, with almost no significant deliberation, it can be regarded as an anomalous case, and one that, considering its comprehensive nature and its impact on civil liberties, deserves more detailed description.

The principal focus of the PATRIOT Act is to provide law enforcement agencies with the proper legal authority to support their efforts to collect information on suspected terrorists, to detain people suspected of being or aiding terrorists and terrorist organizations, to deter terrorists from entering and operating within the borders of the United States, and to further limit the ability of terrorists to engage in money-laundering activities that support terrorist actions. The major provisions of the PATRIOT Act are as follows:

- Relaxes restrictions on information sharing between U.S. law enforcement and intelligence officers on the subject of suspected terrorists.
- Makes it illegal to knowingly harbor a terrorist.

- Authorizes "roving wiretaps," which allows law enforcement officials to get court orders to wiretap any phone a suspected terrorist would use. The provision was needed, advocates said, with the advent of cellular and disposable phones.
- Allows the federal government to detain non-U.S. citizens suspected of terrorism for up to 7 days without specific charges (original versions of the legislation allowed for the holding of suspects indefinitely).
- Allows law enforcement officials greater subpoena power for e-mail records of terrorist suspects.
- Triples the number of border patrol personnel, customs service inspectors, and INS inspectors at the northern border of the United States and provides $100 million to improve technology and equipment on the U.S. border with Canada.
- Expands measures against money laundering by requiring additional record keeping and reports for certain transactions and requiring identification of account holders.
- Eliminates the statute of limitations for prosecuting the most egregious terrorist acts but maintains the statute of limitation on most crimes at 5–8 years.

The PATRIOT Act immediately sparked concern among citizens and organizations involved in protecting the civil rights and liberties of all Americans, although this concern only became more vocal as the time between the attacks increased due to the emotional sensitivities associated with what had transpired. The critics that have emerged, and which continue to emerge in growing numbers as the act is repeatedly renewed, have questioned the constitutionality of several of the act's provisions and have expressed grave concerns regarding the methods by which some of those new authorities will be used by law enforcement agencies in their pursuit of terrorists.

The U.S. attorney general at the time, John Ashcroft, and the DOJ that operated under his direction countered that these authorities are necessary if the U.S. government is to more effectively track and detain terrorists. Regardless, the act very quickly began generating lawsuits, resistance from community officials, and concern about the way its provisions were being used and abused outside of their intended scope in a way that affected everyday Americans with no association with terrorist activities. The position paper titled "Debating the USA Patriotic Act" presents both positive and negative perspectives on the PATRIOT Act.

■ ■ ■ ▬▬▬

Conclusion: An excerpt from "Debating the USA PATRIOT Act," by Donna L. Point

An Army Manual defines terrorism as "the calculated use of violence or threat of violence to attain goals that are political, religious or ideological in nature" (Chomsky 2003 pp. 605–606). This act of terrorism is carried out in various ways such as intimidation, coercion or instilling fear. Being safe and being free are not mutually exclusive. We do not gain one by giving up the other. The Constitution of the United States of America has survived many threats, including civil insurrections and world wars. It is precisely during times of crisis that rights must be most steadfastly defended. The protection of constitutional liberties need not, and indeed should not deprive the government of the authority necessary to vigorously apprehend terrorists, prosecute them and defend the homeland. America's credibility in the world has been dangerously compromised by the Bush administration's blatant disregard for the rule of law. The doctrine of preventive war, which was used to launch the "War on Terror," accords the Bush administration the sovereign right to take military action at will to control and destroy any challenge it perceives (Chomsky 2003). The Bush doctrine is in essence a return to the claim of right to use force or any other means necessary to pursue national interests (O'Connell 2003).

This is not the first time in American history that political leaders advocated and justified the suspension of civil liberties by emphasizing national security and evoking feelings of nationalism. As Benjamin Franklin once noted, "If we surrender our liberty in the name of security, we shall have neither" (Thornburgh 2005). In order to regain respect in the eyes of the world, the president must comply with all international agreements to which the United States is a party. Additionally, the United States must comply with customary international law, including the Geneva Conventions and the Convention Against Torture and Other Cruel, Inhuman or Degrading Treatment or Punishment. When we adopt the principle of universality we adhere to the premise: if an action is right or wrong for others, it is right or wrong for us as well. Those who do not rise to the minimal moral level of applying to themselves the standards they apply to others, cannot be taken seriously when they speak of right and wrong or good and evil. Only by respecting and obeying the law, as we compel other to do, can the United States enlist international cooperation in the "War on Terror"(Center for American Progress 2005; Chomsky 2002).

The USA PATRIOT Act Improvement and Reauthorization Act was signed into law on March 9, 2006. The Bush administration succeeded in avoiding the introduction of any restrictive judicial controls over permanent measures. Many of the provisions that had a "sunset" clause, meaning that once the clear and present danger dissipated they would disappear, did not happen. Instead, 14 temporary measures, adopted in 2001 as emergency procedures, were made a permanent part of the Act. The "new" Act authorizes the imprisonment, for an indefinite period of time, of foreigners suspected of terrorism, without trial or indictment. It also establishes widespread surveillance of the entire population. It left unchecked the provisions that grant "sneak and peek" warrants and National Security Letters among others. Government actions and official proceedings should be as transparent as possible in times of war and peace. The government should be held accountable for its actions through our system of checks and balances as the founding fathers intended. Measures undertaken by the government should be narrowly tailored to the goal of enhancing our security not threatening our civil liberties. President Bush has been quoted as saying that "There's no telling how many wars it will take to secure freedom in the homeland." We are now in the midst of a new political order. We have moved from a state of emergency into a permanent state of exception with no end in sight. It is very difficult to tell if one is a terrorist or not until they have committed a terrorist act. Unwarranted suspicion renders even a perfect procedure useless and may push the associative guilt beyond the legislative intent. This "war" has not divided the terrorists; it has divided the allies (Paye 2006).

Bibliography for Conclusion

Center for American Progress, 2005. Securing America, protecting our freedoms after September 11. In: Progressive Priorities: An Action Agenda for America, pp. 217–234.

Center for Democracy Technology, 2006. The Nature and Scope of Governmental Electronic Surveillance Activity, July 2006. http://www.cdt.org/wiretap/wiretap_overview.html

Chomsky, N., 2003. Commentary: moral truisms, empirical evidence, and foreign policy. Rev. Int. Studies 29, 605–620.

Chomsky, N., 2002. Terror and Just Response. ZNet, July 2, 2002. http://www.chomsky.info/articles/20020702.htm

O'Connell, M.E., 2003. Lawful and unlawful wars against terrorism. Law in the War on International Terrorism, 79–96.

Paye, J.-C., 2006. A permanent state of emergency. Monthly Review, November 2006: 29–37.

Thornburgh, D., 2005. Balancing civil liberties and homeland security: does the USA PATRIOT act avoid Justice Robert H. Jackson's suicide pact? Albany Law Review, September 2005.

Source: Excerpt taken from the following website: http://www.ccclr.org/documents/ccclrpositionpaper.htm. See the companion website for this book for the complete text and full bibliography of this position paper.

▪ ▪ Critical Thinking ▪

Do you feel that the USA PATRIOT Act counters the basic freedoms bestowed upon Americans by the drafters of the Constitution? Why or why not? Would you be willing to give up some of your freedom for increased security from terrorism?

In the 7 years since the act's passage, numerous communities across the country have passed resolutions opposing parts or all of the act's contents. These resolutions began appearing as early as January 2002, when the city of Ann Arbor, Michigan, voiced its opposition to what they saw as an attack on the basic freedoms and rights that Americans considered sacred. As of December 2007, these resolutions continued to appear, with the latest passed in the city of Wichita Falls, Texas on December 4. The American Civil Liberties Union (ACLU), which monitors these actions, registered 414 local, county, and state resolutions that had been passed as of January 1, 2008, with another 275 efforts currently under debate (to see a complete list of resolutions passed, see http://www.bordc.org/list.phpfisortoAlpha51 or http://www.aclu .org/resolutions). Similar resolutions have been passed in the cities of Dallas, Denver, Detroit, Honolulu, Minneapolis, and Seattle, and at the state level in Vermont, Montana, Maine, Hawaii, and Alaska (Bill of Rights Defense Committee, 2007).

Update on the Patriot Act, *New York Times*, Friday, August 12, 2011

A *New York Times* article on Oct. 2, 2001 described its passage as "the climax of a remarkable 18-hour period in which both the House and the Senate adopted complex, far-reaching antiterrorism legislation with little debate in an atmosphere of edgy alarm, as federal law enforcement officials warned that another attack could be imminent." Final passage came on Oct. 24, and President George W. Bush signed it into law two days later.

It has been the subject of debate ever since, as civil liberty advocates have fought to rein in some of the powers it granted. It has been amended but its basic policies have been little changed.

Here is how the Congressional Research Service summarized the law shortly after its passage:

"The Act gives federal officials greater authority to track and intercept communications, both for law enforcement and foreign intelligence gathering purposes. It vests the Secretary of the Treasury with regulatory powers to combat corruption of U.S. financial institutions for foreign money laundering purposes. It seeks to further close our borders to foreign terrorists and to detain and remove those within our borders. It creates new crimes, new penalties, and new procedural efficiencies for use against domestic and international terrorists. Although it is not without safeguards, critics contend some of its provisions go too far. Although it grants many of the enhancements sought by the DOJ, others are concerned that it does not go far enough."

In May 2011, Congress voted to extend three provisions of the law that would have otherwise expired. They allow investigators to get "roving wiretap" court orders allowing them to follow terrorism suspects who switch phone numbers or providers; to get orders allowing them to seize "any tangible things" relevant to a security investigation, like a business's customer records; and to get national security wiretap orders to monitor noncitizen suspects who are not believed to be connected to any foreign power.

The Senate passed the extension 72 to 23 late in the afternoon of the day on which the provision would expire and within hours the House approved it 250 to 153. In an unusual move, a White House spokesman said that President Obama, who was in Europe, would "direct the use" of an autopen machine to sign the bill into law without delay.

During the debate, two senators, Ron Wyden and Mark Udall, claimed that the Justice Department had secretly interpreted the act in a twisted way, enabling domestic surveillance activities that many members of Congress do not understand

In March 2002, President Bush took another major step and signed Homeland Security Presidential Directive 3 (HSPD-3), which stated that:

The Nation requires a Homeland Security Advisory System to provide a comprehensive and effective means to disseminate information regarding the risk of terrorist acts to Federal, State, and local authorities and to the American people. Such a system would provide warnings in the form of a set of graduated "Threat Conditions" that would increase as the risk of the threat increases. At each Threat Condition, Federal departments and agencies would implement a corresponding set of "Protective Measures" to further reduce vulnerability or increase response capability during a period of heightened alert.

This system is intended to create a common vocabulary, context, and structure for an ongoing national discussion about the nature of the threats that confront the homeland and the appropriate measures that should be taken in response. It seeks to inform and facilitate decisions appropriate to different levels of government and to private citizens at home and at work.

The product outcome of this directive was the widely recognizable color-coded Homeland Security Advisory System (HSAS). The HSAS has been called on repeatedly since its inception to raise and lower the nation's alert levels between elevated (yellow) and high (orange), although the frequency of these movements has decreased over time as standards for such movements have been developed.

On November 25, 2002, President Bush signed into law the Homeland Security Act of 2002 (HS Act) (Public Law 107–296), and announced that former Pennsylvania Governor Tom Ridge would become secretary of a new DHS to be created through this legislation. This act, which authorized the greatest federal government reorganization since President Harry Truman joined the various branches of the armed forces under the DOD, was charged with a threefold mission of protecting the United States from further terrorist attacks, reducing the nation's vulnerability to terrorism, and minimizing the damage from potential terrorist attacks and natural disasters.

The sweeping reorganization into the new department, which officially opened its doors on January 24, 2003, joined more than 179,000 federal employees from 22 existing federal agencies under a single, cabinet-level organization. Since that time, there have been many additions, movements, and changes to both the organizational makeup of the department and its leadership. See Chapter 1 for a detailed timeline of the establishment of DHS.

▪ ▪ Critical Thinking ▪

Were members of Congress justified in making such a sweeping reform of the federal government as they did in the aftermath of the September 11 attacks? What could have, or should have, been done differently now that the benefit of hindsight exists?

The 9/11 Commission

As a result of the September 11 attacks, President Bush established the National Commission on Terrorist Attacks Upon the United States, informally known as the 9/11 Commission. He asked former Congressman Lee Hamilton and former New Jersey Governor Thomas Keane to chair the Commission. Members included a broad range of people including former congressmen and senators and officials from previous administrations. The Commission was charged with looking at the events leading up to the September 11 attacks and the actions that were taken immediately following the attack and making recommendations to the President and the Congress. The major finding of the Commission's report was that there were government failures in policy, capabilities, and management. The main areas they focused on were unsuccessful diplomacy, problems within the intelligence community, problems with the FBI, permeable borders and aviation security, lack of command and control in the response, and underfunding of programs to combat terrorism. The intelligence community, the CIA, and the FBI were highly criticized. Congress also came in for criticism for its failure to financially support counterterrorism programs and the confusion over oversight and jurisdictions within its committee structure.

The final report of the 9/11 Commission was issued on July 22, 2004. The specific recommendations were encompassed in the following categories:

- Attack terrorists and their organizations
- Prevent the continued growth of Islamist terrorism
- Protect against and prepare for terrorist attacks
- Establish a National Counterterrorism Center
- Appoint a National Intelligence Director
- Encourage the sharing of information among government agencies and with state and local officials

A copy of the Final Report is available at http://www.9-11commission.gov/report/911report.pdf.

Homeland Security Focus on Terrorism Results in a Disaster: Hurricane Katrina and Its Aftermath

In the first few years following the creation of the DHS, the nation worked through many of the growing pains associated with such a drastic bureaucratic overhaul. The TSA certainly experienced growing pains as the public was faced with ever more restrictive and evasive security policies. Of the many new and changing policies related to both national security and emergency management, one which sparked significant concern was that the focus of emergency management at all levels of government was being led away from the all-hazards philosophy to that of the single terrorism hazard. Floods, tornadoes, and other events continued to occur, although there were several mild hurricane seasons. However, several members of Congress still proposed legislation to remove the FEMA from DHS, although their efforts were ultimately rebuffed.

In late August 2005, Hurricane Katrina veered into the Gulf Coast states of Louisiana, Mississippi, and Alabama, dealing a blow considered by many emergency planners to be a worst-case scenario. At the last minute, the category 5 storm weakened to a category 3, and its track turned just slightly askew, thus preventing a direct hit on the city of New Orleans, but the damage that followed this glancing blow was still enough to completely overwhelm all mitigation and preparative measures that had been taken to protect the city and its residents. The storm's impact covered a broad geographic area stretching from Alabama, across coastal Mississippi and southeast Louisiana, spanning an estimated 90,000 square miles. As of January 2007, the official death toll attributable to the storm stood at 1,836 with another 705 individuals listed as missing (Figure 2–3).

By any account, Hurricane Katrina was a massive storm, both deadly and destructive. But it was the failed response that followed, which exposed severe cracks that had developed in the nation's emergency

FIGURE 2–3 Biloxi, Mississippi, September 3, 2005 — Damage and destruction to houses. Hurricane Katrina caused extensive damage all along the Mississippi Gulf Coast. (Source: Photo by Mark Wolfe/FEMA News Photo)

management system and its ability to respond to a catastrophic event. Both government and independent after-action reports, and several media accounts, judged the overall response an outright failure — with the ongoing recovery phase receiving the same poor evaluation. Many of the problems of the immediate response exposed the impacts of a priority focus on terrorism and homeland security that had developed in preceding years, which had likely been a major contributing factor in the decrease in local, state, and national capacities and capabilities.

Congress immediately tackled the apparent emergency management shortfalls, drawing up legislation aimed at patching many of the holes that had been exposed and developing new systems that were hoped would reduce overall risk for the future. For the moment, at least, it seemed as if the nation's emergency management focus was willing to regain its all-hazards approach. The resulting legislation, the Post-Katrina Emergency Reform Act (PKEMRA), was signed into law by the president on October 4, 2006. This law served to reconfigure the leadership hierarchy of the DHS and to return many functions that were stripped from FEMA back into the agency.

This law established several new leadership positions within the DHS, moved additional functions into (several were simply returned) the FEMA, created and reallocated functions to other components within DHS, and amended the Homeland Security Act in ways that directly and indirectly affected the organization and functions of various entities within DHS. The changes were required to have gone into effect by March 31, 2007. Transfers that were mandated by the Post-Katrina Emergency Management Reform Act included (with the exception of certain offices as listed in the act):

- United States Fire Administration (USFA)
- Office of Grants and Training (G&T)
- Chemical Stockpile Emergency Preparedness Division (CSEP)
- Radiological Emergency Preparedness Program (REPP)
- Office of National Capital Region Coordination (NCRC)

The law determined that the head of FEMA would take on the new title of administrator. This official would now be supported by two deputy administrators. One is the deputy administrator and chief operating officer, who serves as the principal deputy and maintains overall operational responsibilities at FEMA. The other is the deputy administrator for National Preparedness, a new division created within FEMA.

The National Preparedness Division under FEMA included several existing FEMA programs and several programs that were moved into the former Preparedness Directorate. This division focuses on emergency preparedness policy, contingency planning, exercise coordination and evaluation, emergency management training, and hazard mitigation (with respect to the CSEP and REPP programs). The National Preparedness Division oversees two new divisions: Readiness, Prevention, and Planning (RPP) and the National Integration Center (NIC). RPP is now the central office within FEMA handling preparedness policy and planning functions. The NIC maintains the National Incident Management System (NIMS) and the National Response Plan (NRP), and coordinates activities with the U.S. Fire Administration.

The existing Office of Grants and Training was moved into the newly expanded FEMA and was renamed the "Office of Grant Programs." The Training and Systems Support Divisions of the Office of Grants and Training was transferred into the NIC. The Office of the Citizen Corps was transferred into the FEMA Office of RPP.

Additional headquarters' positions created at FEMA by the new law included a Disability Coordinator (located in the FEMA Office of Equal Rights), a Small State and Rural Advocate, a Law Enforcement Advisor to the Administrator, and a National Advisory Council.

This act specifically excluded certain elements of the former DHS Preparedness Directorate from transfer into FEMA. The Preparedness Directorate was renamed the National Protection and Programs Directorate (NPPD), and it remained under the direction of a DHS Under Secretary.

And finally, the law created the Office of Health Affairs (OHA). OHA is led by the chief medical officer, who was given the title of Assistant Secretary for Health Affairs and Chief Medical Officer. The Office of Health Affairs has three main divisions:

- WMD and Biodefense
- Medical Readiness
- Component Services

▪ ▪ Critical Thinking ▪

Several legislators and key emergency management officials proclaimed that, in order to truly reform emergency management in the United States, FEMA would have to be removed from DHS and returned to its cabinet-level status. Do you agree or disagree with their sentiments, and why?

Obama Administration

With the election of President Barak Obama in November 2008, many people expected dramatic change relative to homeland security issues. As a Senator, Mr. Obama voted against the war in Iraq and expressed concerns about civil liberties lost in the aftermath of 9/11. During the campaign, he spoke of wanting to close Guantanamo Bay prison where hundreds of suspected Al-Qaeda conspirators were being kept. There were also some thoughts that the new administration might take FEMA out of DHS and restore it to its independent Agency status. Recognizing that the permeable border remains an issue, President Obama nominated Janet Napolitano, Governor of Arizona, to be Secretary of DHS. She was quickly confirmed by the Senate and was committed to addressing issues facing the Department as well as aggressively tackling the emerging threats such as cybersecurity. Among the high-priority issues were problems with immigration programs, the Transportation Security Administration (TSA) cybersecurity, and critical infrastructure. The TSA was created to address the need for heightened airport security after the hijacking of the planes during 9/11, and has had a mixed record in accomplishing its mission.

On December 25, 2009, a Nigerian national, Umar Farouk Abdulmutallab, on a flight from Amsterdam to Detroit, attempted to explode a plastic device hidden in his underwear. It didn't work and he was immediately arrested when the plane landed. His connections were traced to Yemen and an organized terrorist's organization, possibly Al-Qaeda. This event was a clear blot on the TSA security operations. Initially Secretary Napolitano said the system "worked" but the next day she acknowledged that somewhere the system had failed.

DHS in 2011 published a report on their accomplishments in meeting the recommendations of the 9/11 Commission including in the areas of airline security. Airports now include full body screeners that, hopefully, will prevent any future underwear bombers but these additional security measures are not popular with the general public.

On July 21, 2011, Secretary of DHS Janet Napolitano released a report that highlighted the progress DHS has made in fulfilling the 9/11 Commission recommendations. In releasing the report, the Secretary said, "Now 10 years after the worst terrorist attacks ever on American soil, America is stronger and more resilient than ever before. But threats from terrorism persist. And challenges remain. Over the past decade, we have made great strides to secure our nation against a large attack or disaster, to protect our critical infrastructure and cyber networks, and to engage a broader range of Americans in the shared responsibility for security." (See "Implementing the Recommendations of the 9/11 Commission: Progress Report 2011," http://www.dhs.gov/files/publications/implementing-9-11-commission-recommendations.shtm or access specific recommendations on the companion website for this book.)

The most significant success for the Obama administration and the intelligence community of homeland security was the capture and subsequent killing of Osama bin Laden on May 2, 2011. The U.S. intelligence community, led by the CIA, began an extensive effort starting in 2002 that culminated in a surveillance program on what was thought to be the Al-Qaeda's leader's compound in 2010. Operation Neptune Spear was authorized by President Obama and executed by the CIA and U.S. Navy Seals. The raid on bin Laden's compound in Pakistan started in Afghanistan. After the successful raid, bin Laden's body was taken back to Afghanistan to be verified and then buried at sea. Following this event, other Al-Qaeda operatives were arrested and the general opinion in the intelligence community was that Al-Qaeda was severely wounded and it would be hard to recover. An account of the operation, "Getting Bin Laden" by Nicholas Schmidle (2011), appeared in the August 8, 2011, issue of *The New Yorker*.

Many people have been disappointed by the Obama administration's adoption of Bush-era homeland security practices, including the lack of progress on comprehensive immigration reform, support for continuation of certain segments of the PATRIOT Act, and the failure to resolve issues on the closing of Guantanamo Bay prison. The passage of health care legislation, the problems with unemployment, and a lackluster economy have dominated the administration's agenda, although continuing issues with TSA and airport security, along with significant natural disaster activity, have required some focus on DHS issues.

In May 2011, the Obama administration proposed comprehensive cybersecurity legislation. The highlights in this legislation include consolidating the 47 different state laws that require businesses to report breaches of their cybersystems to consumers and DHS will work with industry to prioritize most important cyberthreats and vulnerabilities; provide clear authority to allow the federal government to provide assistance to state and local governments when there has been a cyberbreach; provide immunity to industry and state and local government when sharing cybersecurity information with DHS; and provide for a new framework to protect individuals' privacy and civil liberties. A more thorough discussion of this legislation is found in Chapter 8.

They also entered into a joint U.S.–U.K. Cooperation on Cyberspace.

Conclusion

The terrorist attacks of September 11 have forever changed America and, in many ways, the world. This event has been termed the most significant disaster since the attack on Pearl Harbor and the first disaster that affected the United States on a national scale. It seemed that every American knew someone or knew of someone who perished in the attacks, and surely every citizen felt the economic impact in the form of lost jobs, lost business, and an immediate reduction in the value of college savings and retirement accounts.

Does the killing of Osama bin Laden negate the need for such a focus on terrorism in homeland security? Terrorist organizations that dislike the U.S. government and its policies exist outside of Al-Qaeda. So being vigilant is important and the intelligence community becomes ever more critical in achieving this goal.

But there are new forms of terrorism — in cybersecurity — with which major corporations such as Sony and Lockheed-Martin have had their systems compromised. The DOD experienced a major cybersecurity attack, when one of its defense contractors with documentation on a new weapon system was hacked into. Environmental terrorism, depending on your political philosophy, has become more prevalent.

Natural hazards continue to beset a good portion of our nation and impact our economic and social stability. In 2011, record floods impacted the Midwest, whereas in 2010 wildfires destroyed forests and threatened communities.

The threat portfolio under the area of terrorism has only expanded, thereby presenting the nation with a whole new set of hazards about which to worry (e.g., biological, chemical, radiological, and nuclear weapons), and which must now be studied and understood in much greater detail in order to best prepare. These significant changes are reflected not only in the daily lives of the American people but also in the way in which the country's government functions.

The concept of homeland security is impacted by each event that happens — natural or man-made, the level of impact of the event has determines its influence, so the concept of homeland security is still, clearly, a work in progress, reacting to events as opposed to strategically anticipating future events.

Key Terms

Cold War: A struggle for power waged between the United States and the Soviet Union, which lasted from the end of World War II until the Soviet Union ultimately collapsed. This war was defined as being "cold" because the aggression was ideological, economic, and diplomatic rather than a direct military conflict.

Critical Infrastructure: Critical infrastructure includes any system or asset that, if disabled or disrupted in any significant way, would result in catastrophic loss of life or catastrophic economic loss. Some examples of critical infrastructure include the following:
Public water systems
Primary roadways, bridges, and highways
Key data storage and processing facilities, stock exchanges, or major banking centers
Chemical facilities located in proximity to large population centers
Major power generation facilities
Hydroelectric facilities and dams
Nuclear power plants

Cybersecurity: The prevention of damage to, unauthorized use of, or exploitation of, and, if needed, the restoration of electronic information and communications systems and the information contained therein to ensure confidentiality, integrity, and availability. Includes protection and restoration, when needed, of information networks and wire line, wireless, satellite, public safety answering points, and 911 communications systems and control systems (NIPP).

Department of Homeland Security: A federal agency whose primary mission is to help prevent, protect against, and respond to acts of terrorism on U.S. soil.

Emergency Management: The discipline dealing with the identification and analysis of public hazards, the mitigation of and preparedness for public risk, and the coordination of resources in response to and recovery from associated emergency events.

Executive Order: A declaration issued by the president or by a governor that has the force of law. Executive orders are usually based on existing statutory authority and require no action by Congress or the state legislature to become effective.

Homeland Security Presidential Directive (HSPD): Policy decisions, issued by the president, on matters that pertain to Homeland Security. As of January 2008, there have been 21 HSPDs issued by the president.

National Incident Management System: This is a system mandated by HSPD-5 that provides a consistent nationwide approach for governments, the private sector, and nongovernmental organizations to work effectively and efficiently together to prepare for, respond to, and recover from domestic incidents, regardless of cause, size, or complexity.

Presidential Directive: A form of executive order issued by the president that establishes an action or change in the structure or function of the government (generally within the Executive Office). Under President Bush, directives have been termed HSPDs and National Security Presidential Directives (NSPDs). Under President Clinton, they were termed PDDs and Presidential Review Directives (PRDs).

Statutory Authority: The legally granted authority, bestowed on the named recipient by a legislature, that provides a government agency, board, or commission the power to perform the various functions, expenditures, and actions as described in the law.

Review Questions

1. What role does the U.S. Constitution define for federal, state, and local governments in the area of emergencies and public safety?
2. What were the first indications that terrorism might be something that the U.S. government had to deal with?
3. What events precipitated President Clinton to sign the Violent Crime Control and Law Enforcement Act of 1994?
4. Was enactment of the Patriot Act justified?
5. What were the areas of recommendations identified by the 9/11 Commission for preventing future attacks?
6. What are the most significant emerging threats to homeland security?

References

City of Oklahoma City Document Management, 1996. Final Report: Alfred P. Murrah Federal Building Bombing April 19, 1995. Stillwater: Department of Central Services Central Printing Division.

Curci, Lt. Col. Michael A. 2004. Transnational terrorism's effect on the U.S. economy. United States Army War College Strategy Research Project. Carlisle Barracks, PA: United States Army.

Federal Emergency Management Agency (FEMA), 2003. A Nation Remembers, A Nation Recovers. FEMA, Washington, DC.

Fusco, A.L., 1993. The World Trade Center Bombing: Report and Analysis. U.S. Fire Administration, Emmitsburg, MD.

Library of Congress. July 21, 2003. www.congress.gov.

Schmidle, N. 2011. Getting Bin Laden. The New Yorker, August 8, 2011. http://www.newyorker.com.reporting/2011/08/110808fa_fact_schmidle.

3

Hazards

What You Will Learn

- The various hazards that often result in major emergencies and disasters, including natural hazards, technological hazards, and terrorism (including chemical, biological, radiological, nuclear, and explosive weapons)
- Why it is so difficult to assess and evaluate the likelihood of terrorist attacks, both within the United States and throughout the world

Introduction

While most Americans associate the Department of Homeland Security with terrorism and the terrorist threat, the Department is actually responsible for the preparation for, the prevention of, the mitigation of, and the response to a much wider portfolio of hazards. Any destabilizing incident or factor, be it human-caused or an act of God, is a threat to the security of the nation. In fact, the United States has suffered countless more deaths, injuries, and dollars in property damage from natural disaster events than those that came at the hands of terrorists. Of course, many will argue that the ever-growing threat of a terrorist's use of weapons of mass destruction provides some parity between natural and man-made events as our cities, states, and our country look to the future.

The nation's natural hazard profile remained relatively unchanged for decades with regard to its makeup. However, due to urbanization, increasing societal complexity, and climate change, both the likelihood and severity of these events that do occur have gradually increased. Today, disasters are happening more frequently, and with greater consequence, thereby demanding greater and greater response capacity and capabilities. What is troubling is that in the United States, just like elsewhere in the world, this trend shows no signs of slowing.

For most of the nation's municipalities, urban and rural alike, the threat or risk posed by terrorism has introduced an expanded set of hazards. These new hazards fall into four principal categories often referred to by the acronym CBRNE: chemical, biological, radiological/nuclear, and explosive. CBRNE hazards must now be considered in concert with the myriad traditional natural and technological hazards that have menaced communities for centuries, and as such further strain the limited financial, equipment, and human resources they possess.

There are two significant differences between these new hazards and the more traditional ones. First, much is known about the traditional hazards as a result of years of research and actual response and recovery from them. For instance, we can now predict with a fair amount of accuracy the track of a hurricane. We know enough about the destructive force of a tornado to design and build safe rooms. We have spent the better part of a century trying, with increasing success, to control flooding. We have developed building codes and standards that protect structures from earthquakes, fires, and wind damage. We have enough experience in responding to disaster events caused by these hazards to ensure that our first responders have effective protective gear and are trained and exercised in the best response protocols and practices. For CBRNE hazards, the knowledge is sparse and the experience is, thankfully, uncommon. Knowledge of the properties and the destructive qualities of the various chemical and biological threats is limited at best, even in the agencies charged with knowing the most about these hazards. The first responder community, the state and local emergency managers, and the general public remain almost completely uninformed about these hazards, and have little or no experience in facing their consequences. The same is largely true with community and national leaders and the news media. It took decades of research and practice for all parties to attain a level of fluency in the traditional mix of natural and technological disasters. Understandably, it will take considerable time before we have reached an adequate level of comfort with regard to our knowledge of the new hazards.

The second notable difference between the traditional hazards and the new hazards of terrorism is the manner in which we encounter each. Traditional hazards occur because of natural processes, whether geological, meteorological, or hydrological, or because of some human accident, oversight, or negligence. Hurricanes, tornadoes, and earthquakes are inherently natural hazards that have existed for eons, regardless of the presence of humans. Technological hazards, including HazMat spills, unintentional releases at nuclear power plants, and transportation accidents, for example, have traditionally been just that — accidents. The new terrorism hazards differ from these natural and technological hazards in that their genesis is intentional, and their primary purpose is maximized death and destruction. These hazards are weapons in every sense of the word, unique in that they primarily target civilian populations instead of military assets, and they are used specifically to advance political, ideological, or religious agendas. No hurricane or earthquake has ever advanced a human agenda.

The Hazards

A *hazard* is defined as a "source of danger that may or may not lead to an emergency or disaster" (National Governors Association, 1982), and it is named after the emergency/disaster that could be so precipitated. Each hazard carries an associated risk, which is represented by the likelihood of the hazard leading to an actual disaster event and the consequences of that event should it occur. The product of realized hazard risk is an emergency event, which is typically characterized as a situation exhibiting negative consequences that require the efforts of one or more of the emergency services (fire, police, emergency medical services [EMS], public health, or others) to manage. When the response requirements of an emergency event exceed the capabilities of those established emergency services in one or more critical areas (e.g., shelter, fire suppression, mass care), the event is classified as a disaster.

Each hazard is distinct with regard to its characteristics. However, there are three umbrella groupings into which all hazards may be sorted that include Natural Hazards, Technological Hazards, and Terrorist Hazards.

Natural Hazards

Natural hazards are those that exist in the natural environment as a result of hydrological, meteorological, seismic, geologic, volcanic, mass movement, or other natural processes, and that pose a threat to human populations and communities. Natural hazards are often intensified in scope and scale by human activities, including development and modification of the landscape and atmosphere. Humans place themselves at risk of natural hazards in order to achieve some other benefit or gain, such as access to land or fisheries, aesthetics, access to commerce and transportation, and many other factors. The following hazards are those with the greatest potential to impact humans on a community-wide or greater scale.

Floods

A flood is an overabundance of water that engulfs dry land and property that is normally dry. Floods may be caused by a number of factors, including heavy rainfall, melting snow, an obstruction of a natural waterway, and other generative factors. Floods usually occur from large-scale weather systems generating prolonged rainfall or onshore winds, but they may also result from locally intense thunderstorms, snowmelt, ice jams, and dam failures. Floods are capable of undermining buildings and bridges, eroding shorelines and riverbanks, tearing out trees, washing out access routes, and causing loss of life and injuries. Flash floods usually result from intense storms dropping large amounts of rain within a brief period, occur with little or no warning, and can reach full peak in only a few minutes.

Floods are the most frequent and widespread disaster in the United States, primarily as a result of human development in the floodplain. The close relationship that exists between societies and water is the result of commerce, agriculture, and access to drinking water. As development and urbanization rates increase, so does the incidence of flooding in large part as a result of this relationship. FEMA estimates that approximately 10 million households are at risk from flooding in the United States, which sustained an average of $2.7 billion each year during the period from 2001 to 2010. Since FEMA's National Flood Insurance Program began in 1978, it has paid out over $37 billion for flood insurance claims and related losses (see sidebar "Flood Facts").

Flood Facts

- Floods and flash floods happen in all 50 states.
- Just an inch of water can cause costly damage to property.
- Flash floods often bring walls of water 10 to 20 ft high.
- A car can easily be carried away by just 2 ft of floodwater.
- Hurricanes, winter storms, and snowmelt are common (but often overlooked) causes of flooding.
- New land development can increase flood risk, especially if the construction changes natural runoff paths.
- Federal disaster assistance is usually a loan that must be paid back with interest. For a $50,000 loan at 4% interest, your monthly payment would be around $240 a month ($2,880 a year) for 30 years. Compare that to a $100,000 flood insurance premium, which is about $400 a year ($33 a month).
- In a high-risk area, homes are more than twice as likely to be damaged by flood than by fire.
- Anyone can be financially vulnerable to floods. People outside of high-risk areas file over 20% of National Flood Insurance Program (NFIP) claims and receive one-third of disaster assistance for flooding.

Source: FEMA, 2011. Flood Facts, National Flood Insurance Program, http://www.floodsmart.gov/floodsmart/pages/flood_facts.jsp.

Floods are typically measured according to their elevation above standard water levels (of rivers or coastal water levels). This elevation is translated into the annualized likelihood of reaching such heights. For example, a flood depth that has a 1% chance of being reached or could be expected to occur once across a 100-year period would be considered a "100-year flood event." Typically, structures that are contained within areas likely to experience flooding in a 100-year flood event are considered to be within the floodplain. River and stream gauges are maintained to monitor floodwater elevations and to provide information on rising water for use in sandbagging and dyke construction. Such information also allows for early warning and evacuation to occur.

Earthquakes

An earthquake is a sudden, rapid shaking of the earth's surface that is caused by the breaking and shifting of tectonic (crustal) plates. This shaking can affect both the natural and built environments, with even moderate events leading to the collapse of buildings and bridges; disruptions in gas, electric, and phone service; landslides; avalanches; fires; and tsunamis. Structures constructed on unconsolidated landfill, old waterways, or other unstable soil are generally at greatest risk unless seismic mitigation has been utilized. Seismicity is not seasonal or climate dependent and can therefore occur at any time of the year.

Earthquakes are sudden, no-notice events despite scientists' and soothsayers' best efforts to predict when they will occur. Seismic sensing technology is effective at measuring and tracking seismic activity, but it has yet to accurately predict a major seismic event with any degree of accuracy.

Each year hundreds of earthquakes occur in the United States, though the vast majority are barely perceptible. As earthquake strength increases, its likelihood of occurrence decreases. Major events, which are greater than 6.5 to 7 on the Richter scale, occur only once every decade or so, but such events have been among the most devastating in the experience of the United States. The Northridge earthquake that struck California in 1994, for instance, is the second most expensive natural disaster to ever occur in the United States as ranked by FEMA relief costs, resulting in almost $7 billion in federal funding (and second only to Hurricane Katrina). It is anticipated that a major earthquake along the New Madrid Fault could cause catastrophic damage across eight states, and result in indirect damages throughout the entire country that would significantly impact the nation's economy.

The strength and effects of earthquakes are commonly described by the Richter and Modified Mercalli Intensity (MMI) scales. The Richter scale, designed by Charles Richter in 1935, assigns a single number to quantify the strength and effect of an earthquake across the entire area affected according to the strength of ground waves at its point of origin (as measured by a seismograph). Richter magnitudes are logarithmic and have no upper limit. The MMI also measures the effects of earthquakes, but rather than applying a single value to the event, it allows for site-specific evaluation according to the effects observed at each location. The MMI (Table 3–1) rates event intensity using Roman numerals I through XII. Determinations are generally made using reports by people who felt the event and observations of damages sustained by structures.

Hurricanes

Hurricanes are cyclonic storms that occur in the Western Hemisphere where the majority of the United States land is located. When these storms affect the Pacific island territories, such as Guam, American Samoa, and the Northern Mariana Islands (among others), they are called *cyclones*. These very strong wind storms begin as tropical waves and grow in intensity and size as they progress to become tropical depressions and tropical storms (as determined by their maximum sustained wind speed). The warm-core

Table 3–1   Modified Mercalli Intensity Scale

MMI Intensity	Damages Sustained and Sensations Experienced	Richter Scale Equivalent
I–IV (instrumental to moderate)	No damage sustained. Sensation ranges from imperceptible to that of a heavy truck striking the building. Standing motor cars may rock.	<4.3
V (rather strong)	Felt by nearly everyone; many awakened. Some dishes, windows broken. Unstable objects overturned. Pendulum clocks may stop.	4.4–4.8
VI (strong)	Felt by all; many frightened. Some heavy furniture moved; a few instances of fallen plaster. Damage slight.	4.9–5.4
VII (very strong)	Damage negligible in buildings of good design and construction; slight to moderate in well-built ordinary structures; considerable damage in poorly built or badly designed structures; some chimneys broken.	5.5–6.1
VIII (destructive)	Damage slight in specially designed structures; considerable damage in ordinary substantial buildings with partial collapse. Damage great in poorly built structures. Fall of chimneys, factory stacks, columns, monuments, walls. Heavy furniture overturned.	6.2–6.5
IX (ruinous)	Damage considerable in specially designed structures; well-designed frame structures thrown out of plumb. Damage great in substantial buildings, with partial collapse. Buildings shifted off foundations.	6.6–6.9
X (disastrous)	Most masonry and frame structures/foundations destroyed. Some well-built wooden structures and bridges destroyed. Serious damage to dams, dikes, embankments. Sand and mud shifting on beaches and flat land.	7.0–7.3
XI (very disastrous)	Few or no masonry structures remain standing. Bridges destroyed. Broad fissures in ground. Underground pipelines completely out of service. Widespread earth slumps and landslides. Rails bent greatly.	7.4–8.1
XII (catastrophic)	Damage nearly total. Large rock masses displaced. Lines of sight and level are distorted. Objects are thrown into the air.	>8.1

Source: USGS, 2009. Magnitude/Intensity Comparison. Earthquake Hazards Program. http://earthquake.usgs.gov/learn/topics/mag_vs_int.php.

depression becomes a tropical storm when the maximum sustained surface wind speeds fall between 39 miles per hour and 73 miles per hour (mph). Tropical cyclonic storms are defined by their low barometric pressure, closed-circulation winds originating over tropical waters, and an absence of wind shear. Cyclonic storm winds rotate counterclockwise in the Northern Hemisphere and clockwise in the Southern Hemisphere.

A *hurricane* is a cyclonic tropical storm with sustained winds measuring 74 mph or more. Hurricane winds extend outward in a spiral pattern as much as 400 miles around a relatively calm center of up to 30 miles diameter known as the *eye*. Hurricanes are fed by warm ocean waters. As these storms make landfall, they often push a wall of ocean water known as a *storm surge* over coastal zones. Once over land, hurricanes cause further destruction by means of torrential rains and high winds. A single hurricane can last for several weeks over open waters and can run a path across the entire length of the eastern seaboard.

Hurricane season runs annually from June 1 through November 30. August and September are peak months during the hurricane season. Hurricanes are commonly described using the Saffir–Simpson scale (Table 3–2). Hurricanes are capable of causing great damage and destruction over vast areas. Hurricane Floyd in 1999 first threatened the states of Florida and Georgia, made landfall in North Carolina, and damaged sections of South Carolina, North Carolina, Virginia, Maryland, Delaware, New Jersey, New York, Connecticut, Massachusetts, and Maine. The damage was so extensive in each of these states that they all qualified for federal disaster assistance. To date, the costliest disaster in U.S. history was Hurricane Katrina that occurred in August of 2005 and required over $29 billion in federal funding. In comparison, the next costliest disaster was the 9/11 attacks on America, which required only $8.8 billion (less than one-third of Katrina's costs). In total dollar figures, this hurricane was estimated to have resulted in over $80 billion in losses (Reuters, 2009) and was one of the deadliest in terms of lives lost (1,836 killed). Six years later, many of the Gulf Coast areas—especially hard-hit New Orleans—are still reeling from this disaster event, with full recovery years or even decades away.

In recent years, significant advances have been made in hurricane tracking technology and computer models. The National Hurricane Center in Miami, Florida, now tracks tropical waves from the moment they form off the coast of West Africa through their development as a tropical depression. Once the tropical

Table 3–2   The Saffir–Simpson Scale

Category	Conditions	Effects
1	Wind speed: 74–95 mph Storm surge: 4–5 feet above normal	Primary damage to unanchored mobile homes, shrubbery, and trees. Some coastal flooding and minor pier damage. Little damage to building structures.
2	Wind speed: 96–110 mph Storm surge: 6–8 ft above normal	Considerable damage to mobile homes, piers, and vegetation. Coastal and low-lying area escape routes flood 2–4 h before arrival of hurricane center. Buildings sustain roofing material, door, and window damage. Small craft in unprotected mooring break moorings.
3	Wind speed: 111–130 mph Storm surge: 9–12 ft above normal	Mobile homes destroyed. Some structural damage to small homes and utility buildings. Flooding near coast destroys smaller structures; larger structures damaged by floating debris. Terrain continuously lower than 5 ft above sea level (ASL) may be flooded up to 6 miles inland.
4	Wind speed: 131–155 mph Storm surge: 13–18 ft above normal	Extensive curtain wall failures, with some complete roof structure failure on small residences. Major erosion of beaches. Major damage to lower floors of structures near the shore. Terrain continuously lower than 10 ft ASL may flood (and require mass evacuations) up to 6 miles inland.
5	Wind speed: Over 155 mph Storm surge: Over 18 ft above normal	Complete roof failure on many homes and industrial buildings. Some complete building failures. Major damage to lower floors of all structures located less than 15 ft ASL and within 500 yards of the shoreline. Massive evacuation of low-ground, residential areas may be required.

Source: FEMA.

depression grows to the strength of a tropical storm, the Hurricane Center assigns the storm a name. After the sustained wind speed exceeds 74 mph, the storm officially becomes a hurricane. The National Hurricane Center uses aircraft to observe and collect meteorological data on the hurricane and to track its movements across the Atlantic Ocean. It also uses several sophisticated computer models to predict the storm's path. These predictions are provided to local and state emergency officials to help them make evacuation decisions and to predeploy response and recovery resources.

Historically, high winds and flood caused by storm surge have been the principal contributors to the loss of life and injuries and the property and infrastructure damage caused by hurricanes. Inland flooding caused by hurricane rainfall has also resulted in large losses of life and severe property damage, especially in zones of hilly or mountainous topography. Damage to the environment is another important factor related to hurricane-force winds and flooding. For instance, storm surges cause severe beach erosion, most notably on fragile barrier islands. Inland flooding from Hurricane Floyd inundated waste ponds on hog farms in North Carolina, washing the hog waste into the Cape Fear River and ultimately into the ocean. The storm surge created by Hurricane Katrina has had a profound impact on the environment—in some cases completely erasing or altering coastal areas. Dauphin Island was literally pushed toward the land by the force of the surge, and the Chandeleur Islands were completely destroyed. Breton National Wildlife Refuge, 1 of 16 wildlife refuges damaged by the storm, lost over half of its area. Much of this land lost served as breeding grounds for marine mammals, reptiles, birds, and fish.

Storm Surges

Storm surges, defined as masses of water that are pushed toward the shore by meteorological forces, are the primary cause of the injuries, deaths, and structural damages associated with hurricanes, cyclones, nor'easters, and other coastal storms. When the advancing surge of water coincides with high tides, the resulting rise in sea level is further exacerbated. Storm surges may reach several dozen feet under the right conditions, as was the case in Hurricane Katrina. Wind-driven turbulence becomes superimposed on the storm tide, thereby causing further damage to structures that are inundated through wave action (each cubic yard of water results in 1,700 lb of pressure on affected structures). The surge height at landfall is ultimately dictated by the expanse and intensity of the storm, the height of the tide at the time of landfall, and the slope of the sea floor approaching land. The longer and shallower the sea floor, the greater the storm surge will be. Because much of the United States' densely populated Atlantic and Gulf Coast coast lines lie less than 10 ft above mean sea level, storm surge risk is extreme.

Tornadoes

A *tornado* is a rapidly rotating vortex or funnel of air extending groundward from a cumulonimbus cloud, exhibiting wind speeds of up to 300 mph. Approximately 1,200 tornadoes are spawned by thunderstorms each year in the United States. Most tornadoes remain aloft, but the few that do touch the ground are devastating to everything in their path. The forces of a tornado's wind are capable of lifting and moving huge objects, destroying or moving whole buildings, and siphoning large volumes from bodies of water and ultimately depositing them elsewhere. Because tornadoes typically follow the path of least resistance, people living in valleys have the greatest exposure to damage.

Tornadoes have been measured using the Fujita–Pearson Tornado Scale since its creation in 1971 (Table 3–3). In 2006, research indicated that tornado damage was occurring from winds of much weaker intensity than previously thought, so the National Weather Service created an enhanced scale to measure them (Table 3–4). First used in January 2007, this scale expands upon the original system's measure of

Table 3–3   Original Fujita–Pearson Tornado Scale

Category	Conditions	Effects
F-0	40–72 mph	Chimney damage, tree branches broken
F-1	73–112 mph	Mobile homes pushed off foundation or overturned
F-2	113–157 mph	Considerable damage, mobile homes demolished, trees uprooted
F-3	158–205 mph	Roofs and walls torn down, trains overturned, cars thrown
F-4	207–260 mph	Well-constructed walls leveled
F-5	261–318 mph	Homes lifted off foundation and carried considerable distances, autos thrown as far as 100 m

Table 3–4   Enhanced Fujita–Pearson Tornado Scale

Category	Conditions	Effects
F-0	65–85 mph	Minor to light damage to structures and vegetation
F-1	85–110 mph	Moderate damage to structures and vegetation
F-2	111–135 mph	Heavy damage to structures and vegetation
F-3	136–165 mph	Severe damage to structures and vegetation
F-4	166–200 mph	Extreme damage to structures and vegetation
F-5	Over 200 mph	Complete destruction of structures and vegetation

damage to homes by adding 18 new damage indicators, including those that affect trees, mobile homes, and several other structures (giving a total of 28 indicators studied in the classification of a tornado). Under the enhanced Fujita–Pearson scale, a tornado that does not affect houses can still be classified.

Tornado damage occurs only when the funnel cloud touches down on land. The states with the greatest tornado risk are Texas, Oklahoma, Arkansas, Missouri, and Kansas, which together occupy what is commonly known as "tornado alley." In recent years, however, tornadoes have struck in cities that are not regularly frequented by tornadoes, including Miami, Nashville, and Washington, DC. Tornadoes can also touch down in several places in succession, as occurred in Washington, D.C., in 2001. In that event, a single tornado first touched down in Alexandria, Virginia, just south of the city and then again in College Park, Maryland, just north of DC. Tornado season generally falls between March and August, although tornadoes can occur at any time of the year. Tornadoes tend to occur in the afternoon and evening, with more than 80% of all tornadoes striking between noon and midnight.

Collapsing buildings and flying debris are the principal factors behind the deaths and injuries tornadoes cause. Early warning is key to surviving tornadoes, as warned citizens can protect themselves by moving to structures designed to withstand tornado-force winds. Doppler radar and other meteorological tools have drastically improved the ability to detect tornadoes and the amount of advance warning time available before a tornado strikes. Improved communications and new technologies have also been critical to giving people advance warning.

Buildings that are directly in the path of a tornado have little chance of surviving unless they are specifically designed to withstand not only the force of the winds but also the force of the debris "missiles" that are thrown about. "Safe room" technology developed by FEMA and Texas A&M University, which retrofits a portion of a structure to withstand such winds through engineered resistant design and special resilient materials, offers those in the path of a tornado much greater survival likelihoods. Safe rooms are often the most cost-effective way to mitigate tornado risk in communities that are already heavily developed, since they can be built into an existing (or new) structure for a small cost (estimated between $3,000 and $5,000).

In order to greatly expand the mitigation benefits of safe rooms, similar technology is being developed for use in community mass-care shelters. New technologies in building design and construction are also being developed by FEMA and others to reduce the damage to buildings and structures not located directly in the path of a tornado. Many of the same wind-resistant construction techniques used effectively in high-risk hurricane areas have been found to be equally effective when applied to new and retrofitted structures located in tornado-prone areas.

Wildfires

Wildfires (often called "wildland fires") are classified into three categories: surface fires, the most common type, which burn along the floor of a forest, moving slowly and killing or damaging trees; ground fires, which are usually started by lightning and burn on or just below the forest floor; and crown fires, which burn through the forest canopy high above the ground and therefore spread much more rapidly due to wind and direct contact with nearby trees. Wildland fires are an annual and increasing hazard due to the air pollution (primarily smoke and ash that travel for miles, causing further hazards to health and mechanical or electrical equipment), risk to firefighters, environmental effects, and property destruction they cause.

As residential areas expand into relatively untouched wildlands (called the *wildland–urban interface*), the threat to the human population increases dramatically. Protecting structures located in or near the wildland poses special problems and often stretches firefighting resources beyond capacity. Wildland fires also cause several secondary hazards. For instance, when heavy rains follow a major fire, landslides, mudflows, and floods can strike on or downhill from the newly unanchored soil. These fires can also severely scorch the land, destroying animal habitats and causing barren patches that may persist for decades, increasing the likelihood of long-term erosion.

Several terms are used to classify the source and behavior of wildland fires:

- *Wildland fires.* Fueled almost exclusively by natural vegetation, these fires typically occur in national forests and parks, where federal agencies are responsible for fire management and suppression.
- *Interface or intermix fires.* These fires occur in or near the wildland–urban interface, affecting both natural and built environments and posing a tactical challenge to firefighters concerned with the often conflicting goals of firefighter safety and property protection.
- *Firestorms.* Events of such extreme intensity that effective suppression is virtually impossible, firestorms occur during extreme weather and generally burn until conditions change or the available fuel is exhausted.
- *Prescribed fires and prescribed natural fires.* These are fires that are intentionally set or selected natural fires that are allowed to burn for the purpose of reducing available natural fuel.

Severe drought conditions and the buildup of large quantities of "fuel" (dead trees and flammable vegetation) on the forest floors have led to a steady increase in the prevalence of wildfires in the United States. Since the National Interagency Fire Center began tracking the number and acreage of fires in 1960, the average number of fires has fallen (presumably due to fire-prevention programs), while the annual acreage burned has risen. In other words, the fewer fires that are occurring are larger and more destructive on average. Before 2004, no year had seen more than 7 million acres burned, and few experienced greater than 4 or 5 million acres burned. Yet, from 2004 to 2007, each year exceeded 8 million, and both 2006 and 2007 exceeded 9 million acres burned. In 2008 the number fell to just over 5 million, and 2009 saw approximately 6 million burned (NIFC, 2009).

Mass Movements

The general category of mass movements includes several different hazards caused by the horizontal or lateral movement of large quantities of physical matter. Mass movements cause damage and loss of life through several different processes, including the pushing, crushing, or burying of objects in their path, the damming of rivers and waterways, the subsequent movement of displaced bodies of water (typically in the form of a tsunami), destruction or obstruction of major transportation routes, and alteration of the natural environment in ways in which humans are negatively impacted. Mass-movement hazards are most prevalent in areas of rugged or varied topography, but they can occur even on level land, as in the case of subsidence. The following are the categories of mass movement hazards:

- *Landslides*. Landslides occur when masses of relatively dry rock, soil, or debris move in an uncontrolled manner down a slope. Landslides may be very highly localized or massive in size, and they can move at a creeping pace or at very high speeds. Many areas have experienced landslides repeatedly since prehistoric times. Landslides are activated when the mechanisms by which the material was anchored become compromised (through a loss of vegetation or seismic activity, for example).
- *Mudflows*. Mudflows are water-saturated rivers of rock, earth, and other debris that are drawn downward by the forces of gravity. These phenomena develop when water rapidly accumulates in the material that is moved, like during heavy rainfall or rapid snowmelt. Under these conditions, solid or loose earth can quickly change into a flowing river of mud, or "slurry." These flows move rapidly down slopes or through channels, following the path of least resistance, and often strike with little or no warning. Mudflows have traveled several miles in many instances, growing in size as they pick up trees, cars, and other materials along the way.
- *Lateral spreads*. Lateral spreads occur when large quantities of accumulated earth or other materials spread downward and outward due to gradual hydrologic and gravitational forces. Spreads can affect rock, but they also occur in fine-grained, sensitive soils such as clays.
- *Liquefaction*. When saturated solid material becomes liquid-like in constitution due to seismic or hydrologic activity, it can exacerbate lateral spreading.
- *Rockfalls*. Rockfalls occur when masses of rock or other materials detach from a steep slope or cliff and descend by freefall, rolling, or bouncing. Topples consist of the forward rotation of rocks or other materials about a pivot point on a hill slope. Rockfalls can occur spontaneously when fissures in rock or other materials cause structural failure or due to seismic or other mechanical activity (including explosions or the movement of heavy machinery).
- *Avalanches*. An avalanche is a mass of ice or snow that moves downhill at a high velocity. Avalanches can shear trees, cover entire communities and highway routes, and level buildings in their path. Avalanches are triggered by a number of processes, including exceeding critical mass on a steep slope or disturbances caused by seismicity or human activity. As temperatures increase and snowpack becomes unstable, the risk of avalanches increases. The primary negative

consequences associated with avalanches are loss of life (mostly to backcountry skiers, climbers, and snowmobilers) and obstruction of major transportation routes. Around 10,000 avalanches are reported each year in the United States. Since tracking began in 1790, an average of 144 people have become trapped in avalanches annually, and of these an average of 14 sustain injuries and 14 die. The average annual value of structural damage is $500,000, though the secondary costs associated with disrupted commerce can be much greater.

- *Land subsidence*. Land subsidence is the loss of surface elevation caused by the removal of subsurface support. Subsidence can range from broad, regional lowering of large landmasses to severe localized collapses. The primary cause of this hazard is human activity, including underground mining, extraction of groundwater or petroleum, and the drainage of organic soils. The average annual damage associated with subsidence in the United States is estimated to be at least $125 million.

- *Expansive soils*. Soils and soft rock that tend to swell or shrink when their moisture content changes are referred to as *expansive soils*. These changes are extremely detrimental to transportation routes (including highways, streets, and rail lines) and structures that are built above the affected soils. The most extensive damage affects highways and streets. Two rock types that are particularly prone to expansion and that are prevalent in the United States (primarily in the West) are aluminum silicates (e.g., ash, glass, and rocks of volcanic origin) and sedimentary rock (e.g., clay and shale).

Tsunamis

A *tsunami* is wave or series of waves that is generated by a mass displacement of sea or lake water. The most common generative factor behind tsunamis is undersea earthquakes that cause ocean floor displacement, but large tsunamis have been caused by volcanic eruptions and landslides as well. Tsunami waves travel outward as movements of kinetic energy (rather than traveling water) at very high speeds in all directions from the area of the disturbance, much like the ripples caused by a rock thrown into a pond. As the waves approach shallow coastal waters, wave speed quickly decreases and the water is drawn upward and onto land. Tsunamis can strike at heights of up to and over 100 ft and extend onto land for a mile or more (depending upon topography). The force of the water causes near total destruction of everything in its path.

The areas at the greatest risk from tsunamis are those lying less than 50 ft above sea level and within 1 mi of the shoreline. Successive crests (high water) and troughs (low water) can occur anywhere from 5 to 90 min apart. Tsunamis travel through deep water at approximately 450 mph, so the areas closest to the point of origin experience the greatest destruction and have the least amount of forewarning. Most tsunami-related deaths are the result of drowning, while the loss of services and related health problems associated with the incredible destruction of the infrastructure (including the loss of hospitals and clinics, water pollution, contaminated food and water stocks, and damaged transmission lines) adds to these statistics.

Volcanic Eruptions

A volcano is a break in the earth's crust through which molten rock from beneath the earth's surface (magma) erupts. Over time, volcanoes will grow upward and outward, forming mountains, islands, or large, flat plateaus called *shields*. Volcanic mountains differ from mountain chains formed through plate tectonics (movement of the earth's crustal plates) because they are built through the accumulation of materials (lava, ash flows, and airborne ash and dust) rather than being pushed up from below. When volcanic material exits the earth, it is called *lava*, and the nature of its exit determines the land formations that result. Thinner lava

68   INTRODUCTION TO HOMELAND SECURITY

typically moves quickly away from the source and becomes a large shield (as in the case of the Hawaiian Islands), while thicker lava and other materials form steeper volcanic formations.

When pressure from gases and molten rock becomes strong enough to cause an explosion, violent eruptions may occur. Gases and rock shoot up through the opening and spill over or fill the air with lava fragments. Volcanoes cause injuries, death, and destruction through a number of processes, including direct burns, suffocation from ash and other materials, trauma from ejected rocks, floods and mudflows from quickly melted snow and ice, burial under burning hot "pyroclastic" burning ash flows, and others. Airborne ash can affect people hundreds of miles away from the eruption and influence global climates for years afterward.

Volcanic ash contaminates water supplies, causes electrical storms, and can cause roofs to collapse under the weight of accumulated material. Eruptions may also trigger tsunamis, flash floods, earthquakes, and rock falls. Sideways-directed volcanic explosions, known as *lateral blasts*, can shoot large pieces of rock at very high speeds for several miles. These explosions can kill by impact, burial, or heat. They have been known to knock down entire forests. Most deaths attributed to the Mount St. Helens volcano were a result of lateral blast and trees that were knocked down. Volcanic ash also has some positive implications because it can be used for construction or road building, as abrasive and cleaning agents, and as raw materials for many chemical and industrial uses. Ash-covered land is also rich in mineral nutrients and ideal for agricultural production.

Severe Winter Storms

Severe winter storms occur when extremely cold atmospheric conditions coincide with high airborne moisture content, resulting in rapid and heavy precipitation of snow and/or ice. When combined with high winds, the event is known as a *blizzard*. In the United States, these hazards originate from four distinct sources:

- In the Northwest, cyclonic weather systems originate in the North Pacific Ocean or the Aleutian Islands region.
- In the Midwest and Upper Plains, Canadian and Arctic cold fronts push ice and snow deep into the heart of the nation—in some instances, traveling as far south as Florida.
- In the Northeast, lake-effect snowstorms develop when cold weather fronts pass over the relatively warm surfaces of the Great Lakes.
- The eastern and northeastern states are affected by extratropical cyclonic weather systems in the Atlantic Ocean and the Gulf of Mexico that produce snow, ice storms, and occasional blizzards.

On January 1, 2006, the federal government began to use a new scale, similar to the scales used to measure the magnitude and intensity of hurricanes and tornadoes, to measure severe winter storms. The Northeast Snowfall Impact Scale (NESIS) provides a numerical value to storms based on the geographical area affected, the amount of snow accumulation, and the number of people affected. The minimum threshold for a storm's inclusion in the scale is 10 in. of snow falling over a wide area.

NESIS values range from 1 to 5 and include associated descriptors (from most to least severe) of Extreme, Crippling, Major, Significant, and Notable. The NESIS scale differs from other meteorological indices in that it considers population data. It uses the following formula:

$$\text{NESIS} = \overset{n=30}{\underset{n=4}{S}}[n/10(A_n/A_{\text{mean}} + P_n/P_{\text{mean}})]$$

Table 3–5   NESIS Values

Category	NESIS Value	Description
1	1–2.499	Notable
2	2.5–3.99	Significant
3	4–5.99	Major
4	6–9.99	Crippling
5	10.0+	Extreme

Source: NOAA, 2006, http://www.ncdc.noaa.gov/oa/climate/research/snow-nesis/.

where *A* equals the area affected and *P* equals the population affected. Table 3–5 shows the categories assigned to severe winter storms using this formula.

Drought

Drought is defined as a prolonged shortage of available water, primarily due to insufficient rain and other precipitation or because exceptionally high temperatures and low humidity cause a drying of agriculture and a loss of stored water resources. Drought hazards differ from other natural hazards in three ways:

1. A drought's onset and conclusion are difficult to determine because the effects accumulate slowly and may linger even after the apparent termination of an episode.
2. There is no precise or universally accepted determination of what conditions constitute official drought conditions or the degree of drought severity.
3. The drought's effects are less obvious and spread over a larger geographic area.

The Climate Prediction Center of the National Weather Service monitors nationwide drought conditions and provides visual reports on a weekly basis and seasonal reports on a monthly basis. A report of current drought conditions in the United States, referred to as the *United States Drought Monitor*, can be viewed at http://www.cpc.noaa.gov/products/expert_assessment/drought_assessment.shtml.

Extreme Temperatures

Major diversions in average seasonal temperatures can cause injuries, fatalities, and major economic impacts when they are prolonged or coincide with other natural or technological events. Extreme heat, called a *heat wave*, occurs when temperatures of 10 or more degrees above the average high temperature persist across a geographic region for several days or weeks. Humid or muggy conditions, which add to the discomfort of high temperatures, can occur when a "dome" of high atmospheric pressure traps hazy, damp air close to the ground. Excessively dry conditions that coincide with extreme heat can provoke wind and dust storms.

When little rain occurs in conjunction with extreme heat, droughts are likely to occur. Prolonged periods of heat have resulted in hundreds of thousands of deaths in single instances, including 600 in the Chicago area in 1995 and almost 37,500 in Europe in 2003. In most years, over 1,500 people die from exposure to excessive heat in the United States, making it the number one weather-related killer of humans.

While there is no widely accepted standard for extreme cold temperatures, periods of colder than normal conditions exhibit a range of negative consequences, depending on where they occur and exactly how cold temperatures fall. Any time temperatures fall below freezing, there is the risk of death from hypothermia to humans and livestock, with the degree to which populations are accustomed to those temperatures a primary factor in resilience. Extreme cold can also lead to serious economic damages from frozen water pipes; the freezing of navigable rivers, which halts commerce and can cause ice dams; and the destruction of crops.

Thunderstorms

Thunderstorms are meteorological events that bring heavy rains, strong winds, hail, lightning, and tornadoes. Thunderstorms are generated by atmospheric imbalance and turbulence caused by a combination of several conditions, including unstable, warm air rising rapidly into the atmosphere; sufficient moisture to form clouds and rain; and upward lift of air currents caused by colliding weather fronts (cold and warm), sea breezes, or mountains.

A thunderstorm is classified as severe if its winds reach or exceed 58 mph, it produces a tornado, or it drops surface hail at least 0.75 in. in diameter. Thunderstorms may occur singly, in clusters, or in lines. Thus, it is possible for several thunderstorms to affect one location in the course of a few hours. These events are particularly devastating when a single thunderstorm affects one location for an extended period. Such conditions lead to oversaturation of the ground and subsequent flash flooding and slope erosion.

Lightning is a major secondary threat associated with thunderstorms. In the United States, between 75 and 100 Americans are hit and killed by lightning each year. Many air disasters have been linked to thunderstorms due to the unpredictable and turbulent wind conditions they cause and the threat of electronic or mechanical failure caused by lightning strikes. When humans or structures are hit by lightning, the effect is devastating to both.

Hail

Hail is frozen atmospheric water that falls to the earth. Moisture in clouds becomes frozen into crystals at high temperatures and begins to fall under its own weight. Typically, these crystals melt at lower temperatures, but in the right conditions they pick up more moisture as they fall and are then lifted to cold elevations, which causes refreezing. This cycle may continue until the individual hailstones reach several inches in diameter under the right conditions. Because of the strength of severe thunderstorms and tornadoes, both can cause this cyclic lifting, and therefore they are often accompanied by hail. Hailstorms occur more frequently during late spring and early summer when the jet stream migrates northward across the Great Plains. When they fall, they can damage crops, break windows, destroy cars and other exposed properties, collapse roofs, and cause other destruction totaling nearly $1 billion each year in the United States.

■ ■ Critical Thinking ■

Why do Americans seem to be more concerned with terrorist hazards than natural hazards? How do our perceptions of risk affect the way that we manage them? Do individuals have a greater personal responsibility to protect themselves from natural hazards than they do from other technological or terrorist hazards?

Technological Hazards

Technological hazards, or "man-made" hazards as they are often called, are an inevitable product of technological innovation and human development. These hazards, which can occur after the failure of or damage to the many structures and systems upon which humans rely, tend to be much less understood than their natural counterparts. Additionally, as technology advances with each passing year, the number of associated disasters increases, and their scope expands. The most common technological hazards arise from systems and structures related to transportation, infrastructure, industry, and construction.

Structural Fires

Studies have shown that civilizations have been fighting structural fires using coordinated governmental resources since the first century AD (Coppola, 2011). Structural fires can be triggered or exacerbated by both natural processes, including lightning, high winds, earthquakes, volcanoes, and floods, or by human origins, including accidents and arson, for example. Lightning is the most significant natural contributor to fires affecting the built environment. Buildings with rooftop storage tanks for flammable liquids are particularly susceptible. There were 1,348,500 fires in the United States in 2009. Of these, 48.1% were outside and "other" fires, 35.6% were structure fires, and 16.2% were vehicle fires.

Residential fires may not typically result in disasters (as defined earlier in this chapter, and by the Department of Homeland Security), but together they result in 85% of the roughly 3,000 civilian deaths that occur each year, and 75% of the 17,000 injuries that occur. They are also a major contributor to the 75,000–85,000 firefighter injuries that occur annually (National Fire Protection Association, 2010).

Transportation Accidents

Transportation is a technology on which the entire world depends for travel, commerce, and industry. The vast system of land, sea, and air transportation involves complex and expensive infrastructure, humans or machines to conduct that infrastructure, and laws and policies by which the whole system is guided. A flaw or breakdown in any one of these components can and often does result in a major disaster involving loss of life, injuries, property and environmental damage, and economic consequences. Transportation accidents can cause mass casualty incidents, as well as major disruptions to society and commerce, when they occur in any of the transportation sectors (including air travel, sea travel, rail travel, bus travel, and roadways). The accidents do not need to be the result of the vehicles themselves. For instance, the collapse of the I-35 Mississippi Bridge in Minneapolis (August 4, 2007) resulted in 13 fatalities, 145 injuries, and severe financial implications given that 140,000 daily commuters had to find alternate means of crossing the river. Transportation systems and infrastructure are considered a top terrorist target due to these severe consequences.

Infrastructure Failures

Infrastructure hazards are another type of technological hazard, and are primarily related to critical systems of utilities, services, and other assets (both state-run and private) that serve the public. The consequences of infrastructure hazards may include loss of vital services, injury, death, property damage, or a combination of these. As technological innovation, global communication, and global commerce increase, nations are becoming much more dependent upon their critical infrastructure. One of the most common types of infrastructure failures, the power outage (or "blackout"), is the number one concern of businesses and the cause of as much as $80 billion in economic losses each year (LaCommare, 2004). The primary types of infrastructure hazards include power failures; telecommunications system failures, computer network failures; critical water or sewer system failures; and major gas distribution line breaks.

Dam Failures

Dams are constructed for many purposes, the most common being flood control and irrigation. When dams retaining large quantities of water fail, there exists the potential for large-scale uncontrolled release of stored water downstream. Dam failures pose the most extreme flood risk due to the sudden and severe impacts that can result. Dams most often fail as a result of maintenance neglect, overtopping (as in the case of a flood), poor design, or structural damage caused by a major event such as an earthquake, collision, or blast. However, dams are also considered a critical terrorist risk due to the fact that dam failure would result in immediate and significant deaths and property destruction, and would provide little hope for warning those in the resulting torrent's path. Dams are both publicly and privately owned and maintained, so their monitoring can pose a challenge to offices of emergency management and homeland security charged with assessing associated hazard risk. The United States as a nation boasts the second greatest number of dams worldwide, exceeded only by China.

Hazardous Materials Incidents

Hazardous materials are chemical substances that if released or misused can pose a threat to people and the environment. Chemicals are prevalent in many industries and products, including agriculture, medicine, research, and consumer product development. These materials may be explosive, flammable, corrosive, poisonous, radioactive, or otherwise toxic or dangerous. Releases typically occur as a result of transportation accidents or accidents at production and storage facilities. Depending on the nature of the chemical, the result of a release or spill can include death, serious injury, long-lasting health effects, and damage to buildings, homes, and other property.

The majority of hazardous materials incidents occur in homes, and the quantities released are almost always too small to cause more than a highly localized hazard. However, it is the transportation or industrial use of these same products that leads to major disaster events when releases occur due to the massive volumes or quantities involved. At present, hazardous materials are manufactured, used, or stored at an estimated 4.5 million facilities in the United States—from major industrial plants to local dry cleaning establishments or gardening supply stores. Since the Oklahoma City and World Trade Center bombings, monitoring of many of these chemicals has increased. However, it was in the wake September 11, with recognition of the terrorist potential at a great many other facility types, that tracking became institutional. This is discussed in greater detail later in this chapter as well as in Chapter 8 (Cybersecurity and Infrastructure Protection).

Nuclear Accidents

Radioactive materials have provided significant benefits since their discovery, including the generation of power, scientific treatments and experiments, new detection, and imaging technologies, among many others. However, because the radiation emitted from these materials can cause immediate and lasting tissue damage to humans and animals upon exposure, these materials must be handled and contained using specialized techniques, materials, and facilities. National and international law strictly dictates who may possess these materials, how they can be used, and how and where they must be disposed of.

Exposure to radiation can be the result of an accidental or intentionally caused spill, breach of the containment vessel, escape of gasses, or an explosion. Nuclear material remains radioactive until it has shed all of its ionizing particles, called *radionuclides*. This process, called *radioactive decay,* is the primary source of health risk to life. When released quickly, dust or gasses may rise into the atmosphere in a characteristic plume, which carries the contaminants far from the point of origin with atmospheric currents, depositing it as radioactive fallout along its course.

In the United States, the greatest threat of exposure to radioactive materials comes from an accident or sabotage at one of the nation's many nuclear power plants. As the distance to a nuclear power plant decreases, the risk of exposure increases, and the likelihood of surviving in the event of a large-scale release of materials decreases. Since 1980, utilities operating commercial nuclear power plants in the United States have been required to maintain on- and off-site emergency response plans as a condition of maintaining their operating licenses. On-site emergency response plans are approved by the Nuclear Regulatory Commission (NRC). Off-site plans (which are closely coordinated with the utility's on-site emergency response plan) are evaluated by FEMA and provided to the NRC, who must consider the FEMA findings when issuing or maintaining a license.

A catastrophic failure of a nuclear reactor is called a *meltdown,* indicative of the failure of the reactor's containment due to the incredibly high heat caused by a runaway nuclear reaction. The worst nuclear accident to date was the result of a reactor core meltdown that occurred in the Chernobyl Nuclear Power Plant in the Ukraine on April 26, 1986. So great was the radioactive plume and resultant fallout, which traveled as far as and landed primarily in neighboring Belarus, that over 336,000 people had to be evacuated and permanently resettled. Over 20 years later, the area is still uninhabitable. The more recent failure of containment vessels at the Fukushima Daiichi nuclear power plant in Japan, which occurred when the plant was inundated in the March 11, 2010, tsunami, highlights the vulnerability of all nuclear plants to the effects of natural disasters. This accident will likely require decades to overcome, with contamination condemning thousands to permanent displacement and possible long-term health effects. It has also caused all nuclear nations to consider the safety of their own plants, and to reconsider whether the risk associated with nuclear power is justified.

In the United States, the most dangerous radioactive event, which was ultimately contained (thereby preventing any realized threat to human life), was the partial core meltdown at the Three Mile Island Nuclear Generating Station in Pennsylvania on March 28, 1979. The accident happened when a system that cooled the nuclear reactor, and therefore controlled the temperature of the reactor core, failed to operate correctly. While some nuclear material was released, the effect on people exposed was similar to that of receiving one or two medical X-rays. The public reaction to this event, however, significantly changed the course of the nuclear power industry in the United States, as expansion abruptly ended. In 2011, in major part due to the events in Japan, the nation turned its attention to two Nebraska-based nuclear power plants located on the banks of the then-flooding Missouri River. Images of the Fort Calhoun Station plant, which was completely surrounded by flood waters, caused understandable concern for nearby residents. In recognition that the Japan incident was caused by a loss of power to cooling systems, the Nebraska plants arranged for multiple backup power systems including newly installed overhead lines and diesel-powered generators.

Terrorism Hazards

Terrorism hazards, or "intentional hazards" as they are often called, are means or mechanisms through which terrorists are able to carry out their attacks. Chapter 2 described the motivational factors behind terrorists' actions, which they feel are justified to achieve their goals. This section describes the mechanisms employed, including what they are, how they function, and the likely consequences that result.

The greatest achievement in managing the consequences of terrorist attacks will come from gaining a better understanding of how these hazards influence risk, how America's society and structures are vulnerable to attacks, and how individuals, communities, and countries can minimize their impacts.

This section presents basic information about the four primary categories of terrorist hazards summarized in the acronym CBRNE, namely, Chemical, Biological, Radiological/Nuclear, and Explosive. Coordinated assaults, which are not typically considered "weapons of mass destruction," will also be addressed. Cyberterrorism, one of the foci of cybersecurity, is addressed in Chapter 8, "Cybersecurity and Infrastructure Protection."

▪ ▪ Critical Thinking ▪

Will it ever be possible to accurately predict terrorist attacks, whether in the United States or elsewhere? Why or why not? What tools, skills, and other options may be used to increase the accuracy of predictions? What is so different about the assessment of terrorist risk versus other hazard types?

Conventional Explosives and Secondary Devices

Conventional explosives have existed for centuries, since explosive gunpowder invented by the Chinese (for use in firecrackers) was modified for use in weaponry. Traditional (manufactured) and improvised explosive devices (IEDs) are generally the easiest weapons to both obtain and use. In fact, instructions for their assembly and deployment are widely available in print and on the Internet, as well as through the transfer of institutional knowledge within informal criminal networks. These widely available weapons, when skillfully used, can inflict massive amounts of destruction to property and can cause significant injuries and fatalities to humans. Conventional explosives are most troubling as weapons of mass destruction (WMD) in light of their ability to effectively disperse chemical, biological, or radiological agents.

Conventional explosives and IEDs can be either explosive or incendiary in nature. Explosives use the physical destruction caused by the expansion of gases that result from the ignition of "high- or low-filler" explosive materials to inflict damage or harm. Examples of explosive devices include simple pipe bombs, made from common plumbing materials; satchel charges, which are encased in a common looking bag such as a backpack, and left behind for later detonation; letter or package bombs, delivered through the mail; or a car bomb, which can be used to deliver a large amount of explosives. Incendiary devices, also referred to as firebombs, rely on the ignition of fires to cause damage or harm. Examples include Molotov cocktails (gas-filled bottles capped with a burning rag), napalm bombs, and fuel-air explosives (thermobaric weapons).

Explosions and conflagrations can be delivered via a missile, or projectile device, such as a rocket, rocket-propelled grenade (RPG), mortar, or air-dropped bomb. Nontraditional explosive delivery methods are regularly discovered, and include the use of fuel-filled commercial airliners flown into buildings as occurred on September 11, 2001. Because these weapons rely on such low technology and are relatively easy to transport and deliver, they are the most common choice of terrorists. Although suicide bombings, in which bombers manually deliver and detonate the device on or near their person, are becoming more common, most devices are detonated through the use of timed, remote (radio, cell phone), or other methods of transmission (light sensitivity, air pressure, movement, electrical impulse, etc.).

Although almost 50% of terrorist attacks involve the use of conventional explosives, less than 5% of actual and attempted bombings are preceded by any kind of threat or warning. These devices can be difficult to detect because most easily attainable explosive materials are untraceable. Commercial explosives in the United States are now required to contain a chemical signature that can be used to trace their source should they be used for criminal means, but this accounts for only a fraction of materials available to terrorists. What is particularly troubling about these devices is that it is easy to detonate multiple explosives in single or multiple municipalities, and secondary explosives can be used to target bystanders and officials who are responding to the initial, often smaller, explosion. Because of the graphic nature of the carnage resulting from explosives, and the widespread fear associated with their historic use, these weapons are very effective as terror-spreading devices (FEMA, 2002).

■ ■ Critical Thinking ■

Conventional explosives can be manufactured using ingredients commonly found in hardware stores, pharmacies, and other sources available to the general public. What can planners do to prevent terrorists from using these much-needed materials for sinister purposes short of banning them entirely?

Chemical Agents

Like explosives, chemical weapons have existed for centuries and have been used repeatedly throughout history. The first organized application and the most significant modern use of chemical weapons occurred during World War I. In Belgium, during a German attack against allied forces in World War I (WWI), German troops released 160 tons of chlorine gas into the air, killing more than 10,000 soldiers and injuring another 15,000. In total, 113,000 tons of chemical weapons were used in WWI, resulting in the deaths of more than 90,000 people and injury to over 1.3 million.

Chemical weapons are created for the sole purpose of killing, injuring, or incapacitating people. They can enter the body through inhalation, ingestion, or the skin or eyes. Many different kinds of chemicals have been developed as weapons, falling under six general categories that are distinguished according to their physiological effects on victims:

1. Nerve agents (Sarin, VX)
2. Blister agents (mustard gas, lewisite)
3. Blood agents (hydrogen cyanide)
4. Choking/pulmonary agents (phosgene)
5. Irritants (tear gas, capsicum [pepper] spray)
6. Incapacitating agents (BZ, Agent 15)

Terrorists can deliver chemical weapons by means of several different mechanisms. Aerosol devices spread chemicals in liquid, solid (generally powdered), or gas form by causing tiny particulates of the chemical to be suspended into the air. Explosives can also be used to disperse the chemicals through the air in this manner. Devices that contain chemicals, either for warfare or everyday use (such as a truck or train tanker), can be breached, thereby exposing the chemical to the air. Chemicals can also be mixed with water or placed into food supplies. Chemicals that are easily absorbed through the skin can be placed directly onto a victim to cause harm or death.

Chemical attacks, in general, are recognized immediately (some indicators of the possible use of chemical agents are listed in the sidebar "General Indicators of Possible Chemical Agent Use"), although it may be unclear to victims and responders until further testing has taken place that an attack has occurred, and whether the attack was chemical or biological in nature. Chemical weapons may be persistent (remaining in the affected area for long after the attack) or nonpersistent (evaporating quickly, due to their lighter-than-air qualities, resulting in a loss of ability to harm or kill after approximately 10 or 15 min in open areas). In unventilated rooms, however, any chemical can linger for a considerable time.

■ ■ ■ ▬▬▬▬▬▬▬▬▬▬▬▬▬▬▬▬▬▬▬▬▬▬▬▬▬▬▬▬▬▬▬▬▬▬▬▬

General Indicators of Possible Chemical Agent Use

- Stated threat to release a chemical agent
- Unusual occurrence of dead or dying animals — for example, lack of insects, dead birds
- Unexplained casualties
- Multiple victims
- Surge of similar 911 calls
- Serious illnesses
- Nausea, disorientation, difficulty breathing, or convulsions
- Definite casualty patterns
- Unusual liquid, spray, vapor, or powder
- Droplets, oily film
- Unexplained odor
- Low-lying clouds/fog unrelated to weather
- Suspicious devices, packages, or letters
- Unusual metal debris
- Abandoned spray devices
- Unexplained munitions

Source: Federal Emergency Management Agency, Interim Planning Guide for State and Local Government: Managing the Emergency Consequences of Terrorist Incidents, Washington, DC: FEMA, July 2002.

▬▬▬▬▬▬▬▬▬▬▬▬▬▬▬▬▬▬▬▬▬▬▬▬▬▬▬▬▬▬▬▬▬▬▬▬ ■ ■ ■

The effect of chemical weapons on victims is usually fast and severe. Identifying what chemical has been used presents special difficulties, and responding officials (police, fire, EMS, HAZMAT) and hospital staff treating the injured are at risk from their effects. Without proper training and equipment, there is little these first response officials can do in the immediate aftermath of a chemical terrorist attack to identify or treat the consequences (FEMA, 2002).

A simple list of agents compiled by the CDC is presented in the sidebar "List of Chemical Agents." Fact sheets about cyanide, sulfur mustard (mustard gas), sarin, ricin, and chlorine, which have been compiled from the CDC website, are presented in five sidebars bearing these chemical names in respective titles. The sidebar "Additional Information on Cyanide, Sulfur Mustard, Sarin, Ricin, and Chlorine" provides sources for further information about these chemical agents.

List of Chemical Agents

- Abrin
- Adamsite (DM)
- Agent 15
- Ammonia
- Arsenic
- Arsine (SA)
- Benzene
- Bromobenzylcyanide (CA)
- BZ
- Cannabinoids
- Chlorine (CL)
- Chloroacetophenone (CN)
- Chlorobenzylidenemalononitrile (CS)
- Chloropicrin (PS)
- Cyanide
- Cyanogen chloride (CK)
- Cyclohexyl sarin (GF)
- Dibenzoxazepine (CR)
- Diphenylchloroarsine (DA)
- Diphenylcyanoarsine (DC)
- Diphosgene (Do P)
- Distilled mustard (HD)
- Ethyldichloroarsine (ED)
- Ethylene glycol
- Fentanyls and other opioids
- Hydrofluoric acid
- Hydrogen chloride
- Hydrogen cyanide (AC)
- Lewisite (L, L-1, L-2, L 3)
- LSD
- Mercury
- Methyldichloroarsine (MD)
- Mustard gas (H) (sulfur mustard)

- Mustard/lewisite (HL)
- Mustard/T
- Nitrogen mustard (HN-1, HN-2, HN-3)
- Nitrogen oxide (NO)
- Paraquat
- Perfluororisobutylene (PHIB)
- Phenodichlorarsine (PD)
- Phenothiazines
- Phosgene (CG)
- Phosgene oxime (CX)
- Phosphine
- Potassium cyanide (KCN)
- Red phosphorus (RP)
- Ricin (considered to be both a chemical and biological weapon)
- Sarin (GB)
- Sesqui mustard
- Sodium azide
- Sodium cyanide (NaCN)
- Soman (GD)
- Stibine
- Strychnine
- Sulfur mustard (H) (mustard gas)
- Sulfur trioxide-chlorosulfonic acid (FS)
- Super warfarin
- Tabun (GA)
- Teflon and perfluororisobutylene (PHIB)
- Thallium
- Titanium tetrachloride (FM)
- VX
- White phosphorus
- Zinc oxide (HC)

Source: Centers for Disease Control and Prevention, www.bt.cdc.gov/agent/agentlistchem.asp.

Biological Agents

Biological or "germ" weapons are live organisms (either bacteria or viruses) or the toxic by-products generated by living organisms that are manipulated in order to cause illness, injury, or death in humans, livestock, or plants. Although awareness of the potential for use of bacteria, viruses, and toxins as weapons existed long before an unknown terrorist used anthrax spores to deliver multiple attacks through the U.S. mail system, this event certainly put them on the forefront of the public and political agendas. Evidence of biological warfare applications exists as early as the 14th century, when the Mongols used plague-infected corpses to spread disease among enemies. Thanks to advances in weapons technology that have allowed much more effective use of bioweapons reaching much greater geographic limits, biological weapons have elicited an increased concern from counterterrorism officials and emergency planners alike.

Bioweapons may be dispersed overtly or covertly by perpetrators. When covertly applied, bioweapons are extremely difficult to recognize because their negative consequences can take hours, days, or even weeks, to emerge. This is especially true with bacteria and viruses, although toxins (which are, in essence, poisons) generally elicit an immediate reaction. Attack recognition is made through a range of methods, including identification of a credible threat, the discovery of weapons materials (dispersion devices, raw biological material, or weapons laboratories), and correct diagnosis of affected humans, animals, or plants. Detection depends on a collaborative public health monitoring system, trained and aware physicians, patients who elect to seek medical care, and equipment suitable for confirming diagnoses. Bioweapons are unique in this regard, in that detection is likely to be made not by a first responder, but by members of the public health community.

The devastating potential of bioweapons is confounded by the fact that people normally have no idea that they have been exposed. During the incubation period, when they do not exhibit symptoms but are contagious to others, they can spread the disease by touch or through the air. Incubation periods can be as short as several hours but as long as several weeks, allowing for wide geographic spreading due to the efficiency of modern travel. The spread of the SARS virus (which was not a terrorist attack) throughout all continents of the world is an evidence of this phenomenon.

Biological weapons are also effective at disrupting economic and industrial components of society, even when they only target animals or plants. Terrorists could potentially spread a biological agent over a large geographic area, undetected, causing significant destruction of crops. If the agent spread easily, as is often the case with natural diseases such as Dutch elm disease, the consequences could be devastating to an entire industry. Cattle diseases such as foot and mouth disease and mad cow disease, which occurs naturally, could be used for sinister purposes with little planning, resources, or technical knowledge. In 1918, the German army did just this, spreading anthrax and other diseases through exported livestock and animal feed. With globalization, such actions would require much less effort to conduct.

The primary defense against the use of biological weapons is recognition, which is achieved through proper training of first responders and public health officials. Early detection, before the disease or illness has spread to critical limits, is key to preventing a major public health emergency.

Biological agents are grouped into three categories, designated A, B, and C. Category A agents are those that have great potential for causing a public health catastrophe, and that are capable of being disseminated over a large geographic area. Examples of Category A agents are anthrax, smallpox, plague, botulism, tularemia, and viral hemorrhagic fevers. Category B agents are those that have low mortality rates, but which may be disseminated over a large geographic area with relative ease. Category B agents include salmonella, ricin, Q fever, typhus, and glanders. Category C agents are common pathogens that have the potential for being engineered for terrorism or weapon purposes. Examples of Category C agents are hantavirus and tuberculosis (FEMA, 2002; Wikipedia, 2005, www.wikipedia.org).

■ ■ Critical Thinking ■

Why do chemical and biological agents instill such fear into the minds of Americans? Do you think that most people overestimate or underestimate their actual risk? What can be done to correct misperceptions of risk? What is most likely causing these misperceptions?

■ ■ ■

Some Indicators of Biological Attack

- Stated threat to release a biological agent
- Unusual occurrence of dead or dying animals
- Unusual casualties
- Unusual illness for region/area
- Definite pattern inconsistent with natural disease
- Unusual liquid, spray, vapor, or powder
- Spraying, suspicious devices, packages, or letters

Source: Federal Emergency Management Agency, Interim Planning Guide for State and Local Anthrax Government: Managing the Emergency Consequences of Terrorist Incidents, Washington, DC: FEMA, July 2002.

■ ■ ■

For indicators of biological attack and a list of biological agents, see the sidebars of the same respective titles. Fact sheets compiled from the CDC website for the following selected biological agents are available as files with matching titles on this book's companion website, together with FEMA information on cyanide, sulfur mustard, sarin, ricin, and chlorine:

- Anthrax
- Smallpox
- Plague
- Botulism
- Tularemia

Next, for a discussion of using vaccines in an emergency-response scenario, see the sidebar "The Difficulties of Preventing or Treating Biological Attacks with Vaccines."

■ ■ ■

List of Biological Agents

- Anthrax (*Bacillus anthracis*)
- Botulism (*Clostridium botulinum* toxin)
- Brucellosis (*Brucella* species)

- Cholera (*Vibricholerae*)
- *E. coli* O157:H7 (*Escherichia coli*)
- Epsilon toxin (*Clostridium perfringens*)
- Emerging infectious diseases such as Nipah virus and hantavirus
- Glanders (*Burkholderia mallei*)
- Melioidosis (*Burkholderia pseudomallei*)
- Typhoid fever (*Salmonella typhi*)
- Typhus fever (*Rickettsia prowazekii*)
- Plague (*Yersinia pestis*)
- Psittacosis (*Chlamydia psittaci*)
- Q fever (*Coxiella burnetii*)
- Ricin (considered to be both a chemical and biological weapon)
- Salmonellosis (*Salmonella* species)
- Smallpox (*Variola major*)
- Staphylococcal enterotoxin B
- Tularemia (*Francisella tularensis*)
- Viral encephalitis (alphaviruses [e.g., Venezuelan equine encephalitis, eastern equine encephalitis, western equine encephalitis])
- Viral hemorrhagic fevers (filoviruses [e.g., Ebola, Marburg] and arenaviruses (e.g., Lassa, Machupo])
- Water safety threats (e.g., Vibricholerae, shigellosis [*Shigella*], *Cryptosporidium parvum*) (Figure 3–1)

Source: Centers for Disease Control and Prevention, www.bt.cdc.gov/agent/agentlist.asp.

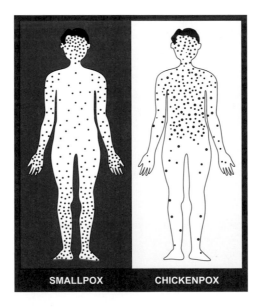

FIGURE 3–1 Rash distribution in (left) smallpox and (right) chickenpox.

The Difficulties of Preventing or Treating Biological Attacks with Vaccines

Unlike chemical, radiological, nuclear, or other WMDs, biological weapons may be prevented before an attack or treated during an attack with the use of vaccines. Vaccines work by helping the body to recognize and destroy a biological agent, thereby developing immunity to it. Vaccines have been used for centuries to prevent or eradicate common diseases, first appearing in 1796 when English physician Edward Jenner developed a vaccine to prevent smallpox. Since then, several diseases have been minimized or eradicated through widespread vaccination programs, including smallpox, polio, measles, rubella, and many other once-common diseases.

Vaccines, however, often come at a high cost. Vaccine development requires significant investments in research, testing, and public relations. For some diseases, including HIV and tuberculosis, expensive, drawn-out campaigns to develop vaccines have thus far proven fruitless despite heavy investment in cash and human resources and decades of time. A second cost of vaccines is the risk associated with administering them. Almost without exception, vaccines carry associated health risks for recipients. For instance, it is estimated that one in every million people given the smallpox vaccine will die as a result of complications directly related to the vaccine itself. In addition to fatalities caused by the vaccine, 1 in 10,000 vaccine recipients experienced one or many other adverse effects directly related to the vaccine itself. These include corneal scarring (blindness), eczema, generalized smallpox-like reaction, and encephalitis.

For many of the biological weapons that are considered to be viable threats, including anthrax and smallpox, there already exist vaccines that could offer a much higher level of resistance in the human population. However, because of the aforementioned costs and risks associated with these vaccines, policymakers are faced with determining whether the vaccine-related injuries and deaths outweigh the potential deaths and injuries that would occur in the event that a terrorist was able to effectively use a biological weapon containing the agent in question. For instance, assuming that approximately 40 million people in the United States would need to be vaccinated (CDC, n.d.), and the administration of the vaccine causes one death for every million people, we should expect that 40 people would die as a result of the vaccine regardless of whether or not an actual smallpox attack ever occurred. Using this baseline, we can then determine whether or not a mass vaccination program is worth the expected vaccine-related fatalities only if we can safely say that the expected result of not vaccinating the population would be a fatality rate greater than 40. To calculate this number, we must first estimate the number of people that would likely be exposed in an attack, multiply this number by 30% (the fatality rate of smallpox), and multiply this again by the expected probability of an attack over the lifetime of the population. So, let's just say that 100,000 people are estimated to be infected in a scenario (a figure chosen for illustrative purposes only). This number would likely lead to 30,000 deaths given the fatality rate of the disease. But if it is determined, for instance, that there is only a 1 in 1,000 chance that an attack like that could happen, then the expected fatality rate based upon the scenario is only 30 deaths — 10 fewer deaths than would be guaranteed in a mass evacuation campaign. Under this scenario the risk associated with the vaccination program is more deadly than the risk associated with an attack.

Because of these and other costs associated with the vaccination of the entire population to certain biological warfare agents, policy has generally dictated that only those specific people who have an individual risk that places the benefit of vaccination greater than the risk of vaccination-related complications (such as active members of the military, public health officials, laboratory workers, and emergency responders), there has never been a single mass vaccination campaign for a biological weapon. Instead, the U.S. government, as well as governments of other countries, has chosen instead to stockpile large amounts of the vaccine to be administered only after an attack is imminent or has already occurred, for the purposes of limiting the spread of the resulting disease. This too has presented problems, however, because the expensive stockpiles quickly expire, and it is doubtful that vaccine programs can be effectively managed in the panic and uncertainty that would result in the aftermath of a biological attack. Further compounding this problem is the fact that weaponized forms of certain biological agents can render the protective benefits of vaccines useless, as is postulated in the case of weaponized anthrax.

For more information on United States efforts to stockpile vaccines against biological weapons, see the CDC article "Developing New Smallpox Vaccines" by Stephen Rosenthal, Michael Merchlinsky, Cynthia Kleppinger, and Karen Goldenthal (http://www.cdc.gov/ncidod/eid/vol7no6/rosenthal.htm).

Nuclear/Radiological

Nuclear and radiological weapons are those that involve the movement of energy through space and through material. There are three primary mechanisms by which terrorists can use radiation to carry out an attack: detonation of a nuclear bomb, dispersal of radiological material, or an attack on a facility housing nuclear material (power plant, research laboratory, storage site, etc.).

Nuclear weapons are the most devastating of the various attack forms listed earlier. They are also the most difficult to develop or acquire, and thus are considered the lowest threat of the three in terms of terrorist potential (likelihood). A nuclear weapon causes damage to property and harm to life through two separate processes. First, a blast is created by the detonation of the bomb. An incredibly large amount of energy is released in the explosion, which is the result of an uncontrolled chain reaction of atomic splitting. The initial shock wave, which destroys all built structures within a range of up to several miles, is followed by a heat wave reaching tens of millions of degrees close to the point of detonation. High winds accompany the shock and heat waves.

The second process by which nuclear weapons inflict harm is through harmful radiation. This radiation and radiological material is most dangerous close to the area of detonation, where high concentrations can cause rapid death, but particles reaching high into the atmosphere can pose a threat several hundreds of miles away under the right meteorological conditions. Radiation can also persist for years after the explosion occurs.

Radiological dispersion devices (RDDs) are simple explosive devices that spread harmful radioactive material upon detonation, without the involvement of a nuclear explosion. These devices are often called "dirty bombs." Radiological dispersion devices also exist that do not require explosives for dispersal. Although illnesses and fatalities very close to the point of dispersal are likely, these devices are more likely to be used to spread terror. Like many biological and chemical weapons, it may be difficult to initially detect that a radiological attack has occurred. Special detection equipment and the training to use it are a prerequisite. See the sidebar "General Indicators of Possible Nuclear Weapon/Radiological Agent Use."

■ ■ ■

General Indicators of Possible Nuclear Weapon/Radiological Agent Use

- Stated threat to deploy a nuclear or radiological device
- Presence of nuclear or radiological equipment
- Spent fuel canisters or nuclear transport vehicles
- Nuclear placards/warning materials along with otherwise unexplained casualties

Source: Federal Emergency Management Agency, "Interim Planning Guide for State and Local Government: Managing the Emergency Consequences of Terrorist Incidents," Washington, DC: FEMA, July 2002.

■ ■ ■

A third scenario involving nuclear/radiological material entails an attack on a nuclear facility. There are many facilities around the country where nuclear material is stored, including nuclear power plants, hazardous materials storage sites, medical facilities, military installations, and industrial facilities. An attack on any of these facilities could result in a release of radiological material into the atmosphere, which would pose a threat to life and certainly cause fear among those who live nearby.

If a radiological or nuclear attack were to occur, humans and animals would experience both internal and external consequences. External exposure results from any contact with radioactive material outside the body, while internal exposure requires ingestion, inhalation, or injection of radiological materials. Radiation sickness results from high doses of radiation, and can result in death if the dosage is high enough. Other effects of radiation exposure can include redness or burning of the skin and eyes, nausea, damage to the body's immune system, and a high lifetime risk of developing cancer (FEMA, 2002).

Information developed by the CDC on a radiation event is presented on the companion website in the document "Facts about a Radiation Emergency."

Preparedness and Sheltering in Place

There are many options for members of the general public who wish to prepare for the effects of terrorist attacks involving the use of chemical, biological, or radiological weapons. In general, these options involve various implements or methods to avoid contact with the agents themselves, or with infected or contaminated individuals. One of the most effective means of preventing exposure to these weapons is to remain indoors after an attack has occurred, termed "sheltering in place," thereby avoiding the likelihood of coming into contact with the pathogen, chemical, or radiation by traveling unprotected through an area of contamination. The federal government, through the Ad Council, has developed and published several options for those wishing to take preparative measures on the Ready.Gov website, as have several other agencies including the Centers for Disease Control and Prevention, the Department of Energy, and many state and local offices of emergency management and homeland security. Levels of actual application of these measures by the general public are assumed to be very low, however, due to a combination of risk perception factors that generate a sense of inability to mitigate WMD effects, and a prioritization of risk reduction measures by these individuals that places such actions lower in priority ranking.

The "Preparedness and Response for a Bioterror or Chemical Attack" fact sheet discusses how the general population can prepare for a bioterror or chemical attack. Preparedness against dispersion of a chemical agent is further discussed in "Chemical Agents: Facts about Sheltering in Place." Both are available on the companion website for this book.

Combined Hazards

By combining two or more methods of attack, terrorists can achieve a synergistic effect. And in doing so, they often increase the efficacy of each agent in terms of its potential to destroy, harm, or kill, thereby creating a sum total consequence much more devastating than had each agent been used independently. The dirty bomb, in which radiological material is added to a conventional explosive, is a perfect illustration of this effect. Explosives function by causing physical damage resulting from the expansion of gases, while the radiological material works by inducing a range of adverse health effects. The combination of the two results in an attack that not only causes both physical damage and harmful radiation, but disperses the radiological material over a much larger area, contaminates both the crime scene and the surrounding structures and environment, and instills a sense of fear into the entire affected population (which can extend to include the entire nation as would likely be the case if a dirty bomb was used anywhere in the country). "Facts about Dirty Bombs," available on the companion website for this book, comprises a fact sheet compiled by the CDC describing dirty bombs and their effects.

Explosives can also be used to deliver chemical or biological weapons in a similar manner. This presents a dangerous scenario in that the trauma resulting from the explosion will demand immediate attention from responders, who may enter a contaminated attack scene without first recognizing or taking the time to check if a biological or chemical agent is present. Victims who are rushed to hospitals can cause secondary infections or injuries to EMS and hospital staff. Additionally, contaminated debris can help to spread certain viruses that may not otherwise have so easily entered the body. There have even been cases of HIV-positive suicide bombers passing their infection to victims struck with bits of shrapnel and bone.

When multiple chemicals, biological agents, or a combination of the two are used in an attack, the consequences can confound even those considered experts. The combination of symptoms resulting from multiple injuries or infections will make diagnosis extremely difficult, because these diagnoses often depend on a defined set of effects. The multiple agents will cause physiological effects in humans, animals, or plants that do not fit any established models. The extra time required for identification of the agents used will undoubtedly cause an overall increase in the efficacy of the terrorist attack.

Other Armed Attacks Using Firearms or Other Tactics

In addition to the CBRNE weapons described above, terrorists may employ tactical methods to instill terror and cause death and destruction. In fact, of the 10,999 attacks that took place in 2009, only 41% of those involved the use of bombs, incendiary devices, or suicide bomb attacks (NCTC, 2009). The remaining 59% of attacks involved armed attacks, assault, kidnapping, other methods, or were unknown. Table 3–6 illustrates how the 2009 attacks were distributed by both method of attack and resulting deaths.

Terrorists generally use the weapons that best meet their budget, expertise, target, and the resources they have accessible. Based on these statistics, it is clear that terrorists favor weapons other than CBRNE weapons, and of the CBRNE weapons that are used, the overwhelming majority are explosive or incendiary in nature. Judging by the number of fatalities caused by these explosive attacks, they are much more effective at causing the fatalities sought by the perpetrators. However, it is undeniable that terrorist

Table 3–6 Worldwide Fatalities by Terrorism Attack Type, 2009

Method of Terrorist Attack	Number of People Killed[a]	Number of Attacks Using the Method[a]
Bombing	7,056	4,050
Armed attack	6,415	4,842
Suicide	3,177	299
Unknown	1,324	709
Assault	1,135	479
Kidnapping	1,017	1,039
Arson/firebombing	981	650
Other	181	172

[a]Note that there is some double counting due to the fact that multiple methods were used in many attacks. The total number of people killed in terrorist attacks in 2009 according to the National Counterterrorism Center was 14,971, and the number of attacks was 10,999. *Source:* National Counterterrorism Center. Report on Terrorist Incidents. Washington, DC, April 30, 2010.

attacks using simpler methods of attack can be devastatingly effective, together causing over 50% of all terrorism fatalities worldwide in 2009. FEMA describes several of these other terrorism hazards in their guide "FEMA 452: Risk Assessment: A How-To Guide to Mitigate Potential Terrorist Attacks," displayed in Table 3–7.

■ ■ Critical Thinking ■

What is the difference between a terrorist attack and an act of war? Do you think that the terrorist attacks that occur in Iraq are terrorism? Why or why not? Will it ever be possible to eradicate terrorism entirely? Why or why not?

Selected Examples of Chemical, Biological, Radiological, and Nuclear Incidents
- **February 2008:** Ricin was discovered in a hotel room occupied by a man who suddenly fell into a coma. The man had produced the toxin years earlier and had been storing it since, but claimed to have never used it for purposes of terrorism.
- **June 2007:** A car bomb rigged with canisters of chlorine gas was detonated outside a U.S. military base located in Diyala, Iraq, sickening 62 soldiers but causing no fatalities.
- **May 2007:** Bombs rigged with chlorine were detonated in two separate incidents in Iraq: one in an open-air market in the Diyala Province, killing 32 and injuring 50 people, and the other at a police checkpoint in the Zangora District, killing as many as 11 people (though most if not all fatalities in both incidents were attributed to the effects of the explosives, not the chemicals).

Table 3–7   Selected Terrorism Hazards

Threat	Application Mode	Duration	Extent of Effects: Static/ Dynamic	Mitigating and Exacerbating Conditions
Armed attack — Ballistics (small arms) — Stand-off weapons (rocket-propelled grenades, mortars)	Tactical assault or sniper attacks from a remote location.	Generally minutes to days.	Varies, based on the perpetrator's intent and capabilities.	Inadequate security can allow easy access to target, easy concealment of weapons, and undetected initiation of an attack.
Cyber attacks	Electronic attack using one computer system against another.	Minutes to days.	Generally no direct effects on built environment.	Inadequate security can facilitate access to critical computer systems, allowing them to be used to conduct attacks.
High-altitude electromagnetic pulse (HEMP)	An electromagnetic energy field produced in the atmosphere by the power and radiation of a nuclear explosion. It can overload computer circuitry with effects similar to, but causing damage much more swiftly than a lightning strike.	It can be induced hundreds to a few thousand kilometers from the detonation.	Affects electronic systems. There is no effect on people. It diminishes with distance, and electronic equipment that is turned off is less likely to be damaged.	To produce maximum effect, a nuclear device must explode very high in the atmosphere. Electronic equipment may be hardened by surrounding it with protective metallic shielding that routes damaging electromagnetic fields away from highly sensitive electrical components.
High-power microwave (HPM) EMP	A non-nuclear radio-frequency energy field. Radio frequency weapons can be hidden in an attaché case, suitcase, van, or aircraft. Energy can be focused using an antenna, or emitter, to produce effects similar to HEMP, but only within a very limited range.	An HPM weapon has a shorter possible range than HEMP, but it can induce currents large enough to melt circuitry, or it can cause equipment to fail minutes, days, or even weeks later. HPM weapons are smaller-scale, are delivered closer to the intended target, and can sometimes be emitted for a longer duration.	Vulnerable systems include electronic ignition systems, radars, communications, data processing, navigation, and electronic triggers of explosive devices. HPM capabilities can cause a painful burning sensation or other injury to a person directly in the path of the focused power beam, or can be fatal if a person is too close to the microwave emitter.	Very damaging to electronics within a small geographic area. A shock wave could disrupt many computers within a 1-mile range. Radio frequency weapons have ranges from tens of meters to tens of kilometers. Unlike HEMP, however, HPM radiation is composed of shorter wave forms at higher frequencies, which make it highly effective against electronic equipment and more difficult to harden against.

Source: FEMA 452: Risk Assessment: A How-To Guide to Mitigate Potential Terrorist Attacks, http://www.fema.gov/plan/prevent/rms/rmsp452.shtm.

- **April 2007:** Three separate incidents involving truck bombs rigged with chlorine occurred in Iraq: one incident at a Ramadi police checkpoint, killing 27 and injuring 30; another at a checkpoint outside Baghdad, killing 1 and injuring 2; and a third near a restaurant in Ramadi, killing 6 and wounding 10 (though most if not all fatalities in all three incidents were attributed to the effects of the explosives, not the chemicals).
- **March 2007:** Four attacks involving the detonation of tankers or other trucks containing chlorine occurred in Iraq: an attack at a Ramadi checkpoint wounded 2 people, an attack in Falluja killed 2 and injured hundreds, an attack in Falluja killed 6 and injured 250, and a fourth injured 71.
- **February 2007:** Three attacks involving the detonation of explosives and the release of chlorine occurred in Iraq: a suicide bomber in Ramadi killed 2 and injured 16, the detonation of a tanker truck near Baghdad killed 9 and injured 148, and a truck bomb in Baghdad killed 5 and hospitalized over 50.
- **January 2007:** A truck bomb in Iraq rigged with chlorine gas canisters was detonated in Ramadi, killing 16.
- **November 2006:** Alexander Litvinenko, a former Russian Federal Security Service official, was poisoned in a suspected assassination in London with radioactive polonium-210.
- **October 2006:** A car bomb rigged with mortar shells and chlorine gas canisters was detonated in Ramadi, wounding four people.
- **February 2004:** U.S. Senate Majority Leader Bill Frist received a letter containing ricin powder. Several staff members needed decontamination, but no injuries or fatalities occurred as a result of the attack.
- **October 2003:** A metallic container was discovered at a Greenville, South Carolina, postal facility with ricin in it. The small container was in an envelope along with a threatening note. Authorities did not believe this was a terrorism-related incident. The note expressed anger against regulations overseeing the trucking industry.
- **August 2002:** Ansar al-Islam, a Sunni militant group, was reported to have tested ricin powder as an aerosol on animals such as donkeys and chickens and perhaps even an unwitting human subject. Additional specific details have not been released.
- **February 2002:** Italian authorities arrested as many as nine Moroccan nationals who may have been plotting to poison the water supply of the U.S. embassy in Rome. Authorities confiscated a detailed map of Rome's underground water system, highlighting the location of the U.S. embassy's pipes. The suspects also had 4 kg potassium ferrocyanide in their possession.
- **December 2001:** According to press reports, the military wing of HAMAS (Palestinian Islamic Resistance Movement) claimed that the bolts and nails packed into explosives detonated by a suicide bomber had been dipped in rat poison.
- **October 2001:** U.S. and international law enforcement authorities stepped up investigations in the United States and abroad to determine the sources of confirmed cases of anthrax exposures in Florida, New York, and Washington, DC. In the past several years, there have been hundreds of hoaxes involving anthrax in the United States. In the aftermath of the September 11 terrorist attacks against the United States, these anthrax scares have spread across the globe and have exacerbated international concerns. The confirmed anthrax cases involved letters sent through the mail to the U.S. Congress and several media organizations. More than 50 individuals were exposed to *B. anthracis* spores, including 18 who became infected, and 5 people died from inhalation anthrax — the first reported cases in the United States in 25 years. U.S. and international health organizations have treated thousands of individuals associated with these incidents.

- **September 2001**: Colombian police accused the Revolutionary Armed Forces of Colombia (FARC) of using improvised grenades filled with poisonous gas during an attack on the city of San Adolfin, Huila Department. According to media accounts, four policemen died and another six suffered respiratory problems from the attack.
- **January 2000**: According to press reports, a Russian general accused Chechen rebels of delivering poisoned wine and canned fruit to Russian soldiers in Chechnya.
- **November 1999**: Raw materials for making ricin were seized by law enforcement authorities during the arrest of a U.S. citizen who threatened to poison two Colorado judges.
- **June 1998**: U.S. law enforcement authorities arrested two members of the violent secessionist group called the Republic of Texas for planning to construct a device with toxins to kill selected government officials. A U.S. federal court convicted them in October 1998 for threatening to use a weapon of mass destruction.
- **December 1996**: Sri Lankan press noted that government authorities warned the military in the northern region not to purchase food or stamps from local vendors, because some stamps had been found laced with cyanide.
- **August 1995**: An MIT Center for Cancer Research employee ingested radioactive phosphorus-32, in what was believed to be a deliberate attempt to poison him.
- **July 1995**: Four improvised chemical devices (ICDs) were found in restrooms at the Kayaba-cho, Tokyo, and Ginza subway stations and the Japanese railway's Shinjuku station. Each device was slightly different but contained the same chemicals.
- **May 1995**: An ICD was left in Shinjuku station in Tokyo. The device consisted of two plastic bags, one containing sodium cyanide and the other sulfuric acid. If the device had not been neutralized, the chemicals would have combined to produce a cyanide gas.
- **May 1995**: A U.S. citizen, and member of the neo-Nazi Aryan Nations, acquired three vials of *Yersinia pestis*, the bacteria that causes plague, from a Maryland lab. Law enforcement officials recovered the unopened material and arrested the individual. No delivery system was recovered, and no information indicated the subject's purpose in obtaining the bacteria.
- **March 20, 1995**: Members of the Japanese cult Aum Shinrikyo used ICDs to release sarin nerve gas in the Tokyo subway station. Twelve people died, and thousands of others were hospitalized or required medical treatment.
- **March 15, 1995**: Three briefcases were left at locations in the Kasumigaseki train station in Tokyo. No injuries resulted, but an Aum Shinrikyo member later confessed that this was a failed biological attack with Botulinum toxin.
- **January 1995**: Tajik opposition members laced champagne with cyanide at a New Year's celebration, killing six Russian soldiers and the wife of another soldier and sickening other revelers.
- **June 27, 1994**: A substance identified as sarin was dispersed using a modified van in a residential area near Matsumoto; 7 people died, and more than 200 people were injured. Reportedly, an Aum Shinrikyo member confessed that the cult targeted three judges who lived there to prevent them from returning an adverse decision against the cult.
- **1993**: A U.S. citizen was detained by the Canadian Customs Service as he attempted to enter Canada from Alaska. A white powdery substance was confiscated and later identified through laboratory analysis as ricin. The individual, traveling with a large sum of cash, told officials that he was carrying the poison to protect his money.
- **1992**: Four individuals were convicted by a U.S. federal court for producing ricin and advocating the violent overthrow of the government. The subjects, who had espoused extremist,

antigovernment, antitax ideals, specifically had targeted a deputy U.S. marshal who previously had served papers on one of them for tax violations.

- **1984:** An outbreak of *Salmonella* poisoning that occurred in Oregon during a two-week period was linked to the salad bars of eight restaurants. More than 700 people were affected, but no fatalities occurred. Investigators of the outbreak determined that two members of the Rajneesh religious sect produced and dispensed *Salmonella* bacteria in the restaurants in order to influence a local election by incapacitating opposition voters.

Sources: CIA, "Terrorism: Guide to Chemical, Biological, Radiological, and Nuclear Weapons Indicators," 2002; CNN, February 4, 2004; CNS Reports, February 3, 2004; BBC News, "Timeline: Iraq," 2007.

Difficulty of Predicting Terror Attacks in the United States

A risk index published on August 18, 2003, by the World Markets Research Center (WMRC), a business intelligence firm based in London, ranked the United States fourth among the top five countries most likely to be targeted for a terrorist attack within the 12-month period that followed (www.wmrc.com). The index also predicted that "another September 11-style terrorist attack in the United States is highly likely." Colombia, Israel, and Pakistan ranked in the top three positions, respectively. After the United States, the Philippines, Afghanistan, Indonesia, Iraq, India, and Britain, which tied with Sri Lanka, rounded out the top 10. North Korea ranked as the least likely country to experience a terrorist attack within that next year. The index, which assessed the risk of terrorism to some 186 countries and their interests, was based on five criteria: "motivation of terrorists; the presence of terror groups; the scale and frequency of past attacks; efficacy of the groups in carrying out attacks; and how many attacks were thwarted by the country." Explaining the U.S. ranking, the index stated that while the presence of militant Islamic networks within the United States is less extensive than in Western Europe, "U.S.-led military action in Afghanistan and Iraq has exacerbated anti-U.S. sentiment" (Homeland Security Monitor, August 19, 2003).

This rank designation made issues such as detection, containment, control, quarantine, and vaccination — to name just a few — significant factors in developing new response and recovery practices for first responders. Political affairs and events across the globe have factored heavily in efforts to prepare populations and to mitigate the impacts of these new hazards on those populations and on critical infrastructure, communities, economies, and the normality of daily life.

During the months that followed the WMRC risk prediction, the actual incidence of terrorism followed drastically different patterns than expected. Who, for instance, could have foreseen that the Maoist insurgency in Nepal would have heated up so quickly, with such deadly consequences? Or who could have guessed that Islamic separatists in the southern provinces of Thailand would have resorted to such brutal measures as to place that country near the top of the terrorism target list for many years to come? The situation in Iraq, by far the ongoing leader in both number of attacks and associated fatalities, spiraled out of control much faster than anyone could have imagined, thanks to the presence of third-world terrorists who imported their deadly methods and materials. The differences in what was predicted and what transpired highlight the difficulty of analyzing and evaluating intentional hazards such as terrorism that are dynamic and that respond to unforeseeable social, political, economic, and other anthropologically generated factors.

Table 3–8 presents the top 15 countries ranked by number of people killed in terrorist attacks in 2005 and 2009, adapted from studies conducted by the National Counterterrorism Center (NCTC) and the Federal Bureau of Investigation (FBI). This table illustrates how great uncertainty factors into any terrorism risk prediction from one year to the next.

A general lack of experience with and knowledge about these new hazards, and the realization that they could be deliberately used to harm or kill U.S. citizens, has resulted in a perception by nearly all Americans that they are potential terrorist targets. (See sidebar "Where Will Terrorists Strike?") And unlike hurricanes or tornadoes, which tend to have geographical boundaries, the general terrorist threat and each of the new hazards must be considered national risks. People in Montana do not worry about hurricanes, and it rarely floods in the desert of Nevada. There have been few if any tornadoes reported in Maine. But residents of all states may consider themselves, however remotely, the next possible victims of terrorism, thereby reinforcing what has become a skewed perception of risk. The open nature of our governance system and our society has resulted in widespread press coverage of WMD risk analyses at the federal level, especially in relation to belief among various government officials that terrorists will not only acquire WMD technologies in the near future, but that the heartland of America (i.e., small towns, shopping malls, restaurants, and other locations away from major, obvious, and hardened targets) is the most likely next target. The appearance of such weapons in literature, in the cinema, and in the media, as actual events occur around the world (a list of selected chemical, biological, radiological, and nuclear incidents compiled by the Central Intelligence Agency [CIA] is presented in the sidebar "Selected Examples of Chemical, Biological, Radiological, and Nuclear Incidents"), buttresses the exaggerated perception of individual risk.

Table 3–8   Top 15 Countries Ranked by Number of Terrorism-Related Fatalities in 2005 and 2009

Country	Rank in 2005	Number of Fatalities	Rank in 2009 (Change)	Number of Fatalities
Iraq	1	8,262	1 (0)	3,654
India	2	1,361	6 (−4)	663
Colombia	3	813	9 (−6)	323
Afghanistan	4	684	2 (+2)	2,778
Thailand	5	498	7 (−2)	401
Nepal	6	485	N/A	N/A
Pakistan	7	338	3 (+4)	2,670
Russia	8	238	8 (0)	337
Sudan	9	157	10 (−1)	255
DPR Congo	10	154	5 (+5)	1,346
Philippines	11	144	11 (0)	241
Algeria	12	132	12 (0)	128
Sri Lanka	13	130	13 (0)	124
Chad	14	109	N/A	N/A
Uganda	15	109	N/A	N/A
Somalia	N/A	N/A	4	1,441
Iran	N/A	N/A	14	114
Yemen	N/A	N/A	15	73

Where Will Terrorists Strike? Different Theories …

One of the greatest problems facing the Department of Homeland Security is trying to determine where terrorists will strike next. Major U.S. cities are considered the most likely targets for terrorist attacks, as evidenced by risk-based funding for terrorism that has clearly targeted urban centers with the greatest amount of counterterrorism-related funding. There are, however, opinions that conflict with this majority assessment.

In 2003, Deputy Secretary of Health and Human Services Claude Allen stated that rural America should be considered among the most likely sites for the next terror attack in the United States, especially a bioterrorism attack. Deputy Secretary Allen stated that "[s]ome rural communities are among the most vulnerable to attack, simply because of their proximity to a missile silo or to a chemical stockpile. Other rural communities are vulnerable simply because they mistakenly believe that terrorism is an urban problem and they are safe from attack." While Allen said the federal government has increased funding for bioterrorism preparedness, he also noted that rural areas are vulnerable given their "limited infrastructure for public health as well as fewer health care providers and volunteer systems."

In March 2004, CSO Online, an industry journal for security executives, conducted a survey that asked where in the United States terrorists would likely strike next. The results of the poll indicated that these industry experts felt the next target would be the airline industry (3%), a seaport (7%), a large public event (23%), an urban mass transit system (27%), or a "different and unexpected target" (41%). Considering the efforts that are under way to block an attack on known or expected targets, it would follow in this line of thinking that terrorists would seek to exploit an unknown target that would likely be "soft," or more vulnerable to attack. Citing another major area of vulnerability, a Princeton University research group found that most Internet experts feel that a devastating cyber attack will occur within the next 10 years, possibly affecting business, utilities, banking, communications, and other Internet-dependent components of society.

On June 23, 2005, the U.S. Senate Foreign Relations Committee released a report stating that there was a 50% chance of a major WMD-based attack, between 2005 and 2010, somewhere in the world. The report was based on a poll of 85 national security and nonproliferation experts. The reports found that the risks of biological or chemical attacks were comparable to or slightly higher than the risk of a nuclear attack, but that there is a "significantly higher" risk of a radiological attack.

As of late 2011, it seems that many of those security experts questioned by CSO Online were correct in their assessments. Although no successful attacks have been carried out since the October 2001 anthrax attacks, there have been at least 30 incidents thwarted in various stages of planning and development. The most significant of these include:

- Shoe Bomber Richard Reid (2001) – Unsuccessful attempt to destroy a commercial airline in flight
- Jose Padilla (2002) – Planning to use a dirty bomb
- Lackawanna Six (2002) – Attended jihadist training in Pakistan to learn how to attack Americans
- Lyman Faris (2003) – Planning to destroy the Brooklyn Bridge
- Virginia Jihad Network (2003) – Planning undetermined attacks against Americans
- Nuradin Abdi (2003) – Planning to bomb a shopping mall
- Dhiren Barot (2004) – Planning to attack the New York Stock Exchange
- James Elshafay and Shahawar Matin Siraj – Planning to bomb a New York subway station
- Yassin Aref and Mohammed Hossein (2004) – Planning to assassinate a Pakistani diplomat in New York City

- Levar Haley Washington, Gregory Vernon Patterson, Hammad Riaz Samana, and Kevin James (2005) – Planning to attack National Guard facilities, synagogues, and other targets in the Los Angeles area
- Michael Reynolds (2005) – Planning to blow up a natural gas refinery in Wyoming
- Narseal Batiste, Patrick Abraham, Stanley Grant Phanor, Naudimar Herrera, Burson Augustin, Lyglenson Lemorin, and Rotschild Augustine (2006) – Planning to destroy the Chicago Sears Tower, FBI offices, and other government buildings
- Assem Hammoud (2006) – Planning to attack underground transit links between New York City and New Jersey
- Derrick Shareef (2006) – Planning to set off hand grenades in a Chicago-area shopping mall
- Fort Dix Plot (2007) – Six men planned to attack Fort Dix Army post in New Jersey using assault rifles and grenades
- JFK Airport Plot (2007) – Four men planned to blow up aviation fuel tanks and pipelines at the John F. Kennedy International Airport in New York City
- Christopher Paul (2008) – Planning to use weapons of mass destruction against Americans
- Synagogue Terror Plot (2009) – Four men planned to attack Jewish centers in New York and planes at a nearby military base
- Najibullah Zazi (2009) – Planning to detonate explosives on the New York City subway
- Hosam Maher Husein Smadi (2009) – Planning to plant a bomb in a Dallas skyscraper
- Michael Finton (2009) – Attempting to detonate a car bomb in downtown Springfield, IL
- Tarek Mehanna and Ahmad Abousamra (2009) – Planning to kill U.S. politicians, American troops in Iraq, and civilians in local shopping malls
- Umar Farouk Abdulmutallab (2009) – Attempted to detonate a bomb hidden in his underwear on a U.S.-bound international flight as the plane began to land

Sources: Homeland Security Monitor, August 28, 2003; ClickZ Network, January 9, 2005; CSO Online, March 25, 2004; Associated Press, June 23, 2005; Haltman, Michael, May 23, 2010.

Conclusion

Terrorism has presented emergency managers in the United States with an expanded range of new hazards — many of which are just now emerging, and many others that have existed elsewhere in the world for centuries but are now legitimate threats to the nation. These hazards have required a significant investment in education of the general public, local officials, the media, and our first responders. This requirement is surpassed in cost by the need to invest in training, protective equipment and gear, specialized technical capabilities, and enhancements of our public health networks. The threat of terrorism in the United States has presented a unique opportunity to integrate many groups responsible for mitigating, preparing, responding to, and recovering from less traditional consequences of disasters, such as the public health service, that will likely assist not only with terrorist hazards but also in just about any devastating disaster event that might occur. It has given us the opportunity to include many of these public health concerns into general disaster planning efforts, and has increased cooperation with the private sector in emergency management systems and efforts (often because privately owned and maintained financial and communications infrastructures are primary terrorist targets). The research and development efforts associated with these new hazards, described in greater detail in Chapter 12, have already begun to result in advances spanning a broad spectrum of human activities from medicine to communications technology, and have led to the development of safer personal protective equipment (PPE), vaccines, and other defenses for the first responders that must manage attack consequences. Most importantly, these new hazards, and the financial resources connected with addressing them, can provide an opportunity to actually embrace and apply an all-hazards approach to achieving a homeland that is more secure from the threat of weapons of mass destruction, technological hazards, and natural hazards alike.

Key Terms

Aerosol Device: A tool, device, or machine that converts liquid or solid matter into a gas or otherwise airborne suspension.

Biological Weapon: A warfare or terrorist device capable of projecting, dispersing, or disseminating a biological warfare agent (bacteria, virus, or toxin).

Blister Agent: Also known as a vesicant, a blister agent is any chemical compound that, upon contact with exposed skin, eyes, or other tissue, causes severe pain and irritation.

Blood Agent: Any chemical compound that is inhaled, ingested, or absorbed, which prevents otherwise normal blood cells from carrying oxygen.

Category A Biological Weapon: Organisms that can be easily disseminated or transmitted from person to person; result in high mortality rates and have the potential for major public health impact; might cause public panic and social disruption; and require special action for public health preparedness.

Category B Biological Weapon: Second-highest-priority agents, including those that are moderately easy to disseminate; result in moderate morbidity rates and low mortality rates; and require specific enhancements of diagnostic capacity and enhanced disease surveillance.

Category C Biological Weapon: Third-highest-priority agents, including emerging pathogens that could be engineered for mass dissemination in the future because of availability; ease of production and dissemination; and potential for high morbidity and mortality rates and major health impact.

CBRNE: Weapons that are chemical, biological, radiological/nuclear, or explosive in nature, often referred to as "weapons of mass destruction" (WMDs).

Chemical Weapon: A warfare or terrorist device capable of projecting, dispersing, or disseminating a chemical warfare agent.

Choking/Pulmonary Agent: A chemical weapon affecting the lungs, designed to impede a victim's ability to breathe (ultimately resulting in their suffocation).

Containment: The prevention of spread of biological, chemical, or radiological materials.

Cyberterrorism: The use or destruction of computing or information technology resources aimed at harming, coercing, or intimidating others in order to achieve a greater political or ideological goal.

Detection: Recognition of the existence of a WMD agent, or the consequences of such an attack. Detection is often achieved through various public health service working together to recognize trends in disease symptoms and geographical coverage.

Drought: A prolonged shortage of available water.

Earthquake: A sudden, rapid shaking of the earth's surface that is caused by the breaking and shifting of tectonic plates.

Explosive Weapon (Conventional Explosives): A device relying on the expansion of gases and/or the propelling of bits of metal, glass, and other materials, to achieve bodily harm, death, and destruction.

Flood: An overabundance of water that engulfs dry land and property that is normally dry.

Hazard: A source of danger that may or may not lead to an emergency or disaster.

Hazardous Materials: Chemical substances that, if released or misused, can pose a threat to people and the environment.

High-Filler Explosive: An explosive that combusts nearly instantaneously, thereby producing a violent, shattering effect. High-filler explosives, which are most often used by the military in shells and bombs, may be detonated by a spark, flame, or by impact, or may require the use of a detonator. Examples include TNT, RDX, and HBX.

Hurricane: A cyclonic atmospheric storm occurring in the Western Hemisphere, characterized by sustained wind speeds exceeding 74 mph.

Incapacitating Agent: A chemical warfare agent that produces a temporary disabling condition (physiological or psychological) that persists. Oftentimes, incapacitating agents result in death to those exposed due to unexpected physical reactions.

Incendiary Weapon: A weapon that disperses a chemical weapon that causes fire. Napalm bombs, used extensively in the Vietnam War to reduce forest coverage, are one example.

Irritant: A noncorrosive chemical that causes a reversible inflammatory effect on living tissue at the site of contact (skin, eyes, or respiratory tract).

Low-Filler Explosives: Also called "low explosives," a low-filler explosive is a mixture of a combustible substance and an oxidant that decomposes rapidly once ignited. Under normal conditions, low explosives undergo combustion rates that vary from a few centimeters per second to approximately 400 m/s. It is possible, however, for low-filler explosives to combust so quickly as to produce an effect similar to detonation (see high-filler explosive) as often occurs when ignited in a confined space. Gunpowder and pyrotechnics (including flares and fireworks) are generally low explosives.

Mass Movement: Hazard characterized by a horizontal or lateral movement of large quantities of physical matter.

Natural Hazard: A hazard that exists in the natural environment as a result of hydrological, meteorological, seismic, geologic, volcanic, mass movement, or other natural processes, and that poses a threat to human populations and communities.

Nerve Agent: A chemical weapon that is absorbed through the skin, eyes, or lungs, that disrupts the body's nervous system.

Nuclear Weapon: A weapon whose destructive force is derived from the energy produced and released during a fission or fusion reaction.

Persistent Chemical: A chemical agent or weapon that maintains its toxic properties for an extended period of time following release into the atmosphere (several hours or days).

Quarantine: The imposed isolation placed upon people, animals, or objects that are confirmed or suspected of being contaminated or infected with a chemical or biological agent, for the purpose of limiting the spread of exposure.

Radiological Dispersion Device: A bomb or other weapon used to spread radiological waste across a wide area for the purpose of causing contamination and bodily harm (often called a "dirty bomb").

Radiological Weapon: See "Radiological dispersion device."

Satchel Charge: A powerful yet portable explosive device traditionally used by infantry forces, but which has become a terrorist weapon of choice in that they blend easily for effective concealment in public places.

Storm Surge: Masses of water that are pushed toward the shore by meteorological forces.

Synergistic Effect: Simultaneous action of separate things that have a greater total effect than the sum of their individual effects.

Tornado: A rapidly rotating vortex or funnel of air extending groundward from a cumulonimbus cloud.

Tsunami: A wave or series of waves generated by a mass displacement of sea or lake water.

Vaccination: The process of administering weakened or dead pathogens to a healthy person or animal, with the intent of conferring immunity against a targeted form of a related disease agent.

Volcano: A break in the earth's crust through which molten rock from beneath the earth's surface erupts.

Wildfire: Large fires which spread throughout the natural environment, whether at the surface, close to the ground, or in the forest crown.

Review Questions

1. Discuss the two major differences between traditional hazards (i.e., hurricanes, floods, tornadoes, earthquakes, hazardous materials incidents) and the new hazards associated with terrorism.
2. What are five major categories of hazards associated with terrorism?
3. Discuss the appropriate responses to the new hazards associated with terrorism. For each hazard, when is it appropriate to shelter in place, evacuate, and/or quarantine?
4. Understanding the new hazards associated with terrorism will be critical to reducing the fear among the public of these hazards. This was done very successfully in the past in understanding and dispelling the fear surrounding traditional hazards. How would you design and implement a public education campaign concerning the new hazards? What information would you present and how?
5. If you were a member of Congress, what role would you foresee for the federal government in researching these new hazards, identifying appropriate response and preparedness measures, and educating the public? What role would you have if you were a governor? What role would you have if you were a mayor or county executive?

References

Coppola, D., 2011. Introduction to International Disaster Management 2nd Edition. Butterworth Heinemann, Burlington, MA.

Federal Emergency Management Agency (FEMA), 2002. Managing the Emergency Consequences of Terrorist Incidents—Interim Planning Guide for State and Local Governments. FEMA, Washington, DC.

Haltman, M., 2010. More Than 30 Incidents of Domestic Terrorism Attacks Thwarted Since 9/11. The Homeland Security Examiner, May 23, http://www.examiner.com/homeland-security-in-national/more-than-30-incidents of-domestic-terrorism-attacks-thwarted-since-9-11.

LaCommare, K., Eto, J., 2004. Understanding the Cost of Power Interruptions to US Electricity Consumers. Ernest Orlando Lawrence Berkeley National Laboratory. http://certs.lbl.gov/pdf/55718.pdf.

NCTC Report, 2009. www.nctc.gov/witsbanner/docs/2009_report_on_terrorism.pdf.

4

Governmental Homeland Security Structures

What You Will Learn

- The individual components that compose the Department of Homeland Security, the function of each component, and other interesting facts and figures about each
- The causes and nature of major structural changes that have occurred within the Department of Homeland Security since it was established in 2002
- The federal agencies, in addition to the Department of Homeland Security, that participate in traditional homeland security activities and the nature of those activities
- The various homeland security-related activities that the nation's state and local organizations participate in, and what types of assistance they provide their constituent members

Introduction

The Department of Homeland Security is a massive agency, juggling numerous responsibilities between a staggeringly wide range of program areas, employing approximately 230,000 people, and managing a massive multibillion-dollar budget and an ambitious list of tasks and goals. The Department leverages resources within federal, state, and local governments, coordinating the ongoing transition of multiple agencies and programs into a single, integrated agency focused on protecting the American people and their homeland.

The function of homeland security, however, is not unique to this one federal department. In fact, there are more than 87,000 different governmental jurisdictions at the federal, state, and local level that have homeland security responsibilities.

This chapter presents the structure and makeup of the Department of Homeland Security as it exists today, explains the organizational positioning of its many components, and details how this organizational structure has changed through time. These components are presented according to three organizational groupings, which include components falling within the Office of the Secretary, preexisting offices (which have maintained their structural integrity within the new Department), and new offices and directorates. This chapter also explains several other areas within the federal government, and at the state and local levels, where homeland security functions exist.

Department of Homeland Security Organizational Chart

At the federal level, the Department of Homeland Security (DHS) organizational composition continues to experience regular transition, and as such remains in a constant state of flux. Several readjustments and reorganizations have occurred during the course of its first decade, with multiple offices and responsibilities being passed between the Departments and many functional components. Though it seemed by the end of first DHS Secretary Tom Ridge's years of service that the basic organizational makeup had been established (see Figure 4–1), incoming DHS Secretary Michael Chertoff proposed several fundamental changes to the Department's organization which were implemented under his widely publicized Reorganization Plan. The Department was again reorganized following the 2005 hurricane season according to the requirements of the Post-Katrina Emergency Management Reform Act (PKEMRA) of 2006.

There are two factors that stand to change the structure of the Department even further as it moves into its second decade. The first is the physical consolidation of the Department's many agencies into a

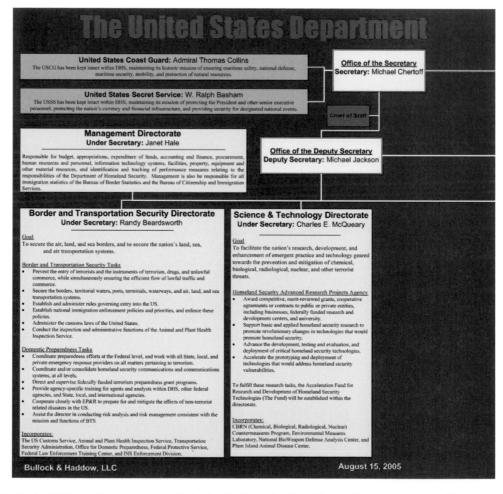

FIGURE 4–1 Original DHS organizational chart, with leadership figures holding office in July of 2005. (Designed by Damon Coppola for Bullock & Haddow, funding provided by the Annie E. Casey Foundation)

new "campus" of buildings that is under construction in the Washington, D.C., area. The Department broke ground for this new massive facility on September 9, 2009, which is being constructed on the site of a former psychiatric institution in the city's southeast. Once the facility is completed, scheduled to occur in 2016, most of the area's 22,000 employees (who are currently scattered across the metropolitan area in dozens of different buildings) will be collocated. It is felt that this will streamline communications and evolve the Department's culture. It may also result in the conglomeration of different offices. The second factor is the completion of the Quadrennial Homeland Security Review which occurred in February 2011. This study was conducted to identify and track all of the Department's functions and to assess how efficiently its various components are carrying out these functions in their present form. Through this study, there will be ongoing efforts to improve upon how the Department does its business, and this will undoubtedly result in the consolidation of various components, the exchange of functions and budgets, and the creation of new offices. The Quadrennial Homeland Security Review states, "The division of operational roles among federal departments and agencies for various homeland security mission goals

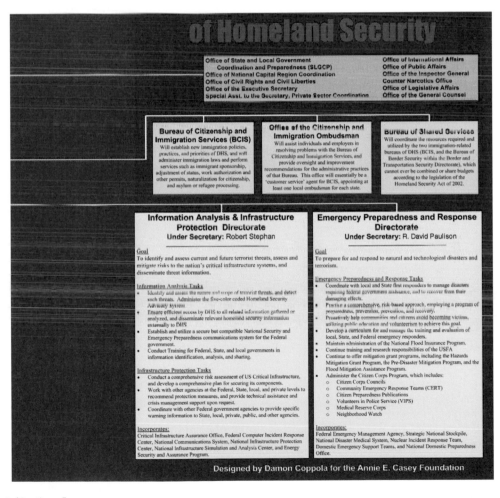

FIGURE 4–1 (Continued)

and objectives [has] emerged as a major area requiring further study[.] . . . Going forward, an analysis of roles and responsibilities across the homeland security missions would help resolve gaps or unnecessary redundancies between departments and agencies" (DHS, 2011). The current organization of the Department is provided in Figure 4–2.

The Office of the Secretary of Homeland Security

The Secretary of Homeland Security is a cabinet-level official, within the executive branch, who leads the department. The first DHS secretary, who served from the department's opening day in March 2003 until February 2005, was former Pennsylvania Governor Tom Ridge. Tom Ridge was followed by Michael Chertoff, who formerly served as a U.S. Circuit Judge for the Third Circuit Court of Appeals and who served as Secretary from February 2005 until January 21, 2009. Former Arizona Governor Janet Napolitano took over the office immediately upon Chertoff's departure and remains in the position as of the publication of this book.

The secretary and his or her staff are responsible for managing the overall direction of the department. This office oversees the activities of the department. In conjunction with other federal, state, local, and private entities, as part of a collaborative effort to strengthen the nation's borders, the Office of the Secretary sets the direction for intelligence analysis and infrastructure protection, improved use of science and technology to counter weapons of mass destruction, and the creation of comprehensive response and recovery initiatives. Within the Office of the Secretary are multiple-program and issue-related offices that contribute to the overall homeland security mission. These offices and their purposes include:

- *The Privacy Office*: This office was created to minimize the impact that the DHS mission has on the privacy of individuals, particularly with respect for their personal information and dignity. Privacy remains a major concern of citizens' advocacy groups due to the types of personally identifiable information that must be gathered in the Department's interaction with American citizens. The DHS privacy office, which is the first in a government agency that is statutorily required, helps to design and implement the means by which the Department handles the information it collects and maintains.

- *Office of Civil Rights and Civil Liberties*: This office provides legal and policy advice to DHS leadership on civil rights and civil liberties issues; investigates and resolves complaints; and provides leadership to Equal Employment Opportunity Programs. Even more so than privacy concerns, civil liberties advocates have argued that the actions of the Department (especially with regard to transportation security, investigations, and counterterrorism measures) have infringed upon the civil liberties and constitutional rights of American citizens. This office tracks those concerns and provides a dedicated staff to the resolution of such issues as they arise, and provides Department-wide training to help manage incidents and reduce the number of incidents that arise.

- *Office of the Inspector General*: This office is responsible for conducting and supervising audits, investigations, and inspections relating to DHS programs and operations, and for recommending ways for DHS to carry out its responsibilities in the most effective, efficient, and economical manner possible. The Inspector General (IG) is a position that is appointed by the President and requires Senate confirmation.

- *Citizenship and Immigration Ombudsman*: This office provides recommendations for resolving individual and employer problems with the U.S. Citizenship and Immigration Services (USCIS) in order to ensure that both the national security and the integrity of the legal immigration system are maintained. The work of this office is a major concern of employers, especially in

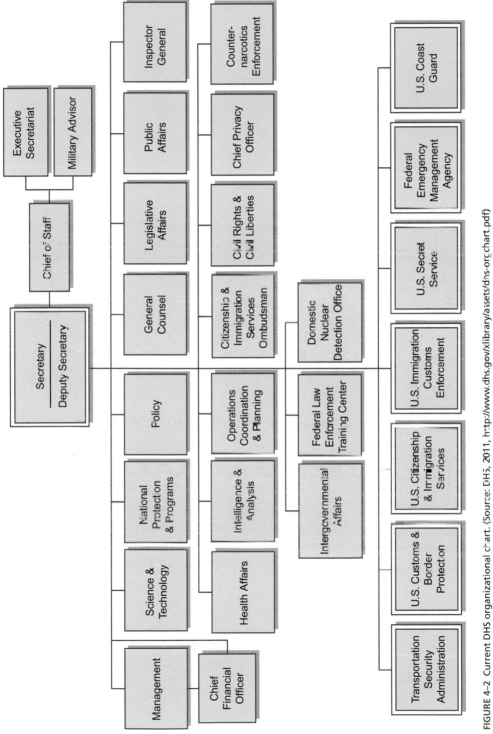

FIGURE 4–2 Current DHS organizational chart. (Source: DHS, 2011, http://www.dhs.gov/xlibrary/assets/dhs-org-chart.pdf)

the agriculture and construction industries, who rely heavily upon a foreign workforce and who have had to dramatically increase their filing and tracking requirements. This office is also tasked with improving the interface that exists between the Department and foreign applicants seeking permission to immigrate to the United States or to become a U.S. citizen.

- *Office of Legislative Affairs*: The staff of this office serve as the primary liaison to members of Congress and their staff, the White House and Executive Branch, and to other federal agencies and governmental entities that have national security roles and concerns. This office is key to ensuring the accurate and effective sharing of information between the department and other key government agencies involved in homeland security.

- *Office of General Counsel*: This office works to integrate the efforts of approximately 1,700 lawyers positioned throughout the Department into what they term to be an "effective, client-oriented, full-service legal team" (DHS, 2007).

- *Office of Public Affairs*: This office is responsible for making sure that the public and the press are informed of the Department's activities and priorities. Because the Federal Emergency Management Agency (FEMA) is now located within the DHS structure, the Department's Office of Public Affairs also serves as the lead Public Information Office (PIO) during a national-level disaster or emergency event. This office is the primary point of contact for the media, outside (nongovernmental and private-sector) organizations, and the general public, when they seek general information about the Department.

- *Office of Counternarcotics Enforcement*: The staff of this office serve as the primary policy advisers to the DHS Secretary for department-wide counternarcotics issues, develop policies that unify DHS counternarcotics activities, and coordinate efforts to monitor and combat connections between illegal drug trafficking and terrorism. Drug interdiction is a function that spans the federal government, existing also within the Department of Justice, the Department of State, the Department of the Treasury, and the White House Office. This office ensures that the DHS efforts support the ongoing government-wide policy and effort.

- *Executive Secretariat*: This office ensures that all DHS officials are included in the correspondence drafting and policymaking process through a managed clearance and control system.

- *Military Advisor's Office*: This office provides sound military advice to the Secretary and other executive staff.

- *The Office of Intergovernmental Affairs*: This office is the primary point of contact with other government agencies at all government levels (including federal, state, local, and tribal governments), integrating the work of the department with that of each of these other entities in their national security efforts.

The Office of the Secretary also maintains a number of advisory panels and committees, which help to form direction and policy on a number of issues deemed critical to the Department's mission. These include:

- The Homeland Security Advisory Council, which provides advice and recommendations to the Secretary on matters related to homeland security. This Council is comprised of leaders from state and local governments, first-responder communities, the private sector, and academia. This council oversees a number of task forces which address topics including border security, community resilience, and Department sustainability and efficiency.

- The National Infrastructure Advisory Council provides advice to the Secretary and the President on the security of information systems for the public and private institutions managing or owning critical infrastructure. Topics addressed include threats to infrastructure, mitigation of infrastructure disruption, establishing resilience standards and goals, understanding and managing infrastructure interdependencies, and the impact of chemical, biological, radiological/nuclear, and explosive (CBRNE) hazards on infrastructure components.

- The Homeland Security Science and Technology Advisory Committee serves as a source of independent scientific and technical planning advice for the Department's Under Secretary for Science and Technology.

- The Critical Infrastructure Partnership Advisory Council was established to facilitate effective coordination between federal infrastructure protection programs and infrastructure protection activities of the private sector and of state, local, territorial, and tribal governments. Committees within this council include Emergency Services; Banking and Finance; Food and Agriculture; Energy, Oil, and Natural Gas Sectors; Freight Rail; Communications; Water; Chemical; Highway; Health Care; Transportation; Nuclear Defense; Dams; Maritime; Mass Transit; Commercial Facilities; and more.

- The Interagency Coordinating Council on Emergency Preparedness and Individuals with Disabilities was established to ensure that the federal government appropriately supports safety and security for individuals with disabilities in disaster situations. This council works to consider how the Department, in their emergency preparedness planning, can accommodate the unique needs of agency employees with disabilities and individuals with disabilities whom the agency serves; to encourage consideration of the unique needs of employees and individuals with disabilities served by state, local, and tribal governments, and private organizations and individuals in emergency preparedness planning; and to facilitate cooperation among federal, state, local, and tribal governments and private organizations and individuals in the implementation of emergency preparedness plans as they relate to individuals with disabilities.

- The Task Force on New Americans leads the interagency effort to develop programs and communication that helps new immigrants to learn English, to embrace American civic culture, and to otherwise become part of the collective American citizenry.

- The DHS Labor Management Forum was established in 2010 according to President Obama's Executive Order 13522 (requiring all executive-level agencies with employees represented by labor organizations to establish Labor-Management Forums) to support cooperative and productive labor-management relations.

Preexisting Offices Moved into DHS in 2002

Several agencies that existed elsewhere in the federal government prior to September 11 were transferred with few or no structural changes into the DHS when it was established. The leadership and staff of each of these agencies now report directly to the Office of the Secretary. Most notable of these agencies are the U.S. Coast Guard (USCG) and the U.S. Secret Service. FEMA was originally integrated into one of four original directorates, but after the bungled response to the post-Katrina 2007 reorganization, FEMA was reinstated as a standalone agency reporting directly to the DHS Secretary. The Federal Law Enforcement Training Center (FLETC) was similarly incorporated into a DHS entity in 2002, but restored to its independent status under the DHS Secretary as part of this 2002 reorganization. These intact agencies are described individually in the following subsections.

The U.S. Coast Guard

The U.S. Coast Guard (USCG), under the direction of Commandant Thad W. Allen, was transferred to the DHS as an intact agency on March 1, 2003. Today, the Coast Guard is led by Admiral Robert J. Papp,

Jr. The primary function of the Coast Guard within the DHS remains consistent with its historic mission, as identified in the following ten mission areas:

- Ports, waterways, and coastal security
- Drug interdiction
- Aids to navigation
- Search and rescue
- Living marine resources
- Defense readiness
- Migrant interdiction
- Marine environment protection
- Ice operations
- Other law enforcement

As lead federal agency for maritime safety and security, the USCG protects several of the nation's vital interests; the personal safety and security of the American population; the natural and economic resources of the United States; and the territorial integrity of the country from both internal and external threats, natural and human-made. As a military, maritime service, the USCG is responsible for a blend of humanitarian, law enforcement, regulatory, diplomatic, and military duties — all for which it is entirely qualified — to provide maritime security, maritime safety, protection of natural resources, maritime mobility, and national defense services (Figure 4–3).

The USCG was recognized after September 11 as being a well-equipped military force with established jurisdiction within U.S. territory. Immediately following September 11, the importance of this fact was not lost on federal government officials who witnessed how, as naval ships were quickly leaving the nation's ports to protect themselves, the Coast Guard's ships were moving into position inside those same ports.

Since entering DHS, the USCG has received a significant boost in its budget allocation, which has been used primarily to update a fleet of ships and aircraft that was considered outdated in relation to the other armed services (as part of the ongoing Integrated Deepwater System project). Additionally, many more employees have been added to the agency's payroll. As of 2010, the Coast Guard employed 42,171 active duty military members and 7,773 civilian employees, for a total of 49,944 people. In addition to these, the USCG maintains 8,100 selected reserve and 30,047 auxiliary employees. Between FY 2004 and FY 2011, the USCG saw its budget rise first from $6.994 billion to $10.078 billion. This represents 18% of the total FY2011 DHS budget authorization (see Figure 4–4).

U.S. Secret Service

The U.S. Secret Service (USSS), under the leadership of Mark J. Sullivan, was transferred to the DHS as an intact agency on March 1, 2003. The Secret Service was able to continue its historic mission of protecting the president and senior executive personnel, in addition to protecting the country's currency and financial infrastructure and providing security for designated national events (e.g., the Super Bowl and the Olympics). The USSS is also responsible for the protection of the vice president, immediate family members of these senior officials, the president-elect, and vice president-elect, or other officers next in the order of succession to the Office of the President and members of their immediate families, presidential candidates, visiting heads of state and their accompanying spouses, and, at the direction of the president, other distinguished foreign visitors to the United States and official representatives of the United States

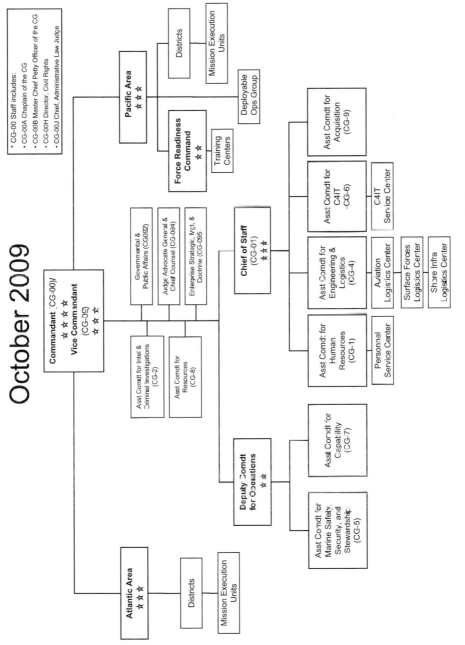

FIGURE 4-3 U.S. Coast Guard organizational chart. (Source: DHS, 2011, http://www.uscg.mil/top/about/organization.asp)

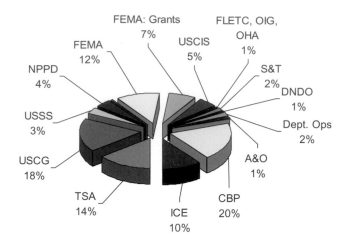

FIGURE 4–4 DHS — Percent of total budget authority by organization. (Source: DHS, 2011, "FY 2012 Budget in Brief," http://www
.dhs.gov/xlibrary/assets/budget-bib-fy2012.pdf)

performing special missions abroad. Former presidents, their spouses, and minor children are also offered
USSS protection for life.

The USSS also protects the executive residence and grounds in the District of Columbia, buildings in
which White House offices are located, the official residence and grounds of the vice president in the District
of Columbia, foreign diplomatic missions located in the Washington metropolitan area, the headquarters
buildings and grounds of the DHS and Treasury Department, and such other areas as directed by the president. The USSS is also responsible for telecommunications fraud, computer and telemarketing fraud, fraud
relative to federally insured financial institutions, and other criminal and noncriminal cases. The Service is
organized into two major components, one focused on protection and the other focused on investigation.

All people, places, and events that are protected represent key components of the nation's government and heritage. They are all, in addition to their intended roles, symbols of the country, and therefore
prime terrorist targets. The loss of any of these, whether due to terrorist or other means, could threaten
the security of the nation, and therefore their protection is considered integral to the homeland security mission. In 2010, the USSS employed 7,014 people. The Secret Service budget allocation has gained
slightly each year, rising from $1.334 billion in FY 2004 to $1.812 billion in FY 2011. This accounts for
about 3% of the total FY 2011 DHS budget.

Federal Emergency Management Agency

The Federal Emergency Management Agency (FEMA) is the government agency responsible for leading
national efforts to mitigate the risk of and prepare for the response to all types of disasters, whether they
are natural, technological, or terrorism related (Figure 4–5). In this effort, FEMA leads several important risk reduction programs including the National Flood Insurance Program, the National Earthquake
Hazards Reduction Program, and others. FEMA is also tasked with managing the federal response and
recovery efforts to support affected states and jurisdictions included in presidentially declared disasters.

FEMA maintains a full-time staff of 7,382 employees (May 2011), of which almost half are funded
through the Disaster Relief Fund (i.e., are associated with the response and recovery of specific disaster
events). These employees work at FEMA headquarters in Washington, D.C., at regional and area offices

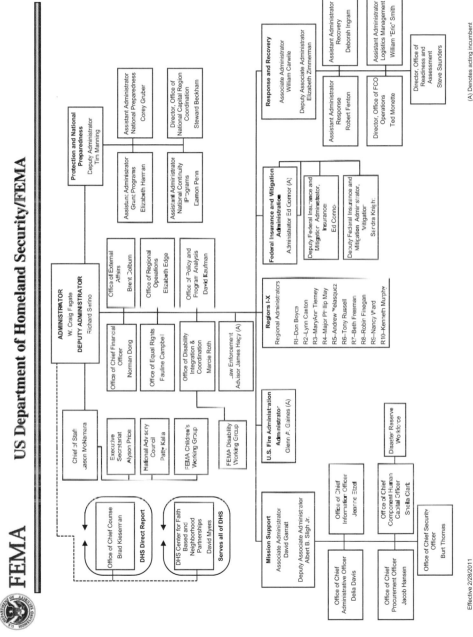

FIGURE 4–5 FEMA organizational chart. (Source: FEMA, 2011, http://www.fema.gov/p3f/about/org_chart.pdf)

across the country (including 10 regional offices, 2 area offices, and 5 recovery offices), at the Mount Weather Emergency Operations Center, and at the National Emergency Training Center in Emmitsburg, Maryland.

While FEMA's central mission has remained the same since it was incorporated into DHS, its various functions have been transferred into and out of the agency during various organizational iterations that have occurred in the intervening years. One of its primary missions, as stated by DHS, is to "further the evolution of the emergency management culture from one that reacts to disasters to one that proactively helps communities and citizens avoid becoming victims." In addition, the directorate develops and manages a national training and evaluation system, designs curriculums, sets standards, and rewards performance in local, state, and federal training efforts.

Through the Disaster Relief Fund, FEMA provides individual and public assistance to help families and communities impacted by disasters rebuild and recover. FEMA also administers hazard mitigation programs to prevent or to reduce the risk to life and property from floods and other hazards. In addition to administering the National Incident Management System (NIMS), in FY 2007, FEMA's role as the lead federal agency for incident management, preparedness, and response was expanded to include the administration of DHS's grant programs and the United States Fire Administration. The inclusion of these programs was intended to reinforce FEMA's ability to provide the United States with a "unified, coordinated, and robust all-hazards preparedness and response capability at all levels of government including federal, state, tribal, and local government personnel, agencies, and regional authorities."

FEMA has been granted the leadership role, through the National Response Framework (NRF) and the Robert T. Stafford Disaster Relief and Emergency Assistance Act, to manage the DHS response to any sort of natural, technological, or terrorist attack disaster. The agency is also in charge of coordinating the involvement of other federal response teams, such as the National Guard, in the event of a major incident. In accordance with the NRF, FEMA also leads federal government relief and recovery efforts that follow major declared disasters. These response and recovery processes are illustrated in much greater detail in Chapter 9.

FEMA also funds and administers the Citizen Corps Program. Citizen Corps funding supports the formation and training of local Citizen Corps Councils (CCCs), which increase local involvement (in CCCs), develop community action plans, help in the performance of threat assessments and the identification of local resources for homeland security, and locally coordinate the Citizen Corps programs. The existing programs, administered by several federal agencies both internal and external to homeland security, involve leaders from law enforcement, fire, and emergency medical services, businesses, community-based institutions, schools, places of worship, health care facilities, public works, and other key community sectors. Current Citizen Corps programs include the following (Citizen Corps activities are documented in greater detail in Chapter 9 of this book):

- Community Emergency Response Teams (CERTs), administered by DHS
- Volunteers in Police Service (VIPS) program, administered by DOJ (Department of Justice)
- Medical Reserve Corps (MRC), administered by HHS (Department of Health and Human Services)
- Neighborhood Watch (USA On Watch) programs, administered by DOJ
- Fire Corps Program, administered by the USA Freedom Corps and several nongovernmental partners
- Citizen-preparedness publications, which are public education guides that seek to increase individual knowledge and preparedness for crime, terrorism, and disasters at home, in neighborhoods, at places of work, and in public spaces

FEMA saw its budget (as a component of the former Emergency Preparedness and Response Directorate until 2006) rise from $5.554 billion in FY 2004 to $7.541 billion in FY 2005, mostly because of biodefense funding. However, biodefense funding was cut from the FEMA budget in FY 2006, dropping the amount the agency received to $5.365 billion. With the introduction of the FEMA Grants

Program in 2008, this amount as requested stood at $9.639 billion. In FY 2011, the FEMA budget stands at $10.528 billion. This amount accounts for 19% of the total DHS budget, of which 7% is real-located outside of FEMA in the form of grants. The FEMA budget can be increased by Congress through emergency appropriations to cover the costs of catastrophic disasters — as was the case following the September 11 attacks and the Hurricane Katrina response.

▪ ▪ Critical Thinking ▪

Do you believe that FEMA is appropriately placed within the DHS bureaucracy in its current position under the Secretary of Homeland Security, or should it have been placed somewhere else within the federal structure outside of DHS? Explain your answer.

Federal Law Enforcement Training Center
The Federal Law Enforcement Training Center (FLETC) serves as the federal government's principal provider of federal law enforcement personnel training. FLETC provides for the training needs of 85 federal agencies that carry out law enforcement responsibilities. The center also provides training and technical assistance to state and local law enforcement entities, and plans, develops, and presents formal training courses and practical exercise applications related to international law enforcement training. The center offers numerous basic law enforcement training programs of varying lengths, designed specif-ically for the duties and responsibilities of the personnel to be trained, and conducts numerous advanced and specialized training programs found nowhere else in the country.

FLETC currently operates four training sites throughout the United States. Its headquarters and primary training site is located in Glynco, Georgia. Two other field locations, both of which provide both basic and advanced training, are located in Artesia, New Mexico, and Charleston, South Carolina. The fourth training site, in Cheltenham, Maryland, provides in-service and requalification training for officers and agents in the Washington, D.C., area. In cooperation with the State Department, FLETC also operates International Law Enforcement Academies in Gabarone, Botswana; San Salvador, El Salvador; Bangkok, Thailand; and through-out the world through collaboration with U.S. embassies and consulates abroad. FLETC maintained a staff of 1,103 in FY 2011, and saw budget allocations rise from $192 million in FY 2004 to $278 million in FY 2011 (representing less than 1% of the DHS budget).

Transportation Security Administration (TSA)

The Transportation Security Administration (TSA) was created just 2 months after the September 11 terrorist attacks (on November 19, 2001), through the Aviation and Transportation Security Act (ATSA — Public Law 107-071). TSA protects the nation's transportation systems in order to ensure the freedom of movement for both people and commercial goods and services. ATSA was created in recognition of failures in private secu-rity systems, and placed overall aviation transportation security under the direction and responsibility of the federal government. TSA's focus is on identifying risks to the transportation sector, prioritizing them, and man-aging them to acceptable levels through a variety of means, while working to mitigate the impact of incidents that may occur (Figure 4–6).

TSA began as an agency focused on airline security, which was understandable considering that the September 11 terrorists capitalized on lax aviation security measures to attack the nation. The agency's focus has steadily expanded to address other transportation modes such as intercity buses, rail travel, and ferry travel, but in terms of both dollars and people, its primary focus clearly remains on aviation security. TSA's specific responsibilities include ensuring thorough and efficient screening of all airline passengers

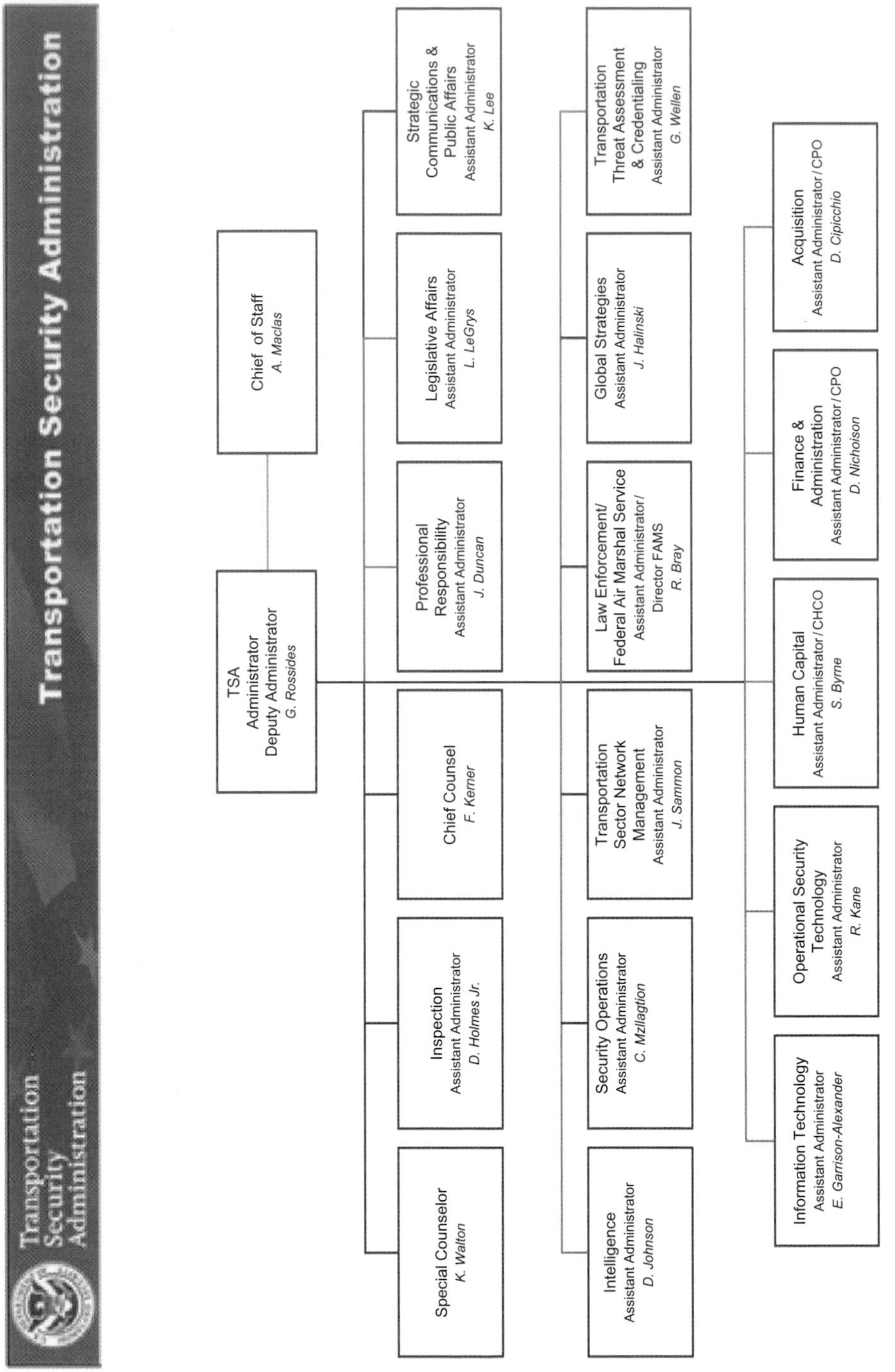

FIGURE 4–6 TSA organizational chart. (Source: TSA, 2011, http://www.tsa.gov/who_we_are/org/editorial_multi_image_with_table_0102.shtm)

and baggage through an appropriate mix of federalized and privatized screeners and technology. This screener workforce consists primarily of 50,000 passenger and baggage screeners located at more than 450 commercial and privatized airports throughout the country.

U.S. air carriers transport approximately 12.5 million tons of cargo, of which 2.8 million tons fly on board commercial passenger planes and 9.7 million tons are shipped in cargo planes (which, still today, are not inspected to the same degree as cargo that is shipped on the passenger carriers). TSA has been given the responsibility to devise and implement a system to screen, inspect, or otherwise ensure the security of all cargo that is to be transported aboard aircraft — a task that will likely require many years and significant financial investment.

TSA is also tasked with managing the security risk to the U.S. surface transportation systems. They are confronted with the paradox of trying to ensure the freedom of movement of people and commerce while preventing the same for terrorists. These transportation systems include approximately 751 million passengers traveling on buses each year, and over 9 billion passenger trips on mass transit per year; over 140,000 mi of railroad (of which 120,000 mi are privately owned); 3.8 million mi of roads (46,717 mi of Interstate highway and 114,700 mi of National Highway System roads), 582,000 bridges over 20 ft of span, 54 tunnels over 19,685 ft in length, and nearly 2.2 million mi of pipeline; and nearly 800,000 shipments of hazardous materials transported every day (95% by truck).

As part of Secretary Chertoff's reorganization plan, the Federal Air Marshals program was transferred from the U.S. Immigration and Customs Enforcement (ICE) office to TSA, where it was originally located before being removed in 2003 under the original framework of DHS.

John Pistole is the current administrator of TSA. The TSA maintained an employee base of 56,221 in FY 2010 (primarily federal airport security screeners), and saw its budget rise steadily from $4.578 billion in FY 2004 to $8.165 billion in FY 2011 (of which $5.560 billion was dedicated to aviation security). The TSA budget represents 14% of the total DHS budget.

New Offices and Directorates

Many new offices have been created within the DHS to manage the wide range of functions that directly and indirectly support national security. Over the past decade, the number of offices has gone up and down as functions arise, are eliminated, or are consolidated. Among these offices, DHS currently maintains three major multifunctional divisions, which have been termed *directorates*. Each directorate is led by an undersecretary. Each of the directorates and offices is described in this section

Directorate for National Protection and Programs

The Directorate for National Protection and Programs serves to accomplish the risk-reduction mission that is central to DHS. This Directorate was newly created in 2007 as a result of the PKEMRA, thereby assuming several functions that had existed previously in other areas spread throughout DHS. This office is led by DHS Undersecretary Rand Beers and maintains a full-time staff of 2,969 employees. The NPPD budget has increased from $1.177 billion in FY 2008 to $2.362 billion in FY 2011, representing 4% of the DHS budget request and an increase of over 100% over FY 2008 amounts.

Prior to NPPD, the DHS Preparedness Directorate fulfilled three critical department-wide needs, namely:

1. To strengthen national risk management efforts for critical infrastructure
2. To define and synchronize DHS-level doctrine for homeland security protection initiatives that entail aggressive coordination internally within DHS, in planning and integration work across the federal government, and with state, communities, and the private sector
3. To deliver grants and related preparedness program and training activities

Of these three functions, the third was transferred to FEMA, while NPPD assumed the status as a "Department-level focal point" for the ongoing management of the first two. In addition, NPPD provides management support and direction for US-VISIT, an immigration tracking and technology program. NPPD is also the lead office for federal efforts to protect and prevent attacks on critical infrastructure, and as such, it works to improve cybersecurity and communications system resilience. NPPD is the office that interacts with the private sector and with state and local government leaders to ensure the full range of department-wide programs and policies are effectively integrated. This office is also working to standardize DHS risk management efforts. The NPPD responsibilities include:

- Identifying threats and vulnerabilities to the nation's cyber infrastructure and mitigating against the consequences of a cyber attack
- Protecting and strengthening the nation's national security and emergency communications capabilities' reliability, survivability, and interoperability at the federal, state, local, and tribal levels
- Integrating and disseminating critical infrastructure and key resources' threat, consequence, and vulnerability information and developing risk mitigation strategies that enhance protection and resilience through coordination with critical infrastructure and key resources owners
- Developing and ensuring implementation of the National Infrastructure Protection Plan (NIPP) for the nation's infrastructure through sector-specific plans
- Ensuring a safe and secure environment in which federal agencies can conduct business by reducing threats posed against approximately 9,000 federal facilities nationwide
- Providing biometric and biographic identity management and screening services to other departmental entities as well as to other federal, state, local, and international stakeholders for immigration and border management
- Leading the Department's effort to develop, implement, and share a common framework addressing the overall analysis and management of homeland security risk

The five components of NPPD include:

- *The Office of Cybersecurity and Communications (CS&C)*: This office works to ensure the security, resiliency, and reliability of the nation's cyber and communications infrastructure in collaboration with the public and private sectors, including international partners. Specifically, CS&C is focused on preparing for and responding to catastrophic incidents that could degrade or overwhelm the networks, systems, and assets that operate our nation's information technology and communications infrastructure. Programs contained within this office include:
  - The National Communications System
  - The National Cybersecurity Division
  - The Office of Emergency Communications
- *The Office of Infrastructure Protection (OIP)*: This office leads the coordinated national effort to reduce risk to critical infrastructures and key resources posed by terrorism. OIP facilitates the identification, prioritization, coordination, and protection of these resources in support of federal, state, local, territorial, and tribal governments, as well as the private sector and international entities. OIP shares this information with "partners" at the state, local, and private levels, communicating threats, vulnerabilities, incidents, potential protective measures, and best practices that enhance protection, response, mitigation, and restoration activities across the nation and the international community. OIP functions are guided by the NIPP (which can be found by accessing http://www.dhs.gov/files/programs/editorial_0827.shtm).

- *The Federal Protective Service (FPS)*: This office provides security and law enforcement services to federally owned and leased buildings, facilities, properties, and other assets nationwide. FPS employs 1,225 federal staff (including 900 law enforcement security officers, criminal investigators, police officers, and support personnel) and 15,000 contract guard staff to secure over 9,000 buildings and safeguard their occupants. FPS was recently transferred into NPPD from U.S. ICE, another DHS component described later in this chapter.
- *The Office of Risk Management and Analysis (RMA)*: This office works to ensure that risk information and analysis are provided to inform a full range of homeland security decisions, including strategy formulation, preparedness priorities, and resource allocations. RMA has two divisions that address critical homeland security needs, the Risk Governance and Support Division and the Risk Analytics Division.
    - *The Risk Governance and Support Division*: This division, through the development of risk processes and capabilities, works to ensure that enterprise decisions are risk-informed and that risk management is executed in an integrated fashion.
    - *The Risk Analytics Division*: This division aims to provide decision support to the homeland security enterprise through the design, execution, and sharing of relevant and technically sound risk and decision analysis.

    RMA supports the Department's Risk Steering Committee, which is comprised of representatives from operational components, governing directorates, and supporting offices. Chaired by the Under Secretary for the National Protection and Programs Directorate, the committee makes decisions on ways to improve and integrate the Department's risk management activities and serves to communicate risk ideas, concepts, and practices.
- *United States Visitor and Immigrant Status Indicator Technology (US-VISIT)*: US-VISIT was established in order to accurately record the entry and exit of travelers to the United States by collecting biographic information and biometric information (such as digital fingerprints and photographs, for example). US-VISIT is part of an ongoing and growing system of security measures that begins overseas and continues through a foreign traveler's arrival in and departure from the United States.

Directorate for Science and Technology

The Directorate for Science and Technology (S&T) provides leadership for directing, funding, and conducting research, development, test, and evaluation (RDT&E), and procurement of technologies and systems that can prevent the importation of chemical, biological, radiological, nuclear, and related weapons and material, and will help the nation protect against and respond to terrorist threats. The S&T Directorate partners and coordinates with federal, state, and local government and private-sector entities in conducting its activities, and is working to establish a system to transfer the fruits of these homeland security developments and technologies into DHS's operational elements. Through S&T research and development activities, DHS hopes to enhance its ability to execute all of its stated missions, now and in the future, and to help the nation meet its homeland security RDT&E needs (Figure 4–7).

The HS Act of 2002 effectively abolished the Office of Science and Technology that existed within the National Institute of Justice (which still exists within the DOJ) and transferred all applicable functions to S&T. The Directorate is comprised of four groups that address basic research through advanced technology development and transition, spanning six primary divisions that address critical homeland security needs. These lead groups include:

- *The Director of Support to the Homeland Security Enterprise and First Responders Group (FRG)*: This group identifies, validates, and facilitates the fulfillment of first-responder requirements

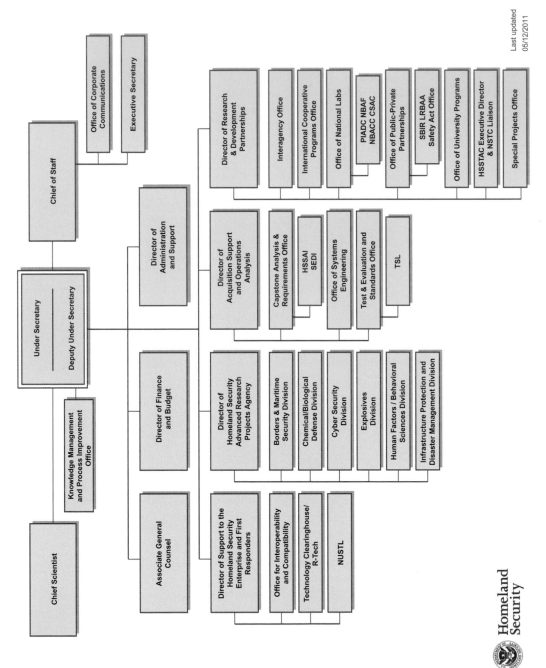

FIGURE 4–7 Science and technology directorate. (Source: DHS, 2011, http://www.dhs.gov/xlibrary/assets/sant-org-chart.pdf)

through the use of existing and emerging technologies, knowledge products, and the acceleration of standards. This organization manages working groups, teams, and stakeholder outreach efforts to better understand the requirements of first responders. FRG manages the following offices:
- Office of Interoperability and Compatibility
- Technology Clearinghouse/R-Tech
- National Urban Security Technology Laboratory (NUSTL)

- *The Director of Homeland Security Advanced Research Projects Agency*: This organization manages a portfolio of highly innovative programs that are transforming the future mission of Homeland Security. Homeland Security Advanced Research Projects Agency (HSARPA) scientific projects address customer-identified needs. HSARPA manages the following technical divisions:
  - *Borders & Maritime Security Division*: Develops and transitions tools and technologies that improve the security of our nation's borders and waterways, without impeding the flow of commerce and travel.
  - *Chemical/Biological Defense Division*: Works to increase the nation's preparedness against chemical and biological threats through improved threat awareness, advanced surveillance and detection, and protective countermeasures.
  - *Cybersecurity Division*: Works to address the security of the nation's computer networks against crime and/or terrorist attacks
  - *Explosives Division*: Develops the technical capabilities to detect, interdict, and lessen the impacts of non-nuclear explosives used in terrorist attacks against mass transit, civil aviation, and critical infrastructure.
  - *Human Factors/Behavioral Sciences Division*: Develops the technical capabilities to detect, interdict, and lessen the impacts of non-nuclear explosives used in terrorist attacks against mass transit, civil aviation, and critical infrastructure.
    - *Infrastructure Protection & Disaster Management Division*: Focuses on identifying and mitigating the vulnerabilities of the 18 critical infrastructure and key assets that keep our society and economy functioning.

- *The Director of Acquisition Support and Operations Analysis (ASOA)*: This office serves as a conduit for Department components seeking support on a range of technical and analytical requirements and document development throughout the acquisition life cycle. ASOA is made up of three primary components including:
  - Office of Systems Engineering (SYS)
  - Capstone Analysis & Requirements Office (CAR)
  - Test & Evaluation and Standards Office (TES)

- *The Director of Research and Development Partnerships (RDP)*: This group conducts stakeholder outreach and engagement through close partnerships with eight Department science and technology groups. The RDP groups include:
  - The Interagency Office
  - The International Cooperative Programs Office
  - The Office of National Laboratories, which includes:
    - Plum Island Animal Disease Center (PIADC)
    - National Biodefense Analysis and Countermeasures Center (NBACC)
    - National Bio- and Agro-Defense Facility (NBAF)
    - Chemical Security Analysis Center (CSAC)
  - *The Office of Public–Private Partnerships,* which includes:
    - Small Business Innovative Research Office (SBIR)

- Long Range Broad Agency Announcement Office (LRBAA)
- SAFETY Act Office
- Commercialization Office
- The Office of University Programs
- The Homeland Security Science and Technology Advisory Committee (HSSTAC)
- The Executive Director & National Science and Technology Council (NSTC) Liaison
- The Special Projects Office

The S&T Directorate maintained a staff of 447 full-time employees in FY 2011. The S&T budget allocation rose steadily from $913 million in FY 2004 to $1.368 billion in FY 2006. In 2007, this amount fell to $968 million, and fell again in FY 2008 to $830 million. In FY 2009, the president requested a slight increase to $869 million. In FY 2011, the budget stood at $1,018 billion, accounting for 2% of the total DHS FY 2011 budget. The S&T directorate is expanded on in much greater detail in Chapter 12.

Directorate for Management

The Undersecretary for Management (USM) is responsible for budget, appropriations, expenditure of funds, accounting, and finance; procurement; human resources and personnel; information technology systems; facilities, property, equipment, and other material resources; and identification and tracking of performance measurements relating to the responsibilities of the DHS. The Office of the USM maintained a budget of $267 million in FY 2011 and a staff of 1046, which represented an increase of approximately 25% over FY 2009 levels. The Office of the USM is but one component of the function termed *Departmental Management and Operations*. This function, which received a budget of $1.270 billion in FY 2011, provides leadership, direction, and management to the whole Department and is comprised of separate appropriations which include (in addition to the Directorate of Management) the following:

- Office of the Secretary and Executive Management (OSEM)
- The Undersecretary for Management (USM)
- Office of the Chief Financial Officer (OCFO)
- Office of the Chief Information Officer (OCIO)
- The National Special Security Events (NSSE) State and Local Fund
- The DHS Headquarters Consolidation Project (HQ)

OSEM provides central leadership, management, direction, and oversight of all the Department's components. The Secretary serves as the top representative of the Department to the President, Congress, and the general public.

USM includes the Immediate Office of the Under Secretary for Management, the Office of the Chief Human Capital Officer, the Office of the Chief Procurement Officer, the Office of the Chief Administrative Officer, and the Office of the Chief Security Officer. USM's primary mission is to deliver administrative support services and provide leadership and oversight for all Departmental Management and Operations functions that include IT, budget and financial management, procurement and acquisition, human capital, security, and administrative services.

OCFO is comprised of the Budget Division, the Program Analysis and Evaluation Division, the Office of Financial Operations Division, the Financial Management and Policy Division, the Internal Control Management Division, the Resource Management Transformation Office (Financial Systems Division), the Grants Policy and Oversight Division, the Departmental Audit Liaison Office, and the Workforce Development Division. OCFO is responsible for the fiscal management, integrity, and accountability of DHS. The mission of the OCFO is to provide guidance and oversight of the Department's budget, financial management, financial operations for all departmental management and operations, the DHS Working Capital Fund, grants and assistance awards, and resource management systems to ensure that funds necessary to carry out the Department's mission are obtained, allocated, and expended in accordance with the Department's priorities and relevant law and policies.

OCIO consists of five program offices: Executive Front Office, Information Security Office, Enterprise Business Management Office, Office of Applied Technology, and the Information Technology Services Office. OCIO is responsible for all the information technology projects in the Department. The OCIO provides information technology leadership, as well as products and services, to ensure the effective and appropriate use of information technology across DHS. The OCIO coordinates acquisition strategies to minimize costs and improve consistency of the information technology infrastructure. The OCIO enhances mission success by partnering with other DHS components to leverage the best available information technologies and management practices. OCIO is the lead organization in providing the capability for DHS to partner in the sharing of essential information to federal, state, tribal, and local governments as well as private industry and regular U.S. citizens for protection of the homeland. OCIO coordinates the planning and design structure to ascertain the best IT practices, processes, and systems to support both OCIO and component missions in accordance with the Department's overall goals. OCIO is the lead organization in developing and maintaining the DHS Information Security Program, which includes oversight and coordination of activities associated with FISMA (Federal Information Security Management Act). OCIO is also responsible for providing performance metrics and overall evaluation of DHS component IT programs as related to DHS and Government Performance and Results Act (GPRA) goals.

NSSE provides funding to state and local governments hosting major events that are considered to be nationally significant by the President, or his representative, the Secretary of DHS. Beginning in September 1998 through February 2008, there have been 28 events designated as NSSEs. Some of these events have included presidential inaugurations, presidential nominating conventions, major sports events, and major international meetings.

The DHS HQ Consolidation Project is responsible for the collocation and consolidation of the Department through lease consolidation and build-out of the St. Elizabeth's campus. The DHS Management Directorate provides the coordination, planning, policy, guidance, operational oversight and support, and innovative solutions for the management needs of the entire Department for the "One DHS" culture.

Office of the Inspector General

The DHS Office of the Inspector General (OIG) was established by the Homeland Security Act of 2002, by amendment to the Inspector General Act of 1978. Inspector General Clark Kent Ervin was the first to hold the post. The inspector general has a dual reporting responsibility, both to the DHS secretary and to Congress. The OIG serves as an independent and objective inspection, audit, and investigative body that safeguards public tax dollars by promoting effectiveness, efficiency, and economy in DHS programs and operations, and by preventing and detecting fraud, abuse, mismanagement, and waste in such programs and operations.

Considering the massive changes that have resulted from the creation of DHS, and the billions of dollars that have been dedicated to the department's mission, an office such as this is critical. In 2011, OIG maintained a staff of 665 people. The OIG budget has remained relatively constant during the period of FY 2004 to FY 2006, with an allocation of approximately $83 million. In FY 2007 this jumped by nearly 25% to $103 million, as the perceived need for greater oversight was confirmed. This amount rose again in FY 2008 to $109 million. The 2011 OIG budget was $130 million, representing less than 1% of the total DHS budget. Clark Kent Ervin left the post of inspector general on December 8, 2004, and was replaced by Assistant Inspector General Richard L. Skinner who has held the office ever since.

United States Citizenship and Immigration Services

The U.S. Citizenship and Immigration Services (USCIS) is the component of DHS that facilitates legal immigration for people seeking to enter, reside, or work in the United States. The office, led by Director Alejandro Mayorkas, is responsible for "ensuring the delivery of the right immigration benefit to the right person at the right time, and no benefit to the wrong person." USCIS has established six strategic goals in accomplishing this task:

1. Strengthening the security and integrity of the immigration system
2. Providing effective customer-oriented immigration benefit and information services
3. Supporting immigrants' integration and participation in American civic culture
4. Promoting flexible and sound immigration policies and programs
5. Strengthening the infrastructure supporting the USCIS mission
6. Operating as a high-performance organization that promotes a highly talented workforce and a dynamic work culture

Before September 11, all immigration issues were handled by the U.S. State Department through their consular services section and by the Immigration and Naturalization Service (INS) of the Department of Justice. The State Department, which handled the granting of permission to apply for entry into the United States from overseas posts, has maintained its role since the government reorganization has taken place. The INS, however, which handled the creation and enforcement of immigration policy within the United States, was absorbed into the DHS and broken into three distinct offices. USCIS was given responsibility for the immigration services (applications for residence, for instance), ICE is responsible for enforcing immigration law within the United States, and Customs and Border Protection (CBP) enforces those same laws at the U.S. ports of entry and the borders (Figure 4–8).

USCIS processes more than seven million applications each year. The office maintained a staff of 10,878 in FY 2011, and saw their budget rise from $1.550 billion in FY 2004 to $2.812 billion in FY 2011. The FY 2011 budget appropriation for USCIS represents 5% of the department's total budget.

United States Customs and Border Protection

U.S. Customs and Border Protection (CBP) is responsible for protecting the nation's borders, at and between official ports of entry. CBP is responsible for ensuring that all persons and cargo entering the United States do so both legally and safely. CBP inspectors are responsible for preventing cross-border smuggling of such contraband as controlled substances, weapons of mass destruction (WMDs), and illegal plants and animals. They also ensure that travelers and immigrants have appropriate documentation necessary to enter the country legally. Other tasks include preventing the illegal export of U.S. currency or other negotiable instruments, the export of stolen goods such as vehicles, and the export of strategically sensitive technologies that could be used overseas to compromise both the security and the strategic and economic position of the United States. The Border Patrol, which operates under the direction of CBP, is responsible for controlling all of America's 7,500 mi of land borders between ports of entry and 95,000 mi of maritime border in partnership with the USCG.

CBP officials are also deployed overseas at major international seaports, through application of the Container Security Initiative (CSI). This project was established to allow agents to prescreen shipping containers in order to detect and interdict WMDs and other illicit material before they arrive in the United States. To date, there are 58 CSI ports throughout the world, covering over 90% of inbound maritime containers. CBP's entry specialists and trade compliance personnel enforce U.S. trade and tariff laws and regulations in order

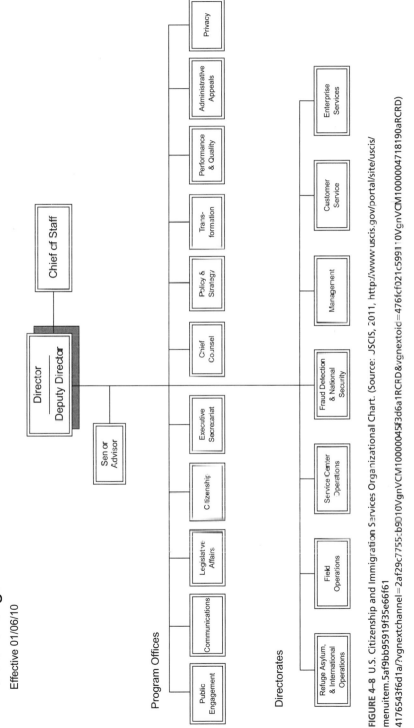

FIGURE 4-8 U.S. Citizenship and Immigration Services Organizational Chart. (Source: USCIS, 2011, http://www.uscis.gov/portal/site/uscis/menuitem.5af9bb95919f35e66f61/?vgnextchannel=2af29c7755cb9010VgnVCM10000045f3d6a1RCRD&vgnextoid=476fcf021c599110VgnVCM1000004718190aRCRD)

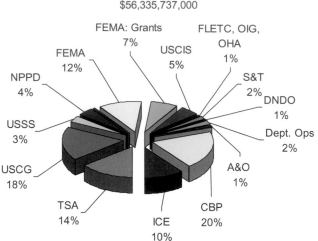

FY 2011
Percent of total budget authority by organization
$56,335,737,000

FIGURE 4–9 DHS FY2011 budget — percent of total budget authority by organization. (Source: DHS, 2010, "FY2011 Budget in Brief," http://www.dhs.gov/xlibrary/assets/budget_bib_fy2011.pdf)

to ensure that a fair and competitive trade environment exists for the United States. CBP's Air and Marine Operations Division patrols the nation's borders to interdict illegal drugs and terrorists before entry into the United States, and provides surveillance and operational support to special national security events.

CBP makes direct contact with more than 500 million people crossing the borders through ports each year, and with tens of thousands of shippers, drivers, pilots, and importers associated with more than 25 million officially declared trade entries. In FY 2011, CBP maintained a staff of 58,575, and saw budgets rise steadily from $5.997 billion in FY 2004 to $11.180 billion in FY 2011. The FY 2011 budget allocation represents the single greatest item on the DHS budget, accounting for 20% of the total (Figure 4–9).

Immigration and Customs Enforcement

As the largest investigative arm of DHS, U.S. Immigration and Customs Enforcement (ICE) enforces federal immigration and customs laws. ICE protects America and upholds public safety by identifying and dismantling criminal organizations that exploit the nation's borders. ICE agents and investigators identify, apprehend, and remove (deport) criminal and other illegal aliens from the United States. The various components of this directorate are as follows:

- The Office of Investigations (OI) is responsible for investigating a broad range of domestic and international activities arising from the illicit movement of people and goods that violate immigration and customs laws and threaten national security. This might include, for example, illegal arms trafficking, intellectual property and financial crime, identity and benefit fraud, commercial fraud, human trafficking, child pornography, and child sex tourism.
- The Office of International Affairs (OIA) expands ICE's law enforcement reach internationally. OIA enhances the ICE mission through international partnerships and the strategic placement of ICE assets to prevent dangerous goods and people from reaching the United States.

- The Office of Detention and Removal Operations (DRO) is responsible for ensuring that aliens ordered for deportation are actually removed from the United States. DRO, in partnership with other ICE programs, targets aliens for removal based upon the risk they present to public safety and national security.

- The Secure Communities/Comprehensive Identification and Removal of Criminal Aliens (SC/CIRCA) Program Office coordinates the planning activities devoted to criminal alien enforcement across ICE. Through SC/CIRCA, ICE leverages technology to increase national security and public safety by prioritizing deployment of resources to areas where criminal aliens present the greatest threat to the public.

- The Office of Intelligence is responsible for the collection, analysis, and dissemination of strategic, operational, and tactical intelligence that directly supports ICE's law enforcement and homeland security mission. Intel is also responsible for sharing potentially critical information developed by ICE's frontline officers and agents with the Intelligence Community (IC) through the production of Homeland Intelligence Reports.

- The Office of the Principal Legal Advisor (OPLA) is the only legal office with authority to represent the United States in removal proceedings before the Executive Office for Immigration Review (EOIR). OPLA also provides legal advice and training to ICE's operational and management programs.

ICE is led by Assistant Secretary John Morton. In FY 2011, ICE employed 20,876 employees, and saw allocations rise steadily from $3.616 billion in FY2004 to $5.835 billion in FY 2011. This allocation represents 10% of the department's 2011 budget (Figure 4–10).

Office of Policy

The Office of Policy, led by Assistant Secretary for Policy David Heyman, formulates and coordinates homeland security policy and procedures for the DHS. This office helps the enormous, widespread department to maintain a centralized, coordinated focus. Through their actions, the Office of Policy coordinates the department's prevention, protection, response, and recovery missions. The Office of Policy:

- Leads coordination of department-wide policies, programs, and planning, which will ensure consistency and integration of missions throughout the entire department

- Provides a central office to develop and communicate policies across multiple components of the homeland security network and strengthens the department's ability to maintain policy and operational readiness needed to protect the homeland

- Provides the foundation and direction for department-wide strategic planning and budget priorities

- Bridges multiple headquarters' components and operating agencies to improve communication among departmental entities, eliminate duplication of effort, and translate policies into timely action

- Creates a single point of contact for internal and external stakeholders that will allow for streamlined policy management across the department

The Office of Policy operates through the actions of the following offices:

- *Office of Policy Development*: Ensures that a coordinated approach to DHS policy is adopted and advocated within its components and that DHS interests are effectively portrayed in national and international efforts

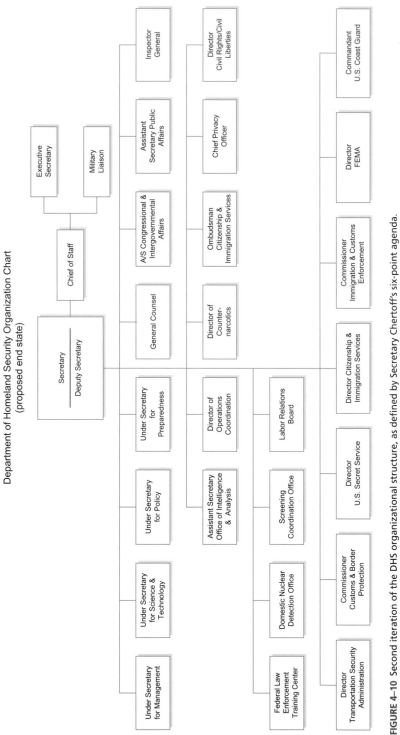

Department of Homeland Security Organization Chart (proposed end state)

FIGURE 4–10 Second iteration of the DHS organizational structure, as defined by Secretary Chertoff's six-point agenda.

- *Office of Strategic Plans*: Maintains what is considered the "long-term view" for DHS and ensures that the DHS Secretary's strategic priorities are incorporated into all planning efforts (especially with regard to integration, component priorities, and resource allocation)
- *Office of State and Local Law Enforcement*: Leads the coordination of department-wide policies relating to state, local, and tribal law enforcement's role in preventing acts of terrorism and also serves as the primary liaison between law enforcement agencies across the country and the Department
- *Office of International Affairs*: Develops DHS's strategy for promoting the department's mission overseas and actively engages foreign allies to improve international cooperation for immigration policy, visa security, aviation security, border security and training, law enforcement, and cargo security
- *Office of Immigration Statistics*: Leads the development of statistical information useful to make decisions and analyze the effects of immigration in the United States
- *Private-Sector Office*: Provides the nation's private sector with a direct line of communication (to DHS), utilizes information received from the private sector, and promotes DHS policies to the private sector
- *Homeland Security Advisory Council*: Leverages the experience, expertise, and national and global connections of its members to provide the DHS Secretary with real-time, real-world, sensing and independent advice to support decision making for homeland security operations

The budget of this new office, created in 2007, falls under the Directorate for Management.

Office of Health Affairs

The Office of Health Affairs (OHA) coordinates all DHS medical activities to ensure appropriate preparation for and response to incidents having "medical significance." OHA serves as the principal medical adviser for the DHS Secretary and FEMA Administrator by providing timely incident-specific management guidance for the medical consequences of disasters. Additionally, OHA leads the department's bio- and chemical defense activities; leads the Department's food, agriculture, and veterinary defense; works with partner agencies to ensure medical readiness for catastrophic incidents; and supports the DHS mission through department-wide standards and best practices for the occupational health and safety of employees. This new office, created in 2007, is led by the Chief Medical Officer, who maintains the title of Assistant Secretary for Health Affairs and Chief Medical Officer. The first person to assume this role was Dr. Jeffrey W. Runge. Today the office is led by Dr. Alex G. Garza.

The OHA has two main divisions:

- *The Health Threats Resilience Division*: Strengthens national capabilities to prepare and secure the nation against the health impacts of CBRN incidents and other intentional and naturally occurring events
- *The Workforce Health and Medical Support Division*: Ensures coordination of medical first responders by providing operational medical support; enhances occupational health in the Department by developing strategy, policy, requirements and metrics for the medical aspects of an occupational health and safety program; and ensures medical quality assurance

The president's FY 2012 budget request for this new office, which maintained a full-time staff of 95 employees in FY 2011, is $213 million.

Offices of Intelligence and Analysis and Operations Coordination

The Office of Intelligence and Analysis (I&A), created in 2007 in response to the changes brought about by the PKEMRA, is responsible for using the information and intelligence gleaned from the myriad sources throughout the federal government to identify and assess current and future threats to the United States. I&A is also responsible for the Department's intelligence and information-gathering and -sharing capabilities for and among all components of DHS, state, local, and private sector partners and the IC. I&A serves as the primary federal interface with state and local fusion centers, providing for reciprocal intelligence and information sharing in support of homeland security operations across all levels of government and the private sector. The Undersecretary for Intelligence and Analysis (ASIS), currently Caryn Wagner, leads this office and serves as the DHS Chief Intelligence Officer (CINT). I&A ensures that information is gathered from all relevant DHS field operations and is fused with information from throughout the IC to produce intelligence reports (and other products) for officials who require them inside and outside of DHS.

The Office of Operations Coordination is responsible for monitoring U.S. security on a daily basis and coordinating activities within DHS and with governors, Homeland Security Advisors, law enforcement partners, and critical infrastructure operators in all 50 states and more than 50 major urban areas nationwide. Information is shared daily by the two halves of the office, referred to as the "Intelligence Side" and the "Law Enforcement side." Each half is identical and functions in tandem with the other but operates under different security clearance standards for information access purposes. The Intelligence Side focuses on pieces of highly classified intelligence and how the information contributes to the current threat picture for any given area. The Law Enforcement Side is dedicated to tracking the different enforcement activities across the country that may have terrorist significance. The two pieces fuse together to create a real-time picture of the nation's threat environment.

Operations Coordination oversees the National Operations Center (NOC), which collects and collates information from more than 35 federal, state, territorial, tribal, local, and private sector agencies. Through the NOC, the office provides real-time situational awareness and monitoring of the nation, coordinates incidents and response activities, and, in conjunction with the I&A, issues advisories and bulletins concerning threats to homeland security, as well as specific protective measures. The NOC — which is always operational — coordinates information sharing to help deter, detect, and prevent terrorist acts and to manage domestic incidents. Information on domestic incident management is shared with Emergency Operations Centers at all levels through the Homeland Security Information Network (HSIN). This office, also created in 2007 in response to the changes brought about by the PKEMRA, is led by Director for Operations Coordination (acting) Richard Chavez.

These two offices operate under a joined budget, termed *Analysis and Operations*, for which $348 million was appropriated in 2011. Together, these offices employed 870 people in FY 2011.

Domestic Nuclear Detection Office

The Domestic Nuclear Detection Office (DNDO) works to enhance the nuclear detection efforts of federal, state, territorial, tribal, and local governments and the private sector and to ensure a coordinated response to such threats. DNDO was established April 15, 2005, to improve the capability of the U.S. government to detect and report unauthorized attempts to import, possess, store, develop, or transport nuclear or radiological material for use against the nation, and to further enhance this capability over time. The objectives of the office are to:

- Develop the global nuclear detection and reporting architecture
- Develop, acquire, and support the domestic nuclear detection and reporting system

- Characterize detector system performance before deployment
- Facilitate situational awareness through information sharing and analysis
- Establish operational protocols to ensure detection leads to effective response
- Conduct a transformational research and development program
- Provide centralized planning, integration, and advancement of U.S. government nuclear forensics programs

The DNDO is led by Director Warren Stern and employed 122 people in FY 2011. The DNDO budget fell from $317 million in FY 2006 to $305 million in FY 2011. The president's FY 2009 budget request for DNDO is $564 million.

■ ■ Critical Thinking ■

Do you believe that it is possible to effectively lead a single federal department like the DHS, with over 220,000 employees, or does its existence combine too many unrelated functions under a single organizational mission? Explain your answer.

Agency Reorganization

At various points throughout the first decade of the Department's existence, reorganizations have been necessary. Offices have been added or expanded and reduced or eliminated. There have been two specific situations, however, where the nature of these organizations was of such great scope as to merit special mention. These include Secretary (Michael) Chertoff's DHS Reorganization Plan and the PKEMRA. Both are described below.

Secretary Chertoff's DHS Reorganization Plan

On July 13, 2005, DHS Secretary Michael Chertoff released a six-point agenda that was used to guide the first of two major reorganizations that have occurred within DHS, in this case aimed at streamlining what were considered inefficient and cumbersome efforts and operations. The agenda followed an initial comprehensive review of operations that Chertoff initiated immediately after assuming his leadership position. The review closely examined the department in search of ways in which leadership could better manage risk in terms of threat, vulnerability, and consequence; prioritize policies and operational missions according to this risk-based approach; and establish a series of preventive and protective steps that would increase security at multiple levels. According to the six-point agenda, changes were focused on the following:

- Increasing overall preparedness, particularly for catastrophic events
- Creating better transportation security systems to move people and cargo more securely and efficiently
- Strengthening border security and interior enforcement and reforming immigration processes
- Enhancing information sharing (with partners)
- Improving financial management, human resource development, procurement, and information technology within the department
- Realigning the department's organization to maximize mission performance

Secretary Chertoff initiated several new policy initiatives that were included in the overhaul of the department, including:

- New border security approaches, accomplished through additional personnel, new technologies, infrastructure investments, and more comprehensive enforcement — coupled with efforts to reduce the demand for illegal border migration by channeling migrants seeking work into regulated legal channels
- Restructuring the current immigration process to enhance security and improve customer service
- Reaching out to the state homeland security officials in order to improve information exchange protocols, refine the Homeland Security Advisory System, and support state and regional data fusion centers
- Investing in DHS personnel by providing professional career training and other development efforts

One of the most significant changes that occurred as result of the six-point agenda was an organizational restructuring of the department (Figure 4–10). Chertoff asserted that these changes were made "to increase [the Department's] ability to prepare, prevent, and respond to terrorist attacks and other emergencies." Changes included the following:

- A new Directorate of Policy was created "to centralize and improve policy development and coordination." This directorate was led by an undersecretary and served as the primary department-wide coordinator for policies, regulations, and other initiatives. This directorate was created to ensure the consistency of policy and regulatory development across various parts of the Department as well as to perform long-range strategic policy planning. This new directorate, which later became the Office for Policy in 2007, included the following offices:
  - Office of International Affairs
  - Office of Private Sector Liaison
  - Homeland Security Advisory Council
  - Office of Immigration Statistics
  - Senior Asylum Officer
- A new Office of Intelligence and Analysis was created to "strengthen intelligence functions and information sharing." This office still exists in the current structure of DHS as previously described.
- A Director of Operations Coordination position was created, with a corresponding Operations Coordination office, which also remains in the current structure of DHS.
- The Information Analysis and Infrastructure Protection Directorate was renamed the Directorate for Preparedness, which consolidated preparedness assets from across the Department. The Directorate for Preparedness was created to facilitate grants and oversee nationwide preparedness efforts supporting first-responder training, citizen awareness, public health, infrastructure security, and cybersecurity and ensure proper steps are taken to protect high-risk targets. Many of this directorate's functions, several of which were removed from FEMA according to Secretary Chertoff's Reorganization Plan, were returned to that and other agencies and offices spread across the Department in 2007 according to the PKEMRA.
- FEMA was removed from the Emergency Preparedness & Response Directorate that was created in the original organization of DHS, and was given a direct reporting responsibility to the Secretary of Homeland Security. This change, which remains in place today, was first made in order to "improve national response and recovery efforts by focusing FEMA on its core functions," and involved drawing many of the preparedness functions from the agency. However, all of these original functions of FEMA were returned to the agency as stipulated by the PKEMRA.

- The Federal Air Marshal Service was moved from the ICE bureau to the TSA (where it was originally housed prior to the creation of DHS in 2002).
- A new Office of Legislative and Intergovernmental Affairs was created, which merged the functions of the original Offices of Legislative Affairs and of State and Local Government Coordination, in an effort to "streamline intergovernmental relations efforts and better share homeland security information with members of Congress as well as state and local officials." This office remains in the new organization of the Department.
- The Office of Security, which develops, implements, and oversees the security policies, programs, and standards within DHS, was moved into the Directorate for Management "in order to better manage information systems, contractual activities, security accreditation, training and resources." This office, led by the Chief Security Officer, remains there today.

Of the changes that were made according to Secretary Chertoff's Reorganization Plan, there was one change that stood out above the rest as being particularly troubling — the disassembly of the Directorate of Emergency Preparedness and Response (EP&R). Although it made perfect sense that FEMA should exist as a standalone agency within the Department — especially considering the fact that the functions of FEMA fully dominated this original directorate — it was somewhat inexplicable as to why FEMA would be stripped of its preparedness and mitigation functions. This action was clearly a complete reversal in the 30-year trend toward the comprehensive approach to emergency management's four functions: mitigation, preparedness, response, and recovery.

United Press International reported that critics both within FEMA and outside of DHS, especially from within the first-responder community, felt that the change was a sure sign that DHS was making a significant departure from the traditional "all hazards" approach to emergency management, which would see terrorism as but one of many hazards encompassing each community's hazard profile. Following the poor response to Katrina, members of Congress redressed this apparent mistake by reinstating all of the functions withdrawn from FEMA back under the direction of its administrator.

■ ■ Critical Thinking ■

Do you believe that the problems attributed to FEMA in the response to Hurricane Katrina would have happened regardless of Secretary Chertoff's reorganization plan, or that it was something about this structure that caused the inefficiencies and shortfalls that were observed? Or were the problems entirely unrelated to the DHS structure? Explain your answer.

The Post-Katrina Emergency Management Reform Act

Hurricane Katrina, which struck on August 29, 2005, and resulted in the death of over 1,800 people (and the destruction of billions of dollars in housing stock and other infrastructure), exposed significant problems with the United States' emergency management framework. Clearly, the terrorism focus had been maintained at the expense of preparedness and response capacity for other hazards, namely, the natural disasters that have proven to be much more likely to occur. FEMA, and likewise DHS, was highly criticized by the public and by Congress in the months following the 2005 hurricane season. In response, Congress passed the Post-Katrina Emergency Management Reform Act (PKEMRA) (H.R. 5441, Public Law 109-295), signed into law by the president on October 4, 2006.

This law established several new leadership positions within DHS, moved additional functions into (several were simply returned) the FEMA, created and reallocated functions to other components within DHS, and amended the Homeland Security Act in ways that directly and indirectly affected the organization and functions of various entities within DHS. The changes were required to have gone into effect by March 31, 2007. Transfers into FEMA that were mandated by PKEMRA included (with the exception of certain offices as listed in the Act):

- United States Fire Administration (USFA)
- Office of Grants and Training (G&T)
- Chemical Stockpile Emergency Preparedness Division (CSEP)
- Radiological Emergency Preparedness Program (REPP)
- Office of National Capital Region Coordination (NCRC)

The law determined that the head of FEMA, at the time R. David Paulison, would take on the new title of administrator. This official would now be supported by two deputy administrators. One is the deputy administrator and chief operating officer, who serves as the principal deputy and maintains overall operational responsibilities at FEMA. The other is the deputy administrator for National Preparedness, a new division created within FEMA. The National Preparedness Division under FEMA included several existing FEMA programs and several programs that were moved into the former Preparedness Directorate. This division focuses on emergency preparedness policy, contingency planning, exercise coordination and evaluation, emergency management training, and hazard mitigation (with respect to the CSEP and REPP programs). The National Preparedness Division oversees two new divisions: Readiness, Prevention and Planning (RPP), and the National Integration Center (NIC). RPP is now the central office within FEMA handling preparedness policy and planning functions. The NIC maintains the NIMS and the National Response Plan (NRP) and coordinates activities with the U.S. Fire Administration.

The existing Office of Grants and Training (OGT) was moved into the newly expanded FEMA and was renamed the "Office of Grant Programs." The training and systems support divisions of the OGT were transferred into the NIC. The Office of the Citizen Corps was transferred into the FEMA Office of Readiness, Prevention and Planning.

Additional headquarters positions created at FEMA by the new law included a disability coordinator (located in the FEMA Office of Equal Rights), a small state and rural advocate, a law enforcement advisor to the administrator, and a national advisory council.

This act specifically excluded certain elements of the former DHS Preparedness Directorate from transfer into FEMA. The Preparedness Directorate was renamed the National Protection and Programs Directorate (NPPD), and it remained under the direction of a DHS Undersecretary (currently Rand Beers).

And finally, the law created the OHA. OHA is led by the Chief Medical Officer, who was given the title of Assistant Secretary for Health Affairs and Chief Medical Officer. This position is currently staffed by Dr. Alex G. Garza.

DHS Budget

Table 4–1 details the FY 2012 DHS budget proposed by department function or component.

Other Agencies Participating in Community-Level Funding

As mentioned in the introduction to this chapter, the DHS may be the most recognized embodiment of federal homeland security action and have the most central role in its implementation, but it is not alone in the federal government by any means in this mission. Several other federal agencies outside of the new department

Table 4–1   FY 2012 Proposed DHS Budget ($ in thousands)

Budget Item	FY 2010	FY 2011	FY 2012 Proposed	Year Over Year Change	Year Over Year (%)
Departmental Operations	809,531	800,931	947,231	146,300	18
Analysis and Operations (A&O)	333,030	335,030	355,368	20,338	6
Office of the Inspector General (OIG)	113,874	129,874	144,318	14,444	11
U.S. Customs & Border Protection (CBP)	11,540,501	11,544,660	11,845,678	301,018	3
U.S. Immigration & Customs Enforcement (ICE)	5,741,752	5,748,339	5,822,576	74,237	1
Transportation Security Administration (TSA)	7,656,066	7,649,666	8,115,259	465,593	6
U.S. Coast Guard (USCG)	10,789,076	10,151,543	10,338,545	187,002	2
U.S. Secret Service (USSS)	1,710,344	1,722,644	1,943,531	220,887	13
National Protection and Programs Directorate (NPPD)	2,429,455	2,432,756	2,555,449	122,693	5
Office of Health Affairs (OHA)	136,850	139,250	160,949	21,699	16
Federal Emergency Management Agency (FEMA)	6,200,618	6,181,718	6,218,433	36,715	1
FEMA: Grant Programs	4,165,200	4,165,200	3,844,663	(320,537)	−8
U.S. Citizenship & Immigration Services (USCIS)	2,870,997	3,054,829	2,906,866	(147,963)	−5
Federal Law Enforcement Training Center (FLETC)	282,812	282,812	276,413	(6,399)	−2
Science & Technology Directorate (S&T)	1,006,471	1,006,471	1,176,432	169,961	17
Domestic Nuclear Detection Office (DNDO)	383,037	383,037	331,738	(51,299)	−13
Total budget authority:	56,169,614	55,728,760	56,983,449	1,254,689	2.25
Mandatory, fee, and trust funds	(10,179,438)	(9,697,347)	(9,578,910)	118,437	−1.22
Discretionary offsetting fees	(3,533,561)	(3,442,780)	(4,180,357)	(737,577)	21
Net discount budget authority	42,456,615	42,588,633	43,224,182	635,549	–
Less rescission of prior-year carryover — regular appropriations	(151,582)	(40,474)	(41,942)	–	0
Adjusted net discount budget authority	42,305,033	42,548,159	43,182,240	634,081	1

have both maintained existing programs and created entirely new programs, each addressing some aspect of homeland security. Many of these also fund or support homeland security efforts at the state and local levels as well. Several of these programs, as discussed next, are either in the transitional or in the developmental phase but have already begun active participation within the greater homeland security context.

The White House (the Executive Office of the President)

The President of the United States and the White House (the Executive Office of the President) play an important homeland security role as the primary drivers of federal policy and as a result of the role of the President as Commander in Chief. Through the National Security and Homeland Security Councils and the National Security Staff, the President provides overall homeland security policy direction and coordination. As a result of Presidential Study Directive 1 (2009), which directed an examination of ways to reform the White House organization for counterterrorism and homeland security, the White House merged the staffs of the National Security Council and the Homeland Security Council into a single new integrated National Security Staff (NSS). The new NSS supports all White House policy-making activities related to international, transnational, and homeland security matters. The NSS was established under the direction of the National Security Advisor. The NSS is maintained as the principal venue for interagency deliberations on national security issues including terrorism, WMDs, and natural disasters, among others. Within the NSS, a number of new directorates and positions were created to deal with new and emerging threats including cybersecurity, WMD terrorism, transborder security, information sharing, and resilience.

U.S. Department of Agriculture

Considering the varied and wide-reaching impacts that both terrorism and other natural disasters (such as plant and animal diseases) could have on the both the U.S. food supply and on the U.S. economy, agriculture has assumed a very important role in the overall homeland security approach of the United States. Shortly after September 11, the U.S. Department of Agriculture (USDA) formed a Homeland Security Council (within USDA) to develop a department-wide plan and coordinate efforts among all USDA agencies and offices. Their efforts have since focused on three key areas of concern:

- Safety and security of the food supply and agricultural production
- Protection of USDA facilities
- USDA staff and emergency preparedness

The USDA contributes to an ongoing DHS effort of protecting the nation's food supply by keeping foreign agricultural pests and diseases from entering the country. In this vein, there has been a drastic increase in the number of veterinarians and food import surveillance officers that have been posted at borders and ports of entry. Although approximately 2,600 members of the USDA border inspection force were transferred to DHS as stipulated in the Homeland Security Act of 2002, USDA has continued to train inspectors and set policy for plants, animals, and commodities entering the United States.

In March 2004, the former DHS Bureau of Customs and Border Protection's Border Patrol (BP) announced the 2004 Arizona Border Control Initiative. This initiative was aimed at securing the border with Mexico. The initiative required increased cooperation between the DHS and the USDA Forest Service in allowing more access to public lands on the border. Forest Service resource managers continue to help DHS enhance border security in such a way as to avoid disturbing the environment, and Forest Service law enforcement personnel have assisted DHS in deterring illegal activities on National Forest System lands.

Protecting the Health and Safety of Farm Animals, Crops, and Natural Resources

The USDA created a National Surveillance Unit within its Animal and Plant Health Inspection Service's (APHIS) Veterinary Services program. The unit provides a focal point for the collection, processing, and delivery of surveillance information used to make risk analyses and to take further action when needed. The unit designs surveillance strategies and coordinates and integrates surveillance activities in order to protect the health of and enhance the marketability of livestock and poultry.

USDA appointed a National Surveillance System Coordinator whose purpose is to more efficiently lead the agency's animal health surveillance efforts. USDA also works with universities and state veterinary diagnostic laboratories to create plant and animal health laboratory networks that help to increase the nation's capability to respond in an emergency. USDA developed guidance documents to help remind farmers and ranchers of steps that they can take to secure their operations.

The Office of Food Defense and Emergency Response (OFDER) was created in 2002 to develop and coordinate all activities of the USDA Food Safety and Inspection Service (FSIS) to prevent, prepare for, respond to, and recover from nonroutine emergencies resulting from intentional and unintentional contamination affecting meat, poultry, and egg products. OFDER serves as the agency's central office for homeland security issues and ensures coordination of its activities with the USDA Homeland Security Office, the DHS, the Food and Drug Administration (FDA) and other federal and state government agencies with food-related responsibilities, and industry.

USDA has provided tens of millions of dollars to states, universities, and tribal lands to increase homeland security prevention, detection, and response efforts. USDA also developed the National Animal Health Reserve Corps, which has resulted in the registration of almost 300 private veterinarians who will assist local communities during times of emergency.

USDA has also continued to perform research on rapid identification tests for biological agents considered to pose the most serious threats to our agricultural system, including foot and mouth disease, rinderpest, and soybean and wheat rust.

Ensuring a Safe Food Supply

The USDA has enhanced security at all food safety laboratories around the country, and expanded its abilities to test for "nontraditional" biological, chemical, and radiological agents. USDA established an Office of Food Security and Emergency Preparedness, which now serves as the lead coordinating body in the development of the infrastructure and capacity to prevent, prepare for, and respond to terrorism aimed at the U.S. food supply. USDA also drafted and distributed guidance for field and laboratory personnel about what to do when the HSAS is raised to either orange or red levels.

New import surveillance liaison inspectors have been hired by the department, who are stationed around the United States to enhance surveillance of imported products. Using a food security plan they developed, USDA has conducted training for employees, veterinarians, and inspectors on threat prevention and preparedness activities. USDA food safety labs have maintained a lead role in creating a network to integrate the U.S. laboratory infrastructure and surge capacity at the local, state, and federal levels.

Protecting Research and Laboratory Facilities

The USDA has provided millions of dollars in grants aimed at security assessments, background investigations, physical security upgrades, and additional security personnel at research and laboratory facilities. Security countermeasures have been implemented based on the findings of these assessments. Furthermore, all USDA laboratories where dangerous agents and toxins are used are held to the requirements of the Agricultural Bioterrorism Protection Act of 2002.

Emergency Preparedness and Response

A department-wide National Interagency Incident Management System (NIIMS), based on the successful system utilized by USDA's Forest Service, is being implemented. This system includes incident command and control systems, coordination systems, training and qualification systems, and publication management systems. USDA's NIIMS uses the same systems within USDA for incident management as those standardized for the nation under the NIMS, which is described in Chapter 7.

The construction of an APHIS Emergency Operations Center (AEOC), which is used to coordinate and support emergency response within APHIS, has been completed. The AEOC, which enhances APHIS's ability to provide leadership during national emergencies, has already been utilized on several occasions, including the exotic Newcastle disease outbreak, the monkey pox outbreak, and the confirmations of bovine spongiform encephalopathy (BSE) in both Canada and the United States.

Protecting Other Infrastructure

The USDA Forest Service's law enforcement officers continue to conduct security assessments of research facilities and air tanker bases nationwide. USDA's Forest Service continues to enhance efforts to protect National Forest System lands and facilities, including dams, reservoirs, pipelines, water treatment plants, power lines, and energy production facilities on government property.

Securing Information Technology

The USDA has conducted tests of its network systems to assess threat levels. USDA upgraded the security status of key information technology personnel and conducted training and planning sessions to strengthen the department's continuity of operations plans.

In addition to these functions, USDA is also the coordinator and primary agency for two Emergency Support Functions: ESF #4 — Firefighting and ESF #11 — Agriculture and Natural Resources. USDA, together with the Department of the Interior (DOI), also operates the National Interagency Fire Center.

Department of Commerce

The Department of Commerce promotes homeland security through actions conducted in three of its many offices and agencies. These include:

- Bureau of Industry and Security
- National Institute for Standards and Technology
- National Oceanographic and Atmospheric Administration

Bureau of Industry and Security

The mission of the Bureau of Industry and Security (BIS) is to advance U.S. national security, foreign policy, and economic interests. BIS's activities include regulating the export of sensitive goods and technologies and enforcing export control and public safety laws; cooperating with and assisting foreign countries on export control; helping U.S. industry to comply with international arms control agreements; and monitoring the U.S. defense industrial base to ensure that it is capable of handling national and homeland security needs. This agency gained more notoriety after September 11, when concerns about certain technologies and arms that could be used by terrorists abroad were raised. The bureau has enjoyed an increase in funding as a result of these changes.

National Institute for Standards and Technology

The National Institute for Standards and Technology (NIST) has provided significant contributions to the homeland security of the nation by assisting in the measurement infrastructure used to establish safety and security standards. NIST labs have enjoyed an increase in funding levels since September 11, and have developed technologies that are used for such actions as establishing standards for and measuring the safety and security of buildings, for the development of biometric identification systems, and for various radiation detection systems utilized at U.S. and foreign ports, among many others. NIST laboratories involved, at least partially, in homeland security include the following:

- Building and Fire Research Laboratory
- Chemical Science and Technology Laboratory

- Materials Science and Engineering Laboratory
- Physics Laboratory
- Technology Services

National Oceanographic and Atmospheric Administration

The National Oceanographic and Atmospheric Administration (NOAA) has been involved in disaster management since long before the creation of DHS. NOAA monitors meteorological conditions, makes forecasts about storm risks, and recommends preparedness measures to FEMA and other federal, state, and local government agencies. The NOAA National Weather Service (NWS), under which the All-Hazards Radio Warning Network is managed, is another vital component to the overall homeland security needs of the nation. Although not focused on terrorism, the weather radio system is capable of being activated in the event of any type of disaster, regardless of its origin, to provide timely warning to people who may be in danger.

Department of Education

The Department of Education is responsible for, among other things, taking a leadership position in establishing standards and technical assistance for school safety. Schools are not only vulnerable to the effects of natural and technological disasters, but have been identified by many terrorism experts to be a primary target for terrorist activities due to the emotional factor involved with the injury or death of children. Both before and since September 11, there have been many terrorist or other attacks in schools throughout the world, including in Beslan, Russia, and in Cambodia — both of which resulted in fatalities — and elsewhere. Attacks on schools, exemplified by the 1999 Columbine attacks, provide further justification of the required homeland security role that is filled by the Department of Education.

The office of Safe and Drug-Free Schools was created in September 2002 to manage all Department of Education activities related to safe schools, crisis response, alcohol and drug prevention, and health and well-being of students. Today, this office is responsible for leading the homeland security efforts of the department. Millions of dollars in funding have been made available to schools by the Department of Education through this office to help them to better address emergency planning issues.

Emergency planning guidance and technical assistance are major concerns of the Department of Education, and this area of expertise is also handled through the Office of Safe and Drug-Free Schools. Through the development and maintenance of a website (http://www2.ed.gov/admins/lead/safety/emergencyplan/index.html), the Department of Education has created what they call a "one-stop shop" for schools to locate information to plan for all types of disasters, whether they are natural, terrorist, or other.

The Environmental Protection Agency

The Environmental Protection Agency (EPA) is charged with protecting human health and the environment. The EPA has played a very important role in emergency management and homeland security for decades, most notably in the water sector. The EPA was one of the signatory agencies of the Federal Response Plan (FRP), and today it plays a major role in the NRF. The EPA is concerned primarily with emergencies involving the release, or threatened release, of oil, radioactive materials, or hazardous chemicals that have the potential to affect communities and the surrounding environment. These releases may be accidental, deliberate, or the result of a natural disaster. EPA works with a variety of private and public entities to prevent, prepare for, and respond to spills and other environmental emergencies. EPA's website provides information for these entities to be able to better prevent spills and releases and to better respond to them when they occur.

The EPA has a responsibility for preparing for and responding to terrorist threats involving WMDs. Because of its inherent role in protecting human health and the environment from possible harmful effects of certain chemical, biological, and nuclear materials, the EPA is actively involved in counterterrorism planning and response efforts. The EPA supports federal counterterrorism programs through the following four mechanisms:

1. Helping state and local responders to plan for emergencies
2. Coordinating with key federal partners
3. Training first responders
4. Providing resources in the event of a terrorist incident

Several offices within the agency are involved in these efforts, including these three:

- Office of Emergency Management
- Office of Superfund Remediation Technology Innovation
- Office of Air and Radiation

Office of Emergency Management

The EPA Office of Emergency Management (OEM) works with other federal partners to prevent accidents as well as to maintain the response capabilities of the Agency. This office is tasked with providing information about response efforts, regulations, tools, and research that will help the regulated community, government entities, and concerned citizens prevent, prepare for, and respond to emergencies. OEM also administers the Oil Pollution Act and several other environmental statutes that relate to environmental emergencies and, more importantly, their prevention.

In 1985, one year after the Bhopal, India, chemical accident that killed thousands of people, the EPA established the Chemical Emergency Preparedness and Prevention Office (CEPPO). Through this office, EPA assumed a leading role within the federal government in building programs to respond to and prevent chemical accidents. CEPPO worked with numerous federal, state, local, and tribal governments; industry groups; environmental groups; labor organizations; and community groups to help them better understand the risks posed by chemicals in their communities, to manage and reduce those risks, and to deal with emergencies.

CEPPO also worked with its state and local partners to develop new approaches to deal with emergency preparedness and accident prevention. They assisted local emergency planning committees (LEPCs) and state emergency response commissions (SERCs) by providing leadership, issuing regulations, developing technical guidance, and enabling these committees to develop their own unique emergency planning systems appropriate to their individual needs.

Today the roles of CEPPO fall within the new Office of Emergency Management. This office addresses a number of areas related to the prevention of and preparedness for hazard events and the response and recovery actions required when events actually occur. These programs include:

- *The Environmental Response Laboratory Network (ERLN)*: The ERLN was established to assist in addressing chemical, biological, and radiological threats during major disaster events. The ERLN is a national network of laboratories that can be ramped up as needed to support large-scale environmental responses by providing analytical capabilities, response capacity, and systematic, coordinated data as needed. The ERLN integrates capabilities of existing public sector laboratories with accredited private sector labs to support environmental responses. ERLN's mission is to provide consistent analytical capabilities, capacities, and quality data to federal, state, and local decision makers.

- *The Emergency Planning and Community Right-to-Know Act (EPCRA) Requirements*: The EPCRA requirements help communities prepare for and respond to chemical accidents by requiring facilities to report chemical storage and release information and communities to develop emergency response plans. EPCRA stipulates that every community in the United States must be part of a comprehensive emergency response plan. SERCs oversee the implementation of EPCRA requirements in each state. LEPCs work to understand chemical hazards in the community, develop emergency plans in case of an accidental release, and look for ways to prevent chemical accidents. LEPCs are made up of emergency management agencies, responders, industry, and the public.

- *Emergency Response and Cleanup Actions*: Each year, more than 20,000 emergencies involving the release (or threatened release) of oil and hazardous substances are reported in the United States, potentially affecting both communities and the surrounding natural environment. Emergencies range from small-scale spills to large events requiring prompt action and evacuation of nearby populations. EPA coordinates and implements a wide range of activities to ensure that adequate and timely response measures are taken in communities affected by hazardous substances and oil releases where state and local first-responder capabilities have been exceeded or where additional support is needed. EPA's emergency response program responds to chemical, oil, biological, and radiological releases and large-scale national emergencies, including homeland security incidents. EPA conducts time-critical and non-time-critical removal actions when necessary to protect human health and the environment by either funding response actions directly or overseeing and enforcing actions conducted by potentially responsible parties.

- *Facility Response Plan (FRP) Rule*: A Facility Response Plan (FRP) demonstrates a facility's preparedness to respond to a worst-case oil discharge. Under the Clean Water Act, as amended by the Oil Pollution Act, certain facilities that store and use oil are required to prepare and submit these plans. As part of the Oil Pollution Prevention regulation, the FRP rule addresses:
  - Who must prepare and submit an FRP
  - What must be included in an FRP
  - Potential to cause "substantial harm" in the event of a discharge

- *Local Government Reimbursement (LGR) Program*: In the event of a release (or threatened release) of hazardous substances, EPA may reimburse local governments for expenses related to the release and associated emergency response measures. The LGR Program provides a safety net of up to $25,000 per incident to local governments that do not have funds available to pay for response actions.

- *National Contingency Plan (NCP) Subpart J*: Subpart J provides for a schedule of dispersants, other chemicals, and other spill-mitigating devices and substances that may be authorized for use on oil discharges.

- *Risk Management Plans (RMPs)*: RMPs require certain facilities to tell the public and the EPA what they are doing to prevent accidents and how they plan to operate safely and manage their chemicals in a responsible way. Under the authority of section 112(r) of the Clean Air Act, the chemical accident prevention provisions require facilities that produce, handle, process, distribute, or store certain chemicals to develop a Risk Management Program, prepare an RMP, and submit the RMP to EPA. Covered facilities were initially required to comply with the rule in 1999, and the rule has been amended on several occasions since then, most recently in 2004.

- *Spill Prevention, Control, and Countermeasures (SPCC) Rule*: The SPCC rule includes requirements for oil spill prevention, preparedness, and response to prevent oil discharges to navigable waters and adjoining shorelines. The rule requires specific facilities to prepare, amend, and implement SPCC plans. The SPCC rule is part of the Oil Pollution Prevention regulation, which also includes the FRP rule.

Office of Superfund Remediation Technology Innovation

The Office of Superfund Remediation Technology Innovation (OSRTI), called the Office of Emergency and Remedial Response (OERR) until 2003, manages the Superfund program. The Superfund program was created to protect citizens from the dangers posed by abandoned or uncontrolled hazardous waste sites. Congress established Superfund in 1980 by passing the Comprehensive Environmental Response, Compensation, and Liability Act (CERCLA). CERCLA gives the federal government the authority to respond to hazardous substance emergencies and to develop long-term solutions for the nation's most serious hazardous waste problems.

Office of Air and Radiation

The Office of Air and Radiation (OAR) develops national programs, technical policies, and regulations for controlling air pollution and radiation exposure. OAR is concerned with energy conservation and pollution prevention, indoor and outdoor air quality, industrial air pollution, pollution from vehicles and engines, radon, acid rain, stratospheric ozone depletion, and radiation protection. With regard to homeland security, this office is responsible for emergency response to radiation disasters, helping to design and implement air protection measures, monitoring ambient air (including project BioWatch and monitoring the air around the World Trade Center disaster), and maintaining a national air monitoring system.

In March 2004, the EPA Homeland Security Collaborative Network (HSCN) was established to facilitate the agency's collective approach to analyzing homeland security issues while formulating policy recommendations and actions cooperatively. The following is a list of EPA program offices that are members of the HSCN and a brief description of their homeland security tasks (where appropriate):

- Office of Air and Radiation (OAR)
  - See earlier description
- Office of Administration and Resource Management (OARM)
  - EPA facilities and employee security
  - Physical critical infrastructure protection
  - Design buildout of sensitive, classified information facilities/secured access facilities (SCIFs/SAFs)
- Monitoring of Homeland Security Advisory System (HSAD) threat conditions
- Office of the Chief Financial Officer (OCFO)
- Office of Enforcement and Compliance Assurance (OECA)
  - Civil and criminal enforcement
  - Incident response
  - Counterterrorism support
  - Forensics
- Office of Environmental Information (OEI)
  - Information protection and access policy
  - Information infrastructure and cyberprotection
  - Information technology
  - Data management

- Office of Prevention, Pesticides, and Toxic Substances (OPPTS)
  - Food and agriculture security support
  - Emergency exemption requests
  - Acute Exposure Guideline Limits (AEGLs)
  - Chemical data/expertise on pesticides and industrial chemicals
  - Licensing authority for antimicrobials to inactivate pathogens and pesticides
  - Establishment of rules for storage/disposal of pesticides and pesticide applicator certification program
- Office of Research and Development (ORD)
  - Water security research
  - Building decontamination
  - Rapid risk assessment
  - Office of Solid Waste and Emergency Response (OSWER)
  - Chemical industry infrastructure support
  - Building and critical infrastructure decontamination
  - Emergency response
  - Lab capacity
  - Continuity of operations plan/continuity of government (COOP/COG)
  - Superfund
- Office of Water (OW)
  - Drinking water and wastewater infrastructure protection
  - Training, simulations, exercises
  - Best water security practices
  - Vulnerability assessments and emergency response plans
  - Tools for preparedness and emergency response
  - Framework for monitoring/surveillance network
  - Financial assistance to states and tribes
  - Information sharing with sector and partners
- Region 6
  - Lead EPA region for homeland security responsibilities

The Department of Justice

The Department of Justice has lead responsibility for criminal investigations of terrorist acts or terrorist threats by individuals or groups inside the United States or directed at U.S. citizens or institutions abroad, as well as for related intelligence collection activities within the United States. Following a terrorist threat or an actual incident that falls within the criminal jurisdiction of the United States, the Attorney General identifies the perpetrators and makes every effort through the various DOJ agencies to bring those perpetrators to justice. These agencies include the Federal Bureau of Investigation (FBI), the Drug Enforcement Administration (DEA), and Bureau of Alcohol, Tobacco, Firearms, and Explosives (ATF), each of which has key homeland security responsibilities.

The Department of State

The Department of State has the responsibility to coordinate activities with foreign governments and international organizations related to the prevention, preparation, response, and recovery from domestic

disasters, and for the protection of U.S. citizens and U.S. interests overseas. The Department of State political officers located at the various embassies and consulates, found throughout all countries of the world
maintaining diplomatic relations with the United States, monitor emerging and known threats through
establishment of local contacts and monitoring of events. The Department of State also provides direction
to the Office of the President on areas where diplomatic pressure may be utilized to control emerging and
known threats to domestic security (see sidebar "Diplomatic Pressure"). The Department of State also has
an important counterterrorism role through its adjudication of visa applications, which helps to prevent
easy access to the nation for possible terrorists (as identified through the various intelligence efforts).

Diplomatic Pressure

Through the U.S. Department of State, the U.S. government works to develop allies in the fight against
terrorism around the world. As a major world power, and the leading provider of international development assistance, the United States is able to influence the actions of other nations through the application of diplomatic pressure when the White House feels that such actions are necessary to maintain
national security. A recent example of this pressure occurred in the summer of 2011 when the U.S.
government threatened to significantly reduce the amount of military aid it provided to Pakistan, a
major ally in the fight against terrorism. Several consecutive events initiated this action, the most significant of which happened in the spring of 2011 when the U.S. military, working in conjunction with
the Central Intelligence Agency, located and killed Al Qaeda leader Osama bin Laden. When it was
discovered that bin Laden had been living unnoticed in the shadow of a significant military facility in
Abbottabad, Pakistan, many U.S. lawmakers felt that Pakistan was not doing enough to battle terrorist extremists. After the military operation took place, Pakistan retaliated against what it called a "vio-
lation of its sovereignty" by refusing entry of various military support personnel and by releasing the
names of key CIA officials operating in the country. These events marked a significant change in the
working relationship that existed between the two countries, and were a sign that Pakistan may not be
taking a hard enough line against terrorism to achieve the outcomes that the U.S. government would
like to see (with regard to a reduction in national security risks). In response, Pakistan was threatened
with a reduction of approximately $800 billion in the ongoing military assistance the United States
had been providing to Pakistan for years. The move was clearly a message to the South Asian country
that their actions were moving away from what was felt by the White House to be in the best interests
of the national security of the United States (Associated Press, 2011).

   For more information, see the article titled "Sixty Years of US Aid to Pakistan" (Guardian, 2011).

The Department of Defense

The Department of Defense (DOD) ensures the security of the United States by acting both as a military
deterrent to nations and groups who might otherwise wish to attack American soil and by pursuing and elimi-
nating threats around the world. DOD military services, defense agencies, and geographic and functional
commands also work to ensure regional stability by participating in conflict around the globe, securing and
assuring access to sea, air, space, and cyberspace, and building the security capacity of key partners. DOD

supports civil authorities in disaster events, at the direction of the Secretary of Defense or the President, when the capabilities of state and local authorities to respond effectively to an event are overwhelmed.

The Department of Health and Human Services

The Department of Health and Human Services (HHS) leads the coordination of all functions relevant to Public Health Emergency Preparedness and Disaster Medical Response. Additionally, HHS incorporates steady-state and incident-specific activities as described in the National Health Security Strategy. HHS is the coordinator and primary agency for NRF Emergency Support Function (ESF) #8 — Public Health and Medical Services, providing the mechanism for coordinated federal assistance to supplement state, local, tribal, and territorial resources in response to a public health and medical disaster, potential or actual incident requiring a coordinated federal response, and/or during a developing potential health and medical emergency.

The Department of the Treasury

The Department of the Treasury (Treasury) works to safeguard the U.S. financial system, combat financial crimes, and cut off financial support to terrorists, WMD proliferators, drug traffickers, and other national security threats. After the 9/11 terrorist attacks, Treasury initiated the Terrorist Finance Tracking Program (TFTP) to identify, track, and pursue terrorists and terror networks (e.g., Al Qaeda). The Treasury Department is uniquely positioned to track terrorist money flows and assist in broader U.S. government efforts to uncover terrorist cells and map terrorist networks here at home and around the world. As the policy development and outreach office for Terrorism and Financing Intelligence (TFI), the Office of Terrorist Financing and Financial Crimes (TFFC) works across all elements of the national security community — including the law enforcement, regulatory, policy, diplomatic, and intelligence communities — and with the private sector and foreign governments to identify and address the threats presented by all forms of illicit finance to the international financial system. TFFC advances this mission by developing initiatives and strategies to deploy a full range of financial authorities to combat money laundering, terrorist financing, WMD proliferation, and other criminal and illicit activities both at home and abroad. These include not only systemic initiatives to enhance the transparency of the international financial system, but also threat-specific strategies and initiatives to apply and implement targeted financial measures to the full range of national security threats.

The Director of National Intelligence

The Director of National Intelligence (DNI) serves as the head of the IC, acts as the principal advisor to the President and National Security Council for intelligence matters relating to national security, and oversees and directs implementation of the National Intelligence Program. The IC, composed of 16 elements across the U.S. Government, functions consistent with law, Executive order, regulations, and policy to support the national security-related missions of the U.S. Government. The homeland security role of DNI is explained in much greater detail in Chapter 5.

Department of Energy

The Department of Energy (DOE) maintains stewardship of vital national security capabilities, from nuclear weapons to research and development programs. DOE is the designated federal agency to provide a unifying structure for the integration of federal critical infrastructure and key resources' protection efforts, specifically for the energy sector. It is also responsible for maintaining continuous and reliable energy supplies for the United States through preventive measures and restoration and recovery actions. DOE is the coordinator and primary agency for ESF #12 (Energy) when disasters are declared by the President.

The Department of Housing and Urban Development

The Department of Housing and Urban Development (HUD) is the coordinator and primary agency for ESF #14 — Long-Term Community Recovery, which provides a mechanism for coordinating federal support to state, tribal, regional, and local governments, nongovernmental organizations (NGOs), and the private sector to enable community recovery from the long-term consequences of extraordinary disasters.

Department of the Interior

The DOI develops policies and procedures for all types of hazards and emergencies that impact federal lands, facilities, infrastructure, and resources; tribal lands; and insular areas. DOI is also a primary agency for ESF #9 (Search and Rescue), providing specialized lifesaving assistance to state, tribal, and local authorities when activated for incidents or potential incidents requiring a coordinated federal response. DOI, together with the Department of Agriculture, also operates the National Interagency Fire Center.

Department of Transportation

The Department of Transportation (DOT) collaborates with DHS on all matters relating to transportation security and transportation infrastructure protection and in regulating the transportation of hazardous materials by all modes (including pipelines). The Secretary of Transportation is responsible for operating the national airspace system. DOT is the coordinating agency for ESF #1 (Transportation) in the event of disasters declared by the president.

The Corporation for National and Community Service

The Corporation for National and Community Service (CNCS) is a government agency that administers several individual volunteer-based but grant-funded programs that contribute to homeland security and emergency management, including AmeriCorps, Senior Corps, and Learn and Serve America.

- AmeriCorps is a network of national service programs that "engage more than 70,000 Americans each year in intensive service to meet critical needs in education, public safety, health, and the environment." AmeriCorps members serve through more than 3,000 nonprofit and nongovernmental agencies, public agencies, and faith-based organizations, tutoring and mentoring youth, building affordable housing, teaching computer skills, cleaning parks and streams, running after-school programs, and helping communities respond to disasters. These programs engage more than two million Americans of all ages and backgrounds in service each year.
- Senior Corps is a network of programs that "tap the experience, skills, and talents of older citizens to meet community challenges." It includes three programs: Foster Grandparents, Senior Companions, and the Retired and Senior Volunteer. More than a half-million Americans ages 55 and older assist local nonprofits, public agencies, and faith-based organizations in carrying out their missions, together having provided over one billion volunteer hours nationwide.
- Learn and Serve America is a program that "supports service-learning programs in schools and community organizations that help nearly one million students from kindergarten through college meet community needs, while improving their academic skills and learning the habits of good

citizenship." Service learning is defined as an educational method by which participants learn and develop through active participation in service that is conducted in and meets the needs of a community.

In July 2002, CNCS awarded 43 grants totaling $10.3 million to increasing citizen participation in homeland security in communities, government agencies, and voluntary organizations. Since that time CNCS has continued to support community-level homeland security projects. In the response to and recovery from the 2005 Gulf Coast hurricanes, CNCS became highly involved in the cleanup and rebuilding of the affected communities through volunteer participation. CNCS grantee programs from throughout the country sent volunteer participants. CNCS volunteers provided millions of hours of service in relief and recovery areas such as "mucking out" flooded houses, demolition, construction, tarping of damaged roofs, victim case management, counseling, and much more. The post-disaster assistance provided by the various CNCS programs is described in the sidebar "National Service Responds to the Gulf Coast Hurricanes."

■ ■ ■

National Service Responds to the Gulf Coast Hurricanes

Since August 2005, the Corporation for National and Community Service has provided more than $200 million worth of resources to Gulf Coast states recovering from the devastation caused by Hurricanes Katrina, Rita, and Wilma. Working in cooperation with FEMA, state and local authorities, and hundreds of nonprofit groups, more than 110,000 national service volunteers have contributed more than 9.6 million hours to the relief, recovery, and rebuilding effort. They also have coordinated an additional 648,000 community volunteers, a major share of the overall volunteer force. Activities have included supporting shelter operations and housing placement; establishing call centers and warehousing sites; assisting with case work and benefits coordination; setting up school and youth programs; blue roofing, debris removal, and mucking out homes; serving on long-term recovery committees; and construction of new homes for low-income families. As a result of its experience with hurricane relief and recovery, the Corporation has established a number of new procedures to provide more effective and timely response to disasters under the authority of FEMA mission assignments. Using lessons learned in Katrina, trained AmeriCorps teams have been deployed to winter ice storms in Missouri; tornadoes in Greensburg, Kansas, and Parkersburg, Iowa; California forest fires; 2008 flooding in Iowa and Missouri; and the BP oil spill, among other disasters. The Corporation continues to shift its resources to support a variety of disaster preparedness and response activities.

In June 2007, the Corporation's board of directors added a new strategic initiative on disaster preparedness and response. This action reflected the agency's growing expertise and increased commitment to help individuals and communities expand their capacity to prepare for and respond to natural disasters.

- **AMERICORPS:** AmeriCorps has been a backbone of Gulf Coast hurricane relief, and continues to be deeply engaged in the long-term recovery effort. More than 17,000 AmeriCorps members have provided 8.5 million hours of service and recruited or coordinated more than 611,000 other volunteers.
- **AMERICORPS NCCC:** More than 5,400 AmeriCorps NCCC members have served on more than 1,040 separate disaster services projects in the Gulf Coast region since September 2005, in coordination with such groups as the American Red Cross, the Salvation Army, Habitat

for Humanity, and state service commissions. In all, NCCC members have contributed more than 2.7 million hours of service, valued at $54 million. They have assisted 3 million people, trained and supervised more than 262,000 community volunteers, completed nearly 55,000 damage assessments, refurbished more than 10,500 homes, constructed 2,000 new homes, served 1.6 million meals, and distributed more than 6,000 tons of food.

- **AMERICORPS STATE AND NATIONAL:** More than 100 grantee programs of AmeriCorps State and National, collectively representing more than 9,000 AmeriCorps members, have provided more than 3.1 million hours in hurricane relief and recovery assistance in the Gulf region. The Corporation has provided more than $78 million in funds to bring thousands of AmeriCorps members to the Gulf region through fiscal year 2010.
- **AMERICORPS VISTA:** More than 2,700 AmeriCorps VISTA members have served in the Gulf Coast, building the capacity of nonprofit organizations and helping low-income people out of poverty. In addition, through its Summer Associate Program, VISTA has sent 246 members to New Orleans to support summer camps for tens of thousands of children in 2007 and 2008.
- **SENIOR CORPS:** More than 18,600 Senior Corps volunteers have served in Gulf Coast hurricane relief efforts, providing food and shelter, coordinating distribution of donated goods, managing community volunteers, meeting the needs of at-risk youth, and more.
- **LEARN AND SERVE AMERICA:** Tens of thousands of students supported by Learn and Serve America raised funds and items needed for hurricane relief, assembled and distributed disaster relief kits, and traveled to the Gulf region to help in the recovery effort. Hundreds of college and high school student groups have traveled to the Gulf Coast to volunteer on spring break and summer trips
- **CHALLENGE GRANT PROGRAM:** The Corporation revised its 2005 Challenge Grant competition to focus on disaster relief, resulting in the approval of $4 million to six multistate projects to recruit nearly 72,000 volunteers, with an emphasis on baby boomers.
- **"SKILLED SERVICE IN THE GULF" GRANTS:** In June 2007, the Corporation announced that Habitat for Humanity International, Xavier University of Louisiana, and Rebuilding Together were selected to receive awards totaling $900,000 to engage skilled volunteers in providing disaster recovery assistance to the Gulf states. The skilled construction volunteers will lead lesser-skilled volunteers and handle the most challenging aspects of rebuilding.
- **COORDINATION AND PLANNING:** To increase coordination at the federal, state, and local levels, the Corporation has worked with the Department of Homeland Security and FEMA on the National Response Framework, created a "Disaster Coordinator Cadre" of specially trained staff available to go to disaster zones to coordinate national service assets and mission assignments with FEMA, and signed a Memorandum of Understanding in January 2007 with the National Voluntary Organizations Active in Disaster to enable smarter, faster cooperation with the group's members.
- **TRAINING AND TECHNICAL ASSISTANCE:** Through its Resource Center, the Corporation offers free online resources on disaster preparedness and response including videos, how-to guides, best practices, and courses. The Corporation also provides in-person training at conferences, including a 2007 national "Disaster Institute" for state service commissions.

Source: CNCS, August 2010, http://www.nationalservice.gov/pdf/09_0829_factsheet_katrina.pdf.

Citizen Corps Program

Citizen Corps is a FEMA-administered program that provides opportunities for citizens who want to help make their communities more secure. Since its January 2002 establishment, tens of thousands of people from all 50 states and U.S. territories have volunteered to work with one or more of the Citizen Corps programs. These include the following:

- Citizen Corps Councils (CCCs) were established at the state and local level to promote, organize, and run the various programs that fall under the Citizen Corps umbrella. Funding for these councils is provided by the federal government through grant awards. As of May 2008, there were CCCs in 56 states and U.S. territories and 1,093 local communities, all of which serve 60% of the total population of the United States.

- Community Emergency Response Teams (CERTs) began in 1983 in Los Angeles, California. City administrators there recognized that in most emergency situations, average citizens — neighbors, coworkers, and bystanders, for example — were often on scene during the critical moments before professional help arrives. These officials acted on the belief that by training average citizens to perform basic search and rescue, first aid, and other critical emergency response skills, they would increase the overall resilience of the community. Additionally, should a large-scale disaster like an earthquake occur, where first response units would be stretched very thin, these trained citizens would be able to augment official services and provide an important service to the community. Beginning in 1993, FEMA began to offer CERT training on a national level, providing funding to cover start-up and tuition costs for programs. By 2008, CERT programs had been established in more than 2,915 communities in all 50 states, the District of Columbia, and several U.S. territories. Today, that number has fallen to 1,790, mostly due to falling funding levels. CERT teams remain active in the community before a disaster strikes, sponsoring events such as drills, neighborhood cleanup, and disaster-education fairs. Trainers offer periodic refresher sessions to CERT members to reinforce the basic training and to keep participants involved and practiced in their skills. CERT members also offer other nonemergency assistance to the community with the goal of improving the overall safety of the community.

- Volunteers in Police Service (VIPS) was created in the aftermath of September 11, 2001, to address the increased demands on state and local law enforcement. The basis of the program is that civilian volunteers are able to support police officers by doing much of the behind-the-scenes work that does not require formal law enforcement training, thereby allowing officers to spend more of their already strained schedules on the street. Although the concept is not new, the federal support for such programs is. VIPS draws on the time and recognized talents of civilian volunteers. Volunteer roles may include performing clerical tasks, serving as an extra set of "eyes and ears," assisting with search-and-rescue activities, and writing citations for accessible parking violations, just to name a few. As of summer 2011, there were 2,177 official VIPS programs registered throughout the United States.

- The Medical Reserve Corps (MRC) was founded after the 2002 State of the Union Address to establish teams of local volunteer medical and public health professionals who can contribute their skills and experience when called on in times of need. The program relies on volunteers who are practicing and retired physicians, nurses, dentists, veterinarians, epidemiologists, and other health professionals, as well as other citizens untrained in public health but who can contribute to the community's normal and disaster public health needs in other ways (which may include interpreters, chaplains, legal advisers, etc.). Local community leaders develop their own MRC units and recruit local volunteers that address the specific community needs. For example, MRC volunteers may deliver necessary public health services during a crisis, assist emergency response teams with patients, and provide care directly to those with less serious injuries and other health-related issues. MRC volunteers may also serve a vital role by assisting their communities with ongoing public health needs (e.g., immunizations, screenings, health and nutrition education, and volunteering in community health centers and local hospitals). The MRC unit decides, in concert with local officials (including the local CCC), on when the community MRC is activated during a local emergency. As of summer 2011, there were 947 MRC programs established throughout the United States.

- The Neighborhood Watch Program has been in existence for more than 30 years in cities and counties throughout the United States. The program is based on the concept that neighbors who join together to fight crime will be able to increase security in their surrounding areas and, as a result, provide an overall better quality of life for residents. Understandably, after September 11, when terrorism became a major focus of the U.S. government, the recognized importance of programs like Neighborhood Watch took on much greater significance. The Neighborhood Watch program is not maintained by the National Sheriff's Association, which founded the program initially. At the local level, the CCCs help neighborhood groups that have banded together to start a program to carry out their mission. Many printed materials and other guidance are available for free to help them carry out their goals. Neighborhood Watch programs have successfully decreased crime in many of the neighborhoods where they have been implemented. In total, as of January 2008, there were 14,791 programs spread out throughout the United States and the U.S. territories. In addition to serving a crime prevention role, Neighborhood Watch has been used as the basis for bringing neighborhood residents together to focus on disaster preparedness and terrorism awareness; to focus on evacuation drills and exercises; and even to organize group training, such as the CERT training.

- Fire Corps was created in 2004 under the umbrella of U.S. Freedom Corps and Citizen Corps. The purpose of the program, like the VIPS program with the police, was to enhance the ability of fire departments to utilize citizen advocates and provide individuals with opportunities to support their local fire departments with both time and talent. Fire Corps was created as a partnership between the International Association of Fire Chiefs' Volunteer Combination Officers Section (VCOS), the International Association of Fire Fighters (IAFF), and the National Volunteer Fire Council (NVFC). By participating in the program, concerned and interested citizens can assist in their local fire department's activities through tasks such as administrative assistance, public education, fund-raising, data entry, accounting, public relations, and equipment and facility maintenance, just to name a few examples. Any fire department that allows citizens to volunteer support service is considered a Fire Corps program, but programs can become official through registering with a local, county, or state CCC, if one exists. Official Fire Corps programs will be provided with assistance on how to implement a nonoperational citizen advocates program or improve existing programs. A Fire Corps National Advisory Committee has been established under the program in order to provide strategic direction and collect feedback from the field. As of summer 2011, there were 1,098 established Fire Corps programs throughout the United States and the U.S. territories. Although some of these programs are relatively new, some, such as Neighborhood Watch, have been in place for more than a decade. More information on these programs is provided in Chapter 9.

NRF Participant Agencies

Many other federal agencies other than those just listed are involved in homeland security efforts, although most of these actions occur as a result of their contractual obligations set out in NRF. Although these actions will be described in greater detail in Chapter 9, the following is a list of the federal agencies that participate in the response to disasters within the United States:

- Corporation for National and Community Service
- Department of Agriculture
- Department of Commerce
- Department of Defense
- Department of Education
- Department of Energy
- Department of Health and Human Services
- Department of Homeland Security
- Department of Housing and Urban Development
- Department of the Interior
- Department of Justice
- Department of Labor
- Department of State
- Department of Transportation
- Department of the Treasury
- Department of Veterans Affairs
- Central Intelligence Agency
- Environmental Protection Agency
- Federal Bureau of Investigation
- Federal Communications Commission
- General Services Administration
- National Aeronautics and Space Administration
- National Transportation Safety Board
- Nuclear Regulatory Commission
- Office of Personnel Management
- Small Business Administration
- Social Security Administration
- Tennessee Valley Authority
- United States Agency for International Development
- U.S. Postal Service

▪▪ Critical Thinking ▪

Why do you think certain homeland security-related functions are still performed by other federal agencies that were not incorporated into DHS? Should they have been? Why or why not?

Activities by State and Local Organizations

State and local governments have expended considerable human and financial resources to secure their jurisdictions from the perceived threat of terrorism. Although considerable amounts of federal funding have gone to helping state and local agencies to better prepare for the terrorist threat, many of these efforts have been performed without any federal compensation. Also, each time a homeland security alert is issued, or when a major event that is identified as being a potential terrorist target is held within a jurisdiction, local leaders must divert sparse financial and human resources from other areas of need to adequately address those threats. These collective strains have prompted the many organizations representative of state and local governments to become actively engaged in the homeland security debate, from the passage of the Homeland Security Act of 2002 until today.

As early as September 2002, the municipal organizations, which include the U.S. Conference of Mayors (USCM), the National League of Cities (NLC), the National Association of Counties (NACo), and the National Governors Association (NGA), and the emergency management organizations, which include the National Emergency Management Association (NEMA) and the International Association of Emergency Managers (IAEM), began fighting for first-responder funding for state and local governments and about the way the money was allocated — whether it would be to the states or directly to the local municipalities. Clearly, these organizations were and continue to be involved in informing the federal government's approach to funding state and local homeland security efforts. Each of these organizations is discussed next.

United States Conference of Mayors

The U.S. Conference of Mayors (USCM) is the official nonpartisan organization of the nation's 1,192 U.S. cities with populations of 30,000 or more. Each city is represented in the conference by its chief elected official, the mayor. The primary roles of the USCM are to:

- Promote the development of effective national urban/suburban policy
- Strengthen federal–city relationships
- Ensure that federal policy meets urban needs
- Provide mayors with leadership and management tools
- Create a forum in which mayors can share ideas and information

The conference has historically assumed a national leadership role, calling early attention to serious urban problems and pressing successfully for solutions.

In December 2001, 3 months after the 9/11 attacks, the USCM released "A National Action Plan for Safety and Security in America's Cities." The document was prepared as part of the Mayors Emergency Safety and Security Summit held in Washington, DC, on October 23–25, 2001. It contained recommendations in four priority areas: transportation security, emergency preparedness, federal–local law enforcement, and economic security. In this document, the mayors made the following critical point:

> It is important to understand that while the fourth area, economic security, is viewed as the ultimate goal of a nation, it cannot be achieved in the absence of the first three. That is, securing our transportation system, maximizing our emergency response capability, and coordinating our law enforcement response to threats and incidents at all levels are viewed as prerequisites to eliminating the anxiety that has accelerated the nation's economic downturn, and to achieving economic security for the nation.

The principal areas of concern in federal–local law enforcement for the mayors are communications, coordination, and border-city security. In the transportation security section, the mayors' paper presents recommendations concerning security issues in each of the major transportation modes: airport, transit, highway, rail, and port.

The USCM leadership has repeatedly expressed concern that a significant amount of funding from the federal government has not reached the cities for combating terrorism. The mayors expressed that they have been working on initiatives related to homeland security, largely without any federal assistance. Select initiatives, related to communities, that they mentioned include the following: (1) conducting exercises to help prepare for emergencies and improve response capabilities, (2) expanding public information and education efforts, and (3) conducting vulnerability assessments of potential key targets.

Funding for cities has remained a principal focus of the USCM in the area of homeland security. In September 2003, the USCM released a report titled, "First Mayors' Report to the Nation: Tracking Homeland Security Funds Sent to the 50 State Governments" (U.S. Conference of Mayors, 2003). Through release of the report, the USCM website announced that 90% of cities had not received funds from the largest federal homeland security program designed to assist first responders by the federally set deadline of August 1, 2003. The report also found that more than half of the cities either had not been consulted or had no opportunity to influence state decision making about how to use and distribute funding.

The USCM established a Homeland Security Monitoring Center (no longer active) to monitor the flow of homeland security funds from the federal government to states and localities. This focus on funding was at the heart of a March 12, 2004, message from Tom Cochran, executive director of the USCM, in a website column that stated, "Our goal is to do one thing: get the money down to our first responders on the front line in cities throughout America" (U.S. Conference of Mayors, 2004a). In June 2004, the USCM released a report of a survey that was conducted to assess the flow of federal homeland security funds through the states to the cities. Their study found that 52% of the 231 cities surveyed had not received any money at all, nor had they been notified that they would receive money from the state block grant program, which is the largest homeland security program designed to assist first responders.

In 2006, the USCM conducted a survey to determine levels of emergency and disaster readiness at the city level in the United States. The results of this survey were issued in a report titled "Five Years Post 9/11 and One Year Post Hurricane Katrina: The State of America's Readiness." Results announced in a press release (see "U.S. Conference of Mayors Press Release" sidebar) showed that cities still have a long way to go. The USCM has continued to fight for municipal homeland security issues in the years since. In January 2007, the mayors released a 10-point legislative agenda that included a section on homeland security. This plan identified three areas of concern for the cities, many of which remain relevant to this day. These included:

- *Interoperable communications*: The mayors called for a well-funded, standalone, federal emergency communications grant program designed to improve interoperable communications, including flexible direct grants to cities and first responders.
- *Transit security*: The mayors called for a flexible federal transit security initiative to improve security in the areas of communications, surveillance, detection systems, personnel, and training. Because of the negative experiences cities had previously encountered trying to find money locally to cover these kinds of expenses, and in trying to receive the actual funds once granted by the federal government, the mayors requested that there be no local or state match and that security funds would go directly to the operator of the system or the jurisdiction providing the security.
- *Funding mechanism*: The mayors contend that improvements must be made in the application process and delivery mechanism for federal homeland security grant resources to make sure that the process is more user-friendly, the funding reaches cities quickly, and the funding is flexible enough to meet local needs.

The mayor's influence was felt by Congress, and many of their 10-Point Plan requests were honored in the 9/11 Bill that was passed on August 3, 2007. For instance, the Urban Area Security Initiative

(UASI), which is designed to assist high-risk urban areas in preventing, preparing for, protecting against, and responding to terrorism, was altered to meet the mayors' preferences. For FY 2008, $850 million was authorized, with an additional $150 million every year thereafter. Eligible city governments were given the opportunity to present what they feel is relevant information about their city's threat, vulnerability, and likely consequences of a terrorist attack, and details about the intended allocation of funds within the local government. If approved, awards are still distributed to the state (a point of contention for the mayors), but the state is required to pass at least 80% of the funds to the appropriate urban area within 45 days. Any remaining amounts retained by the states must be put toward "items, services, or activities that benefit the high-risk urban area." Under the law, the 100 most populous metropolitan areas in the United States are eligible for UASI grants. If a region is not ranked within the 100 most populous metropolitan areas, DHS can still determine it to be a high-risk urban area based on a risk formula, and DHS can designate regions consisting of more than one metropolitan area into several high-risk urban areas. Finally, a high-risk urban area can, with DHS permission, expand its jurisdiction to include additional regions.

The law also changed the Homeland Security Grant Program (HSGP), which seeks to enhance statewide homeland security management, personnel, training, and equipment. The new bill reduced the minimum amount of total funding each state would receive from 0.75% to 0.375% in FY 2008, 0.365% in FY 2009, and 0.360% for FY 2010 on. Like UASI, the state is responsible for allocating at least 80% of the funds to local governments within 45 days of receiving the grant. The factors that will ultimately determine the sums awarded to the states are risk level and the quality of the anticipated effectiveness of the proposal. The most important change to this grant that affects the mayors is the absence of a local match requirement, which had been included in earlier versions of the legislation and was opposed by the Conference of Mayors.

The new 9/11 Bill was to have increased the authorization for the Emergency Management Performance Grant program to $400 million for FY 2008, $535 million in FY 2009, $680 million in FY 2010, $815 million in FY 2011, and $950 million in FY 2012. However, in 2011 those figures fell to $329 million once the budget was approved, rising to $350 million in 2012.

One of the most important changes brought about by the new legislation, in terms of the needs of cities, was the Interoperable Emergency Communications Grant Program. This grant program sought to improve local, tribal, statewide, regional, and national interoperable communications as is needed in collective response to disasters and emergencies. The bill authorized $400 million each fiscal year between 2009 and 2012. However, this grant was lumped into the State Homeland Security Grant Program in 2012. This grant is key for states because they must submit an Interoperable Communication Plan to be approved by the Director of Emergency Communications on the basis of:

1. Risk, including likelihood of a state responding to a nearby jurisdiction, population size, and proximity to international borders
2. Anticipated effectiveness

The USCM also saw its transit security recommendation in the 10-Point Plan integrated in the final version of the 9/11 Bill. Through a partnership between the DHS and the DOT, the bill created the National Strategy for Public Transportation and Security that sought to minimize security threats to the public transportation system and maximize recovery ability. The Public Transportation Security Assistance Program, which has since ended, made grants available for security improvements to transportation agencies that have performed a security assessment or have drawn up a security plan.

National League of Cities

The NLC is the oldest and largest national organization representing municipal governments throughout the United States. The NLC serves as a resource to and is an advocate for the more than 19,000 cities, villages, and towns it represents. More than 1,600 municipalities of all sizes pay dues to NLC and actively participate as leaders and voting members in the organization. The NLC provides numerous benefits to its network of members, including:

- Advocates for cities and towns in the Washington, D.C. area through full-time lobbying and grassroots campaigns
- Promotes cities and towns through an aggressive media and communications program that draws attention to city issues and enhances the national image of local government
- Provides programs and services that give local leaders the tools and knowledge to better serve their communities
- Keeps leaders informed of critical issues that affect municipalities and warrant action by local officials
- Strengthens leadership skills by offering numerous training and education programs
- Recognizes municipal achievements by gathering and promoting examples of best practices and honoring cities and towns with awards for model programs and initiatives
- Partners with state leagues to supplement resources and strengthen the voice of local government in the nation's capital and all state capitals
- Promotes cities and towns through an aggressive media and communications program that draws attention to city issues and enhances the national image of local government

Like the USCM, the NLC has also focused on the first-responder funding issue. It conducted a letter-writing campaign to the White House and Congress to build support for the original allocation of first-responder funds. In 2002, NLC proposed a $75.5 billion stimulus package that would include $10 billion for unmet homeland security needs.

In January 2003, then NLC President Karen Anderson appointed the special Working Group on Homeland Security to serve as NLC's frontline resource on the subject. That group worked to prepare resources to help city officials in carrying out their new roles as the "front line of hometown defense."

The NLC has continued to lobby Congress and the Executive Office to increase or maintain funding support to strengthen "hometown" and homeland security, and develop extensive policy on these issues. The NLC reports the results of surveys on municipal responses to terrorism regarding vulnerable targets and the need for federal guidance and support. A variety of publications that NLC generates offer practical guidance to local officials to assist in their ongoing efforts to develop and refine local and regional homeland security plans.

In 2005, homeland security remained a top priority for the NLC. The two primary NLC issues were first-responder funding and public safety communications. Presented in the "2005 Advocacy Priority" sidebar is text from an NLC document detailing advocacy policy regarding funding for first responders.

In 2005, the NLC developed a policy statement on homeland security that was included in its "National Municipal Policy." The policy statement addresses the following topics:

- Prevention, planning, and mitigation
- Disaster response and recovery
- Training and technical assistance

- Disaster insurance
- Domestic terrorism
- Border security
- Immigration enforcement
- Profiling

In support of these policies, NLC developed a publication, "Protecting Hometown America: Lessons Learned from and for Small Cities and Towns," available on this book's companion website.

2005 Advocacy Priority — The Issue: Funding for First Responders

The nation's cities and towns need a well-funded, improved grant program to respond to terrorism threats in highly populated and high-threat areas. Local governments seek funding that allows jurisdictions to prepare for possible terrorist threats, with flexibility to use the funds for a range of risks based on their state homeland security plans.

Message to Congress
- Preserve direct funding. Preserve direct funding to local governments and regions based on the congressionally mandated 80 percent pass-through requirement from states to local governments.
- Improve homeland and hometown security. Improve security by increasing funding for Urban Area Security Grants and the State Homeland Security Grant program.
- Preserve funding. Preserve funding for both homeland security programs such as Law Enforcement Terrorism Prevention grants, the Urban Search and Rescue program and the Metropolitan Medical Response System, and traditional first-responder and emergency management programs that existed before September 11, 2001.
- Provide flexibility. Provide flexibility for local governments to use homeland security funds to offset overtime expenditures during national high alerts, counterterrorism activities, and training exercises.
- Create a Federal clearinghouse. Create a web-based Federal clearinghouse of best practices and updated voluntary national consensus standards.
- Waive cost-sharing requirements. Waive matching or cost-sharing requirements for local governments.

Request to Congress
- Enact an authorization bill that provides funding for first responders to target terrorism threats in highly populated and high-threat areas, with maximum flexibility to use the funds for a range of risks based on their state homeland security plans.
- Fully fund the State Homeland Security Grant program, Urban Area Security Grants, and other critical homeland security programs.

Source: National League of Cities, http://www.nlc.org/content/Files/PFRHomeland%20Security1.pdf.

The NLC has developed several other publications to assist local governments in participating in homeland security, including:

- "Homeland Security: Practical Tools for Local Governments" (http://www.transit-safety.volpe.dot. gov/security/SecurityInitiatives/Top20/1%20--%20Management%20and%20Accountability/2% 20--%20Updated%20for%20Anti-Terrorism%20Measures/Additional/National_League_of_Cities_ Practical_Tools.pdf#page=6)
- "Why Can't We Talk?" Emergency Communications Interoperability Guide (http://www .safecomprogram.gov/NR/rdonlyres/322B4367-265C-45FB-8EEA-BD0FEBDA95A8/0/Why_cant_ we_talk_NTFI_Guide.pdf)
- "SARS: Lessons Learned for America's Cities and Towns" (http://www.transit-safety.volpe.dot.gov/ security/SecurityInitiatives/Top20/1%20--%20Management%20and%20Accountability/2% 20--%20Updated%20for%20Anti-Terrorism%20Measures/Additional/lessons_sars.pdf)

In July 2007, NLC representatives met with DHS officials to exchange views and perspectives on homeland security in towns and cities. At this meeting, the NLC reiterated that all emergency situations are local events and that local elected officials involved in the day-to-day operations of local government shoulder the burden of ensuring that public safety resources are available to citizens in times of emergency or disaster. At this meeting, NLC highlighted the following seven topics as priorities for local elected officials:

1. Emergency communications
2. Emergency Management Assistance Compacts (EMACs)/Mutual Aid
3. All-hazards planning
4. Federalization of the National Guard
5. Intragovernmental collaboration and communication
6. Full funding of federal mandates
7. Immigration/border security

National Association of Counties

The NACo was created in 1935, and remains the only national organization that represents county governments in the United States. NACo maintains a membership of more than 2,000 counties (over 80% of the U.S. population), but represents all of the nation's 3,068 counties to the White House and to Congress.

NACo is a full-service organization that provides many services to its members, including legislative, research, technical, and public affairs assistance. The association acts as a liaison with other levels of government, works to improve public understanding of counties, serves as a national advocate for counties, and provides them with resources to help them find innovative methods to meet the challenges they face. NACo is involved in a number of special projects that deal with such issues as the environment, sustainable communities, volunteerism, and intergenerational studies.

In 2001, NACo created the "Policy Agenda to Secure the People of America's Counties." This policy paper stated that "[c]ounties are the first responders to terrorist attacks, natural disasters and major emergencies" (National Association of Counties, 2002). NACo established a 43-member NACo Homeland Security Task Force that, on October 23, 2001, prepared a set of 20 recommendations in four general categories concerning homeland security issues: public health, local law enforcement and intelligence, infrastructure security, and emergency planning and public safety. Since that time, NACo has continued to release policy recommendations, with the 2007–2008 Policy Resolutions titled "NACo Homeland Security Policy Resolutions ..." available on this book's companion website.

Like the other municipal organizations listed earlier, NACo is vitally interested in homeland security funding issues and works to help its member counties to locally address the complex issues. In addition to advocacy, NACo develops toolkits and other publications that counties can use to decipher the flood of information that exists. In early 2011, NACo issued a press release that relayed the concerns of counties relative to falling homeland security funding, detailed in the sidebar titled "NACo Fights Massive Cuts to Homeland Security."

NACo Fights Massive Cuts to Homeland Security (Issued May 13, 2011)

WASHINGTON, D.C. – The National Association of Counties (NACo) today warned that proposed cuts to the FY 2012 Department of Homeland Security (DHS) Appropriations Bill would impede progress gained in recent years to effectively and efficiently improve the nation's counties, abilities to protect and serve their communities.

The legislation, which is scheduled to be considered Friday, May 13, in the House of Representatives Appropriations Subcommittee on Homeland Security, proposes massive reductions in grants, technical assistance and programs important to states, local governments and public safety agencies nationwide.

Additionally, the legislation proposes a major change to the current formula for distributing state and local grants; and many counties would presumably be at risk of not receiving any future state and local grant assistance from the DHS.

Specifically, the legislation proposes only $1 billion for DHS Grants, Exercises, and Technical Assistance important to states, local governments and public safety agencies. This is a decrease of $1.2 billion compared to the current year, and the legislation also proposes major reductions in DHS's Fire Grants ($350 million), FEMA Flood Mapping ($120 million), and PreDisaster Mitigation Grants ($40 million).

Additionally, the legislation proposes a major consolidation of programs important to states, local governments and public safety agencies. Specifically, the legislation proposes combining DHS's State Homeland Security Grant Program, Urban Area Security Initiative Grant Program, Metropolitan Medical Response System, Citizen Corp Program, Rail and Transit Grants, Intercity Bus Security Grants, Port Security Grants, Interoperable Emergency Communications Grants and DHS/FEMA Training, Technical Assistance and Exercises into one single line item; and awarding future grants to States, local governments and public safety agencies at the discretion of the DHS Secretary.

"Counties are strongly opposed to any reduction of funds to DHS's State and Local Programs and assert that a minimum level of preparedness must be provided to all communities," said NACo Executive Director Larry E. Naake. "We are asking in the strongest possible terms that members of Congress reject these harmful cuts and continue to work with counties to ensure our communities are well served."

The following is an example of the homeland security toolkits and other relevant publications released by NACo:

- *NIMS Guide for County Officials*: A guide to help county officials understand what NIMS is and the role counties play in planning to prepare for and respond to emergencies of any type and of any scale (http://www.portal.state.pa.us/portal/server.pt/document/783252/nimsguide_pdf)

In February 2004, NACo surveyed several of the nation's "core counties," which are those counties that are most representative of each of the nation's high-threat urban areas included in the DHS Urban Areas Security Initiative (UASI). The survey solicited information about each county's involvement in the UASI and how well the process worked from their perspective. The results of the survey are presented in the sidebar titled "Excerpts from NACo UASI Survey Report."

Excerpts from NAC UASI Survey Report

During FY 2003, the DHS Office of Domestic Preparedness (ODP) created the Urban Areas Security Initiative (UASI). This initiative is designed to combat terrorism in the United States by targeting federal funding to high threat urban areas. These areas have been determined to be high threats because they house significant national, state or business infrastructure, governmental systems and population centers and are considered most vulnerable to terrorist attacks. Each urban area is made up of a core city and county and includes jurisdictions that are contiguous and have established formal mutual aid agreements.

A core county is where the core city of the urban area is located. The funds were to address the unique equipment, training, planning, exercise and operation needs of these large urban areas. After the designation of the 30 urban high threat areas, each state worked with ODP to complete the process to determine the allocation for each urban area. The funds were then awarded to the states, each of which was responsible, through its State Administrative Agency, for managing the submission of assessments and strategies from each urban area that was eligible to receive funds.

In mid-February 2004, the National Association of Counties sent a survey to the core county in each of these high threat urban areas. This survey was designed to find out whether these targeted areas were receiving these much needed funds. In addition, the survey asked each responding county to comment on how the funding distribution process has worked in their states. Fifteen core counties completed the survey, representing 12 of the 20 states that had been awarded at that time.

Findings
Core counties were asked if their states had kept them well informed about the process it followed to submit a plan to the ODP to make their urban area eligible for UASI funds.

- One hundred percent of responding core counties, except Washington, D.C., responded yes to that question.
- When asked if the core county participated in discussions with their states about the distribution of these funds, 80 percent of responding core counties reported discussions with their states.
- Of the three core counties that indicated that they did not participate, all were in states where another core county responded that they had participated in such discussions. The states are California, Ohio, and Texas.

Core counties were next asked if they had participated in discussions with the other participating local governments in their high-threat area. All 15 responding counties (100%) reported having these discussions.

Core counties were asked what percentage of the funds was asked for each of the four major expenditure areas.

- Of the four — training, exercises, equipment, and planning — in 80 percent of the core counties the largest percentage of the funds was requested for equipment. These requests ranged from a low of 30 percent to a high of 100 percent.
- Only Miami-Dade County and Multnomah County requested that the largest percentage of their funds be in the area of training.

Core counties were asked if they had received any of their UASI funds as of the date of their response to this survey.

- Forty-seven percent of responding counties responded yes.
- Fifty-three percent responded that they have not.
- These amounts ranged from a high of $18.5 million down to $40,000.
- When asked what percentage of the anticipated funds they had received, 81 percent reported receiving from 0 to 25 percent.
- Only San Francisco County reported receiving 100 percent of its funds, which amounts to more than $18.5 million.
- Only 47 percent of the core counties, representing six states, said that the state has appropriated its own funds to assist with homeland security efforts.
- Thirty-three percent of core counties did not know whether their states had appropriated these funds.

Among the core counties, 73 percent report that they have used their own general operating funds to enhance homeland security efforts. One hundred percent of the core counties report that the planning and funding process for the UASI grant program has better prepared their counties for responding to a terrorist threat.

Source: National Association of Counties, http://www.naco.org/ContentManagement/ContentDisplay .cfm?ContentID=16077.

National Governors Association

The NGA — the bipartisan organization of the nation's governors — promotes visionary state leadership, shares best practices, and speaks with a unified voice on national policy. Its members are the governors of the 50 states and 5 territories. The NGA bills itself as the collective voice of the nation's governors and one of Washington, D.C.'s most respected public policy organizations. NGA provides governors and their senior staff members with services that range from representing states on Capitol Hill and before the administration on key federal issues to developing policy reports on innovative state programs and hosting networking seminars for state government executive branch officials. The NGA Center for Best Practices focuses on state innovations and best practices on issues that range from education and health to technology, welfare reform, and the environment. NGA also provides management and technical assistance to both new and incumbent governors.

In August 2002, the Center for Best Practices of the NGA released "States' Homeland Security Priorities." A list of 10 major priorities and issues was identified by the NGA center through a survey of states' and territories' homeland security offices (NGA Center for Best Practices, 2002). These priorities clearly illustrated the main concerns of the state leadership in light of the massive changes that were occurring at the federal level and included the following:

- Coordination must involve all levels of government.
- The federal government must disseminate timely intelligence information to the states.
- The states must work with local governments to develop interoperable communications between first responders, and an adequate wireless spectrum must be set aside to do the job.
- State and local governments need help and technical assistance to identify and protect critical infrastructure.
- Both the states and federal government must focus on enhancing bioterrorism preparedness and rebuilding the nation's public health system to address 21st-century threats.
- The federal government should provide adequate federal funding and support to ensure that homeland security needs are met.
- The federal government should work with states to protect sensitive security information, including restricting access to information available through "freedom of information" requests.
- An effective system must be developed that secures points of entry at borders, airports, and seaports without placing an undue burden on commerce.
- The National Guard has proven itself to be an effective force during emergencies and crises. The mission of the National Guard should remain flexible, and Guard units should primarily remain under the control of the governor during times of crises.
- Federal agencies should integrate their command systems into existing state and local incident command systems (ICS) rather than requiring state and local agencies to adapt to federal command systems (NGA Center for Best Practices, Issue Brief, August 19, 2002).

The NGA Center for Best Practices (NGAC) provides support to the governors in their management of new homeland security challenges as they arise and the overall homeland security domain that exists as a result of September 11. NGAC provides these officials with technical assistance and policy research and facilitates their participation in national discussions and initiatives. Center activities focus on states' efforts to protect critical infrastructure, develop interoperable communications capabilities, and prepare for and respond to bioterrorism, agroterrorism, nuclear and radiological terrorism, and cyberterrorism (as it impacts the government's ability to obtain, disseminate, and store essential information). The NGA does recognize that, while terrorism must be a priority, natural and human-made disasters will continue to demand timely and coordinated responses from local, state, and federal government agencies.

The Association's position on homeland security is presented in the sidebar titled "NGA Position on Homeland Security."

NGA Position on Homeland Security

Although the Constitution delegates to Congress the power and responsibility to provide for the common defense, most of the responsibility for providing homeland defense rests with state and local governments. Governors, with the support of the federal government and local jurisdictions, are responsible for ensuring the ability of state, territorial, and local authorities to deal with natural disasters and other types of major emergencies, including a terrorist incident. State homeland security efforts (infrastructure assets, people resources, and coordination) are critical components of the National Strategy for Homeland Security.

NGA policy and positions with regard to Homeland Security issues are guided by the following principles:

- There should be a base capacity in every state, which means that every state should receive some funds.
- The Department of Homeland Security should provide guidance to states for developing equipment and training standards for adequate levels of protection and preparedness.
- There should be flexibility in the allowable uses of grant funds.
- Governors and other high-ranking state and territorial officials need to receive timely and critical intelligence information related to terrorist threats.
- The traditional first responder programs that existed prior to September 11, 2001, should continue to be funded.
- There should be predictable and sustainable long-term funding of homeland security programs.
- All Federal funding, resources, programs and activities involving state and local governments must be coordinated through the nation's Governors for maximum effectiveness and efficiency.
- The role of the business community and the impact on the economic viability of a community when faced with recovery from a terrorist attack must be considered.

Source: National Governors Association, http://www.nga.org/nga/lobbyIssues/1,1169,D_4898,00.html.

Since 2004, the National Governors Association Center for Best Practices (NGA Center) has tracked the states' progress in developing homeland security structures and programs through an annual survey of state homeland security officials. The results of the 2007 survey are listed in the "NGA Survey Results" sidebar.

NGA Survey Results

For the 2007 survey, the NGA Center polled the 56 state and territorial homeland security advisors who, collectively, comprise the Governors Homeland Security Advisors Council. The survey results reflect the participation of roughly 80 percent of those officials; that is, 44 state homeland security officials completed the survey either in whole or in part, although the response rate for some questions was less than the full 80 percent. This year's survey shows that the top five priorities for states in 2007 were, in order:

- Developing interoperable communications
- Coordinating state and local efforts
- Protecting critical infrastructure
- Developing state fusion centers
- Strengthening citizen preparedness

  These priorities have remained stable for several survey years. The survey also revealed that:

- States continue to report unsatisfactory progress in their relationship with the federal government, specifically with the Department of Homeland Security (DHS).
- In the view of the states, federal homeland security grant programs are not adequately funded and do not strike an adequate balance among preparedness, prevention, response, and recovery.
- The majority of states said DHS should coordinate policies with the states prior to the release or implementation of those policies.
- States need federal funding to support personnel to implement and sustain initiatives that are national in scope but that are carried out locally.
- Federal agencies should coordinate their security clearances to ensure that a clearance issued by one agency is recognized by other agencies.
- Only about one-third of states have at least 75 percent of their National Guard forces available to respond to a natural or manmade disaster.
- More than half the states have "significantly" involved local governments in the development of strategic plans, including grant funding allocation plans.

  Full survey results can be found at http://www.nga.org/Files/pdf/0712HOMELANDSURVEY.PDF.

Source: National Governors Association.

National Emergency Management Association

The National Emergency Management Association (NEMA) is a nonpartisan, nonprofit association that works to enhance public safety. NEMA is focused on the all-hazards approach to emergency management. NEMA began in 1974 when state directors of emergency services first united in order to exchange information on common emergency management issues in their constituencies. State emergency management directors form the core membership, but members also include key state staff, homeland security advisers, federal agencies, nonprofit organizations, private-sector companies, and concerned individuals.

NEMA's mission is to:

- Provide national leadership and expertise in comprehensive emergency management
- Serve as a vital emergency management information and assistance resource
- Advance continuous improvement in emergency management through strategic partnerships, innovative programs, and collaborative policy positions

Following September 11, NEMA created the National Homeland Security Consortium, which includes key state and local organizations, elected officials, the private sector, and others with roles and responsibilities for homeland security prevention, preparedness, response, and recovery activities. Participating organizations began meeting in 2002. The consortium is an outgrowth of those initial discussions regarding the need for enhanced communication and coordination between disciplines and levels of government. The consortium is now recognized by DHS and works in partnership with other federal agencies such as the Centers for Disease Control and Prevention. The mission of the consortium is to provide a forum wherein key ideas on homeland security can be shared among and between various levels of government.

International Association of Emergency Managers

The International Association of Emergency Managers (IAEM) is a nonprofit organization dedicated to promoting the goals of saving lives and protecting property during emergencies and disasters. Founded in 1952 as the U.S. Civil Defense Council, it became the National Coordinating Council on Emergency Management in 1985, and changed its name to the IAEM in 1998.

The association brings together emergency managers and disaster response professionals from all levels of government, as well as the military, the private sector, and volunteer organizations in the United States and around the world. The purpose of IAEM is to serve the emergency management community by:

- Encouraging the development of disaster-resistant communities to reduce the effect of disasters on life and property
- Acting as a clearinghouse for information on comprehensive management issues
- Providing a forum for creative and innovative problem-solving on emergency management issues
- Maintaining and expanding standards for emergency management programs and professionals
- Fostering informed decision making on public policy in the emergency management arena

The IAEM often issues policy briefs that relay the position of the nation's and the world's emergency managers about salient issues being debated or considered in Congress.

Homeland Security Activity of State and Tribal Governments

Each governor is responsible for overseeing and ensuring the prevention of hazard risk within that state, including the assessment of threats and vulnerability, the mitigation of hazard risks, the funding and coordination of local offices of emergency management, and the coordination with federal emergency management agencies and entities. The governor is also tasked with leading the state's response to any emergency or disaster, and must therefore take an active role in ensuring that other state officials and agencies are able to address these many hazards and ongoing challenges.

During a disaster event, the governor will likely take on a number of roles, including the state's principal source of information to the public. This might include the issuance of evacuations, details about the scope of the disaster, and the availability of assistance. Governors command the state's National Guard resources and maintain the authority to mobilize them in times of disaster (as stipulated by Title 32 of the U.S. Code). During disasters, it is the responsibility of the governor to assess the need for a disaster declaration and to make that request to the President and/or mutual aid partners if such a determination for need is made.

The state or territorial government itself is tasked with coordinating the activity of cities, counties, and intrastate regions. States administer federal homeland security grants to local and tribal (in certain grant programs) governments, allocating key resources to bolster their prevention and preparedness capabilities. Several state agencies and offices are tasked with ensuring the enforcement of state and federal law and for carrying out other security activities. State government agencies have expanded their roles with regard to the homeland security function since 9/11 as many key components of critical infrastructure, as well as key resources, exist or are maintained at the state level. Moreover, because many risk reduction and other emergency management/homeland security programs are coordinated and funded at the state level, the state government is tasked with providing the necessary direction and guidance for these efforts. During actual disaster events, states must often mobilize their various response resources, as stipulated in the state emergency plan, and help to coordinate federal and other resources as they are provided.

Like governors, tribal leaders are responsible for the public safety and welfare of their membership. They can serve as both key decision makers and trusted sources of public information during incidents. Tribal governments, which have a special status under federal laws and treaties, ensure the provision of essential services to members within their communities and are responsible for developing emergency response and mitigation plans. Tribal governments may coordinate resources and capabilities with neighboring jurisdictions, and establish mutual aid agreements with other tribal governments, local jurisdictions, and state governments. Depending on location, land base, and resources, tribal governments provide law enforcement, fire, and emergency services as well as public safety to their members.

A good indicator of the manner in which each of the state governments approaches the terrorism issue is the priorities set by their emergency managers. A survey of state homeland security structures by NEMA conducted in June 2002 found that all 50 states maintain primary point of contact for antiterrorism/homeland security efforts. At that time, these contacts were located in the following state government offices:

- Governor/Lieutenant Governor's office — 14 states
- Military/adjutant general — 12 states
- Public safety/law enforcement — 12 states
- Office of Homeland Security/Emergency Management — 10 states
- Attorney general — 2 states
- Land commissioner — 1 state (National Conference of State Legislatures, 2005)

In January 2008, these numbers had changed significantly, reflecting an approach that gave much more weight to homeland security as a standalone function in the overall context of state government affairs. Many states had even created dedicated homeland security offices. These figures were as follows:

- Office of Homeland Security/Emergency Management — 34 states
- Military/adjutant general — 8 states
- Public safety/law enforcement — 7 states
- Governor's office — 2 states

However, by August 2011, possibly as a result of shrinking budgets or because of the changing nature of homeland security and emergency management (especially with regard to the nature of natural versus terrorist-based threats), there was a major reversal in the trends toward state government homeland security structuring. NEMA continues to track these structures and reported the following state homeland security and emergency management directorship positioning (not all states listed):

- Governor's Office — 11 states (Alabama, Arkansas, California, Florida, Georgia, Illinois, Louisiana, Mississippi, New York, Oklahoma, Pennsylvania)
- Military/Adjutant General — 17 states (Alaska, Arizona, Hawaii, Idaho, Iowa, Kansas, Kentucky, Maine, Maryland, Montana, Nebraska, North Dakota, Oregon, Rhode Island, South Carolina, Tennessee, Washington, Wisconsin)
- Office of Homeland Security — 1 state (Indiana)
- Office of Public Safety — 12 states (Massachusetts, Minnesota, Missouri, Nevada, New Hampshire, North Carolina, Ohio, South Dakota, Texas, Utah, Vermont, Virginia)
- State Police — 2 states (Michigan, New Jersey)
- Other — 4 states (Colorado, Connecticut, New Mexico, West Virginia) (NEMA, 2011)

Shrinking budgets have been a major concern of state directors of homeland security, who feel that the task of preparing for hazards and maintaining national security is causing incredible strain on state budgets. NEMA reports that the FY 2010 operating budgets for state emergency management were at most $47 million, but that the median budget was $3,300,000. This amount was a reduction from the FY 2009 median of $3,406,500. NEMA also reported that 24 states saw their emergency management budgets shrink in FY 2010, and that such trends are likely to continue. Reductions in dependence on federal funding has become necessary as this funding has decreased and/or been passed through to local agencies. In 2009, 34 states received 60% or more of their homeland security funding from federal dollars. This compares to 36 states in 2008, 39 in 2007, and 46 in 2006. Of the 34 states this year, 13 operate with 100% federal funding, which is down from 18 last year. Staffing of these agencies and offices are seeing similar problems, with the actual number of personnel or full-time equivalents (FTEs) falling, from 5,217 for FY 2009 to 5,020 in FY 2010. At present, many states must rely on volunteers to assist in disaster response and recovery efforts (NEMA, 2011a; NEMA, 2011b).

Local Government Homeland Security Activities

Like their counterpart governors at the state level, mayors and other local elected and appointed officials (such as city managers) are responsible for ensuring the public safety and welfare of their residents. Local chief elected officials serve as their jurisdiction's chief communicator and a primary source of information for homeland security-related information, and ensure their governments are able to carry out emergency response activities. They are typically the key decision makers in times of disaster as stipulated in the local emergency operations plan.

The local government manages a number of key government functions, many of which pertain directly to emergency management and homeland security. These include, for example, law enforcement, fire safety and suppression, public safety, environmental response, public health, and emergency medical services. In times of disaster, this role is put to the forefront as the local government maintains operational control of incidents in accordance with the U.S. federal system of government.

Through individual cooperation, as well as supported by other state and federal programs (such as the UASI program), cities and counties address multijurisdictional planning and operations, equipment support and purchasing, and training and exercises in support of high-threat, high-density urban areas. Federal grant money helps local governments to build and sustain their homeland security capabilities. Local governments coordinate resources and capabilities during disasters with neighboring jurisdictions, NGOs, the state, and the private sector.

County leaders serve as chief operating officers of county governments, in a fashion similar to what exists at the local level. The role of the county (or parish in the case of Louisiana) changes from state to state. This role typically includes supporting and enabling the county governments to fulfill their responsibilities to constituents, including public safety and security. County governments provide frontline leadership for local law enforcement, fire, public safety, environmental response, public health, and emergency medical services for all manner of hazards and emergencies. County governments coordinate resources and capabilities during disasters with neighboring jurisdictions, NGOs, the state, and the private sector.

Emergency preparedness, mitigation, response, and recovery all occur at the local community level. It is at the local level that the critical planning, communications, technology, coordination, command, and spending decisions matter the most. The priorities of groups such as the National Conference of Mayors and the National Association of Counties are to represent these very concerns shared by local communities about what is necessary for them to become resilient from the threat of terrorism. The drive toward a reduction in vulnerability from terrorism has spawned a series of new requirements in preparedness and mitigation planning for most local-level officials that, prior to September 11, rarely considered such issues.

Both NAC and the USCM policy papers identified issues in the areas of command, coordination, communications, funding and equipment, training, and mutual aid. These two organizations recognized and proclaimed the local concerns about protecting critical community infrastructure, including the public health system, most of which is maintained and secured at the local level by local government law enforcement, fire, and health officials.

The events of September 11 brought to the surface the notion that the security of community infrastructure, which was suddenly recognized as a potential target for terrorist attacks, was vital to the security of the nation as a whole. Community infrastructure has always been vulnerable to natural and other technological disaster events — so much so that FEMA's largest disaster assistance program, Public Assistance, is designed to fund the rebuilding of community infrastructure damaged by a disaster event. However, local government officials and local emergency managers were suddenly finding themselves dedicating a greatly increased amount of funding and personnel to protecting and securing community infrastructure from the increased threat of terrorist attack. They have also had to boost the abilities of the local public health system, which has been recognized by the federal government as the most likely area where an outbreak caused by a bioterrorism agent will be identified.

To illustrate several of the new issues that local governments, most notably the smaller, rural governments, have had to consider in light of the new terrorist threat, the following checklist designed for the City of Boone, North Carolina, is provided. This checklist is excerpted from that municipality's technological annex developed for the town's All-Hazards Planning and Operations Manual:

- Identify the types of terrorist events that might occur in the community
- Plan emergency activities in advance to ensure a coordinated response to terrorist attacks
- Build capabilities necessary to respond effectively to the consequences of terrorism
- Identify the type or nature of a terrorist attack when it does happen
- Implement the planned response quickly and efficiently
- Recover from the incident

The response to terrorism is similar in many ways to that of other natural or human-made disasters for which Boone has already prepared. Through additions and modifications, the development of a completely separate system could be avoided. Training and public education have been vital to enhancing preparedness, and understanding the process by which available federal financial assistance is acquired has drastically increased local capacity. The general types of activities that Boone has needed to take to meet the above-mentioned objectives follow:

- Strengthen information and communications technology
- Establish a well-defined incident command structure that includes the FBI
- Strengthen local working relationships and communications
- Educate health-care and emergency response communities about identification of bioterrorist attacks and agents
- Educate health-care and emergency response communities about medical treatment and prophylaxis for possible biological agents
- Educate local health department about state and federal requirements and assistance
- Maintain locally accessible supply of medications, vaccines, and supplies
- Address health care-worker safety issues
- Designate a spokesperson to maintain contact with the public
- Develop comprehensive evacuation plans
- Become familiar with state and local laws relating to isolation/quarantine
- Develop or enhance local capability to prosecute crimes involving WMD or the planning of terrorism events
- Develop, maintain, and practice an infectious diseases' emergency response plan
- Practice with surrounding jurisdictions to strengthen mutual agreement plans
- Outline the roles of federal agency assistance in planning and response
- Educate the public in recognizing events and ways to respond as individuals
- Stay current (Town of Boone, All-Hazards Planning and Operations Manual, Technological Hazards Annex. Boone, NC: Town of Boone, March 2007)

▓ ▓ Critical Thinking ▓

Terrorism prevention and preparedness have added significant strain to already stretched local budgets. Do you feel that the local governments should determine their risk and act accordingly, or should they be expected to prescribe a minimum level of preparedness regardless of the effect it has on other local programs that may suffer as a result of budget reallocations?

Role of Private Sector in Homeland Security and Changes in Business Continuity and Contingency Planning

The terrorist attacks of September 11 affected thousands of private businesses, not just businesses in New York or near the Pentagon, but businesses that were as far away as Hawaii and Seattle. The attacks killed nearly 3,000 people, most of whom were employees of private corporations that had offices in or near the World Trade Center (WTC). Some companies lost hundreds of employees. In downtown Manhattan, almost 34.5 million square feet of office space was destroyed. Totaling $50 billion to $70 billion in insured losses, the WTC attack became one of the costliest disasters in U.S. history. Most of these direct economic losses were incurred by the private sector. In addition to the physical resources and systems lost by businesses in the WTC, changes in public behavior following the attacks had a severe impact on travel, tourism, and other businesses. Because the biggest portion of the impact was absorbed by the private sector, September 11 has been perceived as a sudden wake-up call for disaster preparedness, business continuity planning, and corporate crisis management in the private sector.

The changes in private-sector disaster preparedness after September 11 can be analyzed from two perspectives: (1) the direct involvement of the private sector in disaster preparedness and response in coordination with the DHS and as foreseen by the NRF and the NIMS, and (2) the self-reassessment of the private sector in terms of corporate crisis management and business continuity as a competitive requirement as opposed to cost of business. Our reference point in addressing the changing expectations of the federal government from the private sector will be several major federal documents and strategies, such as the National Strategy for Homeland Security and official press releases from relevant departments and agencies. While addressing the change of internal processes and procedures among the private sector, we will refer to publications and press releases that address changes in particular companies and try to find general trends between different approaches.

Expectations of DHS from the Private Sector

The National Strategy for Homeland Security defines the basic approach of DHS and briefly describes the characteristics of the partnership the department is planning to achieve with the private sector. Given the fact that almost 85% of the infrastructure of the United States is owned or managed by the private sector, there is no doubt that the private sector must be included as a major stakeholder in homeland security. Reducing the vulnerabilities and securing the private sector means the same as securing the vast portion of U.S. infrastructure and economic viability.

According to the National Strategy for Homeland Security, a close partnership between the government and private sectors is essential in ensuring that existing vulnerabilities of critical infrastructures to terrorism are identified and eliminated as quickly as possible. The private sector is expected to conduct risk assessments on their holdings and invest in systems to protect key assets. The internalization of these costs is interpreted by the DHS as not only a matter of sound corporate governance and good corporate citizenship but also an essential safeguard of economic assets for shareholders, employees, and the nation.

The National Strategy for the Protection of Physical Infrastructure and Key Assets provides more direct clues about what the DHS expects from the private sector as a partner and stakeholder in homeland security. The strategy defines the private sector as the owner and operator of the bulk of U.S. critical infrastructures and key assets and mentions that private sector firms prudently engage in risk management planning and invest in security as a necessary function of business operations and customer confidence. Moreover, since in the present threat environment the private sector generally remains the first line of defense for its own facilities, the DHS expects private-sector owners and operators to reassess and adjust their planning, assurance, and investment programs to better accommodate the increased risk presented by deliberate acts of violence (Figure 4–11).

Since the events of September 11, many businesses have increased their threshold investments and undertaken enhancements in security in an effort to meet the demands of the new threat environment. For most enterprises, the level of investment in security reflects implicit risk-versus-consequence trade-offs, which are based on (1) what is known about the risk environment, (2) what is economically justifiable and sustainable in a competitive marketplace or in an environment of limited government resources,

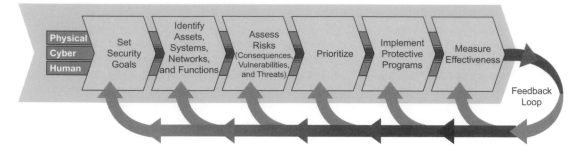

FIGURE 4–11 Operational framework for critical infrastructure and key assets protection. (Source: National Infrastructure Protection Plan)

(3) potential consequences of disasters, and (4) priorities for the protection of human capital, processes, physical infrastructure, organizational reputation, stakeholder confidence, and vital records that require immediate attention. Given the dynamic nature of the terrorist threat and the severity of the consequences associated with many potential attack scenarios, the private sector naturally looks to the government for better information to help make its crucial security investment decisions. The private sector is continuing to look for better data, analysis, and assessment from DHS to use in the corporate decision-making process.

Similarly, the private sector looks to the government for assistance when the threat at hand exceeds an enterprise's capability to protect itself beyond a reasonable level of additional investment. In this light, the federal government promises to collaborate with the private sector (and state and local governments) to ensure the protection of nationally critical infrastructures and assets; provide timely warning and ensure the protection of infrastructures and assets that face a specific, imminent threat; and promote an environment in which the private sector can better carry out its specific protection responsibilities.

A good example of partnership between the private sector and DHS is the sectoral information sharing and analysis centers (ISACs). ISACs are established by the owners and operators of a national critical infrastructure to better protect their networks, systems, and facilities within the coordination of DHS. ISACs serve as central points to gather, analyze, sanitize, and disseminate private-sector information to both industry and DHS. These centers also analyze and distribute information received from DHS to the private sector. The objectives of this program are to seek participation from all sector segments/entities, representation of all segments on ISAC Advisory Board in order to establish a two-way, trusted information sharing program between ISAC entities and DHS, and to provide cleared industry expertise to assist DHS in evaluating threats and incidents. Currently, ISACs exist and are being created in a variety of critical infrastructure sectors. The DHS document that defines the relationships between the private sector and DHS is the National Infrastructure Protection Plan (NIPP) of January 2006 and the subsequent sector-specific annexes that have been developed in 2007. These plans define mechanisms that serve to build those relationships and create a system where the government and private entities can work in harmony to achieve a higher level of protection for critical infrastructures and key resources of the United States. Table 4–2 gives a list of operating ISACs and their dates of establishment.

As mentioned earlier, the primary building block of this relationship is the formation of sectoral ISACs, which promote the coordination, cooperation, best practices, lessons learned, information flow, and information sharing among sector-specific entities. The NIPP defines another coordination body for the achievement of the public–private integration. Those coordinating bodies are called Critical Infrastructure and Key Resources Sector Coordinating Councils. They are private-sector coordinating

Table 4–2   Operating Status of Sectoral ISACs as of 2008

Sector	ISAC	ISAC Established
Agriculture and food	Food	February 2002
Banking and finance	Financial services	October 1999
Chemical	Chemical	April 2002
Commercial facilities	Real estate	February 2003
Drinking water and water treatment systems	Water	December 2002
Emergency services	Emergency management and response	October 2000
Energy	Electric	October 2000
	Energy	November 2001
Government facilities	Multistate	January 2003
Information technology	Information technology	December 2000
	Research and education network	February 2003
Telecommunications	National Coordinating Center for Telecommunications	January 2000
Transportation systems	Public transit	January 2003
	Surface transportation (rail)	May 2002
	Highway	March 2003
	Maritime	February 2003

Source: Government Accountability Office, GAO-07-39, Washington, DC, 2006.
ISAC, Information Sharing and Analysis Center.

mechanisms that comprise private-sector infrastructure owners and operators and supporting associations, as appropriate. Sector coordinating councils bring together the entire range of infrastructure protection activities and issues to a single entity.

The roles of the sector coordinating councils are to identify, establish, and support the information sharing mechanisms (ISMs) that are most effective for their sector, drawing on existing mechanisms (e.g., ISACs) or creating new ones as required. The NIPP also creates Critical Infrastructure and Key Resources Government Coordinating Councils, which are government coordinating councils for each sector comprised of representatives from DHS, the sector specific agency (SSA), and the appropriate supporting federal departments and agencies. The government coordinating councils work with and support the efforts of the sector coordinating councils to plan, implement, and execute sufficient and necessary broad-based sector security, planning, and information sharing to support the nation's homeland security mission.

As indicated by the NIPP, the private sector will be engaged by DHS, in collaboration with the relevant SSAs, to promote awareness of and feedback on the NIPP framework and to solicit their involvement in the national CIP program. The private sector will also be working with the appropriate SSAs to begin implementation of the sector-specific plans (SSPs) for their sectors. As the interim NIPP is implemented, the private sector will be provided with more coordinated data calls from government agencies, enhanced engagement through sector coordinating councils, and subsequent versions of the NIPP and SSPs will reflect discussions among DHS, the SSAs, and other stakeholders, including the private sector. The NIPP serves as a guide for the private sector to identify and implement the procedures to protect the critical infrastructure against specific threats and the general threat environment. There are five major goals identified in the plan, and objectives to meet those goals are also listed. Those goals and the respective objectives are as follows:

- Goal 1: Protect CI/KR against plausible and specific threats. Objectives to meet this goal include:
  - Increase awareness of the threat environment across CI/KR sectors
  - Integrate threat and vulnerability information into specific vulnerability reduction prioritization decisions
  - Use vulnerability assessment information when responding to specific threats
  - Identify and implement protective measures against specific threats
- Goal 2: Long-term reduction of CI/KR vulnerabilities in a comprehensive and integrated manner. Objectives to meet this goal include:
  - Develop and maintain comprehensive national inventory of CI/KR assets and vulnerabilities that includes cyber, physical, and human aspects of each asset, including intangibles
  - Complete mapping of interdependencies among assets and across CI/KR sectors
  - Conduct vulnerability assessments for the nation's critical infrastructure and key resources for both specific and general threats
  - Integrate infrastructure protection activities with those called for in other national-level plans to avoid overlaps and gaps
  - Reduce general vulnerabilities within and across sectors where needed
- Goal 3: Maximize efficient use of resources for infrastructure protection. Objectives to meet this goal include:
  - Prioritize possible protective measures considering return on investment in light of inherent vulnerabilities, existing protective measures, and (when applicable) threat information
  - Encourage and support SSA responsibility for sectors to leverage sector-specific expertise
  - Identify market-based incentives for voluntary action by owners and operators
  - Ensure lessons learned and best practices are captured and shared for evolution into sector-accepted operational practices over time
- Goal 4: Build partnerships among federal, state, local, tribal, international, and private-sector stakeholders to implement CIP programs. Objectives to meet this goal include:
  - Delineate roles, responsibilities, and accountability for actions
  - Develop necessary organizations, staffing, and training to carry out responsibilities
  - Request appropriate authorities and funding to allow actions to be implemented
  - Establish mechanisms for coordination and information exchange among partners
  - Develop mechanisms for tracking involvement and progress
- Goal 5: Continuously track and improve national protection. Objectives to meet this goal include:
  - Develop mechanisms for tracking national- and sector-level vulnerabilities and progress in reducing those vulnerabilities
  - Make infrastructure protection activities and metrics part of the organization's overall operational metrics to reinforce the importance of CIP initiatives and activities
  - Develop a national-risk profile (a high-level summary of the risk and protection for all sectors) to align threats with strategic decision making
  - Develop an information-sharing system to support rapid dissemination of lessons learned

These goals are to be achieved using the national risk management framework as defined by the NIPP. The framework is similar for specific and general threat environments; therefore, we will not address both frameworks separately.

DHS has acknowledged that it is well known that effective protection of the critical infrastructure in the United States is only achievable through direct involvement of and strong partnership with the private sector. The private sector is not only an integral part of the national infrastructure protection effort, but lies in the center of all protection strategies designed by DHS. That said, DHS is responsible for creating the environment where public- and private-sector entities talk to each other and work together to achieve a well-established national goal. Understanding the needs of each sector, building trust among officials and decision makers, making plausible assumptions, and setting realistic milestones are all key success factors. The real challenge is addressing cross-sectoral vulnerabilities due to interdependencies where involvement of multiple sectors is necessary for sustainable protection of a critical infrastructure and creation of realistic recovery objectives and procedures. Creation of cross-sector vulnerability assessment teams and utilization of multiple-sector expertise are critical to successfully plan for contingencies that may simultaneously hit interdependent critical infrastructures.

Corporate Crisis Management, Business Continuity, and Contingency Planning: The New Cost of Doing Business

September 11 was the most devastating day in modern history for American corporations. The attack in New York City was a direct attack on not only the symbols of corporate America, but also on the businesses themselves. The private sector lost human resources, expertise, buildings, office space, data, records, and revenue. Some of these losses were irreplaceable, such as people. The affected companies also suffered time-dependent and continuous losses such as business interruption, loss of customer trust, and employee loyalty. The property and human losses could not have been prevented because the private sector itself could not have stopped the hijacked planes from crashing into the towers. However, effective corporate crisis management and business continuity planning absolutely could have, and in many places did, minimize the continuous losses.

To put this discussion in perspective, the statistics and charts shown in Figure 4–12 illustrate the vulnerability of the private sector in terms of terrorist actions. The Department of State report Patterns of Global Terrorism reports on the total number of facilities struck by international terrorist attacks. The statistics show attacks with respect to the year they occurred and the type of facility struck (e.g., private sector, government, diplomatic, military). These figures are important because they show changing trends in the types of facilities terrorists have chosen to attack. There is a common belief that terrorists are more likely to attack military and government facilities, because of the stated political ideologies of the terrorist groups. However, the facts prove this theory wrong. In actuality, it is the soft-target private-sector facilities that have most commonly been victimized by the scourge of terrorism.

Clearly, a reduction in the number of attacks on businesses worldwide occurred after 2001. This reduction may be attributable to several factors that have changed since that time. One of these factors is the increased global effort to reduce terrorist acts. This effort is primarily led by the United States and its allies, which are the most likely targets but which also have spent billions on preventing such attacks. As terror cells become more and more international and decentralized, international cooperation and intelligence sharing become critical to prevent acts of terrorism. Since 2001, significant amounts of resources have been allocated to achieve this goal, and this may serve as a contributing factor to the reduced number of terrorist attacks.

However, the preceding explanation does not account for why the reduction in the total number of attacks to businesses is steeper compared to other potential targets. As seen in Figure 4–12, the number of terrorist attacks aimed at businesses was reduced from 408 in 2001, to 122 in 2002 and 93 in 2003,

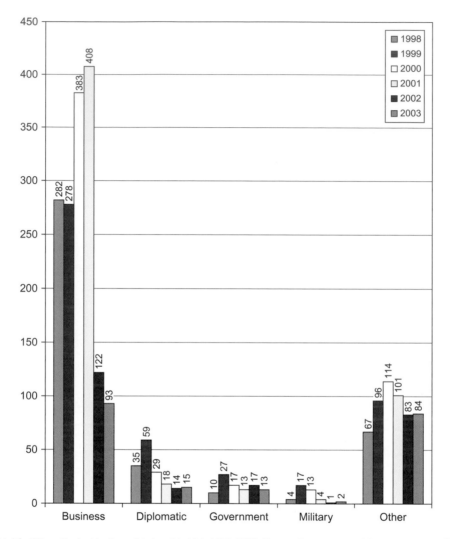

FIGURE 4–12 Total facilities attacked by terrorists (worldwide), 1998–2003. (Source: Department of State, "Patterns of Global Terrorism," 2003)

whereas such reductions were not as significant for diplomatic facilities, government buildings, or military or other facilities.

Businesses have historically been targets of terrorists primarily because they have been perceived as soft targets that are easier to attack and minimally protected. After the 9/11 attacks, the vulnerability of businesses to disasters such as terrorism became obvious. Businesses learned through tragic experience that they constitute a potential target for terrorists. So they began to invest more into their security, risk management, crisis management, and business continuity programs. Research shows that all sophisticated terrorists carefully observe their prospective targets before deciding on their actual target.

ANOTHER VOICE: SAFETY AND SECURITY CONCERNS IN THE PRIVATE SECTOR.

Security in Public vs. Private Sectors

The phone rang at 15 minutes before 3 AM. It was January 26, 2007. Sound asleep, I instinctively reached for my phone, wondering who could be calling at this hour. It was little surprise to me that it was my boss on the line. He was notifying me that an explosion had just occurred outside the entrance of one of our hotels in South Asia. An unidentified man attempted to penetrate hotel security. Strapped with a homemade explosive device, he was confronted by our guards who prevented access to the property. A scuffle ensued and the bomber detonated the device. The security guard was killed instantly alongside the bomber and seven bystanders were injured.

Through the system we had established years earlier, all of our crisis management team members were on a conference call within 15 minutes. We concluded the conference call an hour later with tasks assigned to each member. The team convened again a few hours later to report on their assignments. Since the damage to the hotel's building structure was minimal, the hotel was able to resume its normal operations later that day. Later, a relief fund was set up to help the deceased employee's family.

This is an example of one of those phone calls you do not wish to receive, regardless of the time of day. A phone call like this precipitates a crisis lasting anywhere from one day to several weeks. Everyone in the security department will be tested dealing with this on a 24-hour basis. It is our employee, our company, our reputation, after all.

There is little distinction between the security responsibilities of government agencies and private sector entities. Both protect people, facilities, assets, and reputation. However, the ramifications are far more complex for the private sector when it comes to dealing with the aftermath of a crisis. When working in the government sector, there is little concern about the stock performance, shareholders, a potential increase in insurance premiums, public relations disasters, or lawsuits by customers. These elements can be extremely challenging for someone who makes the decision to cross over into the private sector.

In a corporate crisis environment, pressure comes from many areas. It most often manifests itself from stockholders, legal advisors, consultants, rank-and-file employees, customers and, naturally, competitors. Everyone is a stakeholder.

If FEMA had been a privately owned company and its directors performed in much the same manner that they did during Hurricane Katrina, FEMA's stock would have plunged and no insurance company would have dared to insure them again. Senior executives in the parent company (which would be the Department of Homeland Security in this example) and its board of directors would have fired them all and, needless to say, the PR department would have their own crisis trying to mitigate the negative publicity.

The Hurricane Katrina story could have been very different if it had been handled in an effective and efficient manner. When such disasters occur, mass evacuations and major rescue operations require extensive efforts. In this case, government waste was rampant and communication between agencies broke down. Politics obfuscated good judgment. Conversely, a private company has to be self-sufficient. Its contingency plans need to cover all aspects from start to finish. If a private company fails to manage a crisis effectively, profits will plunge, customers will not return, stock holders will sell, and the company will eventually go under.

Private companies have to have a strategic focus, think ahead, and prepare resources. They should assess the situation from the perspective of each stakeholder. Hurricane plans should include shelters both inside and outside of the facility, prenegotiated contracts with chartered airlines, and

(Continued)

ANOTHER VOICE: SAFETY AND SECURITY CONCERNS IN THE PRIVATE SECTOR (CONTINUED).

---

supplies such as food, beds, and toilets. Having these plans and provisions in place will boost customer confidence, increase business, please shareholders, and drive revenue. Everyone is happy.

Another aspect to consider is that many companies are global, thereby expanding the horizon and adding more elements to the crisis plan. Different parts of the world involve various kinds of threats that might not exist in corporate America. Wars, government instability, foreign languages, customs, laws, and restrictions need to be considered and evaluated in order to allow for fast and seamless reaction during a crisis.

A private company's plan needs to be all encompassing, including preventative methods as well as solutions. A comprehensive review of the business continuity plan is always needed after a crisis comes to an end.

Last but not least, cooperation from company executives is the key. Without it, no crisis plan can function as they always require top down support, money, time, and resources.

Jack Suwanlert
Director — International Loss Prevention
Marriott International Inc.

Corporate Security

Terrorists often select targets they consider to be soft — that is, those that are easy to hit. Therefore, it is not only the operational benefits gained by corporate security programs, but also their visibility, that serves as a deterrent for terrorists. For example, if a terrorist organization aims to damage a country's tourism sector, it may attempt to detonate a bomb in a hotel. As terrorists determine which hotel to attack, they will likely consider several alternatives and select that which has the least visible security. Overall, business sector preparedness is much greater today than it was in 2001, which is one obvious explanation for why attacks on business targets have decreased. This reduction can be attributed to businesses "hardening" themselves against their former "soft target" image.

Another factor that is changing private-sector perceptions is insurance and losses. The Insurance Information Institute has plotted the distribution of different types of insured damages from the September 11 attacks and it presents some interesting facts (see Figure 4–13). The most notable figure in this graph is the amount of damage from business interruption: $9.8 billion (30% of all estimated damage). This is a significant portion of the damage, one over which we have some degree of control if adequate business impact analysis and business continuity planning activities can be established before the crisis. One needs to remember that despite significant losses in the 2001 attack, due to the 1993 WTC bombing and the potential Y2K threat, private-sector members located inside the WTC complex were among the more prepared stakeholders compared to private organizations in other parts of the nation.

Insurance companies are taking into account the existence of preparedness programs as they calculate the premiums and business interruption insurance coverage for private corporations. Due to the heavy losses they incurred after 9/11, insurance companies looked for ways to limit their exposure to potential future catastrophic losses caused by acts of terrorism. Since re-insurers were also hit hard with the costly claims of 9/11, one option was to exclude terrorism coverage completely from the portfolio of available insurance product. At this point, the U.S. government intervened and passed the Terrorism Risk Insurance Act of 2002 (TRIA), which essentially mandated enrolled insurance companies to offer terrorism insurance

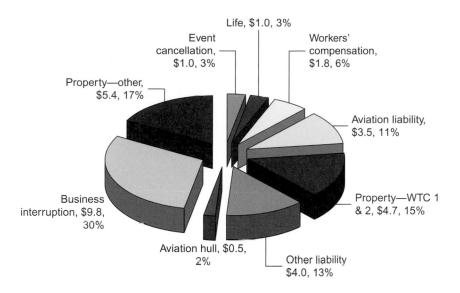

FIGURE 4–13 September 11, 2001, distribution of losses by insurance type ($ in billions). (Source: Insurance Information Institute, 2004)

and in exchange the U.S. government would take the responsibility of paying a significant portion of claims for terrorism incidents that meet a certain criterion. The initial act was designed as a temporary provision to the insurance industry until it figures out a feasible way to offer terrorism insurance and was set to expire by the end of 2005. However, the act was amended in both 2005 and 2007, extending its current benefits to consumers until 2014. The latest version of the act is governed by the following rules:

- The insurance companies enrolled have to make terrorism insurance available to all commercial customers if demanded. The customers may opt to exclude terrorism if they wish to reduce the premiums of their insurance coverage.
- The definition of an "act of terrorism" is that of the Secretary of Treasury.
- The U.S. government is ensuring assistance to the industry of up to $100 billion a year for terrorism-related insurance claims for which the program trigger criteria have been met.
- For a specific incident to qualify for protection by the U.S. government, the combined losses of the incident should exceed $100 million.
- The insurance companies agree to pay up to 20% of the direct earned premium for each year per claim before federal assistance becomes available. The government agrees to pay 85% of the portion of the claim that exceeds the insurer's deductibles.

With the launch of the Terrorism Risk Insurance Act, in a sense the U.S. government has agreed to act as a re-insurer of insurance companies by guaranteeing to absorb a significant amount of losses after terrorist incidents that qualify to trigger the program. One major difference between the 2002 and 2007 versions of the act is that the 2002 version only provided coverage for "international" terrorist attacks, whereas the 2007 version includes acts of "domestic" terrorism (Government Accountability Office, "Terrorism Insurance: Effects of the Terrorism Risk Insurance Act of 2002," 2004; Marsh, 2008).

The "Another Voice" section by Jack Suwanlert provides a comparison of how security is handled differently by public and private entities.

Other Homeland Security Structures

The maintenance of a safe and secure nation depends upon the actions and activities of many more organizations and individuals than those associated with government (as detailed in the preceding text of this chapter). The role of these "other" organizations has been known for quite some time, but was officially recognized in the NRF which expanded its treatment to include nongovernmental groups. These include the private sector, faith-based organizations, community organizations, voluntary organizations, and individuals, among others.

The American Red Cross is probably one of the most significant of these other supporting entities. The American Red Cross is a key player in U.S. emergency management preparedness and response, and is currently a supporting agency to the mass care functions of ESF #6 — Mass Care, Emergency Assistance, Housing, and Human Services under the NRF. As the nation's largest mass care service provider, the American Red Cross provides sheltering, feeding, bulk distribution of needed items, basic first aid, welfare information, and casework, among other services, at the local level as needed. In its role as a service provider, the American Red Cross works closely with local, tribal, and state governments to provide mass care services to victims of every disaster, large and small, in an affected area.

VOADs, or voluntary organizations active in disasters, are associations of NGOs who have a common goal of assisting in major emergencies and who work together to better coordinate their efforts in times of need. At the national level, the National Voluntary Organizations Active in Disaster (NVOAD) is a consortium of approximately 50 national organizations and 55 state and territory equivalents that typically send representatives to the FEMA's National Response Coordination Center to represent the voluntary organizations and assist in response coordination. Members of NVOAD form a coalition of nonprofit organizations that respond to disasters as part of their overall mission. Each state maintains a VOAD which includes organizations that work statewide, and to a growing degree communities are establishing community VOADs.

Individual NGOs are becoming a vital part of the nation's response and recovery network, providing shelter, emergency food supplies, counseling services, and other services to support official emergency management organizations and agencies. They often provide specialized services that help individuals with special needs, including those with disabilities, and provide resettlement assistance and services to arriving refugees. NGOs also play key roles in engaging communities to integrate lawful immigrants into American society and reduce the marginalization or radicalization of these groups. Through the communities, and in some cases official community organizations, many homeland security needs are met. There are a number of established community-based organizations that act toward this common goal, including Neighborhood Watch, the CERTs, and other civic and professional organizations (such as the Lions Club or Rotary International.) These groups may possess the knowledge and understanding of the threats, local response capabilities, and special needs within their jurisdictions and have the capacity necessary to alert authorities of those threats, capabilities, or needs. Additionally, during an incident these groups may be critical in passing along vital incident communications to individuals and families and to supporting critical response activities in the initial stages of a crisis.

Finally, individuals and families take the basic steps to prepare themselves for emergencies, including understanding the threats and hazards that they may face, reducing hazards in and around their homes, preparing an emergency supply kit and household emergency plans (that include care for pets and service animals), monitoring emergency communications carefully, volunteering with established organizations, mobilizing or helping to ensure community preparedness, enrolling in training courses, and practicing what to do in an emergency. These individual and family preparedness activities strengthen community resilience and mitigate the impact of disasters. In addition, individual vigilance and awareness can help communities remain safer and bolster prevention efforts (DHS, 2010).

Conclusion

Emergency management in the United States was forever changed by the events of September 11, 2001, and many would say for the better. This opinion is in wide dispute, however, for a variety of reasons that are unique to each successive level of government, primarily in terms of a loss of dedication to more traditional, nonterrorism hazards. Regardless, it is undeniable that emergency management, and now homeland security, has been thrust to the forefront of the public and the policy agendas, and is one of many primary concerns of federal, state, and local administrators.

For local governments, terrorism is a new threat that greatly expands their already strained safety and security requirements and adds to a long list of needs and priorities. But the threat of terrorism is one that cannot be ignored, and state and local governments have not done so. At these local levels, the dramatic increase in funding that has provided training and equipment to local first responders has been greeted with mixed emotion. Many recipients feel it has remained singular in focus, addressing mainly the terrorism threat. Historically, and including the 2001 terrorist attacks, natural disasters have taken many more lives and have caused much more financial harm. These natural and technological hazards will continue to pose a threat and will continue to result in disaster. It is undeniable that a more comprehensive approach to building the capacity of the local government to respond would provide more long-term benefits. Whether or not these local government agencies will be better prepared overall remains to be seen.

At the state level, governors and state emergency management directors have resisted the push toward local control and have been accused on many occasions of holding out federal homeland security funding from the local governments for which it was intended. In many circumstances it was determined that these accusations were correct. But state officials feel the same concerns about the terrorist threat as do the locals, and have called for better coordination, new communications technologies, and, as always, more and more funding.

At the federal government level, the changes that have resulted with regard to emergency management have been the most visible — and the most dramatic. The creation in 2002 of the DHS, which absorbed FEMA and most of the former federal government disaster management programs, has resulted in DHS taking the lead in addressing these new issues. This new agency has been tested on several occasions, as is displayed throughout this chapter, and has enjoyed relatively mixed but primarily positive success. Under the leadership of DHS, many federal disaster response, recovery, and mitigation programs have so far fared well, although their priorities have seen a drastic shift to accommodate the new terrorist concern. In general, the United States has taken the typical response to a new problem in that it reorganized and committed huge amounts of funding to reducing the newly recognized problem.

The "Select Websites for Additional Information" sidebar lists websites about the organizations discussed in this chapter.

Select Websites for Additional Information

AmeriCorps: http://www.americorps.org
Animal and Plant Health Inspection Service: http://www.aphis.usda.gov
Citizen Corps: http://www.citizencorps.gov
Corporation for National and Community Service: http://www.nationalservice.org
Department of Homeland Security: http://www.dhs.gov
Federal Emergency Management Agency: http://www.fema.gov
Medical Reserve Corps: http://www.medicalreservecorps.gov
Office for Domestic Preparedness: http://www.ojp.usdoj.gov/odp
National Association of Counties: http://www.naco.org
National Governors Association: http://www.nga.org
National League of Cities: http://www.nlc.org
Neighborhood Watch: http://www.usaonwatch.org
Senior Corps: http://www.seniorcorps.org
Transportation Security Administration: http://www.tsa.dot.gov
United States Coast Guard: http://www.uscg.mil
United States Conference of Mayors: http://www.usmayors.org
United States Customs Service: http://www.cbp.gov
United States Secret Service: http://www.secretservice.gov
U.S.A. Freedom Corps: http://www.usafreedomcorps.gov
Volunteers in Police Service: http://www.policevolunteers.org

Key Terms

Adjutant General: The chief administrative officer of a major military unit (the National Guard, in the case of the state government).

Civil Rights: The rights belonging to an individual by virtue of citizenship.

Cybersecurity: The protection of data and systems in networks that are connected to the Internet.

Directorate (DHS): A major division within the Department of Homeland Security that oversees several offices addressing a similar broad-reaching topic (like Science and Technology, for instance).

Ombudsman: A person or an office that investigates complaints and mediates fair settlements.

Superfund: Another name for the Comprehensive Environmental Response, Compensation, and Liability Act of 1980 (CERCLA), which sought to define liability for individual toxic waste sites and then clean up those sites from a fund built from taxes and fines.

Review Questions

1. What is the principal role of emergency management in homeland security? Identify the other major players and their roles in homeland security.

2. Identify the three directorates of the Department of Homeland Security and discuss their respective missions.
3. Discuss the homeland security role of federal agencies other than DHS.
4. Make the case for retaining an all-hazards approach to emergency management that includes terrorism and its associated hazards as one of many hazards. Discuss the pros and cons of such an approach as it relates to all four phases of emergency management: mitigation, preparedness, response, and recovery.
5. If you had been in charge of establishing the Department of Homeland Security (DHS), would you have included the Federal Emergency Management Agency in DHS or would you have retained it as an independent executive branch agency reporting directly to the president? Discuss the possible ramifications of moving FEMA into DHS in terms of FEMA's mission, programs, and reporting structure. The director of FEMA no longer reports directly to the president; will this be a problem in future natural and terrorist-related disasters? What will the impact of FEMA's inclusion in DHS be on the nation's emergency management system?

References

Associated Press. 2011. In sign of tougher line with Pakistan, Obama administration suspends $800 million in military aid. The Washington Post, July 9.

Department of Homeland Security. 2007. Department subcomponents and agencies. http://www.dhs.gov/xabout/structure.

DHS. 2010. Quadrennial Homeland Security Review. February. http://www.dhs.gov/xlibrary/assets/qhsr_report.pdf.

Department of Homeland Security. 2011. Quadrennial Homeland Security Review Report. Department of Homeland Security. http://www.dhs.gov/xlibrary/assets/qhsr_report.pdf.

The Guardian. 2011. Sixty years of US aid to Pakistan: Get the data. Poverty Matters Blog. http://www.guardian.co.uk/global-development/poverty-matters/2011/jul/11/us-aid-to-pakistan.

Guardian. 2011. http://www.guardian.co.uk/global-development/poverty-matters/2011/jul/11/us-aid-to-pakistan.

National Association of Counties (NACo), 2002. Counties and Homeland Security: Policy Agenda to Secure the People of America's Counties. NACo, Washington, DC.

National Association of Counties. 2004. Homeland Security Funding — The Urban Areas Security Initiative: A Survey Report.

National Association of Counties. 2005. Resolution in Support of HHS's State and Local Bioterrorism Grant Program, March 7.

National Conference of State Legislatures. 2005. State offices of homeland security. NCSL Website is no longer available.

National Emergency Management Association. 2001. White Paper on Domestic Preparedness, October 1.

National Emergency Management Association. 2002. NEMA Reports on State Homeland Security Structures, June.

NEMA. 2011. State emergency management organizations. http://www.nemaweb.org/index.php?option=com_content&view=article&id=209&Itemid=377.

NEMA, 2011b. State emergency management staffing. http://www.nemaweb.org/index.php?option=com_content&view=article&id=211&Itemid=383.

NEMA. 2011c. State emergency management agency budgets. http://www.nemaweb.org/index.php?option=com_content&view=article&id=210&Itemid=382.

National Governors Association. 2003. EC-5. Homeland security comprehensive policy. http://www. nga.org/nga/legislativeUpdate/1,1169,C_POLICY_ POSITION%5eD_5102,00.html.

National Governors Association. 2005. Homeland security: NGA position. http://www.nga.org/cms/home/federal-relations/nga-key-committee-issues/page-ec-issues/col2-content/main-content-list/homeland-security.html.

National Governors Association. 2005. Issue brief: Homeland security in the states: much progress, more work, January 24.

National Governors Association Center for Best Practices (NGAC), 2002. Issue Brief: States' Homeland Security Priorities. NGAC, Washington, D.C. August 19.

National League of Cities. 2005. 2005 advocacy priority—the issue: funding for first responders.

National League of Cities. 2011. 2005 National municipal policy. http://www.nlc.org/influence-federal-policy/resources/national-municipal-policy.

U.S. Conference of Mayors. 2001. A national action plan for safety and security in America's cities, December.

U.S. Conference of Mayors. 2003. Homeland Security Report: 90 Percent of Cities Left Without Funds from Largest Federal Homeland Security Program, September 29. http://www.usmayors.org/uscm/us_mayor_newspaper/documents/09_29_03/homeland_report.asp.

U.S. Conference of Mayors. 2004a. Executive director's column, March 12. http://www.usmayors.org/uscm/us_mayor_newspaper/documents/03_15_04/cochran.asp.

U.S. Conference of Mayors. 2004b. 2004 Adopted Resolutions 72nd Annual Meeting, Boston, MA. http://www.usmayors.org/resolutions/72nd_conference/default.asp.

5

Intelligence and Counterterrorism

What You Will Learn

- Elements of the intelligence community and restructuring of statutory authority based on recommendations of the 9/11 Commission
- Detailed overview of essential intelligence agencies such as the CIA, NSA, NRO, and NGA
- New coordination body of national intelligence: Office of the Director of National Intelligence
- Information Sharing and Analysis Centers (ISACs)

Introduction

On September 20, 2001, only 9 days after the 9/11 attacks, President George W. Bush began what would become a major governmental transformation when he announced the establishment of the Office of Homeland Security within the White House, and appointed Tom Ridge, the then governor of Pennsylvania, as homeland security chief. Some months later, after originally rejecting the idea, President Bush proposed the creation of a cabinet-level department of homeland security whose primary purpose would be to unify those agencies responsible for homeland security missions and to achieve greater accountability in the execution of those missions. Driving this effort was a desire among lawmakers to prevent the information sharing failures that occurred prior to the 9/11 attacks, between the many disparate government intelligence agencies, which prevented a complete picture of the pending attacks from being understood. On November 19, 2002, the U.S. Senate voted overwhelmingly to create the Department of Homeland Security (DHS), spurring the most extensive reorganization of the federal government since the 1940s. Despite that so many iterations of this new department's structure centered around the conglomeration of these many intelligence agencies, in the end not one of them was incorporated. Intelligence, however, has remained on the forefront of homeland security and as such is integral to its mission. This chapter explores the role of intelligence in homeland security and describes the various governmental agencies that are involved in intelligence and counterterrorism activities.

The Intelligence Community

The U.S. Intelligence Community is made up of many agencies and organizations that operate within the executive branch and work both independently and collaboratively to gather the intelligence necessary to conduct national security activities (among other activities). The Intelligence Community works to collect and convey essential security-related information to the president and members of the policymaking, law enforcement, and military communities as they need to carry out their required functions and duties.

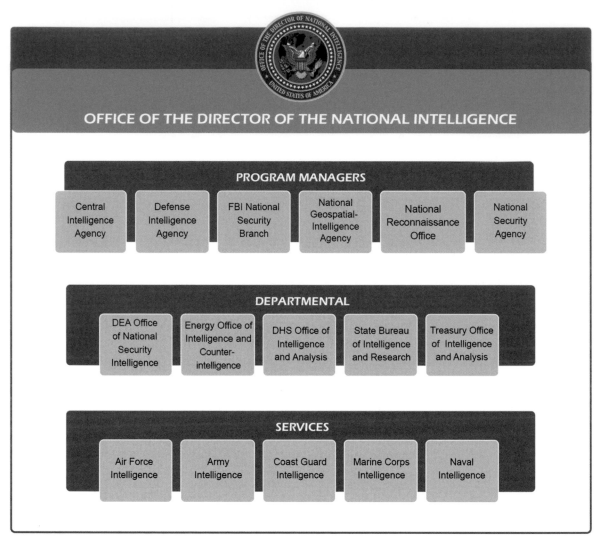

FIGURE 5–1 The U.S. Intelligence Community. (Source: Intelligence.gov, 2011, http://www.intelligence.gov/about-the-intelligence-community/structure/)

Within the U.S. government, the Intelligence Community has developed such that its many components are spread out across the vast range of civilian and military departments (Figure 5–1). While the number of actual agencies has expanded and contracted over time, today 17 agencies perform this function. These agencies include:

- Air Force Intelligence
- Army Intelligence

- Central Intelligence Agency
- Coast Guard Intelligence
- Defense Intelligence Agency
- Department of Energy
- Department of Homeland Security
- Department of State
- Department of the Treasury
- Drug Enforcement Administration
- Federal Bureau of Investigation
- Marine Corps Intelligence
- National Geospatial-Intelligence Agency
- National Reconnaissance Office
- National Security Agency
- Navy Intelligence
- Office of the Director of National Intelligence

These agencies are tasked to varying degrees with the collection and assessment of information regarding national security issues that may include:

- Terrorism
- Weapons (namely nuclear) proliferation, including technologies
- Chemical warfare
- Biological warfare
- Information infrastructure attack
- Narcotics trafficking
- Hostile activities by foreign powers, organizations, persons, and their agents
- Foreign intelligence activities directed against the United States
- Other special activities required to protect U.S. security interests against domestic and foreign threats (as directed by the president)

Like most countries' national governments, the U.S. government has always performed some form of intelligence gathering and analysis activities. However, the extensive Intelligence Community as we know it today is largely the result of expansion during the Cold War era. The cadre of federal employees that form the intelligence function of government grew by the mid-1980s to include more than 100,000 people disbursed throughout 25 organizations and specializing in different aspects of the collection and analysis of information. The amount of the federal budget dedicated to these employees and the activities they conducted grew to more than $30 billion, which was considerable at the time given the relative speed with which these agencies came to prominence. However, considering the highly secretive and critical information needs of the government during this period of showdown among the world's great superpowers, such growth was not surprising.

After the end of the Cold War, the number of agencies and employees was reduced by consolidation of activities and reduction in budgetary allocations. The military intelligence services saw the steepest cuts. Total reductions in the employee base were about 20%. However, because intelligence capacity grew so large during the Cold War era, a vast intelligence capacity remains despite these cuts.

The Intelligence Community was established to identify and head off plans for attacks like the one that occurred on September 11, 2001, but due to obvious shortcomings the attacks were not prevented (or even adequately anticipated). The 9/11 Commission was formed in the aftermath of the attacks to study the existing weaknesses in intelligence structure and effectiveness, to form a better understanding of how the Intelligence Community functions and to identify areas for improvement. The Commission's findings have since profoundly impacted both the Intelligence Community's budgets and the nature of their work and collaboration. Specifically, the Commission found six problems pertaining to the Intelligence Community for which it made recommendations for change. Actions pertaining to these changes include (with commentary drawn from the 9/11 Commission Report) (9/11 Commission, 2004):

1. *Structural barriers to performing joint intelligence work.* National intelligence is still organized around the collection disciplines of the home agencies, not the joint mission. The importance of integrated, all-source analysis cannot be overstated. Without it, it is not possible to "connect the dots." No one component holds all the relevant information.

2. *Lack of common standards and practices across the foreign–domestic divide.* The leadership of the Intelligence Community should be able to pool information gathered overseas with information gathered in the United States, holding the work — wherever it is done — to a common standard of quality in how it is collected, processed, reported, shared, and analyzed. A common set of personnel standards for intelligence can create a group of professionals better able to operate in joint activities, transcending their own service-specific mind-sets.

3. *Divided management of national intelligence capabilities.* While the CIA was once "central" to the national intelligence capabilities, following the end of the Cold War, it has been less able to influence the use of the nation's imagery and signals intelligence capabilities in three national agencies housed within the Department of Defense: the National Security Agency, the National Geospatial-Intelligence Agency, and the National Reconnaissance Office. One of the lessons learned from the 1991 Gulf War was the value of national intelligence systems in precision warfare. Helping to orchestrate this transformation is the undersecretary of defense for intelligence, a position established by Congress after the 9/11 attacks. An unintended consequence of the developments has been the far greater demand made by Defense on technical systems, leaving the Director of Central Intelligence (DCI) less able to influence how these technical resources are allocated and used.

4. *Weak capacity to set priorities and move resources.* The agencies are mainly organized around what they collect or the way they collect it. But the priorities for collection are national. As the DCI makes hard choices about moving resources, he or she must have the power to reach across agencies and reallocate effort.

5. *Too many jobs.* The DCI now has at least three jobs. He or she is expected to run a particular agency, the CIA. He is expected to manage the loose confederation of agencies, that is, the Intelligence Community. He is expected to be the analyst-in-chief for the government, sifting evidence and directly briefing the president as his principal intelligence adviser. No recent DCI has been able to do all three activities effectively. Usually what loses out is the management of the Intelligence Community, a difficult task even in the best case because the DCI's current authorities are weak. With so much to do, the DCI often has not used even the authority he has.

6. *Too complex and secret.* Over the decades, the agencies and the rules surrounding the Intelligence Community have accumulated to a depth that practically defies public comprehension. There are

now 15 agencies or parts of agencies in the Intelligence Community. The Intelligence Community and the DCI's authorities have become arcane matters, understood only by initiates after long study. Even the most basic information about how much money is actually allocated to or within the Intelligence Community and most of its key components is shrouded from public view.

Soon after the 9/11 Commission Report was released, Congress passed the Intelligence Reform and Terrorism Prevention Act (IRTPA) of 2004 (S. 2845, December 7, 2004). This Act prescribed far-reaching reforms for the Intelligence Community, both specific to and in addition to those recommendations made by the 9/11 Commission. Of particular relevance within this Act is the first of its eight sections that is aptly titled "Reform of the Intelligence Community." Of particular note within the verbiage of this section is a call for the creation of two intelligence entities, both of which are described in detail later in this chapter, and which together have helped to address many of the coordination and information-sharing problems that were identified by the Commission. These two entities are:

- Director of National Intelligence
- National Counterterrorism Center

At present, the Intelligence Community is structured to maximize the effectiveness of intelligence collection and dissemination among its 17 member agencies. Each agency is authorized to operate under its own directive, but all share the common intelligence mission as stated in the IRTPA to collect and convey essential information to the president and other key stakeholders. The current structure of the Intelligence Community is represented in the organizational chart shown in Figure 5-1.

The government intelligence capacity involves a full range of activities and operations related to intelligence gathering, analysis, and sharing. Through systems and procedures, the various intelligence agencies convert the information they acquire into clear, comprehensible intelligence and deliver it to end users as required (generally, the president, policy makers, and military commanders). Key to this effort is delivering it in a form they can utilize. The Intelligence Community performs this role according to what is commonly referred to as the "intelligence cycle."

The Intelligence Cycle

The intelligence cycle begins with the identification of key issues that interest policy makers, and defining the answers they require in order to make educated decisions on action and policy. The individual agencies, under the direction of the Office of the Director of National Intelligence, determine how they will acquire needed information and then act on those plans. Once attained, the intelligence is sorted and analyzed, and any necessary reports and recommendations are prepared and delivered. These reports often reveal other areas of concern, which in turn lead to more questions. In this way, the end of one cycle effectively leads to the start of the next.

The steps of the intelligence cycle include (Figure 5-2):

- *Planning*: During the planning step, decisions are made regarding what types of information to collect and how to collect it. The Intelligence Community relies upon the National Intelligence Priorities Framework (NIPF — see sidebar below) to articulate what issues are important, which then determines how to prioritize the use of intelligence resources. The intelligence end users participate in this step by ensuring that their information needs are included in the NIPF process.
- *Collection*: During the collection step, the Intelligence Community gathers the raw data used to produce finished intelligence products. Collection can be from one or more of the source types

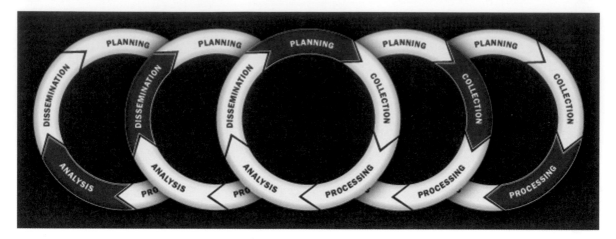

FIGURE 5–2 The intelligence cycle. (Source: Intelligence.gov, 2011, "The Intelligence Cycle")

(listed below), which may be open source or clandestine. End users are able to share their scientific and/or substantive expertise and information in this process.

- *Processing*: In the processing step, information that is collected is converted into a usable format, such as by language translation or decryption.
- *Analysis*: In the analysis step, intelligence officers analyze processed information to turn it into finished intelligence. This may include drafting reports, evaluating the reliability of different sources of information, resolving data conflicts, and other analytic services. Intelligence reports typically integrate multiple sources of intelligence and the experience and knowledge of many different members of the Intelligence Community. Many end user organizations have their own analytic capabilities that better meet internal needs, as well as subject matter experts who have specialized knowledge not typically found in the Intelligence Community. Oftentimes, the intelligence gathered merely supports a much wider understanding held by the end user — an understanding that likely exceeds that of the individuals who collected and processed the data.
- *Dissemination*: In the dissemination step, intelligence products are provided to those who request or otherwise need them.

The Intelligence Community information-gathering effort draws from a number of different source types, which include:

- *Open-source intelligence* (OSINT): This is publicly available information appearing in print or electronic forms, including radio, television, newspapers, journals, the Internet, commercial databases, videos, graphics, and drawings.
- *Human intelligence* (HUMINT): This is intelligence derived from information collected and provided by human sources. This intelligence includes overt data collected by personnel in diplomatic and consular posts, as well as unobtainable information collected via clandestine sources of information, debriefings of foreign nationals and U.S. citizens who travel abroad, official contacts with foreign governments, and direct observation.

- *Signals intelligence* (SIGINT): This is information gathered from data transmissions, including communications intelligence (COMINT), electronic intelligence (ELINT), and foreign instrumentation signals intelligence (FISINT).
- *Geospatial intelligence* (GEOINT): This is information describing, visually depicting, and accurately locating physical features and human activities on the Earth. Examples of GEOINT products include imagery, analyses, maps, and navigation charts. Imagery intelligence (IMINT) is a subset of GEOINT.
- *Measurement and signature intelligence* (MASINT): This is information produced by quantitative and qualitative analysis of physical attributes of targets and events in order to characterize and identify them.

The National Intelligence Priorities Framework (NIPF)

The NIPF is the Director of National Intelligence's guidance to the Intelligence Community on the national intelligence priorities approved by the President.

The NIPF is the DNI's sole mechanism for establishing national intelligence priorities. The NIPF consists of:

- Intelligence topics reviewed by the National Security Council Principals Committee and approved by the President.
- A process for assigning priorities to countries and non-state actors relevant to the approved intelligence topics.
- A matrix showing these priorities. The NIPF matrix reflects consumers' priorities for intelligence support and ensures that long-term intelligence issues are addressed.

The NIPF is updated semiannually in coordination with Intelligence Community elements, the National Intelligence Council, and other internal components of the Office of the Director of National Intelligence. Ad hoc adjustments may also be made to reflect changes in world events and policy priorities.

The Office of the Director of National Intelligence and Intelligence Community elements use the NIPF to guide allocation of collection and analytic resources. In addition, Intelligence Community elements associate intelligence collection requirements and analytic production with NIPF priorities and report to the Director of National Intelligence on their coverage of NIPF priorities.

Source: Office of the Director of National Intelligence, 2009. National Intelligence: A Consumer's Guide. Intelligence Overview.

Intelligence Oversight

The Intelligence Community agencies and offices fall within the executive branch. However, due to the nature of their work, they are subject to external oversight from the executive and legislative branches. The Intelligence Community provides a vital service of ensuring that both policy and decision makers and lawmakers are equally informed of intelligence related to national security issues, and Congress is authorized to maintain oversight of the Intelligence Community intelligence activities. Executive organizations involved in oversight of the Intelligence Community include:

- The President's Foreign Intelligence Advisory Board
- The President's Intelligence Oversight Board
- The Office of Management and Budget

  Within the Congress, principal oversight responsibility rests with the following two entities:

- The Senate Select Committee on Intelligence
- The House Permanent Select Committee on Intelligence

Office of the Director of National Intelligence

The National Commission on Terrorist Attacks upon the United States (the 9/11 Commission) recommended the following in its final report:

> *The current position of Director of Central Intelligence should be replaced by a National Intelligence Director with two main areas of responsibility: (1) to oversee national intelligence centers on specific subjects of interest across the U.S. government and (2) to manage the national intelligence program and oversee the agencies that contribute to it.*

In efforts to move forward with the Commission's recommendation, Senators Susan Collins and Joe Lieberman, and Speaker of the House of Representatives Dennis Hastert, separately introduced legislation to create the Director of National Intelligence (DNI) position. Both bills sought to establish a presidentially nominated, Senate-confirmed position of DNI, who would serve as the head of the Intelligence Community's distinct intelligence agencies. Both bills also sought to establish a separate Senate-confirmed director of central intelligence, who would manage the CIA and would be prohibited from serving simultaneously as the DNI.

The House of Representatives passed the Collins–Lieberman Intelligence Reform and Terrorism Prevention Act on December 7, 2004, by a vote of 336 to 75. On December 8, 2004, the bill was approved by an 89-to-2 vote in the U.S. Senate and was sent to the president for his signature. The president signed the bill and nominated John Negroponte, the former U.S. ambassador to the United Nations and recently the U.S. ambassador to Iraq, for the position of national intelligence director on February 17, 2005. John Negroponte was confirmed by the Senate on April 21, 2005, and was officially sworn in on May 18, 2005.

The primary goal of this new position was to ensure coordination and cooperation among all intelligence communities in the United States and to unify the national intelligence effort in place of the Director of Central Intelligence. The new DNI was given the authority to perform the following critical tasks and activities according to the Act:

- Creating national intelligence centers to incorporate capabilities from across the Intelligence Community in order to accomplish intelligence missions
- Controlling the national intelligence budget in terms of dollar amounts and distribution among different intelligence agencies
- Transferring personnel and funds to ensure that the Intelligence Community is flexible and can respond to emerging threats

- Creating the Privacy and Civil Liberties Board to protect privacy and civil liberties concerns potentially created by proposals to fight terrorism
- Establishing an information-sharing network to break down the stovepipes that currently impede the flow of information between federal, state, and local agencies and the private sector (Congressional Research Service, 2004a; Congressional Research Service, 2004b)

In its first 3 years of existence, the new office accomplished some of the goals mentioned above, but more importantly, this period has been one of transition in the Intelligence Community with the creation of new functions, reshaping of others, and some changes in key officials.

On October 13, 2005, approximately 6 months after taking the office, Director Negroponte together with the Director of Central Intelligence created the National Clandestine Service within the CIA to boost the nation's human intelligence capabilities. Within the same timeframe, the directorate released the National Intelligence Strategy, a document that details the national intelligence framework and established goals, priorities, and measures of effectiveness in adapting to the changing intelligence needs of the United States in the aftermath of the 9/11 attacks. The implementation of the strategy kicked off with the creation of DNI Open Source Center in an attempt to better exploit openly available information (such as websites, reports, videos, radio, television, and books) for intelligence gathering and analysis purposes. Shortly before the end of 2005, the DNI created the DNI National Counterproliferation Center (NCPC). The office is tasked with the unification of efforts to prevent the proliferation of weapons of mass destruction (WMDs) (Office of the Director of National Intelligence, 2008c).

On February 17, 2006, the Drug Enforcement Administration became the 16th member of the Intelligence Community. On May 5, CIA Chief Porter Goss resigned and the media reported that the cause of the resignation was a combination of differences between Goss's and DNI Negroponte's management styles, and the changes made in the direction of the Intelligence Community that Goss did not agree with. Later in the same month, General Mike Hayden (U.S. Air Force) was sworn in as the new chief of CIA. General Hayden previously served as the first principal deputy director of National Intelligence, which is the highest ranking intelligence post within the U.S. Armed Forces (Office of the Director of National Intelligence 2008d).

The year 2007 saw another change of key officials when President Bush announced that DNI John Negroponte would be moving to the State Department as the deputy secretary of state, and nominated Admiral Mike McConnell as his replacement. Although McConnell was holding a senior management position with a private consulting company focusing on intelligence and national security prior to his appointment as the DNI, he had previously served as the director of the National Security Agency (NSA) earlier. As his first major move in his new post, McConnell created the Information Sharing and Steering committee within the DNI to further improve coordination and collaboration among different members of the Intelligence Community. Within this new setting, every member of the Intelligence Community must appoint an information-sharing executive who works closely with the committee to share vital information processed by his or her agency. Just a few days after the announcement of the creation of the new committee, the DOD chief information officer (CIO) and the ODNI CIO signed an agreement that created the Unified Cross Domain Management Office to enhance information sharing between the DOD and the Intelligence Community. On March 27, 2007, the DNI announced the release of the National Counterintelligence Strategy, which details the Intelligence Community's goals and priorities toward a reduction in intelligence threats aimed at the United States (Office of the Director of National Intelligence, 2008e).

Today, the DNI serves as the head of the Intelligence Community and is the principal advisor to the president, the National Security Council, and the Homeland Security Council (HSC) for intelligence matters related to national security. Also, the DNI oversees and directs the implementation of the National Intelligence Program. The DNI's responsibilities, among others, are to:

- Lead the Intelligence Community
- Oversee the coordination of foreign relationships between elements of the Intelligence Community and intelligence services of foreign governments
- Establish requirements and priorities for collection, analysis, production, and dissemination of national intelligence
- Coordinate reform of security clearance and acquisition processes
- Achieve auditable financial statements
- Support legislative, legal, and administrative requirements
- Ensure compliance with statutory and presidentially mandated responsibilities
- Transform the Intelligence Community into a unified, collaborative, and coordinated enterprise

The DNI organization is composed of the DNI staff and Intelligence Community mission and support activities (MSAs). The DNI staff is primarily responsible for Intelligence Community policy and oversight and the preparation of the National Intelligence Program Budget. The MSAs are directly responsible for providing Intelligence Community-wide substantive intelligence, counterintelligence strategy and strategic analysis, research and development, and training and education. The DNI staff is responsible for synchronizing and integrating efforts across the DNI organization.

There are four deputy directors of national intelligence, who serve in the following offices:

- *Office of the Deputy Director for Policy, Plans and Requirements* (DDNI/PPR): This office drives vital intelligence reform by coordinating Intelligence Community-wide policy and strategy, plans, and requirements; modernizing security processes; and strengthening relationships with federal, state, local, foreign, and private sector partners.
- *Office of the Deputy Director for Collection* (DDNI/C): This office coordinates collection throughout the Intelligence Community under the authorities of the DNI. The DDNI/C ensures that the president's and the DNI's priorities are appropriately reflected in future programming and systems acquisition decisions and puts into context for the DNI the way in which actions affect the total collection mission.
- *Office of the Deputy Director for Analysis* (DDNI/A): This office has responsibility for enhancing the quality, timeliness, and utility of analytic support to intelligence consumers. The DDNI/A's approach for achieving this goal is to increase expertise and improve analytic tradecraft at individual, agency, and community levels through specialization, collaboration, and cross-fertilization. The DDNI/A serves concurrently as the chairman of the NIC and manages the production of the President's Daily Brief.
- *Office of the Deputy Director for Future Capabilities* (DDNI/FC): This office is the Intelligence Community's catalyst for technical innovation, responsive stewardship, and acquisition excellence. Its approach is to address the key intelligence challenges by leading advanced research and development focusing on disruptive technology leaps; acting as the DNI's Science and Technology advisor and integrating the Intelligence Community Science and Technology enterprise; developing and evaluating the Intelligence Community-wide, end-to-end collection architecture to promote innovation and responsible financial stewardship; and establishing and maintaining an agile and transparent best practice environment that promotes Intelligence Community acquisition success.

Other elements of the DNI staff include the Civil Liberties Protection Office and the Office of Equal Opportunity and Diversity.

The DNI organization includes ten functional mission support activities, which include:

- *National Counterterrorism Center* (NCTC): It serves as the primary organization in the U.S. government for integrating and analyzing all intelligence pertaining to terrorism possessed or acquired by the U.S. government (except purely domestic terrorism).

- *National Counterintelligence Executive* (NCIX): It is staffed by senior counterintelligence and other specialists from across the national intelligence and security communities. The NCIX mission is to exploit and defeat adversarial intelligence activities directed against U.S. interests; protect the integrity of the U.S. intelligence system; provide incisive, actionable intelligence to decision makers at all levels; protect vital national assets from adversarial intelligence activities; and neutralize and exploit adversarial intelligence activities targeting the armed forces.

- *National Counterproliferation Center* (NCPC): It is responsible for coordinating strategic planning within the Intelligence Community to enhance intelligence support to U.S. efforts to stem the proliferation of WMDs and related delivery systems.

- *Special Security Center's* (SSC): This mission is to assist the DNI in protecting and sharing national intelligence information throughout the Intelligence Community, the U.S. government, U.S. contractors, state, local, and tribal governments, and the foreign partners by conducting assessments of the security of sensitive compartmented information and other intelligence information under the DNI's authority; document overall Intelligence Community security compliance for the DNI; monitor, coordinate, and advise on significant unauthorized disclosures and compromises of classified national intelligence information; and provide feedback to support policy formulation and training initiatives.

- *National Intelligence University* (NIU): It operates under the DNI's authority to establish an integrated framework that brings together the educational components of the Intelligence Community to promote a more effective and productive intelligence community through cross-disciplinary education and joint training. The NIU is made up of the existing Intelligence Community schools and universities, the Office of the Chancellor of the NIU, and the staff and curriculum that support the goals and authority of the DNI.

- *Intelligence Advanced Research Projects Activity* (IARPA): This invests in high-risk/high-payoff research that has the potential to provide the United States with an overwhelming intelligence advantage over the future adversaries.

- *Center for Security Evaluation* (CSE): Its mission is to strengthen overseas security standards, provide for interagency, life-cycle inspections, and aggressively pursue emerging security technologies with security solutions that are risk based and realistic. The CSE is the organization that synchronizes Intelligence Community emergency preparedness activities for the DNI and national leadership.

- *National Intelligence Council* (NIC): It is the Intelligence Community's center for mid-term and long-term strategic analysis. The NIC supports the DNI in his roles as the head of the Intelligence Community and principal advisor for intelligence matters to the president and the National Security and Homeland Security Councils, and serves as the senior intelligence advisor representing the Intelligence Community's views within the U.S. government. The NIC also provides key products and services, such as the National Intelligence Estimates assessing future trends on a wide range of global issues.

- *National Intelligence Coordination Center* (NIC-C): This was established in October 2007 in collaboration with the DOD and several domestic agencies to provide a mechanism to coordinate intelligence activities across the entire U.S. government. The NIC-C works to efficiently coordinate, collaborate, assess, and deploy the nation's total array of intelligence collection capabilities.
- *Mission Support Center*: It provides support services to all DNI staff and mission support activity components.

Central Intelligence Agency

The recognized intelligence needs of modern warfare that surfaced during World War II resulted in the creation of America's first central intelligence organization, the Office of Strategic Services (OSS). The OSS was created to perform a variety of functions, including traditional espionage, covert action (ranging from propaganda to sabotage), counterintelligence, and intelligence analysis. The OSS represented a revolution in U.S. intelligence, not only because of the varied functions performed by a single, national agency, but also because of the breadth of its intelligence interests and its use of scholars to produce finished intelligence.

In the aftermath of World War II, the OSS was disbanded, officially ceasing all operations on October 1, 1945, by executive order from President Truman. However, several of its branches were retained and were distributed among other governmental departments. For instance, the X-2 (Counterintelligence) and Secret Intelligence branches were transferred to the War Department to form the Strategic Services Unit, and the Research and Analysis branch was transferred to the Department of State (Smith, 1983).

As Truman was ordering the termination of the OSS, he was also commissioning studies to determine the requirements of and changes to the U.S. intelligence structure in the post-World War II climate. Based on these studies, the National Intelligence Authority (NIA) and its operational element, the Central Intelligence Group (CIG), were created. The CIG was initially responsible for coordinating and synthesizing the reports produced by the military service intelligence agencies and the FBI, but it soon after assumed the task of secret intelligence collection.

National security needs and the intelligence reorganization were addressed by the National Security Act of 1947. The CIA was established as an independent agency within the executive office of the president to replace the CIG. According to the Act, the CIA was to have five functions:

1. To advise the National Security Council in matters concerning such intelligence activities of the government departments and agencies as related to national security
2. To make recommendations to the National Security Council for the coordination of such intelligence activities of the departments and agencies of the government as related to national security
3. To correlate and evaluate the intelligence relating to national security, and to provide for the appropriate dissemination of such intelligence within the government using, where appropriate, existing agencies and facilities
4. To perform for the benefit of existing intelligence agencies such additional services of common concern as the National Security Council determines can be more effectively accomplished centrally
5. To perform other such functions and duties related to intelligence affecting the national security as the National Security Council may from time to time direct

The organizational structure of the CIA as it exists today began to take shape in the early 1950s under Director Walter Bedell Smith. In 1952, the Office of Policy Coordination was transferred under

CIA control and merged with the secret intelligence-gathering Office of Special Operations to form the Directorate of Plans. That same year, the offices involved in intelligence research and analysis were placed under the Directorate of Intelligence. A third unit, the Directorate of Administration, was established to perform administrative functions.

The principal functions of the Directorate of Plans were clandestine collection and covert action. A separate directorate was later formed to perform technical collection operations, but before that time, the Directorate of Plans was heavily involved in the development and operation of overhead collection systems like the U-2 spy plane and CORONA reconnaissance satellite. In 1973, the Directorate of Plans became the Directorate of Operations. On October 13, 2005, the creation of the National Clandestine Service was announced by the Director of Central Intelligence and the Director of National Intelligence, which absorbed all functions of the Directorate of Operations (Figure 5–3). Today, its functions within the National Clandestine Service include clandestine collection, covert action, counternarcotics and counterterrorism activities, and counterintelligence. On the day of the establishment of this new function within the CIA, John Negroponte, the first Director of National Intelligence, underlined that the National Clandestine Service will significantly improve the HUMINT capability of the nation (Office of the Director of National Intelligence, 2005).

A fourth directorate, the Directorate of Research, was established in 1962. This directorate consolidated into a single-unit all-agency components involved in technical collection activities. In 1963, it was renamed the Directorate of Science and Technology and assumed control of scientific intelligence analysis. Its present functions include the following:

- Developing technical collection systems
- Collecting intelligence from embassy sites (in cooperation with the NSA)
- Recording foreign radio and television broadcasts (through its Foreign Broadcast Information Service)
- Developing and producing technical devices (such as bugging devices, hidden cameras, and weaponry) for agents and officers
- Providing research and development in support of intelligence collection and analysis

Until late 1996, the directorate also managed the National Photographic Interpretation Center (NPIC), which interpreted satellite and aerial reconnaissance imagery. NPIC was absorbed by the newly established National Imagery and Mapping Agency (NIMA) (Richelson et al., 2003).

Another vital directorate of the CIA is the Intelligence and Analysis Directorate (Figure 5–3). This directorate is primarily in charge of analyzing the intelligence data and information collected to make sense out of it for the development of more comprehensive intelligence products. The next section briefly covers the specific duties of different offices within the Intelligence and Analysis Directorate.

Crime and Narcotics Center

The Crime and Narcotics Center (CNC) focuses on international narcotics trafficking and organized crime for policy makers and the law enforcement community. CNC's workforce is diverse, utilizing individuals with a variety of backgrounds, experience, and specialties. The CNC strategic analysts research long-term trends and keep U.S. policy makers informed about new developments. They estimate the impact of the drug trade and of organized crime on U.S. national security, uncover trafficking trends and routes, and monitor relationships among organized crime groups, traffickers, and terrorists. Targeting analysts use technology to identify key people, organizations, trends, and components in criminal organizations. Operational support specialists and program managers provide fast-paced operational research, management, and support to colleagues overseas. They develop substantive expertise on organized crime

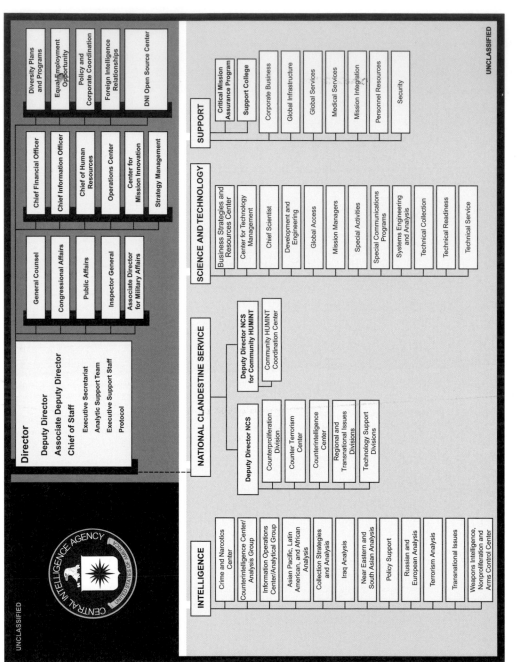

FIGURE 5-3 CIA organizational chart. (Source: CIA, 2011, https://www.cia.gov/library/publications/additional-publications/the-work-of-a-nation/cia-director-and-principles/70040_BLU_SEPT_07_OPA.pdf)

and narcotics issues, and often travel to support operations or collect information. Analysts specializing in technologies such as remote sensing and geographic information systems capitalize on those tools to locate and estimate quantities of illegal crops in countries where those plants are known to be grown (Central Intelligence Agency, 2008c).

Counterintelligence Center/Analysis Group

The Counterintelligence Center/Analysis Group (CIC/AG) identifies, monitors, and analyzes the efforts of foreign intelligence entities against U.S. persons, activities, and interests. The CIC/AG analysts focus on two specific types of counterintelligence threats to U.S. national security: transnational threats, such as the counterintelligence aspect of terrorism, or the threats posed by emerging or changing technologies to the U.S. government's intelligence operations and information systems. The CIC/AG also tracks threats posed by foreign intelligence services and monitors their activities.

Information Operations Center/Analysis Group

The Information Operations Center/Analysis Group (IOC/AG) evaluates foreign threats to U.S. computer systems, particularly those that support critical infrastructures. The group provides its analysis to the president, his senior advisers, high-level officials on cyberissues in the Departments of Defense, State, and Treasury, and to senior private-sector officials responsible for operating critical infrastructures. The IOC/AG analysts consider potential threats from state and nonstate actors and evaluate a wide array of information, including foreign intentions, plans, and capabilities.

Office of Asian Pacific, Latin American, and African Analysis

The Office of Asian Pacific, Latin American, and African Analysis (APLAA) studies the political, economic, leadership, societal, and military developments in Asia, Latin America, and sub-Saharan Africa.

Office of Collection Strategies and Analysis

The Office of Collection Strategies and Analysis (CSAA) provides comprehensive intelligence collection expertise to the DCI, a wide range of senior agency and intelligence community officials, and key national policy makers. The CSAA staff work with analysts in the CIA's National Clandestine Service and Directorate of Science and Technology, the DOD, the NSA, the NGA, the NRO, and other intelligence community agencies to craft new approaches to solving complex collection issues.

Office of Iraq Analysis

The Office of Iraq Analysis is the newest office within the Intelligence and Analysis Directorate. This office was created in November 2003 at a point in time when the collection and analysis of intelligence from Iraq became increasingly important in the aftermath of the war. Since its creation, the analysis workforce of the office has covered important events such as the captures of Saddam Hussein and many other top Iraqi officials, the rise of the Iraqi insurgency, the nation's first post-Saddam elections, and Iraqi economic development (Central Intelligence Agency, 2008b).

Office of Near Eastern and South Asian Analysis

The Office of Near Eastern and South Asian Analysis (NESA) provides policy makers with comprehensive analytic support on Middle Eastern and North African countries, as well as on the South Asian nations of India, Pakistan, and Afghanistan.

Office of Policy Support

The Office of Policy Support customizes defense intelligence analysis and presents it to a wide variety of policy, law enforcement, military, and foreign liaison recipients.

Office of Russian and European Analysis

The Office of Russian and European Analysis (OREA) provides intelligence support on a large set of countries that have long been of crucial importance to the United States as allies or as adversaries and are likely to continue to occupy a key place in U.S. national security policy. OREA officers are a mix of generalists and specialists who concentrate on issues ranging from ethnic conflict in the Balkans to the U.S.–Russian relationship. Previous historical events covered by analysts include the Solidarity movement in Poland, the breakup of the former Soviet Union, the fall of the Berlin Wall, NATO expansion, and numerous wars in the Balkans. Some current focus areas are arms control negotiations and treaty-monitoring efforts, analysis of potential benefits and challenges of EU enlargement, and reporting on the political and economic landscape of central Asia.

Office of Corporate Resources

The Office of Corporate Resources oversees support to the directorate on a wide variety of issues, including budget, contracts, diversity programs, equal employment opportunity, facilities management, human resources, and resource planning.

Office of Terrorism Analysis

The Office of Terrorism Analysis (OTA) is the analytic component of the DCI Counterterrorism Center. The OTA analysts work to inform policy makers and support the intelligence, law enforcement, homeland security, and military communities by performing the following tasks:

- Tracking terrorists and the activities of states that sponsor them, and assessing terrorist vulnerabilities by analyzing their ideology and goals, capabilities, associates, and locations
- Analyzing worldwide terrorist threat information and patterns to provide warnings aimed at preventing terrorist attacks
- Monitoring worldwide terrorism trends and patterns, including emerging and nontraditional terrorist groups, evolving terrorist threats or operational methods, and possible collusion between terrorist groups
- Identifying, disrupting, and preventing international financial transactions that support terrorist networks and operations

Office of Transnational Issues

The Office of Transnational Issues (OTI) produces analytic assessments on critical intelligence-related issues that transcend regional and national boundaries. Drawing on a broad range of experts in engineering, science, and social science disciplines, OTI's analysis addresses energy and economic security, illicit financial activities, societal conflicts, humanitarian crises, and the long-term military and economic strategic environment.

Weapons Intelligence, Nonproliferation, and Arms Control Center

The Weapons Intelligence, Nonproliferation, and Arms Control Center (WINPAC) provides intelligence support aimed at protecting the United States and its interests from all foreign weapons threats.

WINPAC officers are a diverse group with a variety of backgrounds and work experiences, and include mathematicians, engineers (nuclear, chemical/biological, mechanical, and aerospace, among others), physicists, economists, political scientists, computer specialists, and physical scientists. On any given day, those analysts could be answering a question from the president, assessing information about a foreign missile test, or developing new computational models to determine blast effects. A key part of its mission includes studying the development of the entire spectrum of threats, from WMDs (nuclear, radiological, chemical, and biological weapons) to advanced conventional weapons such as lasers, advanced explosives, and armor, as well as all types of missiles, including ballistic, cruise, and surface-to-air missiles. The center studies systems from their earliest development phase to production, deployment, and transfers to other countries, and monitors strategic arms control agreements. The WINPAC also supports military and diplomatic operations.

Today, the CIA is the largest producer of national security intelligence for senior U.S. policy makers. The director of the CIA (DCIA) is the national HUMINT manager and serves on behalf of the DNI as the national authority for coordination, deconfliction, and evaluation of clandestine HUMINT operations across the Intelligence Community, consistent with existing laws, executive orders, and inter-agency agreements.

The CIA is probably the most widely recognized of the various U.S. intelligence agencies, primarily because of its celebrated and cinematized involvement in covert action, and also because of the central role it plays in providing intelligence to the president. However, as noted before, there are several U.S. intelligence agencies, some of which rival the CIA in influence and exceed it in budget. Each of these is described in detail next.

Defense Intelligence Agency

The Defense Intelligence Agency (DIA) is a major producer and manager of foreign military intelligence for the DOD. The DIA was established on October 1, 1961, and was designated a combat support agency in 1986. The DIA's mission is to provide timely, objective, all-source military intelligence to policy makers, to U.S. Armed Forces around the world, and to the U.S. acquisition community and force planners to counter a variety of threats and challenges across the spectrum of conflict.

The director of DIA is a three-star military officer who serves as the principal advisor on substantive military intelligence matters to the secretary of defense and the chairman of the Joint Chiefs of Staff. Additionally, he or she is the program manager for the General Defense Intelligence Program that funds a variety of military intelligence programs at and above the corps level. The director also serves as the program manager for the department's Foreign Counterintelligence Program and is the chairman of the Military Intelligence Board that examines key intelligence issues such as information technology architectures, program and budget issues, and defense intelligence inputs to National Intelligence Estimates.

DIA is headquartered in the Pentagon, but the agency employs more than 15,000 civilian and military personnel around the world. The largest facilities include:

- The Defense Intelligence Analysis Center on Bolling Air Force Base in Washington, D.C.
- The Missile and Space Intelligence Center at Redstone Arsenal in Huntsville, Alabama
- The National Center for Medical Intelligence at Fort Detrick, Maryland

The DIA also deploys military and civilian personnel worldwide during crises or conflicts to support military forces. In December 2007, the DIA established the Defense Intelligence Operations Coordination Center (DIOCC) to seamlessly integrate all defense intelligence resources on the transnational threats to

U.S. national security and to enhance defense intelligence collaboration. The DIOCC collaborates with the DOD and national intelligence resources to manage risk and resource requirements. It integrates and synchronizes all-source military and national-level intelligence capabilities in support of the warfighters. Working closely with the DIOCC to help manage risk and intelligence resources is the Joint Functional Component Command for Intelligence, Surveillance and Reconnaissance (JFCC-ISR). To support DOD efforts in the global war on terrorism, the DIA established the Joint Intelligence Task Force for Combating Terrorism to consolidate and produce all-source terrorism-related intelligence.

The DIA director is the commander of the U.S. Strategic Command organization. The agency is organized as follows:

- The Directorate for Analysis (DI) assesses foreign militaries. Its focuses include WMDs, missile systems, terrorism, infrastructure systems, and defense-related medical issues.
- The Directorate for Intelligence, Joint Staff (J2), provides foreign military intelligence to the Joint Chiefs of Staff and senior DOD officials.
- The Directorate for Human Intelligence (DH) conducts worldwide strategic HUMINT collection operations. The DH oversees the Defense Attache System, which conducts representational duties on behalf of the DOD and advises U.S. ambassadors on military matters.
- The Directorate for MASINT and Technical Collection (DT) is the defense intelligence center for MASINT. It collects and analyzes MASINT and also develops new MASINT capabilities.
- The Directorate for Information Management and Chief Information Officer (DS) serves as DIA's information technology component. It manages the Department of Defense Intelligence Information System (DODIIS) and operates the Joint Worldwide Intelligence Communications System (JWICS).

The Federal Bureau of Investigation (Department of Justice)

The Federal Bureau of Investigation (FBI) is a law enforcement organization that exists at the federal level. However, it is also a threat-based, intelligence-driven national security organization that protects the United States from critical threats while safeguarding civil liberties. As both a component of the Department of Justice and a full member of the U.S. Intelligence Community, the FBI serves as a vital link between intelligence and law enforcement communities.

The FBI's top priorities are combating the threat of terrorism, counterintelligence, and cybercrime. As to counterterrorism, the FBI gives particular attention to terrorist efforts to acquire and use WMDs. FBI agents have been credited with disrupting a number of terrorist plots in various stages of development, and the nature of these threats continues to evolve. In response, the FBI continuously adapts to trends in terrorist recruitment, financing, and training, as well as terrorists' development of new weapons.

The FBI also maintains a counterintelligence role, addressing the threat of foreign intelligence services that attempt to infiltrate the U.S. government. A similar threat comes from foreign business interests and students and scientists seeking to steal technology on behalf of foreign governments or commercial interests. Their investigations include economic espionage, financial crimes, export control violations, cyber intrusions and the compromise of U.S. strategic intellectual property.

Cyberterrorism and crime are on the forefront of the FBI intelligence efforts. Of greatest concern are terrorists or foreign state-sponsored elements targeting national information infrastructure, and criminal enterprises and individuals who illegally access computer systems or spread malicious code. Other areas receiving priority focus are crimes that undermine the health of the economy, including large-scale financial institution frauds, securities and commodities fraud or bank fraud, environmental crimes, health-care fraud, and telemarketing fraud. In the area of violent crimes, the FBI focuses on increasingly sophisticated national and transnational gangs, dangerous fugitives, and kidnappers. The FBI leverages partnerships with over 800,000 state, local, and tribal law enforcement agencies through task forces and fusion centers to collect and disseminate intelligence, serving as a unique link between the intelligence and law enforcement communities.

Federal law, attorney general authorities, and executive orders give the FBI jurisdiction to investigate all federal crimes not assigned exclusively to another federal agency and to investigate threats to the national security. Additionally, there are other laws that give the FBI responsibility to investigate specific crimes. This combination of authorities gives the FBI the unique ability to address national security and criminal threats that are increasingly intertwined, and to shift between the use of intelligence tools such as surveillance or recruiting sources and law enforcement tools of arrest and prosecution. Regardless of which tools are employed, law and policy require that the FBI's information-gathering activities use the least intrusive techniques possible to accomplish the objective and cannot be based solely on activities protected by the First Amendment.

The organization of the FBI intelligence operation is as follows:

- The National Security Branch (NSB) oversees the FBI's national security programs. It includes four divisions plus the Terrorist Screening Center (TSC).
- The Counterterrorism Division (CTD) focuses on both domestic and international terrorism. It oversees the Joint Terrorism Task Forces (JTTFs).
- The Counterintelligence Division (CD) prevents and investigates foreign intelligence activities within the United States and espionage activities in the United States and overseas.
- The Directorate of Intelligence (DI) is the FBI's intelligence analysis component. It has embedded employees at FBI headquarters and in each field office through Field Intelligence Groups (FIGs) and fusion centers.
- The Weapons of Mass Destruction Directorate (WMDD) prevents individuals and groups from acquiring WMD capabilities and technologies for use against the United States, and links all operational and scientific/technology components to accomplish this mission.
- The Terrorist Screening Center (TSC) was created to consolidate the U.S. government's approach to terrorist screening and create a single, comprehensive watch list of known or suspected terrorists. The TSC helps ensure that federal, local, state, and tribal terrorist screeners have ready access to information and expertise.

National Geospatial-Intelligence Agency

By the mid-1990s, imagery was the basis for both imagery intelligence and map-based imagery products, and the Intelligence Community wished to centralize the management of both of these functions. The NIMA, formally proposed by the secretary of defense and the director of the CIA in November 1995, was established on October 1, 1996. Through this creation, the NIMA joined five existing imagery interpretation and mapping organizations: the NPIC, the Defense Mapping Agency, the CIA's Office of Imagery Analysis, the DIA's Office of Imagery Analysis, and the Central Imagery Office. Other offices absorbed into the new agency include the Defense Dissemination Program Office and elements of the Defense Airborne Reconnaissance Office and National Reconnaissance.

Initially, the NIMA was organized into three main directorates: operations, systems and technology, and corporate affairs. Three key units within the Operations Directorate were Imagery Analysis,

Geospatial Information and Services, and the Central Imagery Tasking Office. The latter was responsible for allocating targets to imagery collection systems and determining when the imagery was obtained. Formed from several defense and intelligence agencies, the NIMA merged imagery, maps, charts, and environmental data to produce what has been called *geospatial intelligence*. The Imagery Analysis Unit combined the activities of the NPIC and the CIA and DIA imagery analysis organizations, while the Geospatial Information and Services Unit provided the mapping, charting, and geodesy products formerly provided by the DMA. The unit was responsible for producing strategic and tactical maps, charts, and databases, and specialized products to support current and advanced weapons and navigation systems (Richelson et al., 2003).

Between 1995 and 1998, the NIMA products helped resolve many national and international issues, including long-standing border disputes between Peru and Ecuador, and between Israel and southern Lebanon. The NIMA products also supported the Dayton Peace Accord efforts in the Balkans. In February 2000, the space shuttle Endeavor's Shuttle Radar Topography Mission (SRTM) provided the most detailed measurements of the planet's elevation ever gathered — data that will prove invaluable in supporting the NGA's geospatial-intelligence efforts.

The NIMA played a critical role in homeland security following the attacks of September 11. In the response and recovery phases of the disaster in New York City, the NIMA partnered with the U.S. Geological Survey (USGS) to survey the World Trade Center site and determine the extent of the destruction. Then, in 2002, the NIMA partnered with federal organizations to provide geospatial assistance to the 2002 Winter Olympics in Utah.

On November 24, 2003, the president signed the 2004 Defense Authorization Bill, which included a provision to change the NIMA's name to the National Geospatial-Intelligence Agency (NGA). Today, the NGA develops imagery and map-based intelligence for national defense, homeland security, and navigation safety purposes. The NGA maintains a headquarters in Bethesda, Maryland, and major facilities in Washington, D.C., Northern Virginia, and St. Louis, Missouri. NGA activities are organized under the following components:

- *Source Operations and Management Office*: The Source Directorate discovers, acquires, produces, delivers, and manages the data and information used to produce geospatial intelligence. The Source Directorate manages the end-to-end execution of geospatial intelligence information requirements. This provides the foundation for the "information superiority" needed by the president and Executive Office agencies, Congress, and the military.

- *Enterprise Operations Directorate*: The Enterprise Directorate is responsible for day-to-day systems operations and leveraging technology to ensure and protect the NGA's mission by operating the National System for Geospatial Intelligence (NSG — a unified community of geospatial intelligence experts, producers, and users) and providing enterprise, corporate, dissemination, and information services.

- *Analysis and Production Directorate*: The Production Directorate provides geospatial intelligence and services to policy makers, military decision makers and operational "warfighters," and tailored support to civilian federal agencies and international organizations. This geospatial intelligence is derived from many sources.

- *Acquisition Directorate*: The Acquisition Directorate enables, acquires, and provides systems, supplies, and services that advance NGA's role in geospatial intelligence. This includes imagery, imagery analysis, and geospatial information. The directorate focuses on preacquisition studies; the acquisition program; systems engineering; and the advancement of systems engineering, acquisition/contracting, infrastructure engineering, and imagery and geospatial sciences.

- *InnoVision Directorate*: The InnoVision Directorate forecasts future environments, defines future needs, establishes plans to align resources, and provides technology and process solutions to help NGA, end users, and partners. The InnoVision also provides the focal point in NGA to address the future; leads NGA into the future by developing comprehensive plans and technology initiatives based on analysis of intelligence trends, technology advances, and emerging customer and partner concepts; and helps to guide the agency as it adapts to new needs and the needs of the Intelligence Community.

The NGA also provides imagery in support of major disasters as noted in the following sidebar.

National Geospatial Intelligence Agency Responds to U.S. Disasters

NGA's mission includes the following verbiage: "Know the Earth … Show the Way … Understand the World." The agency lives up to this mission in part by providing geospatial intelligence support for global world events, disasters and military actions. Examples of the natural disasters and other national security related functions served by NGA products include:

- **2008 Midwest Flooding:** In spring 2008, NGA partnered with U.S. Federal Emergency Management Agency (FEMA) to provide direct support for those affected by the Midwest floods. NGA used geospatial information and commercial imagery to determine the extent of the damage. NGA posted imagery and mapping products on our nga-earth.org website for residents and first responders to see the damage and watch recovery efforts.
- **2007 California Wildfires:** In the fall of 2007, NGA provided over 150 geospatial intelligence products to FEMA to lend support in combating the California wildfires. NGA supplied damage assessments of major infrastructure in the area, assessments of areas still on fire and areas where the fire had been extinguished. This information was uploaded to the nga-earth .org website as a way for the public to see the damage without returning to the area. Our products greatly assisted firefighters and other first responders with relief efforts (Figure 5–4).
- **2004 Olympics:** NGA provided substantial support to the Olympic games in Athens, Greece in 2004 and Torino, Italy in 2006. NGA deployed a team of analysts to assist each event with force protection and security issues. NGA lends its geospatial knowledge in helping officials create geospatial products including maps of the locations used for the events and surrounding key infrastructure.
- **Hurricane Katrina:** NGA supported recovery efforts for hurricanes Katrina and Rita in 2005. NGA sent a team of analysts to the region to support FEMA and other first responders. NGA provided imagery from commercial and U.S. government satellites and from airborne platforms. NGA created the NGA-earth.org website to show residents the extent of the damage and progress of the recovery efforts. As a result of our hard work, NGA was highlighted in the U.S. government after action report on Hurricane Katrina under "What was Done Right" (Figure 5–5).

Source: NGA, 2011, What We Do. https://www1.nga.mil/About/WhatWeDo/Pages/default.aspx.

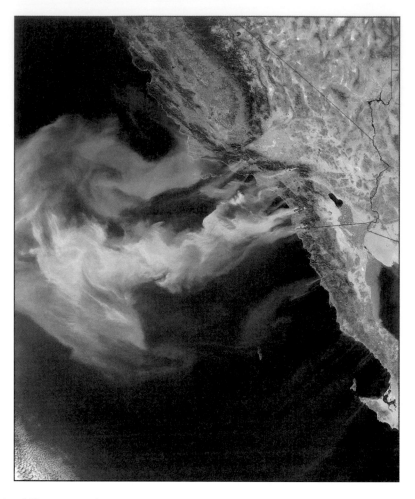

FIGURE 5–4 California wildfire overview. (Source: https://www1.nga.mil/About/WhatWeDo/Pages/default.aspx)

National Reconnaissance Office

The National Reconnaissance Office (NRO) was established on September 6, 1961, to coordinate CIA reconnaissance activities with those of the DOD. The NRO's primary function has been to oversee the research and development, procurement, deployment, and operation of imaging, signals intelligence, and ocean surveillance satellites. It awards contracts, oversees the research and development efforts of contractors, supervises the launch of the payloads, and, in conjunction with the CIA and the NSA, operates these spacecraft. It has also been involved in the research, development, and procurement of selected aerial reconnaissance systems, such as the SR-71. From its inception until September 18, 1992, when its existence was formally acknowledged, the NRO operated as a classified organization. A major restructuring of the NRO also began to be implemented in 1992, which turned the NRO into a functional organization instead of a stand-alone organization (Richelson et al., 2003).

FIGURE 5–5 Hurricane Katrina. (Source: https://www1.nga.mil/About/WhatWeDo/Pages/default.aspx)

In its current setting, the NRO designs, builds, and operates the nation's reconnaissance satellites. NRO products, provided to an expanding list of customers such as the CIA and the DOD, can warn of potential trouble spots around the world, help plan military operations, and monitor the environment. The NRO is a DOD agency and is staffed by DOD and CIA personnel. The NRO has historically been one of the most clandestine intelligence organizations in the United States, but many parts of its operations have now been declassified. For example, the location of its headquarters, in Chantilly, Virginia, was declassified in 1994. In February 1995, CORONA, a photoreconnaissance program in operation from 1960 to 1972, was declassified and 800,000 CORONA images were transferred to the National Archives and Records Administration. The NRO is known as the "nation's eyes and ears in space."

NRO intelligence gathering and analysis activities are conducted at the request of the secretary of defense and/or the DNI. The director of National Reconnaissance Office (DNRO) is selected by the secretary of defense with the concurrence of the DNI and also serves as the assistant to the secretary of the Air Force (Intelligence Space Technology). The NRO's workforce of approximately 3,000 includes personnel primarily from the Air Force, the CIA, and the Navy.

The NRO systems provide the foundation for global situational awareness and address many of the nation's most significant intelligence challenges. For instance, the NRO systems are the only collectors able to access critical areas of interest, and data from overhead sensors provide unique information and perspectives not available from other sources.

The NRO systems provide:

- Monitoring the proliferation of WMDs
- Tracking international terrorists, drug traffickers, and criminal organizations
- Developing highly accurate military targeting data and bomb damage assessments
- Supporting international peacekeeping and humanitarian relief operations
- Assessing the impact of natural disasters, such as earthquakes, tsunamis, floods, and fires

Together with other Defense Department satellites, the NRO systems play a crucial role in providing global communications, precision navigation, early warning of missile launches and potential military aggression, signals intelligence, and near real-time imagery to U.S. forces to support the war on terrorism and other continuing operations. The NRO satellites also support civil customers in response to disaster relief and environmental research. Scientists created a global environment database using NRO imagery to help predict climate change, assess crop production, map habitats of endangered species, track oil spills, and study wetlands. Finally, the NRO data form the basis for products that help depict and assess the devastation in areas affected by natural disasters.

National Security Agency

On May 20, 1949, Secretary of Defense Louis Johnson established the Armed Forces Security Agency (AFSA) and placed it under the command of the Joint Chiefs of Staff. In theory, the AFSA was to direct the communications intelligence and electronic intelligence activities of the military service signals intelligence units (at that time, the Army Security Agency, Naval Security Group, and Air Force Security Service). In practice, however, the AFSA had little power, and its functions were characterized as activities not performed by the service units.

On October 24, 1952 — the same day that he sent a (now-declassified) top-secret eight-page memorandum entitled "Communications Intelligence Activities" to the Secretaries of State and Defense — President Truman abolished the AFSA and transferred its personnel to the newly created National Security Agency (NSA). As its name indicates, the new agency was to have national, not just military, responsibilities. In 1971, the NSA became the National Security Agency/Central Security Service (NSA/CSS). The second half of NSA's title, which is rarely used, refers to its role in coordinating the signals intelligence activities of the military services (Richelson, 1999). Today, the NSA has two primary responsibilities: information assurance and signals intelligence.

The NSA is organized as follows:

- The Information Assurance Directorate (IAD) operates under the authority of the secretary of defense and ensures the availability, integrity, authentication, confidentiality, and nonrepudiation of national security and telecommunications and information systems (national security systems). The IAD is dedicated to providing information assurance solutions that serve to protect U.S. information systems from harm. This mission involves many activities, including the following:
  - Detecting, reporting, and responding to cyberthreats
  - Making encryption codes to securely pass information between systems
  - Embedding information assurance measures directly into the emerging global information grid
  - Building secure audio and video communications equipment
  - Making tamper-proof products
  - Providing trusted microelectronics solutions
  - Testing the security of its partners' and customers' systems
  - Providing operational security assistance
  - Evaluating commercial software and hardware against set standards
- The Signals Intelligence Directorate is responsible for understanding end-users' intelligence information needs, and for the collection, analysis and production, and dissemination of SIGINT. The NSA's SIGINT mission provides military leaders and policy makers with intelligence to ensure national defense and to advance U.S. global interests, and the information attained is specifically limited to that that focuses on foreign powers, organizations, or persons, and international terrorists.

- The Central Security Service (CSS) oversees the function of the military cryptologic system, develops policy and guidance on the contributions of military cryptology to the Signals Intelligence/ Information Security (SIGINT/INFOSEC) enterprise, and manages the partnership of the NSA and the Service Cryptologic Components. The NSA as a whole is known as "NSA/CSS."
- The NSA/CSS Threat Operations Center monitors the operations of the global network to identify network-based threats and protect the United States and allied networks.
- The National Security Operations Center is a 24 hours a day/7 days a week operations center that, on behalf of the NSA/CSS, provides total situational awareness across the NSA/CSS enterprise for both foreign signals intelligence and information assurance, maintains cognizance of national security information needs, and monitors unfolding world events.
- The Research Directorate conducts research on signals intelligence and on information assurance for the U.S. government.

DHS Office of Intelligence and Analysis

The DHS is responsible for leading the unified national effort to secure the United States by preventing and deterring terrorist attacks and responding to threats and hazards. The Intelligence and Analysis (I&A) is a key component of the Intelligence Community. The I&A is DHS's headquarters intelligence element and is led by the undersecretary for Intelligence and Analysis, with guidance from the Homeland Security Council and Homeland Security Intelligence Council. As a member of the Intelligence Community, the I&A is responsible for using information and intelligence from multiple sources to identify and assess current and future threats to the United States. The I&A provides actionable intelligence to support national and DHS decision makers while working closely with state, local, tribal, and private sector partners.

In line with the mission of its umbrella agency, the I&A focuses on threats related to border security; chemical, biological, radiological, and nuclear (CBRN) issues, to include explosives and infectious diseases; critical infrastructure protection; extremists within the homeland; and travelers entering the homeland. Although they are not part of the Intelligence Community, several other DHs subcomponents have extensive interactions with the Intelligence Community, including U.S. Immigration and Customs Enforcement, Customs and Border Protection, Transportation Security Administration, Secret Service, and Citizenship and Immigration Services. In addition, the Coast Guard, a DHS component, is a member of the Intelligence Community.

Department of State Bureau of Intelligence and Research

The Department of State Bureau of Intelligence and Research (INR) provides expert intelligence analysis to the secretary of state and senior policy makers on decisions regarding the protection of American interests around the world. The INR serves as the State Department focal point for all policy issues and activities involving the Intelligence Community. The INR assistant secretary reports directly to the secretary of state and serves as his principal adviser on all intelligence matters.

INR foreign affairs analysts utilize all-source intelligence, diplomatic reporting, public opinion polling, and interaction with U.S. and foreign scholars, in conjunction with intelligence gathered by all Intelligence Community partners, to formulate intelligence products. Their strong regional and functional backgrounds allow them to respond rapidly to changing policy priorities and to provide early warning and analysis of events and trends. The INR analysts — a combination of Foreign Service officers often with extensive in-country experience and Civil Service specialists with in-depth expertise — cover all countries and regional or transnational issues.

The INR provides daily briefings, reports, and memoranda to the secretary of state and other department principals. The INR also briefs members of Congress and their staffs as appropriate. INR products cover the world on foreign relations issues such as political/military developments, terrorism, narcotics, and trade. The INR develops intelligence policy for the Department of State and works to harmonize all agencies' intelligence.

The INR Humanitarian Information Unit (HIU) serves as a nucleus for unclassified information related to complex emergencies and provides a coordinating mechanism for data sharing among the U.S. government, the United Nations, nongovernmental organizations, and foreign governments. The Bureau also administers the Title VIII Grant Program, an initiative funded by Congress for senior-level academic research in Russian, Eurasian, and East European studies.

Conclusion

Despite that Congress and President Bush were not able to consolidate the various intelligence agencies under a single department "roof," there has been significant improvement in the collection, analysis, and dissemination of intelligence since the 9/11 attacks. This coordination among various agencies has also led to some failures that otherwise may not have occurred, such as the 2009 Wikileaks release of over a quarter million diplomatic cables, which was caused by differences in security procedures between the Department of State (whose policies on the handling of classified materials would never have allowed for such a leak to have occurred) and of the Department of Defense (which allowed a low-level employee to not only access information that had no pertinence to his position, but also download the information onto a removable drive without detection). Fortunately, the changes that have occurred thus far appear to have been effective in preventing any additional terrorist attacks in the United States, and the means of and policy for sharing information between these disparate agencies are becoming more and more efficient.

Key Terms

Consequence: The result of a terrorist attack or other hazard that reflects the level, duration, and nature of the loss. For the purposes of the NIPP, consequences are divided into four main categories: public health and safety, economic, psychological, and governance impacts.

Crisis Management: A proactive management effort to avoid crisis, and the creation of strategy that minimizes adverse impacts of crisis to the organization when it could not be prevented. Effective crisis management requires a solid understanding of the organization, its strategy, liabilities, stakeholders, and legal framework combined with advanced communication, leadership, and decision-making skills to lead the organization through the crisis with minimizing potential loss.

Director of Central Intelligence (DCI): Director of the Central Intelligence Agency. In the aftermath of the 9/11 intelligence reform, the DCI is reporting to the Director of National Intelligence for overall intelligence coordination purposes.

Director of National Intelligence (DNI): The statutory authority created on the basis of the recommendations of the 9/11 Commission and tasked by the president to coordinate the holistic intelligence of the United States. Directors of member agencies of the Intelligence Community report to the DNI. The DNI is also responsible for establishing budget priorities for the overall U.S. intelligence effort.

Intelligence: Intelligence is a secret state activity to understand or influence foreign entities (CIA).

Intelligence Community: The collective body of U.S. government agencies that have been tasked with the responsibility of collecting, analyzing, or acting upon intelligence.

Information Sharing and Analysis Center (ISAC): ISACs are sectoral information analysis and sharing centers that bring together representatives and decision makers of a given sector for the purposes of critical infrastructure protection and disaster preparedness.

Unmanned Airborne Vehicles (UAVs): UAVs are airborne vehicles controlled from a ground command center that are used in high-risk intelligence collection efforts and zones as well as in relatively safe target areas where the mission does not require the involvement of a human pilot. UAVs are used in intelligence collection efforts in Iraq as well as for border patrolling activities at the southwest border of the United States.

Review Questions

1. What are the key intelligence agencies in the United States? Briefly comment on their roles in terms of homeland security.
2. Describe how intelligence has evolved in the United States.
3. Is the Office of the National Director of Intelligence a viable alternative for the consolidation of intelligence agencies under one government "roof," as was originally proposed in the early days following the 9/11 attacks?
4. What are the various steps in the intelligence cycle, and what is involved in each?

References

9/11 Commission. 2004. The 9/11 Commission Report. http://govinfo.library.unt.edu/911/report/911Report.pdf.

Blumenthal, H. 2003. Department of Human Services Private Sector Information Sharing: ISAC Program. Government Symposium on Information Sharing and Homeland Security. Pennsylvania.

Central Intelligence Agency. 2007. Offices of CIA. https://www.cia.gov/offices-of-cia/index.html.

Central Intelligence Agency. 2008a. CIA organization chart. https://www.cia.gov/about-cia/leadership/cia-organization-chart.html.

Central Intelligence Agency. 2008b. History of the Intelligence and Analysis Directorate. https://www.cia.gov/offices-of-cia/intelligence-analysis/history.html.

Central Intelligence Agency. 2008c. The CIA Crime and Narcotics Center. https://www.cia.gov/offices-of-cia/intelligence-analysis/organization-1/the-cia-crime-and-narcotics-center.html.

Congressional Research Service. 2004a. RL32506 — The Proposed Authorities of a National Intelligence Director: Issues for Congress and Side-by-Side Comparison of S. 2845, H.R. 10, and Current Law. http://www.fas.org/irp/crs/RL32506.pdf.

Congressional Research Service. 2004b. RS21948 — The National Intelligence Director and Intelligence Analysis. http://www.fas.org/irp/crs/RS21948.pdf.

Department of Homeland Security. 2002. National Strategy for Homeland Security. http://www.dhs.gov/xlibrary/assets/nat_strat_hls.pdf.

Department of Homeland Security. 2004. Agency Responsibilities by Functional Areas, Functions and Tasks. NRP Initial Plan Draft, Appendix A, Table 6.2.

Department of Homeland Security. 2007. Budget in Brief FY 2008. http://www.dhs.gov/xlibrary/assets/budget_bib-fy2008.pdf.

Department of Homeland Security. 2008. Budget in Brief FY 2009. http://www.dhs.gov/xlibrary/assets/budget_bib-fy2009.pdf.

Digital National Security Archive. 2003. Overview of U.S. Intelligence.

Environmental Protection Agency. 2002. FY 2003 Budget in Brief. http://www.epa.gov/ocfo/budget/2003/2003bib.pdf.

Government Accountability Office. 2004. Terrorism Insurance: Effects of the Terrorism Risk Insurance Act of 2002. http://www.gao.gov/new.items/d04806t.pdf.

MILNET. 2006. Changes to the U.S. Intelligence Community. http://www.milnet.com/Changes%20to%20Intelligence%20Community.html.

Office of the Director of National Intelligence. 2005. Establishment of the National Clandestine Service (NCS). http://www.odni.gov/press_releases/20051013_release.htm.

Office of the Director of National Intelligence. 2008a. Members of the Intelligence Community. http://www.intelligence.gov/about-the-intelligence-community/.

Office of the Director of National Intelligence. 2008b. ODNI Organization. http://www.dni.gov/aboutODNI/organization.htm.

Office of the Director of National Intelligence. 2008c. ODNI Press Releases 2005. http://www.odni.gov/press_releases/press_releases_2005.htm.

Office of the Director of National Intelligence. 2008d. ODNI Press Releases 2006. http://www.odni.gov/press_releases/press_releases_2006.htm.

Office of the Director of National Intelligence. 2008e. ODNI Press Releases 2007–2008. http://www.odni.gov/press_releases/press_releases.htm.

Richelson, J.T., 1999. The U.S. Intelligence Community, 4th ed. Westview Press, Boulder, CO.

Richelson, J.T., Gefter, J., Waters, M., et al. 2003. U.S. Espionage and Intelligence, 1947–1996. Digital National Security Archive. Mfiche 2552 GRN–MTXT.

Smith, B.F., 1983. The Shadow Warriors: OSS, and the Origins of the CIA. Basic Books, New York.

6

Border Security, Immigration, and Customs Enforcement

What You Will Learn

- The importance of national borders, and the functions of government that pertain to the movement of people and goods across these borders
- The role of various homeland security organizations in performing immigration and customs enforcement services

Introduction

The borders of any country are strategically important because of the critical role they play in its economic vitality and commerce. Increasing globalization of economic systems and transportation networks has made it possible for every community in the United States to be connected to the outside world through a vast system of airports, seaports, pipelines, roadways, and waterways. Borders are gateways for imported and exported goods; therefore, their effectiveness and efficiency are important measures for the trade capacity and capability of the country. Borders also have an important role for the international tourism and travel capability of the country.

At the same time, borders provide access into the country, through both major and clandestine entry points, for illegal immigrants and goods. Therefore, the security and control of borders is of the utmost importance in the drive to mitigate the risk posed by the penetration of unwanted or dangerous people and goods into the country. Human traffickers, smugglers, drug dealers, criminals, terrorists, illegal drugs, conventional weapons, undeclared or counterfeit products, biological agents, and weapons of mass destruction (WMD) are but a small sample of the many possible individuals and items that together mandate strong national borders.

The Department of Homeland Security (DHS) has been tasked with managing the legal movement of goods and people through the nation's borders, and with protecting these same borders from illegal infiltration. This chapter explores the DHS functions of border protection, immigration, and customs enforcement.

Border Security

The United States shares 5,525 miles of border with Canada and 1,989 miles with Mexico. The maritime border includes 95,000 miles of shoreline and a 3.4-million-square-mile exclusive economic zone. Each year, more than 500 million people cross these borders to enter the United States, and approximately 330 million of them are foreign nationals.

Entry points into the country are not limited to its external borders, however. Sea and airports of entry can be far from the point where the United States territory meets Canada, Mexico, or an international body of water. Each international airport, and each major seaport, serves as a potential doorway for illegal and illicit persons and materials. The border security role, therefore, is not just one of guarding the nation's perimeter and the perimeter of its territories.

The United States has had an active border patrol function since the turn of the 20th century. The first border patrols were conducted by U.S. Immigration Service watchmen on horseback who began curbing illegal border crossings in 1904. At that time, the patrols were unpredictable, irregular, and conducted according to the availability of sporadic resources. Border patrol agents were called Mounted Guards and were based in the city of El Paso, Texas. At most times, approximately 75 Mounted Guards, and oftentimes far fewer, patrolled the length of the Mexican border primarily to stave off illegal immigrants who were coming from China.

Congress authorized a separate group of Mounted Guards in 1915 called the Mounted Inspectors. This unit operated on horseback, in cars, and in boats. Like the Mounted Guards, the Mounted Inspectors focused their efforts on Chinese immigrants. During the same period, U.S. military troops were tasked with patrolling the U.S.–Mexico border as well, in support of the Mounted Guards and Inspectors. When military units interdicted illegal aliens, they brought them to immigration inspection staffed by Mounted Inspectors. Finally, Texas Rangers were assigned to patrol duties in Texas, and it was found that their efforts were highly effective.

In the early 20th century, the government was much more concerned with customs violations and espionage than worrying about the trickle of people who were attempting to enter the country illegally. However, those government agencies charged with inspecting people and products entering and leaving the United States felt that their efforts were ineffective without proper enforcement between the inspection stations. When in 1917 the government issued a higher head tax and literacy requirement on entry into the country, the motive for illegal immigration grew considerably and the number of attempts (and successes) followed suit.

Although most Americans are familiar with the 18th Amendment statutes banning alcohol, most are not aware that this constitutional change also placed finite limits on the number of people who could immigrate to the United States (by the Immigration Acts of 1921 and 1924). As such, the enforcement of the nation's borders received newfound interest among lawmakers and bureaucrats. These new limits dramatically increased the number of people attempting illegal entry, especially those for which legal means proved inadequate or otherwise unsuccessful.

Congress passed the Labor Appropriation Act of 1924 on May 28 of that year, thereby establishing the U.S. Border Patrol for the purpose of securing the borders between inspection stations. In 1925, its duties were expanded to patrol the seacoast. The size of the Border Patrol expanded quickly to 450 as officers were recruited to meet the new demands. Recruitments came from organizations familiar with the task including the Texas Rangers, local sheriffs and deputies, and appointees from the Civil Service Register of Railroad Mail Clerks. The government initially provided the agents a badge and revolver, but they did not begin wearing uniforms until 1928.

In 1932, the Border Patrol split management authority between the Mexican and Canadian borders, with a director-in-charge of each. Because the smuggling of alcohol was the primary concern at this point, most of the Border Patrol's staff were assigned to the Canadian border and headquartered in Detroit.

In 1933, President Franklin D. Roosevelt joined the Bureau of Immigration and the Bureau of Naturalization into the Immigration and Naturalization Service (INS). One year later, the first Border Patrol Academy opened as a training school at Camp Chigas, El Paso. Just 7 years later, the new INS was transferred out of the Department of Labor, where it first existed due to the nature of immigration prior to that time, to the Department of Justice. The employment of the agency more than doubled to 1,531 INS officers, and the Border Patrol had over 1,400 employees in law enforcement and civilian positions by the end of World War II. During World War II, the Border Patrol expanded its duties to include the manning of alien detention camps, guarding diplomats, and assisting the U.S. Coast Guard (USCG) in searching for enemy saboteurs. It was at this time that aircraft became an integral part of operations.

In 1952, new legislation expanded the power of the Border Patrol to include the boarding and search of conveyances for illegal immigrants anywhere in the United States, not just at the points of entry. In that initial year, U.S. agents deported 52,000 illegal immigrants back into Mexico. When the program lost its budget in after just one year, the Mexican government began offering train rides for its deported nationals — yet this program also ended after less than a year. Many more iterations of deportation programs followed within a few years and included planes, trains, and buses, among others. However, it was found that the cost of deportation was prohibitively expensive, and most deportees simply returned soon after deportation due to the poor monitoring of the border.

In the late 1950s, immigrants began turning to private aircraft to enter the United States, and in the decade that followed, this trend moved toward the hijacking of commercial aircraft. Fairly soon after, Border Patrol agents were working the airline industry and accompanying flights to prevent illegal immigrants of taking over the planes. Additionally, the alien smuggling industry came into its own as people looked for experts to help them avoid the growing layers of protection.

Illegal immigration spiraled out of control in the 1980s and 1990s, and the Border Patrol increased in manpower and technology to combat this trend. Through the use of infrared technology (night vision), seismic sensors (to detect walking and vehicle movement), and a modern computing power, the Border Patrol agents were better equipped to locate, apprehend, and process intending illegal immigrants.

The INS initiated a program called "Operation Hold The Line" in 1993 to begin to stave off the unchecked flow of illegal immigrants. This program, which was highly successful, concentrated agents and equipment in high-risk areas, and increased the level of visibility of the agency for deterrence purposes. In 1994, "Operation Gatekeeper" was implemented in San Diego using similar tactics, resulting in a reduction of successful illegal immigrant crossings by 75%. A defined national strategic border control plan was introduced at this time, which established a long-term plan of action for the Border Patrol.

Following the 9/11 terrorist attacks, which exposed weaknesses in the nation's border security and immigration systems, it was recognized that these two functions were vital to national security and therefore a natural match for the new DHS. Like most other agencies moved into DHS, the Border Patrol became part of the new agency on March 1, 2003, in the U.S. Customs and Border Protection (CBP).

Immigration

Immigration is defined as the act of entering and settling permanently in another country, and/or becoming a permanent resident or a legal citizen of that country. The United States is a nation that was founded on the principles of open immigration, and all but a few of its current citizens trace their roots back to immigrants from all countries of the world. Understandably, immigration is closely tied to that of border security, given that a nation's borders exist to ensure that only those transiting legal channels are able to enter the nation. It is through the function of immigration that foreign citizens gain such access.

The granting of residency and citizenship of foreign nationals is guided by the nation's immigration laws. Over the course of the nation's history, these laws have been changed often, reflecting the volatility of national opinions on the value of more open doors in relation to the need for a growing workforce. There has always existed a global demand for U.S. residency and citizenship, given the strength of the U.S.

208 INTRODUCTION TO HOMELAND SECURITY

economy, the high standard of living, the availability of jobs, and the prospect of a better life for many who have struggled back home. At the same time, many U.S. businesses have looked elsewhere for manpower as the strength of the U.S. economy made certain low-wage and seasonal jobs hard to fill, given the ability of most U.S. citizens to find alternate ("desirable") employment.

In the first two hundred years of the nation from about 1600 to 1800, it is estimated that less than one million people migrated to the United States. At this time, law permitted citizenship only to Caucasians (with expansion to other races added in the 19th and 20th centuries). Rates of immigration did not increase until around 1820 with industrialization, and it is estimated that some 30 million people migrated to the United States in the 100 years that followed.

Immigration law aimed at restricting the granting of residency or citizenship to foreign nationals began during this time. The Immigration Act of 1882 levied a tax of 50 cents on each immigrant to the United States, which helped to generate revenue to support the enforcement of immigration provisions through a new Immigration Service. The Immigration Act of 1891 established the Office of the Superintendent of Immigration within the Treasury Department, which was responsible for admitting, rejecting, and processing intending immigrants. Immigration inspectors were recruited and stationed at major U.S. ports of entry (POE) to track passengers as they arrived on incoming ships. The immigration station at Ellis Island in New York, which opened in January 1892, is the most famous of these.

Legislation in March 1895 upgraded the Office of Immigration to the Bureau of Immigration and changed the agency head's title from Superintendent to Commissioner-General of Immigration. The Bureau's first task was to formalize and standardize basic operating and regulatory procedures. For example, inspectors queried arrivals about their suitability for permanent entry and recorded their admission or rejection on manifest records. Detention guards cared for those who were detained until their cases were decided, or, if the decision was negative, until they were deported. Inspectors served on boards of special inquiry that reviewed each exclusion case.

In 1913, the Department of Commerce and Labor reorganized into two separate cabinet departments (as they exist today). The Bureau of Immigration and Naturalization also separated into two distinct bureaus, but they were reunited in 1933 by executive order into today's Immigration and Naturalization Service (INS). President Roosevelt moved the INS from the Department of Labor to the Department of Justice in 1940, thereby changing the nature of immigration to one of national security. In fact, it is the INS that was tasked with organizing and managing the internment camps and detention facilities of aliens and U.S. citizens considered to be from "enemy" nations.

Prior to the creation of the INS, the 1921 Emergency Quota Act was passed, which restricted the number of immigrants annually from any country to 3% of the number of residents from that country already living in the United States (per the most recent census). This was followed by the Immigration Act of 1924, which lowered the 1921 quota to 2%, further restricted immigrants from southern and eastern Europe, and prohibited the immigration of people from East Asia and India. The War Brides Act of 1945 facilitated admission of the spouses and families of returning American soldiers. The Displaced Persons Act of 1948 and the Refugee Relief Act of 1953 allowed many refugees, displaced by the war and unable to enter the United States under regular immigration procedures, to be admitted. With the onset of the Cold War, the Hungarian Refugee Act of 1956, the Refugee-Escapee Act of 1957, and the Cuban Adjustment Program of the 1960s did much the same, offering a new home to the "huddled masses" who sought freedom, opportunity, and escape from tyranny.

In 1965, the Immigration and Nationality Act (INA) Amendments removed any quotas related to specific nationalities. This legislation served to significantly change the nature of the U.S. population in the years to come, with those of European lineage falling from 60% in 1970 to less than 15% in 2000. During the half century that followed this act, immigration grew and grew, doubling in size each decade. However, the Immigration Reform and Control Act of 1986 expanded the INS's responsibilities, giving it more law enforcement powers. One of the most important provisions in this regard was that it charged the agency with enforcing sanctions against American employers who hired undocumented aliens.

In 1990, the Immigration Act of 1990 increased this rate almost overnight by about 40% by raising the statutory limit from 500,000 per year to 700,000 per year, and by instituting a new "visa lottery program" that helped people from poorer countries to attain citizenship. Annual immigration rates continued to rise over time despite recommendations from presidential commissions that recommended curtailing rates significantly, and in the first years of the 21st century, well over 1 million people per year were granted citizenship. In 2010, the most recent year for which records are available, 1,042,625 people were granted permanent residency.

The emphasis on controlling illegal immigration for reasons of economic and national security and crime control fostered INS's growth in the late 20th century. The INS workforce grew from 8,000 in the 1940s to more than 30,000 in 1998. The one-time force of immigrant inspectors became a corps of officers specializing in inspection, examination, adjudication, legalization, investigation, patrol, and refugee and asylum issues. In 2003, as a direct result of the 9/11 terrorist attacks, the INS was transferred to DHS. Rather than transferring as a distinct unit, the INS divisions were broken into three DHS agencies, namely, the U.S. Citizenship and Immigration Service, U.S. Immigration and Customs Enforcement (ICE), and the U.S. Customs and Border Protection (CBP, 2011a).

Immigration enforcement in the United States is conducted through the following functions, each of which is described in the context of specific DHS components in this chapter:

- Inspections
- Border Patrol
- Investigations
- Detention and Removal

Customs Enforcement

Nations protect their national economic interests through the levying of import taxes, called *duties*, on foreign goods, and by controlling the rate of flow and quantity of specific goods that enter the country. The inspection of goods collection of duties is performed by a customs agency or office, which is a traditional function of government.

The United States initiated customs services soon after declaring independence in 1776, as this was a major factor in the declaration itself, and it was also a way for the new government to generate significant revenue. The first official action relevant to customs was the Tariff Act of July 4, 1789, signed by George Washington, and authorizing the collection of duties on imported goods. Only 4 weeks later, Congress established the Customs Service and its POE. Established were 59 collection districts, which were also POE, and 116 ports of delivery. The legislation provided for Presidential appointment of 59 collectors, 10 naval officers and 33 surveyors. The organization fell under the direct authority of the Secretary of the Treasury.

For 125 years, it was this customs function that generated almost all of the government's revenue, and contributed to the fast growth of the young nation. By 1835, revenue collected on imported goods was sufficient to fully eliminate the national debt. The Customs Service funded the functions of all Executive Departments, and paid both military and civil employee salaries. As such, the Customs Service became the largest federal agency at that time, and even in 1792, it represented 80% of the staff of the U.S. Treasury Department (500 employees).

The United States remains a major importer of foreign goods, and at present almost 16% of the national budget is supported by income from customs. The U.S. Customs Service ensures that all imports and exports comply with U.S. laws and regulations. The Customs Service collects and protects the revenue, guards against smuggling, and is responsible for the following:

- Assessing and collecting Customs duties, excise taxes, fees, and penalties due on imported merchandise
- Interdicting and seizing contraband, including narcotics and illegal drugs
- Processing persons, baggage, cargo, and mail, and administering certain navigation laws
- Detecting and apprehending persons engaged in fraudulent practices designed to circumvent Customs and related laws
- Protecting American business and labor and intellectual property rights by enforcing U.S. laws intended to prevent illegal trade practices, including provisions related to quotas and the marking of imported merchandise; the Anti-Dumping Act; and, by providing Customs Recordations for copyrights, patents, and trademarks
- Protecting the general welfare and security of the United States by enforcing import and export restrictions and prohibitions, including the export of critical technology used to develop WMD, and money laundering
- Collecting accurate import and export data for compilation of international trade statistics

Border Security, Immigration, and Customs in the Department of Homeland Security

In its initial organization, DHS consolidated the various agencies responsible for the safety, security, and control of the borders under the Directorate of Border and Transportation Security (BTS). These agencies include the ICE agency (previously the INS), the CBP (previously the Customs Service), the USCG, and the U.S. Customs and Immigration Services (USCIS). With the reorganization effort initiated in the latter half of 2005, the Directorate of Border and Transportation Security was replaced with the Directorate of Policy, and its policy functions were transferred to the new directorate. In today's DHS, the agencies mentioned above have direct reporting responsibility to the secretary of Homeland Security.

The increasing urgency for better customs and border protection has forced government agencies to come up with new initiatives that aim to minimize breaches along the borders to minimize the entry of illegal immigrants and substances into the United States while preserving the efficient travel of legal people and goods into the country.

The three functions described in the preceding text of this chapter (pages 205 to 210) are today managed throughout the DHS, but the most direct responsibilities fall within four specific functional elements, namely:

- U.S. Customs and Border Protection
- U.S. Immigration and Customs Enforcement
- U.S. Coast Guard
- U.S. Citizenship and Immigration Services

U.S. Customs and Border Protection

U.S. Customs and Border Protection (CBP) is the only agency responsible for protecting the sovereign borders of the United States at and between the official POE. CBP is considered the front line in protecting the nation against terrorist attacks. The CBP also ensures national economic security by regulating and facilitating the lawful movement of goods and persons across U.S. borders. CBP is one of DHS's largest and most complex components (Figure 6–1).

The Border Patrol

The mission of the Border Patrol is to prevent terrorists and their weapons (including WMD) from entering the United States, while ensuring that the flow of legal immigration and goods is maintained. The Border Patrol is specifically responsible for patrolling nearly 6,000 miles of Mexican and Canadian international land borders and over 2,000 miles of coastal waters surrounding the Florida Peninsula and the island of Puerto Rico.

As described earlier in this chapter (pages 207 to 208), the Border Patrol has grown from a handful of mounted agents in the early 20th century to a dynamic workforce of over 20,000 agents employed today. Border Patrol agents carry out their mission by maintaining surveillance, following up leads, responding to electronic sensor alarms and aircraft sightings, and interpreting and following tracks. Some of the major activities include maintaining traffic checkpoints along highways leading from border areas and conducting city patrol and transportation checks and antismuggling investigations.

In many places, the U.S. border falls in remote locations, oftentimes in uninhabited deserts, canyons, or mountains. As such, the Border Patrol utilizes specialized equipment and methods to accomplish its mission in these conditions. Electronic sensors are placed at strategic locations along the border to detect people or vehicles entering the country illegally. Video monitors and night vision scopes are also used to detect illegal entries. Border Patrol agents patrol the border in vehicles, boats, and afoot. In some areas, the Border Patrol even employs horses, all-terrain motorcycles, bicycles, and snowmobiles. Examples of tactics used by the Border Patrol to carry out its mission include the following:

- Linewatch operations: Linewatch operations are conducted near international boundaries and coastlines in areas of Border Patrol jurisdiction to prevent the illegal entry and smuggling of aliens into the United States, and to intercept those who do enter illegally before they can escape from border areas.
- Signcutting operations: Signcutting is the detection and the interpretation of any disturbances in natural terrain conditions that indicate the presence or passage of people, animals, or vehicles.
- Traffic checks: Traffic checks are conducted on major highways leading away from the border (1) to detect and apprehend illegal aliens attempting to travel farther into the interior of the United States after evading detection at the border and (2) to detect illegal narcotics.
- Transportation checks: Transportation checks are inspections of interior-bound conveyances, which include buses, commercial aircraft, passenger and freight trains, and marine craft.
- Marine patrol: Along the coastal waterways of the United States and Puerto Rico and interior waterways common to the United States and Canada, the Border Patrol conducts border control activities from the decks of marine craft of various sizes. The Border Patrol maintains over 109 vessels, ranging from blue-water craft to inflatable-hull craft, in 16 sectors, in addition to headquarters' special operations components.
- Horse and bike patrol: Horse units patrol remote areas along the international boundary that are inaccessible to standard all-terrain vehicles. Bike patrol aids city patrol and is used over rough terrain to support linewatch.

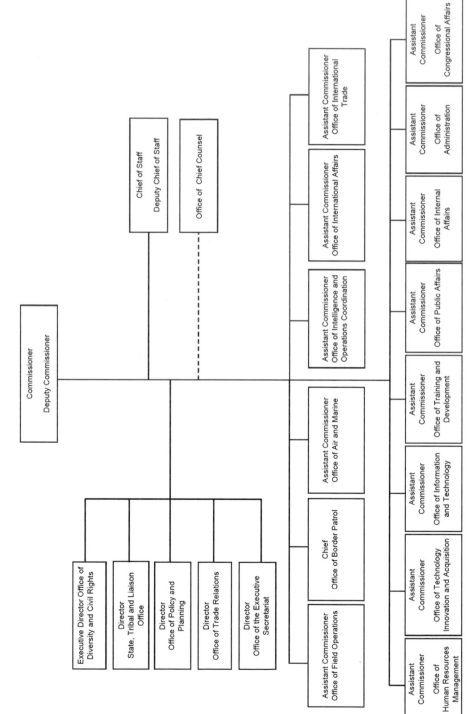

FIGURE 6–1 Customs and Border Protection organizational chart. (Source: CBP, 2011, www.cbp.com)

In FY 2009, Border Patrol agents made over 556,000 arrests of people illegally entering the country. Apprehensions have been on the decline for the past several years as a result of improved enforcement, improved infrastructure, and new technologies.

The once-porous southern border of the country has been shored up considerably in major part because of a number of CBP programs aimed at curbing the ease of movement across the border. These programs include Operation Gatekeeper in San Diego, California, Operation Hold the Line in El Paso, Texas, Operation Rio Grande in McAllen, Texas, Operation Safeguard in Tucson, Arizona, and the Arizona Border Control Initiative (ABCI) along the Arizona border.

An increase in smuggling activities has pushed the Border Patrol to the front line of the U.S. war on drugs. Our role as the primary drug-interdicting organization along the southwest border continues to expand.

The heightened presence of Border Patrol agents along the southwest border has greatly affected narcotics traffickers and alien smugglers. In FY 2009, Border Patrol agents seized more than 10,900 pounds of cocaine and more than 2.6 million pounds of marijuana.

■ ■ Critical Thinking ■

Given the mission of the Border Patrol, do you feel it is appropriately positioned within DHS (as opposed to being an independent agency or under some other federal agency or department)?

CBP Office of Air and Marine

The mission of the CBP Office of Air and Marine (OAM) is to protect people and critical infrastructure through the coordinated use of integrated air and marine forces to detect, interdict, and prevent acts of terrorism and the unlawful movement of people, illegal drugs, and other contraband toward or across U.S. borders. OAM is the world's largest aviation and maritime law enforcement organization, and is a critical part of CBP's enforcement strategy for border security. OAM employs more than 1,200 federal agents and maintains 270 aircraft and 280 marine vessels operating from 80 locations throughout the United States. OAM uses these resources to detect, track, intercept, and apprehend suspected criminals and terrorists at the nation's borders.

During FY 2010, OAM performed the following:

- Conducted approximately 160,000 flight and sea hours
- Contributed to the arrest of 1,975 drug smugglers, the seizure of 831,849 pounds of drugs and $55.3 million in currency, and the apprehension of 62,338 illegal aliens. This included:
  - OAM P-3 aircraft operations accounted for the disruption and seizure of over 148,000 pounds of cocaine, with an estimated street value of $1.8 billion, and intercepted three drug submarines (submersibles).
  - OAM agents interdicted 155 pounds of methamphetamine and 10 pounds of cocaine off the coast of San Diego in August. Valued at more than $3 million, this was the largest methamphetamine seizure at sea by CBP.
- OAM provided significant air security for the State of the Union address in January, the G-20 summit in Pittsburgh in November 2009, and for Super Bowl XLIV in South Florida.
- In support of the response to the Deepwater Horizon oil spill, OAM P-3s flew over 600 hours, providing airspace deconfliction, while the PA-42 aircraft flew close to 800 hours, providing daily aerial mapping services for federal agencies to determine where to place critical assets in the Gulf of Mexico.

OAM operates a number of Predator B unmanned (drone) aircraft in support of law enforcement and homeland security missions at the nation's borders. The CBP drone program focuses operations on helping to identify and intercept potential terrorists and illegal cross-border activity. The system also supports disaster relief efforts of its DHS partners, including the Federal Emergency Management Agency and the USCG. The remotely piloted Predator B allows OAM personnel to safely conduct missions in areas that are difficult to access or otherwise too high risk for manned aircraft or CBP ground personnel.

OAM expects to employ the Predator B throughout the border regions with command and control from a network of ground control stations across the country. The Predator B's capability to provide high-quality streaming video to first responders, and to assess critical infrastructure before and after events, makes it an ideal aircraft to support emergency preparations and recovery operations. The CBP UAS provided emergency support for the 2008 Atlantic hurricane season and the 2009 and 2010 Red River floods in the Midwest (CBP, 2011b; CBP, 2011c).

CBP Office of Technology Innovation and Acquisition (the Secure Border Initiative)

DHS Secretary Michael Chertoff established the Secure Border Initiative (SBI) in 2005 as a comprehensive, multiyear plan to better secure the nation's borders. The SBI program was established within CBP to manage the development, deployment, and integration of SBI acquisition programs, and integrate and coordinate border security programs within CBP.

Today, the SBI mission is to lead the operational requirements support and documentation as well as the acquisition efforts to develop, deploy, and integrate technology and tactical infrastructure in support of CBP's efforts to gain and maintain effective control of U.S. land border areas. Effective control of the border is achieved by knowing what is going on at the border (situational awareness) and having the ability to respond. CBP utilizes a combination of three tools to achieve effective control: personnel, tactical infrastructure, and technology. These include:

- SBInet: SBInet is a program that seeks to deploy modern technology to focus on the areas between the ports of entry on the southwest border. The program's goal is to integrate new and existing border technology into a networked system that will enable CBP personnel to more effectively detect, identify, classify, and respond to border incursions. SBInet is responsible for acquisition, development, and integration of technology solutions to provide:
  - Surveillance and detection tools such as unattended ground sensors, radar, and cameras for comprehensive awareness of the border situation(s) and to give agents the information they need to make deployment and interdiction decisions in their area of responsibility;
  - Command, control, and intelligence tools to help CBP operators manage the large volume of information through a common operating picture (COP), to facilitate tactical decision making, and to coordinate law enforcement responses; and,
  - A communications infrastructure needed to transport sensor information from operational field elements to headquarters.
- SBI Tactical Infrastructure: The Facilities Management and Engineering's Office of Border Patrol (OBP) Program Management Office provides the Border Patrol with long-term planning, construction, and maintenance capabilities — including tactical infrastructure (TI) components such as roads, fencing, lights, electrical components, and drainage structures — to help the Border Patrol achieve its primary homeland security mission. Originally set up under the SBI in 2007, the OBP Program Management Office's most visible construction projects have been, but will not always be, the pedestrian and vehicle fence projects along the southwest border (see Figures 6–2 and 6–3).

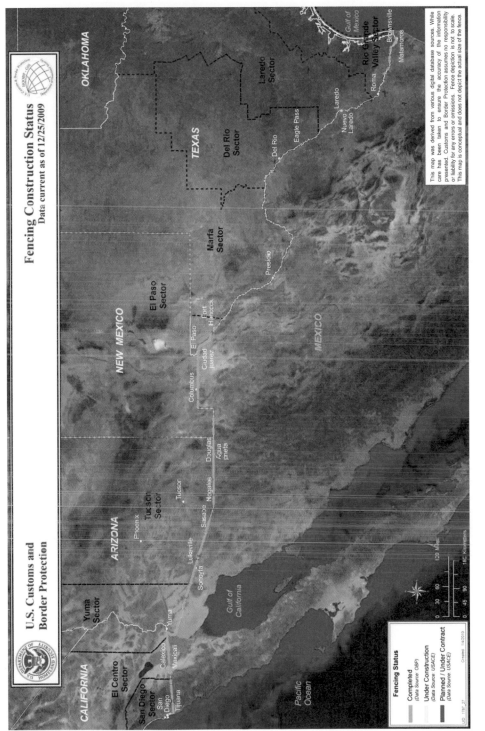

FIGURE 6–2 Southwest border fence. (Source: CBP, 2009)

FIGURE 6–3 Cerrudo services construction workers assemble the southwest border fence in El Paso. (Source: CBP, 2011)

- The Northern Border Project: CBP operations along the northern border are more modest than those on the border with Mexico. However, CPB is deploying integrated technology to meet the needs that exist, including those that address the special vulnerabilities of the northern border maritime (river/lake), cold weather environment. The first phase of this project included the deployment of 16 remote video surveillance systems (RVSS) in the Buffalo and Detroit areas. In addition, three mobile surveillance systems (MSS) were deployed in the Detroit and Swanton areas. In the project's second phase, the NBP will develop and demonstrate an operational integration center that provides opportunities for information sharing and coordination among border security stakeholders.

Secure Freight Initiative

On December 7, 2006, DHS announced the launch of the Secure Freight Initiative (SFI). The purpose of the program is to deploy a network of radiation detection and container imaging equipment to be operated in seaports worldwide for the purpose of preventing terrorists from using nuclear or other radiological materials to attack the global maritime supply chain or using cargo containers to bring the resources for such an attack to the United States.

SFI uses modern imagery and scanning systems to inspect maritime container cargo. Containers arriving at participating seaports overseas are scanned with both nonintrusive radiographic imaging and passive radiation detection equipment placed at terminal arrival gates. Optical scanning technology is used to identify containers and classify them by destination. Relay cargoes (containers being moved from one ship to another) are also inspected with such technology. Sensor and image data gathered in the U.S. ports are encrypted and transmitted near real-time to the CBP National Targeting Center for final assessment and risk classification. If the scanning data indicate concerns, the specific container will be inspected further, based on appropriate response protocols established with the host government authorities. Participating host governments would have immediate access to all scanning data collected, including any scans conducted on non-U.S.-bound containers. If there is a cause for concern, DHS can request the host government to open and inspect U.S.-bound container contents or instruct carriers under existing regulations to refuse to load the container until the risk is fully resolved.

The program's long-term vision is to create a globally networked array of detection equipment that will be configured to enable real-time streaming of container images and radiological detection data to other countries engaged in maritime trade. This government-to-government data sharing will support stronger and more internationally harmonized risk reduction for global freight movement. The overall SFI has two core elements, the first of which has been described above. In addition, DHS is actively preparing a complementary SFI: a next-generation risk-scoring capability to fuse certain existing, but not currently collected, data associated with a container's movement. Taken as a whole, the two-pronged SFI will significantly strengthen maritime security and global nonproliferation efforts (DHS, 2006).

Container Security Initiative

The Container Security Initiative (CSI) was created by the U.S. Customs Service soon after the 9/11 attacks. It was recognized at that time that, like the use of airlines as weapons in 2001, containers could be used by terrorists to easily deliver a WMD device. CSI was created to address the threat to border security and global trade posed by this potential terrorist methodology.

CSI proposes a security regime to ensure all containers that pose a potential risk for terrorism are identified and inspected at foreign ports before they are placed on vessels destined for the United States. CBP has stationed multidisciplinary teams of U.S. officers from both CBP and ICE to work together with the host foreign government counterparts. Their mission is to target and prescreen containers and to develop additional investigative leads related to the terrorist threat to cargo destined to the United States.

The three core elements of CSI are:

- Identify high-risk containers. CBP uses automated targeting tools to identify containers that pose a potential risk for terrorism, based on advance information and strategic intelligence.
- Prescreen and evaluate containers before they are shipped. Containers are screened as early in the supply chain as possible, generally at the port of departure.
- Use technology to prescreen high-risk containers to ensure that screening can be done rapidly without slowing down the movement of trade. This technology includes large-scale X-ray and gamma ray machines and radiation detection devices.

Through CSI, CBP officers work with host customs administrations to establish security criteria for identifying high-risk containers. Those administrations use nonintrusive inspection and radiation detection technology to screen high-risk containers before they are shipped to U.S. ports. CSI offers its participant countries the opportunity to send their customs officers to major U.S. ports to target ocean-going containerized cargo to be exported to their countries. Likewise, CBP shares information on a bilateral basis with its CSI partners. Japan and Canada currently station their customs personnel in some U.S. ports as part of the CSI program.

CSI is now operational at ports in North America, Europe, Asia, Africa, the Middle East, and Latin and Central America. These include the following (* indicates SFI port):

The Americas
- Montreal, Vancouver, and Halifax, Canada
- Santos, Brazil
- Buenos Aires, Argentina
- Puerto Cortes,* Honduras
- Caucedo, Dominican Republic
- Kingston, Jamaica
- Freeport, The Bahamas
- Balboa, Colon, and Manzanillo, Panama
- Cartagena, Colombia

Europe
- Rotterdam, The Netherlands
- Bremerhaven and Hamburg, Germany
- Antwerp and Zeebrugge, Belgium
- Le Havre and Marseille, France
- Gothenburg, Sweden
- La Spezia, Genoa, Naples, Gioia Tauro, and Livorno, Italy
- Felixstowe, Liverpool, Thamesport, Tilbury, and Southampton, United Kingdom
- Piraeus, Greece
- Algeciras, Barcelona, and Valencia, Spain
- Lisbon, Portugal

Asia and the Middle East
- Singapore*
- Yokohama, Tokyo, Nagoya, and Kobe, Japan
- Hong Kong
- Busan* (Pusan), South Korea
- Port Klang and Tanjung Pelepas, Malaysia
- Laem Chabang, Thailand
- Dubai, United Arab Emirates (UAE)
- Shenzhen and Shanghai
- Kaohsiung and Chi-Lung
- Colombo, Sri Lanka
- Port Salalah,* Oman
- Port Qasim, Pakistan
- Ashdod, Israel
- Haifa, Israel

Africa
- Alexandria, Egypt
- Durban, South Africa

The CBP's 58 operational CSI ports now make approximately 86% of all maritime containerized cargo imported into the United States subject to prescreening prior to importation. CSI continues to expand to strategic locations around the world. The World Customs Organization (WCO), the European Union (EU), and the G8 support CSI expansion and have adopted resolutions implementing CSI security measures introduced at ports throughout the world (CBP, 2008).

Agricultural Inspection

CBP agents work in collaboration with inspection agents from the U.S. Department of Agriculture to prevent the introduction of harmful pests into the United States. CBP agricultural specialists have extensive training and experience in agricultural and biological inspection, and are also able to recognize and prevent the entry of organisms that could be used for biological warfare or terrorism.

CBP employs more than 2,000 agriculture specialists who intercept thousands of shipments of prohibited meat, plant materials, or animal products each day at POE. CBP continues to work in close consultation with USDA, both in training the inspection force and in setting regulations and policies for which plants, animals, and other commodities may legally enter the country.

CBP agriculture specialists use detector dogs to sniff out hidden prohibited agricultural items. CBP agriculture specialists and canine teams work at key U.S. POE, including international airports, land borders, and international mail facilities, inspecting both commercial cargo and passengers/pedestrians.

All agricultural items are subject to inspection.

CBP Immigration Inspection Program

Travelers and other individuals seeking to enter the United States must pass through an immigration inspection station at all U.S. POE, including international airports. CBP officers inspect their documents and determine their admissibility. The inspection process includes all work performed in connection with the entry of aliens and U.S. citizens into the United States, including pre-inspection performed by the immigration inspectors outside the United States. The visa process, wherein permission is granted to travel to a U.S. port for entry examination, is conducted by the U.S. Department of State at overseas missions (embassies and consulates). However, it is the DHS that maintains the final say on whether or not the person is able to enter. The CBP officer is responsible for determining the nationality and identity of each person who presents, and must prevent the entry of ineligible aliens, including criminals, terrorists, and drug traffickers, among others. CBP agents will automatically admit U.S. citizens upon verification of citizenship.

Under the authority granted by the INA, as amended, a CBP officer may question, under oath, any person coming into the United States to determine his or her admissibility. In addition, an inspector has authority to search without warrant the person and effects of any person seeking admission, when there is a reason to believe that grounds of exclusion exist, which would be disclosed by such search. The INA is based on the law of presumption: An applicant for admission is presumed to be an alien until he or she shows evidence of citizenship; an alien is presumed to be an immigrant until he or she proves that he or she fits into one of the nonimmigrant classifications.

The mission of the inspections program is to control and guard the boundaries and borders of the United States against the illegal entry of aliens in a way that (CBP, 2011b):

- Functions as the initial component of a comprehensive, immigration enforcement system;
- Prevents the entry of terrorists, drug traffickers, criminals, and other persons who may subvert the national interest;
- Deters illegal immigration through the detection of fraudulent documents and entry schemes;
- Initiates prosecutions against individuals who attempt or aid and abet illegal entry;
- Cooperates with international, federal, state, and local law enforcement agencies to achieve mutual objectives;
- Contributes to the development and implementation of foreign policy related to the entry of persons;
- Facilitates the entry of persons engaged in commerce, tourism, and/or other lawful pursuits;
- Respects the rights and dignity of individuals;
- Examines individuals and their related documents in a professional manner;
- Assists the transportation industry to meet its requirements;
- Responds to private sector interests, in conformance with immigration law;
- Continues to employ innovative methods to improve the efficiency and cost-effectiveness of the inspections process.

CBP maintains a number of "trusted-traveler" programs that allow preapproved, low-risk travelers to expedite their immigration inspection through the use of dedicated lines and kiosks. These include:

- Global Entry (Worldwide) (http://www.globalentry.gov/)
- FAST Driver Cards (between the United States and Canada, and the United States and Mexico) (http://www.cbp.gov/xp/cgov/trade/cargo_security/ctpat/fast/fast_driver/)
- NEXUS (between the United States and Canada) (http://www.cbp.gov/xp/cgov/travel/trusted_traveler/nexus_prog/)
- SENTRI (between the United States and Mexico) (http://www.cbp.gov/xp/cgov/travel/trusted_traveler/sentri/)

CBP FY 2010 YEAR IN REVIEW

Securing America's Borders: CBP Fiscal Year 2010 in Review Fact Sheet

During fiscal year 2010, U.S. Customs and Border Protection made significant progress in securing the border and facilitating legitimate trade and travel — achieving success through targeted operations, enhanced partnerships, and an unprecedented focus on staffing and technology deployment along our borders.

Highlights
- Over the past two years, DHS has dedicated unprecedented manpower, technology and infrastructure to the Southwest border. The Border Patrol is better staffed now than at any time in its 86-year history having doubled the number of agents from 10,000 in FY 2004 to more than

20,500 in FY 2010. In addition to the Border Patrol, CBP's workforce of more than 58,000 employees also includes more than 2,300 agriculture specialists and 20,600 CBP officers at ports of entry.

- Congress provided additional resources in the Emergency Supplemental for Border Security — passed and signed into law in August 2010 — that includes the addition of 1,000 Border Patrol agents, 250 CBP officers, two additional Unmanned Aircraft Systems (UAS), and two new Forward Operating Bases.
- Nationwide Border Patrol apprehensions of illegal aliens decreased from nearly 724,000 in FY 2008 to approximately 463,000 in FY 2010, a 36 percent reduction, indicating that fewer people are attempting to illegally cross the border.
- CBP seized 4.1 million pounds of narcotics, including 870,000 pounds seized at ports of entry, 2.4 million pounds seized in between ports of entry, and 831,000 pounds seized by Air and Marine.
- DHS currently has thousands of technology assets deployed along the southwest border — including mobile surveillance units, thermal imaging systems, and large- and small-scale non-intrusive inspection equipment, as well as 130 aircraft and three Unmanned Aircraft Systems.
- In FY10, CBP deployed 17 new Mobile Non-Intrusive Inspection Systems and 22 additional large-scale Non-Intrusive Inspection (NII) technology imaging systems. The mobile x-ray screening systems allow officers and agents to detect stowaways and materials such as explosives, narcotics and currency in passenger vehicles and cargo. The large-scale systems were used to conduct over 7.3 million examinations at ports of entry that resulted in over 1,300 seizures, including 288,000 pounds of narcotics.
- CBP expanded Unmanned Aircraft Systems (UAS) operations to include a launch and recovery site in Corpus Christi, Texas. This new site allows the UAS program to fly along the entire Southwest border for the first time ever — from the El Centro Sector in California to the Gulf of Mexico in Texas.
- Border Patrol continued to implement the Border Safety Initiative (BSI) to make the border safer for agents, border residents, and legal trade and travel by supporting domestic and foreign media campaigns in countries including Mexico, Guatemala, El Salvador and the Dominican Republic that raise awareness and warn against the dangers of illegally entering the United States through harsh terrain and dangerous environmental conditions.
- CBP officers from the National Targeting Center worked with CBP officers at John F. Kennedy International Airport (JFK) to apprehend Faisal Shahzad, who attempted to detonate a truck bomb in Times Square, as he was attempting to flee the United States on a flight to Dubai.
- CBP officers at Atlanta's Hartfield-Jackson Airport apprehended a suspected Michigan serial killer, Elias Abuelazam, as he was attempting to flee the United States. Abuelazam was suspected in a string of 18 stabbings across Ohio, Michigan and Virginia that left five dead.
- CBP seized $147 million dollars in currency (inbound and outbound) at and between U.S. ports of entry — a more than 30 percent increase from last fiscal year.
- CBP officers at ports of entry apprehended more than 8,400 people wanted for a variety of charges, to include serious criminal crimes such as murder, rape, and child molestation.
- Through our Operation Detour program, CBP has proactively reached out to border communities to help raise awareness among school-age children, parents and faculty about the dangers of smuggling. Results of this ongoing campaign include hosting more than 880 events reaching more than 115,000 students in Texas, Arizona, and California.

(Continued)

CBP FY 2010 YEAR IN REVIEW (CONTINUED)

- CBP Field Operations established emergency operations to expedite the processing of U.S. and Haitian citizens after the earthquake, including deploying 23 CBP officers to Haiti to conduct pre-departure activities for evacuees. CBP, in coordination with ICE and the Department of State, worked with Haitian authorities and other federal agencies to ensure that individuals boarding aircraft destined to the United States had proper documentation and were eligible to depart Haiti on U.S. bound flights.

Organizational Development
- The CBP workforce grew more diverse throughout FY10, with an increase of 7.3 percent in the minority make-up of the CBP workforce compared to FY09. Additionally, nearly one in three CBP employees currently identify as Hispanic American — 35.8 percent of CBP's total workforce.
- CBP graduated 117 CBP officers, 1,215 Border Patrol agents, 48 agriculture specialists, 88 import specialists, 112 Air and Marine agents, 31 entry specialists, 25 regulatory auditors (A), and 37 regulatory auditors (B) from training.
- In FY10, CBP developed and implemented a new National Recruitment Strategy that included recruitment at 133 minority-serving institution events and 403 minority/special-emphasis events. CBP also participated in more than 160 recruitment events directed to veterans and persons with disabilities.
- CBP helped Wounded Warriors connect with hiring officials for fast-track placement within CBP to continue supporting veterans searching for employment with the federal government.
- CBP converted 29 training courses from in-classroom to online, bringing CBP's total FY 2010 savings through online training to more than $318 million.
- CBP has deployed more than 1,500 canine teams throughout the nation, including more than 300 new teams, for human/narcotic detection, search and rescue, agriculture detection, and currency/firearms detection. The Canine Program also increased training partnerships with other agencies, including with the Government of Mexico.

Ports of Entry
- CBP officers at more than 330 ports of entry inspected 352 million travelers and more than 105.8 million cars, trucks, buses, trains, vessels and aircraft.
- More than 100,000 travelers have enrolled in CBP's Global Entry Program — a trusted traveler program designed to expedite screening for low-risk international travelers through biometric identification and rigorous background checks.
- Additionally, more than 800,000 individuals have enrolled in other CBP trusted traveler programs including NEXUS, SENTRI and FAST.
- CBP completed more than 3,200 validations of members of Customs-Trade Partnership Against Terrorism (C-TPAT), a voluntary government-business initiative to strengthen and improve overall international supply chain and U.S. border security. Security conferences held by CBP in California and New York provided information on best practices — including a 5-Step Risk Assessment Guide — to more than 1,500 members to help better secure shipments. CBP conducted a third round of Joint Validations with China Customs which laid the foundation for the signing of a Supply Chain Security Memorandum of Understanding in October.

- CBP deployed 77 new radiation portal monitors (RPMs) in FY10 for a total of 1,428 deployed to land and seaports of entry nationwide. RPMs allow CBP the capability to scan 96 percent of all mail and express consignment mail/parcels; 100 percent of all containerized cargo entering from Canada and Mexico; 100 percent of the personally owned vehicles entering from Canada and Mexico; and 99 percent of all arriving sea-borne containerized cargo for illicit radiological/nuclear materials.
- CBP eliminated the paper arrival/departure I-94W form for travelers from Visa Waiver Program nations. Through the Electronic System for Travel Authorization, DHS receives basic biographical, travel and eligibility information of travelers prior to their departure to the U.S., expediting customs processing while protecting passenger privacy and strengthening global aviation.
- CBP began enforcement of the Importer Security Filing and Additional Carrier Requirements interim final rule (commonly known as "10 + 2" in reference to the data required under the rule)—significantly increasing the scope and accuracy of information gathered on shipments of cargo arriving by sea into the United States and bolstering DHS's layered enforcement strategy to protect against terrorism and other crimes at U.S. ports of entry.

Agriculture Programs and Trade Liaison
- CBP Agriculture Specialists seized more than 1.7 million prohibited plant materials, meat, and animal byproducts in FY 2010, a 9.5 percent increase in seizures compared to FY 2009.
- A CBP agriculture liaison position was established in California to serve as a liaison between CBP, the USDA Animal and Plant Health Inspection Service, and the state-level departments of agriculture to enhance communication and establish interagency partnerships. In fiscal year 2011, additional CBP agriculture liaison positions will be established in key agriculture states, including Florida.
- CBP created and implemented the Agriculture Enforcement Alerts program — an information sharing initiative for state and federal agriculture officials to evaluate trends of plant or animal pests and diseases and identify potential risks to U.S. agriculture.
- CBP, in collaboration with scientists from the USDA, developed an agricultural risk-based passenger flight targeting initiative to detect agricultural pests and contraband. National targeting criteria were developed to select and process passengers on flights with a high probability of having prohibited agriculture items that pose a threat to America's agriculture.
- CBP and the USDA enhanced work with state-level departments of agriculture by refocusing and reinvigorating the joint pest risk committees: expanding discussions on plant pest and foreign animal disease risk mitigation efforts; identifying and reviewing seasonal trends and other real-time data; and conducting special operations.

Office of International Trade
- CBP continued to work closely with our international partners to strengthen the security of the global supply chain.
- CBP initiated nearly 3,700 import safety seizures during FY 2010, an increase of 34 percent over FY 2009; and nearly 20,000 seizures for intellectual property rights (IPR) violations, an increase of 34 percent over FY 2009.
- CBP processed $1.99 trillion in import value and collected $32.3 billion in duties, taxes, and fees — increases of 15.8 percent and 9.5 percent, respectively, compared to FY 2009.

(*Continued*)

CBP FY 2010 YEAR IN REVIEW (CONTINUED)

- CBP responded to 1,600 reported trade violations received through e-Allegations — a web-based system that facilitates public reporting of alleged trade violations — a 60 percent increase over FY 2009.
- CBP made a number of enhancements to the Automated Commercial Environment (ACE) — a commercial trade processing system that facilitates legitimate trade and strengthens border security by modernizing CBP business processes and supporting information technology — allowing for all entries in the system to be assessed for risk and antidumping and countervailing duties and provides enhanced integration with the Commerce Department.
- CBP completed 379 audits of importers and related parties, resulting in the collection of nearly $23 million in revenue.
- CBP established the multi-agency Import Safety Commercial Targeting and Analysis Center in Washington, D.C. For the first time, personnel from ICE, the Food and Drug Administration, the Consumer Product Safety Commission (CPSC), and the Department of Agriculture are working side-by-side to share information that better enables CBP to target and stop unsafe imports before they enter U.S. commerce. In conjunction with the CPSC, CBP also developed an automated system for standardized research and targeting for import safety product recalls.
- CBP's National Targeting and Analysis Groups carried out national operations to enforce trade laws, resulting in the recovery of more than $40 million in lost revenue.
- CBP eliminated its Freedom of Information Act (FOIA) appeals backlog, closing 815 appeals — tripling FY 2009 closures and more than quadrupling FY08 closures.

International Affairs
- CBP's Office of International Affairs led 464 capacity-building sessions for foreign partners, including 23 courses at the International Law Enforcement Academy, as well as CBP border security, customs training, and technical assistance sessions in 91 countries.

Air and Marine Operations
- CBP's Office of Air and Marine contributed to the seizure of more than 800,000 pounds of narcotics and seized nearly $55.3 million in currency. This included the seizure of 155 pounds of methamphetamine and ten pounds of cocaine off the coast of San Diego in August. Valued at more than $3 million, this was the largest meth seizure at sea by CBP.
- In support of essential mission requirements, Air and Marine acquired four "M" model UH-60 Black Hawk helicopters that are capable of reliably operating in a broad spectrum of law enforcement operations and converted three Vietnam-era UH-1 Huey I helicopters to the Huey II model to increase mission capability.
- CBP accepted the first re-winged P-3 Orion Aircraft as part of its Service Life Extension Program (SLEP). The SLEP is replacing the wings of the old airframes to add 15–20 additional years to the life of the aircraft, which will result in significant savings from the more than $3 billion it would cost to replace the fleet of aircraft.
- CBP's P-3s provided critical aerial mapping services during the BP Deepwater Horizon oil spill — allowing federal agencies to determine where to place critical assets in the Gulf of Mexico.
- CBP acquired the maritime variant of the Predator-B. The Guardian, which is based in Cocoa Beach, FL, is equipped with structural, avionics and communications enhancements in addition to a Marine Search Radar and an Electro-optical/Infrared Sensor that is optimized for maritime operations, making it the only one of its kind in the world.

- CBP Air and Marine provided significant air security for the State of the Union address in January, the G-20 summit in Pittsburgh, and for Super Bowl XLIV in South Florida.

Laboratories and Scientific Services
- CBP processed 3,035 forensics cases, including 2,372 for controlled substances, 361 for fingerprint lifts and examinations, 133 for digital data examinations, and 250 audio/video duplications, enhancements, and recoveries.
- CBP used scientific and technological tools to screen nearly 7,000 conveyances going to and from Vancouver, B.C. during the 2010 Winter Olympics.
- CBP's Laboratories and Scientific Services (LSS) provided scientific support in a number of critical trade areas, including 977 shipments of products involved in anti-dumping cases, 484 cases involving IPR enforcement, and other critical trade areas including honey, citric acid, and seafood transshipments as well as counterfeit pharmaceutical importations.
- LSS evaluated 1,776 cases involving the possible importation of products with serious safety issues including antibiotics in honey, flammability of children's wear, cadmium in children's jewelry, and the importation of mislabeled food products.

Source: DHS, 2011.

U.S. Immigration and Customs Enforcement

Immigration and Customs Enforcement (ICE) is the principal investigative arm of DHS and the second largest investigative agency in the federal government. Created in 2003 through a merger of the investigative and interior enforcement elements of the U.S. Customs Service and the INS, ICE now has more than 20,000 employees in offices in all 50 states and 48 foreign countries.

The primary mission of ICE is to promote homeland security and public safety through the criminal and civil enforcement of federal laws governing border control, customs, trade, and immigration. The agency has an annual budget of more than $5.7 billion, primarily devoted to its two principal operating components — Homeland Security Investigations (HSI) and Enforcement and Removal Operations (ERO). Traditionally, the primary mission of the customs enforcement component of ICE was to combat various forms of smuggling. Over time, however, this mission has been expanded to other violations of law involving terrorist financing, money laundering, arms trafficking (including WMD), technology exports, commercial fraud, and child pornography, to name a few.

In total, ICE enforces more than 400 different laws and regulations, including those of 40 other agencies. Within ICE, there are several distinct offices that carry out separate tasks related to the general agency mission. Many of these programs and offices are described below.

ICE Enforcement and Removal Operations

ERO is charged with the enforcement of U.S. immigration laws. It identifies and apprehends removable aliens (see sidebar titled "Definitions of Immigration Enforcement Terms"), detains them if necessary, and removes (deports) them from the country. ERO prioritizes the apprehension, arrest, and removal of convicted criminals who pose a threat to national security, fugitives, and recent illegal border crossers.

ERO staff transport removable aliens from point to point, manage aliens in custody or in an "alternative to detention" program, provide access to legal resources and representatives of advocacy groups, and remove individuals from the United States who have been ordered to be deported. ERO manages six

Service Processing Centers, oversees seven contract detention facilities, and houses aliens in over 240 facilities under intergovernmental service agreements. ERO's mission is broad and requires a diverse workforce made up of law enforcement officers, medical professionals, administrative specialists, and many others to ensure the success of the mission.

The following occur on an average day (relative to ERO operations):

- ERO houses an average of 29,343 illegal aliens.
- ERO personnel manage over 1.64 million aliens in the various stages of immigration removal proceedings.
- ERO processes 1,051 aliens into detention centers. The intake process includes an initial health care screening that is completed within 12 hours of arrival at the facility. This is followed by a comprehensive health assessment that includes a physical examination and the completion of a detailed medical history within 14 days of arrival.
- ERO health care professionals conduct approximately 677 intake health care screenings in facilities staffed by ERO health care providers.
- ERO facilitates 295 physical examinations and 80 dental examinations.
- Health care professionals conduct 303 chronic disease interventions and 144 mental health interventions.
- Facility clinics receive 401 detainees during sick call and fill 848 prescriptions at facilities staffed by ERO health care providers.
- Health care personnel see 37 detainees for urgent care, and there are 33 emergency room or off-site referrals.
- Detainees make 29,311 phone calls.
- ERO employees identify and process 638 criminal aliens in ICE custody for removal.
- ERO personnel monitor 16,346 aliens enrolled in Alternatives to Detention programs, such as Enhanced Supervision Reporting, Electronic Monitoring, or the Intensive Supervision Appearance Program.
- ERO employees procure 352 travel documents.
- ERO employees process 118 bonds.
- ERO removes 1,062 aliens from the United States to countries around the globe, including 651 criminal aliens.
- ERO processes and removes 291 cases as a result of reinstated final orders.
- Forty-two aliens are removed via commercial airlines and 675 aliens are removed via government aircraft.
- Seventeen children are placed with the Office of Refugee Resettlement in the Department of Health and Human Services.
- ERO officers arrest 96 fugitive and nonfugitive aliens, many of whom have been convicted for a multitude of crimes, and eliminate these individuals from the ICE fugitive population.
- ERO works with U.S. Attorneys offices, who accepts 26 cases for criminal prosecution.

The On-Site Detention Compliance Oversight Program was established within ERO to enhance oversight and care of detainees in the ICE custody as part of the agency's commitment to immigration detention reform. The ERO Detention Monitoring Unit conducts compliance monitoring on a continuous or periodic basis. The unit is composed of Detention Service Managers (DSMs) who are embedded in ICE detention facilities, allowing them to assess potential problems and address these problems with the facility and respective field offices before they occur, or to ensure corrective action in a timely manner.

▣ ▣ Critical Thinking ▣

How is the management of lawful immigration efforts related to the security of the nation? How could people harm the country or its citizens by misusing the lawful immigration mechanisms?

▣ ▣ ▣ ▬▬▬▬▬▬▬▬▬▬▬▬▬▬▬▬▬▬▬▬▬▬▬▬▬▬▬▬▬▬▬▬▬▬▬▬▬

Definitions of Immigration Enforcement Terms

- Administrative Removal: The removal of an alien not admitted for permanent residence or an alien admitted for permanent residence on a conditional basis, under a DHS order based on the determination that the individual has been convicted of an aggravated felony. The alien may be removed without a hearing before an immigration court.
- Deportable Alien: An alien who has been admitted into the United States but who is subject to removal under INA § 237.
- Detention: The seizure and incarceration of an alien in order to hold him/her while awaiting judicial or legal proceedings or return transportation to his/her country of citizenship.
- Expedited Removal: The removal of an alien who is inadmissible because the individual does not possess valid entry documents or attempted to enter the United States by fraud or misrepresentation of material fact. The alien may be removed without a hearing before an immigration court.
- Inadmissible Alien: An alien seeking admission into the United States who is ineligible to be admitted according to the provisions of INA § 212.
- Reinstatement of Final Removal Orders: The removal of an alien based on the reinstatement of a prior removal order, where the alien departed the United States under an order of removal and illegally reentered the United States. The alien may be removed without a hearing before an immigration court.
- Removal: The compulsory and confirmed movement of an inadmissible or deportable alien out of the United States based on an order of removal. An alien who is removed has administrative or criminal consequences placed on subsequent reentry owing to the fact of the removal.
- Return: The confirmed movement of an inadmissible or deportable alien out of the United States not based on an order of removal.

Source: Office of Immigration Statistics, 2011. Immigration Enforcement Actions, 2011, Department of Homeland Security Policy Office, http://www.dhs.gov/xlibrary/assets/statistics/publications/enforcement-ar-2010.pdf.

▬▬▬▬▬▬▬▬▬▬▬▬▬▬▬▬▬▬▬▬▬▬▬▬▬▬▬▬▬▬▬▬▬▬▬▬   ▣ ▣ ▣

Secure Communities Program

ICE policy ensures that the removal of criminal aliens, namely, those who pose a threat to public safety, and repeat immigration violators are given priority attention. The Secure Communities program helps the agency to carry out this priority goal. Secure Communities uses an already existing federal information-sharing partnership between ICE and the Federal Bureau of Investigation (FBI) that helps to identify criminal aliens without imposing new or additional requirements on state and local law enforcement. Through

Secure Communities, the FBI sends the fingerprints of arrested individuals that are collected by local jurisdictions (who for decades have shared these with the FBI for cross-checking purposes) to ICE to check against its immigration databases. If these checks reveal that an individual is unlawfully present in the United States or otherwise removable due to a criminal conviction, ICE takes enforcement action. Such people are prioritized for removal, thereby minimizing the threat to public safety caused by illegal aliens.

DHS has expanded Secure Communities from 14 jurisdictions in 2008 to more than 1,300 today, including all jurisdictions along the southwest border where risk is highest. DHS is on track to expand this program to all law enforcement jurisdictions nationwide by 2013. Through April 30, 2011, more than 77,000 immigrants convicted of crimes, including more than 28,000 convicted of aggravated felony (level 1) offenses like murder, rape, and the sexual abuse of children, were removed from the United States after identification through the program. These removals significantly contributed to a 71% increase in the overall percentage of convicted criminals removed by ICE, with 81,000 more criminal removals in FY 2010 than in FY 2008. As a result of the increased focus on criminals, this period also included a 23% reduction or 57,000 fewer noncriminal removals.

Secure Communities is important because ICE only receives enough funding to remove a portion of the more than 10 million individuals estimated to be in the United States illegally or who are removable because of criminal convictions. This program ensures that security is improved, given the nature of how deportation is focused.

ICE Homeland Security Investigations

The ICE Homeland Security Investigations (HSI) Directorate is a critical asset in the ICE mission, responsible for investigating a wide range of domestic and international activities arising from the illegal movement of people and goods into, within, and out of the United States. HSI investigates immigration crime; human rights violations and human smuggling; smuggling of narcotics, weapons, and other types of contraband; financial crimes; cybercrime; and export enforcement issues. ICE special agents conduct investigations aimed at protecting critical infrastructure industries that are vulnerable to sabotage, attack, or exploitation.

In addition to ICE criminal investigations, HSI oversees the agency's international affairs operations and intelligence functions. HSI consists of more than 10,000 employees, consisting of 6,700 special agents, who are assigned to more than 200 cities throughout the United States and 46 countries around the world.

HSI is made up of six key divisions, which include:

- Domestic Operations
- Intelligence
- International Affairs
- Investigative Programs
- Mission Support
- National Intellectual Property Rights (IPR) Coordination Center

ICE Project Shield America

Project Shield America is an ICE program aimed at preventing WMD trafficking by illegal exporters, targeted foreign countries, terrorist groups, and international criminal organizations. This program also works to stop organized criminal and state-sponsored efforts from obtaining and illegally exporting licensable commodities, technologies, conventional munitions and firearms; exporting stolen property; and engaging in financial transactions that support these activities or violate U.S. sanctions and embargoes.

The U.S. government protects both the economic and national security interests of the country in this regard. Foreign adversaries regularly attempt to acquire and steal technologies developed in the United States by both legal and illegal means. Those who succeed in acquiring such technologies often do so without having to expend the great amounts of resources required by the innovative U.S. company or governmental or nongovernmental agency. Moreover, such technologies can be used against the country to jeopardize national security and/or the U.S. economy.

Examples of strategic technology sought by certain proscribed countries include:

- Modern manufacturing technology for the production of microelectronics, computers, digital electronic components, and signal processing systems.
- Technology necessary for the development of aircraft, missile, and other tactical weapon delivery systems.
- All types of advanced signal and weapons detection, tracking, and monitoring systems.
- Technology and equipment used in the construction of nuclear weapons and materials.
- Biological, chemical warfare agents and precursors, and associated manufacturing equipment.

Project Shield America was designed and implemented to work in concert with the three-pronged effort of its Export Enforcement Program, namely:

- *Inspection/Interdiction* — Specially trained U.S. CBP inspectors stationed at high-threat ports selectively inspect suspect export shipments.
- *Investigations* — ICE agents deployed throughout the country initiate and pursue high-quality cases that result in the arrest, prosecution, and conviction of offenders of the Export Administration Act, Arms Export Control Act, Trading with the Enemy Act, International Emergency Economics Powers Act, and other related statutes. ICE investigations aim to detect and disrupt illegal exports before they can cause damage to the national security interests of the United States.
- *International Cooperation* — ICE international attaché offices enlist the support of their host governments to initiate new investigative leads and to develop information in support of ongoing domestic investigations.

The Joint Terrorism Task Force

The National Security Investigation Division's (NSID) National Security Unit (NSU) oversees ICE participation on the Joint Terrorism Task Force (JTTF). The JTTF investigates, detects, interdicts, prosecutes, and removes terrorists and dismantles terrorist organizations. ICE is involved in almost every foreign terrorism investigation related to cross-border crime. ICE is the largest federal contributor to the JTTF through active participation in each of the 104 local JTTFs nationwide. The agency also plays a critical leadership role on the national JTTF. Examples of ICE participation in the JTTF include:

- ICE JTTF agents in Philadelphia led an undercover weapons smuggling investigation resulting in the arrests of 31 subjects, most notably a reputed procurement officer for an overseas terrorist organization.
- ICE JTTF special agents arrested and indicted multiple targets involved in an organized import/export scheme with an OFAC-designated Hezbollah front-company in South America's Tri-Border area, resulting in guilty pleas to export smuggling and conspiracy.

- An ICE JTTF special agent led the investigation, arrest, conviction, and ultimate removal from the United States of the Brooklyn imam accused of tipping off Najibullah Zazi and his coconspirators days prior to the attempted attack against the New York subway system in September 2009. ICE agents in Denver developed immigration fraud charges against Amanullah Zazi, a family member of Najibullah Zazi, and placed him into removal proceedings in November 2009. Amanullah Zazi later pleaded guilty to conspiracy to obstruct justice and abetting others to receive military training from a foreign terrorist organization.

- More than 30 ICE special agents were the first criminal investigators to respond to the attempted Christmas Day attack of Northwest flight #253. They rapidly disseminated lead information to other ICE and JTTF special agents throughout the country.

- ICE JTTF special agents were influential in identifying the would-be Times Square bomber in May 2010 and utilized unique immigration authorities to arrest an alleged hawaladar who allegedly provided funds to execute the attack.

- An ICE JTTF special agent authored the criminal complaint against Brahim Lajqi, a citizen of Kosovo who intended to engage in acts of terrorism targeting four major U.S. cities. Lajqi ultimately pleaded guilty to fraud/misuse of visas.

Border Enforcement Security Task Force

In response to the dramatic increase in cross-border crime and violence in recent years (due in part to feuds between Mexican drug cartels and criminal smuggling organizations), ICE partnered with federal, state, local, and foreign law enforcement counterparts to create the Border Enforcement Security Task Force (BEST). BEST is a series of multiagency teams developed to identify, disrupt, and dismantle criminal organizations posing significant threats to border security. Several international law enforcement agencies serve as key members of the team.

On the southwest border, the participation of the Mexican Secretaria de Seguridad Publica, or SSP, is vital. On the northern border, Canadian law enforcement agencies like the Canada Border Services Agency, the Royal Canadian Mounted Police, the Ontario Provincial Police, the Niagara Regional Police Service, the Toronto Metropolitan Police, the Windsor Police Service, and the Amherstburg Police Service are active members. The Argentinean customs agency is part of the Miami BEST and the Colombian National Police is part of both the Miami and New York–New Jersey BESTs. Currently, there are 21 BESTs with locations around the United States and in Mexico, which include:

- Arizona (Phoenix, Tucson, and Yuma)
- California (Imperial Valley, Los Angeles/Long Beach Seaport, San Diego)
- Florida (Miami Seaport)
- Mexico (Mexico City)
- Michigan (Detroit)
- New Mexico (Albuquerque, Deming, Las Cruces)
- New York (Buffalo, New York Seaport)
- New Jersey (New Jersey Seaport)
- Texas (El Paso, Laredo, Rio Grande Valley)
- Washington (Blaine, Seattle Seaport)
- Gulf Coast (New Orleans Seaport, Mobile Seaport, and Gulfport Seaport)
- Southeast Coastal (Wilmington Seaport, Charleston Seaport, and Savannah Seaport)

Since BEST's inception, investigators have collectively initiated more than 6,400 cases. These actions have resulted in more than:

- 5,200 criminal arrests
- 7,200 administrative arrests
- 12,000 pounds of cocaine
- 300 pounds of heroin
- 300,000 pounds of marijuana
- 2,800 pounds of ecstasy
- 1,800 pounds of meth
- 3,400 weapons
- 455,000 rounds of ammunition
- 1,500 vehicles
- $42.5 million in currency

Counterterrorism and Criminal Exploitation Unit

The Counterterrorism and Criminal Exploitation Unit (CTCEU) prevents terrorists and other criminals from exploiting U.S. immigration. CTCEU staff also review the immigration status of known and suspected terrorists, combat criminal exploitation of the Student and Exchange Visitor Program (SEVP), and leverage HSI's expertise to identify national security threats.

CTCEU is composed of three sections:

- National Security Threat Task Force (NSTTF)
- SEVIS Exploitation Section (SES)
- Terrorist Tracking Pursuit Group (TTPG)

NSTTF identifies, disrupts, and prosecutes people listed in the Terrorist Identities Datamart Environment (TIDE), a database of individuals who have fraudulently obtained U.S. immigration benefits. The task force identifies individuals for TIDE and coordinates their litigation and removal proceedings on behalf of ICE. Identified violators are subject to the full judicial prosecutorial process.

SEVIS SES analyzes and refers educational/school fraud criminal investigation leads to the respective ICE field office. It implements and manages the Agent/SEVIS School Outreach Program that educates others about SEVP exploitation. The program also improves communication between designated school officials and HSI field agents and provides subject matter expertise to partnering agencies when exploitation is suspected.

TTPG leverages ICE expertise across partnering agencies dedicated to promoting national security. This group leads the Targeted Enforcement Program (TEP), an initiative with U.S. CBP that tracks how long individuals identified as security risks stay in the United States. The program works jointly with the FBI's Foreign Terrorist Threat Task Force (FTTTF) that also proactively identifies known or suspected terrorists. TTPG also initiates high-priority nonimmigrant overstay investigations as dictated by the Compliance Enforcement Advisory Panel (CEAP).

Counterproliferation Investigations

ICE is the only federal law enforcement agency with full statutory authority to investigate and enforce criminal violations of all U.S. export laws related to military items, controlled "dual-use" commodities, and sanctioned or embargoed countries. The magnitude and scope of such threats increase significantly each year. ICE agents in the field who conduct counterproliferation investigations (CPI) focus on the trafficking and illegal export of the following commodities and services:

- WMD materials
- Chemical, biological, radiological, nuclear (CBRN) materials
- Military equipment and technology
- Controlled dual-use commodities and technology
- Firearms and ammunition
- Financial and business transactions with sanctioned and embargoed countries and terrorist organizations

The U.S. Coast Guard

The U.S. Coast Guard (USCG) is one of the five armed forces of the United States and the only military organization within the DHS. The Coast Guard protects the maritime economy and the environment, defends the nation's maritime borders, and rescues those in peril. The Coast Guard is simultaneously and at all times an armed force and federal law enforcement agency (Figure 6–4).

The Coast Guard was created on August 4, 1790, by Congressional authorization of the construction of ten vessels to enforce federal tariff and trade laws and to prevent smuggling. Known variously through the 19th and early 20th centuries as the Revenue Marine and the Revenue Cutter Service, the Coast Guard expanded in size and responsibilities as the nation grew. The service received its present name in 1915 under an act of Congress that merged the Revenue Cutter Service with the Life-Saving Service, thereby providing the nation with a single maritime service dedicated to saving life at sea and enforcing the nation's maritime laws. The Coast Guard began to maintain the country's aids to maritime navigation, including operating the nation's lighthouses, when President Franklin Roosevelt ordered the transfer of the Lighthouse Service to the Coast Guard in 1939. In 1946, Congress permanently transferred the Commerce Department's Bureau of Marine Inspection and Navigation to the Coast Guard, thereby placing merchant marine licensing and merchant vessel safety under the Coast Guard purview.

National defense responsibilities remain one of the Coast Guard's most important functions. In times of peace, the agency operates as part of the DHS, serving as the nation's front-line agency for enforcing the nation's laws at sea, protecting the marine environment and the nation's vast coastline and ports, and saving life. In times of war, or at the direction of the President, the Coast Guard serves under the Navy Department.

For over two centuries, the Coast Guard has guarded U.S. maritime interests domestically, in the ports, at sea, and around the globe. The Coast Guard has nearly 42,000 men and women on active duty today. By law, the Coast Guard has 11 missions (three of which are starred, representing an association with border security, customs, or immigration, and which are described in greater detail below). By law, the Coast Guard has 11 missions, which include:

- Ports, waterways, and coastal security
- Drug interdiction
- Aids to navigation
- Search and rescue
- Living marine resources

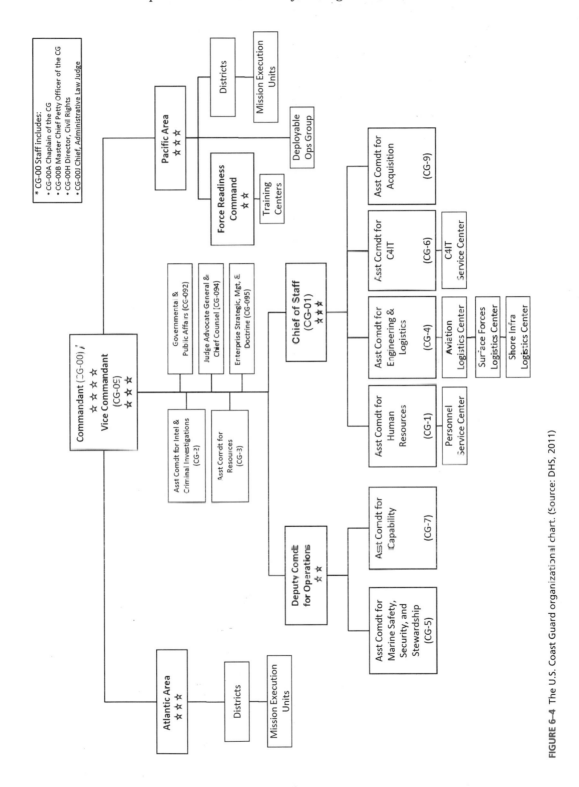

FIGURE 6-4 The U.S. Coast Guard organizational chart. (Source: DHS, 2011)

- Marine safety
- Defense readiness
- Migrant interdiction
- Marine environmental protection
- Ice operations
- Other law enforcement

Drug Interdiction

The Coast Guard is the lead federal agency for maritime drug interdiction and shares lead responsibility for air interdiction with the U.S. Customs Service. As such, it is a key player in combating the flow of illegal drugs to the country. The Coast Guard's drug interdiction mission is to reduce the supply of drugs from the source by denying smugglers the use of air and maritime routes in the Transit Zone, a six-million square-mile area that includes the Caribbean, the Gulf of Mexico, and Eastern Pacific. In meeting the challenge of patrolling this vast area, the Coast Guard coordinates closely with other federal agencies and countries within the region to disrupt and deter the flow of illegal drugs. The Coast Guard drug interdiction accounts for nearly 52% of all U.S. government seizures of cocaine each year.

The Coast Guard has been conducting drug interdiction missions since the late 19th century, when Chinese drug smugglers began illegally importing opium on ships. In the prohibition days, the Coast Guard saw a rather large increase in resources and funding to fight alcohol smuggling, which included the chasing of now-legendary rum-runners. Today, maritime drug smuggling is a very significant problem, and smugglers are using new technologies to evade capture (including submersible ships that are very difficult to detect). Since its first drug seizures in the early 1970s, the Coast Guard has seized well over 1 million pounds of cocaine and marijuana.

Other Border-Area Law Enforcement Roles

Countries need to protect their commercial fishing interests as a matter of economic, environmental, and food supply security. Commercial fishery zones extending from the nation's borders are protected by federal and international laws, and the USCG is tasked with enforcing these laws. Coast Guard vessels prevent illegal foreign fishing vessels from entering and exploiting the U.S. "Exclusive Economic Zone" (EEZ) encroachment as part of the Coast Guard mission. In addition, the Coast Guard is tasked with the duty of enforcing international agreements aimed at controlling illegal, unreported, and unregulated (IUU) fishing activity on the high seas. In 2008, the Coast Guard detected 81 incursions by foreign fishing vessels into the U.S. EEZ. The Coast Guard also participated in the 2008 multinational high seas drift net (HSDN) enforcement campaign, Operation North Pacific Watch. Through this campaign, the Coast Guard interdicted two Chinese HSDN vessels, facilitating their seizure by Chinese officials.

███ ███ ███

An Average Day for the U.S. Coast Guard

In an average day, the U.S. Coast Guard accomplishes the following:

- Saves 13 lives
- Responds to 64 search and rescue cases

- Rescues 77% of mariners in imminent danger
- Keeps 959 pounds of cocaine off the streets
- Saves $260,000 in property
- Interdicts 10 undocumented migrants trying to enter the United States
- Services 49 buoys and fixes 21 discrepancies (such as buoys moved by a hurricane)
- Provides a presence in all major ports
- Screens 679 commercial vessels and 170,000 crew and passengers
- Issues 200 credentials to merchant mariners
- Inspects 70 containers
- Inspects 33 vessels for compliance with air emissions standards
- Performs 30 safety and environmental examinations of foreign vessels entering U.S. ports
- Boards 15 fishing boats to ensure compliance with fisheries laws
- Investigates 12 marine accidents
- Responds to and investigates 10 pollution incidents
- Performs security boardings of 5 high-interest vessels
- Escorts 4 high-value U.S. Navy vessels transiting U.S. waterways
- Identifies one individual with terrorism associations
- Maintains 6 patrol boats and 400 personnel who:
    - Protect Iraq's offshore oil infrastructure
    - Train Iraqi naval forces
    - Keep sea lanes secure in the Arabian Gulf

Source: USCG. 2010. Coast Guard 2010 Snapshot. http://www.uscg.mil/top/about/doc/uscg_snapshot.pdf.

U.S. Citizenship and Immigration Services

U.S. Citizenship and Immigration Services (USCIS) is the DHS component that oversees lawful immigration to the United States. USCIS is tasked with ensuring the security of the nation by providing accurate and useful information to intending immigrants, granting immigration and citizenship benefits, promoting an awareness and understanding of citizenship, and ensuring the integrity of the U.S. immigration system (Figure 6–5).

USCIS currently employs 18,000 people, many of whom are contractors, at approximately 250 locations throughout the world. USCIS employees facilitate the immigration process, which can be cumbersome, time-consuming, and at times technically challenging (due to the requirements under U.S. immigration law). Because intelligence has shown terrorists to be interested in exploiting the U.S. immigration system to gain entry to the United States, USCIS faces an ongoing challenge to maintain system integrity and innovation. At the same time, to serve the millions of people who are adhering to all immigration policies and laws, USCIS must ensure the immigration system is effective, flexible, and customer-oriented.

Services provided by USCIS include:

- Citizenship (including citizenship through naturalization): Intending immigrants who wish to become U.S. citizens submit applications to USCIS. USCIS determines each applicant's eligibility,

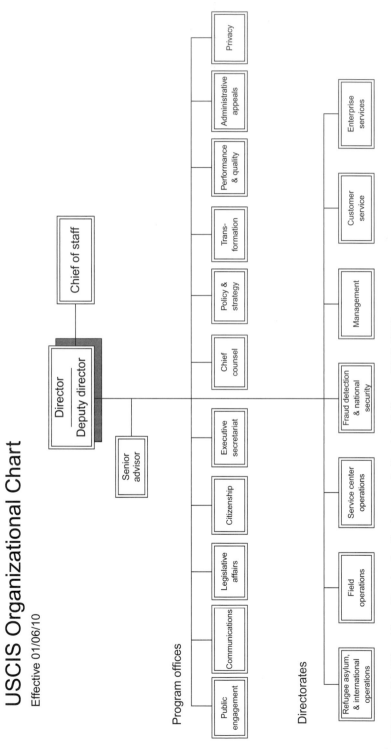

FIGURE 6–5 U.S. Citizenship and Immigration Services organizational chart. (Source: USCIS, 2011)

processes his or her applications, and, if approved, schedules the applicant for a ceremony to take the Oath of Allegiance. USCIS also determines eligibility and provides documentation of U.S. citizenship for people who acquired or derived U.S. citizenship through their parents.

- Family member immigration: USCIS manages the process that allows current permanent residents and U.S. citizens to bring close relatives to live and work in the United States.
- Employment for foreign nationals: USCIS manages the process that allows individuals from other countries to work in the United States.
- Verifying an individual's legal right to work in the United States (e-verify): USCIS maintains the e-verify system, which allows employers to electronically verify an employee's employment eligibility.
- Humanitarian programs: USCIS administers programs that provide protection to individuals inside and outside the United States who are displaced by war, famine, and civil and political unrest, and those who are forced to flee their countries to escape the risk of death and torture.
- Adoptions: USCIS manages the first step in the process for U.S. citizens to adopt children from other countries. Approximately 20,000 adoptions take place each year.
- Civic integration: USCIS promotes instruction and training on citizenship rights and responsibilities and provides immigrants with the information and tools necessary to successfully integrate into American civic culture.

Office of Citizenship

The Office of Citizenship engages and supports the citizenship process by helping new immigrants to succeed in their adoptive country. This includes promotion of the English language and education on the rights and responsibilities of citizenship, for instance. The Office of Citizenship is tasked with the following activities:

- Developing and enhancing educational products and resources that welcome immigrants, promote English language learning and education on the rights and responsibilities of citizenship, and prepare immigrants for naturalization and active civic participation
- Leading initiatives to promote citizenship awareness and demystify the naturalization process for aspiring citizens
- Supporting national and community-based organizations that prepare immigrants for citizenship by providing grants, educational materials, and technical assistance
- Building collaborative partnerships with state and local governments and nongovernmental organizations to expand integration and citizenship resources in communities
- Conducting training workshops and enhancing professional development and classroom resources for educators and organizations preparing immigrants for citizenship
- Promoting integration policy dialogue among different sectors of society and coordinating with stakeholders at all levels to foster integration and community cohesion

The Office of Citizenship is divided into three divisions:

- Testing, Education, and Training
- Policy and Programs
- Grants

Fraud Detection and National Security Directorate

The Fraud Detection and National Security (FDNS) Directorate was created within USCIS in 2004 to strengthen ongoing efforts to ensure that immigration benefits are not granted to individuals who pose a threat to national security or public safety, or who seek to defraud the U.S. immigration system. In 2010, FDNS became a directorate, which elevated the profile of this work within USCIS. FDNS officers are located in every USCIS center, district, field, and asylum office. FDNS officers are also located in other government agencies. FDNS staff enhance USCIS's ability to detect and remove known and suspected fraud from the application process without hampering the process by which legitimate applications are processed. FDNS officers also perform checks of USCIS databases and public information, as well as other administrative inquiries, to verify information provided on, and in support of, applications and petitions. Administrative inquiries may include:

- Fraud assessments (determine the types and volumes of fraud in certain immigration benefits programs)
- Compliance reviews (reviews of certain types of applications or petitions to ensure the integrity of the immigration benefits system)
- Targeted site visits (inquiries conducted in cases where fraud is suspected)

FDNS uses the fraud detection and national security data system (FDNS-DS) to identify fraud and track potential patterns. In July 2009, FDNS implemented the Administrative Site Visit and Verification Program (ASVVP) to conduct unannounced site inspections to verify information contained in certain visa petitions.

Refugee, Asylum, and International Operations Directorate

The Refugee, Asylum, and International Operations (RAIO) Directorate operates both within and outside the United States to provide protection, humanitarian, and other immigration benefits to legitimate foreign citizen applicants, while at the same time ensuring that these benefits are not exploited by terrorists or criminals. Refugees and asylum seekers are people who are typically characterized as:

- Fleeing oppression, persecution, and torture because of their race, religion, nationality, membership in a particular social group, or political opinion
- Confronting an urgent humanitarian situation and needing authorization to enter the United States on a temporary basis

RAIO also provides immigration services to certain groups of foreign citizens who should not or cannot apply for citizenship or immigration permission within the United States itself. These include (for example):

- Active duty members of the U.S. Armed Forces serving overseas who seek to become naturalized citizens
- Lawful permanent residents who are overseas and have lost documentation that would enable them to lawfully return to the United States
- Individuals who live overseas and seek to be reunified with relatives in the United States

RAIO maintains a Washington, D.C. headquarters that is supported by the following:

- 28 overseas field offices
- 8 domestic asylum offices

- 2 domestically located branches of the International Operations (IO) Division tasked with the adjudication of overseas applications not requiring interview
- An IO office in Miami responsible for administering a cooperative agreement that provides resettlement and orientation benefits to Cuban and Haitian parolees
- RAIO officers who deploy on "circuit rides" overseas to adjudicate refugee benefits, frequently in remote locations, and domestically to adjudicate asylum benefits

RAIO is made up of three divisions, which include:

- The Refugee Affairs Division: it is responsible for providing the humanitarian benefit of refugee resettlement to applicants in need of protection throughout the world while diligently protecting the U.S. homeland through careful national security screening
- The Asylum Division: It manages the U.S. affirmative asylum process, which permits individuals already in the United States. or at a port of entry, who are not in immigration proceedings, to request asylum if they are unable or unwilling to return to their country of origin due to past persecution or a well-founded fear of future persecution
- The International Operations Division: It extends immigration benefits to eligible individuals located overseas.

■ ■ ■ ▬▬▬▬▬▬▬▬▬▬▬▬▬▬▬▬▬▬▬▬▬▬▬▬▬▬▬▬▬▬▬▬▬▬▬▬▬

A Typical Day at USCIS

On an average day at USCIS:

- More than a quarter million people visit the USCIS website
- 200 refugee applications are processed around the world, and 4,040 people already in the United States are granted asylum
- 41,000 phone calls to the USCIS toll-free customer service line are answered, and 12,000 customers are served at 84 local offices
- The employment eligibility of more than 80,000 new hires in the United States is verified
- 11,000 applicants are fingerprinted and photographed at 129 Application Support Centers
- 135,000 national security background checks are conducted
- 30,000 applications for various immigration benefits are completed
- 3,700 applications to sponsor relatives and fiancées are processed
- American parents of 125 foreign-born orphans are assisted
- 2,300 petitions filed by employers to bring workers to the United States are processed
- Permanent residence is granted to 3,400 people, and 7,300 Permanent Resident Cards are issued
- 3,000 new citizens are welcomed, 30 of whom are already serving in the U.S. military

Source: USCIS, 2011, http://www.uscis.gov/portal/site/uscis.

■ ■ ■

Office of US-VISIT

The Office of US-VISIT (US-VISIT) is one of five divisions that make up the DHS National Protection and Programs Directorate (NPPD). US-VISIT contributes to border security efforts by providing biometric identification services to federal, state, and local government decision makers to help them accurately identify the people they encounter and determine whether those people pose a risk to the United States.

US-VISIT was created to enhance entry and exit security procedures. It enables consular, border security, and immigration officers to effectively verify the identity of incoming visitors and confirm compliance with visa and immigration policies. The program's goals are to enhance the security of U.S. citizens and visitors who travel in and out of the country, to expedite legitimate travel and trade, and to ensure the integrity of the immigration system while safeguarding the privacy of visitors.

Implementation of the program began in 2004 at 115 airports. Over the years that followed, the biometrics machines were installed at U.S. embassies and consulates throughout the world. Applicants use the machine to digitally scan their fingerprints, and the generated images are saved in a database where other relevant information about the applicants is located. The fingerprints are later used to verify the identity of a visitor when he or she enters or leaves the country.

On arrival in the United States, as part of the enhanced procedures, most visitors traveling on visas will have two fingerprints scanned by an inkless device and a digital photograph taken. All of the data and information are then used to assist the border inspector in determining whether or not to admit the traveler. These enhanced procedures add only seconds to the visitor's overall processing time.

All data obtained from the visitor are securely stored as part of the visitor's travel record. This information is made available only to authorized officials and selected law enforcement agencies on a need-to-know basis in their efforts to help protect against those who intend to harm American citizens or visitors.

The most notable change for international visitors is the new exit procedure. Most visitors who require a visa will eventually need to verify their departure. This checkout process will be completed by use of automated self-service workstations in the international departure areas of airports and seaports. By scanning travel documents and capturing fingerprints on the same inkless device, the system validates the visitor's identity, verifies his or her departure, and confirms his or her compliance with U.S. immigration policy (DHS, 2004, 2011b).

Conclusion

The nation's security and economic stability are contingent upon effective maintenance of secure borders, effective enforcement of immigration laws, and enforceable customs policies and procedures. These three tasks are monumental in their scope, requiring the dedication of hundreds of thousands of government employees, cutting edge technologies, intergovernmental cooperation, and billions upon billions of dollars in budget allocations. By consolidating these functions under the DHS umbrella, the various agencies involved in their conduct have increased the effectiveness of each, and as a result the nation is likely safer and more secure. While legal immigrants and legitimate commerce do form both the foundation and ongoing prosperity of our nation, the truth remains that criminals and terrorists will continue to seek out new and better ways to evade our systems of protection.

Key Terms

Asylum: The protection granted by a nation to a person who has left their native country as a refugee (and would therefore face imminent danger were they to return to that country).

Border: A line that defines geographic and political boundaries or legal jurisdictions.

Containerization: The transportation of cargo in standardized containers that can be seamlessly transferred between ocean-going (ships), rail (trains), and highway (trucks) vehicles without having to unload contents.

Customs: The government function tasked with collecting duties levied on imported goods.

Deportation: The act of forcibly expelling a foreign national from one country to their own country or to a third country willing to accept them.

Drone Aircraft: A powered, pilotless, unmanned aircraft that is typically flown remotely by an operator on the ground.

Duties: Taxes imposed upon goods imported into one country from another, typically imposed for the purposes of protecting domestic business interests, equalizing the charges imposed by other countries on exported goods, and/or generating government revenue.

Excise Tax: Tax imposed on the use or consumption of certain products.

Immigration: The act of a foreign citizen coming to another country for the purposes of residing there permanently, either by legal or by illegal means.

Linewatch Operations: Operations that are conducted near international boundaries and coastlines in areas of Border Patrol jurisdiction to prevent the illegal entry and smuggling of aliens into the United States, and to intercept those who do enter illegally before they can escape from border areas.

Marine Patrol: Border patrol activities conducted along the coastal waterways of the United States and Puerto Rico and interior waterways common to the United States and Canada. Marine patrol activities are typically conducted from the decks of marine craft.

Naturalization: The process under national law by which a foreign-born person is granted citizenship.

Refugee: A person who has been forced to leave their country due to war, persecution, or other reasons for which they fear for their life and safety.

Signcutting Operations: The detection and interpretation of any disturbances in natural terrain conditions that indicate the presence or passage of people, animals, or vehicles.

Visa: An endorsement on a passport that indicates the holder is allowed to enter, exit, and/or stay for a predetermined amount of time in a country. There are numerous classes of visas that each bestow different privileges.

Review Questions

1. How do the nation's borders serve to maintain economic and physical security?
2. What DHS offices are involved in each of the following, and what specific actions do they perform?
   a. Immigration
   b. Border security
   c. Customs enforcement
3. How does DHS balance the protection of the nation's borders with the freedom of movement of legitimate travelers and goods across the borders?

References

CBP, 2008. CSI In Brief. CBP Website. http://www.cbp.gov/xp/cgov/trade/cargo_security/csi/csi_in_brief.xml.

CBP, 2009. Fencing construction status. (December 25). http://www.cbp.gov/linkhandler/cgov/newsroom/highlights/fence_map.ctt/fence_map.pdf.

CBP, 2011a. Immigration inspection program. CBP Website. http://www.cbp.gov/xp/cgov/border_security/port_activities/overview.xml.

CBP, 2011b. Office of air and marine. Fact sheet. http://www.cbp.gov/linkhandler/cgov/newsroom/fact_sheets/marine/air_marine.ctt/air_marine.pdf.

CBP, 2011c. Unmanned aircraft system MQ-9 predator B. CBP fact sheet. http://www.cbp.gov/linkhandler/cgov/newsroom/fact_sheets/marine/uas.ctt/uas.pdf.

Department of Homeland Security, 2004. Fact sheet: Arizona border control initiative. http://www.dhs.gov/xnews/releases/press_release_0520.shtm.

DHS, 2004. US-VISIT program. http://www.dhs.gov/xtrvlsec/programs/content_multi_image0006.htm.

DHS, 2006. Secure freight initiative: vision and operations overview. (December 7). http://www.dhs.gov/xnews/releases/pr_1165943729650.shtm

DHS, 2011a. Securing America's borders: CBP fiscal year 2010 in review fact sheet. (March 15).

DHS, 2011b. Office of US-Visit. http://www.dhs.gov/files/programs/usv.shtm.

The White House, 2005. Border and transportation security. http://www.whitehouse.gov/deptofhomeland/sect3.html.

Transportation Safety and Security

What You Will Learn

- The nature of U.S. transportation systems and infrastructure
- The roles and responsibilities of the Transportation Security Administration

Introduction

Transportation is a general term that refers to the movement of things or people from one location to another. However, in today's modern world, where transportation systems are intertwined into a global network that moves millions of people and products throughout the world on a daily basis, such simple definitions do not give justice to the complexity that exists in this sector. Furthermore, the safety and security needs to address such a complex system are equally complex and interconnected.

Historically, the United States has relied on the private sector for both the transportation network and the promise of domestic transportation safety and security. The events of September 11, 2001, however, illustrated the vulnerabilities of the nation's transportation systems and spurred a massive change in the existing approaches. Transportation security and the identification and reduction of vulnerabilities within the vast transportation networks have since experienced significant challenges and changes. Because of the complexity of these systems as a whole and the complexity of the subsystems included, this has not been an easy task.

In the United States, the Department of Homeland Security Transportation Security Administration (TSA) is the primary government body that addresses the security of transportation systems and infrastructure, while the Coast Guard and the Department of Transportation address it to a lesser degree. This chapter discusses the various components of the nation's transportation network and describes the agencies and programs that exist to ensure their protection.

The Transportation Network

The general term *transportation* refers to a very wide range of systems, structures, vehicles, and actions. The transportation of people and things (namely goods) takes many forms and affects every American's life in some way or another. Disruption of any of these components causes hardship to those impacted when of minor consequence, and severe security and economic impacts when on a large scale. As such, each of the nation's transportation network components is critical to the functioning of American society.

There are a number of distinct components that make up the nation's transportation network, and these include the following.

Freight Rail

The U.S. freight railroad network spans the country and is relied on heavily for the transport of both raw materials and marketable goods. The freight rail network remains a vital component of the U.S. economy as trains still connect many of the nation's distribution hubs and shipping ports. At present, there are approximately 140,000 miles of active railroad track that are utilized by 565 common carrier freight railroads. These railroads serve nearly every industrial, wholesale, retail, and resource-based sector of the U.S. economy, and are responsible for transporting a majority of the goods and commodities Americans depend on.

The current freight rail system is a diverse network of large and small independent companies. In the absence of one single coast-to-coast freight rail operator, these carriers have developed various interchange, joint services, and voluntary access agreements that allow for the transfer of rail cars between carriers, as well as the operation of one carrier's train on the tracks of another. This type of system increases operational efficiency for the railroads and helps to further lower transportation costs, but increases the complexity of the security operation needed to support it.

Freight railroads are divided into three classes based on their size and operating revenues:

- Class I: Railroads that operate over large areas, in multiple states, and concentrate on the long-haul, high-density, intercity traffic lines with annual revenues over $250 million.
- Class II: Railroads that operate on at least 350 miles of active lines and have annual revenues between $20 and $250 million.
- Class III: Railroads that operate on less than 350 miles of line and generate less than $20 million in annual revenues.

Highways, Roadways, and Motor Carrier Networks

All Americans depend on the U.S. highway and roadway systems directly through the facilitation of personal transport, and indirectly through the transport of goods and services upon which they depend. This massive infrastructure network includes:

- 46,934 miles of interstate highway
- 116,813 miles of other National Highway System roads
- 3,884,777 miles of other roads
- 599,766 bridges over 20 feet of span
- 366 U.S. highway tunnels over 100 meters in length

The scope of personal reliance on U.S. roads becomes fully apparent when considering that, through 2007, the total number of vehicles registered in the United States exceeded 254 million. This includes 26.2 million privately owned trucks, 9.0 million commercially owned trucks (with 6 or more tires and/or combination vehicles), 834,000 buses, 136 million passenger cars, 7.1 million motorcycles, and 101 million other 2-axle vehicles.

The motor carrier industry, which does not include intracity or mass transit buses, consists of three primary components, namely:

- *The U.S. Motor Coach Industry*: 3,137 bus companies operate 29,325 motor coach buses. These provide 118,000 jobs (56,000 full-time) and transport 750 million passengers each year.
- *The Pupil Transportation (School Bus) Industry*: The nation's 475,000 school buses represent the largest fleet of public vehicles in the United States. They serve 19,000 U.S. school districts, and transport 25 million students each day. Collectively, these buses conduct 10 billion student trips per year.
- *The Motor Carrier Freight Industry*: In the United States, there are approximately 703,000 active motor carrier companies. These companies employ 4.7 million commercial vehicle drivers, who operate 9.0 million commercial trucks, and 5.1 million commercial trailers. 61,000 of the trucking companies transport 2 billion tons of hazardous materials (HAZMATs) each year.

Ports and Intermodal Freight Transport

In the United States, 99% of imports and exports are conducted by ship through the nation's system of seaports. The U.S. seaport infrastructure is a massive network that is owned and operated by multiple stakeholders at the federal, state, and local levels, and in both the private and public domains. There are 32 states that have active public ports, and there are 327 official ports of entry in the United States and 15 preclearance offices in Canada and the Caribbean. More information about ports is provided later in this chapter under the section "Ports and Shipping Security."

Mass Transit

U.S. law defines *mass transit* to be "transportation by a conveyance that provides regular and continuing general or special transportation to the public, but does not include school bus, charter, or sightseeing transportation" (U.S. Code Title 49, Subtitle III, Chapter 53, §5302). Modes of mass transit in the United States typically include:

- Intercity buses
- Trolleybuses
- Subway and commuter rail
- Demand response services
- Heavy and light rail
- Automated guideway transit
- Cable cars
- Monorails
- Ferries

Each year, almost 10 billion passenger rides are conducted on mass transit systems in the United States. To facilitate these trips, over 144,000 vehicles are required, of which about 56% are buses. The nation's passenger rail system, Amtrak, also operates a nationwide rail transportation network of 22,000 miles of track and serves 21 million passengers per year at more than 500 stations. Interconnectivity of these systems has been fostered such that several different mass transit systems share terminals and other facilities. Ownership of mass transit systems is unique, with many smaller systems independently owned and operated and most medium-to-large size agencies owned and operated by governmental or quasi-governmental organizations.

Ferries continue to serve as a vital component of the U.S. transportation system, with the number of passenger rides provided by almost a quarter-million vehicles approaching 85 million each year. Due to the nature of many waterways, ferries often travel between states, and in certain locations near Mexico and Canada, across international borders. Ferry-related accidents tend to be spectacular in nature given the unique aspect of drowning, and in many historical events dozens and even hundreds to thousands of people have died. As such, ferries have been and continue to be seen as a high-priority target for terrorists throughout the world.

Pipeline Security

As a conveyor of goods from place to place, the oil and gas pipeline network that spans the nation is considered a component of the transportation infrastructure (Figure 7–1). The national pipeline system is somewhat unique with regard to its status as a transportation system, and as such has unique infrastructure security characteristics and requirements. Pipelines have been a regular target of terrorism throughout the world, and intelligence has found evidence that terrorists consider the U.S. pipeline system a high-value target. Additionally, accidents or other disruptions to the pipeline infrastructure can cause significant impacts to property and to humans, and the economic impacts may be far-reaching.

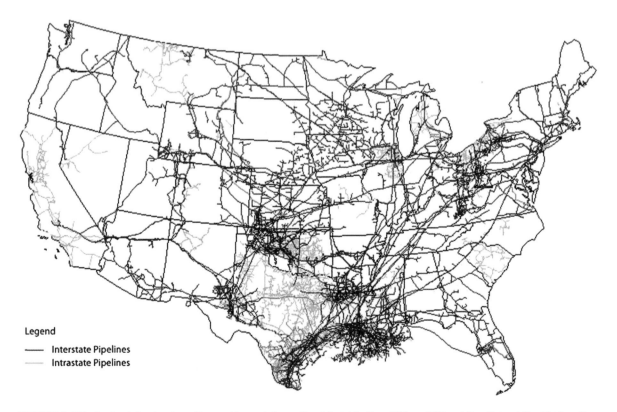

Legend

—— Interstate Pipelines
—— Intrastate Pipelines

FIGURE 7–1 U.S. pipeline infrastructure. (Source: Energy Information Administration, Office of Oil and Gas, Natural Gas Division, Gas Transportation Information System)

Virtually all the critical pipeline infrastructure is owned or operated by private entities. There are:

- 161,189 miles of hazardous liquid pipelines operated by over 200 operators
- 309,503 miles of natural gas transmission pipelines operated by over 700 operators
- 1.9 million miles of natural gas distribution pipelines operated by over 1,300 operators

Air Freight

For the 12 months that ended September 2010, almost 10 million tons of freight was transported within the United States and between the United States and other countries using commercial aircraft. The air freight industry is vital given the speed and efficiency it can provide, both of which are vital for products that are needed immediately or for which the risk of spoilage exists. The top five U.S.–international country gateways for freight in this period included South Korea, Japan, the United Kingdom, Germany, and Taiwan. Air freight presents a unique security challenge due to its sheer quantity and the methods by which it is transported. Air freight is shipped both on dedicated freight-carrying airplanes and on passenger planes in the cargo hold. When transported on passenger aircraft, passengers are exposed to the risk of these goods, which may be used to conduct terrorist attacks.

Commercial and General Aviation

Commercial aviation has been operating in the United States since 1914. At that time, and in the years that followed, the airline industry was accessible only to the most privileged clients and served very few locations. Today, more than 28,000 flights take off or land in the United States each day, representing about half of the world's commercial airline traffic. Of approximately 20,000 airports that are registered in the United States, 599 were certified to serve commercial flights in 2006. These commercial airports serve hundreds of millions of passengers each year, with some of the largest serving tens of millions of passengers each (Atlanta's Hartsfield Jackson International Airport, for instance, serves over 40 million passengers each year) (Reed, 2006).

General Aviation (GA) is a vital component of the aviation sector and the national economy that accounts for some 77% of all flights in the United States. It encompasses a wide range of activities, from pilot training to flying for business and personal reasons, delivery of emergency medical services, and sightseeing. Operations range from short-distance flights in single-engine light aircraft to long-distance international flights in corporate-owned wide-bodies, and from emergency aeromedical helicopter operations to airships seen at open-air sporting events. The sole characteristic that GA operations have in common is that flights are not routinely scheduled; they are on demand.

Transportation Security Domain

The following is a snapshot of the transportation network that exists in the United States:

- 3.9 million miles of public roads
- 1.2 million trucking companies operating 15.5 million trucks including 42,000 HAZMAT trucks
- 10 million licensed commercial vehicle drivers including 2.7 million HAZMAT drivers
- 2.2 million miles of hazardous liquid and natural gas pipeline

- 120,000 miles of major railroads
- Nearly 15 million daily riders on mass transit and passenger rail systems nationwide
- 25,000 miles of commercial waterways
- 361 ports
- 9.0 million containers through 51,000 port of calls
- 11.2 million containers via Canada and Mexico
- 19,576 general aviation airports, heliports, and landing strips
- 459 federalized commercial airports
- 211,450 general aviation aircraft

Source: TSA, 2011.

The Transportation Security Administration

The Aviation and Transportation Security Act (Public Law 107-71), signed by President Bush on November 19, 2001, created the Transportation Security Administration (TSA) within the Department of Transportation. This new office operated in that location until the 2003 opening of the Department of Homeland Security (DHS) when TSA was absorbed into the now-dissolved Directorate for Border and Transportation Security. Since that time, TSA has been returned to its independent status as a standalone agency within DHS.

The 2001 Aviation and Transportation Security Act is notable in that it made many fundamental changes in the way transportation security is performed and managed in the United States. For instance, for the first time this law made aviation security a direct federal responsibility. In addition, it consolidated all transportation security activities under the umbrella of one agency. Because of the nature of the September 11 terrorist attacks, aviation security has received the highest priority among TSA responsibilities (in terms of both staff and budget), and the agency commits significant staff and budget toward developing strategies and implementing necessary technologies to prevent any future terrorist events connected to the abuse of the aviation system and air transportation (Figure 7–2 displays the internal budget allocations of the TSA, illustrating its heavy emphasis toward aviation security). It is likely that in light of the continuing threat posed by terrorists to all public transportation systems, these trends will change and the spending gap between aviation security and other types of transportation security will diminish over time.

Since its initial full year of funding in 2003, TSA has accomplished several important projects that seek to improve air transportation security. The 2003 budget for TSA totaled $4.8 billion, an increase of more than $3.5 billion from 2002 funding levels. The 2003 budget included the costs of well over 30,000 airport security personnel, including screeners, law enforcement personnel, and screener supervisors. The budget also included funding for the purchase of explosive detection systems that had to be in place to screen all checked baggage, and the maintenance of that equipment. The 2003 budget was also the first year reflecting full funding of the greatly expanded federal air marshal program. The president's budget request of $4.82 billion for TSA in FY 2004 was over $1 billion more than the previous year. The FY 2004 budget was spent primarily on four programs, among which the aviation security program was the largest at $4.22 billion (86%) of overall funds. The aviation security program consisted of a passenger screening program for which $1.80 billion was allocated, a baggage screening program with a budget of $944 million, and a security direction and enforcement program for which $1.47 billion was allocated (TSA, 2005).

	FY 2010 Rev. Enacted		FY 2011 Cont. Resolution[1]		FY 2012 Pres. Budget		FY 2012 +/− FY 2011	
	FTE	$000	FTE	$000	FTE	$000	FTE	$000
Aviation Security	49,282	$5,214,040	52,269	$5,214,040	55,284	$5,401,165	3,015	$187,125
Surface Transportation Security	593	110,516	787	110,516	775	134,748	(12)	24,232
Transportation Threat Assessment and Credentialing	246	215,619	252	209,219	481	220,274	229	11,055
Transportation Security Support	1,501	1,001,780	1,517	1,001,780	1,855	1,113,697	338	111,917
Federal Air Marshals	-	860,111	-	860,111	-	991,375	-	131,264
Gross Discretionary	**51,622**	**$7,402,066**	**54,825**	**$7,395,666**	**58,395**	**$7,861,259**	**3,570**	**$465,593**
Mandatory, Fees, & Trust Fund	6	254,000	6	254,000	6	254,000	-	-
Emergency/ Supplemental	-	-	-	-	-	-	-	-
American Reinvestment and Recovery Act (ARRA)	-	-	-	-	-	-	-	-
Total	**51,628**	**$7,656,066**	**54,831**	**$7,649,666**	**58,401**	**$8,115,259**	**3,570**	**$465,593**
Less Prior Year Rescissions	-	(4,000)	-	-	-	-	-	-

[1] The FY 2011 Continuing Resolution funding level corresponds to the FY 2010 Enacted level.

FIGURE 7–2 The TSA budget. (Source: Department of Homeland Security. 2012. Budget in Frief. FY2012. DHS Website. www.dhs.gov/xlibrary/assets/budget-bib-fy2012.pdf.)

When TSA celebrated its fifth anniversary on November 19, 2006, it had accomplished several of its congressionally mandated goals and responsibilities. During that time period, TSA detected and removed more than 40 million items that are prohibited onboard airplanes. TSA installed advanced explosive detection systems in all major airports and redesigned the Air Cargo Rules to ensure that air cargo transported within U.S. airspace on a daily basis is safe. TSA officials assisted the air evacuation of 25,000 hurricane victims in the aftermath of Hurricane Katrina. During that same 5-year period, TSA grew its National Explosives Detection Canine Team Program to 425 teams at more than 80 airports and 11 public transportation systems in the nation (TSA, 2006).

Today, TSA's security focus is on identifying risks, prioritizing them, managing these risks to acceptable levels, and mitigating the impact of potential incidents that may arise as result of these risks. Sharing of information among agencies and stakeholders — including intelligence information — has become a cornerstone of its risk management model. TSA has needed to adapt to the complex and unique requirements of both passenger and cargo security, in recognition of the many differences that exist between transportation modes, and to instill confidence in the security of the transportation system. TSA's stated guiding principle is that it will focus on the leveraging of prevention services, new technologies, best practices, public education, stakeholder outreach, and regulation compliance across transportation modes.

Today, approximately 50,000 Transportation Security Officers (TSOs) provide screening and other security services at approximately 450 airports throughout the United States. They are trained and certified in constantly evolving rules, methods, and technologies that detect the presence of threats against people and the infrastructure required to maintain safe travel for nearly 2 million passengers each day. Additionally, U.S. air carriers annually transport approximately 12.5 million tons of cargo, 2.8 million tons of which is now secured on passenger planes. The remaining 9.7 million tons of freight, which is shipped in cargo planes, also remains a unique threat to the nation given the destructive physical and psychological impact of a large plane crash.

The full scope of TSA's security mandate is staggering and encompasses a jurisdiction that rivals that of any other federal agency. This mandate includes more than 9 billion passenger trips per year on the nation's mass transit systems, more than 161,000 miles of interstate and national highways and their integrated bridges and tunnels, and nearly 800,000 shipments of hazardous materials (95% of which are made by truck). While the United States may not have had another successful attack on its transportation infrastructure in the decade that followed the 9/11 events, these systems remain on the forefront of the security domain in light of the global terrorism experience — much of which has focused on various transportation systems and components (including, for instance, the 2004 Manila ferry bombing, the 2004 Madrid train bombings, the 2005 London subway and bus attacks, the 2006 Mumbai train bombing, the 2010 Moscow subway attack, the 2011 Belarus subway attack, and many, many more).

TSA Transportation Network Management Role

For each of the U.S. transportation systems, TSA addresses these security responsibilities in partnership with other components of the DHS as well as the Department of Transportation and other departments. TSA's Office of Transportation Sector Network Management is tasked with leading the national-level effort to protect and secure U.S. transportation and transport systems. By establishing strategies for protecting and securing each of these different forms of transportation, this office ensures the safe movement of passengers and promotes the free flow of commerce. The Office of Transportation Sector Network Management is developed and is in the process of executing a strategy to ensure effective, efficient, and standardized operations within and among transportation modes. The strategy calls for:

- Completion of transportation industry threat, vulnerability, and consequence assessment
- Development of baseline security standards
- Assessment of operator security status versus existing standards
- Development of plan to close gaps in security standards
- Enhancement of transportation security systems

TSA Components

The TSA ensures transportation security through four mechanisms, each of which is described below. These include:

- Transportation Security Grants
- Law enforcement program
- Security programs
- Security screening

Transportation Security Grants

Since 2006, DHS has awarded over $1.6 billion in special grants that target the nation's transportation systems. TSA maintains the department's Transportation Security Grants, which are provided to mass transit and passenger rail systems, intercity bus companies, freight railroad carriers, ferries, and the trucking industry to help protect the public and nation's critical transportation infrastructure against acts of terrorism and other large-scale events. The grants are designed to support "high-impact" security projects that serve to reduce the risk faced by the various transportation systems.

The Freight Rail Security Grant Program

The Freight Rail Security Grant Program (FRSGP) was created to increase security levels within the freight rail industry by funding vulnerability assessments and security plans, providing funding for security training and exercises for frontline personnel, purchasing and installing global positioning systems (GPS) tracking on railroad cars, and hardening of bridges that are used for freight rail transportation.

The FRSGP received $10 million in funding in FY 2011 for freight railroad carriers and railroad car owners. The focus of this funding is to support security initiatives for freight rail carriers that transport rail security-sensitive materials (RSSM) through designated high-threat urban areas, freight railroad car owners, and offerors that transport bulk poisonous by inhalation/toxic inhalation hazardous (TIH) materials, and owners of rail bridges that are used for freight rail transportation may apply for infrastructure hardening capabilities.

The maximum federal share of any project supported through FRSGP is 75%, with the exception of vulnerability assessments and security plans that have no match requirement. The program funds different project types as determined by the applicant type. Applicants may be:

- Railroad carriers (see above for carrier class descriptions)
  - Class I carriers may request funds to support security awareness and emergency response training for frontline employees, and security-related drills and exercises provided that they have completed an acceptable vulnerability assessment and security plan.
  - Class II and Class III carriers may request funds to conduct a vulnerability assessment and develop a security plan. The carriers may also request funds to support security awareness and emergency response training for frontline employees, and security-related drills and exercises provided that they have completed an acceptable vulnerability assessment and security plan.
- Railroad car owners and offerors may request funds to acquire and install satellite GPS tracking on railroad cars that transport bulk TIH.
- Owners of rail bridges may request funds for infrastructure hardening capabilities.

Eligible applicants for this grant program include the following entities:

- Freight railroad carriers that meet the following criteria are eligible to apply for FRSGP funding:
  - Transport RSSM as defined for this cycle of this grant program.
  - Operate in or through at least one designated HTUA.
  - Certify they have and adhere to a security plan that conforms to federal requirements (49 CFR Part 172)
- Freight railroad car owners that meet the following criteria are eligible to apply for FRSGP funding:
  - Transport bulk rail TIH as defined for this cycle of this grant program.
  - Allow DHS/TSA access to GPS tracking information, as outlined in the grant guidance.

- Owners of rail bridges that meet the following criteria are eligible to apply for FRSGP funding:
  - Own bridges that have a volume exceeding 4.9 MGTM.
  - Commit to and include a monitoring plan describing how security capabilities will be continuously monitored with a 24/7 commitment.

Intercity Bus Security Grant Program

The Intercity Bus Security Grant Program (IBSGP) was created to support the work of operators of fixed-route intercity and charter bus services servicing high-risk urban areas. This grant is designed to strengthen the infrastructure upon which these operators depend, and to protect the traveling public against risks associated with potential terrorist attacks. In FY 2011, DHS committed $4,990,000 to private intercity bus operators under this grant program.

The grant program, at present, supports only operators of "over-the-road" buses, which include:

1. Private operators of fixed-route intercity bus companies serving a defined Urban Areas Security Initiative (UASI) jurisdiction
2. Operators of charter bus services using over-the-road buses that provide a minimum of 50 trips annually to one or more UASI jurisdictions

Under this program, the private operators must provide at least 25% of the project cost through either cash or in-kind contributions. It is important to note that bus operators must have conducted a vulnerability assessment, and developed and/or updated a security plan within the last 3 years, if they are to be eligible for the grant program. Applicants that do not have a current security plan and vulnerability assessment can apply for IBSGP funding to meet that requirement, but are not eligible to apply for other project types. And finally, by accepting one of the IBSGP grant awards, the operator must allow DHS to perform a corporate security review (CSR) and audit upon request, wherein they will be required to provide information concerning critical assets, threat assessments, vulnerability assessments, security plan management, personnel security, training, exercises, cybersecurity, and physical security countermeasures.

The funding priorities for this program (in FY 2011) are:

- Developing a vulnerability assessment and security plan
- Covering operating and capital costs associated with over-the-road bus security awareness, preparedness, and response training (must be DHS-approved)
- Conducting live or simulated exercises (must be DHS-approved)
- Conducting public awareness campaigns (must be DHS-approved)
- Covering operational costs to hire, train, and employ police and security officers, including canine units
- Establishing and improving emergency communications systems
- Implementing and operating passenger screening programs for weapons and explosives
- Protecting or isolating drivers of over-the-road buses
- Conducting chemical, biological, radiological, or explosive detection initiatives
- Acquiring, upgrading, installing, or operating equipment, software, or services for the collection, storage, or exchange of passenger and driver information
- Covering overtime reimbursement for security personnel during periods of high-threat levels
- Modifying over-the-road buses

- Installing cameras and video surveillance equipment on over-the-road buses and at terminals, garages, and bus facilities
- Constructing and modifying terminals, garages, and facilities

Transit Security Grant Program

The Transit Security Grant Program (TSGP) provides funds to owners and operators of transit systems, including intracity bus, commuter bus, certain ferry systems, and all forms of passenger rail. These grants are intended to protect critical surface transportation infrastructure and the traveling public from acts of terrorism. DHS dedicated $235 million to the owners and operators of transit systems under the FY 2011 TSGP. Of this amount, $200 million is provided to the National Passenger Rail Corporation (Amtrak) ($19.96 million), $10 million is for the Freight Rail Security Grant Program, and $4.99 million for the Intercity Bus Security Grant Program.

The Top Transit Asset List (TTAL) assets are considered priority for this program. DHS drafted the TTAL support of the TSGP to identify those things it considers critical to surface transportation. This prioritized list was developed by examining the highest, criticality-type assets at the highest risk regions, and by examining existing intelligence. The assets were analyzed on the basis of threats, vulnerabilities, and consequences. Remediation projects for assets on the TTAL are given priority funding consideration over other capital projects. Priority is also given to "shovel-ready" projects that have complete designs/remediation plans and can be implemented quickly.

Per the grant's appropriation, only up to 10% of total program funding may be used for operational activities, which includes such things as training, drills and exercises, public awareness campaigns, development of security plans, and vulnerability assessments. Program priorities were as follows in FY 2011 under this grant:

- Priority A: Operational Projects (Training, drills/exercises, public awareness, and security planning projects)
- Priority B: Development of new capabilities to enhance visible, unpredictable deterrence efforts in transit, including equipment and other support
- Priority C: "Shovel-ready" capital projects for assets on the TTAL
- Priority D: Remediation plans for assets on the TTAL
- Priority E: Other capital security projects

TSA Law Enforcement Functions

TSA is best known for passenger and baggage screening at airport security checkpoints. However, the agency also maintains a number of law enforcement functions across a fairly wide jurisdiction of transportation infrastructure components. TSA law enforcement also includes the training of transportation employees in the knowledge and skills required to maintain the safety and security of the transportation network.

The Federal Air Marshal Service

The Federal Air Marshal Service is a TSA-managed law enforcement agency charged with securing the civil aviation system from both criminal and terrorist acts. Federal Air Marshals are specially trained federal security officers who travel inconspicuously on commercial flights for the purpose of quickly thwarting an attempted criminal or terrorist attack (or to neutralize a potentially dangerous situation involving unruly passengers). Awareness of the role of Air Marshals, as they are often called, has grown considerably since terrorists overtook four airplanes as part of a concerted attack on America on September 11.

The Federal Air Marshal Service existed long before TSA was created in the aftermath of the September 11 attacks, however. The roots of this organization actually date back to the 1960s and 1970s, when several U.S. commercial flights were hijacked (for both political and asylum-related purposes). To address the growing threat to air travel, the Federal Air Marshal Service was created within the U.S. Customs Service (as the "Customs Air Security Officers Program," or the "Sky Marshal Program"). Under the original program, over 1,700 men and women were given special tactical training at the U.S. Army's Fort Belvoir.

Placed on American aircraft dressed as typical passengers, the Customs Air Security Officers were flying armed and ready. The program lost support, and therefore ceased operations, in mid-1974 when X-ray screening equipment was introduced in the nation's airports.

In 1985, TWA Flight 847 was hijacked, and in response then President Ronald Reagan directed the Secretary of Transportation to explore expansion of the armed Sky Marshal program aboard international flights for U.S. air carriers. Congress responded by passing the International Security and Development Cooperation Act (Public Law 99-83), which provided the statutes that supported the Federal Air Marshal Service. When the terrorists took over the four planes on September 11, 2001, the Air Marshal Program consisted of less than 50 armed marshals who, by statute, flew only on international flights flown by U.S. air carriers. In the aftermath of these events, President George W. Bush quickly enhanced the role of the agency in greatly expanding its ranks to include thousands of new Marshals.

Today, Federal Air Marshals serve as the primary law enforcement entity within TSA. Officers are deployed on flights both within the United States and elsewhere in the world. While their primary mission of protecting air passengers and crew has not changed much over the years, Federal Air Marshals have an ever-expanding role in homeland security and work closely with other law enforcement agencies to accomplish their mission. Currently, air marshals staff several positions at different organizations such as the National Counterterrorism Center, the National Targeting Center, and the FBI's Joint Terrorism Task Forces. In addition, they are also distributed among other law enforcement and homeland security liaison assignments during times of heightened alert or special national events.

Due to the nature of their assignment, Federal Air Marshals operate in almost complete independence, without any chance of calling in additional support if needed. The close quarters of the airplane cabin, where any mistake could easily cost an innocent passenger's health or life, demand a standard of firearms accuracy that exceeds that seen in almost all other law enforcement services. They must remain undercover given the importance of surprise and to prevent intending terrorists from knowing whether or not a Federal Air Marshal is on a particular flight.

National Explosives Detection Canine Team

The TSA National Explosives Detection Canine Team Program is tasked with preparing dogs and their handlers to quickly locate and identify dangerous materials that may present a threat to transportation systems. The threat of a cargo- or luggage-based explosive has mandated the need for increased security measures on both cargo and passenger airplanes, but these measures have come at the cost of shipping speed and efficiency. However, trained explosives detection dogs are able to quickly rule out the presence of dangerous materials in unattended packages, structures, or vehicles, allowing the free and efficient flow of commerce.

Chapter 7 • Transportation Safety and Security 255

The TSA Explosives Detection Canine Handler Course is held at Lackland Air Force Base in San Antonio, Texas. Law enforcement officers from throughout the United States travel to this location for training, and are paired with a dog from the TSA "Puppy Program" at that time (dog breeds used for this function include German Shepherds, Belgian Malanoises, Vizslas, and other types of dogs with exceptional abilities to smell trace amounts of explosive residue). Dogs are given 10 weeks of training, wherein they learn how to locate and identify a wide variety of dangerous materials inclusive of search techniques for aircraft, baggage, vehicles, and transportation structures, as well as procedures for identifying dangerous materials and alerting or letting the handler know when these materials are present.

Crew Member Self-Defense Training Program

The Federal Air Marshal Service manages a program to reduce terrorism risk in airplanes called Crew Member Self-Defense Training (CMSDT). This training, which is available to all U.S. carrier crew members, is provided throughout the country for the convenience of the different airlines and their employees. The course takes just one day and is provided free of charge. Crew members are trained in hand-to-hand combat, self-defense techniques, and other skills such as how to detain an unruly passenger or potential terrorist until the plane has landed. CMSDT is delivered in two parts. First, the participating crew members review a self-paced, interactive DVD and student manual designed to familiarize them with self-defense concepts and techniques. After completing the review, the crew members schedule and attend the one-day hands-on training. Crew members may repeat the training as often as they would like. Crew members trained under this program regularly use their training to restrain intoxicated, belligerent, and otherwise hostile passengers aboard flights originating and/or terminating in the United States.

Armed Security Officer Program

The Armed Security Officer Program is a very specialized transportation security program that focuses on Ronald Reagan Washington National Airport (DCA) in Arlington, Virginia (just minutes to downtown Washington, D.C.). Because of this airport's proximity to the nation's capital and many key U.S. landmarks, there are a number of special security considerations associated with flights in and out of the facility, namely, that it would be very difficult to thwart another attack like occurred on September 11 (given that very little warning would be possible). While commercial flights regularly fly in and out of this airport, general aviation flights require much less security and are therefore more difficult to track, and there remains a concern that terrorists will again try to use aircraft as weapons. In order to allow a small number of general aviation flights to use this facility, the Armed Security Officer Program was created under TSA in partnership with DHS and Department of Defense agencies. The DCA Access Standard Security Program (DASSP), as it is called, allows a total of 48 general aviation flights a day to leave from or fly to designated gateway airports with an Armed Security Officer (ASO) onboard.

Federal Flight Deck Officers Program

The Federal Flight Deck Officers Program further strengthens commercial flights from crime or terrorism by increasing the likelihood that certain cockpit-based flight crew members are able to withstand an attack. Under this program, eligible flight crew members are authorized to use firearms to defend against an act of criminal violence or air piracy attempting to gain control of an aircraft. A flight crew member may be a pilot, flight engineer, or navigator assigned to the flight. This program has since been expanded to include cargo pilots and certain other flight crew members. Each participating crew member is trained by the Federal Air Marshal Service on the use of firearms, use of force, legal issues, defensive tactics, the psychology of survival, and program standard operating procedures.

Law Enforcement Officers Flying Armed Program

Related to the Federal Flight Deck Officers Program is the Law Enforcement Officers Flying Armed training program. This TSA-maintained program is provided to all law enforcement officers who will be flying armed. Under Code of Federal Regulation (CFR) 1544.219 (Carriage of Accessible Weapons), certain law enforcement officers are able to declare their firearms to the airline and bring them onto the flight to increase the security presence that exists. Attendees in the program are given a structured lesson plan that includes protocols in the handling of prohibited items, prisoner transport, and dealing with an act of criminal violence aboard an aircraft.

TSA Security Programs

TSA is also charged with ensuring the secure operation of various transportation networks. The following are examples of these programs:

Air Cargo Security

Air cargo has remained a major security concern since it was discovered that terrorists considered, and even attempted without success, destroying cargo planes over populated areas as an attack method (Associated Press, 2010). The TSA Air Cargo Security Program is composed of two distinct areas, namely:

1. The Transportation Sector Network Management (TSNM) Air Cargo Division (charged with the strategic development of programs)
2. Office of Security Operations (OSO) (charged with program compliance)

The TSA Air Cargo Division is responsible for coordinating the different actions required to bring about a secure air cargo industry, which includes agencies and partners both within and outside of DHS. This division considers a number of threats and systems, both internationally and within the United States, and develops corresponding air cargo regulations, technological solutions, and policies. The challenge is in maintaining constant vigilance while ensuring that commerce is able to continue unimpeded. Examples of the approaches used to secure cargo include:

- Vetting companies that ship and transport cargo on passenger planes to ensure they meet TSA security standards
- Maintaining and staffing Certified Cargo Screening Facilities (CCSFs) that physically screen cargo using approved screening methods and technologies
- Employing random and risk-based assessments to identify high-risk cargo that requires increased scrutiny
- Inspecting industry compliance with security regulations through the deployment of TSA inspectors

TSA worked closely with Congress in 2007 to formulate the components of the 9/11 Bill that relate to air cargo. Since the law went into effect, TSA has increased the amount of cargo currently screened to almost 100% (with 100% of the cargo on 96% of the flights originating in the United States being screened, which means that 85% of passengers flying each day from U.S. airports are on planes where all of the cargo has been fully screened). In late 2008, TSA completed a required milestone of screening 100% of cargo being flown on narrow-body airplanes. TSA conducts surprise cargo security inspections called *strikes*, covert testing, security directives, and 100% screening at 250 smaller airports. In 2008, TSA eliminated all exemptions to screening of air cargo for the first time and increased the amount of cargo that is subject to mandatory screening.

TSA employs 620 Cargo Transportation Security Inspectors (TSIs), who are exclusively dedicated to the oversight of air cargo. TSA also maintains 460 canine teams, of which 120 are specifically assigned to the screening of air cargo at the nation's highest cargo volume airports. This presence has significantly increased the amount of cargo screening TSA is able to conduct.

Flight School Security Awareness Training Program

Federal law (the Interim Final Rule, Flight Training for Aliens and Other Designated Individuals; Security Awareness Training for Flight School Employees) requires flight schools to ensure that their employees who have direct contact with students (including flight instructors, ground instructors, chief instructors, and administrative personnel) receive both initial and recurrent security awareness training. Flight schools may choose either to use TSA's security awareness training program or to develop their own program. If a flight school chooses to develop its own program, the program must adhere to standards in the rule.

For those employees employed by the flight school as of January 18, 2005, initial training must have been completed no later than January 18, 2005. For employees hired after January 18, 2005, initial training must be completed no later than 60 days after the date of hire. Recurrent training must be provided to employees each year in the same month as the month they received initial training. TSA and the Aircraft Owners and Pilots Association (AOPA) have collaborated to create an online General Aviation Security course in order to better facilitate these new security requirements placed on flight schools.

I-STEP Program

The TSA Intermodal Security Training and Exercise Program (I-STEP) provides exercise, training, and security planning tools and services to the transportation community. The program serves the port and intermodal, aviation, mass transit, freight rail, highway and motor carrier, and pipeline industries. This program enables these TSA security partners to:

- Enhance security capabilities through participation in or conduct of exercises and training that strengthen security plans, test emergency procedures, and sharpen skills in incident management
- Build partnerships by collaborating with stakeholder partners, law enforcement personnel, first responders, health and medical professionals, government transportation and homeland security leaders, and industry representatives to address challenges in transportation security
- Gain insights into transportation security by ensuring that needs are aligned with federal grant opportunities, and allowing partners to gain a deeper understanding of lessons learned and best practices

The I-STEP program coordinates public and private sector partners for exercise, training, information sharing and to address transportation security issues focused on protecting travelers, commerce, and infrastructure. TSA is also introducing an online transportation security portal called the Exercise Information System (EXIS) that guides users through a step-by-step exercise planning process, provides exercise planning and evaluation tools, and helps to ensure that lessons learned are shared.

TSA Security Screening

Over 600 million people fly each year and carry with them a quantity of baggage and other items that numbers in the billions. TSA inspectors are responsible for checking each passenger and each item that will be accompanying them onto a commercial aircraft. Screeners work at over 700 security checkpoints and nearly 7,000 baggage screening areas throughout the United States (Figure 7–3).

FIGURE 7–3 New Orleans, Louisiana, August 30, 2008 — TSA officials check evacuees and baggage with security scanners at the airport during Hurricane Gustav. (Photo by Jacinta Quesada/FEMA News Photo)

Passenger Screening

TSA received a legal mandate in 2001, soon after (and as a direct consequence of) the 9/11 terrorist attacks, to screen all air travelers. This role was formerly conducted by private security guards employed by each airport. However, in what is one of the largest single-recruitment campaigns in the civilian government, TSA took over airport passenger screening duties and created a workforce of tens of thousands in just a few months. Today, TSA is best known to Americans through the 43,000 Transportation Security Officers who are stationed at airports throughout the country. In conjunction with over 1,000 credentialed security inspectors, the TSA Transportation Security Officers screen over 2 million passengers each day. TSA Transportation Security Officers also lead and support security operations in other transportation systems, including mass transit and maritime vessels, although these roles cannot be compared in scope to the role of TSA in the airline industry.

In recent years, TSA has attempted to utilize new technologies to detect weapons and other banned items possessed by passengers. Some feel the use of these technologies has come at the expense of civil liberties, and infringes upon the personal rights, privacy, and dignity of passengers. For instance, backscatter devices, which can create imagery that displays what appears underneath a passenger's clothing, have been a matter of contention given the discomfort many passengers have with screeners seeing what they feel to be "pictures of them without their clothes on." Attempts have been made to adapt the technology such that the images do not display anatomical details, but the debate continues (and the devices continue to be used).

Some of the search methods utilized by TSA Transportation Security Officers have also come under scrutiny, including the patting-down of children, senior citizens, and the infirm. Examples of these events, which highlight the sensitive nature of conducting such personal searches, and which have served to mar the TSA image, include:

- March 2011: A cancer survivor who wears a urostomy (urine collection) bag was publicly humiliated when TSA screeners in Detroit burst the bag during a pat-down, causing it to soak his clothing in front of other passengers

- April 2011: Parents of a 6-year-old child videotaped TSA officers patting-down the visibly shaken child at a New Orleans airport
- June 2011: TSA screeners in Florida forced an elderly woman suffering from leukemia to remove her adult diaper when a screening showed what appeared to be a suspicious spot on the undergarment

Baggage Screening

TSA maintains a suite of sophisticated technology and equipment that has been developed in recent years to ensure that luggage and other cargo passengers take onto planes are free from terrorist and other potential hazards (such as flammable liquids, aerosols, and radio equipment that may interfere with the flight). TSA Transportation Security Officers electronically screen millions of bags for explosives and other dangerous items each day at over 7,000 baggage screening locations and at over 450 airports nationwide.

Covert Testing

Covert testing is a process by which trained security officials test the effectiveness of screening systems by attempting to successfully board airplanes (or to check baggage on airplanes) while carrying (or packing) banned substances and devices. This can and does typically involve the use of actual explosives and/or weapons. The purpose of covert testing is to ensure that there are no omissions or unknown loopholes in security systems, and to ensure that employees are maintaining high-security standards at all times. Testers try to think like a terrorist or a criminal, and devise new ways in which to fool current screening systems. Whenever they are successful in moving banned substances and devices past security checkpoints, new processes and procedures are developed to prevent such breaches in the future. The details of covert testing are typically kept secret given the need to maintain an element of surprise for screeners. However, the following are general examples of the types of tests that are employed:

- Threat Image Projection (TIP): The TIP system randomly superimposes images of bombs and bomb parts into real carry-on bags. These images may be superimposed on any of the millions of carry-on bags at checkpoints across the country, at any time of day or night. There are tens of thousands of TIP images and the system is updated with the latest intelligence-driven threats added on a regular basis. Officers are evaluated on the images they detect and training is tailored to drive improvement in detection of threats across the system.
- Aviation Screening Assessment Program (ASAP): ASAP assessments test the screening process by inserting inert bombs, bomb parts, and other threat items into the screening process to identify weaknesses. The assessments test both the technologies and the abilities of the screeners to identify the items. Items are placed on TSA or local, state, and federal employees or in carry-on or checked bags, not on unwitting passengers. Thousands of these assessments are conducted each year.
- TSA's Office of Inspection (TSA OI): TSA's Office of Inspection conducts no-notice covert tests to assess the effectiveness of screening operations. Testers are trained in bomb and weapons smuggling techniques, which are gleaned from intelligence gathered from actual terrorist groups and from actual experience throughout the transportation security system. All airports are subject to no-notice testing by TSA OI. The morning of testing, local police are notified (to protect the testers and passengers in the area), and once testing has begun, the local TSA management are informed of the ongoing process. Upon completion of the test, training is conducted to address any weaknesses in the system that are identified.

- DHS Office of Inspector General (DHS IG) Testing: The DHS IG conducts hundreds of covert tests at airports from coast to coast and acts completely independently from TSA. DHS IG agents measure the effectiveness of screening protocols and communicate these results to TSA and DHS management to increase screening and security effectiveness.
- Government Accountability Office (GAO) Testing: GAO conducts independent tests of airport security to ensure these systems are reviewed by a true independent, external entity. GAO employees report their findings to Congress and share results with TSA. GAO results have led to increases in security through enhanced training and use of technology.

Trucking Security

Security within the nation's commercial trucking industry is a very important component of homeland security given that a significant portion of the nation's hazardous materials (HAZMATs) are transported by these trucks on public highways and roads. Incidents where hazardous materials are spilled or released as a result of commercial truck accidents are fairly common. Moreover, the threat always exists that a terrorist will use a truck carrying some dangerous chemical or other material to cause significant human, property, and environmental damages. Releases involving the volumes or weights of materials contained in these vehicles can have catastrophic effects.

A serious HAZMAT incident is defined by DOT's Research and Special Programs Administration (RSPA) as:

- An incident that involves a fatality or major injury caused by the release of a hazardous material
- The evacuation of 25 or more persons as a result of release of a hazardous material or exposure to fire
- A release or exposure to fire that results in the closure of a major transportation artery
- The alteration of an aircraft flight plan or operation
- The release of radioactive materials from Type B packaging
- The release of over 11.9 gallons or 88.2 pounds of a severe marine pollutant
- The release of a bulk quantity (over 119 gallons or 882 pounds) of a hazardous material

Table 7–1 illustrates the number of these serious incidents that have occurred in all U.S. transportation modes in 2009.

The Office of Hazardous Materials Safety of DOT/RSPA is responsible for coordinating a national safety program for the transportation of hazardous materials by air, rail, highway, and water in the United States. The Code of Federal Regulations (CFR) 49 Part 107 documents the steps being taken to enhance hazardous material transportation security. Subchapter C, Part 107, specifically discusses regulations for HAZMAT transportation on U.S. highways. The subparts of the document include information about regulations for loading and unloading of HAZMAT transportation vehicles, segregation and separation of HAZMAT vehicles and shipments in transit, accidents, and regulations applying to hazardous material on motor vehicles carrying passengers for hire. To supplement safety efforts, the DHS Office of Screening Coordination and Operations (SCO) within the (former) BTS Directorate initiated hazardous materials trucker background checks in 2005 in an effort to secure the highways and trucks. Since then, the office's name has been changed to the Screening Coordination Office and it has been tasked with the coordination of all screening activities and systems administered and maintained by DHS.

Table 7–1   HAZMAT Summary by Mode of Transportation/Cause for 2009

| Mode of Transportation/Cause | Incidents | Serious Incidents[a] | | Fatalities | Damages |
| | | Injuries | | | |
		Hospitalized	Nonhospitalized		
Air					
Defective Component or Device	1	0	0	0	0
Dropped	2	0	0	0	300,000
Forklift Accident	2	0	0	0	0
Impact with Sharp or Protruding Object (e.g., Nail)	1	0	0	0	0
Improper Preparation for Transportation	4	0	0	0	0
Too Much Weight on Package	1	0	0	0	0
Valve Open	1	0	0	0	0
Cause Not Reported	3	0	0	0	0
Highway					
Abrasion	3	0	0	0	553,461
Broken Component or Device	6	0	0	0	122,253
Corrosion — Exterior	1	0	0	0	0
Corrosion — Interior	2	0	0	0	45,200
Defective Component or Device	15	0	0	0	117,588
Deterioration or Aging	7	1	2	0	93,897
Dropped	0	2	2	0	217,388
Fire, Temperature, or Heat	11	2	1	0	1,941,026
Forklift Accident	17	1	3	0	99,789
Freezing	2	0	0	0	4,900
Human Error	38	1	6	0	809,464
Impact with Sharp or Protruding Object (e.g., Nail)	11	0	0	0	393,761
Improper Preparation for Transportation	4	1	0	0	57,100
Inadequate Accident Damage Protection	1	0	0	0	6,900
Inadequate Blocking and Bracing	2	0	0	0	17,000
Inadequate Maintenance	1	0	0	0	45,200
Inadequate Preparation for Transportation	3	0	0	0	58,699
Incompatible Product	1	0	0	0	16,000
Incorrectly Sized Component or Device	1	0	0	0	4,350
Loose Closure, Component, or Device	13	0	3	0	1,634,748
Misaligned Material, Component, or Device	1	0	0	0	0
Overfilled	16	0	0	0	117,880
Rollover Accident	56	1	21	1	8,856,968
Threads Worn or Cross Threaded	1	0	0	0	0
Too Much Weight on Package	3	0	9	0	19,800
Valve Open	3	0	0	0	65,191
Vandalism	2	0	0	0	67,000
Vehicular Crash or Accident Damage	55	3	3	1	8,783,621
Cause Not Reported	70	4	27	4	8,348,960

(Continued)

Table 7–1 (Continued)

Mode of Transportation/Cause	Incidents	Serious Incidents[a]		Fatalities	Damages
		Injuries			
		Hospitalized	Nonhospitalized		
Rail					
Abrasion	1	0	0	0	8,008
Broken Component or Device	1	0	0	0	700
Conveyer or Material Handling Equipment Mishap	1	0	3	0	113,000
Corrosion — Interior	2	0	0	0	40,072
Defective Component or Device	2	0	1	0	6,000
Derailment	11	2	6	1	13,197,309
Deterioration or Aging	3	1	0	0	4,242
Human Error	3	0	0	0	94,904
Improper Preparation for Transportation	2	0	0	0	19,334
Inadequate Preparation for Transportation	2	4	1	0	7,503
Loose Closure, Component, or Device	2	0	0	0	13,401
Misaligned Material, Component, or Device	1	0	0	0	704
Missing Component or Device	4	1	0	0	22,664
Overpressurized	2	2	0	0	3,500
Rollover Accident	3	0	0	0	1,045,000
Stub Sill Separation from Tank (Tank Cars)	1	0	0	0	37,000
Valve Open	1	0	0	0	147,000
Cause Not Reported	2	0	0	0	539,958
Water					
Inadequate Blocking and Bracing	1	0	0	0	89,527
Overfilled	1	0	0	0	0
Cause Not Reported	1	0	0	0	600
Totals by Mode					
Air Incidents	15	0	0	0	300,000
Highway Incidents	354	16	77	6	32,528,144
Rail Incidents	44	10	11	1	15,300,299
Water Incidents	4	0	0	0	90,727
Total — 2009	**416**	**26**	**88**	**7**	**48,218,570**

[a]PHMSA revised the definition of a serious incident in 2002. This is the current definition:

- A fatality or major injury caused by the release of a hazardous material,
- The evacuation of 25 or more persons as a result of release of a hazardous material or exposure to fire,
- A release or exposure to fire that results in the closure of a major transportation artery,
- The alteration of an aircraft flight plan or operation,
- The release of radioactive materials from Type B packaging,
- The release of over 11.9 gallons or 88.2 pounds of a severe marine pollutant, or
- The release of a bulk quantity (over 119 gallons or 882 pounds) of a hazardous material.

Source: Hazardous Materials Information System, U.S. Department of Transportation. Data as of January 6, 2010.
Note: Due to multiple causes being involved in a single incident, the totals above may not correspond to the totals in the other reports.

In fiscal years 2005 and 2006, TSA provided grants through the Trucking Security Program (TSP) totaling $4.8 million to trucking companies. This funding level increased to $11.6 million in fiscal year (FY) 2007, and again to $15.5 million for FY 2008.

The funding priorities for 2008 were the following:

- Participant Identification and Recruitment: Identification and recruitment of highway professionals, such as truckers, school bus drivers, motor coach drivers, highway workers, and first responders to participate in highway security efforts; and development of a 5-year strategic plan
- Planning: Development of emergency response and contingency plans based on identified high-risk scenarios (e.g., truck hijacking, HAZMAT) and conducting hazard analysis and risk assessment in an effort to improve the plan
- Training: Development of a web-based security training system to train highway professionals, specialized HAZMAT drivers, and state and local law enforcement organizations. Design of an evaluation methodology for all training programs, and the development of a 5-year strategic plan for training
- Communications: Maintain a full-service (24/7) communications/call center staffed with well-trained responders who will provide nationwide first responder/enforcement contact numbers and electronic linkage to registered participants, and the development of a 5-year strategic plan for communications
- Information Analysis and Distribution: The applicant will provide management consulting services and oversight in cooperation with ODP leadership to maintain the Highway Information Sharing and Analysis Center (ISAC), located at the Transportation Security Operations Center (TSOC) in Herndon, Virginia. This center is dedicated exclusively to highway and highway transport-related security needs and issues. The applicant will provide recommendations, implementation strategies, and a completed plan for continued Highway ISAC operations. Responsibilities may include identification of the appropriate role of a highway-specific ISAC, identification of benefits of highway-specific ISAC separation from existing rail or other centers, optimal configuration and location of a new ISAC, and optimal staffing or implementation strategies (DHS, 2005b, 2006b, 2007f; Transportation Security Administration, 2007e).

In 2009, the Trucking Security Grant Program funding fell to $7 million, and in 2010 direct funding for the program was eliminated altogether.

Ports and Shipping Security

DHS considers the securing of goods imported and exported via maritime transport to be a critical task. Given the significance of containerization and maritime commerce on the U.S. economy, it is clear that a successful terrorist attack on a major U.S. port could result in not only significant loss of life and tremendous physical damage, but also serious disruption to the economy of the United States and its trade partners. The SAFE Port Act of October 2006 tasked DHS with the responsibility of assuring maritime transport security and protecting the nation's ports. This is accomplished through risk mitigation, vulnerability analysis, and the establishment of preventive measures in those facilities. The SAFE Port Act also tasked DHS with the creation of a resumption plan to minimize the disruption to economic activity in the case of a major terrorist attack on these seaports.

The USCG is the lead federal agency for maritime homeland security efforts, and is integral to DHS's port and shipping security efforts. The USCG even has its own maritime homeland security strategy wherein duties, responsibilities, and strategic missions are clearly defined. The USCG states its homeland security mission to be the protection of the U.S. maritime domain and the U.S. marine transportation system, the denial of their use and exploitation by terrorists as a means for attacks on U.S. territory, population, and critical infrastructure, and the preparation for and, in the event of attack, conduct of emergency response operations. In accomplishing its homeland security mission, the strategic goals of the Coast Guard are as follows:

- Increasing maritime domain awareness
- Conducting enhanced maritime security operations
- Closing port security gaps
- Building critical security capabilities
- Leveraging partnerships to mitigate security risks
- Ensuring readiness for homeland defense operations

The maritime and port security role of TSA has been to provide grants to support port security and related issues. In 2011, over $235 million was available to 52 port areas considered of highest risk (with the opportunity for others to apply as well as a "third tier" applicant). From 2002 until 2011, DHS awarded more than $2 billion in grants to many port owners, operators, and service providers as part of the Port Security Grant Program. While the focus of these grants changes from year to year, the 2011 priorities indicate the maturity of this effort. The 2011 priorities include:

- Enhancing Maritime Domain Awareness (MDA)
- Enhancing Improvised Explosive Device (IED) and CBRNE prevention, protection, response, and recovery capabilities
- Port resilience and recovery capabilities
- Training and exercises
- Efforts supporting implementation of the Transportation Worker Identification Credential (TWIC)

Assuring the security of seaports is a unique challenge due to the importance of commerce that passes through them and the relatively complex supply chain operations involved. This complexity is the result of both a multistep process required of each cargo item navigating its way to a recipient and the nature of the various stakeholders involved that include private companies and foreign governments. Figure 7–4 provides a simplified overview of the process for a typical container shipped to the United States from a foreign destination.

A careful examination of the cargo transit process reveals that nine of 16 typical security steps involved occur outside the jurisdiction of U.S authorities. However, security assurance through the detection and mitigation of actual threats to containers in transit require all 16 steps be performed. To account for this challenge, DHS maintains a cooperative security-focused relationship with foreign governments and their corresponding port authorities, under which each government allows the other to inspect facilities and carry out specific counterterrorism and other inspection measures, as the materials weave their way through the shipment process. For instance, in many key foreign ports, DHS officials perform daily audits and inspections of containers bound for the United States, and work with their foreign counterparts to ensure that chemicals, biological agents, nuclear materials, and explosives that may be hidden in containers are detected and interdicted before they pose a threat to life and commerce. While partner government agencies are invited to conduct the same level of inspection at U.S. ports for materials bound for their own ports, only a handful actually accept.

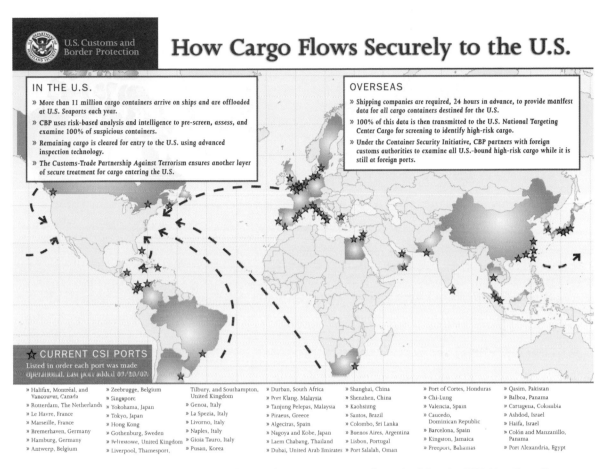

FIGURE 7-4 How cargo flows securely to the United States. (Source: Department of Homeland Security. 2007 How Cargo Flows Securely to the United States. US Customs and Border Protection Website: http://www.cbp.gov/linkhandler/cgov/trade/cargo_security/cargo_control/cargo_flow_map.ctt/cargo_flow_map.pdf.)

In light of these challenges, the risk intervention and port security efforts of DHS may be grouped into three distinct phases, namely:

- Overseas vulnerability reduction efforts
- In-transit vulnerability reduction
- Vulnerability reduction in U.S. waters and on U.S. shores

Examples of the various initiatives that occur in each phase are the following:

Initiatives That Address Overseas Vulnerability Reduction

1. The 24-Hour Advance Manifest Rule: All sea carriers with the exception of bulk carriers and approved break bulk cargo are required to provide proper cargo descriptions and valid consignee addresses 24 hours before a cargo is loaded at the foreign port for shipment to the United States through the Sea Automated Manifest System. Failure to meet the 24-hour Advanced Manifest Rule

results in a "do not load" message and other penalties. The information collected by the Customs and Border Patrol (CBP) is analyzed and the cargo deemed as high risk is inspected at the port of origin before it starts its journey into the United States.

2. Container Security Initiative (CSI): The screening of containers that pose a risk for terrorism is accomplished by teams of CBP officials deployed to work in concert with their host nation counterparts through the CSI program. As of 2011, there were 58 international ports participating in CSI, accounting for 90% of all trans-Atlantic and trans-Pacific cargoes imported into the United States subject to preload screening. A full list of all participating CSI ports is given in Table 7–2.

3. Customs–Trade Partnership against Terrorism (C-TPAT): C-TPAT is a voluntary government-business initiative aimed at strengthening and improving international supply chain and U.S. border security. Through this initiative, DHS asks businesses to ensure the integrity of their security practices and to communicate and verify the security guidelines of their business partners within the supply chain. Thousands of importers, carriers, brokers, forwarders, ports and terminals, and foreign manufacturers, most of whom are private companies, have participated. In turn, business participants providing verifiable security information are eligible for special benefits, including more expeditious transit of goods through a reduction in the number of inspections, priority processing, specially assigned C-TPAT inspectors who work directly with the company, eligibility in a self-inspection program, and invitations to security seminars. Through C-TPAT efforts, CBP is able to devote its resources to high-risk shipments. As of 2011, more than 10,000 companies had enrolled in the program.

4. International Ship and Port Facility Security (ISPS) Code: The ISPS Code requires large vessels operating internationally and port facilities that serve them to conduct security assessments, to develop security plans, and to hire security officers. By establishing a standard for security, the world trade community has increased its ability to prevent maritime-related attacks by making ports around the world more aware of unusual or suspicious activity. In the United States, the code is followed by the enactment of provisions of the Marine Transportation Security Act of 2002, and by aligning domestic marine security regulations with the guidelines of ISPS.

5. International Port Security Program (IPS): The objective of the ISP program is to engage in bilateral or multilateral discussions with trading nations around the world to exchange information and share best practices to align port security programs through implementation of the ISPS Code and other international maritime security standards. Under this effort, the U.S. Coast Guard and foreign nations work jointly to evaluate trade partner countries' overall compliance with the ISPS Code. The Coast Guard uses the information gained from site visits to improve the United States' own security practices and to determine if additional security precautions are required for vessels arriving in the United States from other countries, such as boarding the vessel. The program allows reciprocity from participating countries, who may apply the same standards to U.S. ships entering their own ports.

6. Secure Freight Initiative (SFI): The Secure Freight Initiative was launched in 2006 through partnership with DHS and the Department of Energy to prevent terrorists' use of global commerce to carry out a nuclear or radiological attack. Through the program, containers are scanned using special imaging and detection equipment while they are still at foreign ports, and inspected further while still overseas if concerns arise. The first countries that participated in the program were Honduras and Pakistan, and since then several others have joined (including the United Kingdom, Hong Kong, and Singapore.)

7. Operation Safe Commerce (OSC): Operation Safe Commerce is a program funded by Congress that seeks to improve methods of analyzing security in the commercial supply chain and testing

Table 7–2   Ports in CSI

Currently Operational Ports

In the Americas and Caribbean
- Montreal, Vancouver, and Halifax, Canada
- Santos, Brazil
- Buenos Aires, Argentina
- Puerto Cortes, Honduras
- Caucedo, Dominican Republic
- Kingston, Jamaica
- Freeport, The Bahamas
- Balboa, Colón and Manzanillo, Panama
- Cartagena, Colombia

In Europe
- Rotterdam, The Netherlands
- Bremerhaven and Hamburg, Germany
- Antwerp and Zeebrugge, Belgium
- Le Havre and Marseille, France
- Gothenburg, Sweden
- La Spezia, Genoa, Naples, Gioia Tauro, and Livorno, Italy
- Felixstowe, Liverpool, Thamesport, Tilbury, and Southampton, United Kingdom (U.K.)
- Piraeus, Greece
- Algeciras, Barcelona, and Valencia, Spain
- Lisbon, Portugal

In Asia and the East
- Singapore
- Yokohama, Tokyo, Nagoya, and Kobe, Japan
- Hong Kong
- Pusan, South Korea
- Port Klang and Tanjung Pelepas, Malaysia
- Laem Chabang, Thailand
- Dubai, United Arab Emirates (UAE)
- Shenzhen and Shanghai
- Kaohsiung and Chi-Lung
- Colombo, Sri Lanka
- Port Salalah, Oman
- Port Qasim, Pakistan
- Port of Ashdod, Israel
- Port in Haifa, Israel

In Africa
- Durban, South Africa
- Alexandria, Egypt

Source: U.S. Customs and Border Protection, 2011, http://www.cbp.gov/xp/cgov/trade/cargo_security/csi/ports_in_csi.xml.

new security technologies and solutions. Technologies tested through CSI enhance maritime cargo security, protect the global supply chain, and facilitate the flow of commerce. The ports of Seattle and Tacoma, Los Angeles, and Long Beach, and the Port Authority of New York/New Jersey as well as selected international ports participated in the program. OSC was completed in 2004, after over $200 million in grants had been awarded. The findings, outcomes, and lessons learned in the pilot project have been largely incorporated into DHS safe commerce strategies.

Initiatives That Address "In-Transit" Vulnerability Reduction

1. Smart Box Initiative: Through CSI, smarter, tamper-evident containers that better secure containerized shipping have been developed. Designed to be "tamper evident," Smart Boxes couple an internationally approved mechanical seal affixed to an alternate location on the container door with an electronic container security device designed to deter and detect tampering. If someone attempts to open the cargo door after it has been sealed, the smart box device on the door records the attempted or successful intrusion. The container security market has grown rapidly since the initiative began, and today there are a wide selection of smart box devices available on the market with different capabilities and technologies (radio frequency, cellular, satellite). More recent options allow for identification of the container's contents, the exporter's shipping patterns, and even to identify atypical movements of the container.
2. Ship Security Alert System (SSAS): Like a silent alarm in a bank, an SSAS allows a vessel operator to send a covert alert to shore for incidents involving acts of violence (such as piracy or terrorism), indicating the security of the ship is under threat or has been compromised. The International Maritime Organization requires all vessels of 500 gross tons or larger to have SSAS onboard to ensure covert alerting of a designated authority, ensuring a timely response during a threat.
3. Automated Targeting System (ATS): CBP's ATS serves as the premier tool for performing transactional risk assessments and evaluating potential national security risks posed by cargo and passengers arriving by sea, air, truck, and rail. Using prearrival information and input from the intelligence community, this rule-based system identifies high-risk targets before they arrive in the United States. ATS consists of six modules that provide selectivity and targeting capability to support CBP inspection and enforcement activities. These include:
   a. ATS-Inbound: Inbound cargo and conveyances (rail, truck, ship, and air)
   b. ATS-Outbound: Outbound cargo and conveyances (rail, truck, ship, and air)
   c. ATS-Passenger (ATS-P): Travelers and conveyances (air, ship, and rail)
   d. ATS-Land (ATS-L): Private vehicles arriving by land
   e. ATS-International (ATS-I): Cargo targeting for CBP's collaboration with foreign customs authorities
   f. ATS-Trend Analysis and Analytical Selectivity Program (ATS-TAP) (analytical module)
4. 96-Hour Advance Notice of Arrival: Foreign ships must notify the Coast Guard 96 hours before arriving in a U.S. port and provide detailed information on the crew, passenger, cargo, and voyage history. This information is analyzed using databases and intelligence information, including reviewing previous security problems with the vessel or illegal activity on the part of the crew. Part of this analysis will also account for the security environment in previous ports of call. By obtaining this information well in advance of a vessel's arrival, the U.S. Coast Guard is able to make determinations about which vessels require additional attention, including security precautions such as an at-sea boarding or armed escort during transit to and from port.

Initiatives That Address Vulnerability Reduction "in U.S. Waters and on U.S. Shores"
1. National Targeting Center (NTC): The priority mission of CBP's NTC is to provide tactical targeting and analytical research support for CBP antiterrorism efforts. Experts in passenger and cargo targeting at the NTC operate around the clock using tools like the Automated Targeting System (ATS) to identify tactical targets and support intradepartmental and interagency antiterrorist operations. The NTC also supports operations in the field, including the Container Security Initiative (CSI) personnel stationed at critical foreign ports throughout the world.
2. Maritime Intelligence Fusion Centers: Located in Norfolk, Virginia, and Alameda, California, these units compile and synthesize intelligence products from the federal, state, and local levels dealing with maritime security. The intelligence is then disseminated to homeland security professionals across the country responsible for securing ports and waterways to more effectively perform their security functions.
3. High-Interest Vessel Boarding: Before they are allowed to enter port, all vessels are screened for the security risk they pose to the United States based on information about the vessel's cargo, size, voyage, security history, and any intelligence information. Those identified as higher risk are targeted for offshore boarding to ensure potential security issues are addressed prior to entry into port. In addition, the Coast Guard randomly selects vessels for security boarding to ensure an element of unpredictability and thus deterrence. Specially trained Coast Guard teams board the boats through traditional water-based methods or via fast roping from helicopters.
4. Automatic Identification System (AIS): Through AIS, detailed ship information and tracking data are automatically sent to other ships and shore-based agencies, allowing for comprehensive, virtually instantaneous vessel tracking and monitoring. This program effectively increases security and safety in shipping channels. The International Maritime Organization's (IMO) International Convention for the Safety of Life at Sea (SOLAS) requires AIS equipment to be fitted on international voyaging ships with a gross weight exceeding 300 tons, and all passenger ships regardless of size. It is estimated that more than 40,000 ships currently carry AIS equipment. Most vessels required to use this technology are large vessels on international voyages. The Coast Guard's goal is to complete the implementation of a Nationwide Automatic Identification System by 2014.
5. Area Maritime Security Committees: The Coast Guard has established committees in all the nation's ports to coordinate the activities of all port stakeholders, including other federal, local, and state agencies, industry, and the boating public. These groups are tasked with collaborating on plans to secure their ports so that the resources of an area can be best used to deter, prevent, and respond to terror threats.
6. Port Security Assessment Program: This program is aimed at increasing the information and best practices available to port officials across the country to help them make decisions about how to reduce the vulnerability of their ports. The Coast Guard prioritized the examination of key infrastructure in the nation's 55 most economically and strategically important ports for potential vulnerabilities. Some ports have also used DHS Port Security grant funds to perform risk assessments and vulnerability analysis of their facilities. In addition to these assessments, the Coast Guard is creating a geographic information systems (GIS) database that can be easily searched for national, regional, and local information. A Government Accountability Office study identified inadequate project planning and delayed implementation regarding the USCG GIS project.
7. Nonintrusive Inspection (NII) Technology: NII technologies allow U.S. Customs and Border Protection to screen a larger portion of the stream of commercial traffic in less time while facilitating legitimate trade. CBP officers use large-scale gamma ray and X-ray imaging systems to

safely and efficiently screen conveyances for contraband, including weapons of mass destruction. These units can scan the interior of a full-size 40-foot container within a minute. Inspectors also use personal radiation detectors to scan for signs of radioactive materials, as well as special high-tech tools such as density meters and fiber-optic scopes to peer inside suspicious containers. Finally, if necessary, containers are opened and unloaded for a more intensive manual inspection.

8. Maritime Safety and Security Teams (MSSTs): MSSTs are a Coast Guard rapid response force assigned to vital ports and capable of nationwide deployment via air, ground, or sea transportation to meet emerging threats. MSSTs were created in direct response to the terrorist attacks on September 11, 2001, through the Maritime Transportation Security Act of 2002. They have unique capabilities, including explosives detection dogs, personnel trained to conduct fast-roping deployments from a helicopter to a hostile vessel, and antiterrorism/force protection small boat handling training. As of 2006, there are 12 distinct MSSTs within the U.S. Coast Guard, each with approximately 75 personnel (an Anchorage, AK-based team was dismantled in 2011).

9. Guarding in-between the Ports: Coast Guard, U.S. CBP, and U.S. Immigration and Customs Enforcement's Air and Marine Operations units are responsible for patrolling and securing the nation's borders between the ports of entry.

10. Transportation Workers Identity Card (TWIC): Through the TWIC program, a secure uniform credential has been developed for the transportation system to prevent potential terrorist threats from entering sensitive areas. The TWIC program ensures that credentials are accompanied by biometric identifiers to positively authenticate identities of TWIC holders. By having one universally recognized credential, workers avoid paying for redundant cards and background investigations to enter secure areas at multiple facilities. TSA kicked off the first TWIC credentialing in October 2007 at Port of Wilmington, Delaware, and since then expanded throughout the nation to over 165 enrollment centers. As of late 2011, over 1.9 million people were enrolled in the program, and over 1.8 million cards had been issued.

ANOTHER VOICE: VB-IEDS BY DON GOFF (C-STAR SYSTEMS).

The initial attack on December 7, 1941, came not, as we usually think, by aircraft, but from five small two-man submarines that tried to enter Pearl Harbor ahead of the planes. More recently, attacks on the M/S Achille Lauro and the USS Cole, piracy off of Somalia, and the terrorist incursion in Mumbai remind us that sea-borne attacks by small craft remain a real threat. Within the continental United States, the convergence of transportation, energy, and communication systems provide potential terrorists with numerous targets accessible by small boat. As in the attack on the USS Cole, a small boat filled with explosives maneuvered alongside a target can inflict substantial damage. Obtaining and operating a small boat is both affordable and easily learned. Termed "Vessel-borne Improvised Explosive Devices" or VB-IEDs, this attack vector creates a highly challenging scenario and causes more than a few sleepless nights for those charged with maritime defense and law enforcement.

Vulnerabilities

Attacks across water can, of course, occur anywhere along the United States' Atlantic, Pacific, Caribbean, and Great Lakes coast lines — some 88 thousand miles long, including Alaska and Hawaii. The vulnerabilities of the great port cities have been looked at in terms of point targets such as container facilities, nuclear plants, and liquid natural gas (LNG) terminals. A great deal of effort has gone on post 9/11 to identify, assess, and prioritize such vulnerability points. Less obvious are the cities on the inland waters. Of all the major cities in the U.S., only Indianapolis is not positioned on a navigable body of water. All of these cities, both coastal and inland, have a large concentration of critical infrastructure, and most are transportation hubs for air, rail, and motor transport, as well as for communications, energy, and power distribution.

Using open source materials, it is relatively easy to identify critical points in the transportation, energy, and communication infrastructure which, if attacked, could create not only chaos and physical damage, but also lead to substantial economic and environmental problems, using relatively small quantities of conventional explosives. Many of these open-source materials that can be used for target analysis are unclassified online resources that are just as readily available to potential terrorists as to casual surfers.

Examples of such convergence points are fairly intuitive. In the past several decades, railroads have struggled to remain profitable. Since at least the 1980s, they have augmented their revenue by leasing out their rights-of-way to other carriers such as telecommunications and gas and oil pipelines. When railroad bridges cross waterways, they may have cables and pipes attached to them or channeled under them. These points of infrastructure convergence exist in numerous locations around the country. Using global information system freeware on the Internet, it is fairly easy to spot these particular vulnerabilities. Current satellite photography resolution openly published allows even a casual observer to see these points with great ease and clarity.

Threats

We have seen such attacks in other instances, but not in the U.S. to date. The ready availability of small recreational watercraft and the shortage of law enforcement and Coast Guard coverage of all possible avenues of approach create great difficulties for detection. The ability of the potential terrorist to be "hiding in plain sight" makes this a particularly onerous threat. Think about the crowds of recreational boaters on the waterway on a given weekend driving small, white, fiberglass outboard runabouts. Think about the difficulty of detecting a specific such boat within those crowds of weekend sailors and you get a sense for the law enforcement challenges, though as we will see below, a number of countermeasures and mitigations are in play.

What is less clear is whether a potential terrorist would want to attack such targets simply because they are available. To date, most attacks have been included within a fairly narrow target window. The terrorists appear to believe they will score more political points by attacking symbolic targets than by imposing substantial physical damage to property. Lives matter more than things, fortunately. But the human impact of infrastructure damage could create a more significant impact, leaving longer term consequences.

Consequences

Conducting a kinetic attack against a single point of failure could not only produce damage at that point, but could trigger a cascading effect. Attacks on the telecommunications infrastructure are relatively self-healing. Attacks on the energy distribution system are more problematic. In addition to the loss of a power cable or a gas pipeline, the impact of a sea-borne attack could also produce ecological consequences, such as pollution of a river or bay, fouling of water intake ducts for public water supplies, or destroying wetlands.

With modern "just-in-time" delivery methods, the disruption of energy and transportation has a rapid and growing effect on manufacturing processes, food distribution, and other aspects of the economy which are dependent on those infrastructures. In studies simulating the importation of a series of "dirty bombs" through a west coast port, the economic impact grew steadily while the port was

(Continued)

---

closed, with economic effects felt for several weeks and even months after the port was reopened. One study identified port closures as costing the U.S. economy about $1 billion for each of the first five days, and then rising exponentially.

Risk Mitigation

The Maritime Transportation Security Act of 2002 (MTSA) was enacted to address port and waterway security. It focuses on vessels and port facilities conducting vulnerability assessments and developing security methods related to screening procedures, security patrols, restricted areas, personnel identification, access controls and surveillance equipment. It is primarily focused on the ocean ports.

The MTSA security regulations use risk-management methods to identify, prioritize and focus on those sectors of maritime industry with a higher risk of involvement in a transportation security incident, such as offshore oil and gas platforms, fuel terminals and port facilities that handle certain kinds of dangerous cargo or service the vessels that carry such cargoes.

MTSA also created Area Maritime Security Committees (AMSCs) to coordinate the activities of all maritime stakeholders, including other federal, local, and state agencies, industry, and recreational and commercial boaters. The AMSCs collaborate on identifying key locations that would present a risk, evaluate and prioritize those risks, and develop mitigation plans to deter, prevent, and respond to terror threats.

A large number of these area studies of sea-borne attacks have been conducted by the Coast Guard, ports authorities, and Area Maritime Security Committees; however, the inland waters have more limited security coverage and critical points are often at the jurisdictional boundaries of federal, state, and local governments. Entities such as the U.S. Coast Guard, Customs and Border Protection, the Federal Emergency Management Agency and state and local law enforcement and emergency planners collaborate to focus preventive measures on key points of vulnerability and to maximize the effectiveness of response.

Additional legislation was adopted four years later called the Security and Accountability For Every Port Act of 2006 (SAFE Port Act). This Act added certain requirements to prevent foreign ownership of U.S. ports, required worker identification measures, and created a grant program.

It also clarified the responsibilities of the Coast Guard's companion agencies within the Department of Homeland Security, Customs and Border Patrol (CBP), and the Transportation Security Administration (TSA).

CBP has added to efforts to counter terrorist efforts by creating the Container Security Initiative (CSI) and the Customs Trade Partnership against Terrorism (C-TPAT). These programs provide incentives to shippers to increase their security procedures and to focus on containers.

In addition, the Maritime Administration in the Department of Transportation has regulatory authority over both vessels and nonvessel operating container cargo, that is, the companies which own the containers but not the ships hauling them.

Finally, the Coast Guard has organized America's Waterways Watch, a sort of marine neighborhood watch, to encourage recreational and commercial boaters to develop situational awareness and to report suspicious behaviors through a toll free telephone number. This program is really the only program focused on the threat from VB-IEDs.

The primary focus of these government actions has been upon the major ports and upon container cargo and individual screenings. The problem is that none of these programs have focused on or provided major resources to analyze the threat and identify mitigation procedures for VB-IEDs, merely to look for them incidentally.

Don Goff has over forty years experience in business, education and public policy. He is a nationally recognized subject matter expert on security and critical infrastructure issues and has served on the Area Maritime Security Committees for the National Capital Region and for Maryland and the Chesapeake Bay. He is currently President of CSTAR Systems, Inc. Dr. Goff holds a Ph.D. from Northwestern University.

Bus Transportation Security

Bus transportation safety is an often-neglected link in the nation's transportation infrastructure and represents a substantial homeland security vulnerability. In the first edition of this book, we described the issue of bus transportation security as follows: "The bus transportation system is likely to eventually become a target of terrorists because the system has comparatively less protection against terrorist attacks, which makes it 'soft' for terrorists searching for less risky but high-consequence attacks." On July 7, 2007, a terrorist detonated a bomb in a London double-decker bus in a coordinated attack on the bus and rail networks of that city, killing 13 people and injuring many more. The incident highlighted the vulnerability of the bus transportation system, despite that the majority of transportation security efforts focus on air and sea transport. Securing the bus system is an extremely challenging task as public ground transportation is much more dynamic and state-changing than other types of transport. With multiple stops and frequently changing passengers over short periods of time, securing the bus system becomes a very resource intensive and, in some instances, impractical process. However, there are ways to reduce the vulnerabilities even if the security risks of bus transport cannot be eliminated to the degree as exists in other transportation sectors.

To support the intercity bus transportation sector, DHS established the Intercity Bus Security Grant Program under its Infrastructure Protection Program, as described before in this chapter. DHs uses this program to provide funding to intercity bus companies for the improvement of their transport security measures. In FY 2011, the Bus Security Grant Program was funded at $4.99 million.

Railway Transportation Security

The railroad system is another highly utilized and valuable component of the U.S. transportation infrastructure that requires protective measures to address the growing threat of terrorist attacks and other hazard-related vulnerabilities. DHS made its most noticeable references to the protection of the railway system in the National Strategy for the Physical Protection of Critical Infrastructure and Key Assets and in the announcement of Operation Liberty Shield. This national strategy document refers to potential vulnerabilities of the rail system and expands upon possible terrorist attack scenarios. In light of this, four priorities for improvement in the railroad security are identified, including:

1. The need to develop improved decision-making criteria regarding the shipment of hazardous materials: DHS and DOT, coordinating with other federal agencies, state and local governments, and industry, have facilitated the development of an improved process to ensure informed decision making with respect to hazardous materials shipments.
2. The need to develop technologies and procedures to screen intermodal containers and passenger baggage: DHS and DOT have worked with sector counterparts to identify and explore technologies

and processes to enable efficient and expeditious screening of rail passengers and baggage, especially at intermodal stations.

3. The need to improve security of intermodal transportation: DHS and DOT continue to work with sector counterparts to identify and facilitate the development of technologies and procedures to secure intermodal containers and detect threatening content. DHS and DOT have worked with the rail industry to devise or enable a hazardous materials identification system that supports the needs of first responders, yet avoids providing terrorists with easy identification of a potential weapon.

4. The need to clearly delineate roles and responsibilities regarding surge requirements: DHS and DOT have worked with industry to delineate infrastructure protection roles and responsibilities to enable the rail industry to address surge requirements for resources in the case of catastrophic events. Costs and resource allocation remain a contentious issue for the rail sector. DHS and DOT convened a working group consisting of government and industry representatives to identify options for the implementation of surge capabilities, including access to federal facilities and capabilities in extreme emergencies.

The national physical protection strategy clearly identifies the transportation of HAZMAT within the railroad infrastructure as the greatest vulnerability of the system. This assessment was reiterated by Admiral James Loy, former TSA administrator, in a meeting with the North American Rail Shippers Association where he identified the following as the primary threats to the railway system: (1) hazardous material, (2) nuclear and radiological material, (3) food and livestock, and (4) intermodal containers. In response to Admiral Loy's assessment, DOT and DHS released a document regarding the HAZMAT transportation vulnerability and measures to be taken to minimize the terrorist threat to the system. This document provides background information on the improvements accomplished in the railroad system since September 11. It discusses the security task force established by the Association of American Railroads (AAR) to assess vulnerabilities in several critical areas, such as physical assets, information technology, chemicals and hazardous materials, defense shipments, train operations, and passenger security. In March 2003, DHS announced Operation Liberty Shield, which included the following steps to enhance railway security:

1. To improve rail bridge security: State governors were asked to provide additional police or National Guard forces at selected bridges.

2. To increase railroad infrastructure security: Railroad companies were asked to increase security at major facilities and key rail hubs.

3. AMTRAK security measures: AMTRAK implemented security measures consistent with private rail companies.

4. To increase railroad hazardous material safety: At the request of the Department of Transportation, private railroad companies will monitor shipments of hazardous material and increase surveillance of trains carrying this material.

On April 8, 2004, the Senate's Commerce, Science, and Transportation Committee approved the Rail Security Act of 2004, which authorized an increase in rail security funding by $1.1 billion, over the initial funding of only $65 million. The Rail Security Act, as proposed, required DHS to conduct a vulnerability assessment of the nation's rail systems and report back to Congress with its findings. The vulnerability assessment requires a review of freight and passenger rail transportation, including the identification and evaluation of critical assets and infrastructures; threats to those assets and infrastructures; vulnerabilities that are specific to rail transportation of hazardous materials; and security weaknesses. Based on the assessment, DHS developed prioritized recommendations for improving the security of rail infrastructure and facilities, terminals, tunnels, bridges, and other at-risk areas; deploying weapons detection and surveillance equipment; training employees; and conducting public outreach campaigns. The results of the DHS freight and passenger rail transportation vulnerability assessment are also used to distribute future funding for the Rail Security Grant Program.

The Association of American Railroads coordinated and conducted a comprehensive risk analysis covering the entire railway industry. The scope of this risk assessment included the train operations, communication and cybersecurity aspects, identification and protection of critical assets, transportation of hazardous materials, and identification of a military liaison. The association worked closely with the federal intelligence community and security experts and identified and prioritized more than 1,300 critical assets. As a result of the vulnerability analysis, more than 50 permanent changes were made to procedures and operations, including restricted access to facilities, increased tracking of certain shipments, enhanced employee security training, and cybersecurity improvements. In addition to those measures, it was decided that one rail police officer should sit on the FBI's National Joint Terrorism Task Force, and two rail analysts should sit in the DHS intelligence offices to help evaluate data at the top-secret level. The association created a DOD-certified, full-time operations center, working at the secret level to monitor and evaluate intelligence on potential threats and communicate with railroads through the Railway Alert Network (RAN). A Surface Transportation Information Sharing and Analysis Center (ST-ISAC) — operating at the top secret level — was also created to collect, analyze, and disseminate information on physical and cybersecurity threats (Association of American Railroads, 2004).

As rail security grew in stature following the 9/11 attacks, TSA provided the top 10 mass transit and passenger rail agencies with TSA-certified explosives detection canine teams to aid in the identification of explosives materials within the mass transit/rail transportation system. The pilot inspection program was named the Transit and Rail Inspection Pilot (TRIP), which is a first-time rail security technology study conducted by DHS in cooperation with several other entities. TRIP was conducted in three phases. TRIP Phase I occurred at the New Carrollton, Maryland, rail station and evaluated the use of technologies for screening rail passengers and their baggage prior to boarding a train. TRIP Phase II occurred at Union Station in Washington, D.C., and tested the use of screening equipment for checked baggage and cargo prior to their loading onto an Amtrak passenger train, as well as screening of unclaimed baggage and temporarily stored items inside Union Station. TRIP Phase III occurred onboard a Shoreline East commuter rail car. The goal of Phase III was to evaluate the use of existing technologies installed on a rail car to screen passengers and their baggage for explosives, while the rail car is in transit. By 2007, DHS increased its deployment and coverage of explosives detection and canine teams to 13 mass transit systems and a total of 53 canine teams. In addition to the TRIP program, TSA hired and deployed 100 surface transportation (rail) inspectors to enhance the level of national transportation security by leveraging private and public partnerships through a consistent national program of compliance reviews, audits, and enforcement actions pertaining to required standards and directives.

The DHS FY 2011 Freight Rail Security Program was appropriated with total funds of $10 million. The funding priorities for the program were as follows:

1. *GPS tracking*: Owners and offerors of railroad cars used in the transportation of poisonous by inhalation/toxic inhalation hazardous (TIH) materials may apply for funds to acquire, install, and operate satellite GPS tracking on those railroad cars for the period of performance.
2. *Infrastructure hardening on rail bridges*: Owners of rail bridges that are used for freight rail transportation may apply for infrastructure hardening capabilities. Infrastructure hardening is defined as the act of applying security to the infrastructure including but not limited to access control systems, video monitoring systems, and physical barriers.

3. *Vulnerability assessments and security plans*: Freight railroad vulnerability assessments provide a broader picture of the mode's preparedness, as well as security risks that need to be mitigated. Security plans help target resources and mitigation strategies toward gaps in the mode's security identified by the vulnerability assessments. The information captured in the vulnerability assessments and security plans (including any mitigation strategies) can be used to form the basis of funding priorities for this grant program in future years, as appropriate. Only Class II and Class III railroad carriers are eligible to apply for vulnerability assessment and security planning funds.

4. *Security training and exercises for railroad frontline employees*: Effective employee training programs address individual employee responsibilities and provide heightened security awareness. Training should cover assessment and reporting of incidents, employee response, crew communication and coordination, and incident evacuation procedures.

Conclusion

Transportation safety and security are key concepts in the scope of homeland security given the high valuation of these systems to terrorists, the importance of the systems to freedom of movement and the U.S. economy, and because of the high vulnerability these systems have with regard to natural hazards (out of their sheer scope and size). The complexity of each of these systems and their related infrastructure, and the interconnectedness of each of these systems upon which we depend each day, increases our overall vulnerability and increases the difficulty of mitigating the risks we face. In dealing with those distinct vulnerabilities, homeland security agencies at all government levels, and security agencies within the transit authorities and in the private sector, must coordinate on a level that surpasses most other areas of security. The proportional budget appropriation dedicated to transportation security is indicative of these challenges and the growing risk we face as infrastructure ages, as populations move and expand, and as climate change brings about more frequent and devastating events.

Key Terms

Hazardous Material (HAZMAT): Materials, substances, or chemicals that are deemed to have adverse effects on human health and the environment. Typical examples of HAZMAT include but are not limited to biological, chemical, and radiological agents and materials. HAZMAT incidents may be intentional (terrorism) or unintentional (man-made/technological). Oil spills, poisonous gas releases, nuclear waste incidents, and dirty bombs are examples of HAZMAT-related incidents.

Smart Box: Designed to be "tamper evident," the Smart Box couples an internationally approved mechanical seal affixed to an alternate location on the container door with an electronic container security device designed to deter and detect tampering of the container door.

Transportation Workers Identity Card (TWIC): TWICs are tamper-resistant biometric credentials that will be issued to workers who require unescorted access to secure areas of ports, vessels, outer-continental-shelf facilities, and all credentialed merchant mariners.

Review Questions

What are the different transportation modes in the United States? How does the U.S. government protect each? Discuss what types of criteria should be used for prioritizing budgets for protecting different transportation modes.

References

American Petroleum Institute. 2005. Security guidelines for the petroleum industry. http://api.org/policy/otherissues/upload/SecurityGuideEd3.pdf.

American Petroleum Institute. 2008. Energy security: help reduce the threat. http://www.api.org/ehs/partnerships/community/energy-security.cfm.

American Society of Civil Engineers/American Water Works Association. 2006. Guidelines for the physical security of water utilities. http://www.asce.org/static/1/redirect.cfm?prmType=WISE&prmFile=20061/00_Complete_Document.

Association of American Railroads. 2004. Freight raill security briefing. http://www.aar.org/Rail_Safety/Security.pdf.

Association of Metropolitan Sewage Agencies (AMSA). 2004. Wastewater sector security link, vol. 1, no. 1. http://newsmanager.commpartners.com/amsawssl/issues/2004-06-17.html.

Associated Press. 2010. US knew for years that cargo planes were terror targets. (November 9). http://www.foxnews.com/us/2010/11/09/knew-cargo-planes-vulnerable-years/.

Blumenthal, H. 2003. Department of Human Services private sector information sharing: ISAC program. Government Symposium on Information Sharing and Homeland Security, Pennsylvania.

Central Intelligence Agency. 2007. Offices of CIA. https://www.cia.gov/offices-of-cia/index.html.

Central Intelligence Agency. 2008a. CIA organization chart. https://www.cia.gov/about-cia/leadership/cia-organization-chart.html.

Central Intelligence Agency. 2008b. History of the intelligence and analysis directorate. https://www.cia.gov/offices-of-cia/intelligence-analysis/history.html.

Central Intelligence Agency. 2008c. The CIA crime and narcotics center. https://www.cia.gov/offices-of-cia/intelligence-analysis/organization-1/the-cia-crime-and-narcotics-center.html.

Communications Sector Coordinating Council. 2007. Communications sector specific infrastructure protection plan. http://www.dhs.gov/xlibrary/assets/nipp-ssp-communications.pdf.

Communications Sector Coordinating Council. 2008. What is the CSCC? http://www.commscc.org/.

Congressional Research Service. 2004a. Border security and unmanned aerial vehicles. http://www.fas.org/irp/crs/RS21698.pdf/.

Congressional Research Service. 2004b. RL32506 — the proposed authorities of a national intelligence director: issues for Congress and side-by-side comparison of S. 2845, H.R. 10, and current law. http://www.fas.org/irp/crs/RL32506.pdf.

Congressional Research Service. 2004c. RS21948 — the national intelligence director and intelligence analysis. http://www.fas.org/irp/crs/RS21948.pdf.

Congressional Research Service. 2006. Border security: barriers along the U.S. international border. http://fas.org/sgp/crs/homesec/RL33659.pdf.

Congressional Research Service. 2007a. Terrorism and security issues facing the water infrastructure sector. http://www.fas.org/irp/crs/RL32189.pdf.

Congressional Research Service. 2007b. Terrorism and security issues facing the water infrastructure sector. http://www.fas.org/sgp/crs/terror/RL32189.pdf.

Congressional Research Service. 2008. FY 2009 appropriations for state and local homeland security. http://www.fas.org/sgp/crs/homesec/RS22805.pdf.

Coppola, D., 2003. Annotated Organizational Chart for the Department of Homeland Security. Bullock & Haddow, LLC., Washington, DC.

Department of Energy. 2007. Energy sector specific infrastructure plan. ftp://ftp.nerc.com/pub/sys/all_updl/cip/Energy_Redacted_All.pdf.

Department of Homeland Security. 2002. National strategy for homeland security. http://www.dhs.gov/xlibrary/assets/nat_strat_hls.pdf.

Department of Homeland Security. 2003. National strategy for the protection of physical infrastructure and key assets. http://www.dhs.gov/xlibrary/assets/Physical_Strategy.pdf.

Department of Homeland Security. 2004a. Agency responsibilities by functional areas, functions and tasks. NRP Initial Plan Draft, Appendix A, Table 6.2.

Department of Homeland Security. 2004b. Fact sheet: Arizona border control initiative. http://www.dhs.gov/xnews/releases/press_release_0520.shtm.

Department of Homeland Security. 2004c. The national plan for research and development in support of critical infrastructure protection. http://www.dhs.gov/xlibrary/assets/ST_2004_NCIP_RD_PlanFINALApr05.pdf.

Department of Homeland Security. 2004d. Fiscal year 2005 freight rail security program application kit. http://www.ojp.usdoj.gov/odp/docs/FY2005FRSP.pdf.

Department of Homeland Security. 2005a. Fact sheet: Arizona border control initiative — phase II. https://www.dhs.gov/xnews/releases/press_release_0646.shtm.

Department of Homeland Security. 2005b. FY 2006 critical infrastructure protection program. http://www.ojp.usdoj.gov/odp/newsreleases/FY06_IPP_PressKit.pdf.

Department of Homeland Security. 2006a. DHS releases cyber storm public exercise report. http://www.dhs.gov/xnews/releases/pr_1158341221370.shtm.

Department of Homeland Security. 2006b. FY 2007 critical infrastructure protection program. http://www.dhs.gov/xlibrary/assets/grants-2007-infrastructure-protection.pdf.

Department of Homeland Security. 2007a. Budget in brief FY 2008. http://www.dhs.gov/xlibrary/assets/budget_bib-fy2008.pdf.

Department of Homeland Security. 2007b. DHS moves forward on border fencing and technology improvements. http://www.dhs.gov/xnews/releases/pr_1197058374853.shtm.

Department of Homeland Security. 2007c. Overview: FY 2007 infrastructure protection program final awards. http://www.dhs.gov/xlibrary/assets/grants_ippawardsfy07.pdf.

Department of Homeland Security. 2007d. Strategy to enhance international supply chain security. http://www.dhs.gov/xlibrary/assets/plcy-internationalsupply-chainsecuritystrategy.pdf.

Department of Homeland Security. 2007e. The national response framework ESF#10 annex. http://www.fema.gov/pdf/emergency/nrf/nrf-annexes-all.pdf.

Department of Homeland Security. 2007f. FY 2008 critical infrastructure protection program. http://www.fema.gov/government/grant/ipp/index.shtm#tsp/.

Department of Homeland Security. 2007g. Overview: FY 2007 infrastructure protection program awards. http://www.dhs.gov/xlibrary/assets/grants-2007-infrastructure-protection.pdf.

Department of Homeland Security. 2008a. Budget in brief FY 2009. http://www.dhs.gov/xlibrary/assets/budget_bib-fy2009.pdf.

Department of Homeland Security. 2008b. FY 2008 port security grant program. http://www.fema.gov/government/grant/psgp/index.shtm.

Department of Homeland Security. 2008c. Cyber storm: securing cyber space. http://www.dhs.gov/xprepresp/training/gc_1204738275985.shtm.

Department of Homeland Security. 2008d. National cybersecurity division. http://www.dhs.gov/xabout/structure/editorial_0839.shtm.

Department of Transportation Maritime Administration. 2002. U.S. waterborne foreign trade containerized cargo stats. https://www.marad.dot.gov/Marad_Statistics/Con-Pts-02.htm.

Digital National Security Archive. 2003. Overview of U.S. intelligence. http://nsarchive.chadwyck.com/esp_essay.htm.

Environmental Protection Agency. 1998. How wastewater treatment works: the basics. http://www.epa.gov/npdes/pubs/bastre.pdf.

Environmental Protection Agency. 2002. FY 2003 budget in brief. http://www.epa.gov/ocfo/budget/2003/2003bib.pdf.

Environmental Protection Agency. 2006a. EPA budget in brief FY 2007. http://www.epa.gov/budget/2007/2007bib.pdf/.

Environmental Protection Agency. 2006b. EPA water security initiative (WaterSentinel). http://www.epa.gov/safewater/watersecurity/pubs/fs_watersecurity_securityinitiative.pdf.

Environmental Protection Agency. 2007a. EPA budget in brief FY 2008. http://www.epa.gov/budget/2007/2008bib.pdf.

Environmental Protection Agency. 2007b. Water sector specific infrastructure protection plan. http://www.dhs.gov/xlibrary/assets/Water_SSP_5_21_07.pdf.

Environmental Protection Agency. 2008. EPA budget in brief FY 2009. http://www.epa.gov/budget/2007/2009bib.pdf.

Government Accountability Office. 2004a. GAO-04-1062 maritime security. http://www.gao.gov/new.items/d041062.pdf.

Government Accountability Office. 2004b. Terrorism insurance: effects of the terrorism risk insurance act of 2002. http://www.gao.gov/new.items/ d04806t.pdf.

Government Accountability Office. 2006a. GAO-07-39 critical infrastructure protection: progress coordinating government and private sector efforts varies by sectors' characteristics. http://www.gao.gov/new.items/d0739.pdf.

Government Accountability Office. 2006b. Securing wastewater facilities. http://www.gao.gov/new.items/d06390.pdf.

Government Accountability Office. 2007a. GAO-07-412 port risk management. http://www.gao.gov/new.items/d07412.pdf.

Government Accountability Office. 2007b. Passenger rail security — federal strategy and enhanced coordination needed to prioritize and guide security efforts. http://www.gao.gov/cgi-bin/getrpt?GAO-07-583T.

Greenberg, W.J. 2003. September 11, 2001: a CEO's story. *Harvard Business Review*, vol. 10.1225/R0210D, pp. 7–8.

Harrald, C., Coppola, D.P., Yeletaysi, S. 2003. Assessing the financial impacts of the World Trade Center attacks on publicly held corporations. TIEMS Conference Proceedings, Provence, France.

Kavanaugh, P. 2002. Current state of crisis management as an industry in Canada. The Health Canada Emergency Preparedness Forum, October 28, 2002.

Lerbinger, O., 1997. The Crisis Manager. Lawrence Erlbaum Associates, New York.

Marsh & Mclennan Company 2008. Terrorism Risk Insurance Act (TRIA) is extended by Congress. http://global.marsh.com/documents/TRIA_Is_Extended_2nd_Edition.pdf.

McDaniel, G. (Ed.), 1994. IBM Dictionary of Computing. McGraw-Hill, New York.

Medical News Today. 2006. Landfills, chemical weapon debris possibly a good match, computer model suggests. http://www.medicalnewstoday.com/articles/46108.php.

MILNET. 2006. Changes to the U.S. Intelligence Community. http://www.milnet.com/Changes%20to%20Intelligence%20Community.html.

Minuteman Civil Defense Corps. 2008. Volunteer saves illegal alien from certain death. http://bborderops.com/index.php?option5com_content&task5view&id541&Itemid52.

National Coordination Center for Telecommunications. 2008. Program information. http://www.ncs.gov/ncc/.

Northrop Grumman. 2004. Press release: HSDN. http://www.it.northropgrumman.com/pressroom/press/2004/pr151.html.

Office of the Director of National Intelligence. 2005. Establishment of the national clandestine service (NCS). http://www.odni.gov/press_releases/20051013_release.htm

Office of the Director of National Intelligence. 2008a. Members of the intelligence community. http://www.intelligence.gov/1-members.shtml.

Office of the Director of National Intelligence. 2008b. ODNI organization. http://www.dni.gov/aboutODNI/organization.htm.

Office of the Director of National Intelligence. 2008c. ODNI press releases 2005. http://www.odni.gov/press_releases/press_releases_2005.htm.

Office of the Director of National Intelligence. 2008d. ODNI press releases 2006. http://www.odni.gov/press_releases/press_releases_2006.htm.

Office of the Director of National Intelligence. 2008e. ODNI press releases 2007–2008. http://www.odni.gov/press_releases/press_releases.htm.

Reed, D. 2006. US airports, by the numbers. USA Today (September 27). http://www.usatoday.com/travel/flights/2006-09-26-airport-numbers_x.htm.

Richelson, J.T., 1999. The U.S. Intelligence Community, 4th ed. Westview Press, Boulder, CO.

Richelson, J.T., Gefter, J., Waters, M., et al. 2003. U.S. espionage and intelligence, 1947–1996. Digital National Security Archive. Mfiche 2552 GRN–MTXT.

Smith, B.F., 1983. The Shadow Warriors: OSS, and the Origins of the CIA. Basic Books, New York.

The White House. 2003. National strategy to secure cyberspace. http://www.whitehouse.gov/pcipb/cyberspace_strategy.pdf.

The White House. 2005. Border and transportation security. http://www.whitehouse.gov/deptofhomeland/sect3.html/.

Transportation Sector Government Coordinating Council. 2007. Transportation systems specific infrastructure protection plan. http://www.dhs.gov/xlibrary/assets/nipp-ssp-transportation.pdf.

Transportation Security Administration. 2005. TSA FY 2004 budget briefing. (June 2005). http://www.tsa.gov/public/interweb/assetlibrary/TSA_FY2004_budget_briefing_(public).ppt.

Transportation Security Administration. 2006. TSA turns five. http://www.tsa.gov/5th/index.shtm.

Transportation Security Administration. 2007a. DHS agencies announce enrollment dates for TWIC in 10 ports. http://www.tsa.gov/press/releases/2008/0304.shtm.

Transportation Security Administration. 2007b. Fact sheet: FY 2008 freight rail security grant program. http://www.tsa.gov/assets/pdf/fy_2008_frsgp_fs.pdf.

Transportation Security Administration. 2007c. FAQ: transportation worker identification credential (TWIC). http://www.tsa.gov/what_we_do/layers/twic/twic_faqs.shtm.

Transportation Security Administration. 2007d. FY 2008 freight rail security grant program. http://www.tsa.gov/assets/pdf/fy_2008_frsgp.pdf.

Transportation Security Administration. 2007e. FY 2008 trucking security program fact sheet. http://www.tsa.gov/assets/pdf/fy_2008_tsp_fs.pdf.

Transportation Security Administration. 2008. FY 2008 intercity bus security grant program. http://www.tsa.gov/assets/pdf/fy_2008_ibsgp_fs.pdf.

TSA. 2011. Transportation sector network management. http://www.tsa.gov/what_we_do/tsnm/index.shtm.

U.S. Customs and Border Protection. 2006a. Border patrol overview. http://www.cbp.gov/xp/cgov/border_security/border_patrol/border_patrol_ohs/overview.xml.

U.S. Customs and Border Protection. 2006b. SBInet: securing U.S. borders. http://www.dhs.gov/xlibrary/assets/sbinetfactsheet.pdf.

U.S. Customs and Border Protection. 2008a. FY 2007 performance and accountability report. http://www.cbp.gov/linkhandler/cgov/toolbox/publications/admin/fiscal_2007.ctt/fiscal_2007.pdf.

U.S. Customs and Border Protection. 2008b. Ports in CSI. http://www.cbp.gov/xp/cgov/border_security/international_activities/csi/ports_in_csi.xml.

U.S. Department of Transportation. 2008. Serious HAZMAT incidents in the U.S. 1997–2006. http:/hazmat.dot.gov/pubs/inc/data/tenyr_new_serious.pdf.

U.S. Immigration and Customs Enforcement. 2008a. ICE FY 2007 accomplishments. http://www.ice.gov/doclib/pi/news/factsheets/fy07accmplshmntsweb.pdf.

U.S. Immigration and Customs Enforcement. 2008b. ICE operations. http://www.ice.gov/about/operations.htm.

U.S. Coast Guard. 2004. Secure seas, open ports. http://www.piersystem.com/go/doc/586/41841/.

U.S. Coast Guard. 2007. Coast Guard announces record drug seizures. http://www.piersystem.com/go/doc/786/184995/.

U.S. Congress, 1983. Compilation of Intelligence Laws and Related Laws and Executive Orders of Interest to the National Intelligence Community. U.S. Government Printing Office, Washington, DC.

USA Today. 2005. Border patrols growing in Arizona (March 29). http://www.usatoday.com/news/nation/2005-03-29-borders_x.htm.

Water Environment Research Foundation. 2008. WERF research projects online database. http://www.werf.org/.

Water ISAC. 2008. What is water ISAC? http://www.waterisac.org/cs/what_is_waterisac.

8

Cybersecurity and Critical Infrastructure Protection

What You Will Learn

- The meaning of the terms *cybersecurity* and *critical infrastructure*
- The roles of various federal government agencies in maintaining cybersecurity and protecting critical infrastructure
- Local and state government cybersecurity responsibilities
- Private sector cybersecurity and critical infrastructure protection responsibilities
- What programs exist to help entities respond to cybersecurity and critical infrastructure issues
- Recent ideas surrounding the possibility of cyber war

Introduction

Cybersecurity is defined by *Webster's Dictionary* as "measures taken to protect a computer or computer system (as on the Internet) against unauthorized access or attack." *Cyberterrorism* is the newest of all terrorist attack methods, and it is defined as the use or destruction of computing or information technology resources aimed at harming, coercing, or intimidating others in order to achieve a greater political or ideological goal (thus differentiating cyberterrorism from cybercrime, which seeks only personal gain or notoriety).

Cyberterrorism has more recently become a major threat, one which continues to increase in severity with each passing year as our nation's and the world's reliance on information technology, computers, and the Internet grows. This reliance has come to exist in virtually all sectors of society, beginning with our economic engines, spanning through almost every component of our critical and other infrastructure systems (including communication systems, power generation facilities, water treatment plants, dams, transportation, and many other areas), and even including the nation's military command and control mechanisms and facilities. The current systems are inherently insecure as demonstrated by the hacking into the systems of the Pentagon and of the defense contractor Lockheed Martin. Adding to the threat are individuals and nations who are adversaries of the U.S. and thus seek to exploit our dependence on cyberspace. While much action has already been taken to protect these systems, whether foreign or domestic, our growing reliance on technology greatly increases the potential consequences were these systems to be compromised, disrupted, or destroyed. Criminals and terrorists are constantly developing new and innovative ways to compromise these ever-more complex systems on which we rely.

Critical infrastructure refers to those assets, systems, and networks that are essential to preserving national security, public safety, economic health, and the social security of our citizens and our communities. Cybersecurity — or protection of the information technology sector — is part of the critical infrastructure matrix. Homeland Security Presidential Directive (HSPD) 7: Critical Infrastructure Identification, Prioritization, and Protection established U.S. policy for enhancing protection of critical infrastructure.

The intent of this chapter is to discuss current policies, programs, and actions that have been undertaken in the areas of cybersecurity and critical infrastructure. Because of the technical nature of these subjects, some materials in this chapter are derived directly from publications of the DHS. We have also included a cross-reference to the 9/11 Commission report, as several recommendations included in the report applied to cybersecurity and critical infrastructure.

Cybersecurity

Cybersecurity and cyberterrorism have been concerns of the private sector and government agencies, including the military and the FBI, since the 1980s. Following the September 11 terrorist attacks, cybersecurity as a terrorist risk was pushed closer into the limelight and was referred to directly in the National Strategy for Homeland Security as a national concern, and again as a central component of the subsequent National Strategy to Secure Cyberspace. The Comprehensive National Cybersecurity Initiative (CNCI) is an essential part of this strategy as is Presidential Directive 54. Additionally, it was addressed through the executive office by means of the issuance of Homeland Security Presidential Directive (HSPD) 7: Critical Infrastructure Identification, Prioritization, and Protection.

Cybersecurity has a prominent role in the National Security Strategy published by the White House in May 2010, and the Obama Administration has moved aggressively to identify emerging issues and to work with the international community to address cybersecurity.

Excerpts from the White House Cyber Policy Review

Cyberspace touches practically everything and everyone. It provides a platform for innovation and prosperity and the means to improve general welfare around the globe. But with the broad reach of a loose and lightly regulated digital infrastructure, great risks threaten nations, private enterprises, and individual rights. The government has a responsibility to address these strategic vulnerabilities to ensure that the United States and its citizens, together with the larger community of nations, can realize the full potential of the information technology revolution.

The architecture of the nation's digital infrastructure, based largely upon the Internet, is not secure or resilient. Without major advances in the security of these systems or significant change in how they are constructed or operated, it is doubtful that the United States can protect itself from the growing threat of cybercrime and state-sponsored intrusions and operations. Our digital infrastructure has already suffered intrusions that have allowed criminals to steal hundreds of millions of dollars, and nation-states and other entities to steal intellectual property and sensitive military information. Other intrusions threaten to damage portions of our critical infrastructure. These and other risks have the potential to undermine the Nation's confidence in the information systems that underlie our economic and national security interests.

The Federal government is not organized to address this growing problem effectively now or in the future. Responsibilities for cybersecurity are distributed across a wide array of federal departments and agencies, many with overlapping authorities, and none with sufficient decision authority to direct actions that deal with often conflicting issues in a consistent way. The government needs to integrate competing interests to derive a holistic vision and plan to address the cybersecurity-related issues confronting the United States. The Nation needs to develop the policies, processes, people, and technology required to mitigate cybersecurity-related risks.

Information and communications networks are largely owned and operated by the private sector, both nationally and internationally. Thus, addressing network security issues requires a public-private partnership as well as international cooperation and norms. The United States needs a comprehensive framework to ensure coordinated response and recovery by the government, the private sector, and our allies to a significant incident or threat.

The United States needs to conduct a national dialogue on cybersecurity to develop more public awareness of the threat and risks and to ensure an integrated approach toward the Nation's need for security and the national commitment to privacy rights and civil liberties guaranteed by the Constitution and law.

Research on new approaches to achieving security and resiliency in information and communications infrastructures is insufficient. The government needs to increase investment in research that will help address cybersecurity vulnerabilities while also meeting our economic needs and national security requirements.

The Nation is at a crossroads. The globally interconnected digital information and communications infrastructure known as "cyberspace" underpins almost every facet of modern society and provides critical support for the U.S. economy, civil infrastructure, public safety, and national security. This technology has transformed the global economy and connected people in ways never imagined. Yet, cybersecurity risks pose some of the most serious economic and national security challenges of the 21st Century. The digital infrastructure's architecture was driven more by considerations of interoperability and efficiency than of security. Consequently, a growing array of state and non-state actors are compromising, stealing, changing, or destroying information and could cause critical disruptions to U.S. systems. At the same time, traditional telecommunications and Internet networks continue to converge, and other infrastructure sectors are adopting the Internet as a primary means of interconnectivity. The United States faces the dual challenge of maintaining an environment that promotes efficiency, innovation, economic prosperity, and free trade while also promoting safety, security, civil liberties, and privacy rights.[1] It is the fundamental responsibility of our government to address strategic vulnerabilities in cyberspace and ensure that the United States and the world realize the full potential of the information technology revolution.

The status quo is no longer acceptable. The United States must signal to the world that it is serious about addressing this challenge with strong leadership and vision. Leadership should be elevated and strongly anchored within the White House to provide direction, coordinate action, and achieve results. In addition, federal leadership and accountability for cybersecurity should be strengthened. This approach requires clarifying the cybersecurity-related roles and responsibilities of federal departments and agencies while providing the policy, legal structures, and necessary coordination to empower them to perform their missions. While

---

[1] Internet Security Alliance, *The Cyber Security Social Contract: Policy Recommendations for the Obama Administration and 111th Congress,* at 5.

efforts over the past two years started key programs and made great strides by bridging previously disparate agency missions, they provide an incomplete solution. Moreover, this issue transcends the jurisdictional purview of individual departments and agencies because, although each agency has a unique contribution to make, no single agency has a broad enough perspective or authority to match the sweep of the problem.

The national dialogue on cybersecurity must begin today. The government, working with industry, should explain this challenge and discuss what the Nation can do to solve problems in a way that the American people can appreciate the need for action. People cannot value security without first understanding how much is at risk. Therefore, the Federal government should initiate a national public awareness and education campaign informed by previous successful campaigns. Further, similar to the period after the launch of the Sputnik satellite in October, 1957, the United States is in a global race that depends on mathematics and science skills. While we continue to boast the most positive environment for information technology firms in the world, the Nation should develop a workforce of U.S. citizens necessary to compete on a global level and sustain that position of leadership.

The United States cannot succeed in securing cyberspace if it works in isolation. The Federal government should enhance its partnership with the private sector. The public and private sectors' interests are intertwined with a shared responsibility for ensuring a secure, reliable infrastructure. There are many ways in which the Federal government can work with the private sector, and these alternatives should be explored. The public-private partnership for cybersecurity must evolve to define clearly the nature of the relationship, including the roles and responsibilities of each of the partners.[2,3,4] The Federal government should examine existing public–private partnerships to optimize their capacity to identify priorities and enable efficient execution of concrete actions.[5,6,7]

The Nation also needs a strategy for cybersecurity designed to shape the international environment and bring like-minded nations together on a host of issues, such as technical standards and acceptable legal norms regarding territorial jurisdiction, sovereign responsibility, and use of force. International norms are critical to establishing a secure and thriving digital infrastructure. In addition, differing national and regional laws and practices — such as laws concerning the investigation and prosecution of cybercrime; data preservation, protection, and privacy; and approaches for network defense and response to cyberattacks — present serious challenges to achieving a safe, secure, and resilient digital environment. Only by working with international partners can the United States best address these challenges, enhance cybersecurity, and reap the full benefits of the digital age.

The Federal government cannot entirely delegate or abrogate its role in securing the Nation from a cyber incident or accident. The Federal government has the responsibility to protect and

[2] Written testimony of Scott Charney (Microsoft) to the House Committee on Homeland Security, Subcommittee on Emerging Threats, Cybersecurity, and Science and Technology, March 10, 2009, at 4.
[3] Cross-Sector Cyber Security Working Group (CSCSWG) Response to 60-day Cyber Review Questions, March 16, 2009, at 2.
[4] Information Technology & Communications Sector Coordinating Councils, March 20, 2009, at 2.
[5] Center for Strategic and International Studies (CSIS) Commission on Cybersecurity for the 44th Presidency, *Securing Cyberspace for the 44th Presidency*, December 2008, at 43.
[6] TechAmerica, Response to 60-Day Cyber Security Review, at 6.
[7] Business Software Alliance, *National Security & Homeland Security Councils Review of National Cyber Security Policy*, March 19, 2009, at Q3.

defend the country, and all levels of government have the responsibility to ensure the safety and wellbeing of citizens. The private sector, however, designs, builds, owns, and operates most of the digital infrastructures that support government and private users alike. The United States needs a comprehensive framework to ensure a coordinated response by the Federal, State, local, and tribal governments, the private sector, and international allies to significant incidents. Implementation of this framework will require developing reporting thresholds, adaptable response and recovery plans, and the necessary coordination, information sharing, and incident reporting mechanisms needed for those plans to succeed. The government, working with key stakeholders, should design an effective mechanism to achieve a true common operating picture that integrates information from the government and the private sector and serves as the basis for informed and prioritized vulnerability mitigation efforts and incident response decisions.

Working with the private sector, performance and security objectives must be defined for the next-generation infrastructure. The United States should harness the full benefits of technology to address national economic needs and national security requirements. Federal policy should address requirements for national security, protection of intellectual property, and the availability and continuity of infrastructure, even when it is under attack by sophisticated adversaries. The Federal government through partnerships with the private sector and academia needs to articulate coordinated national information and communications infrastructure objectives. The government, working with State and local partners, should identify procurement strategies that will incentivize the market to make more secure products and services available to the public. Additional incentive mechanisms that the government should explore include adjustments to liability considerations (reduced liability in exchange for improved security or increased liability for the consequences of poor security), indemnification, tax incentives, and new regulatory requirements and compliance mechanisms.[8,9]

The White House must lead the way forward. The Nation's approach to cybersecurity over the past 15 years has failed to keep pace with the threat. We need to demonstrate abroad and at home that the United States takes cybersecurity related issues, policies, and activities seriously. This requires White House leadership that draws upon the strength, advice, and ideas of the entire Nation.

Table 8–1 Near-Term Action Plan

---

1. Appoint a cybersecurity policy official responsible for coordinating the Nation's cybersecurity policies and activities; establish a strong NSC directorate, under the direction of the cybersecurity policy official dual-hatted to the NSC and the NEC, to coordinate interagency development of cybersecurity-related strategy and policy.
2. Prepare for the President's approval an updated national strategy to secure the information and communications infrastructure. This strategy should include continued evaluation of CNCI activities and, where appropriate, build on its successes.
3. Designate cybersecurity as one of the President's key management priorities and establish performance metrics.

---

[8] Jim Harper, *Government-Run Cybersecurity? No Thanks.* Cato Institute March 13, 2009.
[9] Internet Security Alliance. *Issue Area 3; Norms of Behavior—Hathaway Questions,* March 24, 2009, at 2. 4–7.

Table 8–1 (Continued)

4. Designate a privacy and civil liberties official to the NSC cybersecurity directorate.
5. Convene appropriate interagency mechanisms to conduct interagency-cleared legal analyses of priority cybersecurity-related issues identified during the policy-development process and formulate coherent unified policy guidance that clarifies roles, responsibilities, and the application of agency authorities for cybersecurity-related activities across the Federal government.
6. Initiate a national public awareness and education campaign to promote cybersecurity.
7. Develop U.S. Government positions for an international cybersecurity policy framework and strengthen our international partnerships to create initiatives that address the full range of activities, policies, and opportunities associated with cybersecurity.
8. Prepare a cybersecurity incident response plan; initiate a dialog to enhance public-private partnerships with an eye toward streamlining, aligning, and providing resources to optimize their contribution and engagement
9. In collaboration with other EOP entities, develop a framework for research and development strategies that focus on game-changing technologies that have the potential to enhance the security, reliability, resilience, and trustworthiness of digital infrastructure; provide the research community access to event data to facilitate developing tools, testing theories, and identifying workable solutions.
10. Build a cybersecurity-based identity management vision and strategy that addresses privacy and civil liberties interests, leveraging privacy-enhancing technologies for the Nation.

Source: www.whitehouse.gov/issues/cybersecurity.

Components of Cybersecuity

Cyberinfrastructure includes electronic information and communication systems, and the information contained in these systems. Computer systems, control systems such as Supervisory Control and Data Acquisition (SCADA) systems, and networks such as the Internet are all part of the cyberinfrastructure.

Information and communications systems are composed of hardware and software that process, store, and communicate data of all types. Processing includes the creation, access, modification, and destruction of information. Storage includes paper, magnetic, electronic, and all other media types. Communications include sharing and distribution of information.

Information technology (IT) critical functions are sets of processes that produce, provide, and maintain products and services. IT critical functions encompass the full set of processes (e.g., R&D, manufacturing, distribution, upgrades, and maintenance) involved in transforming supply inputs into IT products and services.

DHS Cybersecurity Efforts

Through Presidential directives, the Department of Homeland Security (DHS) was tasked with leading and managing the nation's cyberterrorism threat through its risk management division, the Directorate for National Protection and Programs. In the Quadrennial Homeland Security Review published by DHS in February 2010, the fourth stated mission of the Department was Safeguarding and Securing Cyberspace. In this document, they state, "Our vision is a cyberspace that supports a secure and resilient infrastructure, that enables innovation and prosperity, and that protects privacy and other civil liberties by design. It is one in which we can use cyberspace with confidence to advance our economic interests and maintain national security under all conditions. We will achieve this vision by focusing on two goals: (1) helping to create a safe, secure, and resilient cyber environment; and (2) promoting cybersecurity knowledge and innovation. We must enhance public awareness and ensure that the public both recognizes cybersecurity challenges and is empowered to address them. We must create a dynamic cyber workforce across government with sufficient capacity and expertise to manage current and emerging risks. We must invest in the innovative technologies, techniques, and procedures necessary to sustain a safe, secure, and resilient cyber environment. Government must work creatively and collaboratively with the private sector to identify solutions that take into account both public and private interests, and the private sector and academia must be fully empowered to see and solve ever larger parts of the problem set. Finally, because cybersecurity is an exceedingly dynamic field, we must make specific efforts to ensure that the nation is prepared for the cyber threats and challenges of tomorrow, not only of today. To do this, we must promote cybersecurity knowledge and innovation. Innovation in technology, practice, and policy must further protect — not erode — privacy and civil liberties."

Safeguarding and Securing Cyberspace: Mission Goals and Objectives

Our security and way of life depend upon a vast array of interdependent and critical networks, systems, services, and resources. To have an infrastructure that is secure and resilient, enables innovation and prosperity, and protects privacy and other civil liberties by design, we must secure cyberspace and manage other risks to its safe use.

Key Strategic Outcomes

- Critical information systems and information and communications services are secure, reliable, and readily available.
- Homeland security partners develop, update, and implement guidelines, regulations, and standards that ensure the confidentiality, integrity, and reliability of systems, networks, and data.
- Cyber disruptions or attacks are detected in real-time, consequences are mitigated, and services are restored rapidly.
- Academic institutions produce and homeland security partners sustain a cybersecurity workforce that meets national needs and enables competitiveness.
- Critical infrastructure sectors adopt and sector partners meet accepted standards that measurably reduce the risk of cyber disruption or exploitation.

Goal 4.1: Create a Safe, Secure, and Resilient Cyber Environment

Ensure malicious actors are unable to effectively exploit cyberspace, impair its safe and secure use, or attack the nation's information infrastructure.

Objectives

- **Understand and prioritize cyber threats**: Identify and evaluate the most dangerous threats to Federal civilian and private-sector networks and the Nation.
- **Manage risks to cyberspace**: Protect and make resilient information systems, networks, and personal and sensitive data.
- **Prevent cybercrime and other malicious uses of cyberspace**: Disrupt the criminal organizations and other malicious actors engaged in high-consequence or wide-scale cybercrime.
- **Develop a robust public–private cyber incident response capability**: Manage cyber incidents from identification to resolution in a rapid and replicable manner with prompt and appropriate action.

Goal 4.2: Promote Cybersecurity Knowledge and Innovation: Ensure that the Nation is prepared for the cyber threats and challenges of tomorrow.

Objectives

- **Enhance public awareness**: Ensure that the public recognizes cybersecurity challenges and is empowered to address them.
- **Foster a dynamic workforce**: Develop the national knowledge base and human capital capabilities to enable success against current and future threats.
- **Invest in innovative technologies, techniques, and procedures**: Create and enhance science, technology, governance mechanisms, and other elements necessary to sustain a safe, secure, and resilient cyber environment.

CASE STUDY: HACKERS INFILTRATE SEARCH ENGINES, SOCIAL NETWORKS

By Jon Swartz,
USA TODAY
(Published April 9, 2008)

SAN FRANCISCO — Consumers who use search engines, online social networks, browsers and the like face a gantlet of viruses and malicious software code, according to a cybersecurity report from Symantec, issued Tuesday as security experts gather here for the sprawling RSA Conference on tech security.

The repercussions go beyond the loss of personal data, security experts say. As more consumers are victimized, it could undercut their confidence in legitimate websites, says Billy Hoffman, manager of Hewlett-Packard Security Labs.

Previously, hackers were more likely to use e-mail with attachments to steer victims to virus-tainted websites. Now, they are implanting their links on legitimate websites.

In all, Symantec detected 711,912 threats last year, compared with 125,243 in 2006. The malicious attacks – including recent exploits of users of Google, Facebook, search engine Mozilla and others – are designed to steal user credentials or launch bigger attacks through the victim's social network of contacts, says Alfred Huger, vice president of engineering at Symantec.

"Rather than set a bear trap – a porn or get-rich-quick site loaded with malicious code – to entice users, hackers are actively hunting by injecting their bad stuff on trustworthy sites," Hoffman says.

Among the most frequent targets:

Search engines. Cybercriminals are using a chink in Google's website to redirect unsuspecting PC users to sites containing malicious software. When someone does a Google search, they are redirected to what appears to be a legitimate website. The site, in fact, is tainted with malware. Google says it is fixing the problem. Mozilla, considered a safer alternative to Microsoft's Internet Explorer, is not immune. In the last six months of 2007, there were 88 vulnerabilities reported in Mozilla browsers, compared with 34 in the first half, says Symantec's report.

uSocial networks. Hackers are intensifying their efforts to compromise social-networking sites using unsecure Web 2.0 technologies to load malware onto the PCs of consumers. Indeed, the number of compromised sites is "slowly outnumbering malicious ones created specifically by cybercriminals," the report says.

In one breach, a widget application on Facebook that promised to tell members who had a secret crush on them instead tried to trick them into downloading spyware. The scam was discovered by security firm Fortinet.

Meanwhile, the latest of three computer worms wriggled into Google's social-networking service, Orkut, in February. Like a worm in December, this one spreads through comments that are typically posted on a user's profile, says Robert McArdle, an anti-virus specialist at Trend Micro.

uCalendar. Scammers are sending personalized e-mail as meeting invitations in Google Calendar. Since each e-mail has a different link for each recipient, it is harder for spam filters to detect anything wrong, says Jamz Yaneza, research project manager at Trend Micro.

The e-mail informs victims that they have inherited or are due a large amount of money from an unlikely source. The spammer asks the victim to pay a nominal fee to cover the transfer of the alleged inherited funds. Google support has been notified by security firms, and it is blocking accounts used in the scam.

While other federal agencies and the private sector are extremely active in this area, DHS has been in the lead in the federal government's efforts to respond to this issue. DHS is responsible for helping Federal Executive Branch civilian departments and agencies secure their unclassified networks (.gov). DHS also works with owners and operators of critical infrastructure and key resources (CIKR) — whether private sector, state, or municipality — to support their cybersecurity preparedness. DHS has created an intricate and complex array of programs and organizations. In a June, 2011 report on the DHS website, a summary of their activities in cybersecurity lists numerous organizations, partnerships, and activities that they are engaged in. Based on this report, the following programs and initiatives are being undertaken in support of federal cybersecurity efforts.

National Cyber Incident Response Plan

The President's Cybersecurity Policy Review called for "a comprehensive framework to facilitate coordinated responses by Government, the private sector, and allies to a significant cyber incident." DHS coordinated the interagency, state and local governments, and private sector working group that developed the National Cyber Incident Response Plan.

The plan enables DHS to coordinate the response of multiple federal agencies, state and local governments, international partners, and private industry to incidents at all levels. It is designed to be flexible and adaptable to allow synchronization of response activities across jurisdictional lines. The NCIRP was tested during the Cyber Storm III national exercise, which simulated a large-scale attack on the nation's critical information infrastructure. Seven Cabinet agencies, eleven states, twelve international partners, and sixty private-sector companies participated in the Cyber Storm III exercise.

Cyber Storm III Exercise

Cyber Storm III

In September 2010, DHS hosted Cyber Storm III, a response exercise in which members of the cyberincident response community address the scenario of a coordinated cyberevent in which the National Cyber Incident Response Plan is activated, testing the National Cybersecurity and Communications Integration Center and the federal government's full suite of cybersecurity response capabilities.

National Cybersecurity and Communications Integration Center (NCCIC)

The NCCIC is a 24-hour, DHS-led coordinated watch and warning center that will serve as the nation's principal hub for organizing cyberresponse efforts and maintaining the national cyber and communications common operational picture.

The NCCIC combines two of DHS's operational organizations: the U.S. Computer Emergency Readiness Team (US-CERT) and the National Coordinating Center for Telecommunications (NCC), the operational arm of the National Communications System. It integrates the efforts of DHS's National Cybersecurity Center (NCSC), which coordinates operations among the six largest federal cybercenters, the DHS Office of Intelligence and Analysis, and private-sector partners. Additional representatives from federal agencies, the private sector, and state and local governments are also collocated at the NCCIC.

U.S. Computer Emergency Readiness Team

US-CERT is the operational arm of National Cybersecurity Division (NCSD) that provides response support and defense against cyberattacks for the Federal Civilian Executive Branch (.gov) networks. US-CERT also collaborates and shares information with state and local governments, industry, and international partners to address cyberthreats and develop effective security responses. US-CERT is a partnership between DHS and the public and private sectors. The team was established in 2003 to protect the nation's Internet infrastructure. The team is charged with protecting the nation's Internet infrastructure by coordinating defense against and response to cyberattacks. It is responsible for analyzing and reducing cyberthreats and vulnerabilities, disseminating cyberthreat warning information, and coordinating incident response activities. US-CERT interacts with federal agencies, industry, the research community, state and local governments, and others to disseminate reasoned and actionable cybersecurity information to the public. The National Cyber Response Coordination Group (NCRCG), made up of 13 federal agency representatives, acts as the principal federal agency mechanism for cyberincident response. In the event of a nationally significant cyber-related incident, the NCRCG will help to coordinate the federal response, with representatives from US-CERT, law enforcement, and the intelligence community. One of the tools created and used by US-CERT to create public awareness and to disseminate information about known cyberthreats is the Cyber Security Preparedness and the National Cyber Alert System where both technical and nontechnical computer users can stay prepared for these threats by receiving current information by signing up to receive automatic notifications from the system. Another initiative of the National Cybersecurity Division is the "Cyber Cop Portal" which is an Internet portal where more than 5,300 cybercrime investigators worldwide can share information and collaborate.

What Is DHS Doing about Phishing?

US-CERT is collecting phishing email messages and web site locations so that we can help people avoid becoming victims of phishing scams.

You can report phishing to us by sending email to phishing-report@us-cert.gov.

What is Phishing?

Phishing is an attempt by an individual or group to solicit personal information from unsuspecting users by employing social engineering techniques. Phishing emails are crafted to appear as if they have been sent from a legitimate organization or known individual. These emails often attempt to entice users to click on a link that will take the user to a fraudulent web site that appears legitimate. The user then may be asked to provide personal information such as account usernames and passwords that can further expose them to future compromises. Additionally, these fraudulent web sites may contain malicious code.

Learn More about Phishing

The following documents and web sites can help you learn more about phishing and how to protect yourself against phishing attacks.

- Avoiding Social Engineering and Phishing Attacks
- Protecting Your Privacy
- Understanding Web Site Certificates
- Anti-Phishing Working Group (APWG)
- Federal Trade Commission, Identity Theft
- Recognizing and Avoiding Email Scams

Methods of Reporting Phishing Email to US-CERT

- In Outlook Express, you can create a new message and drag and drop the phishing email into the new message. Address the message to phishing-report@us-cert.gov and send it.

- In Outlook Express you can also open the email message* and select *File>Properties>Details.* The email headers will appear. You can copy these as you normally copy text and include it in a new message to phishing-report@us-cert.gov.
- If you cannot forward the email message, at a minimum, please send the URL of the phishing web site.

---

* If the suspicious mail in question includes a file attachment, it is safer to simply highlight the message and forward it. Some configurations, especially in Windows environments, may allow the execution of arbitrary code upon opening and viewing a malicious email message.

Source: http://www.uscert.gov/cas/alldocs.html.

To ensure the systems that support CIKR — the essential functions that underpin American society — are protected from cyberthreats, the Industrial Control Systems Cyber Emergency Response Team (ICS-CERT) provides onsite support to owners and operators of critical infrastructure for protection against and response to cyberthreats, including incident response, forensic analysis, and site assessments.

In August 2009, DHS and the Information Technology Sector Coordinating Council released the IT Sector Baseline Risk Assessment (ITSRA) to identify and prioritize national-level risks to critical sector-wide IT functions while outlining strategies to mitigate those risks and enhance national and economic security.

National Cyber Alert System

Four products in the National Cyber Alert System offer a variety of information for users with varied technical expertise. Those with more technical interest can read the Technical Cyber Security Alerts or the Cyber Security Bulletins. Users looking for more general-interest pieces can read the Cyber Security Alerts and Cyber Security Tips. All past issues of the following products are available:

- Technical Cyber Security Alerts provide timely information about current security issues, vulnerabilities, and exploits.
- Cyber Security Bulletins provide weekly summaries of new vulnerabilities. Patch information is provided when available.
- Cyber Security Alerts provide timely information about current security issues, vulnerabilities, and exploits. They outline the steps and actions that non-technical home and corporate computer users can take to protect themselves from attack.
- Cyber Security Tips provide advice about common security issues for the general public.

Source: http://www.uscert.gov/cas/alldocs.html.

The EINSTEIN Program

The EINSTEIN system is designed to provide the U.S. Government with an early warning system for intrusions to Federal Executive Branch civilian networks, near real-time identification of malicious activity, and automated disruption of that malicious activity.

EINSTEIN 1: The first iteration of the EINSTEIN system was developed in 2003. It automates the collection and analysis of computer network security information from participating agency and government networks to help analysts identify and combat malicious cyberactivity that may threaten government network systems, data protection, and communications infrastructure.

EINSTEIN 2: The second phase of EINSTEIN was developed in 2008. It incorporated intrusion detection capabilities into the original EINSTEIN system. DHS is currently deploying EINSTEIN 2 at federal Executive Branch civilian agencies and Networx Managed Trusted Internet Protocol Services (MTIPS) providers, private Internet service providers that serve federal agencies to assist them with protecting their computers, networks, and information.

EINSTEIN 2 has now been deployed at 15 of 19 departments and agencies. In addition, the four MTIPS providers currently service to seven federal agencies.

In 2010, EINSTEIN 2 sensors registered 5.4 million hits, an average of over 450,000 hits per month. A hit is an alert triggered by a predetermined intrusion detection signature that corresponds to a known threat.

EINSTEIN 3: DHS is developing the third phase of the EINSTEIN system — an intrusion prevention capability which will provide DHS with the ability to automatically detect and disrupt malicious activity before harm is done to critical networks and systems.

National Strategy for Trusted Identities in Cyberspace

In July 2010, the White House published a draft National Strategy for Trusted Identities in Cyberspace — which seeks to secure the identities of individuals, organizations, services, and devices during online transactions, as well as the infrastructure supporting the transaction — fulfilling one of the near-term action items of the President's *Cyberspace Policy Review*. The Strategy supports the protection of privacy and civil liberties by enabling only the minimum necessary amount of personal information to be transferred in any particular transaction.

In March 2010, Secretary Napolitano launched the National Cybersecurity Awareness Challenge, which called on members of the public and private sector companies to develop creative and innovative ways to enhance awareness of the importance of cybersecurity and safeguard America's computer systems and networks from attacks.

In July 2010, seven of the more than 80 proposals were selected and recognized at a White House ceremony. The winning proposals helped inform the National Cybersecurity Awareness Campaign, ***Stop. Think. Connect.***

Private Cyber Infrastructure Protection

Private industry owns and operates the vast majority of the nation's critical infrastructure and cyber-networks. Consequently, the private sector plays an important role in cybersecurity. DHS is engaged in several pilot programs to promote public–private-sector collaboration. In 2010, DHS launched two critical initiatives with the private sector. Along with Department of Defense (DOD) and the Financial Services Information Sharing and Analysis Center, DHS launched a pilot program designed to help protect key critical networks and infrastructure within the financial services sector by sharing actionable, sensitive information. In June 2010, DHS implemented the Cybersecurity Partners Local Access Plan, which allows security-cleared owners and operators of CIKR, as well as state technology officials and law enforcement officials, to access secret-level cybersecurity information and video teleconference calls via local fusion centers.

■ ■ Critical Thinking ■

Based on what you have read, do you think that DHS is the appropriate federal entity to lead the government's cybersecurity programs? If so, why; if not, what other Agency would be more appropriate and what is your reasoning?

Based on your knowledge, what do you think are the biggest cybersecurity threats to the United States and why?

A Focus on China

The Defense Department and federal intelligence agencies are on the warpath against increasing numbers of cyberattacks.

To combat the threat, the government is rolling out a system this year that reduces external connections to the Internet, detects intrusions in and out of federal networks, and enables faster patching of holes.

Even so, the Government Accountability Office reported this week that 20 of 24 major federal agencies are deficient in protecting against cyberattacks. Gregory Wilshusen, the GAO's director of information security issues, cited past instances in which the State Department network was breached by a malicious code inside an e-mail; a Transportation Security Administration hard drive with employment records was found missing; and an idled nuclear power plant's private computer network was infected by a virus, disabling a safety monitoring system.

Deputy Defense Secretary Gordon England noted last week that Estonia was victimized by a series of attacks for three weeks in 2007 that forced its largest bank to shut down its online banking network. "Cyberwarfare is already here," England told a Veterans of Foreign Wars conference.

Much of the attention focuses on China, which could be infiltrating U.S. government information technology systems despite denials by Beijing. In its annual report to Congress last week on China's military power, the Pentagon said several cyberspace attacks around the world in 2007 were sourced back to China. Director of National Intelligence Mike McConnell told the Senate Intelligence Committee last month that several nations, including China and Russia, "have the technical capabilities to target and disrupt elements of the U.S. information infrastructure and for intelligence collection." He recommended "proactive measures to detect and prevent intrusions from whatever source, as they happen, and before they can do significant damage." "The Chinese have a lot of resources, and they're willing to spend it to break in," says James Lewis, a cybersecurity expert at the Center for Strategic and International Studies.

Alan Paller, director of research at the SANS Institute, which specializes in information security research and training, says preventing cyberattacks is as important as preventing physical attacks. "Owning our computers is a powerful weapon in a war," Paller says. "We need to get them out."

Source: Times Online: "China's cyber army is preparing to march on America, says Pentagon," http://technology.timesonline.co.uk/tol/news/tech_and_web/the_web/article2409865.ece.

DOD Cybersecurity Efforts

In July 2011, the DOD announced their first comprehensive strategy on cybersecurity entitled Department of Defense's Strategy for Operating in Cyberspace. The strategy covers both cybersecurity and cyberwar. The blueprint was produced by the U.S. Cyber Command, a new military unit with the mission to protect military networks from attack. Much of the recent DOD activity can be traced to an incident in which 24,000 files documenting a new weapons system being developed for DOD were stolen from the federal contractor doing the work. DOD officials believed it was the work of a foreign intelligence organization.

The strategy has five components: (1) cyberspace as an operational domain, (2) new defenses and operating concepts for DOD networks, (3) partnerships with DIIS and the private sector to support critical infrastructure, (4) international cooperation, and (5) research and development.

There is some controversy over the decision to identify cyberspace as a military domain, the same as land or sea. In March 2011, the White House prepared draft guidance to assist agencies in the careful application of the use of the word, indicating its preference for the use of the term *cyberspace*.

DOD has already developed systems that are used to deter an adversary from using computer hacking or other computer means to attack the United States. They have developed viruses that can be used to corrupt critical networks outside of the United States.

CASE STUDY: CYBERSECURITY BEST PRACTICES AT DEFENSE

Aliya Sternstein, 08/01/2011

The U.S. military's computer systems are probed by outsiders millions of times a day, while insiders, like a soldier who allegedly extracted heaps of classified files for public consumption on the WikiLeaks website, also pose threats.

In mid-July, the Pentagon released an unprecedented cybersecurity strategy that formally branded cyberspace as a domain of warfare, akin to land, sea, air, and space. But, instead of outlining offensive measures, the framework focuses on how to deter the enemy from ever attempting an attack.

As part of this plan, the military is employing "active cyber defense" – an amalgamation of sensors, software, and intelligence reports aimed at instantly blocking malicious activity.

(Continued)

Active cyber defense will build off existing methods of tracking vulnerabilities, according to the strategy. Perhaps an Army model under development, commonly known as continuous monitoring, will be one such building block.

Challenge

The Army requires constant visibility into the security status of all computing assets to be able to get the military the information it needs at the moment it needs it.

"The beauty of the design for continuous monitoring is you get to see, know and do," says Michael J. Jones, chief of the emerging technologies division within the Army's CIO/G6 Cyber Directorate. The "know" elements "give the commander a better understanding of which vulnerabilities are a priority." As for "do," he adds, "that's where the leaders in the Army get paid the big bucks."

Currently, the Army has scanning machinery in place to collect security stats from most information technology assets. That's the seeing part. The Army's network operations and security centers watch each technology's rate of compliance with security standards.

But center staff can't possibly tackle all abnormal findings at once and some weaknesses are less important than others. The Army needed a way to prioritize action.

Progress

"Continuous monitoring is expected to deliver center commanders a means of understanding the nature of risks and who is on the hook for mitigating them," Jones says.

Every weakness identified by the surveillance equipment is given a risk score — the higher the score, the greater the threat. This is the "knowing" part of the see, know and do.

For instance, if an IT system's antivirus program has not been updated in more than seven days, it gets a bad score. If a system does not have the proper configuration settings, a high risk score is tabulated. And if a system is missing the latest patches, or bug fixes, the risk score increases.

Last fall, the Army conducted a "know" pilot and was successful in scoring the threat intensity of more than 20,000 IT assets.

But the test revealed that the scores aren't that useful for responding — the "doing" part — without having someone to call to fix the problems. "One of the lessons learned from the pilot was the need to identify who, which Army organization, is responsible for ensuring the security of IT devices identified as not meeting specific compliance standards," Jones says.

He anticipates continuous monitoring to be fully deployed and operational in 2013.

Key Issues

– Apply scanners and sensors to all IT assets to keep tabs on potential vulnerabilities.
– Ensure the data culled by the surveillance tools feeds into a central location.
– Develop a scoring mechanism to quantify the severity of each security risk.
– Prioritize fixes according to risk score. Respond to the big numbers first.
– Assign specific staff to oversee the security posture of each asset.
– When the monitoring machinery detects trouble, managers should dispatch the group responsible for bringing the network component into compliance.

Cybersecurity Efforts of Other Federal Agencies

Each federal agency is responsible for protecting their own networks and vary in the level of their cybersecurity efforts. For example, the Department of Commerce is responsible for establishing standards and issuing guidelines through the National Institute of Standards and Technology, and has issued some preliminary guidelines. The Department of State handles international efforts in coordination with DOD. The National Science Foundation supports research and development in concert with the National Telecommunications and Information Administration.

The Department of Education has been particularly active in this area. In partnership with DHS, they have established the National Initiative for Cybersecurity Education (NICE) from the CNCI. In May 2010, the NICE extended the scope of cybereducation beyond the federal workplace to include the public and students in kindergarten through post-graduate school. The goal of NICE is to establish an operational, sustainable, and continually improving cybersecurity education program for the nation to promote the use of sound cyberpractices that will enhance the nation's security. NICE has since grown to include over 20 federal departments and agencies, to ensure coordination, cooperation, focus, public engagement, technology transfer, and sustainability.

The Environmental Protection Agency (EPA) has developed several cybersecurity road maps including for the water sector, green building, and the emerging technology of smart grids.

■ ■ Critical Thinking ■

Based on what you have read, does the proliferation of government committees and initiatives in cybersecurity make sense and do you think there are other actions that they should consider taking? What are your thoughts on DOD making cyberspace a new area, or domain, requiring military vigilance?

DHS Response to the 9/11 Commission Recommendations

On July 21, 2011, DHS Secretary Napolitano announced the release of a report highlighting DHS progress in fulfilling the 9/11 Commission Recommendations. Several of these recommendations applied to cybersecurity and critical infrastructure. What follows are pertinent excerpts of the DHS progress report, entitled Department of Homeland Security: Progress in Implementing 9/11 Commission Recommendations, 2011.

Recommendation: Assess Critical Infrastructure and Readiness

Over the past ten years, DHS has made significant strides in enhancing the security of the nation's critical physical infrastructure as well as its cyber infrastructure and networks. Key tools include the National Cybersecurity Protection System (NCPS) — of which the EINSTEIN cyber intrusion detection system is a key component — and the NCCIC, a DHS-led coordinated watch and warning center that serves as the nation's principal hub for organizing cyber response efforts. In addition, DHS and DOD signed a landmark memorandum of agreement to align and enhance America's capabilities to protect against threats to critical civilian and military computer systems and networks. Further, DHS led the effort to develop the National Infrastructure Protection Plan (NIPP), a comprehensive risk management framework for all levels of government, private industry, nongovernmental entities, and tribal partners, while implementing the Chemical Facility Anti-Terrorism Standards (CFATS) to regulate security at high-risk chemical facilities.

In Safeguarding Cyber Infrastructure and Networks

DHS is responsible for protecting the federal executive branch civilian agencies and guiding the protection of the nation's critical infrastructure and connections to cyberspace. This includes the dot-gov world, where the government maintains essential functions that provide services to the American people as well as the systems and networks that support the financial services, energy, and defense industries.

In October 2010, Secretary Napolitano and Secretary of Defense Robert Gates signed a Memorandum of Agreement to align and enhance America's capabilities to protect against threats to critical civilian and military computer systems and networks. The Agreement embeds DOD cyber analysts within DHS and sends DHS privacy, civil liberties, and legal personnel to DOD's National Security Agency to strengthen the nation's cybersecurity posture and ensure the protection of fundamental rights.

In November 2010, the Multi-State Information Sharing and Analysis Center, funded in part by DHS, opened the Cyber Security Operations Center, a 24-hour watch and warning facility, to enhance situational awareness at the state and local level and allow the federal government to quickly and efficiently provide critical cyber risk, vulnerability, and mitigation data to state and local governments.

In partnership with the private sector, US-CERT takes proactive measures to stop possible threats from reaching an even broader audience. US-CERT hosts the Joint Agency Cyber Knowledge Exchange Program, an analyst-to-analyst information-sharing forum for the exchange of classified and unclassified cyber threat information and techniques for mitigating and defending against cyber threats.

Protecting Critical Infrastructure and Its Connections to Cyberspace

DHS developed the first-ever National Cyber Incident Response Plan in September 2010 to coordinate the response of multiple federal agencies, state and local governments, and hundreds of private firms, to incidents at all levels. DHS tested this plan during the Cyber Storm III national exercise, which simulated a large-scale attack on the nation's critical information infrastructure.

In October 2009, DHS opened the new NCCIC — a 24-hour, DHS-led coordinated watch and warning center to serve as the nation's principal hub for organizing cyber response efforts and maintaining the national cyber and communications common operational picture. DHS also implemented the Cybersecurity Partners Local Access Plan, which allows security-cleared owners and operators of CIKR, as well as state technology officials and law enforcement officials, to access secret level cybersecurity information via local fusion centers.

Protecting the dot-gov World

In close partnership with other federal agencies and the private sector, DHS utilizes NCPS, of which the EINSTEIN intrusion detection system is a key component, to protect the dot-gov domains. The EINSTEIN system, initially deployed in 2004, helps block malicious actors from accessing federal executive branch civilian agencies, while working closely with those agencies to bolster their defensive capabilities. Recently, DHS deployed EINSTEIN 2 — an automated cyber surveillance system that monitors federal Internet traffic for malicious intrusions — at 15 departments and agencies and four MTIPS providers. At full operational capability, EINSTEIN 3 will provide DHS with the ability to detect malicious activity and disable attempted intrusions automatically, a significant improvement in the Department's ability to prevent cyber intrusions on federal executive branch civilian networks and systems. Once fully deployed, EINSTEIN 2 and EINSTEIN 3 will provide cyber protection capabilities to more than 110 federal civilian executive branch departments and agencies.

Intelligence and Cybersecurity

By embedding intelligence analysts at US-CERT, the ICS-CERT, and the NCCIC, I&A is able to analyze intrusion detection information gathered from DHS sensors like EINSTEIN as well as investigative information from DHS components to provide a national intelligence perspective to cyber incidents. Analysis is then shared with the federal, state, local, and tribal government agencies in the form of Homeland Intelligence Reports. Additionally, I&A integrates all-source intelligence from the intelligence community with information provided by private sector owners and operators of CIKR to provide a more comprehensive tactical and strategic understanding of cyber threats. I&A disseminates this information through regular intelligence products and briefings to the private sector.

Recent Initiatives

In an address in 2009, President Obama announced that cybersecurity was one of the top priorities of his administration. He said they were seeking "a new comprehensive approach to securing America's digital infrastructure." To support this, he later released the *Cyberspace Policy Review* which built upon the CNCI. He appointed a cybersecurity advisor at the White House and created a cybersecurity directorate within the National Security Council (NSS), charging them to update the national strategy initially promulgated under Presidential Directive 54. The administration proposed comprehensive cybersecurity legislation in May 2011. Among the highlights in this legislation include consolidating the 47 different state laws that require businesses to report breaches of their cybersystems to consumers — DHS will work with industry to prioritize the most important cyberthreats and vulnerabilities — provide clear authority to allow the federal government to provide assistance to state and local governments when there has been a cyberbreach, provides immunity to the industry, state and local governments when sharing cybersecurity information with DHS, and provides for a new framework to protect individuals' privacy and civil liberties.

THE WHITE HOUSE FACT SHEET ON THE CYBERSECURITY LEGISLATIVE PROPOSAL, MAY 12, 2011

We count on computer networks to deliver our oil and gas, our power and our water. We rely on them for public transportation and air traffic control.... But just as we failed in the past to invest in our physical infrastructure – our roads, our bridges and rails – we've failed to invest in the security of our digital infrastructure.... This status quo is no longer acceptable – not when there's so much at stake. We can and we must do better. – President Obama, May 29, 2009

Our critical infrastructure – such as the electricity grid, financial sector, and transportation networks that sustain our way of life – have suffered repeated cyber intrusions, and cybercrime has increased dramatically over the last decade. The President has thus made cybersecurity an Administration priority. When the President released his *Cyberspace Policy Review* almost two years ago, he declared that the "cyber threat is one of the most serious economic and national security challenges we face as a nation." The Administration has since taken significant steps to better protect America against cyber threats. As part of that work, it has become clear that our Nation cannot fully defend against these threats unless certain parts of cybersecurity law are updated.

(Continued)

THE WHITE HOUSE FACT SHEET ON THE CYBERSECURITY LEGISLATIVE PROPOSAL, MAY 12, 2011 (CONTINUED)

Members of both parties in Congress have also recognized this need and introduced approximately 50 cyber-related bills in the last session of Congress. Senate Majority Leader Reid and six Senate committee chairs thus wrote to the President and asked for his input on cybersecurity legislation. The Administration welcomed the opportunity to assist these congressional efforts, and we have developed a pragmatic and focused cybersecurity legislative proposal for Congress to consider. This legislative proposal is the latest achievement in the steady stream of progress we are making in securing cyberspace and completes another near-term action item identified in the *Cyberspace Policy Review*.

The proposed legislation is focused on improving cybersecurity for the American people, our Nation's critical infrastructure, and the Federal Government's own networks and computers.

Protecting the American People

1. **National Data Breach Reporting.** State laws have helped consumers protect themselves against identity theft while also incentivizing businesses to have better cybersecurity, thus helping to stem the tide of identity theft. These laws require businesses that have suffered an intrusion to notify consumers if the intruder had access to the consumers' personal information. The Administration proposal helps businesses by simplifying and standardizing the existing patchwork of 47 state laws that contain these requirements.

2. **Penalties for Computer Criminals.** The laws regarding penalties for computer crime are not fully synchronized with those for other types of crime. For example, a key tool for fighting organized crime is the Racketeering Influenced and Corrupt Organizations Act (RICO). Yet RICO does not apply to cybercrimes, despite the fact that cybercrime has become a big business for organized crime. The Administration proposal thus clarifies the penalties for computer crimes, synchronizes them with other crimes, and sets mandatory minimums for cyber intrusions into critical infrastructure.

Protecting Our Nation's Critical Infrastructure

Our safety and way of life depend upon our critical infrastructure as well as the strength of our economy. The Administration is already working to protect critical infrastructure from cyber threats, but we believe that the following legislative changes are necessary to fully protect this infrastructure:

1. **Voluntary Government Assistance to Industry, States, and Local Government.** Organizations that suffer a cyber intrusion often ask the Federal Government for assistance with fixing the damage and for advice on building better defenses. For example, organizations sometimes ask DHS to help review their computer logs to see when a hacker broke in. However, the lack of a clear statutory framework describing DHS's authorities has sometimes slowed the ability of DHS to help the requesting organization. The Administration proposal will enable DHS to quickly help a private-sector company, state, or local government when that organization asks for its help. It also clarifies the type of assistance that DHS can provide to the requesting organization.

2. **Voluntary Information Sharing with Industry, States, and Local Government.** Businesses, states, and local governments sometimes identify new types of computer viruses or other cyber threats or incidents, but they are uncertain about whether they can share this information with the Federal Government. The Administration proposal makes clear that these entities can share information about cyber threats or incidents with DHS. To fully address these entities' concerns, it provides them with immunity when sharing cybersecurity information with DHS. At the

same time, the proposal mandates robust privacy oversight to ensure that the voluntarily shared information does not impinge on individual privacy and civil liberties.

3. **Critical Infrastructure Cybersecurity Plans.** The Nation's critical infrastructure, such as the electricity grid and financial sector, is vital to supporting the basics of life in America. Market forces are pushing infrastructure operators to put their infrastructure online, which enables them to remotely manage the infrastructure and increases their efficiency. However, when our infrastructure is online, it is also vulnerable to cyberattacks that could cripple essential services. Our proposal emphasizes transparency to help market forces ensure that critical-infrastructure operators are accountable for their cybersecurity.

The Administration proposal requires DHS to work with industry to identify the core critical-infrastructure operators and to prioritize the most important cyber threats and vulnerabilities for those operators. Critical infrastructure operators would develop their own frameworks for addressing cyber threats. Then, each critical-infrastructure operator would have a third-party, commercial auditor assess its cybersecurity risk mitigation plans. Operators who are already required to report to the Security and Exchange Commission would also have to certify that their plans are sufficient. A summary of the plan would be accessible, in order to facilitate transparency and to ensure that the plan is adequate. In the event that the process fails to produce strong frameworks, DHS, working with the National Institute of Standards and Technology, could modify a framework. DHS can also work with firms to help them shore up plans that are deemed insufficient by commercial auditors.

Protecting Federal Government Computers and Networks

Over the past five years, the Federal Government has greatly increased the effort and resources we devote to securing our computer systems. While we have made major improvements, updated legislation is necessary to reach the Administration goals for Federal cybersecurity, so the Administration's legislative proposal includes:

1. **Management.** The Administration proposal would update the Federal Information Security Management Act (FISMA) and formalize DHS' current role in managing cybersecurity for the Federal Government's civilian computers and networks, in order to provide departments and agencies with a shared source of expertise.

2. **Personnel.** The recruitment and retention of highly qualified cybersecurity professionals is extremely competitive, so we need to be sure that the government can recruit and retain these talented individuals. Our legislative proposal will give DHS more flexibility in hiring these individuals. It will also permit the government and private industry to temporarily exchange experts, so that both can learn from each others' expertise.

3. **Intrusion Prevention Systems.** Intrusion detection systems are automated sensors that identify cyber intrusions and attacks. Intrusion prevention systems can actually block cyber intrusions and attacks. DHS' Einstein system is one example of an intrusion prevention system, and the proposal makes permanent DHS's authority to oversee intrusion prevention systems for all Federal Executive Branch civilian computers. Internet Service Providers (ISPs) implement these systems on behalf of DHS, blocking attacks against government computers. The Attorney General currently reviews and provides immunity for those ISPs, as necessary, to provide that service, and the proposal streamlines that process. This only applies to intrusion prevention systems that protect government computers, and the proposal also codifies or adds: strong privacy and civil liberties protections, congressional reporting requirements, and an annual certification process.

(Continued)

THE WHITE HOUSE FACT SHEET ON THE CYBERSECURITY LEGISLATIVE PROPOSAL, MAY 12, 2011 (CONTINUED)

4. **Data Centers**. The Federal Government has embraced cloud computing, where computer services and applications are run remotely over the Internet. Cloud computing can reduce costs, increase security, and help the government take advantage of the latest private-sector innovations. This new industry should not be crippled by protectionist measures, so the proposal prevents states from requiring companies to build their data centers in that state, except where expressly authorized by federal law.

New Framework to Protect Individuals' Privacy and Civil Liberties
The Administration's proposal ensures the protection of individuals' privacy and civil liberties through a framework designed expressly to address the challenges of cybersecurity.

- It requires DHS to implement its cybersecurity program in accordance with privacy and civil liberties procedures. These must be developed in consultation with privacy and civil liberties experts and approved by the Attorney General.
- All federal agencies who would obtain information under this proposal will follow privacy and civil liberties procedures, again developed in consultation with privacy and civil liberties experts and with the approval of the Attorney General.
- All monitoring, collection, use, retention, and sharing of information are limited to protecting against cybersecurity threats. Information may be used or disclosed for criminal law enforcement, but the Attorney General must first review and approve each such usage.
- When a private-sector business, state, or local government wants to share information with DHS, it must first make reasonable efforts to remove identifying information unrelated to cybersecurity threats.
- The proposal also mandates the development of layered oversight programs and congressional reporting.
- Immunity for the private-sector business, state, or local government is conditioned on its compliance with the requirements of the proposal.

Taken together, these requirements create a new framework of privacy and civil liberties protection designed expressly to address the challenges of cybersecurity.

Source: White House Fact Sheet: Cybersecurity Legislative Proposal, May 12, 2011.

Critical Infrastructure Protection

The DHS defines *critical infrastructure* as " the assets, systems and networks, whether physical or virtual, so vital to the United States that their incapacitation or destruction would have a debilitating effect on security, national economic security, public health or safety, or any combination thereof."

Before the creation of DHS, the Clinton Administration was concerned about issues of the U.S. critical infrastructure. This concern became heightened after bombings of U.S. embassies and facilities. In 1998, President Clinton issued Presidential Decision Directive/NSC-63, May 22, 1998.

The comprehensive nature of the Clinton Directive formed the backbone of federal government actions to preserve and protect the nation's critical infrastructure. Many of the ideas and programs established by PDD-63 were carried over into the Bush Administration, although it took the events of September 11 to add a new criticality to the U.S. efforts in critical infrastructure protection. The full text is available online at http://www.fas.org/irp/offdocs/pdd-63.

After September 11, two major documents provided significant authority for the federal government to develop critical infrastructure protections, the Homeland Security Act of 2002 and the Homeland Security Presidential Directive 7 (HSPD-7).

The Homeland Security Act of 2002 provides primary authorization for DHS, assigning DHS the responsibility for developing a comprehensive plan to secure critical infrastructure. It also required that DHS recommend measures to protect the key resources and critical infrastructure of the United States.

HSPD 7 establishes a framework for DHS and partners to identify, prioritize, and protect the critical infrastructure in their communities from terrorist attacks. The directive identified 17 critical infrastructure sectors and, for each sector, designates a federal sector-specific agency (SSA) to lead protection and resilience-building programs and activities. The directive requires DHS to identify gaps in existing sectors and establish new sectors to fill the gaps. For example, in March 2008, DHS established the Critical Manufacturing Sector as the 18th sector.

In 2009, DHS published a revised NIPP, which was originally published by DHS in 2006. The NIPP provides the structure for coordination and integration of the wide range of efforts to enhance protection and resiliency of the nation's CIKR into a single national program. The goal of the NIPP is to "build a safer, more secure and resilient America by preventing, deterring, neutralizing, or mitigating the effects of deliberate efforts by terrorists to destroy, incapacitate or exploit elements of our nation's CIKR and to strengthen national preparedness, timely response, and rapid recovery of CIKR in the event of an attack, natural disaster or other emergency."

In the context of the NIPP, this includes actions to deter the threat, mitigate vulnerabilities, or minimize the consequences associated with a terrorist attack or other man-made or natural disaster. Protection can include a wide range of activities such as improving security protocols, hardening facilities, building resiliency and redundancy, incorporating hazard resistance into facility design, initiating active or passive countermeasures, installing security systems, leveraging "self-healing" technologies, promoting workforce surety programs, implementing cybersecurity measures, training, and exercises, and business continuity planning, among others. Protection includes actions to mitigate the overall risk to CIKR assets, systems, networks, functions, or their interconnecting links resulting from exposure, injury, destruction, incapacitation, or exploitation (Figure 8–1).

To achieve the goal of building a safer, more secure, and more resilient America, the NIPP has established the following objectives:

1. Understanding and sharing information about terrorist threats and other hazards
2. Building partnerships to share information and implement CIKR protection and resiliency programs
3. Implementing a long-term risk management program that includes:
   a. Hardening, distributing, diversifying, and otherwise ensuring the resiliency of CIKR against known threats and hazards, as well as other potential contingencies
   b. Developing processes to interdict human threats to prevent potential attacks

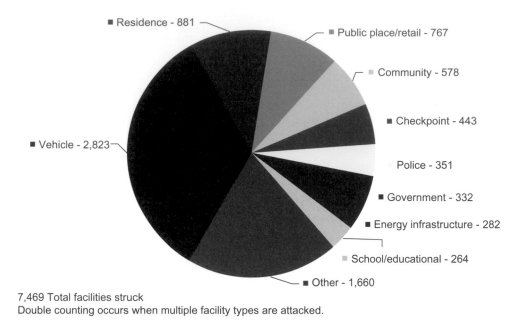

7,469 Total facilities struck
Double counting occurs when multiple facility types are attacked.

FIGURE 8–1 Total facilities attacked by terrorists (worldwide), 2009. (Source: National Counterterrorism Center)

    c. Planning for rapid response to CIKR disruptions to limit the impact on public health and safety, the economy, and government functions

    d. Planning for rapid CIKR recovery for those events that are not preventable

  4. Maximizing the efficient use of resources for CIKR protection (Figure 8–2)

The basic framework of the NIPP focuses on managing risk, organizing and partnerships, information sharing and program sustainability. To support managing risks, the plan defines a process that includes steps to identify, assess, and prioritize risks; implement protective measures; and measure the effectiveness of those measures.

The NIPP has an extensive network for coordination among the levels of government and the private sector and among the sectors. Elements of this network include a national-level coordination council, sector partnership councils, regional coordination councils, and international protocols, all of which emphasize the information-sharing aspects of the CIKR. The NIPP supports the development of sector-specific plans (SSPs), which detail the application of the NIPP framework to the unique characteristics of their sector. The NIPP promotes a series of activities to support program sustainability, including building national awareness through education, training, and exercises, supporting research and development, building and protecting databases and systems such as the National CIKR Protection Data System, and organizational exercises (Figure 8–3).

There are very fundamental reasons for the federal government to make a substantial and coordinated effort to protect this nation's infrastructure. Attacks on critical infrastructure could significantly disrupt the functioning of both government and industry and provide cascading effects beyond the original target, for example, disruption of the Alaska pipeline. Terrorist attacks or natural or technological

FIGURE 8–2 La Canada Flintridge, CA, August 2, 2010 – The Big Tujunga Dam is under construction to reinforce the walls due to an increased debris flow from recent severe winter storms. Under the declaration DR 1884 for Public Assistance, FEMA funds emergency protective measures for critical infrastructure such as roads, bridges, and dams. (Source: Photo by Adam DuBrowa/FEMA)

hazards can cause dramatic loss of life, injuries, property damage, and severe economic and social disruption, for example, Hurricane Katrina. An attack using components of the nation's critical infrastructure as weapons of mass destruction would have devastating physical and psychological consequences, for example, blowing up a nuclear power plant.

The current critical infrastructure sectors number 18 and each has a single designated SSA or some have multiple agencies working in partnership. The sectors are listed below with the designated SSA(s):

- *Agriculture and Food*: Department of Agriculture (DOA) and Health and Human Services (HHS)
- *Banking and Finance*: Department of the Treasury (Treasury)
- *Chemical*: DHS
- *Commercial Facilities*: DHS
- *Communications*: DHS
- *Critical Manufacturing*: DHS
- *Dams*: DHS
- *Defense Industrial Base*: DOD

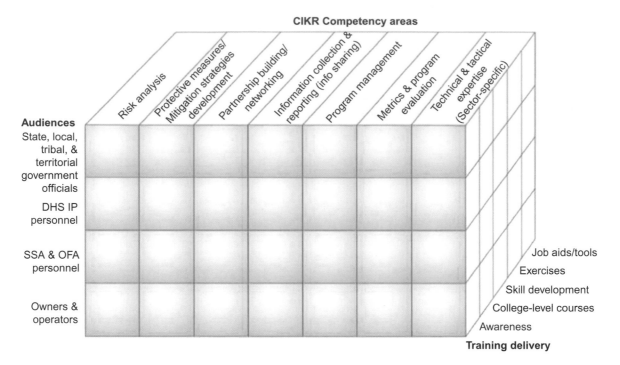

FIGURE 8–3 Developing NIPP CIKR Core Competencies. (Source: NIPP, 2009, p. 83; http://www.dhs.gov/xlibrary/assets/NIPP_Plan.pdf)

- *Emergency Services*: DHS
- *Energy*: Department of Energy (DOE)
- *Government Facilities*: DHS
- *Health Care and Public Health*: HHS
- *Information Technology*: DHS
- *National Monuments and Icons*: Department of the Interior (DOI)
- *Nuclear Reactors, Materials, and Waste*: DHS
- *Postal and Shipping*: DHS
- *Transportation Systems*: DHS
- *Water*: Environmental Protection Agency (EPA)

■ ■ Critical Thinking ■

Under the Clinton PDD-63, sector responsibility was spread among the federal agencies but now the DHS has assumed lead responsibilities for many of the CIKR sectors. Do you have an opinion on which approach is better?

Under the DHS approach, do you think any of these could be better done by another agency? For example, assigning Nuclear Reactors, Materials, and Waste to the Nuclear Regulatory Commission.

State and Local Governments

The NIPP established a partnership framework that allows federal, state, local, tribal, and territorial governments to work with each other and private sector partners.

Under the NIPP, state, local, tribal, and territorial governments are responsible for implementing the homeland security mission, protecting public safety and welfare, and ensuring the provision of essential services to communities and industries within their jurisdictions. They play a very important and direct role in enabling CIKR protection and resilience, including CIKR under their control, as well as that owned and operated by other NIPP partners within their jurisdictions. The efforts of these public entities are critical to the effective implementation of the NIPP, SSPs, and various jurisdictionally focused protection and resiliency plans. They are equally critical in terms of enabling time-sensitive, post-event CIKR response and recovery activities.

To permit effective NIPP implementation and performance measurement at each jurisdictional level, protection programs have been established that reference all core elements of the NIPP framework, where appropriate, including key cross-jurisdictional security and information-sharing linkages, as well as specific CIKR protection programs focused on risk management. These programs play a primary role in the identification and protection of CIKR regionally and locally and also support DHS and SSA efforts to identify, ensure connectivity with, and enable the protection of CIKR of national-level criticality within the jurisdiction.

State (and territorial, where applicable) governments are responsible for establishing partnerships, facilitating coordinated information sharing, and enabling planning and preparedness for CIKR protection within their jurisdictions. They serve as crucial coordination hubs, bringing together prevention, protection, response, and recovery authorities, capabilities, and resources among local jurisdictions, across sectors, and between regional entities. States and territories also act as conduits for requests for federal assistance when the threat or incident situation exceeds the capabilities of public and private sector partners at lower jurisdictional levels. States receive CIKR information from the federal government to support national and state CIKR protection and resiliency programs.

Among the responsibilities for protection of the CIKR that exist at the state and territorial levels include:

- Acting as a focal point for and promoting the coordination of protective and emergency response activities, preparedness programs, and resource support among local jurisdictions, regional organizations, and private sector partners
- Developing a consistent approach to CIKR identification, risk determination, mitigation planning, and prioritized security investment, and exercising preparedness among all relevant stakeholders within their jurisdictions
- Identifying, implementing, and monitoring a risk management plan and taking corrective actions, as appropriate
- Participating in significant national, regional, and local awareness programs to encourage appropriate management and security of cybersystems
- Facilitating the exchange of security information, including threat assessments and other analyses, attack indications and warnings, and advisories, within and across jurisdictions and sectors therein
- Participating in the NIPP sector partnership model, including: sector-specific GCCs; the State, Local, Tribal, and Territorial Government Coordinating Council (SLTTGCC); SCCs; and other CIKR governance and planning efforts relevant to the given jurisdiction

- Ensuring that funding priorities are addressed and that resources are allocated efficiently and effectively to achieve the CIKR protection mission in accordance with relevant plans and strategies
- Sharing information on CIKR deemed to be critical from national, state, regional, local, tribal, and/ or territorial perspectives to enable prioritized protection and restoration of critical public services, facilities, utilities, and functions within the jurisdiction
- Addressing unique geographical issues, including trans-border concerns, dependencies, and interdependencies among the sectors within the jurisdiction
- Identifying and implementing plans and processes for increasing protective measures that align to all-hazards warnings; specific threats, as appropriate; and each level of the HSAS
- Providing response and protection, as appropriate, where there are gaps and where local entities lack the resources needed to address those gaps

Automated Critical Asset Management System (ACAMS)

The Automated Critical Asset Management System (ACAMS) is a web-based information services portal that helps state and local governments build CIKR protection programs in their local jurisdictions. ACAMS allows its users, who are emergency management personnel, law enforcement, public safety, and first responders, to:

- Collect and use CIKR asset data
- Assess CIKR asset vulnerabilities
- Develop all-hazards incident response and recovery plans
- Build public–private partnerships

The key features included in ASCAS are:

- Comprehensive CIKR asset inventory, inventory management, and assessment tools
- Sector-specific protection measures recommended by DHS
- Automatic generation of standardized reports
- DHS-approved CIKR asset taxonomy classification tool
- Integrated mapping and geospatial functionality
- CIKR reference document library

ACAMS is provided to state and local jurisdictions at no charge and is accessible via an unclassified password-protected Internet portal.

Critical Thinking

Consider the community you live in and identify the CIKR that exist within that community. Choose one CIKR asset and describe its potential vulnerabilities.

Private Sector

The private sector is especially critical since significant portions of the United States's critical infrastructure is owned or managed by the private sector. The issue of a private company sharing information with the federal government has not been completely resolved. Since the events of September 11, many businesses have increased their threshold investments and undertaken enhancements in security in an effort to meet the demands of the new threat environment. For most enterprises, the level of investment in security reflects implicit risk-versus-consequence trade-offs, which are based on (1) what is known about the risk environment, (2) what is economically justifiable and sustainable in a competitive marketplace or in an environment of limited government resources, (3) potential consequences of disasters, and (4) priorities for the protection of human capital, processes, physical infrastructure, organizational reputation, stakeholder confidence, and vital records that require immediate attention. Given the dynamic nature of the terrorist threat and the severity of the consequences associated with many potential attack scenarios, the private sector naturally looks to the government for better information to help make its crucial security investment decisions. The private sector is continuing to look for better data, analysis, and assessment from DHS to use in the corporate decision-making process. See Figure 8–4.

Similarly, the private sector looks to the government for assistance when the threat at hand exceeds an enterprise's capability to protect itself beyond a reasonable level of additional investment. In this light, the federal government promises to collaborate with the private sector (and state and local governments) to ensure the protection of nationally critical infrastructures and assets; to provide timely warning and ensure the protection of infrastructures and assets that face a specific, imminent threat; and to promote an environment in which the private sector can better carry out its specific protection responsibilities.

Private owners have an economic interest in protecting their investments and ensuring a continuity of operations of their facilities and systems from a variety of threats both internal and external. Private owners and operators are usually best able to assess what risks they face and how to set some priorities

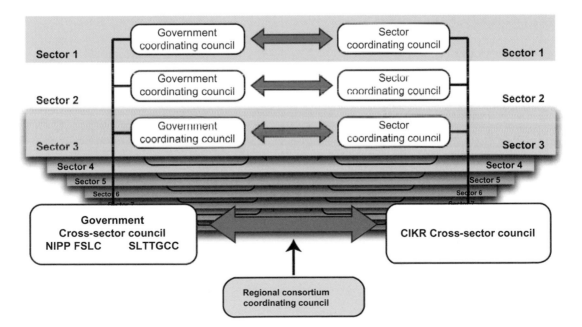

FIGURE 8–4 Sector Partnership Model. (Source: NIPP, 2009, p. 50; http://www.dhs.gov/xlibrary/assets/NIPP_Plan.pdf)

among the risks for prevention purposes. For many private sector enterprises, the level of investment in security reflects risk-versus-consequence trade-offs that are based on two factors: (1) what is known about the risk environment, and (2) what is economically justifiable and sustainable in a competitive marketplace or within resource constraints. Within this context, the NIPP suggests that the private sector can better protect their CIKR assets by taking the following steps:

- Performing comprehensive risk assessments on their specific sector, enterprise, or facility risk landscape
- Implementing protective actions and programs to reduce identified vulnerabilities appropriate to the level of risk presented
- Participating in the NIPP sector partnership model (including SCCs and information-sharing mechanisms)
- Developing an awareness of critical dependencies and interdependencies at the sector, enterprise, and facility levels
- Assisting and supporting federal, state, local, and tribal government CIKR data collection and protection efforts
- Developing and coordinating CIKR protective and emergency response actions, plans, and programs with appropriate federal, state, and local government authorities
- Establishing continuity plans and programs that facilitate the performance of critical functions during an emergency or until normal operations can be resumed
- Establishing cybersecurity programs and associated awareness training within the organization
- Adhering to recognized industry best business practices and standards, including those with a cybersecurity nexus
- Promoting CIKR protection education, training, and awareness programs
- Adopting and implementing effective workforce security assurance programs to mitigate potential insider threats
- Providing technical expertise to the SSAs and DHS
- Establishing resilient, robust, and/or redundant operational systems or capabilities associated with critical functions
- Promoting CIKR protection education, training, and awareness programs
- Adopting and implementing effective workforce security assurance programs to mitigate potential insider threats
- Providing technical expertise to the SSAs and DHS
- Participating in regular CIKR protection-focused training and exercise programs with other public and private sector partners
- Identifying and communicating requirements to DHS and/or the SSAs and state and local governments for CIKR protection-related R&D
- Sharing security-related best practices and entering into operational mutual-aid agreements with other industry partners
- Working to identify and reduce barriers to public–private partnerships

The Critical Infrastructure Partnership Advisory Council (CIPAC) provides a legal framework for collaboration and coordination. Through CIPAC there is enhanced communication, planning, and implementation and improved incident response and recovery.

ANOTHER VOICE: SAFETY AND SECURITY CONCERNS IN THE PRIVATE SECTOR.

Security in Public vs. Private Sectors

The phone rang at 15 minutes before 3 AM. It was January 26, 2007. Sound asleep, I instinctively reached for my phone, wondering who could be calling at this hour. It was little surprise to me that it was my boss on the line. He was notifying me that an explosion had just occurred outside the entrance of one of our hotels in South Asia. An unidentified man attempted to penetrate hotel security. Strapped with a homemade explosive device, he was confronted by our guards who prevented access to the property. A scuffle ensued and the bomber detonated the device. The security guard was killed instantly alongside the bomber and seven bystanders were injured.

Through the system we had established years earlier, all of our crisis management team members were on a conference call within 15 minutes. We concluded the conference call an hour later with tasks assigned to each member. The team convened again a few hours later to report on their assignments. Since the damage to the hotel's building structure was minimal, the hotel was able to resume its normal operations later that day. Later, a relief fund was set up to help the deceased employee's family.

This is an example of one of those phone calls you do not wish to receive, regardless of the time of day. A phone call like this precipitates a crisis lasting anywhere from one day to several weeks. Everyone in the security department will be tested dealing with this on a 24-hour basis. It is our employee, our company, our reputation, after all.

There is little distinction between the security responsibilities of government agencies and private sector entities. Both protect people, facilities, assets, and reputation. However, the ramifications are far more complex for the private sector when it comes to dealing with the aftermath of a crisis. When working in the government sector, there is little concern about the stock performance, shareholders, a potential increase in insurance premiums, public relations disasters, or lawsuits by customers. These elements can be extremely challenging for someone who makes the decision to cross over into the private sector.

In a corporate crisis environment, pressure comes from many areas. It most often manifests itself from stockholders, legal advisors, consultants, rank-and-file employees, customers and, naturally, competitors. Everyone is a stakeholder.

If FEMA had been a privately owned company and its directors performed in much the same manner that they did during Hurricane Katrina, FEMA's stock would have plunged and no insurance company would have dared to insure them again. Senior executives in the parent company (which would be the Department of Homeland Security in this example) and its board of directors would have fired them all and, needless to say, the PR department would have their own crisis trying to mitigate the negative publicity.

The Hurricane Katrina story could have been very different if it had been handled in an effective and efficient manner. When such disasters occur, mass evacuations and major rescue operations require extensive efforts. In this case, government waste was rampant and communication between agencies broke down. Politics obfuscated good judgment. Conversely, a private company has to be self-sufficient. Its contingency plans need to cover all aspects from start to finish. If a private company fails to manage a crisis effectively, profits will plunge, customers will not return, stock holders will sell, and the company will eventually go under.

Private companies have to have a strategic focus, think ahead, and prepare resources. They should assess the situation from the perspective of each stakeholder. Hurricane plans should include shelters both inside and outside of the facility, prenegotiated contracts with chartered airlines, and

(Continued)

ANOTHER VOICE: SAFETY AND SECURITY CONCERNS IN THE PRIVATE SECTOR (CONTINUED).

---

supplies such as food, beds, and toilets. Having these plans and provisions in place will boost customer confidence, increase business, please shareholders, and drive revenue. Everyone is happy.

Another aspect to consider is that many companies are global, thereby expanding the horizon and adding more elements to the crisis plan. Different parts of the world involve various kinds of threats that might not exist in corporate America. Wars, government instability, foreign languages, customs, laws, and restrictions need to be considered and evaluated in order to allow for fast and seamless reaction during a crisis.

A private company's plan needs to be all encompassing, including preventative methods as well as solutions. A comprehensive review of the business continuity plan is always needed after a crisis comes to an end.

Last but not least, cooperation from company executives is the key. Without it, no crisis plan can function as they always require top down support, money, time, and resources.

Jack Suwanlert
Director — International Loss Prevention
Marriott International Inc.

International

The federal government and private sector corporations have a significant number of facilities located outside the United States that may be considered CIKR. The NIPP addresses international CIKR protection, including interdependencies and vulnerabilities based on threats (and associated consequences) that originate outside the country or pass through it. The federal government and the private sector work with foreign governments and international/multinational organizations to enhance the confidentiality, integrity, and availability of cyberinfrastructure and products. High priority is placed on the protection of assets, systems, and networks that operate across or near the borders with Canada and Mexico, or rely on other international aspects to enable critical functionality. These also include any assets that require coordination with and planning and/or sharing resources among neighboring governments at all levels, as well as private sector CIKR owners and operators.

The NIPP recognizes several areas where special considerations exist: first, when CIKR is extensively integrated into an international or global market (e.g., financial services, agriculture, energy, transportation, telecommunications, or information technology) or when a sector relies on inputs that are not within the control of U.S. entities; and second, when government facilities and functions are directly affected by foreign-owned and -operated commercial facilities.

The federal government, working in close coordination and cooperation with the private sector, launched the Critical Foreign Dependencies Initiative in 2007 to identify assets and systems located outside the United States, which, if disrupted or destroyed, would critically affect public health and safety, the economy, or national security. The initiative produced a strategic compendium which guides the engagement with foreign countries in the CIKR protection mission.

Response to the 9/11 Commission Recommendations

Recommendation: Assess Critical Infrastructure and Readiness

Since fiscal year 2006, DHS has provided more than $3.6 billion in grant funding through the Port Security, Transit Security, and Buffer Zone Protection grant programs to protect critical infrastructure from terrorism. These grants support security plans, facility security upgrades, training, exercises, law enforcement anti-terrorism operations, and capital projects for risk mitigation of high-threat infrastructure.

DHS developed an annual National Risk Profile that provides a multi-hazard assessment of risks facing critical infrastructure, including terrorist threats, cyber risks, and natural disasters.

To date, the Department has reviewed an estimated 40,000 consequence assessment questionnaires submitted by potentially high-risk chemical facilities. Of these, approximately 4,500 facilities have been preliminarily identified as high-risk, resulting in the development and submission of Security Vulnerability Assessments. Of those facilities, nearly all have received final high-risk determinations and are in the process of completing Site Security Plans to bolster safety and security measures.

The Department's Office of Infrastructure Protection (IP) has conducted more than 1,900 security surveys and more than 2,500 vulnerability assessments of the nation's critical infrastructure to identify security gaps and potential vulnerabilities and provide protective measures recommendations to enhance the protection and resilience of the nation's critical infrastructure. IP has also conducted more than 1,400 capability assessments of state and local bomb squads, explosives detection canine teams, dive teams, and SWAT teams to identify potential gaps and provide recommendations to mitigate vulnerabilities.

IP has also worked with state and local partners to develop 20 Multi-Jurisdiction IED Security Plans for high-risk urban areas that outline specific bombing prevention actions that reduce vulnerabilities and mitigate the risk of IED attacks.

U.S. Coast Guard has assessed over 28,000 potential terrorist targets, spanning all 18 critical infrastructure sectors, including waterside commercial nuclear facilities. Under the Maritime Transportation Security Act, maritime CIKR are required to have facility security plans which the USCG must approve.

The Federal Protective Service also provides risk assessment and mitigation, physical security, and Federal law enforcement training and oversight to enhance protection at more than 9,000 federally owned and leased facilities in all 50 states and the U.S. territories.

To facilitate the implementation of the NIPP and to support efforts to develop and implement critical infrastructure protection and resilience capabilities, DHS has established new technologies and tools for use by DHS and its federal, state, local and private sector partners. These capabilities include:

Automated Critical Asset Management System (ACAMS): ACAMs is a secure, web-based portal developed in partnership with the State, Local, Tribal, Territorial Government Coordinating Council to help local communities build critical infrastructure protection programs in their local jurisdictions and implement the NIPP

Infrastructure Information Collection System (IICS): IICS allow users to easily access, search, retrieve, and export infrastructure data contained within disparate IP systems/datasets and other federal, state, and local systems, enabling information sharing across organizations.

Integrated Rapid Visual Screening Tool for Tunnels and Mass Transit Stations: Assesses the level of risk for buildings and infrastructure from terrorist attacks and natural disasters and helps design professionals, building owners, and first responders understand the risk and resilience of buildings and infrastructure. The tool is currently used by TSA and local law enforcement agencies;

Resilient Tunnel Project: Develops innovative, feasible, and cost efficient solutions to limit water flow in case of a mass transit tunnel breach and is currently evaluating inflatable tunnel plugs.

Blast/Projectile – Protective Measures and Design Tool Project: Develops mitigation schemes for critical transit infrastructure such as underwater tunnels, transit stations, and ventilation structures as well as towers, cables, suspenders, and other critical bridge components;

Bridge Vulnerability Project: Collects vintage components from long-span bridges and evaluates their vulnerability to an explosive attack in order to refine blast modeling tools;

Unified Blast Analysis Tool Project: Predicts blast pressures in transportation tunnel systems, determining possible structural failures;

Geospatial Location Accountability and Navigation Systems for Emergency Responders (GLANSER): Enables incident commanders to locate and track first responder personnel during an incident through locators, alarms, communications, and visualizations that can be integrated into Personal Protection Equipment; and

Controlled Impact Rescue Tool: Breaches reinforced concrete walls in minutes in order to significantly decrease the time needed to perform urban search and rescue operations. FEMA plans to deploy this tool in support of its Urban Search and Rescue teams in 2011.

Source: DHS.2011. Implementing 9/11 Commission Recommendations. Progress Report 2011. http://www.dhs.gov/xlibrary/assets/implementing-9-11-commission-report-progress-2011.pdf. Nagesh, Gauthem. 2011. Cyber-Attackson US Grow, Experts Say. Hillicon Valley. July 26. http://thehill.com/blogs/hillicon-valley/technology/173595-experts-say-cyber-attacks-on-us-more-frequent-and-sophisticated.

Conclusion

It is clear that cybersecurity continues to be the next frontier of homeland security. A frontier where new questions and challenges arise each day and where computers and computer systems run many aspects of our daily lives including most of our transportation systems, our power supplies, banking and ATM machines, etc., and even what is available on the shelves of our grocery stores. The newest elements of the federal government's research agenda are looking for trustworthy spaces, which means creating different security levels on the Internet and identifying economic incentives to promote adoption of cybersecurity defense systems by individuals and businesses.

"Department of Internet Defense" by David Ignatius, *The Washington Post*, August 12, 2011

"Cybersecurity" is one of those hot topics that has launched a thousand seminars and strategy papers without producing much in the way of policy. But that's beginning to change, in one of 2011's most important but least noted government moves.

This summer, with little public fanfare, the Obama administration rolled out a strategy for cybersecurity that couples the spooky technical wizardry of the National Security Agency with the friendly, cops-and-firefighters ethos of the Department of Homeland Security. This partnership may be the smartest aspect of the policy, which has so far avoided the controversies that usually attach themselves like viruses to anything involving government and the Internet.

The new initiative was explained at a conference here last week sponsored by the Aspen Strategy Group, a forum that has been meeting each summer for 30 years to discuss defense issues. Among the participants were the two people who helped frame the plan, William Lynn and Jane Holl Lute, the deputy secretaries of defense and homeland security, respectively.

What's driving the policy is a growing recognition that the Internet is under attack — right now, every day — by foreign intelligence agencies and malicious hackers alike. Experts cite some frightening examples: An attack in May on Citigroup, in which hackers stole credit card information on 360,000 clients; a still-mysterious assault last October on the Nasdaq stock exchange; a 2009 breach of the U.S. electrical grid by Russian and Chinese intruders; and a 2009 heist of plans for the F-35 joint strike fighter.

And that's just what's public.... But classified estimates are said to be much scarier — with a hundred attacks for every one that's publicly disclosed. It's good to be skeptical about such unspecified threats — when officials warn direly, "If only you knew what we know" but in this case, the danger is obviously real. The question is what to do about it.

The heart of the new cyberdefense strategy is to spread the use of secret tools developed by the NSA....

What made this recipe powerful was that the NSA provided what officials like to call its "special sauce," in the form of electronic signatures of malicious software, which the NSA gathers 24-7 through its intelligence network.

The experiment has been running for 90 days now, and officials say that it's working....

The National Security Council soon will be debating whether to extend this pilot program to other sectors of critical infrastructure....

Here's what I took from five days of discussion: The Internet was deliberately built with an open architecture, which was once its greatest strength but is now a vulnerability. Regulatory norms may be useful (just like fire codes and clean-water standards). But real security will come when it's a moneymaker for private companies that want to satisfy public demand for an Internet that isn't crawling with bugs.

The NSA can help by sharing its secret tools. But it needs a civilian interface, in Homeland Security, to reassure the public that this is about security, not spying.

Source: D. Ignatius, *The Washington Post*, August 12, 2011. http://www.washingtonpost.com/opinions/department-of-internet-defense/2011/08/12.

You know the issue/problem has arrived when Congress is considering creating a new Committee to provide oversight. In June 2011, Senator John McCain (R-AZ) wrote to his fellow senators proposing the creation of a Select Committee on Cybersecurity and Electronic Intelligence Leaks. He was not the first to do so as Majority Leader Harry Reid (D-NV) proposed the idea in 2009 but could not find support for the idea and it was actively opposed (as is the current suggestion) by Senators Lieberman (I-CT) and Collins (R-ME) who rule the Homeland Security and Governmental Affairs Committee.

All levels of government are actively engaged with dealing with the issues surrounding cybersecurity and CIKR. The coordinating mechanisms established by DHS to work with other federal agencies, state and local governments, and the private sector are comprehensive and appear to be working. CIKR sectors are making progress at varying levels. This may be one of the areas where the government is actually working as fast as the private sector in looking for solutions to problems and anticipating the next major breakthrough. However, the General Accounting Office (GAO) has told Congress that progress has been slower than expected because agencies lack cybersecurity officials with defined roles and responsibilities.

Privacy and the issues of civil liberties remain a major issue when discussing cyberspace. The legislation proposed by the Obama Administration in 2011 includes a framework that ensures the protection of individuals' privacy and liberties while dealing with the challenges presented by cybersecurity.

Richard Clarke, the prescient and brilliant former National Security Advisor to Presidents Clinton and Bush, along with Robert Knake, a fellow at the International Council on Foreign Relations, have recently published a book entitled *Cyber War*, which sets out an agenda for what the United States should be doing to protect its national security from a cyberattack. His book provides some chilling examples of previous, real-life cyberattacks on DOD systems and U.S. infrastructure systems. Among other thing they call for the creation of a Defensive Triad. The Triad would "stop malware on the Internet, hardens the controls of the electric grid, and increase the security of the Defense Department's networks and the integrity of its weapons." They also suggest the possibility of establishing a Cyber Defense Administration within DHS to allow DHS to better operate as part of the Triad. Both ideas warrant careful consideration as we move homeland security into the next frontier.

Key Terms

ACAMS: A web-enabled information services portal that helps state and local governments build CIKR programs.

CFATS: The Chemical Facilities Anti-Terrorism Standards (CFATS) were established by DHS to provide guidance on hardening the facilities that produce, utilize, or store chemical substances, both public and private, throughout the United States.

Consequence: The result of a terrorist attack or other hazard that reflects the level, duration, and nature of the loss resulting from the incident. For the purposes of the NIPP, consequences are divided into four main categories: public health and safety, economic, psychological, and governance impacts. (*Source*: NIPP)

Crisis Management: A proactive management effort to avoid crisis, and the creation of strategy that minimizes adverse impacts of crisis on the organization when it could not be prevented. Effective crisis management requires a solid understanding of the organization, its strategy, liabilities, stakeholders, and legal framework combined with advanced communication, leadership, and decision-making skills to lead the organization through the crisis while minimizing potential loss.

Critical Infrastructure: Assets, systems, and networks, whether physical or virtual, so vital to the United States that the incapacity or destruction of such assets, systems, or networks would have a debilitating impact on security, national economic security, public health or safety, or any combination of those matters. (*Source*: NIPP)

Critical Infrastructure (and Key Resources) Government Coordinating Council (GCC): The GCC brings together diverse federal, state, local, and tribal interests to identify and develop collaborative strategies that advance critical infrastructure protection. GCCs serve as a counterpart to sector coordinating councils for each CIKR sector. They provide interagency coordination around CIKR strategies and activities, policy and communication across government, and between government and the sector to support the nation's homeland security mission. Government coordinating councils for each sector are comprised of representatives from DHS, the SSA, and the appropriate supporting federal departments and agencies. (*Source*: DHS)

Cybersecurity: The prevention of damage to, unauthorized use of, or exploitation of, and, if needed, the restoration of electronic information and communications systems and the information contained therein to ensure confidentiality, integrity, and availability. Includes protection and restoration, when needed, of information networks and wire line, wireless, satellite, public safety answering points, and 911 communications systems and control systems. (*Source*: NIPP)

Environmental Protection Agency (EPA): The U.S. Environmental Protection Agency is an agency of the federal government of the United States responsible for protecting the natural environment (i.e., air, water, and land) and therefore the health of citizens.

Federal Energy Regulatory Commission (FERC): The FERC regulates and oversees energy industries in the economic, environmental, and safety interests of the American public.

Information and communications systems are composed of hardware and software that process, store, and communicate data of all types.

Information Technology (IT) critical functions are sets of processes that produce, provide, and maintain products and services. IT critical functions encompass the full set of processes (e.g., R&D, manufacturing, distribution, upgrades, and maintenance) involved in transforming supply inputs into IT products and services.

Information Sharing and Analysis Center (ISAC): ISACs are sectorial information analysis and sharing centers that bring together representatives and decision makers of a given sector for the purposes of critical infrastructure protection and disaster preparedness.

National Infrastructure Protection Plan (NIPP): U.S. government plan that lays the framework for critical infrastructure and key asset protection activities. The plan is complemented with sector-specific annexes that detail sector-specific planning, response, and coordination bodies for effective disaster preparedness and incident response.

National Response Coordination Center (NRCC): The NRCC is FEMA's primary operations center during disaster response. The center is also vital for resource coordination between different emergency support functions.

National Response Team (NRT): The U.S. National Response Team is an organization of 16 federal departments and agencies responsible for coordinating emergency preparedness and response to oil and hazardous substance pollution incidents. The Environment Protection Agency (EPA) and the U.S. Coast Guard (USCG) serve as chair and vice chair, respectively.

Sector-Specific Agency (SSA): The federal agency designated to lead identification, assessment, protection, and resilience-building programs and activities for each CI sector.

Sector Coordinating Council: These councils are private sector counterparts to the GCCs. They are self-organized, self-run, and self-governed organizations that are representative of a spectrum of key stakeholders within a sector. SCCs serve as the government's principal point of entry into each sector for developing and coordinating a wide range of CIKR protection activities and issues. (*Source*: NIPP)

U.S. Computer Emergency Readiness Team (US-CERT): Established in 2003 to protect the nation's Internet infrastructure, US-CERT coordinates defense against and responses to cyberattacks across the nation.

Vulnerability: The vector of physical, social, geographical, and political factors that influence or define the combined susceptibility to a disaster of a given person, place, or other physical entity.

Review Questions

1. Who has the lead role for cybersecurity in the federal government?
2. What is unique about how DOD is characterizing cyberspace/security?
3. What is the role of the private sector in cybersecurity? What are your suggestions to improve private sector participation and coordination with the DHS in cybersecurity?
4. What is INSTEIN?
5. Identify three different forms of critical infrastructure. For each, name who is the SSA, and what is being done at the federal level to reduce these vulnerabilities?
6. What is ACAMS?
7. What Senate Committee has authorization for cybersecurity issues?

Further Reading

Blumenthal, H., 2003. Government Symposium on Information Sharing and Homeland Security, Department of Human Services Private Sector Information Sharing: ISAC Program, Pennsylvania.

Clarke, R., 2010. Cyber War: The Next Threat to National Security and What to Do about it. Ecco, New York.

Communications Sector Coordinating Council, 2007. Communications sector specific infrastructure protection plan. http://www.dhs.gov/xlibrary/assets/nipp-ssp-communications.pdf.

Communications Sector Coordinating Council, 2008. What is the CSCC? http://www.commscc.org/.

Congressional Research Service, 2007a. Terrorism and security issues facing the water infrastructure sector. http://www.fas.org/sgp/crs/terror/RL32189.pdf.

Congressional Research Service, 2007b. Terrorism and security issues facing the water infrastructure sector. http://www.fas.org/sgp/crs/terror/RL32189.pdf.

Congressional Research Service, 2008. FY 2009 appropriations for state and local homeland security. http://www.fas.org/sgp/crs/homesec/RS22805.pdf.

Coppola, D., 2003. Annotated Organizational Chart for the Department of Homeland Security. Bullock & Haddow, LLC, Washington, DC.

Department of Homeland Security, 2002. National strategy for homeland security. http://www.dhs.gov/xlibrary/assets/nat_strat_hls.pdf.

Department of Homeland Security, 2003. National strategy for the protection of physical infrastructure and key assets. http://www.dhs.gov/xlibrary/assets/Physical_Strategy.pdf.

Department of Homeland Security, 2004. The national plan for research and development in support of critical infrastructure protection. http://www.dhs.gov/xlibrary/assets/ST_2004_NCIP_RD_PlanFINALApr05.pdf.

Department of Homeland Security, 2005. FY 2006 critical infrastructure protection program. http://www.ojp.usdoj.gov/odp/newsreleases/FY06_IPP_PressKit.pdf.

Department of Homeland Security, 2006a. DHS releases cyber storm public exercise report. http://www.dhs.gov/xnews/releases/pr_1158341221370.shtm.

Department of Homeland Security, 2006b. FY 2007 critical infrastructure protection program. http://www.dhs.gov/xlibrary/assets/grants-2007-infrastructure-protection.pdf.

Department of Homeland Security, 2007a. FY 2008 critical infrastructure protection program. http://www.fema.gov/government/grant/ipp/index.shtm#tsp.

Department of Homeland Security, 2007b. Overview: FY 2007 infrastructure protection program awards. http://www.dhs.gov/xlibrary/assets/grants-2007-infrastructure-protection.pdf.

Department of Homeland Security, 2009a. National infrastructure protection plan. http://www.dhs.gov/files/programs/editorial/gc_1204738275985.shtm.

Department of Homeland Security, 2009b. NIPP: sector specific plans. http://www.dhs.gov/files/programs/gc_1179866197607.shtm.

Department of Homeland Security, 2010. Quadrennial homeland security review report: a strategic framework for a secure homeland. http://www.dhs.gov/xlibrary/assets/qhsr_report.pdf.

Department of Homeland Security, 2011. Implementing the recommendations of the 9/11 commission, a progess report. http://www.dhs.gov/xlibrary/assets/progress_report.pdf.

Government Accountability Office, 2006. GAO 07 39 critical infrastructure protection: progress coordinating government and private sector efforts varies by sectors' characteristics. http://www.gao.gov/new.items/d0739.pdf.

Greenberg, W.J., 2003. September 11, 2001: a CEO's story. Harvard Business Review, vol.10.1225/R0210D, pp. 7–8.

Harrald, C., Coppola, D.P., and Yeletaysi, S., 2003. Assessing the Financial Impacts of the World Trade Center Attacks on Publicly Held Corporations. TIEMS Conference Proceedings. Provence, France.

Ignatius, D., 2011. Department of internet defense. The Washington Post. http://www.washingtonpost.com/opinions/department-of-internet-defense/2011/08/12.

Lerbinger, O., 1997. The Crisis Manager. Lawrence Erlbaum Associates, New York.

Nagesh, G., 2011. Cyber attacks on U.S. grow. Hillicon Valley Blog, http://thehill.com/blogs/hillcon-valley/technology/173595.

National Commission on Terrorist Attacks Upon the United States, 2004, Final report of the National Commission on Terrorists Attacks upon the United States.

Pincus, W., 2010. Government devotes more money to cybersecurity. *The Washington Post*. http://www.washingtonpost.com/wp-dyn/content/article/2010/06/22.

The White House, 2003. National strategy to secure cyberspace. http://www.whitehouse.gov/pcipb/cyberspace_strategy.pdf.

The White House, 2011. Fact sheet: cybersecurity legislative proposal. http://www.whitehouse.gov/the-press-office/2011/05/12/fact-sheet.pdf.

Symantec, 2010. The Symantec Internet Security Threat Report. http://www.symantec.com/business/theme%20jsp?themeid−threatreport.

u SD Times, Expert backs new security certification for coders. http://www.sdtimes.com/EXPERT_BACKS_NEW_SECURITY_CERTIFICATION_FOR_CODERS/About_SECURITY_and_SOFTWAREDEVELOPMENT_and_ISC2/32912.

Times Online, 2007. China's cyber army is preparing to march on America, says Pentagon. http://www.technology.timesonline.co.uk/tol/news/tech_and_web/the_web/article2409865.ece.

9

All-Hazards Emergency Response and Recovery

What You Will Learn

- How large-scale emergencies are declared at each level of government, and what kinds of declarations are made
- Legislative actions taken since the September 11 terrorist attacks that affect the nation's response capabilities
- The many federal homeland security grant programs that are available to states and local communities
- The response roles assumed by each level of government, from local to national (including those of the Department of Homeland Security as well as other federal agencies and offices), and by private and nonprofit organizations
- What homeland security volunteer programs exist, what each does, and how they are distributed across the country
- How the National Incident Management System and the National Response Framework guide all-hazards emergency response to major incidents in the United States

Introduction

When a natural disaster such as a flood, earthquake, or hurricane occurs, or when a technological incident or terrorist attack happens, local police, fire, and emergency medical personnel are generally the first to respond. Their mission is to rescue and attend to victims, suppress any secondary fires that may have resulted, secure and police the disaster area, and begin the process of restoring order. They are supported in this effort by local emergency management personnel and community government officials.

The adage that "practice makes perfect" comes to mind when considering the unprecedented number of natural and man-made disasters the past decade has presented, which have together tested the capacity of these first responders and the nation's response system as a whole. In the vast majority of cases, both the systems in place and the participants responding were considered efficient and effective. However, the unexpected terrorist attacks of September 11, 2001, the anthrax events that followed shortly thereafter, and the poor response to Hurricane Katrina, all revealed certain weaknesses in this system that clearly needed to be addressed. Although the immediate responses to the World Trade Center attacks were

FIGURE 9–1 New York City, New York, September 27, 2001 — An aerial view of the rescue and recovery operations under way in lower Manhattan at the site of the collapsed World Trade Center. (Source: Photo by Bri Rodriguez/FEMA News Photo)

typical of an effective national response system (the most advanced in the world at the time), there still followed an unprecedented loss of lives among both civilians and first responders (Figure 9–1). Several of the primary support systems in place at the time performed far below expectations, and many established procedures were not followed or were not deemed suitable for the catastrophic scenario that presented. Hurricane Katrina, just 4 years later, exposed yet more remaining and several new systemic shortfalls that the terrorism-focused efforts could not have possibly addressed.

The 9/11 attacks were truly a watershed event in emergency management history. In their shadow, agencies at the national, state, and local government levels were prompted to initiate evaluations that sought to improve existing response procedures and protocols in light of the vast new knowledge and experience that had been attained. The spectacular nature of the attacks, and the apparent threat of subsequent events of equal or greater magnitude, mandated the generation of after-action reports that spurred many changes and improvements in the procedures and protocols that first responders have since applied to their emergency management efforts. Considering the devious and dangerous potential posed by future terrorism events, many of these evaluations focused their attention on what appeared to be a relatively new concept for most of the agencies involved: how best to protect first responders from harm in future attacks.

The federal government responded to this shift in response procedures by updating the Federal Response Plan (FRP). A new prescriptive and functional document, the National Response Plan (NRP), was the product of these efforts. This change was justified under the belief that, because the nature of threats facing the United States had become more complex, and because the effect of future natural, technological, and terrorist events could cause detriment to the American way of life, a unified national effort was required to prepare for the response to these events before they occur again. The team members assembled to create this document were charged with making this new national response system as efficient and effective as possible, and to focus on utilizing a unified approach to managing incidents that would result in a significant reduction in the vulnerability of the United States to all hazards.

The NRP, which resulted from these collective efforts, and which was released in January 2005, was billed as an all-discipline, all-hazards plan. The NRP was designed to establish a single, comprehensive framework for the management of domestic incidents, which would likely involve many participants from all government levels. The plan directly addressed the prevention of terrorist attacks, as well as the reduction in vulnerability to all natural and man-made hazards. Finally, it attempted to offer guidance on minimizing the damage and assisting in the recovery from any type of incident that occurred.

Although the plan placed a clear emphasis on retaining the primary responsibility for initial incident response at the local level, with the locally available assets and special capabilities for prevention, it included a more aggressive integration between agencies in charge and sought to establish a workable, unified approach to the management of incidents, especially those involving the criminal element of terrorism.

To carry out the coordinated response approach prescribed in the NRP, the federal government created the National Incident Management System (NIMS). On March 1, 2004, former Department of Homeland Security (DHS) Director Tom Ridge announced the release of NIMS and stated that it was created in order to "provide a consistent nationwide approach for federal, state, and local governments to work effectively and efficiently together to prepare for, respond to, and recover from domestic incidents, regardless of cause, size, or complexity."

Hurricane Katrina (2005) exposed several problems that existed within the new NRP, the most significant reported to be its sheer length. In response, the federal government developed a much more concise National Response Framework (NRF), based heavily upon the systems and organization contained within the original NRP. Upon draft release in early September 2007, the NRF came under heavy criticism due to the fact that it had been created largely devoid of local or state response agency involvement, and many emergency managers felt that it lacked the detailed operational guidance they had hoped for. After a period of comment and adjustment that was expanded far beyond its initial 30 days, a final NRF was released on January 22, 2008. It remains to be seen what improvements this progression, from FRP, to NRP, to NRF, will have with regard to streamlining the multiagency response that is required during major national-level disasters, including those involving terrorist intent.

Overall, the changing nature of the terrorist threat (e.g., greater population exposure, possible use of weapons of mass destruction [WMDs]) has been the motivator for developing a new approach to response operations. This new approach has sought to initiate a profound transformation on the response community at the state and local levels through implementation of the following four goals:

- To unify crisis and consequence management (CM) as a single, integrated function, rather than two separate functions, and integrate all existing federal emergency response plans into a single document (the NRF)
- To provide interoperability and compatibility among federal, state, and local capabilities (through NIMS)
- To enhance response and preparedness capabilities of first responders and state and local governments against all kinds of hazards and threats by providing extensive funding for equipment, training, planning, and exercises
- To integrate the private sector and the business communities at a greater extent into response activities and responsibilities in order to increase resources in hand

It is the purpose of this chapter to describe the functional and operational performance of the U.S. response system, to identify and describe the changes brought about by the creation of the DHS and the actions of DHS and Congress, and to discuss their consequences. The chapter highlights in this regard include legislative and budgetary issues, local and state response capacities, volunteer group response mechanisms, an overview of the Incident Command System (ICS) and the NIMS, NRP, and NRF, and the recovery function including various programs available to assist in recovery.

■ ■ Critical Thinking ■

Should the federal emergency management role be crafted by the Department of Homeland Security, by the state and local emergency management organizations that ultimately benefit from the federal assistance provided, or by collaboration among all levels? What benefits and shortcomings would result from each of these three different planning scenarios?

Response Processes

Whenever the national emergency number 911 is called, in any event ranging from a simple traffic accident, to a tornado sighting, or for someone showing signs of a viral disease, the first responders that answer the call are always local officials. But when the size of the incident grows so large that response requirements exceed these local capabilities, and the costs of inflicted damage surpass what the local government can manage, the mayor or county executive must turn to the governor and state government resources for assistance in responding to the event and in helping the community to recover. Each state then calls upon an established system whereby the governor crafts a response that combines various personnel (including the state emergency management agency and the state National Guard), equipment, and funding. And should the disaster exceed the state's abilities to manage, then it is likely that a national disaster has occurred and federal emergency management efforts are required.

The new NRF, like that of its predecessors, dictates the rules by which states initiate an appeal for assistance, and by which that assistance is granted should the president choose to declare a disaster. The new disaster reporting process is similar to that which was stipulated under the original FRP, although fundamental changes have certainly occurred. The following gives a brief overview of the declaration process that exists under the NRF, which is described in much greater detail later in this chapter.

Should the governor decide, based on information and damage surveys generated by community and state officials, or predictions of impending disaster or terrorist threat, that the size of the actual or anticipated disaster event has exceeded or will exceed the state's capacity to respond, the governor will make a formal request to the president for a presidential major disaster declaration or an emergency declaration. This request is prepared by state officials in cooperation with regional staff from the Federal Emergency Management Agency (FEMA).

At the federal level, the governor's request is analyzed first by FEMA's regional administrator, who evaluates the damage and requirements for federal assistance and makes a recommendation to the FEMA administrator. The FEMA administrator, acting through the Secretary of Homeland Security, may then recommend a course of action to the president.

The president considers the FEMA administrator's recommendation, and decides whether or not to declare the disaster a presidential major disaster declaration or an emergency declaration. What constitutes each of these is described in the sidebar "Types of Presidential Declarations."

Types of Presidential Declarations

Presidential Major Disaster Declaration

A Presidential Major Disaster Declaration (Major Declaration) is defined by FEMA to be "any natural catastrophe (including any hurricane, tornado, storm, high water, wind-driven water, tidal wave, tsunami, earthquake, volcanic eruption, landslide, mudslide, snowstorm, or drought), or, regardless of cause, any fire, flood, or explosion, in any part of the United States, which in the determination of the President causes damage of sufficient severity and magnitude to warrant major disaster assistance under the [Stafford] Act to supplement the efforts and available resources of States, local governments, and disaster relief organizations in alleviating the damage, loss, hardship, or suffering caused thereby."

A Presidential major disaster declaration puts into motion long-term Federal recovery programs, some of which are matched by State programs, and designed to help disaster victims, businesses, and public entities.

Emergency Declaration

An Emergency Declaration is defined by FEMA to be "any occasion or instance for which, in the determination of the President, Federal assistance is needed to supplement State and local efforts and capabilities to save lives and to protect property and public health and safety, or to lessen or avert the threat of a catastrophe in any part of the United States."

An emergency declaration is more limited in scope and without the long-term Federal recovery programs of a major disaster declaration. Generally, Federal assistance and funding are provided to meet a specific emergency need or to help prevent a major disaster from occurring.

Sources: Federal Emergency Management Agency (FEMA), "Number of Declarations per Calendar Year Since 1998," Washington, DC: FEMA, 2008; FEMA, "National Response Framework (DRAFT)," Washington, DC: FEMA, 2007.

Once a presidential declaration has been made, the FEMA administrator, acting on behalf of the Secretary of Homeland Security and/or senior staff designated by the FEMA administrator determines the need to activate components of the NRF to conduct further assessment of the situation, initiate interagency coordination, share information with affected jurisdictions, and/or initiate the deployment of resources. At this time, federal departments and agencies are notified by the DHS National Operations Center (NOC), and may be called on to staff the National Response Coordination Center (NRCC) or the National Infrastructure Coordinating Center (NICC).

If an incident has already occurred, the NRF priority shifts to immediate and short-term response activities. The purpose of these activities is to preserve lives, protect property, and prevent further harm to the environment. The social, economic, and political structures of the affected community or communities are protected as well. Response actions could include the participation of law enforcement officers, fire officials, emergency medical services (mass care, public health, and medical services), officials involved in infrastructure restoration, environmental protection officials, and more.

Either during (if appropriate) or immediately following the response phase, the long-term recovery is initiated (Figure 9–2).

FIGURE 9–2 Tuscaloosa, AL, May 25, 2011 — FEMA Community Relations (CR) Specialists Aron Thompson (far left), and Tony Bronk (center) are providing FEMA disaster recovery information at a disaster benefit concert. FEMA CR outreach efforts attempt to get FEMA registration and other helpful recovery information to survivors of the deadly April tornado. (Source: Photo by George Armstrong/FEMA)

When a major disaster strikes in the United States, or when the threat of disaster is imminent, the aforementioned chronology describes how the most sophisticated and advanced emergency management system in the world responds and begins the recovery process. The fundamental pillars on which the system is built are, and continue to be, coordination and cooperation among a significant number of federal, state, and local government agencies, volunteer organizations, and, more recently, the business community.

■ ■ Critical Thinking ■

When the Federal Response Plan (FRP) was replaced by the National Response Plan (NRP), the president gained the power to initiate a federal response in support of the states, under specific circumstances as outlined in the plan, regardless of a request from a governor. This power was transferred into the new National Response Framework (NRF). Do you feel that this takes too much authority away from the states or that this is a necessary tool?

Legislative Actions

The establishment of the state of homeland security as it exists today involved several bills and laws, essentially determined by homeland and national security presidential directives delivered during the years following the 9/11 attacks. The most significant include the following:

- The USA PATRIOT Act of 2001
- The Aviation and Transportation Security Act of 2001

- The SA 4470 Amendment
- The Public Health Security and Bioterrorism Preparedness and Response Act of 2002
- The Enhanced Border Security and Visa Entry Reform Act of 2002
- The Maritime Transportation Security Act of 2002
- The Homeland Security Act of 2002

These laws, among many other goals, attempted to clearly define the mission and organization of emergency management and terrorism preparedness in the United States. The single greatest change that resulted from these laws in the spectrum of emergency management — and also in terms of the changes that have occurred within the federal government itself — was the creation of the DHS. The new department, which integrated 22 existing federal agencies under the direction of a single cabinet-level official for the purpose of streamlining emergency management and counterterrorism activities, was vigorously debated, but finally came into existence in March 2003.

FEMA, which was included in this transfer, and which retained its pre-DHS trademark name, was transferred largely intact to form one of five directorates that existed under the original DHS organization, the Directorate of Emergency Preparedness and Response (EP&R). The EP&R mission as defined by the Homeland Security Act of 2002 was similar to that of FEMA prior to its incorporation (to ensure that the nation is prepared for catastrophes — whether natural or technological disasters or terrorist assaults), although there was clearly a new focus that considered more carefully the terrorism hazard. This new directorate supported the original federal government national response and recovery strategy, and dedicated much of its resources to enhancing the abilities of first responders at the local level to carry out that same mission. For several years, however, many of its original (and central) mitigation and preparedness functions were removed from the agency and transferred elsewhere within DHS, only to be returned to FEMA per legislation passed in the aftermath of Hurricane Katrina.

DHS has emphasized through its public relations efforts that it continues to make every effort to support FEMA's original mission of comprehensive emergency management. They assure that FEMA, within DHS, will continue in its efforts to reduce the loss of life and property and to protect the nation's institutions from all types of hazards through risk-based emergency management. In a continuation of FEMA's mitigation role, but using new nomenclature, DHS has asserted it will further the evolution of the emergency management culture from one that reacts to disasters to one that proactively helps communities and citizens avoid becoming victims — with *prevention* being the term of choice to replace *mitigation*.

The Homeland Security Act of 2002 describes the responsibilities of FEMA, within DHS, as follows:

- Helping to ensure the preparedness of emergency response providers for terrorist attacks, major disasters, and other emergencies
- Establishing standards, conducting exercises and training, evaluating performance, and providing funds in relation to the Nuclear Incident Response Team (defined in Section 504 of the bill)
- Providing the federal government's response to terrorist attacks and major disasters
- Aiding the recovery from terrorist attacks and major disasters
- Working with other federal and nonfederal agencies to build a comprehensive national incident management system
- Consolidating existing federal government emergency response plans into a single, coordinated national response plan

- Developing comprehensive programs for developing interoperable communications technology and ensuring that emergency response providers acquire such technology

The responsibility of providing the federal government's response to terrorist attacks and major disasters — item 3 above — is explained in detail in the act, and includes the following:

- Coordinating the overall response to terrorist attacks
- Directing the Domestic Emergency Support Team (DEST), the Strategic National Stockpile (SNS), the National Disaster Medical System (NDMS), and the Nuclear Incident Response Team (each described later in this chapter)
- Overseeing the Metropolitan Medical Response System (MMRS) and coordinating other federal response resources

It is important to note that the new responsibilities of FEMA are not intended to detract from other important functions transferred to DHS, such as those of the U.S. Fire Administration (USFA). In almost all areas, DHS has fully preserved the authority to carry out the original functions of FEMA, including support for community initiatives that promote homeland security.

The following agencies were transferred to DHS, and were integrated into FEMA as a result, through the provisions of the Homeland Security Act of 2002:

- The Integrated Hazard Information System of the National Oceanic and Atmospheric Administration (NOAA), which was renamed "FIRESAT"
- The National Domestic Preparedness Office (NDPO) of the Federal Bureau of Investigation (FBI)
- The Domestic Emergency Support Teams (DEST) of the Department of Justice (DOJ)
- The Office of Emergency Preparedness (OEP), the National Disaster Medical System (NDMS), and the Metropolitan Medical Response System (MMRS) of the Department of Health and Human Services (HHS) (the NDMS was transferred back into HHS in 2007)
- The Strategic National Stockpile (SNS) of HHS

Other legislation that addresses local response issues is presented briefly in Table 9–1.

Budget

The DHS receives one of the largest shares of the federal budget. Each year since its creation, its associated budget requests and funds granted have only increased in size. In 2004, this amounted to $35.6 billion, rising to $38.5 billion in 2005, to $40.4 billion in 2006, again to $43.0 billion in 2007, again to $47.0 billion in 2008, again to $52.7 billion in FY 2009, to $56 billion in FY 2010, and down to $55.6 in FY 2011. The presidential budget request for FY 2012 sought $56.9 billion for DHS. Of this total allocation, approximately $10 billion is targeted for emergency management through FEMA. A breakdown of the various components that make up the FEMA budget, including changes from the period FY 2010 through FY 2012 (as proposed) can be found online in the DHS Budget Overview (p. 137).

Local Response

On an operational level, minor disasters occur daily in communities around the United States. Local fire, police, and emergency medical personnel respond to these events in a routine, systematic, and well-planned

Table 9–1 Local Response-Related Legislation

Bill	Title	Homeland Purpose
HR 3153	State Bioterrorism Preparedness Act of 2001	To assist states in preparing for, and responding to, biological or chemical terrorist attacks.
HR 3435	Empowering Local First Responders to Fight Terrorism Act of 2001	To provide for grants to local first-responder agencies to combat terrorism and be a part of homeland defense.
HR 3615	Protecting Our Schools Homeland Defense Act of 2002	To amend the Public Health Service Act to direct the Secretary of Health and Human Services to make grants to train school nurses as "first responders" in the event of a biological or chemical attack.
HR 5169	Wastewater Treatment Works Security Act of 2002	To improve the defense and response of publicly owned water treatment plants against terrorist attacks by assessing risks and locating vulnerabilities.
S 1520	State Bioterrorism Preparedness Act of 2002	To assist states in preparing for, and responding to, biological or chemical attack.
S 1602	Chemical Security Act of 2001	To protect the public against the threat of a chemical terrorist attack.
S 1746	Nuclear Security Act of 2001	To strengthen security at sensitive nuclear facilities.
S 2664	First Responder Terrorism Preparedness Act of 2002	To establish an Office of National Preparedness to coordinate terrorism preparedness and response.
HR 727	Trauma Care Systems Planning and Development Act of 2007	To amend the Public Health Service Act to add requirements regarding trauma care, and for other purposes.
HR 1	Implementing Recommendations of the 9/11 Commission Act of 2007	To provide for implementation of the recommendations of the National Commission on Terrorist Attacks upon the United States.
HR 1674	Tsunami Warning and Education Act	To authorize and strengthen the tsunami detection, forecast, warning, and mitigation program of the National Oceanic and Atmospheric Administration, to be carried out by the National Weather Service, and to establish tsunami warning centers, among other things, to disseminate forecasts and tsunami warning bulletins to federal, state, and local government officials and the public.
HR 5136	National Integrated Drought Information System Act of 2006	To establish a National Integrated Drought Information System that (1) provides an effective drought early warning system; (2) coordinates, and integrates as practicable, federal research in support of such a system; and (3) builds on existing forecasting and assessment programs and partnerships.
HR 23	Tornado Shelters Act	To amend the Housing and Community Development Act of 1974 to authorize communities to use community development block grant funds for construction of tornado-safe shelters in manufactured home parks.

(Continued)

Table 9–1 (Continued)

Bill	Title	Homeland Purpose
HR 5419	Commercial Spectrum Enhancement Act	To amend the National Telecommunications and Information Administration Organization Act to facilitate the reallocation of spectrum from governmental to commercial users; to improve, enhance, and promote the nation's homeland security, public safety, and citizen-activated emergency response capabilities through the use of enhanced 911 services, to further upgrade Public Safety Answering Point capabilities and related functions in receiving E-911 calls, and to support in the construction and operation of a ubiquitous and reliable citizen-activated system.
S 3678	Pandemic and All-Hazards Preparedness Act	A bill to amend the Public Health Service Act with respect to public health security and all-hazards preparedness and response, and for other purposes.
S 1152	Firefighting Research and Coordination Act	A bill to reauthorize the United States Fire Administration, and for other purposes (including directs the administrator to (1) provide technical assistance and training to state and local fire service officials to establish nationwide and state mutual aid systems for dealing with national emergencies and (2) develop and make model mutual aid plans for both intrastate and interstate assistance available to state and local fire service officials).
S. 2735	Dam Safety Act of 2006	A bill to amend the National Dam Safety Program Act to reauthorize the national dam safety program, and for other purposes.

Source: Association of Corporate Counsel, 2002, http://www.acca.com/infopaks/homeland/legislativechart.pdf and http://www.govtrack.us.

course of action (Figure 9–3). Firefighters, police officers, and emergency medical technicians respond to the scene and take immediate actions. Their job is to secure the scene and maintain order, rescue and treat those who are injured, contain and suppress fire or hazardous conditions, and retrieve the dead. Some notable facts about first responders who assert their role as the real front line in the nation's defense from disasters of all categories follow:

- There are more than 1 million firefighters in the United States, of whom approximately 750,000 are volunteers.
- Local police departments have an estimated 556,000 full-time employees, including about 436,000 sworn enforcement personnel.
- Sheriffs' offices reported about 291,000 full-time employees, including about 186,000 sworn personnel.
- There are more than 155,000 nationally registered emergency medical technicians (EMTs) (Department of Homeland Security, www.dhs.gov).

FIGURE 9–3 New York City, NY, October 5, 2001 — Rescue workers continue their efforts at the World Trade Center. (Source: Photo by Andrea Booher/FEMA News Photo)

▪▪ Critical Thinking ▪

The nation's system of emergency management relies predominantly upon the efforts of unpaid volunteer first responders. Is this type of system sustainable? Why or why not? What could be done to improve it, and at what cost?

The actions of local first responders are driven by procedures and protocols developed by the responding agencies themselves (e.g., fire, police, and emergency medical). Most communities in the United States have developed community-wide emergency plans, mandated by the Disaster Mitigation Act of 2000 (DMA, 2000), which incorporate these procedures and protocols. In the aftermath of the September 11 terrorist events, many communities have reworked or are reviewing and reworking their community emergency plans to include new and improved methodologies for responding to all forms of terrorist attacks including bioterrorism and other WMDs. These changes are most often driven by available federal and state funds (including grants that require such changes for funds eligibility) and to mirror new programs that have been designed at these two higher levels of government (see "2011 HSGP allocation by Program," http://www.fema.gov/pdf/government/grant/2011/fy11_hsgp_factsheet.pdf; FEMA, 2010, "2010 HSGP fact sheet," http://www.fema.gov/pdf/government/grant/HSGP.pdf; FEMA, 2009, "2009 HSGP fact sheet," http://dema.delaware.gov/Docs/wmd/FY2009%20HSGP_FAQ.pdf.

The federal government has continued to support local-level first responders heavily through funding, as described earlier in the discussion of budgets. This funding support has been provided to address four primary areas of focus, including:

- *Planning*: Support of state and local governments in developing comprehensive plans to prepare for and respond to a terrorist attack
- *Equipment*: Assistance for state and local first-responder agencies for the purchase of a wide range of equipment needed to respond effectively to a terrorist attack, including personal protective equipment, chemical and biological detection systems, and interoperable communications gear

- *Training*: Resources to train firefighters, police officers, and emergency medical technicians to respond and operate in response to terrorist attacks, most notably for those that result in a chemically or biologically hazardous environment
- *Exercises*: Support for a coordinated, regular program of exercises that improve response capabilities, practice mutual aid, and assess operational improvements and deficiencies

First-Responder Roles and Responsibilities

The roles and responsibilities of first responders are usually detailed in the community emergency operations plan (EOP). Citing the responsibilities of first responders after a terrorist incident provides a useful example of the scope of the changes that these officials are experiencing, as displayed in the following list detailing several of the main objectives for the first responders to a terrorist incident:

- Protect the lives and safety of the citizens and other first responders
- Isolate, contain, and/or limit the spread of any cyber, nuclear, biological, chemical, incendiary, or explosive devices
- Identify the type of agent and/or devices used
- Identify and establish control zones for the suspected agent used
- Ensure emergency responders properly follow protocol and have appropriate protective gear
- Identify the most appropriate decontamination and/or treatment for victims
- Establish victim services
- Notify emergency personnel, including medical facilities, of dangers and anticipated casualties and proper measures to be followed
- Notify appropriate state and federal agencies
- Provide accurate and timely public information
- Preserve as much evidence as possible to aid in the investigation process
- Protect critical infrastructure
- Oversee fatality management
- Develop and enhance medical EMS
- Protect property and environment (Bullock & Haddow, LLC, 2003)

Local Emergency Managers

It is primarily the responsibility of the designated local emergency manager to develop and maintain community-level emergency plans. Often, this individual shares a dual responsibility in local government, such as fire or police chief, and serves only part-time as the community's emergency manager. The emergency management profession, and the professional skill and knowledge of the local emergency manager, has progressively matured since the 1980s. Today, there are far more opportunities for individuals to receive formal training in emergency management than ever before, including as recently as 5 years ago. There are currently more than 227 junior college, undergraduate, and graduate programs that offer courses and degrees in emergency management and 105 Homeland Security/Defense and Terrorism Higher Education Programs. Additionally, FEMA's Emergency Management Institute (EMI) located in Emmitsburg, Maryland, offers emergency management courses on campus and through distance learning programs. EMI has also worked closely with junior colleges, colleges, universities, and graduate schools to develop course work and curriculums in emergency management. Details of EMI's Certified Emergency Manager Program are as follows:

- The International Association of Emergency Managers (IAEM) created the Certified Emergency Manager (CEM) Program to raise and maintain professional standards. It is an internationally recognized program that certifies achievements within the emergency management profession.
- CEM certification is a peer-review process administered through the IAEM. An individual does not have to be an IAEM member to be certified. Certification is maintained in 5-year cycles.
- The CEM program is served by a CEM commission that is composed of emergency management professionals, including representatives from allied fields, education, the military, and private industry.
- Development of the CEM program was supported by FEMA, the National Emergency Management Association (NEMA), and a host of allied organizations (International Association of Emergency Managers, www.iaem.org).

The roles and responsibilities of the county emergency manager are defined by the County EOP. The job descriptions of these individuals exhibit the same levels of variance as those in the local first-responder community, primarily on account of the broadening incident threat spectrum that likewise poses a threat at the county level. Although no specific guidelines are given for the new roles of either local or county emergency managers, the essential differences between legacy and more modern EOPs are based on the following requirements:

- Changes in established procedures for handling terrorist incidents
- Changes in necessary response equipment
- Changes in the structure of responding agencies and protocols of operations and interagency cooperation
- Changes in neighboring local, state, and federal emergency operation plans

Funding for First Responders

As of early 2008, the federal government had spent more than $16 billion on funding for first responders since the September 11 terrorist attacks. This funding has come not only in clear recognition of the importance of first responders in managing the new terrorist risk, but also in acknowledgment of their role in protecting citizens from all forms of disaster. Since 2001, this support has come through the provision of several grant programs, which often change from year to year as needs and priorities are evaluated, adjusted, and reevaluated. Several of these programs and their associated funding levels from recent years are discussed below.

The administration authority for the various first-responder and other state homeland security and emergency management grant programs has been transferred time and again since the establishment of DHS. Before its creation, this funding (which existed at much lower levels) was administered through several different federal agencies — the most significant portion of which was managed by FEMA. After the 2002 establishment of DHS, funding was consolidated under the EP&R Directorate. In 2004, the Office of State and Local Government Coordination and Preparedness (SLGCP) was established within DHS to streamline and coordinate all homeland security-based funding to the states and territories — which included first-responder grant programs. Grants were managed by an office within this office, appropriately titled the Office for Domestic Preparedness (ODP). One of the greatest accomplishments of ODP was the consolidation of six individual grant programs, including the State Homeland Security Program (SHSP), the Urban Areas Security Initiative (UASI), the Law Enforcement Terrorism Prevention Program (LETPP), the Citizen Corps Program (CCP), the Emergency Management Performance Grants (EMPG), and the Metropolitan Medical Response System Program Grants. All six programs were integrated into the Homeland Security Grant Program (HSGP). Finally, in 2007, when DHS was reorganized yet again according to the post-Katrina Emergency Management Reform Act of 2006, grant administration authority was once again returned to the newly reestablished FEMA.

First-responder grant amounts have varied significantly from year to year. The federal government provided a total of $5.056 billion in grants to state and local governments during FY 2003, but this amount dropped to $4.366 billion during FY 2004. These grants targeted state and local responders, public health agencies, and emergency managers, in their efforts to prepare for disasters. There was considerable dispute between the states during these years, addressed at the congressional level, about how this funding should be disbursed among the states and territories. There existed two schools of opposing thought — one that felt funding should include a minimum amount per state, based on the assumption that nobody can say for sure where the terrorists will strike next, and another that felt funding should be risk based, going to those states with populated urban centers containing obvious terrorist targets. The calculation that determined the amount allocated to each state as a factor of how many people reside in that state — the "per capita funding" — was often used to illustrate how states like Alaska were receiving much more funding per person than states believed to be obvious targets, such as New York or California. In 2005, it was decided by Congress that risk factors would be considered in the determination of funding levels for each state. The amount of funding, however, has wavered since its record high in FY 2003, with funding levels totaling $4.192 billion in FY 2004, $3.985 billion in FY 2005, $3.377 billion in FY 2006, $3.398 billion in FY 2007, and a request of $3.196 billion in FY 2008.

FY 2011 Homeland Security Grant Program (HSGP)

State Homeland Security Program (SHSP)

- Total Funding Available in FY 2011: $526,874,100
- Purpose: The FY 2011 SHSP provides funding to support the implementation of State Homeland Security Strategies to address the identified planning, organization, equipment, training, and exercise needs at the state and local levels to prevent, protect against, respond to, and recover from acts of terrorism and other catastrophic events. SHSP also provides funding to implement initiatives in the State Preparedness Report. Consistent with the Implementing Recommendations of the 9/11 Act of 2007 (Public Law 110-53) ("hereafter "9/11 Act"), states are required to ensure that at least 25 percent (25%) of SHSP appropriated funds are dedicated towards law enforcement terrorism prevention-oriented planning, organization, training, exercise, and equipment activities, including those activities which support the development and operation of fusion centers.
- Eligible Applicants: The State Administrative Agency (SAA) is the only entity eligible to apply to FEMA for SHSP funds. Recipients include all 50 states, the District of Columbia, Puerto Rico, American Samoa, Guam, the Northern Mariana Islands, and the U.S. Virgin Islands.

- Awards: FY 2011 SHSP allocations will be made based on three factors: minimum amounts as legislatively mandated, DHS's risk methodology, and effectiveness. Each state and territory will receive a minimum allocation under SHSP using the thresholds established in the 9/11 Act. All 50 states, the District of Columbia, and Puerto Rico will receive 0.355 percent of the total funds allocated for grants under Section 2004 of the Homeland Security Act of 2002 (6 U.S.C. §101 et seq.), as amended by the 9/11 Act. Four territories (American Samoa, Guam, the Northern Mariana Islands, and the U.S. Virgin Islands) will receive a minimum allocation of 0.08 percent of the total funds allocated for grants under Section 2004 of the Homeland Security Act of 2002, as amended by the 9/11 Act. Per the 9/11 Act, states are required to ensure that at least 25 percent (25%) of SHSP appropriated funds are dedicated towards law enforcement terrorism prevention activities.

Urban Areas Security Initiative (UASI)

- Total Funding Available in FY 2011: $662,622,100
- Purpose: The UASI Program provides funding to address the unique planning, organization, equipment, training, and exercise needs of high-threat, high-density urban areas, and assists them in building an enhanced and sustainable capacity to prevent, protect against, respond to, and recover from acts of terrorism. Per the 9/11 Act, states are required to ensure that at least 25 percent (25%) of UASI appropriated funds are dedicated towards law enforcement terrorism prevention activities.
- Eligible Applicants: The SAA is the only entity eligible to apply to FEMA for UASI funds. The 31 high risk urban areas eligible for funding under the FY 2011 UASI program are the only urban areas that may apply.
- Program Awards: The 11 highest risk urban areas, designated Tier I urban areas, will be eligible for $540,696,100. The remaining 20 Urban Areas, designated Tier II urban areas, will be eligible for $121,926,000. Funds will be allocated based on DHS's risk methodology and effectiveness.

Operation Stonegarden (OPSG)

- Total Funding Available in FY 2011: $54,890,000
- Purpose: The OPSG Program provides funding to enhance cooperation and coordination among local, tribal, territorial, state, and federal law enforcement agencies in a joint mission to secure the United States' borders along routes of ingress from international borders to include travel corridors in states bordering Mexico and Canada, as well as states and territories with international water borders.
- Eligible Applicants: The SAA is the only entity eligible to apply to FEMA for OPSG funds. Local units of government at the county level and federally recognized tribal governments in the states bordering Canada (including Alaska), southern states bordering Mexico, and states and territories with International water borders may apply for FY 2011 OPSG funds through their SAA.
- Program Awards: FY 2011 OPSG allocations will be made competitively to designated localities within U.S. border states based on risk analysis and the anticipated feasibility and effectiveness of proposed investments by the applicants.

Metropolitan Medical Response System (MMRS) Program

- Total Funding Available in FY 2011: $34,929,932
- Purpose: The MMRS Program provides funding to support the integration of emergency management, health, and medical systems into a coordinated response to mass casualty

incidents caused by any hazard. Successful MMRS grantees reduce the consequences of a mass casualty incident during the initial period of a response by having augmented existing local operational response systems before an incident occurs.

- Eligible Applicants: The SAA is the only entity eligible to apply to FEMA for MMRS funds. The 124 MMRS jurisdictions eligible for funding under the FY 2011 MMRS Program are the only jurisdictions that may apply.
- Program Awards: Each of the 124 MMRS jurisdictions will receive $281,693 to establish or sustain local capabilities.

Citizen Corps Program (CCP)

- Total Funding Available in FY 2011: $9,980,000
- Purpose: CCP provides funding to bring community and government leaders together to coordinate the involvement of community members and organizations in emergency preparedness, planning, mitigation, response, and recovery.
- Eligible Applicants: The SAA is the only entity eligible to apply to FEMA for CCP funds. Recipients for the CCP include all 50 states, the District of Columbia, Puerto Rico, American Samoa, Guam, the Northern Mariana Islands, and the U.S. Virgin Islands.
- Program Awards: FY 2011 CCP allocations will be determined using a formula, which specifies that all 50 states, the District of Columbia, and the Commonwealth of Puerto Rico will receive a minimum of 0.75 percent (.75%) of the total available grant funding, and that four territories (American Samoa, Guam, the Northern Mariana Islands, and the U.S. Virgin Islands) will receive a minimum of 0.25 percent (.25%) of the total available grant funding. The balance of CCP funds will be distributed on a population-match basis. In addition to CCP allocations, states and urban areas are encouraged to fully leverage HSGP resources to accomplish the Citizen Corps mission.

Source: FEMA, 2011, "FY 2011 Homeland Security Grant Program (HSGP)," http://www.fema.gov/government/grant/hsgp/; FEMA, 2011, "FY 2011 — Homeland Security Grant Program Guidance and Application Kit."

▪▪ Critical Thinking ▪

If you could design any grant program to increase the nation's preparedness to cope with all forms of hazards, what types of items or actions would that grant program support? How would you craft the program regarding eligibility? At what levels would your program need to be funded in order for it to make an actual difference in performance levels nationwide?

State Response

States make up the second tier of emergency response in the United States. State emergency management provides mitigation and preparedness support throughout the year, but comes into play only when called upon by an overwhelmed community, county, or region. Each of the 50 states and 6 territories that make up the United States maintains a state government Office of Emergency Management. However, where the emergency management office resides within the government structure varies from state to state. In California, the California Emergency Management Agency reports to the Governor's office. In Tennessee, the Tennessee Emergency Management Agency (TEMA) reports to the adjutant general. In Florida, the emergency management function is located in the Office of Community Affairs. Today, National Guard adjutant generals manage state emergency management offices in less than one-quarter of the states and territories, a number that has fallen from more than 50% only 5 years ago. Civilian employees lead all other state emergency management offices, a growing trend that recognizes the comprehensive intergovernmental organizational role that is central to the office of emergency management.

Funding for state emergency management offices is provided principally through a combination of DHS support and state budgets. In recent years, FEMA has provided up to $340 million annually to the states to fund state and local government emergency management activities. This money is used by state emergency management agencies to hire staff, conduct training and exercises, and purchase equipment. A segment of this funding is targeted for local emergency management operations as designated by the state. State budgets provide funding for emergency management operations, but this funding historically has been inconsistent, especially in those states with minimal annual disaster activity. The principal resource available to governors in responding to a disaster event in their state is the National Guard. The resources of the National Guard that are used for disaster response include personnel, communications systems and equipment, air and road transport, heavy construction and earth moving equipment, mass care and feeding, equipment, and emergency supplies such as beds, blankets, and medical supplies.

Not surprisingly, response capabilities and capacities are strongest in those states and territories that experience the highest levels of annual disaster activity. All states and territories, however, being in possession of critical assets and resources, find themselves suddenly striving to reinforce their capabilities against the possibility of a terrorist incident. North Carolina is a state that regularly manages the risk of and response to hurricanes and floods. How the North Carolina Department of Emergency Management describes its response process presents a good example of some of the individual aspects of a mature state response function. The sidebar titled "North Carolina State Emergency Management Response Process" details that function.

North Carolina State Emergency Management Response Process

The [State's] emergency response functions are coordinated in a proactive manner from the State Emergency Operations Center located in Raleigh, North Carolina. Proactive response strategies used by the division include the following:

- Area commands that are strategically located in an affected region to assist with local response efforts using state resources
- Central warehousing operations managed by the state that allow for immediate delivery of bottled water, ready-to-eat meals, blankets, tarps, and the like; field deployment teams manned by division and other State agency personnel that assist severely affected counties; coordinate and prioritize response activity
- Incident action planning that identifies response priorities and resource requirements 12 to 24 hours in advance

The State Emergency Response Team (SERT), which is comprised of top-level management representatives of each State agency involved in response activities, provides the technical expertise and coordinates the delivery of the emergency resources used to support local emergency operations.

When resource needs are beyond the capabilities of State agencies, mutual aid from other unaffected local governments and States may be secured using the Statewide Mutual Aid agreement or Emergency Management Assistance compact. Federal assistance may also be requested through the Federal Emergency Response Team, which collocates with the SERT during major disasters.

Source: North Carolina Department of Emergency Management, www.dem.dcc.state.nc.us.

The changes that continue to occur regarding the roles and responsibilities of the state emergency managers are based on the same principles as those occurring at the local level (i.e., changes in procedures to handle terrorist incidents, response equipment, responding agencies and protocols of cooperation, and in local/state/federal operation plans). The sidebar "State, Territorial, or Tribal Emergency Management Responsibilities ..." summarizes the responsibilities of the various political entities for the public safety and welfare of the residents of each, as stated in the NRF.

State, Territorial, or Tribal Emergency Management Responsibilities as Described in the National Response Framework

States, territories, and tribal nations have the primary responsibility for the public health and welfare of their citizens (under the NRF, the term "State" and discussion of the roles and responsibilities of States typically include those responsibilities that apply to U.S. territories and possessions and tribal nations). State and local governments are closest to those impacted by natural disasters, and have always had the lead in response and recovery. States are sovereign entities, and the Governor has the primary responsibility for the public safety and welfare of residents. U.S. territories and possessions and tribal nations also have sovereign rights and hold special responsibilities.

States have significant resources of their own, including State emergency management and homeland security agencies, State Police, health agencies, transportation agencies, and the National Guard. The role of the State government in incident response is to supplement local efforts before, during, and after incidents. During incident response, States play a key role coordinating resources and capabilities from across the State and obtaining resources and capabilities from other States. If a State anticipates that its resources may become overwhelmed, each Governor can request assistance from the Federal government or from other States through mutual aid and assistance agreements such as the Emergency Management Assistance Compact.

A primary role of State government in incident management is to supplement and facilitate local efforts before, during, and after incidents. The State provides direct and routine assistance to its local jurisdictions through emergency management program development, coordinating routinely in these efforts with Federal preparedness officials. States must be prepared to maintain or accelerate services and to provide new services to local governments when local capabilities fall short of demands.

States are also responsible for requesting Federal emergency assistance for communities and tribes within their area of responsibility. Thus, States help by coordinating federal assistance to the local level. In response to an incident, the State helps coordinate and integrate resources and applies them to local needs.

As a State's chief executive, the Governor is responsible for the public safety and welfare of the people of his or her State. The Governor (for the purposes of the NRF, any reference to a State Governor also references the chief executive of U.S. territories):

- Is responsible for coordinating State resources needed to prevent, prepare for, respond to and recover from emergency incidents of all types.
- In accordance with State law, may be able to make, amend or suspend certain orders or regulations in support of the incident response.
- Communicates to the public and helps people, businesses and organizations cope with the consequences of any type of emergency.
- Commands the State military forces (National Guard and State militias).
- Arranges help from other States through interstate mutual aid and assistance compacts, such as the Emergency Management Assistance Compact (EMAC).
- Requests federal assistance including, if appropriate, a Stafford Act Presidential declaration of an emergency or disaster, when it becomes clear that State or interstate mutual aid capabilities will be insufficient or have been exceeded.
- Coordinates with impacted tribal nations within the State and initiates requests for a Stafford Act Presidential emergency or disaster declaration on behalf of an impacted tribe when appropriate.

Before being sworn in, each new Governor should:

- Avoid vacancies in key homeland security positions such as the State homeland security director or the State emergency manager. A newly elected Governor should work with his or her transition team to identify these key personnel early to minimize vacancies and encourage overlap with the outgoing administration. As soon as a new Governor selects people for these positions, the department or agency they are about to lead should be informed.
- Ensure that a staff able to manage a disaster response operation is in place on their inauguration day.
- Task their incoming gubernatorial staff, particularly the legal counsel, with reviewing the procedures necessary for them to declare a State emergency and use their emergency powers.

The State Homeland Security Advisor serves as counsel to the Governor on homeland security issues and serves as a liaison between the Governor's office, the State homeland security structure, DHS and other organizations both inside and outside of the State. The advisor often chairs a committee composed of representatives of relevant State agencies, including public safety, the National Guard, emergency management, public health and others charged with developing preparedness and response strategies.

All States have laws mandating establishment of a State emergency management agency and the EOP coordinated by that agency. The Director of the State emergency management agency ensures that the State is prepared to deal with large-scale emergencies and is responsible for coordinating the State response in any major emergency or disaster. This includes supporting local governments as needed or requested, and coordinating assistance with the federal government. If the community's resources are not adequate, local authorities can seek additional assistance from the county or State emergency manager. The State emergency management agency may dispatch personnel to the scene to assist in the response and recovery effort. If a community requires resources beyond those available in the State, local agencies may request certain types of federal assistance directly. For example, under the Oil Protection Act or the Comprehensive Environmental Response, Compensation, and Liability Act (CERCLA), local and tribal governments can request assistance directly from the Environmental Protection Agency and/or the U.S. Coast Guard without having to go through the State. However, only the Governor can request a Presidential declaration under the Stafford Act.

Heads of other State departments and agencies and their staff develop and train to internal policies and procedures to meet response and recovery needs. They should also participate in inter-agency training and exercising to develop and maintain the necessary capabilities.

Source: Department of Homeland Security (DHS), "The National Response Framework," Washington, D.C.: DHS, 2008.

Critical Thinking

Should the states take a more active role in emergency management at the local level? Do you feel there is anything that the states could do to improve local capacities without infringing on their jurisdictional rights?

Volunteer Group Response

Volunteer groups are often on the front line of disaster response. National groups such as the American Red Cross and the Salvation Army maintain rosters of local chapters of volunteers who are trained in emergency response. These organizations work collaboratively with local, state, and federal authorities to address the immediate needs of disaster victims. They provide shelter, food, and clothing to disaster victims who have had to evacuate or lost their homes to disasters large and small. Each year, the range of response and recovery functions assumed by volunteer groups in lieu of traditional government response agency efforts only grows.

In addition to the Red Cross and the Salvation Army, there are numerous volunteer groups across the country that provide aid and comfort to disaster victims. The National Volunteer Organizations Against Disasters (NVOAD) is composed of an association of 50 national member organizations, 56 state and territorial VOADs, and a quickly growing number of county, community, regional, and other local VOADs that are involved in disaster response and recovery operations around the country and abroad. Formed in 1970, NVOAD helps member groups at a disaster location to coordinate and communicate in order to provide the most efficient and effective response. A list of the NVOAD member organizations follows:

- ACTS World Relief (Foundation of Hope)
- Adventist Community Services
- All Hands Volunteers, Inc.
- Alliance of Information and Referral Systems (AIRS)
- American Baptist Men
- American Radio Relay League, Inc.
- American Red Cross
- Billy Graham Rapid Response Team
- Brethren Disaster Ministries
- Buddhist Tzu Chi Foundation
- Catholic Charities USA Learn More
- Christian Reformed World Relief Committee
- Churches of Scientology Disaster Response
- Church World Service
- City Team Ministries
- Convoy of Hope
- Cooperative Baptist Fellowship
- Episcopal Relief and Development
- Feeding America
- Feed the Children
- Habitat for Humanity International
- Hands on Network generated by Points of Light Foundation
- Hope Coalition America (Operation Hope)
- HOPE Worldwide, Ltd.
- Humane Society of the United States
- International Critical Incident Stress Foundation
- International Relief and Development
- The Jewish Federations of North America
- Latter-Day Saints Charities
- Lutheran Disaster Response
- Mennonite Disaster Service
- Mercy Medical Airlift
- National Association of Jewish Chaplains
- National Baptist Convention USA
- National Organization for Victim Assistance
- Nazarene Disaster Response
- NECHAMA — Jewish Response to Disaster
- Noah's Wish

- Operation Blessing
- Presbyterian Church in America — Mission North America
- Presbyterian Disaster Assistance
- Samaritan's Purse
- Save the Children
- Society of St. Vincent DePaul
- Southern Baptist Convention/North American Mission Board
- The Salvation Army
- United Church of Christ
- United Methodist Committee on Relief
- United Way Worldwide
- World Vision (NVOAD, 2011, http://www.nvoad.org/member/national-members)

DHS Volunteer Programs

Volunteerism has been an integral part of life in the United States for decades. After the September 11, 2001, terrorist attacks, this attribute only expanded. What also occurred was that many people who already volunteered in their communities, and many people who had not volunteered but were suddenly drawn to do so, sought out ways in which they could contribute to making their communities more secure. The federal government responded to their outpouring of concern through the creation of U.S. Freedom Corps, which was created "in an effort to capture those opportunities [to contribute to community security] and to foster a culture of service, citizenship, and responsibility."

Citizen Corps is the arm of U.S. Freedom Corps that provides opportunities for citizens who want to help make their communities safer and more secure. In the first 5 years of its existence, following a call by President George W. Bush for 2 years of volunteer service from every American citizen, almost 24,000 people from all 50 states and U.S. territories volunteered to work with one or more of the Citizen Corps programs. Since then, the numbers have increased. The programs contained within Citizen Corps include:

- Citizen Corps Councils
- Community Emergency Response Teams (CERT)
- Volunteers in Police Service (VIPS)
- Medical Reserve Corps
- Neighborhood Watch
- Fire Corps

Although some of these programs are new, others, such as Neighborhood Watch, have been in place for more than a decade. Brief information about the programs and their response component follow, along with the sidebar "Citizen Corps Facts," which includes various facts about the Corps reported by DHS.

CITIZEN CORPS FACTS

- Volunteerism jumped significantly in the United States in the years following the September 11 terrorist attacks, with the greatest single increase coming between 2002 and 2003 when rates rose by about 4 million people. These rates remained high until 2006, when they began falling to levels just above what they were in 2002 (61.2 million people, or 26.7%) (Bureau of Labor Statistics, 2007, http://www.bls.gov/news.release/volun.nr0.htm).
- There are currently more than 244,000 volunteers registered with the Volunteers in Police Service program and over 2,180 registered programs. Volunteers provide well over 1 million hours of service a year.
- Since its inception in 2002, the Medical Reserve Corps has grown to over 147,000 volunteer members. There are 952 communities with federally funded Medical Reserve Corps units.
- There are now 14,791 Neighborhood Watch groups registered on www.usaonwatch.org.
- Fire Corps was started in May 2004. It its first year of existence, almost 300 Fire Corps programs were created. Today there are 1,098 throughout the United States.

Source: FEMA, 2011, http://www.citizencorps.gov/cc/CouncilMapIndex.do?nationalCouncilMapForPDFPartner.3.x = 39&nationalCouncilMapForPDFPartner.3.y − 23&nationalCouncilMapForPDFPartner.3 = Volunteers + In + Police + Service#map

Citizen Corps Councils

Citizen Corps Councils (CCCs) are established at the state and local levels to promote, organize, and run the various programs that fall under the Citizen Corps umbrella. Funding for these councils is provided by the federal government through grant awards. As of August 2011, there were CCCs in 56 states and U.S. territories, and 1,101 local communities, all of which serve 61% of the total population of the United States. Figure 9–4 displays the geographic coverage of the CCCs.

Community Emergency Response Teams

The Community Emergency Response Team (CERT) program began in Los Angeles, California, in 1983. City administrators there recognized that in most emergency situations, average citizens — neighbors, co-workers, and bystanders, for example — were often on the scene during the critical moments before professional help arrived. These officials acted on the belief that, by training average citizens to perform basic search and rescue, first aid, and other critical emergency response skills, they would increase the overall resilience of the community. Additionally, should a large-scale disaster like an earthquake occur, where first-response units would be stretched very thin, these trained citizens would be able to augment official services and provide an important service to the community.

Beginning in 1993, FEMA began to offer CERT training on a national level, providing funding to cover start-up and tuition costs for programs. As of August 2011, CERT programs had been established in more than 1,807 communities in all 50 states, the District of Columbia, and several U.S. territories. CERT

Total Active Statewide Councils	56
Total Active Countywide/Local/Tribal Councils	1123
Population Served, based on 2000 Census Data	173699288 (61% of total US population)

FIGURE 9-4 Map of Citizen Corps Councils in the United States and its territories. (Source: Citizen Corps, 2011)

teams remain active in the community before a disaster strikes, sponsoring events such as drills, neighborhood cleanup, and disaster-education fairs. Trainers offer periodic refresher sessions to CERT members to reinforce the basic training and to keep participants involved and practiced in their skills. CERT members also offer other nonemergency assistance to the community with the goal of improving the overall safety of the community. Figure 9-5 illustrates the geographic coverage of CERT in the United States.

Volunteers in Police Service Program

Since September 11, 2001, the demands on state and local law enforcement have increased dramatically. Limited resources at the community level have resulted from these increased demands, and regular police work has ultimately suffered. To address these shortfalls, the Volunteers in Police Service (VIPS) program was created. The basis of the program is that civilian volunteers are able to support police officers by doing much of the behind-the-scenes work that does not require formal law enforcement training, thereby allowing officers to spend more of their already strained schedules on the street. Although the concept is not new, federal support for such programs is.

The VIPS draws on the time and recognized talents of civilian volunteers. Volunteer roles may include performing clerical tasks, serving as an extra set of eyes and ears, assisting with search and rescue activities,

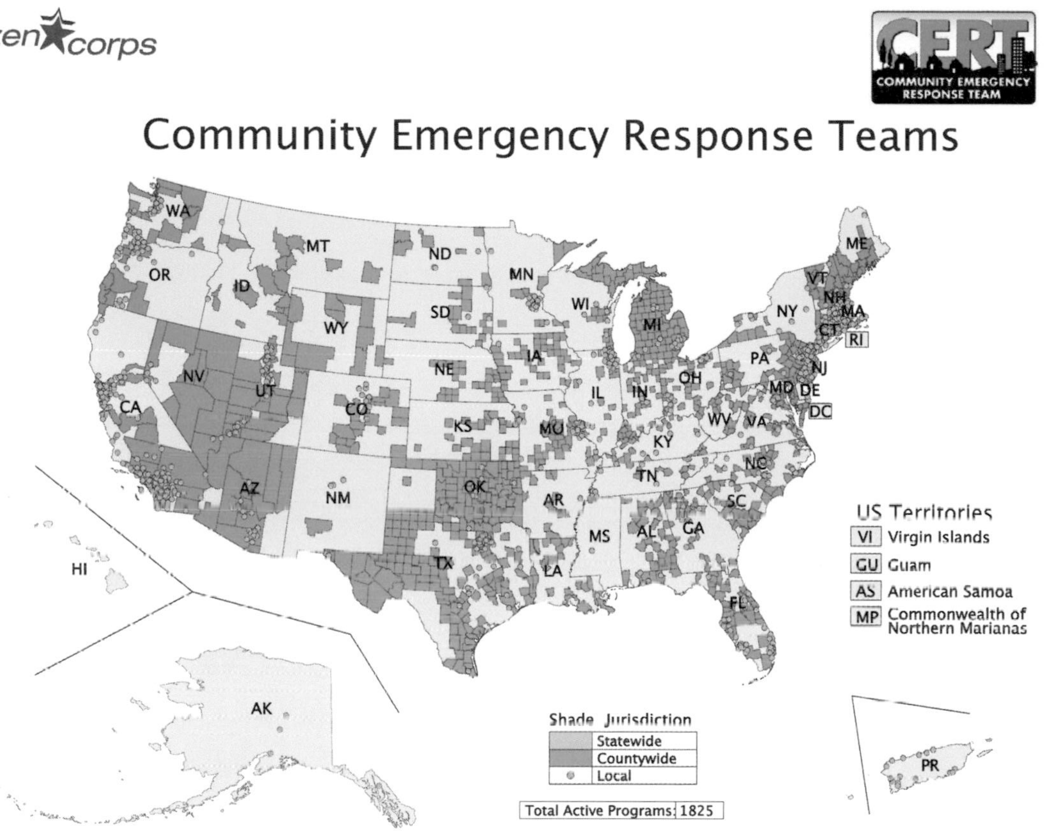

Community Emergency Response Teams

FIGURE 9–5 CERT programs in the United States and its territories. (Source: Citizen Corps, 2011)

and writing citations for accessible parking violations, just to name a few. As of August 2011, there were 2,180 official VIPS programs registered throughout the United States. Figure 9–6 illustrates the geographic coverage of VIPS in the United States.

Medical Reserve Corps Program

The Medical Reserve Corps (MRC) was founded after the 2002 State of the Union Address, to establish teams of local volunteer medical and public health professionals who can contribute their skills and experience when called on in times of need. The program relies on volunteers who are practicing and retired physicians, nurses, dentists, veterinarians, epidemiologists, and other health professionals, as well as other citizens untrained in public health but who can contribute to the community's normal and disaster public health needs in other ways (which may include interpreters, chaplains, legal advisers, etc.).

Local community leaders develop their own MRC units and recruit local volunteers who address the specific community needs. For example, MRC volunteers may deliver necessary public health services during a crisis, assist emergency response teams with patients, and provide care directly to those with less serious injuries and other health-related issues. MRC volunteers may also serve a vital role by assisting their communities with ongoing public health needs (e.g., immunizations, screenings, health and nutrition

FIGURE 9–6 VIPS programs in the United State and its territories. (Source: Citizen Corps, 2011)

education, and volunteering in community health centers and local hospitals). The MRC unit decides, in concert with local officials (including the local CCC), on when the community MRC is activated during a local emergency. As of August 2011, there were 952 MRC programs established throughout the United States.

Neighborhood Watch Program

The Neighborhood Watch program has been in existence for more than 30 years in cities and counties throughout the United States. The program is based on the concept that neighbors who join together to fight crime will be able to increase security in their surrounding areas and, as a result, provide an overall better quality of life for residents. Understandably, after September 11, 2001, when terrorism became a major focus of the U.S. government, the recognized importance of programs like Neighborhood Watch took on much greater significance.

The Neighborhood Watch program is not maintained by the National Sheriff's Association, which founded the program initially. At the local level, the CCCs help neighborhood groups who have banded together to start a program to carry out their mission. Many printed materials and other guidance are available for free to help them carry out their goals.

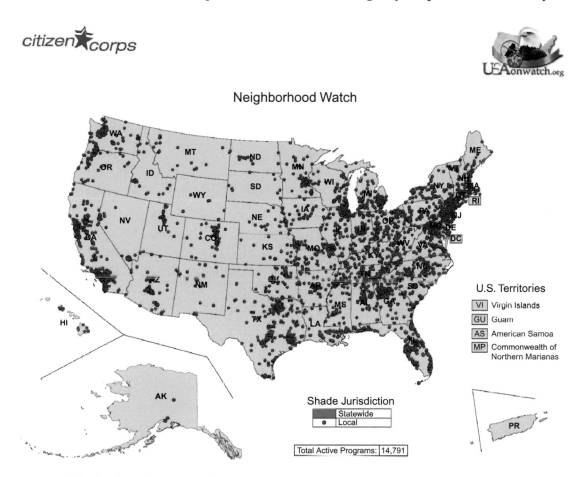

FIGURE 9-7 Neighborhood Watch programs in the United States and its territories. (Source: FEMA, 2008)

Neighborhood Watch programs have successfully decreased crime in many of the neighborhoods where they have been implemented. In total, as of January 2008, there were 14,791 programs spread out throughout the United States and the U.S. territories. In addition to serving a crime prevention role, Neighborhood Watch has also been used as the basis for bringing neighborhood residents together to focus on disaster preparedness and terrorism awareness; to focus on evacuation drills and exercises; and even to organize group training, such as the CERT training. Figure 9-7 illustrates the geographic coverage of Neighborhood Watch programs in the United States.

Fire Corps

The Fire Corps was created in 2004 under the umbrella of U.S. Freedom Corps and Citizen Corps. The purpose of the program, like the VIPS program with the police, was to enhance the ability of fire departments to utilize citizen advocates and provide individuals with opportunities to support their local fire departments with both time and talent.

Fire Corps was created as a partnership between the International Association of Fire Chiefs' Volunteer Combination Officers Section (VCOS), the International Association of Fire Fighters (IAFF), and the National Volunteer Fire Council (NVFC). By participating in the program, concerned and interested citizens can assist in their local fire department's activities through tasks such as administrative assistance, public education, fund-raising, data entry, accounting, public relations, and equipment and facility maintenance, to name just a few.

Any fire department that allows citizens to volunteer support service is considered a Fire Corps program, but programs can become official through registering with a local, county, or state CCC, if one exists. Official Fire Corps programs will be provided with assistance on how to implement a nonoperational citizen advocates program or how to improve existing programs. A Fire Corps National Advisory Committee has been established under the program in order to provide strategic direction and collect feedback from the field. As of August 2011, there were 1,098 established Fire Corps programs throughout the United States and U.S. territories. Figure 9–9 illustrates the geographic coverage of Fire Corps programs in the United States.

DHS Response Agencies

With the passage of the Homeland Security Act of 2002, several government agencies and offices that managed components of the nation's response framework were consolidated into the DHS. Originally, these various components were brought into DHS and merged together to form an EP&R Directorate, composed most prominently by the functions of the original FEMA. During the course of the DHS's thus-far-brief history, several of these components have moved within the structure of DHS — many falling under the direction of the newly reformed FEMA while others have since been removed from the Department entirely or are facing permanent closure. These agencies and offices, each of which is described in detail below, include:

> Federal Emergency Management Agency (FEMA)
> Integrated Hazard Information System of the National Oceanic and Atmospheric Administration
> National Domestic Preparedness Office of the Federal Bureau of Investigation
> Domestic Emergency Support Teams of the Department of Justice
> Office of Emergency Preparedness
> National Disaster Medical System
> Metropolitan Medical Response System
> Strategic National Stockpile

Federal Emergency Management Agency

The Federal Emergency Management Agency — a former independent agency that became part of the new DHS in March 2003 — is tasked with responding to, planning for, recovering from, and mitigating against disasters. The FEMA Response Division provides the core operational and logistical disaster response capability of the federal government, which is called upon to save and sustain lives, minimize suffering, and protect property in a timely and effective manner in communities that become overwhelmed by natural disasters, acts of terrorism, or other emergencies. FEMA response program activities encompass the coordination of all federal emergency management response operations, response planning, and logistics programs and integration of federal, state, tribal, and local disaster programs. This coordination is designed to facilitate the delivery of immediate emergency assistance to individuals and communities impacted and overwhelmed by emergency and disaster events (see Figure 9–8).

FIGURE 9–8 Joplin, MO, August 3, 2011 — Damage sustained at St. John's Regional Medical Center after the May 22 EF-5 tornado that struck the city. FEMA is working to provide assistance to those affected by the tornado. (Source: Photo by Elissa Jun/FEMA)

FEMA's disaster response responsibilities within DHS, which are very similar to those maintained by the agency prior to its incorporation into DHS, include (among others).

- Coordinating with local and state first responders to manage disasters requiring federal assistance and to recover from their effects (as stipulated in the NRF)
- Administering the Disaster Relief Fund
- Maintaining administration of the National Flood Insurance Program
- Administering the training and other responsibilities of the U.S. Fire Administration
- Offering mitigation grant programs, including the Hazards Mitigation Grant Program, the Pre-Disaster Mitigation Program, and the Flood Mitigation Assistance Program
- Administering the Citizen Corps Program

Integrated Hazard Information System

The Integrated Hazard Information System (IHIS) was transferred from the NOAA into the DHS EP&R Directorate. At the time of transfer, its name was changed to "FIRESAT." IHIS, originally named the Hazards Support System (HSS), was a classified information system developed by the Department of Defense (DOD) in 1997 to compile data obtained from various satellites and sensors, such as those used to detect ballistic missiles and others that continuously monitor weather conditions in the United States. In late 2000, after DOD tested the system, HSS was turned over to the U.S. Geological Survey (USGS) in the Department of the Interior and renamed IHIS, where it would be used to detect wildfires and volcanic eruptions around the world. However, Congress directed USGS to cease expenditures on IHIS, apparently because of concerns about unauthorized reprogramming of those funds. Since then, no funding has been authorized for IHIS. The agreement by Congress and the administration to move IHIS to DHS included "the transfer of workstations, software, documentation, and its communications component." However, the president did not request funding for FIRESAT for FY 2004 (Bea et al., 2003).

National Domestic Preparedness Office

The National Domestic Preparedness Office (NDPO), within the DOJ, coordinated all federal efforts, including those of the DOD, FEMA, the HHS, the Department of Energy (DOE), and the Environmental Protection Agency (EPA), to assist state and local first responders with planning, training, equipment, and exercises necessary to respond to a conventional or nonconventional WMD incident.

NDPO's various functions were transferred into the new DHS and placed under the direction of the FEMA-dominated EP&R Directorate. Among the functions of the NDPO transferred were:

- Serve as a single program and policy office for WMD to ensure that federal efforts are in harmony and represent the most effective and cost-efficient support to the state and local first-responder community
- Coordinate the establishment of training curriculum and standards for first-responder training to ensure consistency based on training objectives and to tailor training opportunities to meet the needs of the responder community
- Facilitate the efforts of the federal government to provide the responder community with detection, protection, analysis, and decontamination equipment necessary to prepare for, and respond to, an incident involving WMD
- Provide state and local governments with the resources and expertise necessary to design, conduct, and evaluate exercise scenarios involving WMD
- Communicate information to the state and local emergency response community

Domestic Emergency Support Team

The Domestic Emergency Support Team (DEST) is designed to be an interagency team of experts, operating on a stand-by basis, which can be quickly mobilized. This team, even within DHS (and directed by FEMA per the Stafford Act), is led by the FBI to provide an on-scene commander (OSC) (special agent in charge) with advice and guidance in situations involving WMDs, or other significant domestic threats. The DEST guidance can range from information management and communications support to instructions on how to best respond to the detonation of a chemical, biological, or nuclear weapon, or a radiological dispersal device (RDD). As specialized predesignated teams, DEST has no permanent staff at DHS, the FBI, or any other federal agency.

Office of Emergency Preparedness

The Office of Emergency Preparedness (OEP) was responsible for oversight, coordination, and management of EP&R and recovery activities in the HHS prior to its transfer to DHS. There were two principal programs of OEP that now exist within DHS under separate functional units. They are the NDMS and the MMRS and are described in further detail later.

Before its move into DHS, OEP served as the lead for Emergency Support Function (ESF) #8 within the FRP — Health and Medical. Under the NRF, HHS has maintained this responsibility under the new

ESF #8, Public Health and Medical Services. The tasks performed by the NDMS and MMRS, which were fulfilled within ESF #8, are still performed as before but under different direction.

National Disaster Medical System

The National Disaster Medical System (NDMS), which originally resided within the Office of Emergency Preparedness of HHS, was transferred to the DHS EP&R Directorate per the Homeland Security Act of 2002, but now falls back under the direction of HHS as stipulated in the post-Katrina Emergency Management Reform Act of 2006 (including its $33.8 million budget). NDMS is a federally coordinated system that is responsible for supporting federal agencies in the management and coordination of the federal medical response to major emergencies and federally declared disasters. In doing so, it establishes a single, integrated national medical response capability for assisting state and local authorities in dealing with the medical and health effects of major disasters. NDMS also cares for casualties of U.S. military operations overseas who have been airlifted back to the United States.

NDMS consists of more than 8,000 volunteer health professionals and support personnel organized into disaster assistance teams that can be activated and deployed anywhere in the country to assist state and local emergency medical services. Several operational units within NDMS assist in this function:

- *Disaster Medical Assistance Team (DMAT)*: A DMAT is a group of professional and para-professional medical personnel, supported by logistical and administrative staff, designed to provide medical care during a disaster or other event. Each team has a sponsoring organization, such as a major medical center, public health or safety agency, nonprofit, public, or private organization that signs a Memorandum of Agreement (MOA) with DHS. The DMAT sponsor organizes the team and recruits members, arranges training, and coordinates the dispatch of the team.
- *Disaster Mortuary Operational Response Team (DMORT)*: DMORTs, like DMATs, are composed of private citizens, each with a particular field of expertise, who are activated in the event of a disaster. During an emergency response, DMORTs work under the guidance of local authorities by providing technical assistance and personnel to recover, identify, and process deceased victims. Teams are composed of funeral directors, medical examiners, coroners, pathologists, forensic anthropologists, medical records technicians and transcribers, fingerprint specialists, forensic odontologists, dental assistants, X-ray technicians, mental health specialists, computer professionals, administrative support staff, and security and investigative personnel. Their duties include setting up temporary morgue facilities, victim identification, forensic dental pathology, forensic anthropology, and processing, preparation, and disposition of remains.
- *Veterinary Medical Assistance Team (VMAT)*: VMATs are composed of private citizens who are activated in the event of a disaster. During an emergency response, VMATs work under the guidance of local authorities by providing technical assistance and veterinary services. Teams are composed of clinical veterinarians, veterinary pathologists, animal health technicians (veterinary technicians), microbiologist/virologists, epidemiologists, toxicologists, and various scientific and support personnel. Their tasks include assessing the medical needs of animals, medical treatment and stabilization of animals, animal disease surveillance, zoonotic disease surveillance and public health assessments, technical assistance to ensure food and water quality, hazard mitigation, animal decontamination, and biological and chemical terrorism surveillance.
- *Federal Coordinating Centers (FCCs)*: FCCs recruit hospitals and maintain local nonfederal hospital participation in the NDMS, coordinate exercise development and emergency plans with participating hospitals and other local authorities in order to develop patient reception,

transportation, and communication plans, and during system activation, coordinate the reception and distribution of patients being evacuated to the area.

- *National Pharmacy Response Team (NPRT)*: NPRTs are located in each of the 10 DHS regions. NPRTs are activated in times of disaster to assist in chemo-prophylaxis (preventive medicine) or the vaccination of hundreds of thousands, or even millions of Americans. They may be activated in any scenario that is expected to require the assistance of hundreds of pharmacists, pharmacy technicians, and students of pharmacy.

- *National Nurse Response Team (NNRT)*: NNRTs are specialty DMATs designed for use in scenarios expected to require the activation of hundreds of nurses to assist in chemoprophylaxis, a mass vaccination program, or a scenario that overwhelms the nation's supply of nurses in responding to a WMD event. The NNRTs are directed by the NDMS in conjunction with a regional team leader in each of the 10 standard federal regions. Each NNRT is composed of approximately 200 civilian nurses. National Nurse Response Team members are required to maintain appropriate certifications and licensure within their discipline, stay current in treatment recommendations for diseases compatible with WMDs, complete web-based training courses in disaster response, humanitarian relief, bioterrorism, and other relevant training, participate in regular training exercises, and be available to deploy when needed.

Metropolitan Medical Response System

The Metropolitan Medical Response System (MMRS) provides funding to cities that upgrade and improve their own planning and preparedness to respond to mass casualty events. The concept for the program began in 1995 in the Washington, D.C., metropolitan area with the creation of the Metropolitan Medical Strike Team (MMST). This first team, which pooled resources from several adjoining jurisdictions, was created primarily for the response to chemical incidents, but was able to provide on-site emergency health and medical services following WMD terrorist incidents.

The MMST concept was expanded to several cities under the guidance and funding of the federal government through the authority of the Defense against Weapons of Mass Destruction Act of 1996 (Nunn-Lugar-Domenici legislation). The program's name was changed to the Metropolitan Medical Response System to highlight its national system-oriented approach. The program has grown from the 25 teams created in 1995 to almost 124 municipalities.

The sidebar titled "MMRS Capabilities and Impacts" provides a detailed description of capabilities and the difference the MMRS makes at the local level.

MMRS Capabilities and Impacts

MMRS Capabilities

- Initial identification of agents
- Ability to perform operations in OSHA levels A, B, and C personal protective equipment, avoiding secondary responder casualties
- Enhanced triage, treatment, and decontamination capabilities at the incident site and definitive care facilities

- Maintenance of local caches sufficient to treat 1,000 patients exposed to chemical agents
- Ability to transport uncontaminated/decontaminated patients to area hospitals for definitive care
- Ability to maintain a viable health system
- Ability to transport patients to participating NDMS hospitals throughout the nation
- Mechanisms to activate mutual aid support from local, state, and federal emergency response agencies
- Ability to integrate additional response assets into the ongoing incident command structure

MMRS Local Level Impacts

- Requires development of response plans unique for each city
- Creates integrated immediate response structure
- Creates additional local and regional support networks
- Integrates with local mass casualty plans
- Brings together and encourages city planning agencies to interact where they never interacted before
- Encourages and initiates hospital WMD planning
- Encourages local health-care providers to develop appropriate medical treatment protocols

Source: HHS, www.hhs.gov.

Strategic National Stockpile

The Strategic National Stockpile (SNS) began in 1999, when Congress charged HHS and Centers for Disease Control and Prevention (CDC) with the establishment of the capability to provide a resupply of large quantities of essential medical material to states and communities during an emergency within 12 hours of the federal decision to deploy to that region. The system that was developed was called the National Pharmaceutical Stockpile (NPS).

As stipulated in the Homeland Security Act of 2002, on March 1, 2003, the NPS was transferred from HHS to DHS, and was given the new title, Strategic National Stockpile. The program was established so that it could be managed jointly by DHS and HHS and be able to work with governmental and nongovernmental partners to continually seek ways to upgrade the nation's public health capacity to respond to national emergencies. With the signing of the BioShield legislation, however, the SNS program was returned to HHS for oversight and guidance.

During a national emergency, state, local, and private stocks of medical material will be depleted quickly. The SNS is designed to help all state and local first responders bolster their response to a national emergency, through the provision of specially designed 12-hour Push Packages, private vendors, or a combination of both, depending on the situation. Like most federal response programs, the SNS is not a first-response tool, but one that supplements the initial local response efforts.

The SNS is a national repository of antibiotics, chemical antidotes, antitoxins, life-support medications, IV administration supplies, airway maintenance supplies, and medical/surgical items. The SNS is designed to supplement and resupply state and local public health agencies in the event of a national emergency anywhere and at any time within the United States or its territories. The system is also set up to allow for the acquisition of additional pharmaceuticals and/or medical supplies not maintained directly by the SNS through the use of private vendors (which can ship supplies to arrive within 24–36 hours of the request). In some areas, the vendors, which are preregistered under the program, can actually provide the first wave of supplies that arrive.

The sidebar "The Strategic National Stockpile" gives an overview of how the SNS functions, and how its components interact with local and state organizations.

The Strategic National Stockpile

The Strategic National Stockpile (SNS) program is committed to have 12-hour Push Packages delivered anywhere in the United States or its territories within 12 hours of a Federal decision to deploy. The 12-hour Push Packages have been configured to be immediately loaded onto either trucks or commercial cargo aircraft for the most rapid transportation. Concurrent to SNS transport, the SNS program will deploy its Technical Advisory Response Unit (TARU). The TARU staff will coordinate with State and local officials so that the SNS assets can be efficiently received and distributed on arrival at the site.

DHS will transfer authority for the SNS materiel to the State and local authorities once it arrives at the designated receiving and storage site. State and local authorities will then begin the breakdown of the 12-hour Push Package for distribution. SNS TARU members will remain on-site in order to assist and advise State and local officials in putting the SNS assets to prompt and effective use.

The decision to deploy SNS assets may be based on evidence showing the overt release of an agent that might adversely affect public health. It is more likely, however, that subtle indicators, such as unusual morbidity and/or mortality identified through the nation's disease outbreak surveillance and epidemiology network, will alert health officials to the possibility (and confirmation) of a biological or chemical incident or a national emergency. To receive SNS assets, the affected State's Governor's office will directly request the deployment of the SNS assets from CDC or DHS. DHS, HHS, CDC, and other Federal officials will evaluate the situation and determine a prompt course of action.

The SNS program is part of a nationwide preparedness training and education program for State and local health-care providers, first responders, and governments (to include Federal officials, Governors' offices, State and local health departments, and emergency management agencies). This training explains the SNS program's mission and operations and also alerts State and local emergency response officials to the important issues they must plan for in order to receive, secure, and distribute SNS assets.

To conduct this outreach and training, CDC and SNS program staff are currently working with DHS, HHS agencies, regional emergency response coordinators at all of the U.S. Public Health Service regional offices, State and local health departments, State emergency management offices, the Metropolitan Medical Response System cities, the Department of Veterans Affairs, and the Department of Defense.

Source: Centers for Disease Control and Prevention, www.cdc.gov.

Urban Search and Rescue

The concept of formally maintained Urban Search and Rescue (US&R or USAR) teams was introduced in the early 1980s. The Fairfax County (Virginia) Fire and Rescue and the Metro-Dade County (Florida) Fire Department each created specialized search and rescue teams trained for rescue operations in collapsed buildings. US&R involves the location, rescue (extrication), and initial medical stabilization of victims trapped in confined spaces. Structural collapse is most often the cause of victims being trapped, but victims may also be trapped in transportation accidents, mines, and collapsed trenches. The initial teams created to carry out these tasks were so successful in this specialty that they were often sent abroad on missions, representing the U.S. government relief efforts, through support of the Department of State and the Office of Foreign Disaster Assistance (OFDA) of the U.S. Agency for International Development (USAID). These teams have deployed to Mexico City, the Philippines, and Armenia, providing vital search and rescue support in earthquake-induced disasters in each of these areas (see Figure 9–9).

Beginning in 1991, US&R became a component of federal response operations under the FRP, when the US&R concept was incorporated as an individual ESF. From that starting point, the size of the US&R system grew considerably, with FEMA sponsoring the creation of 25 national US&R task forces. There are now a total of 28 national task forces, staffed and equipped to conduct around the clock search and rescue operations following any disaster that requires their specialized talents and equipment. In 2003, when FEMA was transferred into DHS, the US&R system transferred with FEMA, intact. FEMA, under DHS, maintains its primary agency designation under ESF #9, Search and Rescue.

How the teams are structured and operate is discussed in the sidebar "Urban Search and Rescue (US&R) Teams."

FIGURE 9–9 Sabine Pass, TX, September 14, 2008 — Members of the FEMA Urban Search and Rescue team, Indiana Task Force 1 go into neighborhoods impacted by Hurricane Ike to search for people needing help getting out of the area. (Source: Photo by Jocelyn Augustino/FEMA)

Urban Search and Rescue (US&R) Teams

- If a disaster event warrants national US&R support, DHS will deploy the three closest task forces within 6 hours of notification and additional teams as necessary. The role of these task forces is to support State and local emergency responders' efforts to locate victims and manage recovery operations.
- Each task force consists of two 31-person teams, four canines, and a comprehensive equipment cache. For every US&R task force, there are 62 positions. To ensure that a full team can respond to an emergency, the task forces have at the ready more than 130 highly trained members.
- A task force is really a partnership between local fire departments, law enforcement agencies, Federal and local governmental agencies, and private companies.
- A task force is totally self-sufficient for the first 72 hours of a deployment.
- The equipment cache used to support a task force weighs nearly 60,000 pounds and is worth about $1.4 million. Add the task force members to the cache, and you can completely fill a military C-141 transport or two C-130s.
- US&R task force members work in four areas of specialization: search, to find victims trapped after a disaster; rescue, which includes safely digging victims out of tons of collapsed concrete and metal; technical, made up of structural specialists who make rescues safe for the rescuers; and medical, which cares for the victims before and after a rescue.
- In addition to search and rescue support, the DHS provides hands-on training in search and rescue techniques and equipment, technical assistance to local communities, and in some cases Federal grants to help communities better prepare for US&R operations.
- The bottom line in US&R: Some day, lives may be saved because of the skills these rescuers gain. These first responders consistently go to the front lines when the nation needs them most.
- Not only are these first responders a national resource that can be deployed to a major disaster or structural collapse anywhere in the country, they are also the local firefighters and paramedics who answer local 911 calls.
- Events such as the 1995 bombing of the Alfred P. Murrah Federal Office Building in Oklahoma City, the Northridge earthquake, the Kansas grain elevator explosion in 1998, and earthquakes in Turkey and Greece in 1999 underscore the need for highly skilled teams to rescue trapped victims.
- What the task force can do: Conduct physical search and rescue in collapsed buildings; provide emergency medical care to trapped victims; deploy search and rescue dogs; assess and control gas, electric service, and hazardous materials; and evaluate and stabilize damaged structures.

Sources: Federal Emergency Management Agency, www.fema.gov; Department of Homeland Security, www.dhs.gov.

Maritime Search and Rescue

The USCG is one of only two federal agencies (including the U.S. Secret Service) that transferred into the new DHS as an independent entity, thus reporting directly to the Secretary of Homeland Security as opposed to one of the five directorates. The USCG maintains several distinct missions within DHS, but one of those, search and rescue, has resulted in strong cooperation with FEMA and the EP&R Directorate. Specifically, USCG maintains the authority and responsibility for the various tasks related to maritime search and rescue.

Maritime search and rescue (SAR) is one of the Coast Guard's oldest missions. Minimizing the loss of life, injury, property damage, or loss by rendering aid to persons in distress and property in the maritime environment has always been a Coast Guard priority. Coast Guard SAR response involves multiple-mission stations, cutters, aircraft, and boats linked by communications networks. The Coast Guard is the SAR coordinator for U.S. aeronautical and maritime search and rescue regions that are near America's oceans, including Alaska and Hawaii. To meet this responsibility, the Coast Guard maintains SAR facilities on the East, West, and Gulf coasts; in Alaska, Hawaii, Guam, and Puerto Rico; and on the Great Lakes and inland U.S. waterways.

The USCG maintains that, in performing their SAR goal, they are guided by two program objectives:

1. Save at least 93% of those people at risk of death on waters over which the Coast Guard has SAR responsibility.
2. Prevent the loss of at least 80% of the property that is at risk of destruction on the waters over which the Coast Guard has SAR responsibility.

Additionally, the USCG maintains standards of operation by which they plan to fulfill these goals and objectives:

Readiness: Search and rescue unit ready to proceed within 30 minutes of notification of a distress.

Transit: Search and rescue unit on scene, or within the search area, within 90 minutes of getting under way.

VHF FM Distress Net Standard: 100% VHF-FM continuous coverage to receive a 1-W signal out to 20 nautical miles around the U.S. Atlantic, Pacific, Gulf of Mexico, and Great Lakes coasts. This is the primary distress alerting and SAR communications method for U.S. coastal waters.

406-MHz Emergency Position Indicating Radio Beacon (EPIRB): Maximum use of the 406-MHz EPIRB in the offshore environment. The beacon's superior alerting, position indicating, and signaling capabilities significantly improve system effectiveness and efficiency. Beacon registration provides useful SAR response information and mitigates false alarm response costs. Currently about 70% of U.S. beacons are registered.

Command and Control Standard: Initiate action within 5 minutes of initial notification of a distress incident. Process and evaluate information about the SAR incident and determine appropriate action.

Computer-Assisted Search Planning (CASP) System Standard: Use CASP for planning guidance for all cases involving incidents outside the 30 fathom mark when:
- The duration of an incident has or could have exceeded 24 hours
- There is uncertainty concerning the incident time, incident location, or type of search object(s) involved

Automated Mutual-Assistance Vessel Rescue (AMVER) System Standard: Use AMVER for identification of rescue resources for all cases involving incidents on the high seas. The Coast Guard actively seeks to increase participation in this voluntary reporting system. Each year, more vessels participate in the system and more lives are saved.

SAR Planner Training Standard for SAR Mission Coordinators: 100% attendance and completion of resident SAR planner training at the National SAR School for Area, District, Section, and Group SAR planners.

The Coast Guard currently maintains six separate programs under the SAR, as briefly described in the sidebar "U.S. Coast Guard Search and Rescue Programs."

U.S. Coast Guard Search and Rescue Programs

Rescue 21

The Coast Guard currently uses the National Distress and Response System to monitor for maritime distress calls and coordinate response operations. The system consists of a network of VHF-FM antenna sites with analog transceivers that are remotely controlled by regional communications centers and rescue boat stations providing coverage out to approximately 20 nautical miles from the shore in most areas.

Salvage Assistance and Technical Support

The Marine Safety Center Salvage Assistance and Response Teams provide on-scene technical support during maritime catastrophes in order to predict events and mitigate their impact.

Operational Command, Control, and Communications

The National Strike Force Coordination Center (NSFCC) provides oversight and strategic direction to the strike teams, ensuring enhanced interoperability through a program of standardized operating procedures for response, equipment, training, and qualifications. The NSFCC conducts at least six major government-led spill response exercises each year under the National Preparedness for Response Exercise program; maintains a national logistics network, using the Response Resource Inventory; implements the Coast Guard Oil Spill Removal Organization program; and administers the National Maintenance Contract for the Coast Guard's $30 million inventory of prepositioned spill response equipment.

AMVER

AMVER (Automated Mutual-Assistance Vessel Rescue) is a ship-reporting system for search and rescue. It is a global system that enables identification of other ships in the area of a ship in distress, which could then be sent to its assistance. AMVER information is used only for search and rescue, and is made available to any rescue coordination center in the world responding to a search and rescue case. The Coast Guard actively seeks to increase participation in this voluntary reporting system. Each year, more vessels participate in the system and more lives are saved. Currently, ships from more than 143 nations participate.

AMVER represents "free" safety insurance during a voyage by improving the chances for aid in an emergency. By regular reporting, someone knows where a ship is at all times on its voyage in the event of an emergency. AMVER can reduce the time lost for vessels responding to calls for assistance by orchestrating a rescue response, utilizing ships in the best position or with the best capability to avoid unnecessary diversions in response to a Mayday or SOS call.

Pollution Control

The Response Operations Division develops and maintains policies for marine pollution response. They also coordinate activities with the international community, intelligence agencies, and the Federal government in matters concerning threats or acts of terrorism in U.S. ports and territorial waters.

National Strike Force

The National Strike Force (NSF) was established in 1973 as a direct result of the Federal Water Pollution Control Act of 1972. The NSF's mission is to provide highly trained, experienced personnel and specialized equipment to Coast Guard and other Federal agencies to facilitate preparedness and response to oil and hazardous substance pollution incidents in order to protect public health and the environment. The NSF's area of responsibility covers all Coast Guard districts and Federal response regions.

The strike teams provide rapid response support in incident management, site safety, contractor performance monitoring, resource documentation, response strategies, hazard assessment, oil spill dispersant and operational effectiveness monitoring, and high-capacity lightering and offshore-skimming capabilities.

Source: Department of Homeland Security, www.dhs.gov

Other Response Agencies

Each of the agencies listed in the preceding section operates under the management of DHS, and in several cases, under FEMA, regardless of whether or not a disaster declaration has occurred. However, there are several other agencies within the federal government that bring emergency response capabilities to the federal response system, in many cases operating in their respective organizations without any clear day-to-day contact with DHS outside of a declared disaster. As stipulated in the NRF, these agencies can all be called upon to provide their services in times of need, under the coordination efforts of FEMA, in response to major disasters that require federal support (namely, presidentially declared disasters and emergencies). These departments and agencies are discussed individually.

Federal Bureau of Investigation

The Federal Bureau of Investigation (FBI), part of the Department of Justice, is the lead federal agency (LFA) for crisis management and investigation of all terrorism-related matters, including incidents involving a WMD. Within the FBI's role as LFA, the FBI federal on-scene commander (OSC) coordinates the overall federal response until the attorney general transfers the LFA role to FEMA (Figure 9–10). The primary response-related units within the FBI include:

- *FBI Domestic Terrorism/Counterterrorism Planning Section (DTCTPS)*: The DTCTPS serves as the point of contact (POC) to the FBI field offices and command structure as well as other federal

FIGURE 9–10 New York City, NY, September 18, 2001 — FBI members look toward the wreckage at the World Trade Center. (Source: Photo by Andrea Booher/FEMA News Photo)

agencies in incidences of terrorism, the use or suspected use of WMDs, and/or the evaluation of threat credibility. If the FBI's Strategic Information and Operations Center (SIOC) is operational for exercises or actual incidents, the DTCTPS will provide staff personnel to facilitate the operation of SIOC.

- *FBI Laboratory Division*: Within the FBI's Laboratory Division reside numerous assets, which can deploy to provide assistance in a terrorism/WMD incident. The Hazardous Materials Response Unit (HMRU) personnel are highly trained and knowledgeable and are equipped to direct and assist in the collection of hazardous and/or toxic evidence in a contaminated environment.
- *FBI Critical Incident Response Group (CIRG)*: The Crisis Management Unit (CMU), which conducts training and exercises for the FBI and has developed the concept of the Joint Operations Center (JOC), is available to provide on-scene assistance to the incident and integrate the concept of the JOC and the ICS to create efficient management of the situation.

Department of Defense

In the event of a terrorist attack or an act of nature on American soil resulting in the release of chemical, biological, radiological, or nuclear material or high-yield explosive (CBRNE) devices, the local law enforcement, fire, and emergency medical personnel who are first to respond may become quickly overwhelmed by the magnitude of the attack. The Department of Defense (DOD) has many unique war-fighting support capabilities, both technical and operational, that could be used in support of state and local authorities, if requested by DHS, as the LFA, to support and manage the consequences of such a domestic event.

When requested, the DOD will provide its unique and extensive resources in accordance with the following principles. First, DOD will ensure an unequivocal chain of responsibility, authority, and accountability for its actions to ensure the American people that the military will follow the basic constructs of lawful action when an emergency occurs. Second, in the event of a catastrophic CBRNE event, DOD will always play a supporting role to the LFA in accordance with all applicable law and plans. Third, DOD support will emphasize its natural role, skills, and structures to mass mobilize and provide logistical support. Fourth, DOD will purchase equipment and provide support in areas that are largely related to its war-fighting mission. Fifth, reserve component forces are DOD's forward-deployed forces for domestic CM.

All official requests for DOD support to CBRNE consequence management (CM) incidents are made by the LFA to the Executive Secretary of the DOD. Although the LFA may submit the requests for DOD assistance through other DOD channels, immediately upon receipt, any request that comes to any DOD element shall be forwarded to the Executive Secretary. In each instance the Executive Secretary will take the necessary action so that the Deputy Secretary can determine whether the incident warrants special operational management. In such instances, upon issuance of Secretary of Defense guidance to the chairman of the Joint Chiefs of Staff (CJCS), the Joint Staff will translate the Secretary's decisions into military orders for these CBRNE-CM events, under the policy oversight of the ATSD(CS). If the Deputy Secretary of Defense determines that DOD support for a particular CBRNE-CM incident does not require special CM procedures, the Secretary of the Army will exercise authority as the DOD executive agent through the normal director of Military Support and Military Support to Civil Authorities (MSCA) procedures, with policy oversight by the ATSD(CS).

Additionally, DOD has established 10 Weapons of Mass Destruction Civil Support Teams (WMD-CSTs), each composed of 22 well-trained and equipped full-time National Guard personnel. Upon Secretary of Defense certification, one WMD-CST will be stationed in each of the 10 FEMA regions around the country, ready to provide support when directed by their respective governors. Their mission is to deploy rapidly, assist local responders in determining the precise nature of an attack, provide expert technical advice, and help pave the way for the identification and arrival of follow-up military assets. By congressional direction, DOD is in the process of establishing and training an additional 17 WMD-CSTs to support the U.S. population. Interstate agreements provide a process for the WMD-CST and other National Guard assets to be used by neighboring states. If national security requirements dictate, these units may be transferred to federal service.

In August 2005, the DOD announced that it had, for the first time, created operational plans of war that included U.S. territory, primarily for use in the response to a major terrorist attack within the nation's borders. The plans are based on 15 possible attack scenarios that assume simultaneous attacks throughout the country. Northern Command, a new military sector created in 2002 whose territory includes the United States, developed these domestic war plans. In the event of military involvement in a domestic disaster, as stipulated in these plans, ground troop responsibilities would range from crowd control to high-end, full-scale disaster management following attacks that utilize WMDs. What is important to note about these plans, which are the first of their kind, is that they maintain in explicit verbiage that military assets utilized in a domestic incident will be provided in support of civilian response units, including police, fire, and EMS officials. They do allow, however, for the military to assume command in mass casualty situations where local response units are clearly overwhelmed and no longer able to adequately perform their duties.

These military plans are based on two separate documents, entitled CONPLAN 2002 and CONPLAN 0500 (CONPLAN is short for "Concept Plan"). CONPLAN 2002 was drafted to centralize missions of domestic basis into a single document, covering land, sea, and air operations. The plan covers the pre- and post-attack timeframes, which enables the military to help prevent terrorist attacks from occurring (either within or outside the United States). CONPLAN 0500, on the other hand, covers the organizational response to the 15 hypothetical scenarios mentioned earlier. These two plans have yet to gain approval of the Secretary of Defense.

These plans represent a great advancement for military involvement in domestic disaster response. Though it was always assumed that the military may have to lend support in response to a large-scale terrorist attack within the United States, no formalized plans had been created to dictate how that would be carried out. Through these plans, the military will be able to formalize both its responsibilities and its capabilities, and will likely be able to exercise in this role before its members are required to perform.

Organizations that are concerned with civil liberties have raised alarm about the idea of greater military involvement in homeland security operations. These groups feel that such defined military involvement would run counter to the 1878 Posse Comitatus Act, which prevents military forces from participating in domestic law enforcement in any form (this act was reiterated in the Homeland Security Act of 2002). However, military drafters of the two CONPLANs assert that the military role would fall under Article 2 of the Constitution, which allows the president to use the military to defend the nation as he or she sees fit, which is allowable under the Posse Comitatus Act (Washington Post, 2005).

Department of Energy

Through its Office of Emergency Response, the Department of Energy (DOE) manages radiological emergency response assets that support both crisis and CM response in the event of an incident involving a WMD. DOE is prepared to respond immediately to any type of radiological accident or incident with its radiological emergency response assets.

Through its Office of Nonproliferation and National Security, DOE coordinates activities in nonproliferation, international nuclear safety, and communicated threat assessment. DOE maintains the following capabilities that support domestic terrorism preparedness and response:

- *Aerial Measuring System (AMS)*: AMS is an aircraft-operated radiation detection system that uses fixed-wing aircraft and helicopters equipped with state-of-the-art technology instrumentation to track, monitor, and sample airborne radioactive plumes and/or detect and measure radioactive material deposited on the ground.

- *Atmospheric Release Advisory Capability (ARAC)*: ARAC is a computer-based atmospheric dispersion and deposition modeling capability operated by Lawrence Livermore National Laboratory (LLNL), and its role in an emergency begins when a nuclear, chemical, or other hazardous material is, or has the potential of being, released into the atmosphere. ARAC consists of meteorologists and other technical staff using three-dimensional computer models and real-time weather data to project the dispersion and deposition of radioactive material in the environment.

- *Accident Response Group (ARG)*: ARG is DOE's primary emergency response capability for responding to emergencies involving U.S. nuclear weapons. ARG members will deploy with highly specialized, state-of-the-art equipment for weapons' recovery and monitoring operations. ARG advance elements focus on initial assessment and provide preliminary advice to decision makers.

- *Federal Radiological Monitoring and Assessment Center (FRMAC)*: For major radiological emergencies affecting the United States, the DOE established an FRMAC. The center is the control point for all federal assets involved in the monitoring and assessment of off-site radiological conditions. FRMAC provides support to the affected states, coordinates federal off-site radiological environmental monitoring and assessment activities, maintains a technical liaison with tribal nations and state and local governments, responds to the assessment needs of the LFA, and meets the statutory responsibilities of the participating federal agency.

- *Nuclear Emergency Search Team (NEST)*: NEST is DOE's program for dealing with the technical aspects of nuclear or radiological terrorism. Response teams vary in size from a five-person technical advisory team to a tailored deployment of dozens of searchers and scientists who can locate and then conduct or support technical operations on a suspected nuclear device.

- *Radiological Assistance Program (RAP)*: Under RAP, DOE provides, upon request, radiological assistance to DOE program elements, other federal agencies, state, tribal, and local governments, private groups, and individuals. RAP provides resources (trained personnel and equipment) to evaluate, assess, advise, and assist in the mitigation of actual or perceived radiation hazards and risks to workers, the public, and the environment.
- *Radiation Emergency Assistance Center/Training Site (REAC/TS)*: The REAC/TS is managed by DOE's Oak Ridge Institute for Science and Education in Oak Ridge, Tennessee, and it maintains a 24-hour response center staffed with personnel and equipment to support medical aspects of radiological emergencies.
- *Communicated Threat Credibility Assessment*: DOE is the program manager for the Nuclear Assessment Program (NAP) at LLNL. The NAP is a DOE-funded asset specifically designed to provide technical, operational, and behavioral assessments of the credibility of communicated threats directed against the U.S. government and its interests.
- *Nuclear Incident Response*: This program provides expert personnel and specialized equipment to a number of federal emergency response entities that deal with nuclear emergencies, nuclear accidents, and nuclear terrorism. The emergency response personnel are experts in such fields as device assessment, device disablement, intelligence analysis, credibility assessment, and health physics.

Department of Health and Human Services

The Department of Health and Human Services (HHS), as the LFA for ESF #8 (health and medical services), provides coordinated federal assistance to supplement state and local resources in response to public health and medical care needs following a major disaster or emergency. Additionally, HHS provides support during developing or potential medical situations and has the responsibility for federal support of food, drug, and sanitation issues. Resources are furnished when state and local resources are overwhelmed and public health and/or medical assistance is requested from the federal government.

HHS, in its primary agency role for ESF #8, coordinates the provision of federal health and medical assistance to fulfill the requirements identified by the affected state/local authorities having jurisdiction. Included in ESF #8 are overall public health response; triage, treatment, and transportation of victims of the disaster; and evacuation of patients out of the disaster area, as needed, into a network of military services, veterans affairs, and pre-enrolled nonfederal hospitals located in the major metropolitan areas of the United States.

ESF #8 utilizes resources primarily available from:

1. Within HHS
2. ESF #8 support agencies
3. The National Disaster Medical System
4. Specific nonfederal sources (major pharmaceutical suppliers, hospital supply vendors, international disaster response organizations, and international health organizations)

Other than the agencies integrated under FEMA, the CDC may also be used in response activities. CDC is the federal agency responsible for protecting the public health of the country through prevention and control of diseases and response to public health emergencies. CDC works with national and international agencies to eradicate or control communicable diseases and other preventable conditions. The CDC's Bioterrorism Preparedness and Response Program oversees the agency's effort to prepare state and local governments to respond to acts of bioterrorism. In addition, CDC has designated emergency response personnel throughout the agency who are responsible for responding to biological, chemical, and radiological terrorism. CDC has epidemiologists trained to investigate and control outbreaks or illnesses, as well as laboratories capable of quantifying an individual's exposure to biological or chemical agents.

Environmental Protection Agency

The Environmental Protection Agency (EPA) is chartered to respond to WMD releases under the National Oil and Hazardous Substances Pollution Contingency Plan (NCP) regardless of the cause of the release. EPA is authorized by the Comprehensive Environmental Response, Compensation, and Liability Act (CERCLA); the Oil Pollution Act; and the Emergency Planning and Community Right-to-Know Act to support federal, state, and local responders in counterterrorism.

EPA will provide support to the FBI during crisis management in response to a terrorist incident. In its crisis management role, the EPA on-scene commander (OSC) may provide the FBI special agent in charge (SAC) with technical advice and recommendations, scientific and technical assessments, and assistance (as needed) to state and local responders. The EPA's OSC will support DHS during consequence management for the incident. EPA carries out its response according to the FRP's ESF #10, Hazardous Materials. The OSC may request an environmental response team that is funded by the EPA if the terrorist incident exceeds available local and regional resources. The EPA chairs the National Response Team (NRT).

Department of Agriculture

It is the policy of the U.S. Department of Agriculture (USDA) to "be prepared to respond swiftly in the event of national security, natural disaster, technological, and other emergencies at the national, regional, state, and county levels to provide support and comfort to the people of the United States." USDA has been charged with ensuring the safety of the nation's food supply. Since September 11, the concern that bioterrorism will impact agriculture in rural America, namely, crops in the field, hoofed animals, and food-safety issues in the food chain between the slaughterhouse and/or processing facilities and the consumer, has only grown. USDA offices that address this concern include:

- *Office of Crisis Planning and Management (OCPM)*: This USDA office coordinates the emergency planning, preparedness, and crisis management functions and the suitability for employment investigations of the department.
- *USDA State Emergency Boards (SEBs)*: The SEBs have responsibility for coordinating USDA emergency activities at the state level.
- *Farm Service Agency*: This USDA agency develops and administers emergency plans and controls covering food processing, storage, and wholesale distribution; distribution and use of seed; and manufacture, distribution, and use of livestock and poultry feed.
- *Food and Nutrition Service (FNS)*: This USDA agency provides food assistance in officially designated disaster areas on request by the designated state agency. Generally, the food assistance response from FNS includes authorization of Emergency Food Stamp Program benefits and use of USDA-donated foods for emergency mass feeding and household distribution, as necessary. FNS also maintains a current inventory of USDA-donated food held in federal, state, and commercial warehouses and provides leadership to the FRP under ESF #11, Food.

- *Food Safety and Inspection Service*: This USDA agency inspects meat and meat products, poultry and poultry products, and egg products in slaughtering and processing plants; assists the Food and Drug Administration in the inspection of other food products; develops plans and procedures for radiological emergency response in accordance with the Federal Radiological Emergency Response Plan (FRERP); and provides support, as required, to the FRP at the national and regional levels.

- *Natural Resources Conservation Service*: This USDA agency provides technical assistance to individuals, communities, and governments relating to proper use of land for agricultural production; provides assistance in determining the extent of damage to agricultural land and water; and provides support to the FRP under ESF #3, Public Works and Engineering.

- *Agricultural Research Service (ARS)*: This USDA agency develops and carries out all necessary research programs related to crop or livestock diseases; provides technical support for emergency programs and activities in the areas of planning, prevention, detection, treatment, and management of consequences; provides technical support for the development of guidance information on the effects of radiation, biological, and chemical agents on agriculture; develops and maintains a current inventory of ARS-controlled laboratories that can be mobilized on short notice for emergency testing of food, feed, and water safety; and provides biological, chemical, and radiological safety support for USDA.

- *Economic Research Service*: This USDA agency, in cooperation with other departmental agencies, analyzes the impacts of the emergency on the U.S. agricultural system, as well as on rural communities, as part of the process of developing strategies to respond to the effects of an emergency.

- *Rural Business-Cooperative Service*: This USDA agency, in cooperation with other government agencies at all levels, promotes economic development in affected rural areas by developing strategies that respond to the conditions created by an emergency.

- *Cooperative State Research, Education, and Extension Service (CSREES)*: This USDA agency coordinates use of land-grant and other cooperating state college and university services and other relevant research institutions in carrying out all responsibilities for emergency programs.

- *Rural Housing Service*: This USDA agency will assist the Department of Housing and Urban Development by providing living quarters in unoccupied rural housing in an emergency situation.

- *Rural Utilities Service*: This USDA agency will provide support to the FRP under ESF #12, Energy, at the national level.

- *Office of Inspector General (OIG)*: This USDA office is the department's principal law enforcement component and liaison with the FBI. OIG, in concert with appropriate federal, state, and local agencies, is prepared to investigate any terrorist attacks relating to the nation's agriculture sector, to identify subjects, interview witnesses, and secure evidence in preparation for federal prosecution. As necessary, OIG will examine USDA programs regarding counterterrorism-related matters.

- *Forest Service (FS)*: This USDA agency will prevent and control fires in rural areas in cooperation with state, local, and tribal governments and appropriate federal departments and agencies. They will determine and report requirements for equipment, personnel, fuels, chemicals, and other materials needed for carrying out assigned duties.

Nuclear Regulatory Commission

The Nuclear Regulatory Commission (NRC) is the LFA (in accordance with the FRERP) for facilities or materials regulated by NRC or by an NRC agreement. NRC's counterterrorism-specific role, at these facilities or material sites, is to exercise the federal lead for radiological safety while supporting other federal, state, and local agencies in crisis and CM. Emergency management assistance that is provided by the NRC includes:

- *Radiological Safety Assessments*: NRC provides facilities (or materials users) with technical advice to ensure on-site measures are taken to mitigate negative "off-site" consequences. NRC serves as the primary federal source of information regarding on-site radiological conditions and off-site radiological effects. The commission supports the technical needs of other federal agencies by providing descriptions of devices or facilities containing radiological materials and assessing the safety impact of terrorist actions and of proposed tactical operations of any responders. Safety assessments are coordinated through an NRC liaison at the Domestic Emergency Support Team (DEST), Strategic Information and Operations Center (SIOC), Command Post (CP), and Joint Operations Center (JOC).

- *Protective Action Recommendations*: NRC contacts state and local authorities and offers them advice and assistance on the technical assessment of radiological hazards and, if requested, provides advice on protective actions for the public. NRC coordinates any recommendations for protective actions through an NRC liaison at the CP or JOC.

- *Responder Radiation Protection*: NRC assesses the potential radiological hazards to any responders and coordinates with the radiation protection staff of an affected facility (or disaster site) to ensure that personnel responding to the scene are observing the appropriate precautions.

- *Information Coordination*: NRC supplies other responders and government officials with timely information concerning the radiological aspects of an event. NRC liaises with the Joint Information Center (JIC) to coordinate information concerning the federal response.

▪ ▪ Critical Thinking ▪

How does the involvement of the Department of Defense in the nation's emergency management system differ from all other federal agencies? Why is this difference significant? Do you feel that anything should be done to change the way the military supports domestic emergency management?

National Incident Management System (NIMS)

A difficult issue in any response operation is determining who is in charge of the overall response effort at the incident. This concept of control, or leadership, is most commonly referred to in the emergency management community as *incident command*. With the significant shift in legislation brought about by the creation of DHS, and the new emphasis on terrorism, the issue of incident command was in danger of becoming even more difficult and, likewise, confusing and even conflicting. To address the concerns that many officials at the local, state, and federal levels expressed in light of the changes that were occurring in the emergency management world, President George W. Bush called on the Secretary of Homeland Security, by means of Homeland Security Presidential Directive (HSPD)-5, to develop a nationally based ICS. The purpose of this system, it was assumed, was to provide a consistent nationwide approach for federal, state, tribal, and local governments to work together to prepare for, prevent, respond to, and recover from domestic incidents — regardless of their cause, size, or complexity.

On March 1, 2004, following the collective efforts of state and local government officials, representatives from a wide range of public safety organizations, and DHS, the product result of HSPD-5 was released. The NIMS, as it is called, incorporated existing knowledge, lessons learned, and best practices into a new comprehensive national approach to domestic incident management and command that appeared to fully account for the many recent changes in federal response requirements that resulted for the reasons mentioned above. This document was created such that it addressed all jurisdictional levels and all functional disciplines involved in emergency management.

The NIMS represents a core set of doctrine, principles, terminology, and organizational processes to enable the management of disasters at all government levels. One very important aspect of this new framework is that it recognized the value of an existing system, the ICS, and stressed the importance of effective incident command as a way of better managing disaster events. The well-known National Commission on Terrorist Attacks Upon the United States (the 9/11 Commission) identified ICS as an answer to many of the coordination problems that arose during the response to the September 11 attacks, and recommended a national adoption of ICS to enhance command, control, and communications capabilities during disaster response (Figure 9–11).

To better understand the processes by which NIMS helps in the management of events requiring multiple levels of government, it is necessary to have a brief understanding of the ICS. The ICS was developed in California in 1970 after a devastating wildfire. During the after-action analysis of the response to the fire, which caused hundreds of millions of dollars in damage, killed 16 people, and left hundreds of families without homes, it was recognized that problems with communications and with coordination between different agencies made operations much less effective than they could have been. Following this analysis, Congress mandated that a system be created to address these coordination issues, and the result

FIGURE 9–11 New York City, NY, September 21, 2001 — Rescue operations continue far into the night at the World Trade Center. (Source: Photo by Andrea Booher/FEMA News Photo)

was a system called FIRESCOPE ICS, developed by the U.S. Forest Service, the California Department of Forestry and Fire Protection, the Governor's Office of Emergency Services, and several local and county fire departments.

FIRESCOPE ICS effectively standardized the response to wildfires in California. It resulted in a common terminology being used by all responding agencies, which significantly reduced the confusion. It established common procedures to be applied to firefighting, which significantly reduced the amount of time needed to coordinate between two or more agencies that would be working together on attacking a fire. Several field tests had shown that the system was effective, and by 1981 it was being applied throughout Southern California. So effective was FIRESCOPE ICS at standardizing coordination to wildfire events that departments began to apply its methods to other events unrelated to wildfires. It was soon recognized as being effective for the response to floods, hazardous materials' spills and leaks, earthquakes, and even major transportation accidents.

There are multiple functions in the ICS, including common use of terminology, integrated communications, a unified command (UC) structure, resource management, and action planning. A planned set of directives includes assigning one coordinator to manage the infrastructure of the response, and assigning personnel, deploying equipment, obtaining resources, and working with the numerous agencies that respond to the disaster scene. In most instances, the local fire chief or fire commissioner is designated the incident commander.

The ICS was designed to remain effective at each of the following three levels of incident escalation:

1. Single jurisdiction and/or single agency
2. Single jurisdiction with multiagency support
3. Multijurisdictional and/or multiagency support

There are five major management systems within the ICS. They include command, operations, planning, logistics, and finance. Each is described here:

- *Command*: The command section includes developing, directing, and maintaining communication and collaboration with the multiple agencies on site, as well as working with local officials, the public, and the media to provide up-to-date information regarding the disaster.
- *Operations*: The operations section handles the tactical operations, coordinates the command objectives, develops tactical operations, and organizes and directs all resources to the disaster site.
- *Planning*: The planning section provides the necessary information to the command center to develop the action plan to accomplish the objectives. This section also collects and evaluates information as it is made available.
- *Logistics*: The logistics section provides personnel, equipment, and support for the command center. This section handles the coordination of all services that are involved in the response from locating rescue equipment to coordinating the response for volunteer organizations such as the Salvation Army and the Red Cross.
- *Finance*: The finance section is responsible for the accounting for funds used during the response and recovery aspect of the disaster. This section monitors costs related to the incident and provides accounting procurement time recording cost analyses.

Under the ICS, there is almost always a single incident commander. However, even under this single command figure, the ICS allows for something called a *unified command* (UC). UC is often used when there is more than one agency with incident jurisdiction or when incidents cross multiple political jurisdictions. Within this UC framework, agencies are able to work together through the designated members of the UC, often with a senior official from each agency or discipline participating in the UC, to establish a common set of objectives and strategies and a single plan of action. Due to the nature of disasters, multiple government agencies often need to work together to monitor the response and manage a large number of personnel responding to the scene. ICS allows for the integration of the agencies to operate under a single response management.

Although NIMS was built upon this ICS system, the new system extends far beyond the initial scope of ICS. This is to be expected, of course, considering the exponentially greater size of the incidents regularly managed under NIMS (despite that NIMS was designed to be effectively used to manage small, single-jurisdictional events such as house fires or automobile accidents). NIMS establishes standardized incident management processes, protocols, and procedures that all responders, whether they are federal, state, tribal, or local, can use to coordinate and conduct their cooperative response actions. Using these standardized procedures, it is presumed that all responders will be able to share a common understanding and will be able to work together with very little mismatch. The following are the key components of the new incident management system:

- *Incident Command System (ICS)*: NIMS establishes ICS as a standard incident management organization with five functional areas — command, operations, planning, logistics, and finance/administration — for management of all major incidents. To ensure further coordination, and during incidents involving multiple jurisdictions or agencies, the principle of UC has been universally incorporated into NIMS. This UC not only coordinates the efforts of many jurisdictions, but also provides for and ensures joint decisions on objectives, strategies, plans, priorities, and public communications.

- *Communications and Information Management*: Standardized communications during an incident are essential, and NIMS prescribes interoperable communications systems for both incident and information management. NIMS recognizes that responders and managers across all agencies and jurisdictions must have common access to the full operational picture, thereby allowing for efficient and effective incident response.

- *Preparedness*: Preparedness incorporates a range of measures, actions, and processes accomplished before an incident happens. NIMS preparedness measures include planning, training, exercises, qualification and certification, equipment acquisition and certification, and publication management. NIMS stresses that each of these measures helps to ensure that preincident actions are standardized and consistent with mutually agreed-on doctrine. NIMS further places emphasis on mitigation activities to enhance preparedness. Mitigation includes public education and outreach; structural modifications to reduce the loss of life or destruction of property; code enforcement in support of zoning rules, land management, and building codes; and flood insurance and property buy-out for frequently flooded areas.

- *Joint Information System (JIS)*: The Joint Information System provides the public with timely and accurate incident information and unified public messages. This system employs JICs and brings incident communicators together during an incident to develop, coordinate, and deliver a unified message. This is performed under the assumption that it will ensure that federal, state, and local levels of government are releasing the same information during an incident.

- *NIMS Integration Center (NIC)*: To ensure that NIMS remains an accurate and effective management tool, a NIMS NIC will be established by the DHS Secretary to assess proposed changes to NIMS, capture and evaluate lessons learned, and employ best practices. The NIC will provide strategic direction and oversight, supporting both routine maintenance and continuous refinement of the system and its components over the long term. It will also develop and facilitate national standards for NIMS education and training, first-responder communications and equipment, typing of resources, qualification and credentialing of incident management and responder personnel, and standardization of equipment maintenance and resources. Finally, the NIC will continue to use the collaborative process of federal, state, tribal, local, multidisciplinary, and private authorities to assess prospective changes to NIMS.

Figure 9–12 illustrates how NIMS was developed on the structure originally outlined in the ICS. The NRP, which guides the federal support of state, county, tribal, and local response to disasters, was built on the NIMS framework. Together, these three coordinated concepts have likely helped to further eliminate coordination problems that may have existed before in the absence of such complementary systems.

Federal Response

Almost every facet of the nation's emergency response system has undergone change to some degree as a result of the reaction to the September 11 terrorist attacks on America. Although some of the more

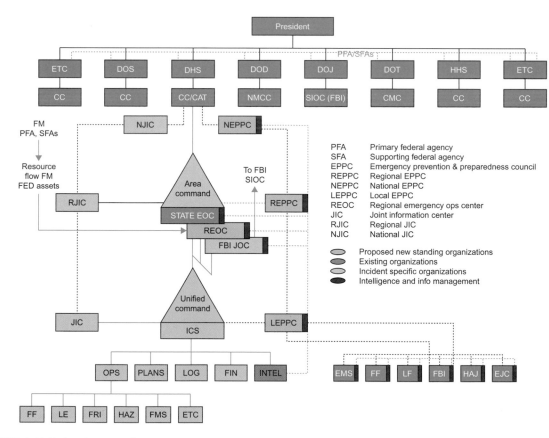

FIGURE 9–12 National structure for NIMS operations.

significant adjustments have occurred at the federal level — most notably the creation of DHS — all state and most local agencies have followed this lead. As for the response to major disasters, namely, those requiring action by multiple levels of government, these changes have resulted in a shift toward increased federal control and direction. This shift is most notable with regard to events that involve a criminal element such as exists with intentional disasters (e.g., sabotage or civil unrest) and terrorist-driven threats or events. These changes have all been formalized through the transformation of the federal response framework from the old Federal Response Plan (FRP), which was successfully applied during several terrorist event responses including the Murrah Federal Building bombing and the September 11 attacks, to the National Response Plan (NRP) in the years immediately following the September 11 attacks, to the National Response Framework (NRF), released January 2008 in response to criticisms and shortcomings of the NRP.

It has traditionally been the case that a federal response may be initiated in two ways: a governor can request a presidential disaster declaration or the president can declare a presidential emergency upon damage to federal entities (as was the case for the *Discovery* tragedy). Today, however, there is a third mechanism. The president, through FEMA, can predeploy resources (personnel and equipment) to a location where a disaster declaration is imminent due to an impending disaster. These authorities first appeared in the NRP, and remain unchanged under the NRF. It is important to note that, although a formal declaration does not have to be signed by the president for the federal government to begin response, the governor of the affected state must make a formal request for assistance to occur and must specify in the request the specific needs of the disaster area. Under the new NRF, the president may unilaterally declare a major disaster or emergency if extraordinary circumstances exist. For summaries of procedures on disaster declaration by the president and assistance without the president's declaration, see the sidebars "Presidential Major Disaster Declaration Process Guidelines" and "Federal Assistance without a Presidential Declaration," respectively.

Presidential Major Disaster Declaration Process Guidelines

- The Stafford Act (§401) requires that: "All requests for a declaration by the President that a major disaster exists shall be made by the Governor of the affected State." A State also includes the District of Columbia, Puerto Rico, the Virgin Islands, Guam, American Samoa, and the Commonwealth of the Northern Mariana Islands. The Marshall Islands and the Federated States of Micronesia are also eligible to request a declaration and receive assistance.
- Contact is made between the Governor of the affected State (including the District of Columbia), or territory, and the FEMA Regional Administrator. This contact may take place prior to or immediately following the disaster.
- State and Federal officials conduct a preliminary damage assessment (PDA) to estimate the extent of the disaster and its impact on individuals and public facilities. This information is included in the Governor's request to show that the disaster is of such severity and magnitude that effective response is beyond the capabilities of the State and the local governments and that Federal assistance is necessary. Normally, the PDA is completed prior to the submission of the Governor's request. However, when an obviously severe or catastrophic event occurs, the Governor's request may be submitted prior to the PDA. Nonetheless, the Governor must still make the request.

- Based on the PDA findings, the Governor submits a request to the president through the FEMA Regional Administrator for either a major disaster or an emergency declaration and identifies the affected counties. As part of the request, the Governor must take appropriate action under State law and direct execution of the State's emergency plan. The Governor has to provide in the request information on the nature and amount of State and local resources that have been or will be committed to alleviating the results of the disaster, provide an estimate of the amount and severity of damage and the impact on the private and public sector, and provide an estimate of the type and amount of assistance needed under the Stafford Act.
- The completed request, addressed to the President, is submitted through the FEMA Regional Administrator, who evaluates the damage and requirements for Federal assistance and makes a recommendation to the FEMA Administrator.
- The FEMA Administrator, acting through the Secretary of Homeland Security, may then recommend a course of action to the President.
- Based on the Governor's request, the president may declare that a major disaster or emergency exists, thereby activating the NRP and setting in motion the full array of available Federal programs to assist in the response and recovery effort. The Governor, appropriate Members of Congress, and Federal departments and agencies are immediately notified of a Presidential declaration.

Source: Federal Emergency Management Agency, "National Response Framework," 2008, http://www.fema .gov/emergency/nrf/.

Federal Assistance Without a Presidential Declaration

In many cases, assistance may be obtained from the Federal government without a Presidential declaration. For example, FEMA places liaisons in State EOCs and moves commodities near incident sites that may require Federal assistance prior to a Presidential declaration. Additionally, some types of assistance, such as Fire Management Assistance Grants — which provide support to States experiencing severe wildfires — are performed by Federal departments or agencies under their own authorities and do not require Presidential approval. Finally, Federal departments and agencies may provide immediate lifesaving assistance to States under their own statutory authorities without a formal Presidential declaration.

Source: Federal Emergency Management Agency, "National Response Framework," 2008, www.fema.gov.

Under the NRF, the president maintains the ultimate discretion in making a disaster declaration. There are no set criteria by which he or she is bound and no government regulations to guide which events are declared disasters and which are not. FEMA has developed a number of factors it considers in making its recommendation to the president, including individual property losses per capita, level of damage to existing community infrastructure, level of insurance coverage, repetitive events, and other subjective factors. But in the end, the decision to make the declaration is the president's alone. One major change in the verbiage of the plan, as changed in the NRP, concerns the prevention of terrorist attacks. In situations where the Homeland Security Operations Center determines that a terrorist threat exists for which federal intervention is required to prevent an incident from occurring, DHS provides support as necessary under the direction of the attorney general, through the FBI.

A presidential disaster declaration can be made in as short a time as a few hours, as was the case in the 1994 Northridge earthquake, the 1995 Oklahoma City bombing, and the September 11 World Trade Center attacks. Sometimes it takes weeks for damages to be assessed and the capability of state and local jurisdictions to fund response and recovery efforts to be evaluated. Should the governor's request be turned down by the president, the governor has the right to appeal, an appeal that will be considered, especially if new damage data become available and are included in the appeal.

Presidential declarations are routinely sought for such events as floods, hurricanes, earthquakes, and tornadoes. In recent years, governors have become more inventive and have requested presidential disaster declarations for snow removal, drought, West Nile virus, and economic losses caused by failing industries, such as the Northwest salmon-spawning decline.

Once a disaster declaration has been made, the full range of federal government resources becomes available to assist the affected state or states. The federal assistance is guided through the invocation of the NRP, which is detailed later in this chapter. Through this plan, and under the guidance of the DHS, 32 signatory federal agencies and the American Red Cross provide all forms of assistance as dictated under the 15 ESFs (also detailed later in this chapter). A declaration also paves the way for federal funding to pay for response activities at all government levels (including reimbursing the expenses of federal agencies that do respond) and certain recovery costs to individuals, businesses, nonprofit agencies, and public entities.

From January 1953 to July 2011, there have been 1,999 presidential disaster declarations, averaging 34 declarations per year (Table 9–2). As an illustration of disaster declaration activity in a single year, in 1999 there were 50 major disaster declarations in 38 states:

- 18 for hurricanes (13 alone for Hurricane Floyd)
- 11 for tornadoes
- 7 for floods
- 6 for winter storms
- 6 for severe storms
- 1 for a flash flood
- 1 for winter freeze

Before the creation of the NRP, and subsequent NRF, there were several individual response plans that guided the government response to several different kinds of emergencies or disasters. However, HSPD-5 directed DHS to develop the NRP such that all existing federal plans were integrated into that one document or directly linked through formal coordination mechanisms — giving it the distinction of

Table 9–2 Total Major Disaster Declarations, 1953–2011 (as of July)

Year	Declarations
1953	13
1954	17
1955	18
1956	16
1957	16
1958	7
1959	7
1960	12
1961	12
1962	22
1963	20
1964	25
1965	25
1966	11
1967	11
1968	19
1969	29
1970	17
1971	17
1972	48
1973	46
1974	46
1975	38
1976	30
1977	22
1978	25
1979	42
1980	23
1981	15
1982	24
1983	21
1984	34
1985	27
1986	28
1987	23
1988	11
1989	31
1990	38
1991	43
1992	45
1993	32
1994	36
1995	32

Table 9–2 (Continued)

Year	Declarations
1996	75
1997	44
1998	65
1999	50
2000	45
2001	45
2002	49
2003	46
2004	68
2005	48
2006	52
2007	63
2008	75
2009	59
2010	81
2011 (as of July)	60
Total	**1,999**
Average	**34**

Source: FEMA, 2011, http://www.fema.gov/news/disaster_totals_annual.fema

serving as the single guide for federal response. The following list contains the various plans and operation guidelines integrated or linked under the NRP:

- Federal Response Plan (FRP)
- Federal Radiological Emergency Response Plan (FRERP)
- Domestic Terrorism Concept of Operations Plan (CONPLAN)
- Mass Mitigation Emergency Plan (Distant Shore)
- National Oil Spill and Hazardous Substances Pollution Contingency Plan (NCP)

The NRP essentially replaced the FRP, and accommodated the needs of events covered under the FRERP, CONPLAN, Distant Shore, and NCP, as well as several newly identified or newly addressed issues through the development of various *incident annexes*. These annexes, which have not yet been developed for the new NRF and are therefore still applicable in their original NRP format, include the following (described in much greater detail later in this chapter):

- Biological incident
- Catastrophic incident
- Cyber incident
- Food and agriculture incident
- Nuclear/radiological incident

- Oil and hazardous materials incident
- Terrorism incident law enforcement and investigation

National Response Framework (NRF)

The National Response Framework (NRF) was developed to be a single document by which emergency management efforts at all levels of government could be structured. The NRF has been described by FEMA as being "a guide to how the Nation conducts all-hazards response." It is meant to be scalable, flexible, and adaptable in coordinating the key roles and responsibilities of response participants throughout the country, at all levels of government. It describes specific authorities and practices for managing incidents that range from serious local events to large-scale national-level terrorist attacks or catastrophic natural disasters. The NRF was built directly upon the structure of the NIMS, itself developed to provide a consistent template for managing incidents.

The NRF is the latest iteration in a progression of emergency response documents guiding federal emergency management action. The first in this series of documents was the FRP, released in 1992, which focused most specifically on the roles and responsibilities of the federal government in assistance to overwhelmed state and local jurisdictions. Following the 9/11 attacks, it was determined that the document guiding national response required a more comprehensive approach in order to define the state, local, and other roles in the greater scheme of major disaster response and recovery. As a result, the NRP was released in 2004, thereby replacing the FRP. Nine months after Katrina's landfall, however, a notice of change to the NRP was released, incorporating preliminary lessons learned from the 2005 hurricane season. These changes were based upon suggestions of various emergency management stakeholders, many of whom felt that the NRP was overly bureaucratic, repetitive, and national in focus. FEMA officials felt that one of the greatest criticisms was that users did not consider the NRP to be a "plan" as its name suggested, but rather a framework guiding the types of actions that could be taken in response to the variety of possible incidents that might occur. In response, the DHS developed and released the NRF in September of 2007, and provided a period for comments by local and state stakeholders. Changes were made to the draft framework based upon these comments, and on January 22, 2008, the final NRF was released. The document became official 60 days following its release, thereby superseding the NRP.

The NRF is built upon the template established under the NIMS, which was called for by HSPD-5 in the aftermath of the September 11 terrorist attacks. NIMS enables all levels of government, the private sector, and nongovernmental organizations (NGOs) to work together during an emergency or disaster event. The NRF and NIMS, working together, seek to ensure that all stakeholders are operating under a common set of emergency management principles.

The NRF can be either partially or fully implemented in the lead-up or response to an emergency or disaster threat, thereby allowing for what is considered a "scaled" response that tasks only those agencies and resources that are actually needed.

Organization of NRF

The NRF is composed of:

- *A core document*: Describes the principles that guide national response roles and responsibilities, response actions, response organizations, and planning requirements that together work to achieve an effective national response to any incident that occurs

- *Emergency Support Function (ESF) Annexes*: Group federal resources and capabilities into functional areas that are most frequently needed in a national response (e.g., transportation, firefighting, mass care)
- *Support Annexes*: Describe essential supporting aspects that are common to all incidents (e.g., financial management, volunteer and donations management, private-sector coordination)
- *Incident Annexes*: Address the unique aspects of how we respond to seven broad incident categories (e.g., biological, nuclear/radiological, cyber, mass evacuation)
- *Partner Guides*: Provide ready references describing key roles and actions for local, tribal, state, federal, and private-sector response partners

The NRF describes the roles and responsibilities not only of public-sector agencies, but also of the private sector, NGOs, and individuals and households. Communities, tribes, states, the federal government, NGOs, and the private sector are each informed of their respective roles and responsibilities, and how their actions complement each other. Each governmental level is tasked with developing capabilities needed to respond to incidents, including the development of plans, conducting assessments and exercises, providing and directing resources and capabilities, and gathering lessons learned.

The scope of the NRF includes domestic incidents of all sizes, regardless of state or federal involvement. The NRF can be partially or fully implemented in response to or anticipation of a natural or technological hazard, or a terrorist threat. By defining what is called *selective implementation*, the NRF allows for a scaled response. In this manner, events that start out small but grow larger in scope can be applicable to the plan from the moment they begin. This also allows for what is considered a more seamless transition from local, to state, and ultimately to federal involvement as incidents grow in size. One of the greatest changes between the NRF and previous versions of the response document is that no formal declaration is required before the NRF may be invoked. For the NRF doctrine and nature of assistance available, see the sidebars "National Response Framework Response Doctrine" and "Types of Federal Disaster Assistance Available under the NRF," respectively.

National Response Framework Response Doctrine

The response doctrine of the NRF defines basic roles, responsibilities, and operational concepts for response across all levels of government and with NGOs and the private sector. The overarching objective of response activities contained within the NRF centers upon saving lives and protecting property and the environment.

Five key operations principles define response actions in support of the nation's response mission. Taken together, these five principles constitute the national response doctrine. The response doctrine is rooted in America's federal system and the Constitution's division of responsibilities between federal and state governments. Because this doctrine reflects the history of emergency management and the distilled wisdom of responders and leaders at all levels, it gives elemental form to the NRF. This doctrine evolved in response to changes in the political and strategic landscape, lessons learned from operations, and the introduction of new technologies. The doctrine influences the way in which policy and plans are developed, forces are organized and trained, and equipment is procured. It promotes unity of purpose, guides professional judgment, and enables responders to best fulfill their responsibilities." Response doctrine is comprised of five key principles:

- Engaged partnership
- Tiered response
- Scalable, flexible, and adaptable operational capabilities
- Unity of effort through unified command
- Readiness to act

Source: DHS, National Response Framework, 2008, www.dhs.gov.

Types of Federal Disaster Assistance Available under the NRF

The National Response Framework (NRF) makes available the following types of assistance.

Preincident Services

- Interagency information and intelligence sharing is conducted to enable counterterrorism activities.
- Resources and staff can be prepositioned to ensure effective response in anticipation of a disaster.

Immediate Relief Delivery — Response Actions

- Assets are mobilized and resources are deployed to support the incident.
- Teams with specialized capabilities such as the NDMS, the HHS Secretary's Emergency Response Team, the Epidemic Intelligence Service, HHS behavioral health response teams, the U.S. Public Health Service Commissioned Corps, and Urban Search and Rescue teams are deployed.
- A Joint Field Office (JFO) and other field facilities are established to provide incident management, public health, and other community support.
- Assistance is provided to support immediate law enforcement, fire, ambulance, and emergency medical service actions; emergency flood fighting; evacuations; transportation system detours; emergency public information; actions taken to minimize additional damage; urban search and rescue; the establishment of facilities for mass care; the provision of public health and medical services, food, ice, water, and other emergency essentials; debris clearance; the emergency restoration of critical infrastructure; control, containment, and removal of environmental contamination; and protection of responder health and safety.
- During the response to a terrorist event, law enforcement actions to collect and preserve evidence and to apprehend perpetrators are conducted.

Assistance to Speed Recovery and Reduce Damage from Future Occurrences
- Loans and grants to repair or replace damaged housing and personal property are provided.
- Grants to repair or replace roads and public buildings, incorporating to the extent practical hazard-reduction structural and nonstructural measures, are provided.
- Technical assistance to identify and implement mitigation opportunities to reduce future losses is provided.
- Other assistance, including crisis counseling, tax relief, legal services, and job placement may also be provided.

Source: Department of Homeland Security (DHS), "The National Response Plan," Washington, D.C.: DHS, 2005.

Roles and Responsibilities Defined by the NRF

The NRF Core Document provides an overview of the roles and responsibilities of key emergency management stakeholders at the local, tribal, state, and federal levels who are involved in the implementation of the NRF, including the private sector and NGOs. The following section describes exactly who is involved with the NRF at each jurisdictional level, and what each must do to build and maintain emergency response capabilities.

Local Level
Disaster response almost always begins locally, and remains local In terms of actual incident command and control responsibility. This responsibility rests both with the individual members of the community themselves and with the public officials elected by them in the county and city governments. The responsibilities of the following individuals are specifically mentioned in the NRF.

Chief Elected or Appointed Official
A mayor, city manager, or county manager, as a jurisdiction's chief executive officer, is responsible for ensuring the public safety and welfare of the people of that jurisdiction. Specifically, this official provides strategic guidance and resources during preparedness, response, and recovery efforts by:

- Establishing strong working relationships with local jurisdictional leaders and core private-sector organizations, voluntary agencies, and community partners. This official must get to know, coordinate with, and train with local partners in advance of an incident and to develop mutual aid and/or assistance agreements for support in response to an incident.
- Leading and encouraging local leaders to focus on preparedness by participating in planning, training, and exercises.
- Supporting participation in local mitigation efforts within the jurisdiction and, as appropriate, with the private sector.
- Understanding and implementing laws and regulations that support emergency management and response.
- Ensuring that local emergency plans take into account the needs of:
  - The jurisdiction, including persons, property, and structures

- Individuals with special needs, including those with service animals
- Individuals with household pets
- Encouraging residents to participate in volunteer organizations and training courses
- Working closely with members of Congress during incidents and on an ongoing basis regarding local preparedness capabilities and needs

Emergency Manager

The local emergency manager has the day-to-day authority and responsibility for overseeing emergency management programs and activities. They must work with chief elected and appointed officials to ensure that there are effective emergency plans in place and activities being conducted. Their role includes:

- Coordinating all components of the local emergency management program, to include assessing the availability and readiness of local resources most likely required during an incident and identifying and correcting any shortfalls
- Coordinating the planning process and working cooperatively with other local agencies and private-sector organizations
- Developing mutual aid and assistance agreements
- Coordinating damage assessments during an incident
- Advising and informing local officials about emergency management activities during an incident
- Developing and executing public awareness and education programs
- Conducting exercises to test plans and systems and obtain lessons learned
- Involving the private sector and NGOs in planning, training, and exercises

Department and Agency Heads

The local emergency manager is assisted by, and coordinates the efforts of, employees in departments and agencies that perform emergency management functions. The emergency management responsibilities of department and agency heads include:

- Collaborating with the emergency manager during the development of local emergency plans and providing key response resources
- Participating in the planning process to ensure that specific capabilities (e.g., firefighting, law enforcement, emergency medical services, public works, environmental and natural resources agencies) are integrated into a workable plan to safeguard the community
- Developing, planning, and training to internal policies and procedures to meet response and recovery needs safely
- Participating in interagency training and exercises to develop and maintain the necessary capabilities

Individuals and Households

Although not formally a part of emergency management operations, individuals and households are considered as playing an important role in the overall emergency management strategy under the NRF. Specifically, the NRF states that community members can contribute by:

- Reducing hazards in and around their homes
- Preparing an emergency supply kit and household emergency plan

- Monitoring emergency communications carefully
- Volunteering with an established organization
- Enrolling in emergency response training courses

Private Sector and NGOs

In almost every large-scale emergency incident, and some small-scale ones, the government must work together with private-sector and NGO groups as partners in emergency management. The roles of private-sector organizations include:

- Providing for the welfare and protection of their employees in the workplace
- Private-sector components of the nation's critical infrastructure, including water, power, communications, transportation, medical care, security, and numerous other services, must work together with emergency managers to ensure effective response and recovery
- Planning for the protection of information and the continuity of business operations
- Planning for, responding to, and recovering from incidents that impact their own infrastructure and facilities
- Collaborating with emergency management personnel before an incident occurs to ascertain what assistance may be necessary and how they can help
- Developing and exercising emergency plans before an incident occurs
- Establishing mutual aid and assistance agreements, where appropriate, to provide specific response capabilities
- Providing assistance (including volunteers) to support local emergency management and public awareness during response and throughout the recovery process

Participation of the private sector varies based on the nature of the organization and the nature of the incident. The five distinct roles that private-sector organizations play are summarized in Table 9–3.

The NRF states that NGOs play "enormously important roles before, during, and after an incident." NGOs provide sheltering, emergency food supplies, counseling services, and other vital support services to support response and promote the recovery of disaster victims. These groups often provide specialized services that help individuals with special needs, including those with disabilities. NGOs bolster and support government efforts at all levels — for response operations and planning. NGOs impacted by a disaster may also need government assistance. NGOs collaborate with responders, governments at all levels, and other agencies and organizations. Examples of NGO and voluntary organization contributions include:

- Training and managing volunteer resources
- Identifying shelter locations and needed supplies
- Providing critical emergency services to those in need, such as cleaning supplies, clothing, food and shelter, or assistance with postemergency cleanup
- Identifying those whose needs have not been met and helping coordinate the provision of assistance

State, Territorial, and Tribal Governments

The primary emergency management role of state, territorial, and tribal governments is to supplement and facilitate local efforts before, during, and after an emergency incident occurs. These government agencies provide direct and routine assistance to their local jurisdictions through emergency management program

Table 9–3 Private-Sector Response Role under NRF

Category	Role in This Category
Impacted organization or infrastructure	Private-sector organizations may be impacted by direct or indirect consequences of the incident. These include privately owned critical infrastructure, key resources, and other private-sector entities that are significant to local, regional, and national economic recovery from the incident. Examples of privately owned infrastructure include transportation, telecommunications, private utilities, financial institutions, and hospitals. Critical infrastructure and key resources (CIKR) are grouped into 17 sectors that together provide essential functions and services supporting various aspects of the American government, economy, and society.
Regulated and/or responsible party	Owners/operators of certain regulated facilities or hazardous operations may be legally responsible for preparing for and preventing incidents from occurring and responding to an incident once it occurs. For example, federal regulations require owners/operators of nuclear power plants to maintain emergency plans and facilities and to perform assessments, prompt notifications, and training for a response to an incident.
Response resource	Private-sector entities provide response resources (donated or compensated) during an incident — including specialized teams, essential service providers, equipment, and advanced technologies — through local public–private emergency plans or mutual aid and assistance agreements, or in response to requests from government and nongovernmental-volunteer initiatives.
Partner with state/local emergency organizations	Private-sector entities may serve as partners in local and state emergency preparedness and response organizations and activities.
Components of nation's economy	As the key element of the national economy, private-sector resilience and continuity of operations planning, as well as recovery and restoration from an actual incident, represent essential homeland security activities.

development and by routinely coordinating these efforts with federal officials. They must be prepared to maintain or accelerate the provision of commodities and services to local governments when local capabilities fall short of demands. The roles and responsibilities of the following individuals are described in greater detail in the NRF.

Governor

The public safety and welfare of a state's citizens are fundamental responsibilities of the governor. The governor:

- Is responsible for coordinating state resources and providing the strategic guidance needed to prevent, mitigate, prepare for, respond to, and recover from incidents of all types
- May be able to make, amend, or suspend, in accordance with state law, certain orders or regulations associated with response
- Communicates to the public and helps people, businesses, and organizations cope with the consequences of any type of incident
- Commands the state military forces (National Guard personnel not in federal service and state militias)
- Coordinates assistance from other states through interstate mutual aid and assistance compacts, such as the EMAC

- Requests federal assistance including, if appropriate, a Stafford Act presidential declaration of an emergency or major disaster, when it becomes clear that state capabilities will be insufficient or have been exceeded
- Coordinates with impacted tribal governments within the state and initiates requests for a Stafford Act presidential declaration of an emergency or major disaster on behalf of an impacted tribe when appropriate

State Homeland Security Advisor

The State Homeland Security Advisor serves as a counsel to the governor on homeland security issues and may serve as a liaison between the governor's office, the state homeland security structure, DHS, and other organizations both inside and outside of the state. The adviser often chairs a committee composed of representatives of relevant state agencies, including public safety, the National Guard, emergency management, public health, and others charged with developing prevention, protection, response, and recovery strategies. This also includes preparedness activities associated with these strategies.

Director, State Emergency Management Agency

All states have laws mandating establishment of a state emergency management agency and the emergency plans coordinated by that agency. The state Director of Emergency Management ensures that the state is prepared to deal with large-scale emergencies and is responsible for coordinating the state response in any incident. This includes supporting local governments as needed or requested and coordinating assistance with other states and/or the federal government. If local resources are not adequate, authorities can seek additional assistance from the county emergency manager or the state Director of Emergency Management. The state emergency management agency may dispatch personnel to the scene to assist in the response and recovery effort.

Other State Departments and Agencies

State department and agency heads and their staffs develop, plan, and train to internal policies and procedures to meet response and recovery needs safely. They also participate in interagency training and exercises to develop and maintain the necessary capabilities. They are vital to the state's overall emergency management and homeland security programs, as they bring expertise spanning the NRF's ESFs and serve as core members of the state emergency operations center (EOC).

Indian Tribes

The U.S. government has a trust relationship with Indian tribes and recognizes their right to self-government. As such, tribal governments are responsible for coordinating resources to address actual or potential incidents. When local resources are not adequate, tribal leaders seek assistance from states or the federal government. For certain types of federal assistance, tribal governments work with the state, but as sovereign entities they can elect to deal directly with the federal government for other types of assistance. To obtain federal assistance via the Stafford Act, a state governor must request a presidential declaration on behalf of a tribe. The tribal leader is responsible for the public safety and welfare of the people of that tribe. As authorized by tribal government, the tribal leader:

- Is responsible for coordinating tribal resources needed to prevent, protect against, respond to, and recover from incidents of all types. This also includes preparedness and mitigation activities
- May have powers to amend or suspend certain tribal laws or ordinances associated with response

- Communicates with the tribal community, and helps people, businesses, and organizations cope with the consequences of any type of incident
- Negotiates mutual aid and assistance agreements with other tribes or jurisdictions
- Can request federal assistance under the Stafford Act through the governor of the state when it becomes clear that the tribe's capabilities will be insufficient or have been exceeded
- Can elect to deal directly with the federal government. Although a state governor must request a presidential declaration on behalf of a tribe under the Stafford Act, federal departments or agencies can work directly with the tribe within existing authorities and resources

Federal Government

When an incident occurs that exceeds or is anticipated to exceed local or state resources — or when an incident is managed by federal departments or agencies acting under their own authorities — the federal government uses the NRF to involve all necessary department and agency capabilities, organize the federal response, and ensure coordination with response partners. Under the NRF, the federal government's response structures are adaptable specifically to the nature and scope of a given incident. The principles of UC are applied at the headquarters, regional, and field levels to enable diverse departments and agencies to work together effectively. Using UC principles, participants share common goals and synchronize their activities to achieve those goals.

Coordination of Federal Responsibilities

The president leads the federal government response effort to ensure that the necessary coordinating structures, leadership, and resources are applied quickly and efficiently to large-scale and catastrophic incidents. The president's Homeland Security Council (HSC) and National Security Council (NSC), which bring together cabinet officers and other department or agency heads as necessary, provide national strategic and policy advice to the president during large-scale incidents that affect the nation.

Federal assistance can be provided to state, tribal, and local jurisdictions, and to other federal departments and agencies, in a number of different ways through various mechanisms and authorities. Federal assistance does not require coordination by DHS, and can be provided without a presidential major disaster or emergency declaration (as is the case with the National Oil and Hazardous Substances Pollution Contingency Plan, the Mass Migration Emergency Plan, the National Search and Rescue Plan, and the National Maritime Security Plan).

When the overall coordination of federal response activities is required, it is implemented through the Secretary of Homeland Security. Other federal departments and agencies carry out their response authorities and responsibilities within this authority and direction. Several presidential directives outline the following primary lanes of responsibility that guide federal support at national, regional, and field levels.

Incident Management

The Secretary of Homeland Security is the principal federal official for domestic incident management. By presidential directive and statute, the Secretary is responsible for coordination of federal resources utilized in the prevention of, preparation for, response to, or recovery from terrorist attacks, major disasters, or other emergencies. The role of the Secretary of Homeland Security is to provide the president with an overall architecture for domestic incident management and to coordinate the federal response, when required, while relying upon the support of other federal partners. Depending on the incident, the Secretary also contributes elements of the response consistent with DHS's mission, capabilities, and authorities.

The FEMA administrator, as the principal advisor to the President, the Secretary, and the HSC on all matters regarding emergency management, helps the Secretary in meeting these responsibilities. Federal assistance for incidents that do not require DHS coordination may be led by other federal departments and agencies consistent with their authorities. The Secretary of Homeland Security may monitor such incidents and may activate specific NRF mechanisms to provide support to departments and agencies without assuming overall leadership for the federal response to the incident. The following four criteria define situations for which DHS shall assume overall federal incident management coordination responsibilities within the NSF and implement the NSF's coordinating mechanisms:

- A federal department or agency acting under its own authority has requested DHS assistance.
- The resources of state and local authorities are overwhelmed and federal assistance has been requested.
- More than one federal department or agency has become substantially involved in responding to the incident
- The Secretary has been directed by the President to assume incident management responsibilities

Law Enforcement

- The attorney general is the chief law enforcement officer of the United States. Generally acting through the FBI, the attorney general has the lead responsibility for criminal investigations of terrorist acts or terrorist threats by individuals or groups inside the United States or directed at U.S. citizens or institutions abroad, as well as for coordinating activities of the other members of the law enforcement community to detect, prevent, and disrupt terrorist attacks against the United States. This includes actions that are based on specific intelligence or law enforcement information. In addition, the attorney general approves requests submitted by state governors pursuant to the Emergency Federal Law Enforcement Assistance Act for personnel and other federal law enforcement support during incidents. The attorney general also enforces federal civil rights laws and will provide expertise to ensure that these laws are appropriately addressed.

National Defense and Defense Support of Civil Authorities

The primary mission of the DOD and its components is national defense. Because of this critical role, resources are committed after approval by the Secretary of Defense or at the direction of the president. Many DOD components and agencies are authorized to respond to save lives, protect property and the environment, and mitigate human suffering under imminently serious conditions, as well as to provide support under their separate established authorities, as appropriate. The provision of Defense support is evaluated by its legality, lethality, risk, cost, appropriateness, and impact on readiness. When federal military and civilian personnel and resources are authorized to support civil authorities, command of those forces will remain with the Secretary of Defense. DOD elements in the incident area of operations and National Guard forces under the command of a governor will coordinate closely with response organizations at all levels.

International Coordination

The Secretary of State is responsible for managing international preparedness, response, and recovery activities relating to domestic incidents and the protection of U.S. citizens and U.S. interests overseas.

Intelligence

The Director of National Intelligence leads the intelligence community, serves as the President's principal intelligence advisor, and oversees and directs the implementation of the National Intelligence Program.

Other Federal Departments and Agencies

Under the NRF, various federal departments or agencies may play primary, coordinating, and/or support roles based on their authorities and resources and the nature of the threat or incident. In situations where a federal department or agency has responsibility for directing or managing a major aspect of a response being coordinated by DHS, that organization is part of the national leadership for the incident and is represented in the field at the JFO in the Unified Coordination Group, and at headquarters through the NOC and the NRCC, which is part of the NOC. In addition, several federal departments and agencies have their own authorities to declare disasters or emergencies. For example, the Secretary of Health and Human Services can declare a public health emergency. These declarations may be made independently or as part of a coordinated federal response. Where those declarations are part of an incident requiring a coordinated federal response, those federal departments or agencies act within the overall coordination structure of the NSF.

Response Actions under the NRF

The NRF was created to strengthen, organize, and coordinate emergency response actions across all levels of government and with all involved stakeholders. The NRF reiterates the long-standing notion that incident response should begin and continue at the lowest jurisdictional level capable of handling the required actions. The NRF applies to incidents of all types, including acts of terrorism, major disasters, and other emergencies. The NRF core document describes and outlines key tasks related to the three phases of an effective response capacity, namely, prepare, respond, and recover. An overview of the key tasks associated with response is provided below.

Depending on the size, scope, and magnitude of an incident, communities, states, and, in some cases, the federal government will be called to action. Four key actions typically occur in support of a response.

Gain and Maintain Situational Awareness
Baseline Priorities

Situational awareness requires continuous monitoring of relevant sources of information regarding actual and developing incidents. The scope and type of monitoring vary based on the types of incidents being evaluated and needed reporting thresholds. Critical information is passed through established reporting channels according to established security protocols. Priorities are summarized as follows.

> *Providing the right information at the right time*: For an effective national response, jurisdictions must continuously refine their ability to assess the situation as an incident unfolds and rapidly provide accurate and accessible information to decision makers in a user-friendly manner. It is essential that all levels of government, the private sector (in particular, owners/operators of critical infrastructure and key resources [CIKR]), and NGOs share information to develop a common operating picture and synchronize their response operations and resources.
>
> *Improving and integrating national reporting*: Situational awareness must start at the incident scene and be effectively communicated to local, tribal, state, and federal governments and the private sector, to include CIKR. Jurisdictions must integrate existing reporting systems to develop an information and knowledge management system that fulfills national information requirements.

Linking operations centers and tapping subject-matter experts: Local governments, tribes, states, and the federal government have a wide range of operations centers that monitor events and provide situational awareness. Based on their roles and responsibilities, operations centers should identify information requirements, establish reporting thresholds, and be familiar with the expectations of decision makers and partners. Situational awareness is greatly improved when experienced technical specialists identify critical elements of information and use them to form a common operating picture.

Local, Tribal, and State Actions

Local, tribal, and state governments can address the inherent challenges in establishing successful information-sharing networks by:

- Creating fusion centers that bring together into one central location law enforcement, intelligence, emergency management, public health, and other agencies, as well as private-sector and NGOs when appropriate, and that have the capabilities to evaluate and act appropriately on all available information
- Implementing the National Information Sharing Guidelines to share intelligence and information and improve the ability of systems to exchange data
- Establishing information requirements and reporting protocols to enable effective and timely decision making during response to incidents. Terrorist threats and actual incidents with a potential or actual terrorist link should be reported immediately to a local or regional Joint Terrorism Task Force

Federal Actions

The NOC serves as the national fusion center, collecting and synthesizing all source information, including information from state fusion centers, across all-threats and all-hazards information covering the spectrum of homeland security partners. Federal departments and agencies should report information regarding actual or potential incidents requiring a coordinated federal response to the NOC. Such information may include:

- Implementation of a federal department or agency emergency plan
- Actions to prevent or respond to an incident requiring a coordinated federal response for which a federal department or agency has responsibility under law or directive
- Submission of requests for coordinated federal assistance to, or receipt of a request from, another federal department or agency
- Requests for coordinated federal assistance from state, tribal, or local governments, the private sector, and NGOs
- Suspicious activities or threats, which are closely coordinated among the DOJ/FBI SIOC, the NOC, and the National Counterterrorism Center (NCTC)

The primary reporting method for information flow is the Homeland Security Information Network (HSIN). Additionally, there are threat-reporting mechanisms in place through the FBI where information is assessed for credibility and possible criminal investigation. Each federal department and agency must work with DHS to ensure that its response personnel have access to and are trained to use the HSIN common operating picture for incident reporting.

Alerts

When notified of a threat or an incident that potentially requires a coordinated federal response, the NOC evaluates the information and notifies appropriate senior federal officials and federal operations centers: the NRCC, the FBI SIOC, the NCTC, and the National Military Command Center (NMCC). The NOC serves as the primary coordinating center for these and other operations centers. The NOC alerts department and agency leadership to critical information to inform decision making. Based on that information, the Secretary of Homeland Security coordinates with other appropriate departments and agencies to activate plans and applicable coordination structures of the NRF as required. Officials should be prepared to participate, either in person or by secure video teleconference, with departments or agencies involved in responding to the incident. The NOC maintains the common operating picture that provides overall situational awareness for incident information. Each federal department and agency must ensure that its response personnel are trained to utilize these tools.

Operations Centers

Federal operations centers maintain active situational awareness and communications within and among federal departments and agency regional, district, and sector offices across the country. These operations centers are often connected with their state, tribal, and local counterparts, and can exchange information and draw and direct resources in the event of an incident.

Activate and Deploy Resources and Capabilities
Baseline Priorities

When an incident or potential incident occurs, responders assess the situation, identify and prioritize requirements, and activate available resources and capabilities to save lives, protect property and the environment, and meet basic human needs. In most cases, this includes development of incident objectives based on incident priorities, development of an incident action plan by the incident command in the field, and development of support plans by the appropriate local, tribal, state, and/or federal government entities. Key activities are summarized in the following:

> *Activating people, resources, and capabilities*: Across all levels, initial actions may include activation of people and teams and establishment of incident management and response structures to organize and coordinate an effective response. The resources and capabilities deployed and the activation of supporting incident management structures should be directly related to the size, scope, nature, and complexity of the incident. All responders should maintain and regularly exercise notification systems and protocols.
>
> *Requesting additional resources and capabilities*: Responders and capabilities may be requested through mutual aid and assistance agreements, the state, or the federal government. For all incidents, especially large-scale incidents, it is essential to prioritize and clearly communicate incident requirements so that resources can be efficiently matched, typed, and mobilized to support operations.
>
> *Identifying needs and pre-positioning resources*: When planning for heightened threats or in anticipation of large-scale incidents, local or tribal jurisdictions, states, or the federal government should anticipate resources and capabilities that may be needed. Based on asset availability,

resources should be pre-positioned and response teams and other support resources may be placed on alert or deployed to a staging area. As noted above, mobilization and deployment will be most effective when supported by planning that includes prescripted mission assignments, advance readiness contracting, and staged resources.

Local, Tribal, and State Actions

In the event of, or in anticipation of, an incident requiring a coordinated response, local, tribal, and state jurisdictions should:

- Identify staff for deployment to the EOC, which should have standard procedures and call-down lists to notify department and agency points of contact
- Work with emergency management officials to take the necessary steps to provide for continuity of operations
- Activate incident management teams (IMTs) as required. IMTs are incident command organizations made up of the command and general staff members and appropriate functional units of an ICS organization. The level of training and experience of the IMT members, coupled with the identified formal response requirements and responsibilities of the IMT, are factors in determining the "type," or level, of the IMT
- Activate specialized response teams as required. Jurisdictions may have specialized teams including search and rescue teams, crime scene investigators, public works teams, hazardous materials response teams, public health specialists, or veterinarians/animal response teams
- Activate mutual aid and assistance agreements as required

Federal Actions

In the event of, or in anticipation of, an incident requiring a coordinated federal response, the NOC, in many cases acting through the NRCC, notifies other federal departments and agencies of the situation and specifies the level of activation required. After being notified, departments and agencies should:

- Identify and mobilize staff to fulfill their department's or agency's responsibilities, including identifying appropriate subject-matter experts and other staff to support department operations centers.
- Identify staff for deployment to the NOC, the NRCC, FEMA Regional Response Coordination Centers (RRCCs), or other operations centers as needed, such as the FBI's Joint Operations Center. These organizations have standard procedures and call-down lists, and will notify department or agency points of contact if deployment is necessary.
- Identify staff who can be dispatched to the JFO, including federal officials representing those departments and agencies with specific authorities, lead personnel for the JFO sections (Operations, Planning, Logistics, and Administration and Finance), and the ESFs.
- Begin activating and staging federal teams and other resources in support of the federal response as requested by DHS or in accordance with department or agency authorities (Figure 9–13).
- Execute prescribed mission assignments and readiness contracts, as directed by DHS.

FIGURE 9–13 Joplin, MO, May 25, 2011 — An Applicant Services Specialist assists one of the survivors of the Joplin tornado with the FEMA registration process. Disaster Recovery Centers, like this one in a local Methodist church, are set up for survivors to register for assistance and get questions answered about the recovery process. Registering with FEMA starts the process for survivors to receive aid. (Source: Photo by Jace Anderson/FEMA)

Coordinate Response Actions
Baseline Priorities

Coordination of response activities occurs through response structures based on assigned roles, responsibilities, and reporting protocols. Critical information is provided through established reporting mechanisms. The efficiency and effectiveness of response operations are enhanced by full application of the NIMS with its common principles, structures, and coordinating processes. Specific priorities include the following.

Managing emergency functions: Local, tribal, and state governments are responsible for the management of their emergency functions. Such management includes mobilizing the National Guard, pre-positioning assets, and supporting communities. Local, tribal, and state governments, in conjunction with their voluntary organization partners, are also responsible for implementing plans to ensure the effective management of the flow of volunteers and goods in the affected area.

Coordinating initial actions: Initial actions are coordinated through the on-scene incident command and may include immediate law enforcement, rescue, firefighting, and emergency medical services; emergency flood fighting; evacuations; transportation detours; and emergency information for the public. As the incident unfolds, the on-scene incident command develops and updates an incident action plan, revising courses of action based on changing circumstances.

Coordinating requests for additional support: If additional resources are required, the on-scene incident command requests the needed support. Additional incident management and response structures and personnel are activated to support the response. It is critical that personnel understand roles, structures, protocols, and concepts to ensure clear, coordinated actions.

Resources are activated through established procedures and integrated into a standardized organizational structure at the appropriate levels.

Identifying and integrating resources and capabilities: Resources and capabilities must be deployed, received, staged, and efficiently integrated into ongoing operations. For large, complex incidents, this may include working with a diverse array of organizations, including multiple private-sector entities and NGOs through prearranged agreements and contracts. Large-scale events may also require sophisticated coordination and time-phased deployment of resources through an integrated logistics system. Systems and venues must be established to receive, stage, track, and integrate resources into ongoing operations. Incident command should continually assess operations and scale and adapt existing plans to meet evolving circumstances.

Coordinating information: Effective public information strategies are essential following an incident. Incident command may elect to establish a JIC, a physical location where the coordination and dissemination of information for the public and media concerning the incident are managed. JICs may be established locally, regionally, or nationally depending on the size and magnitude of an incident. In the event of incidents requiring a coordinated federal response, JICs are established to coordinate federal, state, tribal, local, and private-sector incident communications with the public. By developing media lists, contact information for relevant stakeholders, and coordinated news releases, the JIC staff facilitates dissemination of accurate, consistent, accessible, and timely public information to numerous audiences.

Local, Tribal, and State Actions

Within communities, NIMS principles are applied to integrate response plans and resources across jurisdictions and departments and with the private sector and NGOs. Neighboring communities play a key role in providing support through a framework of mutual aid and assistance agreements. These agreements are formal documents that identify the resources that communities are willing to share during an incident. Such agreements should include:

- Definitions of key terms used in the agreement
- Roles and responsibilities of individual parties
- Procedures for requesting and providing assistance
- Procedures, authorities, and rules for allocation and reimbursement of costs
- Notification procedures
- Protocols for interoperable communications
- Relationships with other agreements among jurisdictions
- Treatment of workers' compensation, liability, and immunity
- Recognition of qualifications and certifications

States provide the majority of the external assistance to communities. The state is the gateway to several government programs that help communities prepare. When an incident grows beyond the capability of a local jurisdiction, and responders cannot meet the needs with mutual aid and assistance resources, the local emergency manager contacts the state. Upon receiving a request for assistance from a local government, immediate state response activities may include:

- Coordinating warnings and public information through the activation of the state's public communications strategy and the establishment of a JIC

- Distributing supplies stockpiled to meet the emergency
- Providing needed technical assistance and support to meet the response and recovery needs of individuals and households
- Suspending existing statutes, rules, ordinances, and orders by the governor for the duration of the emergency, to the extent permitted by law, to ensure timely performance of response functions
- Implementing state donations management plans and coordinating with NGOs and the private sector
- Ordering the evacuation of persons from any portions of the state threatened by the incident, giving consideration to the requirements of special needs populations and those with household pets or service animals
- Mobilizing resources to meet the requirements of people with special needs, in accordance with the state's preexisting plan and in compliance with federal civil rights laws

In addition to these actions, the Governor may activate elements of the National Guard. The National Guard is a crucial state resource, with expertise in communications, logistics, search and rescue, and decontamination. National Guard forces employed under State Active Duty or Title 32 status are under the command and control of the governor of their state and are not part of federal military response efforts. Title 32 Full-Time National Guard Duty refers to federal training or other duty, other than inactive duty, performed by a member of the National Guard. Title 32 is not subject to Posse Comitatus restrictions, and allows the governor, with the approval of the president or the Secretary of Defense, to order a guard member to:

- Perform training and other operational activities
- Conduct homeland defense activities for the military protection of the territory or domestic population of the United States, or of the infrastructure or other assets of the United States determined by the Secretary of Defense to be critical to national security, from a threat or aggression against the United States

State-to-State Assistance

If additional resources are required, the state should request assistance from other states by using interstate mutual aid and assistance agreements such as the EMAC. Administered by the NEMA, EMAC is a congressionally ratified organization that provides form and structure to the interstate mutual aid and assistance process. Through EMAC or other mutual aid or assistance agreements, a state can request and receive assistance from other member states. Such state-to-state assistance may include:

- Invoking and administering a statewide mutual aid agreement, as well as coordinating the allocation of resources under that agreement
- Invoking and administering EMAC and/or other compacts and agreements, and coordinating the allocation of resources that are made available to and from other states

Requesting Federal Assistance

When an incident overwhelms or is anticipated to overwhelm state resources, the Governor may request federal assistance. In such cases, the affected local jurisdiction, tribe, state, and the federal government will collaborate to provide the necessary assistance. The federal government may provide assistance in the form of funding, resources, and critical services. Federal departments and agencies respect the sovereignty and responsibilities of local, tribal, and state governments while rendering assistance. The intention of the federal government in these situations is not to command the response, but rather to support the affected local, tribal, and/or state governments.

Robert T. Stafford Disaster Relief and Emergency Assistance Act

When it is clear that state capabilities will be exceeded, the governor can request federal assistance, including assistance under the Robert T. Stafford Disaster Relief and Emergency Assistance Act (Stafford Act). The Stafford Act authorizes the president to provide financial and other assistance to state and local governments, certain private nonprofit organizations, and individuals to support response, recovery, and mitigation efforts following presidential emergency or major disaster declarations. The Stafford Act is triggered by a presidential declaration of a major disaster or emergency, when an event causes damage of sufficient severity and magnitude to warrant federal disaster assistance to supplement the efforts and available resources of state, local governments, and the disaster relief organizations in alleviating the damage, loss, hardship, or suffering.

Proactive Response to Catastrophic Incidents

Prior to and during catastrophic incidents, especially those that occur with little or no notice, the state and federal governments may take proactive measures to mobilize and deploy assets in anticipation of a formal request from the state for federal assistance. Such deployments of significant federal assets would likely occur for catastrophic events involving chemical, biological, radiological, nuclear, or high-yield explosive WMDs, large-magnitude earthquakes, or other catastrophic incidents affecting heavily populated areas. The proactive responses are utilized to ensure that resources reach the scene in a timely manner to assist in restoring any disruption of normal function of state or local governments. Proactive notification and deployment of federal resources in anticipation of or in response to catastrophic events will be done in coordination and collaboration with state, tribal, and local governments, and private-sector entities when possible.

Federal Assistance Available without a Presidential Declaration

In many cases, assistance may be obtained from the federal government without a presidential declaration. For example, FEMA places liaisons in state EOCs and moves commodities near incident sites that may require federal assistance prior to a presidential declaration. Additionally, some types of assistance, such as Fire Management Assistance Grants — which provide support to states experiencing severe wildfires — are performed by federal departments or agencies under their own authorities and do not require presidential approval. Finally, federal departments and agencies may provide immediate lifesaving assistance to states under their own statutory authorities without a formal presidential declaration.

Other Federal or Federally Facilitated Assistance

The NRF covers the full range of complex and constantly changing requirements in anticipation of, or in response to, threats or actual incidents, including terrorism and major disasters. In addition to Stafford Act support, the NRF may be applied to provide other forms of support to federal partners. Federal departments and agencies must remain flexible and adaptable in order to provide the support that is required for a particular incident.

Federal-to-Federal Support

Federal departments and agencies execute interagency or intra-agency reimbursable agreements, in accordance with the Economy Act or other applicable authorities. The NRF's Financial

Management Support Annex contains additional information on this process. Additionally, a federal department or agency responding to an incident under its own jurisdictional authorities may request DHS coordination to obtain additional federal assistance. In such cases, DHS may activate one or more ESF to coordinate required support. Federal departments and agencies must plan for federal-to-federal support missions, to identify additional issues that may arise when providing assistance to other federal departments and agencies, and to address those issues in the planning process. When providing federal-to-federal support, DHS may designate a federal resource coordinator to perform the resource coordination function.

International Assistance

A domestic incident may have international and diplomatic implications that call for coordination and consultations with foreign governments and international organizations. An incident may also require direct bilateral and multilateral actions on foreign affairs issues related to the incident. The Department of State has responsibility for coordinating bilateral and multilateral actions and for coordinating international assistance. International coordination within the context of a domestic incident requires close cooperative efforts with foreign counterparts, multilateral/international organizations, and the private sector. Federal departments and agencies should consider in advance what resources or other assistance they may require or be asked to accept from foreign sources and address issues that may arise in receiving such resources. Detailed information on coordination with international partners is further defined in the International Coordination Support Annex.

Response Activities

Specific response actions will vary depending on the scope and nature of an incident. Response actions are based on the objectives established by the incident command and JFO's Unified Coordination Group. Detailed information about the full range of potential response capabilities is contained in the Emergency Support Function Annexes, Incident Annexes, and Support Annexes.

Department and Agency Activities

Federal departments and agencies, upon receiving notification or activation requests, implement their specific emergency plans to activate resources and organize their response actions. Department and agency plans should incorporate procedures for:

- Designation of department or agency representatives for interagency coordination, and identification of state, tribal, and local points of contact
- Activation of coordination groups managed by the department or agency in accordance with roles and responsibilities
- Activation, mobilization, deployment, and ongoing status reporting for resource-typed teams with responsibilities for providing capabilities under the NRF
- Readiness to execute mission assignments in response to requests for assistance (including prescripted mission assignments), and to support all levels of department or agency participation in the response, at both the field and the national levels
- Ensuring that department or agency resources (e.g., personnel, teams, or equipment) fit into the interagency structures and processes set out in the framework

Regional Response Activities

The FEMA regional administrator deploys a liaison to the state EOC to provide technical assistance and also activates the RRCC. Federal department and agency personnel, including ESF primary and support agency personnel, staff the RRCC as required. The RRCCs:

- Coordinate initial regional and field activities
- Deploy regional teams, in coordination with state, tribal, and local officials, to assess the impact of the event, gauge immediate state needs, and make preliminary arrangements to set up operational field facilities
- Coordinate federal support until a JFO is established
- Establish a JIC to provide a central point for coordinating emergency public information activities

Incident Management Assistance Team

In coordination with the RRCC and the state, FEMA may deploy an Incident Management Assistance Team (IMAT). IMATs are interagency teams composed of subject-matter experts and incident management professionals. IMAT personnel may be drawn from national or regional federal department and agency staff according to established protocols. IMAT teams make preliminary arrangements to set up federal field facilities and initiate establishment of the JFO.

Emergency Support Functions

The NRCC or RRCC may also activate specific ESFs by directing appropriate departments and agencies to initiate the initial actions delineated in the ESF Annexes.

Demobilize

Demobilization is the orderly, safe, and efficient return of a resource to its original location and status. It should begin as soon as possible to facilitate accountability of the resources and be fully coordinated with other incident management and response structures.

Local, Tribal, and State Actions

At the local, tribal, and state levels, demobilization planning and activities should include:

- Provisions to address and validate the safe return of resources to their original locations
- Processes for tracking resources and ensuring applicable reimbursement
- Accountability for compliance with mutual aid and assistance provisions

Federal Actions

The Unified Coordination Group oversees the development of an exit strategy and a demobilization plan. As the need for full-time interagency response coordination at the JFO wanes, the Unified Coordination Group plans for selective release of federal resources, demobilization, transfer of responsibilities, and closeout. The JFO, however, continues to operate as needed into the recovery phase to coordinate those resources that are still active. ESF representatives assist in demobilizing resources and organizing their orderly return to regular operations, warehouses, or other locations.

Key NRF Concepts

The key concepts, systems, and components upon which the NRF was built were drawn directly from the NIMS. This close association has resulted in a core set of common concepts, principles, terminology, and technologies that exist throughout both documents. These key concepts, systems, and components are described in the following sections.

Incident Command System

The NIMS concept is modeled upon the Incident Command System (ICS), which was developed by the federal, state, and local wildland fire agencies during the 1970s. ICS is structured to facilitate activities in five major functional areas: command, operations, planning, logistics, and finance/administration. In some circumstances, intelligence and investigations may be added as a sixth functional area.

Multiagency Coordination System

The Multiagency Coordination System (MACS) is designed to help coordinate activities that occur above the field level, and to prioritize demands for critical or competing resources. Examples of multiagency coordination include a state or county EOC, a state intelligence fusion center, the NOC, the FEMA National Response Coordination Center, the DOJ/FBI SIOC, the FBI Joint Operations Center, and the National Counterterrorism Center.

Unified Command

Unified command allows for more efficient multijurisdictional or multiagency management of emergency events. It enables agencies with different legal, geographic, and functional responsibilities to coordinate, plan, and interact with each other in an effective manner. UC allows all agencies with jurisdictional authority or functional responsibility for the incident to jointly provide management direction to an incident through a common set of incident objectives and strategies and a single Incident Action Plan. Under unified command, each participating agency maintains its authority, responsibility, and accountability.

Field-Level Incident Command

Under the NRF, local responders use ICS to manage response operations. ICS is designed to enable effective incident management by integrating a combination of facilities, equipment, personnel, procedures, and communications operating within a common organizational structure. A basic strength of ICS is that it is already widely adopted and used in incidents of any size. Typically, the incident command is structured to facilitate activities in five major functional areas: command, operations, planning, logistics, and finance/administration. ICS defines certain key roles for managing an ICS incident, as follows.

> The incident commander is the individual responsible for all response activities, including the development of strategies and tactics and the ordering and release of resources. The incident commander has overall authority and responsibility for conducting incident operations and is responsible for the management of all incident operations at the incident site.
> When multiple command authorities are involved, the incident may be led by a UC composed of officials who have jurisdictional authority or functional responsibility for the incident under an appropriate law, ordinance, or agreement. The UC provides direct, on-scene control of tactical operations.

The command staff consists of a public information officer, safety officer, liaison officer, and other positions. The command staff reports directly to the incident commander.

The general staff normally consists of an operations section chief, planning section chief, logistics section chief, and finance/administration section chief. An intelligence/investigations section may be established, if required, to meet response needs.

At the tactical level, on-scene incident command and management organization are located at an incident command post, which is typically composed of local and mutual aid responders.

Field-Level Area Command

If necessary, an area command may be established to assist the executive official that is responsible for providing management oversight for multiple incidents being handled by separate incident command posts or to oversee management of a complex incident dispersed over a larger area. The area command does not have operational responsibilities and is activated only if necessary, depending on the complexity of the incident and incident management span-of-control considerations. The area command or incident command post provides information to, and may request assistance from, the local EOC.

Local Emergency Operations Center

Local EOCs are the physical locations where multiagency coordination occurs. EOCs are used to establish an operational "picture" of the incident, provide external coordination for OSCs, and secure additional resources as needed. The core functions of an EOC include coordination, communications, resource allocation and tracking, and information collection, analysis, and dissemination. EOCs may be permanent organizations and facilities staffed 24 hours a day, 7 days a week, or they may be established only as required. Standing EOCs are typically directed by a full-time emergency manager. EOCs may be organized by major discipline (fire, law enforcement, medical services, etc.), by jurisdiction (city, county, region, etc.), by ESF (communications, public works, engineering, transportation, resource support, etc.), or, more likely, by some combination thereof. The chief elected or appointed official provides policy direction and supports the incident commander and emergency manager, as needed.

State Emergency Operations Center

State EOCs are the physical location where state agency emergency management coordination efforts occur. Every state maintains an EOC that can expand as necessary to manage events requiring state-level assistance. The local incident command structure directs on-scene emergency management activities and maintains command and control of on-scene incident operations, whereas state EOCs are activated only in support of local EOCs. The key function of state EOC personnel is to ensure that state agency personnel who are located at the scene have the necessary response resources.

Joint Information Center

To coordinate the release of emergency information and other public affairs functions, a JIC may be established. The JIC serves as a focal point for coordinated and timely release of incident-related information to the public and the media. Information about where to receive assistance is communicated directly to victims and their families in an accessible format and in appropriate languages.

Joint Field Office

Federal incident support to the state is generally coordinated through a JFO. The JFO provides the means to integrate diverse federal resources and engage directly with the state. Within the JFO, there is one key operational group and two key officials.

Unified Coordination Group

The Unified Coordination Group is composed of senior officials from the state and key federal departments and agencies, and is established at the JFO. Using UC principles, this group provides national support to achieve shared emergency response and recovery objectives.

State Coordinating Officer

The SCO plays a critical role in managing the state response and recovery operations following presidential disaster declarations. The governor of the affected state appoints the SCO, and lines of authority flow from the governor to the SCO, following the state's policies and laws. For events in which a declaration has not yet occurred but is expected (such as with an approaching hurricane), the Secretary of Homeland Security or the FEMA administrator may predesignate one or more federal officials to coordinate with the SCO to determine resources and actions that will likely be required and begin deployment of assets. The specific roles and responsibilities of the SCO include:

- Serving as the primary representative of the governor for the affected state or locality with the RRCC (see above) or within the JFO once it is established
- Working with the federal coordinating officer to formulate state requirements, including those that are beyond state capability, and to set priorities for employment of federal resources provided to the state
- Ensuring coordination of resources provided to the state via mutual aid and assistance compacts
- Providing a linkage to local government
- Serving in the Unified Coordination Group in the JFO

Governor's Authorized Representative

As the complexity of the response dictates, the NRF recognizes that the governor may empower a governor's authorized representative to:

- Execute all necessary documents for disaster assistance on behalf of the state, including certification of applications for public assistance
- Represent the governor of the impacted state in the Unified Coordination Group, when required
- Coordinate and supervise the state disaster assistance program to include serving as its grant administrator
- Identify, in coordination with the SCO, the state's critical information needs for incorporation into a list of essential elements of information (critical items of specific information required to plan and execute an operation)

Homeland Security Council and National Security Council

The Homeland Security Council (HSC) and National Security Council (NSC) advise the president on national strategic policy during large-scale incidents. These councils ensure coordination for all homeland and national security-related activities among executive departments and agencies and promote effective development and implementation of related policy. The HSC and NSC ensure unified leadership across the federal government. The Assistant to the President for Homeland Security and Counterterrorism and the Assistant to the President for National Security Affairs coordinate interagency policy for domestic and international incident management, respectively, and convene interagency meetings to coordinate policy issues. Both councils use well-established policy development structures to identify issues that require interagency coordination. To support domestic interagency policy coordination on a routine basis, HSC and NSC deputies and principals convene to resolve significant policy issues. They are supported by the two policy coordination committees at the assistant Secretary level.

Domestic Readiness Group

The Domestic Readiness Group (DRG) is an interagency body convened on a regular basis to develop and coordinate preparedness, response, and incident management policy. This group evaluates various policy issues of interagency importance regarding domestic preparedness and incident management and makes recommendations to senior levels of the policymaking structure for decision. During an incident, the DRG may be convened by DHS to evaluate relevant interagency policy issues regarding response and develop recommendations as may be required.

Counterterrorism Security Group

The Counterterrorism Security Group (CSG) is an interagency body convened on a regular basis to develop terrorism prevention policy and to coordinate threat response and law enforcement investigations associated with terrorism. This group evaluates various policy issues of interagency importance regarding counterterrorism and makes recommendations to senior levels of the policymaking structure for decision.

National Operations Center

The National Operations Center (NOC) is the primary national hub for situational awareness and operations coordination across the federal government for incident management. It provides the Secretary of Homeland Security and other key officials with information necessary to make critical national-level incident management decisions. The NOC is a permanent, nonstop multiagency operations center. NOC staff monitor threat and hazard information from across the United States and abroad, supported by a 24/7 watch officer contingent, including:

- NOC managers
- Selected federal interagency, state, and local law enforcement representatives
- Intelligence community liaison officers provided by the DHS Chief Intelligence Officer
- Analysts from the Operations Division's interagency planning element
- Watch standers representing dozens of organizations and disciplines from the federal government and others from the private sector

The NOC facilitates information sharing and operations coordination with other federal, state, tribal, local, and nongovernmental partners. During emergency response, the NOC develops and distributes spot reports, situation reports, and other information-sharing tools. The following operational components of the NOC provide integrated mission support.

National Response Coordination Center

The National Response Coordination Center (NRCC) is FEMA's primary emergency management operations and resource coordination center. The NRCC constantly monitors potential or developing incidents and supports the efforts of regional and field components as needs arise. The NRCC can increase staffing in anticipation of or in response to an emergency by activating ESFs and other personnel in order to provide resources and policy guidance to a JFO or other local incident management structure. The NRCC conducts operational planning, deploys national-level entities, and collects and disseminates incident information as it is analyzed.

National Infrastructure Coordinating Center
The NICC monitors the nation's CIKR on an ongoing basis. During an incident, the NICC allows the sharing of information across the various components of critical infrastructure and key sectors through entities such as information sharing and analysis centers and sector coordinating councils.

National Military Command Center

The National Military Command Center (NMCC) is the nation's focal point for continuous monitoring and coordination of worldwide military operations. It directly supports key military officials, including the chairman of the CJCS, the Secretary of Defense, and the president. The center participates in a wide variety of activities, ranging from missile warning and attack assessment to management of peacetime contingencies such as Defense Support of Civil Authorities (DSCA) activities. In conjunction with monitoring the current worldwide situation, the center alerts the Joint Staff and other national agencies to developing crises and will initially coordinate any military response required.

National Counterterrorism Center

The National Counterterrorism Center (NCTC) integrates and analyzes all intelligence pertaining to terrorism and counterterrorism for the federal government, and conducts strategic operational planning using this information.

Strategic Information and Operations Center

The FBI SIOC is the focal point and operational control center for all federal intelligence, law enforcement, and investigative law enforcement activities related to domestic terrorist incidents or threats. The SIOC maintains direct communication with the NOC and serves as an information clearinghouse to help collect, process, vet, and disseminate information relevant to law enforcement and criminal investigation efforts.

Other DHS Operations Centers

Depending on the type of incident, the operations centers of other DHS operating components may serve as the primary operations management center in support of the Secretary. These include the USCG, Transportation Security Administration, U.S. Secret Service, and U.S. Customs and Border Protection operations centers.

NRF Emergency Support Functions
Through the NRF, FEMA coordinates response support from across the federal government and certain NGOs by calling up, as needed, one or more of the 15 ESFs. The ESFs are coordinated by FEMA through its NRCC. ESFs are used to coordinate specific functional capabilities and resources provided by federal departments and agencies and with certain private-sector and NGOs when applicable. ESF functions are coordinated by a single agency but may rely on several agencies to provide resources specific to each functional area. The mission of the ESFs is to provide the greatest possible access to capabilities of the federal government regardless of which agency has those capabilities.

For each ESF there is an ESF coordinator, a primary agency, and several support agencies (based upon authorities, resources, and capabilities). The categories of resources provided under the ESFs are consistent with those identified in the NIMS. ESFs may be selectively activated for both presidentially declared and nondeclared incidents as circumstances require, although not all incidents requiring federal support result in the activation of ESFs. FEMA has the ability to deploy assets and emergency management capabilities through the ESFs into an area in anticipation of an approaching storm or event that is expected to cause severe negative consequences.

A list of the 15 ESFs and a description of the scope of each are found in Table 9–4.

Table 9–4 NRF Emergency Support Functions and Primary Responsibilities

ESF #1 — Transportation
ESF Coordinator: Department of Transportation
Aviation/airspace management and control
Transportation safety
Restoration and recovery of transportation infrastructure
Movement restrictions
Damage and impact assessment

ESF #2 — Communications
ESF Coordinator: DHS (National Communications System)
Coordination with telecommunications and information technology industries
Restoration and repair of telecommunications infrastructure
Protection, restoration, and sustainment of national cyber and information technology resources
Oversight of communications within the federal incident management and response structures

ESF #3 — Public Works and Engineering
ESF Coordinator: Department of Defense (U.S. Army Corps of Engineers)
Infrastructure protection and emergency repair
Infrastructure restoration
Engineering services and construction management
Emergency contracting support for lifesaving and life-sustaining services

ESF #4 — Firefighting
ESF Coordinator: Department of Agriculture (U.S. Forest Service)
Coordination of federal firefighting activities
Support to wildland, rural, and urban firefighting operations

ESF #5 — Emergency Management
ESF Coordinator: DHS (FEMA)
Coordination of incident management and response efforts
Issuance of mission assignments
Resource and human capital
Incident action planning
Financial management

ESF #6 — Mass Care, Emergency Assistance, Housing, and Human Services
ESF Coordinator: DHS (FEMA)
Mass care
Emergency assistance
Disaster housing
Human services

ESF #7 — Logistics Management and Resource Support
ESF Coordinator: General Services Administration and DHS (FEMA)
Comprehensive, national incident logistics planning, management, and sustainment capability
Resource support (facility space, office equipment and supplies, contracting services, etc.)

(Continued)

Table 9–4 (Continued)

ESF #8 — Public Health and Medical Services
ESF Coordinator: Department of Health and Human Services
Public health
Medical
Mental health services
Mass fatality management
ESF #9 — Search and Rescue
ESF Coordinator: DHS (FEMA)
Lifesaving assistance
Search and rescue operations
ESF #10 — Oil and Hazardous Materials Response
ESF Coordinator: Environmental Protection Agency
Oil and hazardous materials (chemical, biological, radiological, etc.) response
Environmental short- and long-term cleanup
ESF #11 — Agriculture and Natural Resources
ESF Coordinator: Department of Agriculture
Nutrition assistance
Animal and plant disease and pest response
Food safety and security
Natural and cultural resources and historic properties protection
Safety and well-being of household pets
ESF #12 — Energy
ESF Coordinator: Department of Energy
Energy infrastructure assessment, repair, and restoration
Energy industry utilities coordination
Energy forecast
ESF #13 — Public Safety and Security
ESF Coordinator: Department of Justice
Facility and resource security
Security planning and technical resource assistance
Public safety and security support
Support to access, traffic, and crowd control
ESF #14 — Long-Term Community Recovery
ESF Coordinator: DHS (FEMA)
Social and economic community impact assessment
Long-term community recovery assistance to states, tribes, local governments, and the private sector
Analysis and review of mitigation program implementation
ESF #15 — External Affairs
ESF Coordinator: DHS
Emergency public information and protective action guidance
Media and community relations
Congressional and international affairs
Tribal and insular affairs

Once ESFs are activated, they may have a headquarters, regional, and field presence. At FEMA headquarters, the ESFs support decision making and coordination of field operations within the NRCC. The ESFs deliver regional-level technical support and other services in the RRCs, and in the JFO and incident command posts. At all levels, FEMA issues mission assignments to obtain resources and capabilities from across the ESFs in support of the affected states. At the headquarter, regional, and field levels, ESFs provide staff to support the incident command sections for operations, planning, logistics, and finance/administration, as requested, which enables the ESFs to work collaboratively. Similar structures organize response at the field, regional, and headquarters levels.

The emergency support functions of the NRF are, in order:

- ESF #1, Transportation (Coordinator: Department of Transportation)

ESF #1 supports DHS by assisting federal, state, tribal, and local governmental entities, voluntary organizations, NGOs, and the private sector in the management of transportation systems and infrastructure during domestic threats or in response to incidents. ESF #1 also participates in prevention, preparedness, response, recovery, and mitigation activities. It carries out the Department of Transportation's (DOT's) statutory responsibilities, including regulation of transportation, management of the nation's airspace, and ensuring the safety and security of the national transportation system.

- ESF #2, Communications (Coordinators: DHS/National Protection and Programs/Cybersecurity and Communication/National Communications System)

ESF #2 supports the restoration of the communications infrastructure, facilitates the recovery of systems and applications from cyberattacks, and coordinates federal communications support to response efforts during incidents requiring a coordinated federal response. ESF #2 implements the provisions of the Office of Science and Technology Policy (OSTP) National Plan for Telecommunications Support (NPTS) in Non-Wartime Emergencies. ESF #2 also provides communications support to federal, state, tribal, and local governments and first responders when their systems have been impacted, and provides communications and information technology (IT) support to the JFO and JFO field teams. The National Communications System (NCS) and the National Cybersecurity Division (NCSD) work closely to coordinate the ESF #2 response to cyber incidents.

- ESF #3, Public Works and Engineering (Coordinator: U.S. Army Corps of Engineers)

ESF #3 assists DHS by coordinating and organizing the capabilities and resources of the federal government to facilitate the delivery of services, technical assistance, engineering expertise, construction management, and other support to prepare for, respond to, and/or recover from a disaster or an incident requiring a coordinated federal response. Activities within the scope of this function include conducting preincident and postincident assessments of public works and infrastructure; executing emergency contract support for lifesaving and life-sustaining services; providing technical assistance to include engineering expertise, construction management, and contracting and real estate services; providing emergency repair of damaged public infrastructure and critical facilities; and implementing and managing the DHS/FEMA Public Assistance Program and other recovery programs.

- ESF #4, Firefighting (Coordinator: U.S. Forest Service)

ESF #4 provides federal support for the detection and suppression of wildland, rural, and urban fires resulting from, or occurring coincidentally with, an incident requiring a coordinated federal response for assistance.

- ESF #5, Emergency Management (Coordinator: FEMA)

ESF #5 supports overall activities of the federal government for domestic incident management. ESF #5 serves as the coordination ESF for all federal departments and agencies across the spectrum of domestic incident management from hazard mitigation and preparedness to response and recovery. ESF #5 identifies resources for alert, activation, and subsequent deployment for quick and effective response. During the postincident response phase, ESF #5 is responsible for the support and planning functions. ESF #5 activities include those functions that are critical to support and facilitate multiagency planning and coordination for operations involving incidents requiring federal coordination. This includes alert and notification; staffing and deployment of DHS and FEMA response teams, as well as response teams from other federal departments and agencies; incident action planning; coordination of operations; logistics management; direction and control; information collection, analysis, and management; facilitation of requests for federal assistance; resource acquisition and management; federal worker safety and health; facilities management; financial management; and other support as required.

- ESF #6, Mass Care, Emergency Assistance, Housing, and Human Services (Coordinator: FEMA)

ESF #6 coordinates the delivery of federal mass care, emergency assistance, housing, and human services when local, tribal, and state response and recovery needs exceed their capabilities. When directed by the president, ESF #6 services and programs are implemented to assist individuals and households impacted by potential or actual disaster incidents (see Figure 9–14). ESF #6 is organized into four primary functions:

Mass care: Includes sheltering, feeding operations, emergency first aid, bulk distribution of emergency items, and collecting and providing information on victims to family members.

Emergency assistance: Assistance required by individuals, families, and their communities to ensure that immediate needs beyond the scope of the traditional "mass care" services provided at the local level are addressed. These services include support to evacuations (including registration and tracking of evacuees); reunification of families; provision of aid and services to special needs populations; evacuation, sheltering, and other emergency services for household pets and service animals; support to specialized shelters; support to medical shelters; nonconventional shelter management; coordination of donated goods and services; and coordination of voluntary agency assistance.

Housing: Includes housing options such as rental assistance, repair, loan assistance, replacement, factory-built housing, semipermanent and permanent construction, referrals, identification and provision of accessible housing, and access to other sources of housing assistance. This assistance is guided by the National Disaster Housing Strategy.

Human services: Includes the implementation of disaster assistance programs to help disaster victims recover their nonhousing losses, including programs to replace destroyed personal property, and obtain disaster loans, food stamps, crisis counseling, disaster unemployment, disaster legal services, support and services for special needs populations, and other federal and state benefits.

- ESF #7, Logistics Management and Resource Support (Coordinators: General Services Administration, FEMA)

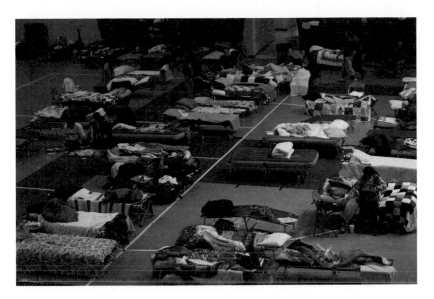

FIGURE 9–14 Minot, ND, June 24, 2011 — Red Cross shelter in an auditorium that housed flood evacuees. Burleigh and Ward counties were designated a federal disaster area, opening the way for federal disaster assistance from FEMA. (Source: Photo by Andrea Booher/FEMA)

Assists DHS by:

(FEMA) Providing a national disaster logistics planning, management, and sustainment capability that harnesses the resources of federal logistics partners, key public and private stakeholders, and NGOs to meet the needs of disaster victims and responders

(GSA) Supporting federal agencies and state, tribal, and local governments that need resource support prior to, during, and/or after incidents requiring a coordinated federal response

- ESF #8, Public Health and Medical Services (Coordinator: HHS)

Provides the mechanism for coordinated federal assistance to supplement state, tribal, and local resources in response to a public health and medical disaster, potential or actual incidents requiring a coordinated federal response, and/or during a developing potential health and medical emergency. Public Health and Medical Services includes responding to medical needs associated with mental health, behavioral health, and substance abuse considerations of incident victims and response workers. Services also cover the medical needs of members of the "at risk" or "special needs" population. Public Health and Medical Services includes behavioral health needs consisting of both mental health and substance abuse considerations for incident victims and response workers and, as appropriate, medical needs groups defined in the core document as individuals in need of additional medical response assistance, and veterinary and/or animal health issues. ESF #8 provides supplemental assistance to state, tribal, and local governments in the following core functional areas:

Assessment of public health/medical needs
Health surveillance
Medical care personnel

Health/medical/veterinary equipment and supplies
Patient evacuation
Patient care
Safety and security of drugs, biologics, and medical devices
Blood and blood products
Food safety and security
Agriculture safety and security
All-hazard public health and medical consultation, technical assistance, and support
Behavioral health care
Public health and medical information
Vector control
Potable water/wastewater and solid waste disposal
Mass fatality management, victim identification, and decontaminating remains
Veterinary medical support

- ESF #9, Search and Rescue (SAR) (Coordinator: FEMA)

Rapidly deploys components of the federal SAR response system to provide specialized lifesaving assistance to state, tribal, and local authorities when activated for incidents or potential incidents requiring a coordinated federal response. The federal SAR response system is composed of the primary agencies that provide specialized SAR operations during incidents or potential incidents requiring a coordinated federal response. This includes:

Structural Collapse (Urban) Search and Rescue (US&R)
Waterborne Search and Rescue
Inland/Wilderness Search and Rescue
Aeronautical Search and Rescue

- ESF #10, Oil and Hazardous Materials Response (Coordinator: EPA)

Provides federal support in response to an actual or potential discharge and/or uncontrolled release of oil or hazardous materials when activated. Response to oil and hazardous materials incidents is generally carried out in accordance with the National Oil and Hazardous Substances Pollution Contingency Plan (NCP). Appropriate general actions under this ESF can include, but are not limited to, actions to prevent, minimize, or mitigate a release; efforts to detect and assess the extent of contamination (including sampling and analysis and environmental monitoring); actions to stabilize the release and prevent the spread of contamination; analysis of options for environmental cleanup and waste disposition; implementation of environmental cleanup; and storage, treatment, and disposal of oil and hazardous materials. In addition, ESF #10 may be used under appropriate authorities to respond to actual or threatened releases of materials not typically responded to under the NCP but that pose a threat to public health or welfare or to the environment.

- ESF #11, Agriculture and Natural Resources (Coordinator: Department of Agriculture)

Supports state, tribal, and local authorities and other federal agency efforts to provide nutrition assistance; control and eradicate, as appropriate, any outbreak of a highly contagious or economically devastating animal or zoonotic disease, or any outbreak of an economically devastating plant pest or disease; ensure the safety and security of the commercial food supply; protect natural and cultural resources and historic properties (NCH); and provide for the safety and well-being of household pets during an emergency response or evacuation situation.

- ESF #12, Energy (Coordinator: DOE)

Facilitates the restoration of damaged energy systems and components when activated for incidents requiring a coordinated federal response. ESF #12 is an integral part of the larger DOE responsibility of maintaining continuous and reliable energy supplies for the United States through preventive measures and restoration and recovery actions. ESF #12 collects, evaluates, and shares information on energy system damage and estimations on the impact of energy system outages within affected areas. Additionally, this function provides information concerning the energy restoration process such as projected schedules, percent completion of restoration, and geographic information on the restoration. It facilitates the restoration of energy systems through legal authorities and waivers. It also provides technical expertise to the utilities, conducts field assessments, and assists government and private-sector stakeholders to overcome challenges in restoring the energy system.

- ESF #13, Public Safety and Security (Coordinator: Department of Justice)

Provides a mechanism for coordinating and providing federal-to-federal support; federal support to state, tribal, and local authorities; and/or support to other ESFs, consisting of law enforcement, public safety, and security capabilities and resources during potential or actual incidents requiring a coordinated federal response.

- ESF #14, Long-Term Community Recovery (Coordinator: FEMA)

Provides a mechanism for coordinating federal support to state, tribal, regional, and local governments, NGOs, and the private sector to enable community recovery from the long-term consequences of extraordinary disasters. ESF #14 accomplishes this by identifying and facilitating availability and use of sources of recovery funding, and providing technical assistance for community recovery and recovery planning support. The function support will vary depending on the magnitude and type of incident.

- ESF #15, External Affairs (Coordinator: DHS)

Ensures that sufficient assets are deployed to provide accurate, coordinated, timely, and accessible information to the various groups affected by the disaster. ESF #15 provides the resource support and mechanisms to implement the NRF Incident Communications Emergency Policy and Procedures (ICEPP) described in the Public Affairs Support Annex. ESF #15 coordinates federal actions to provide the required external affairs support to federal, state, tribal, and local incident management elements to coordinate communications to their audiences. The JIC ensures the coordinated release of information under ESF #15. The planning and products component of External Affairs develops all external and internal communications strategies and products for the ESF #15 organization. And finally, ESF #15 provides the resources and structure for the implementation of the ICEPP.

NRF Support Annexes

The NRF Support Annexes describe how federal departments and agencies; state, tribal, and local entities; the private sector; volunteer organizations; and NGOs coordinate and execute the functional processes and administrative requirements necessary for the management of emergency and disaster incidents. The actions described in these annexes are applicable to nearly every type of incident that may occur, whether natural, technological, or intentional in origin. The annexes, which may be fully or partially implemented, may each support several ESFs, as needed.

As was true with the ESFs, there are roles and responsibilities assumed by federal departments and agencies, NGOs, and the private sector for each support annex. The overarching nature of functions covered by the annexes frequently involves either the support to, or the cooperation of, all departments and agencies involved in incident management efforts to ensure seamless transitions between preparedness, response, and recovery activities. Each annex is managed by one or more coordinating agencies and is supported by various cooperating agencies. The responsibilities of coordinating and cooperating agencies are identified below.

Coordinating Agency

Coordinating agencies are responsible for implementing the processes detailed in the annexes. These federal agencies support DHS incident management efforts by providing the leadership, expertise, and authority to implement critical and specific aspects of the response. When the functions of a particular support annex are required, the agency serving as the coordinator is responsible for:

- Orchestrating a coordinated delivery of those functions and procedures identified in the annex
- Providing staff for operations functions at fixed and field facilities
- Notifying and subtasking cooperating agencies
- Managing tasks with cooperating agencies, as well as appropriate state, tribal, or local agencies
- Working with appropriate private-sector organizations to maximize use of available resources
- Supporting and keeping ESFs and other organizational elements informed of annex activities
- Planning for short- and long-term support to incident management and recovery operations
- Conducting preparedness activities such as training and exercises to maintain personnel who can provide appropriate support

Cooperating Agencies

Cooperating agencies have specific expertise and capabilities that allow them to assist the coordinating agency in executing incident-related tasks or processes. When the procedures within a support annex are needed to support elements of an incident, the coordinating agency will notify cooperating agencies of the circumstances. Cooperating agencies are responsible for:

- Conducting operations, when requested by DHS or the coordinating agency, consistent with their own authority and resources
- Participating in planning for short- and long-term incident management and recovery operations and the development of supporting operational plans, standard operating procedures, checklists, or other job aids, in concert with existing first-responder standards
- Furnishing available personnel, equipment, or other resource support as requested by DHS or the support annex coordinator
- Participating in training and exercises aimed at continuous improvement of response and recovery capabilities

When requested, and upon approval of the Secretary of Defense, the DOD provides defense support of civil authorities during domestic incidents. Accordingly, DOD is considered a cooperating agency for the majority of support annexes.

The support annexes of the NRF are summarized next.

- Critical Infrastructure and Key Resources (Coordinator: DHS)

Describes policies, roles and responsibilities, and the concept of operations for assessing, prioritizing, protecting, and restoring critical infrastructure and key resources (CIKR) during actual or potential domestic incidents. Specifically, this annex does the following:

> Describes roles and responsibilities for CIKR preparedness, protection, response, recovery, restoration, and continuity of operations
>
> Establishes a concept of operations for incident-related CIKR preparedness, protection, response, recovery, and restoration
>
> Outlines incident-related actions to expedite information sharing and analysis of actual or potential impacts to CIKR and facilitate requests for assistance and information from public- and private-sector partners

- Financial Management (Coordinator: FEMA and others)

Provides basic financial management guidance for all NRF departments and agencies providing assistance for incidents requiring a coordinated federal response. The financial management function is a component of ESF #5 (Emergency Management). The processes and procedures described ensure that funds are provided expeditiously and that financial operations are conducted in accordance with established federal laws, policies, regulations, and standards.

- International Coordination (Coordinator: Department of State)

Provides guidance on carrying out responsibilities for international coordination in support of the federal government's response to a domestic incident with an international component. The NRF role of the Department of State is to fully support federal, state, tribal, and local authorities in effective incident management and preparedness planning. A domestic incident will have international and diplomatic impacts and implications that call for coordination and consultations with foreign governments and international organizations. An incident may also require direct bilateral and multilateral actions on foreign affairs issues related to the incident, for which DOS has independent and sole responsibility.

- Private-Sector Coordination (Coordinator: DHS)

Describes the policies, responsibilities, and concept of operations for incident management activities involving the private sector during emergencies and disasters. The annex describes the activities necessary to ensure effective coordination and integration with the private sector, both for-profit and not-for profit, including the nation's critical infrastructure, key resources, other business and industry components, and NGOs engaged in response and recovery. This annex applies incidents that involve the private sector in any of the following ways:

> Impacted organization or infrastructure
> Response resource
> Regulated and/or responsible party
> Member of the state emergency management organization

- Public Affairs (Coordinator: DHS)

Describes the policies and procedures used to mobilize federal assets to prepare and deliver risk and emergency communications messages to the public. The annex is applicable to all federal departments and agencies responding under the NRF.

- Tribal Relations (Coordinator: DHS)

Describes the policies, responsibilities, and concept of operations for coordination and interaction of federal incident management activities with those of tribal governments and communities during incidents requiring a coordinated federal response. Because tribal governments are fully integrated into the NRF, this annex addresses only those factors in the relationship between federal departments and agencies and the federally recognized tribes.

- Volunteer and Donations Management (Coordinator: FEMA)

Describes the coordination processes used to support the state in ensuring the most efficient and effective use of unaffiliated volunteers, unaffiliated organizations, and unsolicited donated goods to support all ESFs, including offers of unaffiliated volunteer services and unsolicited donations to the federal government.

- Worker Safety and Health (Coordinator: Department of Labor/Occupational Safety and Health Administration)

Provides federal support to response and recovery organizations in assuring response and recovery worker safety and health during emergency incidents. This annex describes the technical assistance resources, capabilities, and other support to ensure that response and recovery worker safety and health risks are anticipated, recognized, evaluated, communicated, and consistently controlled.

NRF Incident Annexes

The incident annexes address contingency or hazard situations requiring specialized application of the NRF. These annexes, which were not reengineered when the NRF was released and are therefore a carryover from the legacy NRP, describe the following components for each of the specialized incident types:

Policies: Each annex explains unique authorities pertinent to that incident, the special actions or declarations that may result, and any special policies that may apply.

Situation: Each annex describes the incident situation as well as the planning assumptions, and outlines the approach that will be used if key assumptions do not hold (e.g., how authorities will operate if they lose communication with senior decision makers).

Concept of operations: Each annex describes the concept of operations appropriate to the incident, integration of operations with NRF elements, unique aspects of the organizational approach, notification and activation processes, and specialized incident-related actions. Each annex also details the coordination structures and positions of authority that are unique to the type of incident, the specialized response teams or unique resources needed, and other special considerations.

Responsibilities: Each incident annex identifies the coordinating and cooperating agencies involved in an incident-specific response; in some cases this responsibility is held jointly by two or more departments.

As is true with the support annexes described above, there are coordinating and cooperating agencies that have been identified for each incident annex. The responsibilities of these agencies in the incident annexes are identical to those detailed in the support annexes. Each of the incident annexes is described below.

- Biological Incident Annex (Coordinator: HHS)

Outlines the actions, roles, and responsibilities associated with response to a disease outbreak of known or unknown origin requiring federal assistance, including threat assessment notification procedures, laboratory testing, joint investigative/response procedures, and activities related to recovery. The broad objectives of the federal government's response to a biological terrorism event, pandemic influenza, emerging infectious disease, or novel pathogen outbreak are to:

Detect the event through disease surveillance and environmental monitoring
Identify and protect the population(s) at risk
Determine the source of the outbreak
Quickly frame the public health and law enforcement implications
Control and contain any possible epidemic (including providing guidance to state and local public health authorities)
Augment and surge public health and medical services
Track and defeat any potential resurgence or additional outbreaks
Assess the extent of residual biological contamination and decontaminate as necessary

- Catastrophic Incident Annex (Coordinator: DHS)

Establishes the context and overarching strategy for implementing and coordinating an accelerated, proactive national response to a catastrophic incident (a more detailed NRF Catastrophic Incident Supplement (NRF-CIS), designated "For Official Use Only," has not been released for public view). A catastrophic incident is any natural or man-made incident resulting in extraordinary levels of mass casualties, damage, or disruption severely affecting the population, infrastructure, environment, economy, national morale, and/or government functions. Recognizing that federal and/or national resources are required to augment overwhelmed state, local, and tribal response efforts, the NRF-CIA establishes protocols to pre-identify and rapidly deploy key essential resources (e.g., medical teams, US&R teams, transportable shelters, and medical and equipment caches) that are expected to be urgently needed/required to save lives and contain incidents. Accordingly, upon designation by the Secretary of Homeland Security of a catastrophic incident, federal resources — organized into incident-specific "packages" — deploy in accordance with the NRF-CIS and in coordination with the affected state and incident command structure. An important factor associated with NRF-CIA-designated disasters is that federal assets unilaterally deployed in accordance with the NRF-CIS do not require a state cost-share. Departments and agencies assigned primary responsibility for one or more functional response areas under the NRF-CIS appendixes include:

Mass care: American Red Cross
Search and rescue: Department of Homeland Security
Decontamination: Department of Homeland Security, Environmental Protection Agency, and Department of Health and Human Services
Public health and medical support: Department of Health and Human Services
Medical equipment and supplies: Department of Health and Human Services
Patient movement: Department of Health and Human Services and Department of Defense
Mass fatality: Department of Health and Human Services
Housing: Department of Homeland Security
Public and incident communications: Department of Homeland Security
Transportation: Department of Transportation
Private-sector support: Department of Homeland Security
Logistics: Department of Homeland Security

- Cyber Incident Annex (Coordinators: DHS, DOD, and DOJ)

Discusses policies, organization, actions, and responsibilities for a coordinated approach to prepare for, respond to, and recover from cyber-related emergency incidents impacting critical national processes and the national economy. A cyber-related emergency may take many forms: an organized cyberattack, an uncontrolled exploit such as a virus or a worm, a natural disaster with significant cyberconsequences, or other incidents capable of causing extensive damage to critical infrastructure or key assets. Federal government responsibilities include:

Providing indications and warning of potential threats, incidents, and attacks
Information sharing both inside and outside the government, including best practices, investigative information, coordination of incident response, and incident mitigation
Analyzing cyber vulnerabilities, exploits, and attack methodologies
Providing technical assistance
Conducting investigations, forensics analysis, and prosecution
Attributing the source of cyberattacks
Defending against the attack
Leading national-level recovery efforts

- Food and Agriculture Incident Annex (Coordinators: Department of Agriculture and HHS)

Describes how the various involved agencies will respond to emergency incidents involving the nation's agriculture and food systems. A food and agriculture incident may threaten public health, animal nutrition, food production, aquaculture, livestock production, wildlife, soils, rangelands, and agricultural water supplies. Responding to the unique attributes of this type of incident requires separate planning considerations that are tailored to specific health and agriculture concerns and effects of the disease (e.g., deliberate contamination versus natural outbreaks, plant and animal versus processed food, etc.). The objectives of a coordinated federal response to an incident impacting food and agriculture are to:

Detect the event through the reporting of illness, disease/pest surveillance, routine testing, consumer complaints, and/or environmental monitoring
Establish the primary coordinating agency
Determine the source of the incident or outbreak
Control and contain the distribution of the affected source
Identify and protect the population at risk
Assess the public health, food, agriculture, and law enforcement implications
Assess the extent of residual biological, chemical, or radiological contamination and decontaminate and dispose as necessary
Support effective and coordinated communication between federal, state, and local responders to a potential or actual incident that requires a coordinated federal response impacting food and agriculture
Minimize public health and economic impacts of a food- and agriculture-related incident
Specify roles and responsibilities of coordinating federal agencies and departments
Provide transition from response to rapid recovery following a food- and agriculture-related incident

- Nuclear/Radiological Incident Annex (Coordinators: DHS, DOD, DOE, EPA, National Aeronautics and Space Administration, and Nuclear Regulatory Commission)

Facilitates an organized and coordinated response by federal agencies to terrorist incidents involving nuclear or radioactive materials, and accidents or incidents involving such material. These nuclear/radiological incidents, which include sabotage and terrorist incidents, involve the release or potential release of radioactive material that poses an actual or perceived hazard to public health, safety, national security, and/or the environment (including the terrorist use of RDDs), or "dirty bombs," or improvised nuclear devices (INDs), reactor plant accidents (commercial or weapons production facilities), lost radioactive material sources, transportation accidents involving nuclear/radioactive material, and foreign accidents involving nuclear or radioactive material. This annex:

> Provides planning guidance and outlines operational concepts for the federal response to any nuclear/radiological incident, including a terrorist incident that has actual, potential, or perceived radiological consequences within the United States or its territories, possessions, or territorial waters and that requires a response by the federal government
> Describes federal policies and planning considerations on which this annex and federal agency-specific nuclear/radiological response plans are based
> Specifies the roles and responsibilities of federal agencies for preventing, preparing for, responding to, and recovering from nuclear/radiological incidents
> Includes guidelines for notification, coordination, and leadership of federal activities, and coordination of public information, congressional relations, and international activities
> Provides protocols for coordinating federal government capabilities to respond to radiological incidents. These capabilities include, but are not limited to:
>
>> The Interagency Modeling and Atmospheric Assessment Center (IMAAC), which is responsible for production, coordination, and dissemination of consequence predictions for an airborne hazardous material release
>> The Federal Radiological Monitoring and Assessment Center (FRMAC), established at or near the scene of an incident to coordinate radiological assessment and monitoring
>> The Advisory Team for Environment, Food, and Health (known as "the Advisory Team"), which provides expert recommendations on protective action guidance

- Oil and Hazardous Materials Incident Annex (Coordinators: EPA and USCG)

Describes the roles, responsibilities, and coordinating mechanisms for managing major oil and hazardous materials pollution incidents. This annex addresses those oil and hazardous materials incidents that are managed through concurrent implementation of the NRF and the National Oil and Hazardous Substances Pollution Contingency Plan (NCP), but are not ESF #10 (Oil and Hazardous Materials Response) activations. The NCP provides the organizational structure and procedures for federal response to releases of oil and hazardous materials, and addresses incident prevention, planning, response, and recovery. The hazardous materials addressed under the NCP include certain substances considered weapons of mass destruction (i.e., chemical agents, biological agents, and radiological/nuclear material). The NCP establishes structures at the national, regional, and local levels that are used to respond to thousands of incidents annually. When an NRF incident does occur, these NCP structures remain in place to provide hazard-specific expertise and support. This annex describes how the NCP structures work with NRF coordinating structures during major emergency or disaster incidents.

- Terrorism Incident Law Enforcement and Investigation Annex (Coordinator: FBI)

Facilitates a federal law enforcement and investigative response to all threats or acts of terrorism within the United States, regardless of whether they are deemed credible and/or whether they are major or minor in scope. This annex provides planning guidance and outlines operational concepts for the federal law enforcement and investigative response to a threatened or actual terrorist incident, and acknowledges and outlines the unique nature of each threat or incident, the capabilities and responsibilities of the local jurisdictions, and the law enforcement and investigative activities necessary to prevent or mitigate a specific threat or incident. The law enforcement and investigative response to a terrorist threat or incident within the United States is a highly coordinated, multiagency state, local, tribal, and federal responsibility. The attorney general holds the lead responsibility for criminal investigations of terrorist acts or terrorist threats by individuals or groups inside the United States, or directed at U.S. citizens or institutions abroad, under HSPD-5. Acting through the FBI, the attorney general, in cooperation with other federal departments and agencies engaged in activities to protect national security, also coordinates the activities of the other members of the law enforcement community to detect, prevent, preempt, and disrupt terrorist attacks. Although not formally designated under this annex, other federal departments and agencies may have authorities, resources, capabilities, or expertise required to support terrorism-related law enforcement and investigation operations. Agencies may be requested to participate in federal planning and response operations, and may be requested to designate liaison officers and provide other support as required.

Partner Guides

Response Partner Guides were developed in conjunction with the NRF in order to provide local, tribal, state, federal, and private-sector response stakeholders with a reference of their key roles and actions in coordinated response. The Partner Guides include:

- Local Government Response Partner Guide
- State Response Partner Guide
- Private-Sector and Nongovernmental Response Partner Guide
- Federal Response Partner Guide

    See the sidebar "NRF Federal-Level Operations Coordination" for a summary of overall coordination.

■ ■ ■ ▬▬▬▬▬▬▬▬▬▬▬▬▬▬▬▬▬▬▬▬▬▬▬▬▬▬▬▬▬▬▬▬▬▬▬▬▬▬

NRF Federal-Level Operations Coordination

- The Secretary of Homeland Security is the principal federal official responsible for domestic incident management.
- All Federal departments and agencies may play significant roles in incident management and response activities, depending on the nature and size of an event. The policies, operational structures, and capabilities to support an integrated federal response are defined in the Emergency Support Functions (see below), and are coordinated through prescribed mission assignments, and formalized in interagency agreements.
- The FEMA administrator is the principal advisor to the president, the Secretary of Homeland Security, and the Homeland Security Council regarding emergency management. The FEMA administrator's duties include operation of the National Response Coordination Center, the effective support of all emergency support functions, and, more generally, preparation for, protection against, response to, and recovery from all-hazards incidents. Reporting to the Secretary of Homeland Security, the administrator also is responsible for management of the core DHS grant programs supporting homeland security.
- Other DHS agency heads have a lead response role or an otherwise significant role, depending on the type and severity of the event. For example, the U.S. Coast Guard commandant has

statutory lead authority for certain mass migration management scenarios and significant oil/hazardous substance spill incidents in the maritime environment.
- The DHS director of operations coordination is the Secretary's principal advisor for the overall departmental level of integration of incident management operations and oversees the National Operations Center.

Source: FEMA, "National Response Framework," Washington, DC, 2008.

■ ■ Critical Thinking ■

The NRF is a comprehensive document, but it cannot possibly cover every possible need that may arise in every emergency incident. In light of the wide array of emergencies and disasters that could occur in your community, are there any specific community-level needs that might fall outside the spectrum of the NRF that are not explicitly detailed (e.g., the needs of children in emergencies)?

Recovery

The recovery function is not easy to classify; it often begins in the initial hours and days following a disaster event and can continue for months and in some cases years, depending on the severity of the event. Unlike the response function, where all efforts have a singular focus, the recovery function or process is characterized by a complex set of issues and decisions that must be made by individuals and communities. These issues include the following:

- Rebuilding homes
- Replacing property
- Resuming employment
- Restoring businesses
- Permanently repairing and rebuilding infrastructure

Since the establishment of DHS, the recovery function has remained relatively unchanged, although minor changes affecting the nomenclature and classification of the available assistance, as well as some relief programs and grants, have occurred. Because the recovery function has such long-lasting impacts and usually high costs, the participants in the process are numerous. They include all levels of government, the business community, political leadership, community activists, and individuals. The major players and programs will be listed here and changes, if any, will be described.

Given that the federal government plays the largest role in providing the technical and financial support for recovery, this section focuses on the federal role. It discusses the structure and the various programs available to assist individuals and communities in the postdisaster environment and will briefly reference the various national voluntary organizations that provide some assistance for recovery. See the sidebar "Quick Facts on Recovery" for a brief historical summary.

Quick Facts on Recovery

Since March 2003, FEMA has responded to 454 major natural disaster and emergency declarations.

In 2009, FEMA responded to 54 new presidential major disaster declarations and 7 new presidential emergency declarations across 28 States and Territories, including the recent tsunami that affected American Samoa obligating $11.4B in assistance, primarily for Individual Assistance (i.e., housing and other needs assistance) and Public Assistance (i.e., reimbursement to clear debris and rebuild roads, schools, libraries, and other public facilities).

In FY 2007, 68 major disasters and 11 emergencies were declared in 36 states. For Katrina alone, $607 million has been provided for housing and other needs assistance in FY 2007, and $2.6 billion has been obligated to continue to provide reimbursement to clear debris and rebuild roads, schools, libraries, and other public facilities.

In the year since Katrina made landfall, FEMA provided nearly $6.3 billion directly to some 1.7 million households for housing and other needs—the most provided by the agency for any single natural disaster. FEMA also provided more than $7 billion in Public Assistance to clear debris and rebuild roads, schools, libraries, and other public facilities.

The 2005 hurricane season was the most active and devastating in U.S. history. Within 100 days of Hurricane Katrina's striking the Gulf Coast, FEMA provided nearly $5.2 billion to more than 1.4 million households impacted by Hurricanes Katrina and Rita; figures unmatched in the Agency's history. More than 130 Disaster Recovery Centers were stretched across Texas, Louisiana, Mississippi, Alabama, and Florida, serving the needs of an unprecedented number of people displaced from their homes. Working through the American Red Cross, FEMA supported the Nation's largest-ever sheltering operation, with more than 320,000 evacuees at its peak, and paid to house 85,000 families in emergency hotel housing. FEMA also provided rental assistance to more than 653,000 families who were displaced. More than 40,000 manufactured homes or travel trailers provided through FEMA were occupied by families in the Gulf Coast, and more than 140,000 temporary roofs were put on damaged homes through the U.S. Army Corps of Engineers. As of January 1, 2006, FEMA and its Federal partners removed nearly 60 million cubic yards of debris, and FEMA approved over $392 million in Community Disaster Assistance Loans and over $205 million in unemployment insurance.

2004 Hurricane Recovery: Building on its response to Hurricanes Charley, Frances, Ivan, and Jeanne, FEMA continued its support and contribution to the long-term recovery of communities in the impacted states. In Florida, which was hit by all four hurricanes, FEMA has provided more than $5.6 billion in Federal assistance to date, including nearly $1.2 billion for housing and other needs assistance awarded to individuals; nearly $1.2 billion for contracted goods and services needed when the hurricanes hit; and more than $1.8 billion in U.S. Small Business Administration loans to homeowners, renters, and owners of businesses of any size that sustained uninsured or underinsured damage or loss because of the disasters.

By November 2002, FEMA had given a total of $306,102,000 in disaster recovery funding for the victims of September 11 attacks. The distribution among programs follows:

- Temporary housing: mortgage and rental assistance ($76,275,000), minimal home repair ($1,450,000), transient accommodations ($1,225,000), rental assistance ($26,150,000)
- Individual family grants ($25,400,000)

- Crisis counseling assistance and training program ($162,400,000)
- Unemployment assistance ($13,200,000)
- Legal services ($2,000)

Source: DHS, 2011, http://www.dhs.gov/xlibrary/assets/budget_bib_fy2011.pdf; http://www.dhs.gov/xlibrary/assets/budget_bib_fy2010.pdf; http://www.dhs.gov/xlibrary/assets/budget_bib-fy2009.pdf; http://www.dhs.gov/xlibrary/assets/budget_bib-fy2008.pdf; http://www.dhs.gov/xlibrary/assets/Budget_BIB-FY2007.pdf; http://www.dhs.gov/xlibrary/assets/FY_2005_BIB_4.pdf.

Disaster Recovery Operations in the National Response Framework

The NRF addresses the need for structured principles and procedures by which individuals, communities, and the nation recover from the consequences of emergencies and disasters. Recovery operations may require significant contributions from all sectors of society, each of which is addressed. There are two phases of recovery identified in the NRF, including:

Short-term recovery: This is the period when recovery actions that begin immediately upon occurrence of the disaster, which overlap with response actions, are taken. This phase includes actions such as providing essential public health and safety services, restoring interrupted utility and other essential services, reestablishing transportation routes, and providing food and shelter for those displaced by the incident. Although called "short term," some short-term recovery activities may last for weeks. Short-term recovery actions are addressed in several functional areas of the NRF.

Long term recovery: This is the period that involves the restoration of lives and livelihoods beyond the emergency phase of the disaster, once lifelines and critical societal components have been restored or replaced. This phase falls squarely within the direction of ESF #14, "Long-Term Community Recovery," and often continues for several months or years after the disaster has ended.

Recovery can include the development, coordination, and execution of service- and site-restoration plans; reconstitution of government operations and services; programs to provide housing and promote restoration; long-term care and treatment of affected persons; and additional measures for social, political, environmental, and economic restoration. Under the NRF, recovery operations and programs:

- Identify needs and resources
- Provide accessible housing and promote restoration
- Address care and treatment of affected persons
- Provide recovering victims with appropriate recovery information
- Facilitate community restoration
- Incorporate mitigation measures and techniques, as feasible

Recovery Coordination

As in the response phase, the JFO serves as the central coordination point among local, tribal, state, and federal governments, as well as private-sector and nongovernmental entities that are providing recovery assistance. The NRF outlines several recovery actions that may take place under this structure, including:

Coordinating assistance programs to help individuals, households, and businesses meet basic needs and return to self-sufficiency. Such programs include housing assistance, other needs assistance (ONA), crisis counseling services, disaster legal services, and unemployment or reemployment programs. Other activities include coordinating with local and tribal governments the need for and locations of disaster recovery centers (DRCs).

Establishing DRCs. Federal, state, tribal, local, voluntary, and NGOs determine the need for and location of DRCs. DRC staff provide recovery and mitigation program information, advice, counseling, and related technical assistance.

Coordinating with private-sector and NGOs involved in donations management and other recovery activities. Donations and volunteer management in the past have been chaotic and disorganized, often leading to what is called "the second disaster." The NRF addresses these issues by tasking various federal agencies and offices with the management of these two functions.

Coordinating public assistance grant programs authorized by the Stafford Act. These programs aid local, tribal, and state governments and eligible private nonprofit organizations with the cost of emergency protective services, debris removal, and the repair or replacement of disaster-damaged public facilities and associated environmental restoration.

Coordinating with the private sector on restoration and recovery of CIKR. Activities to restore and facilitate the recovery of CIKR are primarily the responsibilities of the private sector, who owns the majority of these components. The restoration and repair of these facilities is integral to the recovery of the community, and therefore almost always require the assistance of the federal and state governments. The NRF guides the emergency management stakeholders in working with the owners and operators of these facilities to ensure that critical services return (which include, e.g., water, power, natural gas and petroleum, emergency communications, and health care).

Coordinating mitigation grant programs to help communities reduces the potential impacts of future disasters. The NRF addresses the most important concept behind recovery, which is to ensure that new disaster information is applied such that preexisting hazard vulnerabilities are effectively reduced.

At a certain point in the recovery operation, it will be determined that operations no longer require the services of a full JFO and that office will be closed. At this point, ongoing activities are led by the individual agencies that hold recovery responsibilities under the NRF. Federal partners then work directly with their regional or headquarter offices to administer and monitor recovery programs, support, and technical services.

Each of the primary and support agencies of ESF #14 has distinct programs aimed at facilitating recovery, based on their individual agency-specific expertise. The following subsections describe each agency's recovery function.

Coordination of Disaster Recovery

The practical work of implementing the recovery process occurs at the JFO. Two organizational structures, or branches, divide the recovery assistance functions. These branches assess state and local recovery needs at the outset of the disaster and relevant time frames for program delivery. The human services branch coordinates assistance programs to help individuals, families, and businesses meet basic needs and return to self-sufficiency. It is responsible for the donations management function. The infrastructure support branch coordinates assistance programs to aid state and local governments and eligible private nonprofit organizations to repair or replace damaged public facilities. The two branches assist in identifying appropriate agency assistance programs to meet applicant needs, synchronizing assistance delivery and encouraging incorporation of mitigation measures where possible. In addition to the work of the DRCs, applicant briefings are conducted for local government officials and certain private nonprofit organizations to inform them of available recovery assistance and how to apply.

Federal disaster assistance available under a major disaster falls into three general categories: individual assistance, public assistance, and hazard mitigation assistance. Individual assistance is aid to individuals, families, and business owners. Public assistance is aid to public and certain private nonprofit entities for emergency services and the repair or replacement of disaster-damaged public facilities. Hazard mitigation assistance is funding available for measures designed to reduce future losses to public and private property. A detailed description of the first two types of assistance follows.

FEMA'S Individual Assistance Recovery Programs

Individual assistance programs are oriented to individuals, families, and small businesses, and the programs include the Individuals and Households Program (IHP), SBA loans, disaster unemployment assistance (DUA), legal services, special tax considerations, and crisis counseling. The disaster victim must first register for assistance and establish eligibility before receiving this assistance. These programs are described next.

Individuals and Households Program

The Individuals and Households Program (IHP) is a program coordinated jointly by FEMA and the affected states. When a major disaster is declared, the IHP provides both money and services to people in the declared areas whose property has been damaged or destroyed and whose losses are not covered by insurance. To receive assistance under this program, disaster victims must register for assistance and first have their eligibility established.

IHP has two separate programs that address the needs of individuals and households. The housing assistance program works to ensure that people whose homes are damaged by a disaster have a safe place to live while it is repaired or replaced. The ONA program provides financial assistance to individuals and households who have disaster-related expenses or serious needs, but who do not qualify for Small Business Administration (SBA) loans (see next subsection). These two programs are designed to provide funds for expenses that are not covered by insurance. They are available only to U.S. citizen homeowners and renters, noncitizen nationals, or qualified aliens. The following is a list of the types of assistance available through this program and what each provides:

Temporary housing: Funding that covers the cost of renting an alternate house or apartment when a victim's residence is uninhabitable due to disaster damage.
Repair: Funding that covers the cost of repair to damage that was caused by the disaster, but which was not covered by insurance. These repairs must be geared toward making the home "safe and sanitary" to qualify.
Replacement: Funding to cover the cost of replacing a home destroyed by a disaster.
Permanent housing construction: Funding for the construction of a new home. This type of assistance occurs only in very unusual situations, in remote locations where no other type of housing is possible.

Other needs assistance (ONA): Funding for necessary and serious needs caused by the disaster. This includes medical, dental, funeral, personal property, transportation, moving and storage, and other expenses that FEMA approves. To receive ONA, the victim may first need to apply for an SBA loan.

Small Business Administration Disaster Loans

Following federally declared disasters, the U.S. Small Business Administration (SBA) normally provides federally subsidized loans to repair or replace homes, personal property, or businesses that sustained damages not covered by insurance. For many individuals, the SBA disaster loan program is the primary form of disaster assistance. The SBA can provide three types of disaster loans to qualified homeowners and businesses:

- Home disaster loans to homeowners and renters to repair or replace disaster-related damage to home or personal property
- Business physical disaster loans to business owners to repair or replace disaster-damaged property, including inventory and supplies
- Economic injury disaster loans, which provide capital to small businesses and to small agricultural cooperatives to assist them through the disaster recovery period

Disaster Unemployment Assistance

The Disaster Unemployment Assistance (DUA) program provides unemployment benefits and re-employment services to individuals who have lost their jobs as a result of the disaster. Benefits begin with the date the job was lost, and can be continued for up to 26 weeks after the presidential declaration date. The DUA program is available to people who are not covered by other unemployment insurance programs or who cannot qualify for other unemployment compensation.

Legal Services

Following a disaster, the Young Lawyers Division of the American Bar Association may be contracted by FEMA to provide free legal assistance to disaster victims. These services are provided to low-income individuals who, prior to or because of the disaster, are unable to afford adequate legal services to meet their postdisaster-related needs. Legal advice under this program is limited to cases that will not result in any attorney or other fees. The assistance that participating lawyers provide typically includes the following:

- Assistance with insurance claims (life, medical, property, etc.)
- Counseling on landlord/tenant problems
- Assisting in consumer protection matters, remedies, and procedures
- Replacement of wills and other important legal documents destroyed in a major disaster

Special Tax Considerations

Taxpayers who have sustained a casualty loss from a declared disaster may deduct that loss on the federal income tax return for the year in which the casualty actually occurred, or elect to deduct the loss on the tax return for the preceding tax year. To qualify, victims' losses must be greater than 10% of the adjusted gross income for the tax year by at least $100. Additionally, the Internal Revenue Service (IRS) can expedite refunds due to taxpayers in a federally declared disaster area. This service is available to any taxpayer in a federally declared disaster area.

Crisis Counseling

The Crisis Counseling Assistance and Training Program (CCP) is designed to provide supplemental funding to states for short-term crisis counseling services. Two separate portions of the CCP can be funded: immediate services and regular services. A state may request either or both types of funding. The immediate services program is intended to enable the state or local agency to respond to the immediate mental health needs with screening, diagnostic, and counseling techniques, as well as outreach services such as public information and community networking. The regular services program is designed to provide up to 9 months of crisis counseling, community outreach, and consultation and education services to people affected by the disaster. To be eligible for crisis counseling services funded by this program, the person must be a resident of the designated area or must have been located in the area at the time the disaster occurred. The person must also have a mental health problem that was caused or aggravated by the disaster or its aftermath, or he or she must benefit from services provided by the program.

Public Assistance Programs

Public assistance, oriented to public entities, is designed to facilitate the repair, restoration, reconstruction, or replacement of public facilities or infrastructure damaged or destroyed by a federally declared disaster. Eligible applicants include state governments, local governments, and any other political subdivision of a state, Native American tribes, and Alaska Native villages. Certain private nonprofit (PNP) organizations may also receive assistance, including educational, utility, irrigation, emergency, medical, rehabilitation, and temporary or permanent custodial care facilities, and other PNP facilities that provide essential services of a governmental nature to the general public.

As soon as is possible and practical following a disaster declaration, the state, assisted by FEMA, briefs state, local, and PNP officials to inform them of the assistance available and how to apply for it (Figure 9–15). To receive this assistance, a Request for Public Assistance must be filed with the state within 30 days of the time the area is designated as eligible. Following the briefing, a "Kickoff Meeting" is conducted where damages are discussed, needs assessed, and a plan of action put in place. A team made up of federal, state, and local representatives initiates the project, including documenting the eligible facilities, the eligible work, and the eligible cost for fixing the damages to every public or PNP facility identified by state or local representatives. The team prepares a project worksheet (PW) for each project. Projects are grouped into the following categories:

- *Category A*: Debris removal
- *Category B*: Emergency protective measures
- *Category C*: Road systems and bridges
- *Category D*: Water control facilities
- *Category E*: Public buildings and contents
- *Category F*: Public utilities
- *Category G*: Parks, recreational, and other

FEMA reviews and approves the PWs and obligates the federal share of the costs (75% or more) to the state. The state then disburses funds to local applicants.

FIGURE 9–15 Birmingham, AL, June 17, 2011 — FEMA Associate Administrator William Carwile (center) listens to a report during a general staff meeting at the Joint Field Office, along with Alabama State Coordinating Officer Jeff Byard (left) and Federal Coordinating Officer Mike Byrne. The meetings help coordinate all of the state and federal resources to continue the recovery process. (Source: FEMA photo/Tim Burkitt)

Other Federal Agency Disaster Recovery Funding

Other federal agencies have programs that contribute to social and economic recovery. Most of these additional programs are triggered by a presidential declaration of a major disaster or emergency under the Stafford Act. However, the Secretary of the Department of Agriculture and the administrator of the SBA have specific authority relevant to their constituencies to declare a disaster and provide disaster recovery assistance. All of the agencies are part of the structure of the NRF.

Conclusion

The motives behind the establishment of the DHS are almost as numerous as the number of agencies it involves, and include politics, power, public relations, or a real need to improve the federal response and recovery systems because of the new spectrum of threats made apparent by the September 11 attacks. For whatever reason or combination of reasons, a system that had demonstrated its operational capabilities in both natural disasters and terrorism events in Oklahoma City, New York, and the Pentagon became subject to significant and ongoing change. As a result of the integration of different agencies and the need for new procedural systems to operate together, the NRP was developed with the NIMS. NIMS and the NRF (that has since replaced the NRP) together serve as references and guidelines to determine how the nation's first responders and agencies involved in response operate.

The effort to include citizens and the private sector as active partners is commendable. Programs developed under the CCCs provide the opportunity to build strong communities. However, they have been poorly supported by the political leadership and are underfunded. Further collaboration with the business sector will allow for enhanced preparedness and protection of the critical infrastructure and provide a better understanding of its vulnerabilities and how to respond if it is attacked.

As a final point, it is essential to bear in mind that the massive integration of many agencies into one has its drawbacks: independence is compromised and the overall redundancy of the system decreases. The NRF and NIMS define how different agencies operate together but it should not jeopardize or change the agencies' own integrity and mission. Although redundancy is an attribute that all organizations try to get rid of, it is also what often saves the day during a crisis situation. "Too efficient" systems with minimal backup, no duplication of function, and low flexibility/adaptability have been shown to be more vulnerable to unexpected situations, to fail in a worse manner, and to be less agile when responding to and dealing with an emergency. Thus, an excessive integration to reduce redundancy can cause the involved agencies to depend on each other rather than empower each other — and this might lead the way for a catastrophic chain reaction of failure to occur in certain conditions.

CASE STUDY: THE LONDON TERROR ATTACKS, JULY 7, 2005

On Thursday, July 7, 2005, just before 9 AM, four suicide bombers blew themselves up   three on London subway trains and one on a bus. The explosions resulted in the deaths of 56 people, including the bombers, and injured more than 700 others. The entire London subway system was closed for the remainder of the day, and cellular telephone systems were jammed, leading to commuter chaos. The following timeline illustrates the attacks and the step-by-step response by British authorities.

8:50 AM — Three explosions occur almost simultaneously on three London underground trains: between Aldgate and Liverpool Street stations on the Circle Line, between Russell Square and King's Cross stations on the Piccadilly Line, and at Edgware Road station on the Circle Line. At first, police are only aware of the Aldgate/Liverpool Street train attack. The Russell Square/King's Cross blast was not reported until 8:56, and the Edgware blast at 9:17. A review of technical data and witness accounts showed that the three bombs actually went off within about 50 seconds of each other.

9:47 — The No. 30 bus on Upper Woburn Place near Tavistock Square is destroyed by a fourth explosion. Pictures show the roof of the double-decker bus ripped off and witnesses report seeing body parts in the road, Reuters reports.

10:02 — Scotland Yard says it is dealing with a "major incident."

10:20 — Metropolitan Police post a message on their website reporting that a major transportation incident has happened in London and that it is responding to six metro stations and one confirmed explosion in a public bus. Cause, severity, and impact of the explosions are not known at this point.

10:47 — Home Secretary Charles Clarke says multiple London blasts have caused "terrible injuries."

11:15 — European Union commissioner for justice and security affairs Franco Frattini tells reporters in Rome that the blasts in London are terrorist attacks.

11:35 — London police chief tells Reuters news agency there are "indications of explosives" at one of the blast sites.

12:00 PM — British Prime Minister Tony Blair says the "barbaric" London blasts are terrorist attacks and were designed to coincide with the G8 summit in Scotland. He will return to London.

(Continued)

CASE STUDY: THE LONDON TERROR ATTACKS, JULY 7, 2005 (CONTINUED)

12:15 — A group calling itself the Group of al-Qaeda of Jihad Organization in Europe lays claim to the blasts, posting a statement on an Islamist website. The claim cannot be independently verified.

12:27 — Police and hospital officials tell Reuters that a total of 185 people are wounded across London, 10 of them seriously and 7 critically.

12:30 — Metropolitan Police confirmed explosions in three metro stations and one public bus and continues its presence on the incident sites. At the time the police do not provide numbers of casualties but underline that there are many.

12:51 — Emergency services personnel tell CNN writer William Chamberlain that all survivors had been evacuated from King's Cross station, leaving the dead below ground "in the double digits."

12:53 — Britain's Home Secretary Charles Clarke tells the House of Commons there were four explosions in central London and the underground system will be closed all day. They would decide later in the day whether to resume bus services. Earlier six attacks were reported.

2:38 — U.S. law enforcement sources cite the British government as saying that at least 40 people have been killed. London hospitals report at least 300 wounded, the Associated Press reports.

3:26 — London deputy police chief Brian Paddick says police had no warning of the attacks and have not received any claims of responsibility. He says police are keeping an open mind over who carried out the attacks and that it is unclear whether a claim of responsibility by al-Qaeda is genuine or whether suicide bombers were involved. No arrests have been made in connection with the attacks.

3:41 — Assistant chief ambulance officer Russell Smith says the service has treated 45 patients with serious or critical injuries. A further 300 patients have been treated for minor injuries.

4:30 — London Police announce that the Metropolitan Police Service Casualty Bureau has been opened and ask the public to call the hotline if they are concerned about their loved ones who may have been affected by the incidents. The police announced the number of the confirmed fatalities as 33 for the first time and mentioned that the incidents were caused by terrorists.

4:32 — Transport authorities say Docklands Light Railway services in east London and mainline rail services have resumed, except out of King's Cross and Victoria stations. Buses in central London are also returning to service. All underground services remain suspended.

5:43 — Prime Minister Tony Blair says that Britain will not be intimidated by terrorism and promises intense police and security services action to bring those behind the bombings to justice. "I would also pay tribute to the stoicism and resilience of the people of London who have responded in a way typical of them," says Blair.

5:49 — The United Nations Security Council passes a resolution condemning the London attacks and expressing "outrage and indignation at today's appalling terrorist attacks against the people of the United Kingdom that cost human life and caused injuries and immense human suffering."

7:15 — Metropolitan police updates the number of confirmed fatalities as 37 and confirms that the incidents involved four explosive devices.

This timeline is based on multiple sources including CNN, and the London Metropolitan Police media releases:
www.cnn.com/2005/WORLD/europe/07/07/london.timeline/index.html,
www.met.police.uk/news/op_theseus/response1.htm,

www.met.police.uk/news/op_theseus/response2.htm,
www.met.police.uk/news/op_theseus/response3.htm, and
www.met.police.uk/news/op_theseus/response4.htm.

Observations and Comments on Incident

London Metropolitan Police: London Metropolitan Police immediately responded to all potential incident scenes and fulfilled their first-response responsibility. The unique aspect of the incident management by the Metropolitan Police was consistent and persistent behavior in terms of releasing information to the media and the public. The department did not speculate on the incidents and their outcomes and public impacts at any time. The Metropolitan Police chose to release factual information only when the validity of the information was confirmed by credible sources, in many cases its investigators or cooperating government officials. The first casualty numbers were announced about 4:30 PM by the department. Until then various sources in the media were reporting a range of casualty numbers (between 2 and 90) (based on Multiple London Metropolitan Police Press Releases and media coverage on July 7, 2005).

London Fire Brigade: Around 200 firefighters were called to explosions at Aldgate, Edgware Road, and King's Cross London underground stations and an explosion on a bus at Tavistock Square on Thursday, July 7. Twelve fire appliances with 60 firefighters attended the incident at Edgware Road, 12 fire appliances with 60 firefighters attended the incident at King's Cross, 10 fire appliances with 50 firefighters attended the Aldgate incident, and 4 fire appliances with 20 firefighters were called to Tavistock Square. Throughout the morning, several new specialist fire rescue units were deployed to work with the other emergency services to evacuate casualties and make the incident locales safe (London Fire Brigade, http://www.london-fire.gov.uk/news/statement.asp).

London Emergency Medical Services: The response of the emergency medical service units to the bomb attacks in London has generally been assessed as "adequate" by experts. The incident claimed more than 50 lives, left more than 700 hurt, and kept about 100 overnight in hospital, 22 of whom were in critical condition as of July 8. Hospitals responding to the crisis included St. Mary's hospital in Paddington, the Royal Free hospital in Hampstead, St. Thomas's hospital, and Great Ormond Street children's hospital, which does not have an emergency department but took in 22 patients. Hospitals in London were put on major incident alert within minutes of the first explosion, which occurred at 0851 BST in the third carriage of an underground train traveling in a tunnel 100 meters from Liverpool Street station. Less than a mile away, at the Royal London hospital in Whitechapel, medical staff implemented a well-rehearsed strategy to cope with the first of 208 patients. The shock waves from the blast were the cause of the most frequently seen injuries on that day, which are particularly traumatic for air-filled parts of the body. The waves can cause perforated eardrums, collapsed lungs, and perforated bowels. But the force can also devastate soft tissue — the blast was responsible for many of the limbs lost during the attacks. Smoke inhalation resulting in lung damage, burns, and ripped skin caused by debris such as glass shards were also common injuries ("Medical Teams Praised for Reaction to Bombings," www.newscientist.com/article.ns?id = dn7649).

Leadership and Crisis Communications

U.K. Prime Minister Tony Blair was participating in the G8 summit in Gleneagles, Scotland, when he learned about the terror attacks. At 12 PM that day, Blair appeared before the media in Gleneagles and gave a three-and-a-half-minute-long speech about the day's terrorist incidents.

(*Continued*)

CASE STUDY: THE LONDON TERROR ATTACKS, JULY 7, 2005 (CONTINUED)

Mr. Blair's style of communication on that day has demonstrated his leadership skills and expertise in crisis communications. An analytical piece about the way he delivered his speech marks the following nuances in his speech as critical to conveying the right message in the right way:

- He demonstrated his passion for his people and did not choose to hide his emotions.
- He shared his emotions (grief), but also presented a strong image that communicated he and his government were there and ready to deal with the problem.
- He improvised his speech instead of reading it, which proved that it was not "business as usual" for him.
- He used many long pauses to communicate the gravity of the situation.
- He avoided speculations and focused on stating the limited number of facts he was informed about.
- He sincerely communicated his condolences to the families who lost loved ones in the attacks.
- He used strong and direct vocabulary to describe the events ("barbaric").

The analysis above is based on analysis by T.J. Walker ("Crisis Communications with Class," http://www.mediatrainingworldwide.com). For the video of the complete speech, see http://relay.westminsterdigital.co.uk/demand.php?c=number10/statements&m=statementFull2005-07-07.wmv&.wvx. For a transcript of the speech, see www.number-10.gov.uk/output/Page7853.asp.

Conclusion

As a test of response capabilities, many have argued that the Department of Homeland Security was given an easy assignment — there were only seven initial fatalities, no injuries, and very little destruction. However, from a coordination standpoint, the event was colossal. As previously mentioned, it was the single greatest mobilization of civil service employees in the history of the nation, and with very few exceptions, the operation was carried off without a hitch. All local and state costs were reimbursed by the federal government, and many working relationships were created in the response and recovery phases when counterparts were able to work face to face in a relatively low-stress environment. The event proved that FEMA had retained its agency status within DHS, and was able to continue functioning as it had before the Homeland Security Act was signed just 4 months earlier.

References

Bullock & Haddow, LLC, 2003. North Carolina: Madison County Terrorism Annex to Basic Emergency Response Plan, unpublished operational planning document.

Environmental Protection Agency 2003. Response to the Columbia space shuttle incident. http:// www.epa.gov/columbia.

Federal Emergency Management Agency, 2003a. President declares emergency in Texas and Louisiana in response to space shuttle tragedy. FEMA Press Release, February 1. http://www.fema.gov/news/newsrelease.fema?id=2406.

Federal Emergency Management Agency, 2003b. FEMA to lead search, find, and secure mission following space shuttle tragedy. FEMA Press Release, February 1. http://www.fema.gov/news/newsrelease.fema?id=2405.

Federal Emergency Management Agency, 2003c. FEMA puts federal resources into action to assist state and local authorities in search, find, and secure mission for *Columbia* debris. FEMA Press Release, February 2. http://www.fema .gov/news/newsrelease.fema?id=2407.

Federal Emergency Management Agency, 2003d. FEMA establishes joint information center for *Columbia* debris search, find, and secure mission at Lufkin civic center. FEMA Press Release, February 3. http://www.fema.gov/news/ newsrelease.fema?id=2409.

Federal Emergency Management Agency, 2003e. *Columbia* material collection guidelines: fact sheet. FEMA Press Release, February 5. http://www.fema.gov/news/ newsrelease.fema?id=2414.

Federal Emergency Management Agency, 2003f. President amends *Columbia* emergency declaration to include all states. FEMA Press Release, February 6. http://www.fema .gov/news/newsrelease.fema?id=2416.

Federal Emergency Management Agency, 2003g. FEMA updates search, find, and secure activities for *Columbia*

emergency. FEMA Press Release, February 6. http://www .fema.gov/news/newsrelease.fema?id=2415.

Federal Emergency Management Agency, 2003h. Good progress made in one month of shuttle recovery. FEMA Press Release, March 1. http://www.fema.gov/news/ newsrelease.fema?id=2458.

Federal Emergency Management Agency, 2003i. FEMA will hand on-going recovery operations to NASA April 30. FEMA Press Release, April 17. http://www.fema.gov/news/ newsrelease.fema?id=2534.

Federal Emergency Management Agency, 2003j. Recap of the search for *Columbia* shuttle material. FEMA Press Release, May 5. http://www.fema.gov/news/newsrelease. fema?id=2808.

Wikipedia, 2005. Space shuttle Columbia disaster. http:// en.wikipedia.org/wiki/Space_Shuttle_Columbia_disaster.

Key Terms

Demobilization: The orderly, safe, and efficient return of a resource or resources to their original location and status.

Disaster Declaration: The process by which the chief executive official of a jurisdiction (e.g., the mayor, governor, or president) identifies a situation as being beyond the capacity of that particular jurisdiction to be responsed. Under established statutory authorities at the state and federal levels, disaster declaration frees up various resources in support of the affected governments.

Emergency Declaration: Any occasion or instance for which, in the determination of the president, federal assistance is needed to supplement state and local efforts and capabilities to save lives and to protect property and public health and safety, or to lessen or avert the threat of a catastrophe in any part of the United States. An emergency declaration is more limited in scope and without the long-term federal recovery programs of a major disaster declaration. Generally, federal assistance and funding are provided to meet a specific emergency need or to help prevent a major disaster from occurring.

Emergency Support Function (ESF): Used by the federal government and many state governments as the primary mechanism at the operational level to organize and provide assistance. ESFs align categories of resources and provide strategic objectives for their use. ESFs exist within the NRF, and in most state and local emergency operations plans. ESFs utilize standardized resource management concepts such as typing, inventorying, and tracking to facilitate the dispatch, deployment, and recovery of resources before, during, and after an incident.

Federal Response Plan: A plan guiding the overall delivery of federal assistance in Stafford Act (presidentially declared) disasters that was replaced by the National Response Plan in 2004.

Incident Command System (ICS): A system by which emergency incidents of all sizes are managed, developed by the federal, state, and local wildland fire agencies during the 1970s. ICS is structured to facilitate activities in five major functional areas: command, operations, planning, logistics, and finance/administration. In some circumstances, intelligence and investigations may be added as a sixth functional area.

Individual Assistance: Individual assistance programs are oriented to individuals, families, and small businesses, and the programs include the Individuals and Households Program, Small Business Administration loans, disaster unemployment assistance, legal services, special tax considerations, and crisis counseling. The disaster victim must first register for assistance and establish eligibility before receiving this assistance.

Joint Field Office: The JFO coordinates federal incident support to the state, allowing the integration of diverse federal resources. Within the JFO, there is one key operational group and two key officials, including the Unified Coordination Group and the State Coordinating Officer.

Joint Information Center (JIC): A JIC may be established in emergency situations in order to coordinate the release of emergency information and other public affairs functions. The JIC serves as a focal point for coordinated and timely release of incident-related information to the public and the media. Information about where to receive assistance is communicated directly to victims and their families in an accessible format and in appropriate languages.

Long-Term Recovery: This is the period that involves the restoration of lives and livelihoods beyond the emergency phase of the disaster, once lifelines and critical societal components have been restored or replaced. This phase falls squarely within the direction of Emergency Support Function #14, "Long-Term Community Recovery," and often continues for several months or years after the disaster has ended.

Multiagency Coordination System (MACS): A system designed to help coordinate activities that occur above the field level, and to prioritize demands for critical or competing resources. Examples of multiagency coordination include a state or county emergency operations center, a state intelligence fusion center, the National Operations Center, the FEMA National Response Coordination Center, the Department of Justice/FBI Strategic Information and Operations Center, the FBI Joint Operations Center, and the National Counterterrorism Center.

National Incident Management System (NIMS): A system that provides a proactive approach guiding government agencies at all levels, the private sector, and nongovernmental organizations to work seamlessly to prepare for, prevent, respond to, recover from, and mitigate the effects of incidents, regardless of cause, size, location, or complexity, in order to reduce the loss of life or property and harm to the environment.

National Response Framework (NRF): A document released in 2008 to replace the National Response Plan that guides how the nation conducts all-hazards response. The framework documents the key response principles, roles, and structures that organize national response. It describes how communities, states, the federal government, and private-sector and nongovernmental partners apply these principles for national response. It also describes special circumstances where the federal government must exercise a larger role, including incidents where federal interests are involved and catastrophic incidents where a state would require significant support. It was designed to allow all response stakeholders to provide a unified national response.

National Response Plan: A plan released in 2004 to replace the Federal Response Plan that guided the response actions of local, state, and federal resources to major "incidents of national significance." This plan was replaced in 2008 by the NRF.

NRF Cooperating Agency: Cooperating agencies have specific expertise and capabilities that allow them to assist the coordinating agency in executing incident-related tasks or processes. When the procedures within a support annex are needed to support elements of an incident, the coordinating agency will notify cooperating agencies of the circumstances.

NRF Coordinating Agency: Coordinating agencies are responsible for implementing the processes detailed in NRF annexes. These federal agencies support DHS incident management efforts by providing the leadership, expertise, and authorities to implement critical and specific aspects of the response. When the functions of a particular support annex are required, the agency serving as the coordinator must carry out various responsibilities as stipulated in the NRF.

Posse Comitatus Act: A law passed in 1878 that restricts the use of the armed forces to perform domestic law enforcement.

Presidential Major Disaster Declaration: Any natural catastrophe (including any hurricane, tornado, storm, high water, wind-driven water, tidal wave, tsunami, earthquake, volcanic eruption, landslide, mudslide, snowstorm, or drought), or, regardless of cause, any fire, flood, or explosion, in any part of the United States that in the determination of the president causes damage of sufficient severity and magnitude to warrant major disaster assistance under the Stafford Act to supplement the efforts and available resources of states, local governments, and disaster relief organizations in alleviating the damage, loss, hardship, or suffering caused thereby.

Public Assistance: Public assistance, oriented to public entities, is designed to facilitate the repair, restoration, reconstruction, or replacement of public facilities or infrastructure damaged or destroyed by a federally declared disaster. Eligible applicants include state governments, local governments and any other political subdivision of a state, Native American tribes, and Alaska Native villages. Certain private nonprofit (PNP) organizations may also receive assistance, including educational, utility, irrigation, emergency, medical, rehabilitation, and temporary or permanent custodial care facilities, and other PNP facilities that provide essential services of a governmental nature to the general public.

Short-Term Recovery: This is the period when recovery actions that begin immediately upon occurrence of the disaster, which overlap with response actions, are taken. This phase includes actions such as providing essential public health and safety services, restoring interrupted utility and other essential services, reestablishing transportation routes, and providing food and shelter for those displaced by the incident. Although called *short term*, some short-term recovery activities may last for weeks. Short-term recovery actions are addressed in several functional areas of the NRF.

State Coordinating Officer (SCO): The SCO plays a critical role in managing the state response and recovery operations following presidential disaster declarations. The governor of the affected state appoints the SCO, and lines of authority flow from the governor to the SCO, following the state's policies and laws. For events in which a declaration has not yet occurred but is expected (such as with an approaching hurricane), the Secretary of Homeland Security or the FEMA administrator may predesignate one or more federal officials to coordinate with the SCO to determine resources and actions that will likely be required, and begin deployment of assets.

Strategic National Stockpile: CDC's Strategic National Stockpile (SNS) consists of strategically placed repositories of medicine and medical supplies that can be called on to protect the public in the event of a public health emergency severe enough to deplete local supplies. Once federal and local authorities agree that the SNS is needed, medicines will be delivered to any state in the United States within 12 hours. Each state has plans to receive and distribute SNS medicine and medical supplies to local communities as quickly as possible.

Unified Command: A system that allows for more efficient multijurisdictional or multiagency management of emergency events by enabling agencies with different legal, geographic, and functional responsibilities to coordinate, plan, and interact with each other in an effective manner. Unified command allows all agencies with jurisdictional authority or functional responsibility for the incident to jointly provide management direction to an incident through a common set of incident objectives and strategies and a single incident action plan. Under unified command, each participating agency maintains its authority, responsibility, and accountability.

Unified Coordination Group: The Unified Coordination Group is comprised of senior officials from the states and key federal departments and agencies, and is established at the JFO. Using unified command principles, this group provides national support to achieve shared emergency response and recovery objectives.

Urban Search and Rescue: Urban search and rescue (US&R) involves the location, rescue (extrication), and initial medical stabilization of victims trapped in confined spaces. Although structural collapse is the most common origin of trapped victims, transportation accidents, mines, and collapsed trenches may also cause such to occur. US&R is considered a "multihazard" discipline, as it may be needed for a variety of emergencies or disasters, including earthquakes, hurricanes, typhoons, storms and tornadoes, floods, dam failures, technological accidents, terrorist activities, and hazardous materials releases.

Zoonotic: A disease that can be spread between animals and people.

Review Questions

1. In your opinion, what are the most important differences between the NRF, the NRP, and the FRP?
2. Do you feel that the creation of the Department of Homeland Security has improved emergency response in the United States? Why or why not?
3. If you were an appointed local emergency manager, would you be satisfied with the actions of the federal government in terms of preparedness for large-scale emergency events? What would be the greatest benefits and problems for you under this new structure (the NRF) from a response perspective? Answer the same question from a regional emergency manager officer and a FEMA high-level officer point of view.
4. What was the basis of the decision to create the National Incident Management System (NIMS)? Why wasn't the ICS used instead? What benefits are gained by having an NRF that is based on the NIMS?
5. The establishment of the Department of Homeland Security, and the many subsequent changes to the national emergency management framework, are seen by many local emergency managers as inhibiting their efforts to establish an effective all-hazards emergency response capacity. What are your opinions on this stance? Explain your answer.

References

American Corporate Council Association (ACCA), 2002. 107th Congress Homeland Security Legislation. http://www.acc.com/infopaks/homeland/legislativechart.pdf.

Bea, Keath, W. Krouse, D. Morgan, W. Morrissey, and C. Redhead. 2003. Emergency Preparedness and Response Directorate of the Department of Homeland Security.

Congressional Research Service. http://www.fas.org/sgp/crs/RS21367.pdf.

Bullock & Haddow, LLC, 2003. Personal interviews with the Chief of Staff and Deputy Chief of Staff of the Federal Emergency Management Agency, unpublished.

Department of Homeland Security, 2007. FY 2007 Homeland Security Grant Program. http://www.dhs.gov/ xlibrary/assets/grants_st-local_fy07.pdf.

Environmental Protection Agency, 2008. "National Oil and Hazardous Substances Pollution Contingency Plan." http:// www.epa.gov/OEM/content/lawsregs/ncpover.htm.

Federal Bureau of Investigation, 2001. Domestic Terrorism Concept of Operations Plan. http://www.fbi.gov/ publications/conplan/conplan.pdf.

Federal Emergency Management Agency, 1992. Federal Response Plan. http://www.library.findlaw.com/1992/ Apr/1/127810.html.

Federal Emergency Management Agency, 2001. Federal Radiological Emergency Response Plan. http://www.fas.org/ nuke/guide/usa/doctrine/national/frerp.htm.

Federal Emergency Management Agency, 2004. National Response Plan. http://www.dhs.gov/xlibrary/assets/ NRPbaseplan.pdf.

Federal Emergency Management Agency, 2008. National Response Framework. http://www.fema.gov/emergency/nrf/.

Federal Emergency Management Agency. 2008. Number of Declarations per Calendar Year Since 1998. Washington, DC. http://www.fema.gov/government/grant/pa/ stat1.shtm.

Washington Post. 2005. War plans drafted to counter terror attacks in U.S. *The Washington Post*, August 8, p. A1. http://www.washingtonpost.com/wp dyn/content/ article/2005/08/07/AR2005080700843_pf.html.

10
Mitigation, Prevention, and Preparedness

What You Will Learn

- The definitions of mitigation, preparedness, and prevention
- Overview of mitigation and preparedness programs
- Where terrorism fits in the classical life cycle of emergency management
- Preparedness for chemical, biological, and radiological incidents
- Community issues in preparedness
- Private-sector involvement in mitigation and preparedness

Introduction

Mitigation and preparedness constitute one-half of the classic emergency management cycle, with response and recovery completing the sequence (Figure 10–1). Mitigation and preparedness generally occur before a disaster ever occurs, although postdisaster mitigation and preparedness, conducted in recognition that similar events are likely in the future, make these two activities somewhat general to the entire emergency management cycle. This is in contrast to response and recovery, which by definition are only possible in the aftermath of a disastrous event.

In its classical meaning, *mitigation* refers to a sustained action taken to reduce or eliminate risk to people and property from hazards and their effects. Mitigation activities address either or both of the two components of risk, which are probability (likelihood) and consequence. By mitigating either of these components, the risk becomes much less of a threat to the affected population. In the case of natural disasters, the ability of humans to limit the probability of a hazard is highly dependent on the hazard type, with some hazards such as hurricanes or tornadoes impossible to prevent, while avalanches, floods, and wildfires are examples of hazards for which limiting the rate of occurrence is possible.

In general, however, mitigation efforts for natural hazards tend to focus on improved consequence management. In terms of man-made disasters, however, there is a much greater range of opportunities to minimize both the probability and the consequences of potential incidents, and both are applied with equal intensity. Mitigation in terms of terrorism, which is a much more complicated process, is discussed later in this chapter.

Preparedness can be defined as a state of readiness to respond to a disaster, crisis, or any other type of emergency situation. In general, preparedness activities can be characterized as the human component

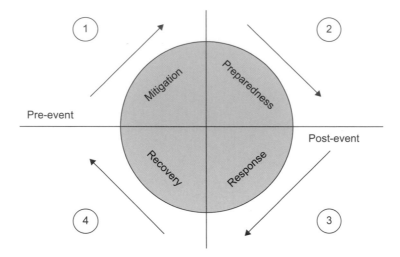

FIGURE 10–1 The four classical phases of disaster management.

of predisaster hazard management. Training and public education are the most common preparedness activities, and, when properly applied, they have great potential to help people survive disasters. Although preparedness activities do little to prevent a disaster from occurring, they are very effective at ensuring that people know what to do once the disaster has happened.

The concepts of mitigation and preparedness have been altered since September 11, 2001, when terrorism became viewed as the primary threat facing America. As such, terms like *terrorism prevention* and *terrorism preparedness* have become more popular. One must question, in light of these new terms, whether there is any real difference between the traditional definitions of *preparedness* and *mitigation* and what is being conducted in light of the new terrorism hazard.

The National Response Plan (NRP), released in December 2004 to replace the Federal Response Plan (FRP) as the operating plan for managing the response to major disasters by all federal government departments and agencies in support of state and local emergency managers, provided insight into this issue. Although this new plan did not directly define the phases of incident management, it introduced to users the sequential terminology of prevention, preparedness, response, recovery, and mitigation. The use of this terminology reflects two major changes with respect to the classical incident management approach in the United States. The first change is that mitigation is placed last in this cycle of incident management, which could indicate to readers that the activity (in the context of the plan) is perceived as a postincident one. This is significant mainly because it is altering a set terminology, which has already been widely understood and accepted within the emergency management discipline, feasibly resulting in unnecessary confusion. The second change, which is surely the more radical of the two, is the introduction of the term *prevention*, not only as a concept but also as a distinct phase in the incident management cycle. The plan defined prevention as "actions taken to avoid an incident or to intervene to stop an incident from occurring, which involve actions taken to protect lives and property." The NRP, like the FRP, was a comprehensive plan developed according to the all-hazards approach, but the inclusion of prevention as a separate incident phase (especially in light of the preceding definition) gave rise to the question of whether the NRP was focused primarily on terrorism incident management. Prevention does not seem applicable to most natural disasters.

In January 2008, the NRP was replaced by the National Response Framework (NRF), and as such much of the emergency management terminology and functions have changed accordingly. The following section describes several of these changes as they relate to mitigation, prevention, and preparedness.

First, the document's title has been changed appropriately to reflect its true nature — namely, that it provides guidelines, rules of engagement, and an organizational framework for all stakeholders of a disaster response involving the federal government rather than offering specific steps of action as is typical in an EOP.

Second, the NRF does not attempt to redefine the phases of emergency management as occurred in the NRP. In the NRP, prevention was introduced as a distinct phase in the incident management cycle, and in many (but not all) references, as a replacement for mitigation. The NRF makes no direct reference to the emergency management cycle, and refers more sensibly to the terms *prevention* and *mitigation*. *Mitigation* is used comfortably and consistently as part of the all-hazards approach, thereby providing clarity throughout the document. The choice not to push prevention as a distinct emergency management phase is consistent with former Department of Homeland Security (DHS) Secretary Michael Chertoff's vision to establish DHS as managing all hazards rather than having a distinct focus on terrorism. The term *prevention* is most closely associated with terrorism, and therefore finds little applicability in any generalized emergency management approach.

The third major difference relates to the adjustments made to general terms that better accommodate the involvement and partnership of nonfederal stakeholders. These entities are better defined in terms of their role with regard to the emergency support functions (ESFs). The final difference is that the framework commits the federal government to the development of specific emergency response plans based on the 15 incident scenarios identified by the Homeland Security Council. Because incident scenario planning tends to create a rigid response functionality, it is difficult to agree with the approach taken. In such an approach, flexibility is sacrificed and problems may arise when real incidents do not fit the expected parameters. Additionally, this should be seen as a departure from the all-hazards approach as so many of the scores of known hazards are omitted or disregarded, though it is true that these 15 scenarios may be useful as an exercise tool. (For more complete information regarding the NRF and the changes it brings, see DHS, 2011a; Public Broadcasting System, 2006.)

Whether we call it prevention or mitigation, proactive incident management is crucial for minimizing the loss of human life, injuries, financial losses, property damage, and interruption of business activities. Specific methods of prevention and mitigation change from hazard to hazard, and incident to incident, but the goals are the same.

Using the all-hazards approach, whether you are mitigating for earthquakes or floods or preparing for a potential terrorist threat, the classic mitigation planning process is an effective guide for the overall process. The traditional mitigation planning process, still conducted by the Federal Emergency Management Agency (FEMA) today under its DHS umbrella, consists of four stages: (1) identifying and organizing resources; (2) conducting a risk or threat assessment and estimating losses; (3) identifying mitigation measures that will reduce the effects of the hazards and creating a strategy to deal with the mitigation measures in priority order; and (4) implementing the measures, evaluating the results, and keeping the plan up-to-date. This chapter expands on these concepts.

Mitigation and preparedness are vital for sustainable emergency management because strategies geared strictly toward post disaster response tend to be costlier than those accounting for predisaster opportunities. However, it can be difficult to convince decision makers to invest in mitigation and preparedness activities. (See "Another Voice: Why Is Mitigation and Preparedness the Only Sustainable, Cost-Effective Way of Dealing with Emergencies?")

The next section focuses on mitigation, prevention, and preparedness activities in an effort to identify ongoing programs, as well as new developments as they fit into each subject.

Mitigation Plans, Actions, and Programs

Mitigation activities include many different methods and strategies that have the common goal of reducing the risk associated with potential hazards. To provide a deeper understanding of mitigation, it is important to first understand the nature of natural, man-made, and terrorism risk.

There are many different definitions of *risk*, each of which may be appropriate within specific circumstances. Kaplan 1997, an acclaimed risk management expert, argues that rather than providing a full definition of *risk*, one must ask three major questions in considering a specific hazard: (1) What can happen? (2) How likely is it? (3) What are the consequences? This indirect definition provides a much more flexible starting point with which to begin our discussion of risk and how to mitigate it. It also sheds additional light on the complexity of treating risks, which are clearly dynamic in nature. How we consider those risks — and rank them according to our concern — is a factor of the combined answers of those three questions. For instance, although traffic accidents occur on a daily basis, their consequences tend to be relatively minor. Very large meteor strikes, on the other hand, are very rare, but when they do occur, their consequences are globally catastrophic. Each hazard must be considered for its individual characteristics, and it is up to the individual, community, or society that is making the analysis to determine what level of effort will be made to address each according to these individual risk components.

The uncertainty component of risk, contained within the probability of disastrous event occurrence, places the greatest burden on those who are treating a full portfolio of risks that must be compared in relation to each other. Uncertainty forces us to ask ourselves questions that are often difficult and based more on expert judgment than on concrete evidence, such as, "What is the probability that a 7.0-magnitude earthquake will happen in San Francisco Bay within the next 10 years?" or "What is the probability that terrorists will attack and damage a nuclear power plant in the United States?" The probability component of risk is important because it is an equally weighted parameter that helps us to quantify and prioritize mitigation actions when dealing with multiple risks. The determination of probabilities for events is often a difficult and complicated process. Although several quantitative methods and tools are available that can be used to determine probabilities, these often tend to be too complex for communities to use. Qualitative methods have been developed to ease this problem, which in turn allows for much easier comparison of risk by communities that attempt treating their risks. The sidebar titled, "Qualitative Representation of Likelihood" illustrates but one example of a system of estimation used to establish qualitative risk likelihood rankings.

Qualitative Representation of Likelihood

This particular qualitative representation system uses words to describe the chance of an event occurring. Each word or phrase has a designated range of possibilities attached to it. For instance, events could be described as follows:

- Certain: 99% chance of occurring in a given year (one or more occurrences per year)
- Likely: 50%–99% chance of occurring in a given year (one occurrence every 1 to 2 years)
- Possible: 5%–49% chance of occurring in a given year (one occurrence every 2 to 20 years)
- Unlikely: 2%–5% chance of occurring in a given year (one occurrence every 20 to 50 years)
- Rare: 1%–2% chance of occurring in a given year (one occurrence every 50 to 100 years)
- Extremely rare: 1% chance of occurring in a given year (one occurrence every 100 or more years)

Note that this is just one of a limitless range of qualitative terms and values assigned that can be used to describe the likelihood component of risk. As long as all hazards are compared using the same range of qualitative values, the actual determination of likelihood ranges attached to each term does not necessarily matter.

■ ■ ■

The second component of risk, hazard consequence, is a detailed examination of the total unwanted impact of the disaster to the community, government, or the interested stakeholders. Consequence is often given an assigned monetary value in order to facilitate comparison with other hazards, but there are many intangible consequences that are very difficult to quantify in such absolute terms but which have to be considered as well if a comprehensive risk analysis is expected (Table 10–1). Interestingly, the consequences of disasters also have a probabilistic nature. In practice, it is quite hard to assign a single monetary value to the expected damage; probability distributions are used to model the most likely damage estimates. For this reason, qualitative applications of consequence estimation have also been developed. An example is presented in the sidebar "Qualitative Representation of Consequence."

Table 10–1 Tangible and Intangible Consequences of Disasters

Consequences	Measure	Tangible Losses	Intangible Losses
Deaths	Number of people	Loss of economically active individuals	Social and psychological effects on remaining community
Injuries	Number and injury severity	Medical treatment needs, temporary loss of economic activity by productive individuals	Social and psychological pain and recovery
Physical damage	Inventory of damaged elements by number and damage level	Replacement and repair cost	Cultural losses
Emergency operations	Volume of manpower, person-days employed, equipment, and resources expended to relief mobilization cost, investment in preparedness capability	Stress and overwork in relief participants	
Disruption to economy	Number of working days lost, volume of production lost	Value of lost production opportunities, and in competitiveness and reputation	
Social disruption	Number of displaced persons, homeless	Temporary housing, relief, economic production	Psychological, social contacts, cohesion, community morale
Environmental impact	Scale and severity	Cleanup costs, repair costs	Consequences of poorer environment, health risks, risk of future disaster

Source: United Nations Development Programme, *Vulnerability and Risk Assessment*, 2nd ed., Cambridge: Cambridge Architectural Research Limited, 1994.

Qualitative Representation of Consequence

As was true with the qualitative representation of likelihood, words or phrases that have associated meanings can be used to describe the effects of a past disaster or the anticipated effects of a future one. These measurements can be assigned to deaths, injuries, or costs (often, the qualitative measurement of fatalities and injuries is combined). The following is one example of a qualitative measurement system for injuries and deaths:

- Insignificant: No injuries or fatalities
- Minor: Small number of injuries but no fatalities; first-aid treatment required
- Moderate: Medical treatment needed but no fatalities; some hospitalization
- Major: Extensive injuries, significant hospitalization; fatalities
- Catastrophic: Large number of fatalities and severe injuries; extended and large numbers requiring hospitalization

Once both of these factors (probability and consequence) have been determined, it is possible to compare risks against each other, primarily for the purposes of treating the risks through intervention measures. Normally, only limited funds exist for this purpose and, as such, not all risks can be treated. Risk comparison allows for a prioritization of risk, which can help those performing mitigation and preparedness ensure that they are spending their limited funds most wisely. Table 10–2 provides one example of a risk matrix that can be used to compare risks to each other.

Having provided a basic description of the components of risk, it is appropriate to move on to the mitigation of risk. In applying mitigation, risk managers try to minimize probability or consequence or both. In practice, however, it is not always easy, or even possible, to address both. And because each risk is unique, there are different strategies that must be identified, assessed, and applied for successful risk intervention. For example, assume one seeks to minimize the risk of an earthquake. How can one minimize the probability of its happening? In terms of modern science, unfortunately, there is no known way

Table 10–2 Example of a Qualitative Risk-Level Analysis Matrix

Likelihood	Consequences				
	Insignificant	**Minor**	**Moderate**	**Major**	**Catastrophic**
Almost certain	High	High	Extreme	Extreme	Extreme
Likely	Moderate	High	High	Extreme	Extreme
Possible	Low	Moderate	High	Extreme	Extreme
Unlikely	Low	Low	Moderate	High	Extreme
Rare	Low	Low	Moderate	High	High

Source: Emergency Management Australia, "Emergency Risk Management: Application's Guide," Australian Emergency Manual Series, 2000.

of doing so, and this is true for many natural hazards despite humankind's best efforts. However, one can still mitigate the risk of an earthquake by minimizing its consequences. For the earthquake risk, several known and proven strategies are available to minimize such consequences, such as adopting and enforcing earthquake-resistant building codes, educating the public about earthquakes, and developing robust earthquake response plans.

In dealing with the newly expanded terrorism risk, the mitigation strategy would likely take on a much different approach. In this case, the opportunity to minimize the likelihood of the event's occurrence is very possible, and has been done countless times with great success. Through actionable intelligence collection on terrorist activity, and by infiltration of its social and communication networks, it is possible to stop terrorists before they proceed with their plots. Therefore, theoretically, the probability component of terrorism risk can be reduced through mitigation (or "prevention"). Of course, minimizing this likelihood component is a very complex task, requiring governments to allocate significant resources to build and manage necessary systems, establish international partnerships, and build networks to identify and detain terrorists.

The consequence component of terrorism risk can also be mitigated. However, unlike most natural disasters that have a limited range of possible consequences, the options available to terrorists are limited only by their imagination. Terrorists have limitless targets, including facilities, infrastructures, and organizations, so many different strategies must be employed to minimize the impacts of terrorist attacks to each of these potential targets. DHS has developed a manual titled *Reference Manual to Mitigate Potential Terrorist Attacks against Buildings* (the sidebar "FEMA 426"). This manual discusses the importance of minimizing the impacts of potential terrorist attacks against buildings. Buildings, however, are but one target. Presumably, it may be impossible to mitigate all possible consequences only because to do so would surely exhaust even the richest nation's financial resources. It would seem, then, that the best measures would seek multiple-use solutions, such as building a robust mass-casualty public health system that would not only serve to mitigate the impact of terrorism on humans but also mitigate the consequences of other natural and technological hazards that also may affect the population.

■ ■ ■ ━━

FEMA 426: Reference Manual to Mitigate Potential Terrorist Attacks against Buildings

The Federal Emergency Management Agency (FEMA) developed the Reference Manual to Mitigate Potential Terrorist Attacks against Buildings to provide information on how to mitigate the effects of potential terrorist attacks. The intended audience includes the building sciences community of architects and engineers working for private institutions. The manual supports FEMA's mission (to lead America to prepare for, prevent, respond to, and recover from disasters) and the Strategic Plan's Goal 3 (to prepare the nation to address the consequences of terrorism), all of which will be done within the all-hazards framework and the needs of homeland security.

The building science community, as a result of FEMA's efforts, has incorporated extensive building science into designing and constructing buildings against natural hazards (earthquake, fire, flood, and wind). To date, the same level of understanding has not been applied to man-made hazards (terrorism/intentional acts) and technological hazards (accidental events). Since September 11, 2001, terrorism has become a dominant domestic concern. Security can no longer be viewed as a stand-alone capability that can be purchased as an afterthought and put in place. Life, safety, and security issues must become a design goal from the beginning.

The objective of this manual is to reduce physical damage to structural and nonstructural components of buildings and related infrastructure and also to reduce resultant casualties during conventional bomb attacks, as well as attacks using chemical, biological, and radiological agents. Although the process is general in nature and applies to most building uses, this manual is most applicable for six specific types of facilities:

- Commercial office facilities
- Retail commercial facilities
- Light industrial and manufacturing facilities
- Health care facilities
- Local schools (K-12)
- Higher education (university) facilities

Chapter 1 presents selected methodologies to integrate threat/hazard, asset criticality, and vulnerability assessment information. This information becomes the input for determining relative levels of risk. Higher risk hazards require mitigation measures to reduce risk. The chapter also provides an assessment checklist that compiles many best practices to consider during the design of a new building or renovation of an existing building.

Chapter 2 discusses architectural and engineering design considerations (mitigation measures), starting at the perimeter of the property line, and includes the orientation of the building on the site. Therefore, this chapter covers issues outside the building envelope.

Chapter 3 provides the same considerations for the building — its envelope, systems, and interior layout.

Chapter 4 provides a discussion of blast theory to understand the dynamics of the blast pressure wave, the response of building components, and a consistent approach to define levels of protection.

Chapter 5 presents chemical, biological, and radiological measures that can be taken to mitigate vulnerabilities and reduce associated risks for these terrorist tactics or technological hazards.

Appendices A, B, and C contain acronyms, general definitions, and CBR definitions, respectively.

Appendix D describes electronic security systems and design considerations.

Appendices E and F present a comprehensive bibliography of publications and the associations and organizations capturing the building security guidance needed by the building sciences community, respectively.

Source: FEMA 426, June 2003, http://www.fema.gov/pdf/plan/prevent/rms/426/fema426.pdf.

The threat of terrorism is not new. Throughout history there have been terrorist organizations and terrorist attacks in all parts of the world, including North America, Europe, and Australia; however, the September 11 attacks resulted in such severe consequences that, not unexpectedly, terrorism became the primary issue on the U.S. government's agenda.

Mitigating the terrorism risk is important in order to minimize potential damage that may result from what is known to be a very real threat, but it is vital to remember that combating terrorism is a complex and long-term task, one that requires both patience and sacrifice. Therefore, all stakeholders — including the government, the public, the private sector, the media, and academia — need to appreciate the benefit of applying mitigation on an all-hazards approach such that all known risks are treated, not only terrorism. Clearly, as has been shown in the years following the September 11 attacks, there are much more likely hazards — hurricanes and floods being the greatest — that have much greater potential to cause harm in terms of both likelihood and consequence. Hurricanes Katrina and Rita and the 2011 tornadoes that struck Joplin, MO, and Tuscaloosa, AL, are just some of many recent examples.

DHS continues to provide funding for predisaster and postdisaster mitigation projects through FEMA and its other relevant directorates. Details of those initiatives are provided in the next sections.

Federal Insurance and Mitigation Administration (FIMA)

The Federal Insurance and Mitigation Administration (FIMA) is responsible for a vast majority of the U.S. government's hazard mitigation activities, including the National Flood Insurance Program (NFIP). FIMA performs several organizational activities that serve to promote protection, prevention, and partnerships at the federal, state, local, and individual levels. The overall mission of FIMA is to protect lives and prevent the loss of property from natural and other hazards. FIMA employs the all-hazards approach through a comprehensive risk-based emergency management program. (See sidebar "What FIMA does and Mitigation Value to Society.")

■ ■ ■ ■ ▬▬▬▬▬▬▬▬▬▬▬▬▬▬▬▬▬▬▬▬▬▬▬▬▬▬▬▬▬▬

What FIMA Does and Mitigation Value to Society

What FIMA Does

FIMA manages the National Flood Insurance Program (NFIP) and a range of programs designed to reduce future losses to homes, businesses, schools, public buildings, and critical facilities from floods, earthquakes, tornadoes, and other natural disasters.

Mitigation focuses on breaking the cycle of disaster damage, reconstruction, and repeated damage. Mitigation efforts provide value to the American people by creating safer communities and reducing loss of life and property. Mitigation includes such activities as:

- Complying with or exceeding NFIP floodplain management regulations.
- Enforcing stringent building codes, flood-proofing requirements, seismic design standards, and wind-bracing requirements for new construction or repairing existing buildings.
- Adopting zoning ordinances that steer development away from areas subject to flooding, storm surge, or coastal erosion.
- Retrofitting public buildings to withstand hurricane-strength winds or ground shaking.
- Acquiring damaged homes or businesses in flood-prone areas, relocating the structures, and returning the property to open space, wetlands, or recreational uses.
- Building community shelters and tornado-safe rooms to help protect people in their homes, public buildings, and schools in hurricane- and tornado-prone areas.

Mitigation's Value to Society

1. Mitigation creates safer communities by reducing losses of life and property.
2. Mitigation enables individuals and communities to recover more rapidly from disasters.
3. Mitigation lessens the financial impact of disasters on individuals, the Treasury, and state, local, and tribal communities.

Source: FEMA, 2011, Federal Insurance and Mitigation Administration (FIMA), http://www.fema.gov/about/divisions/mitigation.shtm.

FIMA administers the nationwide risk-reduction programs authorized by the U.S. Congress and is composed of the following divisions:

The Risk Analysis Division applies engineering and planning practices in conjunction with advanced technology tools to identify hazards, assess vulnerabilities, and develop strategies to manage the risks associated with natural hazards. The division runs the following FEMA mitigation programs:

- Flood Map Modernization
- National Dam Safety Program
- Mitigation Planning

The Risk Reduction Division works to reduce risk to life and property through the use of land use controls, building practices, and other tools. These activities address risk in both the existing built environment and future development, and they occur in both pre- and postdisaster environments. The division is in charge of the following programs:

- National Earthquake Hazards Reduction Program (NEHRP)
- Hazard Mitigation Grant Program (HMGP)
- Flood Mitigation Assistance Program (FMA)
- Pre-Disaster Mitigation Program (PDM)
- Severe Repetitive Loss Program (SRL)
- Repetitive Flood Claims Program (RFC)
- Building Science
- Community Rating System (CRS)

The *Risk Insurance Division* helps reduce flood losses by providing affordable flood insurance for property owners and by encouraging communities to adopt and enforce floodplain management regulations that mitigate the effects of flooding on new and improved structures. The Division's prime responsibility is to run the NFIP, through which affordable flood insurance is provided to communities vulnerable to flood hazards, and impacts of floods are minimized through enforcement of floodplain management for new and altered buildings and structures (FEMA, 2011a). FEMA mitigation programs and their funding levels are described in subsequent sections.

Flood Map Modernization

Flood Map Modernization is a multiyear program to improve existing flood maps in the United States and to create new maps based on new technology and standards for those localities that require flood maps for which no previous maps exist. The need for flood map modernization arises because of the dynamic nature of flood hazards that change with geography. Changing information management standards, improvements in information delivery methods such as the Internet, and advances in technologies such as GIS (geographical information systems) are other drivers behind flood map modernization. Conventional flood maps involve paper-based cartographic maps that may be many years old, providing limited accuracy in a quickly changing physical environment. To make the updating, sharing, collaboration, and delivery of those maps more efficient, Flood Map Modernization is creating electronic maps based on GIS that adhere to newest data management standards (i.e., GIS data models and meta-data).

The resulting maps and data better serve the needs of all parties that use those maps. FEMA Risk Analysis Division takes the lead in this program and acts as the main integrator of data, creator of geographic maps, and the clearinghouse for the dissemination of all flood map products. Community planners, public policymakers, local officials, developers, builders, insurance companies, and individual property owners can all benefit from those map products made available by the program. The improved flood maps provide more reliable information on flood risks and therefore help stakeholders make better informed decisions related to their vulnerability to floods. In the long run, the use of those maps is expected to reduce total costs of flood disasters, as communities and service providers make it a habit to check flooding risks before making land use decisions.

Flood Map Modernization is a multiyear program that started in 2004 and sustained its funding levels throughout the years that followed. In FY 2006 and 2007, the program enjoyed a funding level of $198 million, and was funded at $220 million for FY 2008, 2009, 2010, and 2011, respectively. The president's FY 2012 budget includes approximately $102 million to fund the activities of the program (FEMA, 2011e).

National Dam Safety Program

National Dam Safety Program is an initiative of the FEMA Risk Analysis Directorate. The program was created by the Water Resources and Development Act of 1996 and has since been reauthorized twice with new legislation introduced in 2002 and 2006.

The primary goal of the program is to provide funding for states to be used in dam safety-related activities. In that scope, states use program funds to provide dam safety training, increase the frequency of dam safety inspections, create and test emergency response plans, and promote dam safety awareness through videos and other educative material. Between FY 1998 and FY 2004, the program provided approximately $22 million to states. Other components of the program include dam safety research and dam safety training.

As confirmed by the National Dam Safety Act of 2006 (Public Law 109–460), the program will continue to provide $38.7 million to states as dam safety grants, $9 million for dam safety research, and $3.25 million for dam safety training for FY 2007 to 2011 (Association of State Dam Safety Officials, 2005; FEMA, 2011b; American Society of Civil Engineers, 2007; Congressional Research Service, 2007a).

Mitigation Planning Program

The Mitigation Planning Program administered by FEMA's Risk Analysis Division creates multihazard mitigation planning manuals, how-to guidelines, and best-practice documents. Since the program has an all-hazards mitigation scope, it works closely with several partners in different areas of interest and expertise. Some of the program partners include the American Planning Association, Association of State Floodplain Managers, Institute for Business and Home Safety, and National Institute for Building Sciences.

The program also works closely with the (postdisaster) HMGP and the PDM administered by FEMA's Risk Reduction Division (FEMA, 2011d).

National Earthquake Hazards Reduction Program

The NEHRP was established by the Earthquake Hazards Reduction Act of 1977 to "reduce the risks of life and property from future earthquakes in the United States." In 1980, the act was amended to include the National Institutes of Standards and Technology (NIST, then the National Bureau of Standards) and to designate the newly created FEMA as the lead agency. FEMA coordinated NEHRP until 2003, when legislation transferred FEMA's management role in the program to NIST. In this capacity, FEMA planned and managed the federal response to earthquakes, funded state and local preparedness exercises, and supported seismic design and construction techniques for new buildings and retrofit guidelines for existing buildings.

As part of this program, the U.S. Geological Survey (USGS) conducts and supports earth science investigations into the origins of earthquakes, predicts earthquake effects, characterizes earthquake hazards, and disseminates earth science information. Additionally, the National Science Foundation (NSF) provides funding to earthquake engineering research, basic earth science research, and earthquake-related social science.

In addition to its lead management role for the program, NIST conducts and supports engineering studies to improve seismic provisions of building codes, standards, and practices for buildings and lifelines (FEMA, "NEHRP," 2007).

Total combined NEHRP funding to the four lead agencies from FY 2005 to FY 2008 rose $127.1 million, to $118.5 million, to $118 million, and finally to $119 million. The FY 2009 budget was $129 million, the FY 2010 budget was $131 million, and the president's FY 2011 budget request included $129 million for NEHRP (NEHRP, 2011).

The roles of the four NEHRP agencies were further clarified in the 1990 NEHRP Reauthorization Act, which cast their primary responsibilities as follows:

Federal Emergency Management Agency

- Translates research results into technical publications
- Supports state and local governments by providing multiple-hazard loss estimation capability for use in planning and response
- Prepares technical documents aimed at improving the seismic safety of new and existing buildings
- Works with national standards organizations to develop seismic standards for new and existing lifelines
- Prepares and disseminates information about building codes and practices

National Institutes of Standards and Technologies

- Promotes better building practices among architects and engineers
- Works with national standards organizations to develop improved seismic standards for new and existing lifelines
- Chairs and provides the secretariat for the Interagency Committee on Seismic Safety in Construction (ICSSC), which recommends practices and policies to reduce earthquake hazards in federally owned, leased, assisted, and regulated facilities

National Science Foundation

- Supports research on plate tectonics
- Funds engineering research on geotechnical, structural, architectural, and lifeline systems
- Supports research on the social and economic aspects of earthquake hazard mitigation
- Supports the education of new scientists and engineers in the field

United States Geological Survey

- Provides national and regional seismic hazard and risk maps
- Conducts engineering seismology studies of the ground-shaking phenomenon
- Develops methods and standardized procedures for forecasting earthquakes
- Supports an external cooperative grants research program
- Operates national seismograph networks

NEHRP is an essential program because of the susceptibility of the entire geography of the United States to earthquake disasters. Relative earthquake risks of U.S. states can be viewed at the following website: http://www.fema.gov/hazard/earthquake/risk.shtm. There are multiple active faults throughout the United States. The San Andreas fault in California and New Madrid fault crossing parts of Illinois, Missouri, Arkansas, Kentucky, and Tennessee are but two examples. These faults are known to have the potential to generate very strong earthquakes. Had the 1906 San Francisco earthquake occurred today, it has been estimated that it would have affected nearly 10 million residents within a 19-county area, and would have caused economic losses ranging from $90 to $120 billion. The earthquake could damage as many as 90,000 buildings and depending on the time of the day, 800 to 3,400 people may lose their lives in collapsed buildings. Many of those consequences are preventable through effective earthquake hazard mitigation, thus the importance of the NEHRP (FEMA, 2007b).

FEMA's Mitigation Grant Programs

FEMA currently has five mitigation grant programs: the Hazards Mitigation Grant Program, Pre-Disaster Mitigation Grant Program, Flood Mitigation Assistance Grant Program, Severe Repetitive Loss Grant Program (SRL), and Repetitive Flood Claims Grant Program (RFC), all of which are administered by the Risk Reduction Division of the Mitigation Directorate. (A table of Historic HMS Funding is available online — see p. 5 of "JUNE 1, 2010 HMA GUIDANCE": http://www.fema.gov/library/viewRecord .do?id = 4225.)

Hazards Mitigation Grant Program

Authorized under Section 404 of the Stafford Act, the Hazard Mitigation Grant Program (HMGP) provides grants to states and local governments to implement long-term hazard-mitigation measures after a major disaster declaration. The purpose of the program is to reduce the loss of life and property due to natural disasters and to enable mitigation measures to be implemented during the immediate recovery from a disaster declaration. HMGP funding is only available in states following a presidential disaster declaration. Eligible applicants follow:

- State and local governments
- Indian tribes or other tribal organizations
- Certain private nonprofit organizations

Individual homeowners and businesses may not apply directly to the program; however, a community may apply on their behalf. HMGP funds may be used to fund projects that will reduce or eliminate the losses from future disasters. Projects must provide a long-term solution to a problem — for example, elevation of a home to reduce the risk of flood damages as opposed to buying sandbags and pumps to fight the flood. In addition, a project's potential savings must be more than the cost of implementing the project. Funds may be used to protect either public or private property or to purchase property that has been subjected to, or is in danger of, repetitive damage.

The HMGP is directly funded by FEMA's Disaster Relief Fund. The amount of HMGP funds that will be made available depends on the combined funding made available from the Disaster Relief Fund for the Public Assistance Program and the Individual Assistance Program. The Public Assistance Program makes funds available to communities in repairing or replacing roads, bridges, and other public infrastructure after a disaster occurs. The Individual Assistance Program provides grants for individuals and families in the aftermath of disasters.

According to FEMA's "Hazard Mitigation Assistance Unified Guidance: June 1, 2010," "HMGP funding is allocated using a "sliding scale" formula based on a percentage of the estimated total federal assistance under the Stafford Act, excluding administrative costs for each presidential major disaster declaration. Applicants with a FEMA-approved State or Tribal Standard Mitigation Plan may receive

- Up to 15% of the first $2 billion of the estimated aggregate amount of disaster assistance;
- Up to 10% for the next portion of the estimated aggregate amount more than $2 billion and up to $10 billion; and
- 7.5% for the next portion of the estimated aggregate amount more than $10 billion and up to $35.333 billion.

Applicants with a FEMA-approved State or Tribal Enhanced Mitigation Plan are eligible for HMGP funding not to exceed 20% of the estimated total federal assistance under the Stafford Act, up to $35.333 billion of such assistance, excluding administrative costs authorized for the disaster" (FEMA, 2010).

In the aftermath of the severe 2004 hurricane season, which included Hurricanes Frances, Jeanne, Ivan, and Charley, FEMA provided a record $359 million in mitigation funding to the State of Florida through the HMGP. As of November 26, 2007, Hurricane Katrina- and Rita-related HMGP grants exceeded $1.47 billion (FEMA, 2011c, 2011j, 2011k).

Pre-Disaster Mitigation Program

The Pre-Disaster Mitigation (PDM) Program was authorized by Section 203 of the Robert T. Stafford Disaster Assistance and Emergency Relief Act (as amended by Section 102 of the Disaster Mitigation Act of 2000). Funding for the program is provided through the National Pre-Disaster Mitigation Fund to assist state and local governments (including Indian tribal governments) in implementing cost-effective hazard mitigation activities that complement a comprehensive mitigation program. Recipients of this grant must be participating in the NFIP if they have been identified as being at special risk from flood hazards (i.e., have a "Special Flood Hazard Area"), and must have a mitigation plan in effect. The PDM was funded in FY 2006, FY 2007, and FY 2008 at $49.5 million, $100 million, $114 million, respectively. FY 2009 funding was $90 million, FY 2010 was $100 million, and FY 2011 was $100 million, respectively. The president's FY 2012 budget request included $84.9 million for the program (DHS, 2011a; DHS, 2012; FEMA, 2011f).

Flood Mitigation Assistance Program

The Flood Mitigation Assistance (FMA) Program provides funding to assist states and communities in implementing measures to reduce or eliminate the long-term risk of flood damage to buildings, manufactured homes, and other structures insurable under the NFIP. Three types of grants are available under FMA: planning, project, and technical assistance grants. FMA planning grants are available to states and communities to prepare flood mitigation plans. NFIP-participating communities with approved flood mitigation plans can apply for FMA project grants. FMA project grants are available to states and NFIP-participating communities to implement measures to reduce flood losses. Ten percent of the project grant is made available to states as a technical assistance grant. These funds may be used by the state to help administer the program. Communities receiving FMA planning and project grants must be participating in the NFIP. An example of eligible FMA projects includes the elevation, acquisition, and relocation of NFIP-insured structures. FMA program priority for FY 2007 and 2008 is the funding of mitigation projects that minimize or eliminate the long-term risk of flood damage to properties insured by NFIP. In FY 2007, the program was funded at $31 million inclusive of all types of grants, and in FY 2008 funding included $34 million. However, the president's FY 2009 budget did not request any funding for the FMA program (see FEMA, 2008c).

Severe Repetitive Loss Program

The Severe Repetitive Loss Program (SLP) is a proactive mitigation initiative of the NFIP to reduce or eliminate flood-related damages and insurance claims for the approximately 83,000 residential properties that qualify as structures with severe repetitive flood damage potential. Structures with severe repetitive flood loss potential are defined as structures that meet the following criteria:

- Have four or more NFIP claim payments over $5,000 each, given that at least two such claims have occurred within 10 years of each other, and the total amount paid to the policy holder exceeds $20,000; or
- Have two or more separate claims payments where the total amount paid for the building portion of such claims exceeded the value of the property, given that two such claims have occurred within 10 years of each other.

The SLP has been in effect since the Flood Insurance Reform Act of 2004. This program reduces the cost of NFIP claims made by owners of highly vulnerable structures by funding mitigation projects that strengthen those structures against flood damage. Among qualifying projects are flood proofing (historical properties only), relocation, elevation, acquisition, mitigation reconstruction (demolition rebuild), and minor physical localized flood control projects. The program is funded at $40 million per fiscal year from 2005 to 2009 (FEMA, 2011h).

Repetitive Flood Claims Program

Another program introduced by the Flood Insurance Reform Act of 2004 is the RFC. The program is conceptually similar to the SLP, but the criterion to qualify for the program is more relaxed. Any state or community that had at least one claim to the NFIP can apply for RFC funding to finance projects to reduce the vulnerability of properties against floods. RFC funds can only be spent to improve structures that are located within a state or community that is ineligible for the FMA due to cost share or capacity to manage the activities.

In FY 2007, 11 states applied for RFC funding for a total of 24 projects covering 118 properties. A total of $33.7 million in funding was requested. FEMA selected 15 of these projects, covering 41 properties, which were funded by the program's $10 million annual budget (FEMA, 2008b, 2008e, 2008f).

Other FEMA Mitigation Directorate Programs

National Flood Insurance Program

Congress established the National Flood Insurance Program (NFIP) with the passage of the National Flood Insurance Act of 1968. The NFIP is a federal program enabling property owners in participating communities to purchase insurance as a protection against flood losses in exchange for state and community floodplain management regulations that reduce future flood damages. Flood insurance is designed to provide an alternative to disaster assistance to reduce the escalating costs of repairing damage to buildings and their contents caused by floods. Flood damage is reduced by nearly $1 billion a year through communities implementing sound floodplain management requirements and property owners' purchasing of flood insurance. Additionally, buildings constructed in compliance with NFIP building standards suffer approximately 80% less damage annually than those not built in compliance. And, every $3 paid in flood insurance claims reduces $1 in disaster assistance payments (FEMA, 2005).

The importance of flood insurance was again proven following Hurricanes Katrina, Rita, and Wilma in 2005, when the NFIP paid more than $16 billion in claims (Figure 10–2). As more communities

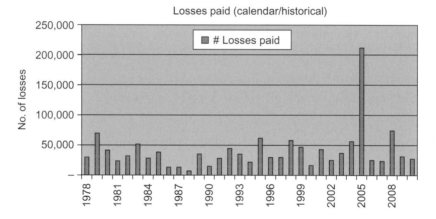

FIGURE 10–2 Losses paid by National Flood Insurance by year. (Source: FEMA, 2011, "Number of Losses Paid by Calendar Year," http://www.fema.gov/business/nfip/statistics/cy2010_lossespaid.shtm)

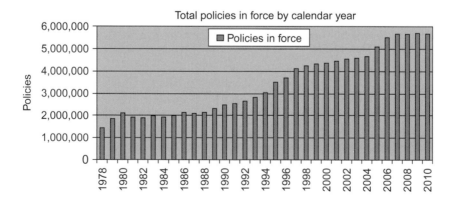

FIGURE 10–3 Growth in national flood insurance policies since 1978. (Source: FEMA, 2011, "Total Policies in Force by Calendar Year" from this site — http://www.fema.gov/business/nfip/statistics/cy2010_totpif.shtm)

meet floodplain management eligibility requirements and participate in the program, they will continue to minimize flood risk, while enjoying greater financial protection from inevitable flood damages. As these benefits become more and more apparent to homeowners with each disaster that occurs, participation in the NFIP should continue to increase over time. Figure 10–3 provides an overview of the growth in the number of flood insurance policies issued by the NFIP. NFIP funding increased from $2.5 billion to $2.8 billion from FY 2006 to FY 2008. The president's FY 2009 budget request included $3.16 billion in mandatory and discretionary funding for the program (NFIP, 2008; Insurance Information Institute, 2008; FEMA, 2011g; DHS, 2008).

Prevention Actions and Programs

Prevention refers to actions taken to avoid an incident or to intervene in an effort to stop an incident from occurring in order to protect lives and property. The draft National Incident Management System of August 2007 defines prevention as follows:

> *Actions to avoid an incident or to intervene to stop an incident from occurring. Prevention involves actions to protect lives and property. It involves applying intelligence and other information to a range of activities that may include such countermeasures as deterrence operations; heightened inspections; improved surveillance and security operations; investigations to determine the full nature and source of the threat; public health and agricultural surveillance and testing processes; immunizations, isolation, or quarantine; and, as appropriate, specific law enforcement operations aimed at deterring, preempting, interdicting, or disrupting illegal activity and apprehending potential perpetrators and bringing them to justice. (FEMA, 2007a, p. 156)*

According to DHS, the NRP (now called the National Response Framework) may be implemented for threats or potential incidents of national significance to prevent or intervene in order to lessen the impact of an incident. Prevention activities may include heightened inspections; improved surveillance and security operations; public health and agricultural surveillance and testing; immunizations, isolation, or quarantine; and, as appropriate, specific law enforcement operations aimed at deterring, preempting, interdicting, or disrupting illegal activity and apprehending potential perpetrators and bringing them to justice (FEMA, 2005).

As the prevention activities described by DHS imply, most of these activities are related to the prevention of terrorist incidents. Prevention actions related to terrorism threats and incidents include law enforcement activities and protective activities. All federal law enforcement activities are coordinated by the attorney general, generally acting through the FBI. During an incident, initial prevention efforts include, but are not limited to, the following actions:

- Collecting, analyze, and apply intelligence and other information.
- Conducting investigations to determine the full nature and source of the threat.
- Implementing countermeasures such as surveillance and counterintelligence.
- Conducting security operations, including vulnerability assessments, site security, and infrastructure protection.
- Conducting tactical operations to prevent, interdict, preempt, or disrupt illegal activity.
- Conducting attribution investigations, including an assessment of the potential for future-related incidents.

- Conducting activities to prevent terrorists, terrorist weapons, and associated materials from entering or moving within the United States.

As defined within the NRP, any activity that attempts to prevent terrorist attacks can be considered a prevention measure. Several specific DHS prevention programs are discussed in greater detail in Chapter 5.

Several of the recommendations made by the 9/11 Commission, discussed in Chapter 2, also include prevention components. The following examples are provided:

Prevention of proliferation of weapons of mass destruction and their acquisition by terrorist groups: The 9/11 Commission underlines that about two dozen terrorist groups including al-Qaeda have attempted to acquire or develop chemical, biological, radiological, and nuclear weapons. Most of those weapons can be developed relatively inexpensively if the necessary knowledge is available to terrorists. The possible consequences of an attack involving those weapons are very likely to be devastating. Therefore, preventing the proliferation of such weapons or materials that are necessary in their development is a critical task that needs to be performed. The commission recommends that the United States has to work with the international community to get this done. The commission recommends that the United States should sustain its support for the Cooperative Threat Reduction Program, which aims to secure the weapons and highly dangerous materials still scattered in Russia and other countries of the Soviet Union.

Prevention of financial strength and flexibility of terrorist organizations: The United States and its allies made an effort to paralyze the financial networks of terrorists in the recent aftermath of 9/11. This effort aimed to reduce or eliminate the ability of terrorist groups to support their operations and maintain their existence. The experience showed that tracking and blocking of money that is potentially connected to terrorist groups is a very difficult job that demands not only international cooperation but also the convenience of national laws of international partners. Therefore, other innovative ways of reducing the financial strength and flexibility of terrorist organizations are necessary.

Prevention of terrorist travel: With the advancements in and increased frequency of international travel, terrorist groups were able to gain the mobility to conduct attacks in different parts of the world. This gives an opportunity to governments to identify the terrorist as they enter the transportation system or the country through its border checkpoints. This is a critical task that may prevent some terrorist attacks or at least the penetration of terrorists from one country to another one. But the fact that terrorists also use local resources and people in their activities makes the challenge even tougher.

Prevention of terrorist access to critical infrastructures and key assets: The 9/11 Commission recommends that the improvements being made to protect U.S. borders such as use of terrorist lists, biometric screening, biometric passports, and other threat-related information be shared with and implemented at access points to critical infrastructures and key assets. Such assets may include nuclear power plants, dams, and other infrastructures of national significance and consequences (9/11 Commission, 2004).

Preparedness Actions and Programs

Preparedness within the field of emergency management can best be defined as a state of readiness to respond to a disaster, crisis, or any other type of emergency situation. It includes those activities, programs, and systems that exist before an emergency that are used to support and enhance response to an emergency or disaster.

FIGURE 10–4 Mays Landing, NJ, April 17, 2010 — Community Relations Specialists Paul Williams and Joseph Bonaccorse (right) team up with Community Emergency Response Team Nancy E. Neglia (left) and Dwight L. Neglia to inform residents of the flood-affected area of the FEMA registration process. FEMA Community Relations specialists are going door to door to inform residents about the assistance available. (Source: Photo by Michael Medina-Latorre/FEMA)

Preparedness is important to the overall emergency management cycle because it provides for the readiness and testing of all actions and plans before actual application occurs in response to a real incident or disaster. There is a close connection between mitigation and preparedness. Often, emergency managers argue over whether a specific action should be considered mitigation or preparedness. Oftentimes the lines of distinction become fuzzy, and exact determination impossible. In its most simple terms, preparedness is more about planning for the best response, whereas mitigation includes all the actions that are attempts to prevent the need for a disaster response or to minimize the scope of the needed response.

Examples of preparedness for natural hazards are organizing evacuation drills from buildings in case of fires or other threats, providing first-response training to employees so that they can assist each other and their neighbors in small emergencies (Figure 10–4), and preparing a family disaster plan that covers topics such as the designation of a location where family members will meet if they get separated during an event and what personal papers (e.g., prescriptions and insurance records) they might need in the aftermath of an event. More specific examples include the logistical planning for tugboats operating around oil refineries such that they become responsible for responding to fire emergencies in the refinery, or providing training and relocating necessary hazardous materials (HAZMAT) teams to areas where the risk of radiological emergencies is higher, such as nuclear power plants.

In the aftermath of September 11, terrorism preparedness has become a more pressing issue. The risk of terrorists gaining access to and using weapons of mass destruction (WMDs), such as biological, chemical, and radiological agents, forced the U.S. government to establish an adequate response capability, capacity, and expertise to protect American citizens against a potential attack and respond to it in case these weapons are used. Citizens, who are the most likely targets of these attacks, must be adequately prepared if any response effort is to be successful. DHS has been given the responsibility for this task, although several other federal government agencies, including the Centers for Disease Control and

Prevention (CDC) and the Department of Education, for example, provide guidance on a full range of terrorism preparedness activities.

FEMA is responsible for preparing for and responding to natural and technological disasters and terrorism. As such, FEMA produces and publishes several documents that help citizens and businesses to take preparative action against each of these threats, including the new terrorism risk. Unfortunately, the arsenal of weapons available to the growing cadre of international terrorists is expanding — and as new weapons are identified and understood, the public must be educated accordingly. The sidebars "CDC Guidance for Evacuation Preparedness for Chemical Weapons," "FEMA 'Are You Ready' Protective Measures for a Nuclear Blast," and "DHS Ready.Gov Guidance on Explosions" presented in this chapter provide examples of the guidance provided by DHS, CDC, and FEMA for citizen preparedness against such weapons.

CDC Guidance for Evacuation Preparedness for Chemical Weapons

Some kinds of chemical accidents or attacks may make staying put dangerous. In such cases, it may be safer for you to evacuate or leave the immediate area. You may need to go to an emergency shelter after you leave the immediate area.

How to Know If You Need to Evacuate

You will hear from the local police, emergency coordinators, or government on the radio or television if you need to evacuate. If there is a "code red" or "severe" terror alert, you should pay attention to radio and television broadcasts so that you will know right away if an evacuation order is made for your area.

What to Do

Act quickly and follow the instructions of local emergency coordinators. Every situation can be different, so local coordinators may give you special instructions to follow for a particular situation. Local emergency coordinators may direct people to evacuate homes or offices and go to an emergency shelter. If so, emergency coordinators will tell you how to get to the shelter. If you have children in school, they may be sheltered at the school. You should not try to get to the school if the children are being sheltered there.

The emergency shelter will have most supplies that people need. The emergency coordinators will tell you which supplies to bring with you. Be sure to bring any medications you are taking. If you have time, call a friend or relative in another state to tell him or her where you are going and that you are safe. Local telephone lines may be jammed in an emergency, so you should plan ahead to have an out-of-state contact with whom to leave messages. If you do not have private transportation, make plans in advance of an emergency to identify people who can give you a ride.

Evacuating and sheltering in this way should keep you safer than if you stayed at home or at your workplace. You will most likely not be in the shelter for more than a few hours. Emergency coordinators will let you know when it is safe to leave the shelter.

Source: Centers for Disease Control and Prevention, 2005, www.cdc.gov.

FEMA "Are You Ready" Protective Measures for a Nuclear Blast

Before a Nuclear Blast

To prepare for a nuclear blast, you should do the following:

- Find out from officials if any public buildings in your community have been designated as fallout shelters. If none have been designated, make your own list of potential shelters near your home, workplace, and school. These places would include basements or the windowless center area of middle floors in high-rise buildings, as well as subways and tunnels.
- If you live in an apartment building or high-rise, talk to the manager about the safest place in the building for sheltering and about providing for building occupants until it is safe to go out.
- During periods of increased threat increase your disaster supplies to be adequate for up to two weeks.
- Taking shelter during a nuclear blast is absolutely necessary. There are two kinds of shelters: blast and fallout:
    - Blast shelters are specifically constructed to offer some protection against blast pressure, initial radiation, heat, and fire. But even a blast shelter cannot withstand a direct hit from a nuclear explosion.
    - Fallout shelters do not need to be specially constructed for protecting against fallout. They can be any protected space, provided that the walls and roof are thick and dense enough to absorb the radiation given off by fallout particles.

During a Nuclear Blast

The following are guidelines for what to do in the event of a nuclear explosion.

If an attack warning is issued:

- Take cover as quickly as you can, below ground if possible, and stay there until instructed to do otherwise.
- Listen for official information and follow instructions.

If you are caught outside and unable to get inside immediately:

- Do not look at the flash or fireball — it can blind you.
- Take cover behind anything that might offer protection.
- Lie flat on the ground and cover your head. If the explosion is some distance away, it could take 30 seconds or more for the blast wave to hit.
- Take shelter as soon as you can, even if you are many miles from ground zero where the attack occurred — radioactive fallout can be carried by the winds for hundreds of miles. Remember the three protective factors: distance, shielding, and time.

After a Nuclear Blast

Decay rates of the radioactive fallout are the same for any size of nuclear device. However, the amount of fallout will vary based on the size of the device and its proximity to the ground. Therefore, it might be necessary for those in the areas with highest radiation levels to shelter for up to a month. The heaviest fallout would be limited to the area at or downwind from the explosion, and 80% of the fallout would occur during the first 24 hours. People in most of the areas that would be affected could be allowed to come out of shelter within a few days and, if necessary, evacuate to unaffected areas.

Returning to Your Home

Remember the following:

- Keep listening to the radio and television for news about what to do, where to go, and places to avoid.
- Stay away from damaged areas. Stay away from areas marked "radiation hazard" or "HAZMAT." Remember that radiation cannot be seen, smelled, or otherwise detected by human senses.

Source: Federal Emergency Management Agency, 2005, www.fema.gov.

DHS Ready.Gov Guidance on Explosions

If There Is an Explosion

- Take shelter against your desk or a sturdy table.
- Exit the building ASAP.
- Do not use elevators.
- Check for fire and other hazards.
- Take your emergency supply kit if time allows.

If There Is a Fire

- Exit the building ASAP.
- Crawl low if there is smoke.
- Use a wet cloth, if possible, to cover your nose and mouth.
- Use the back of your hand to feel the upper, lower, and middle parts of closed doors.
- If the door is not hot, brace yourself against it and open slowly.
- If the door is hot, do not open it. Look for another way out.
- Do not use elevators.
- If you catch fire, do not run. Stop-drop-and-roll to put out the fire.
- If you are at home, go to a previously designated meeting place.
- Account for your family members and carefully supervise small children.
- Never go back into a burning building.

If You Are Trapped in Debris

- If possible, use a flashlight to signal your location to rescuers.
- Avoid unnecessary movement so that you don't kick up dust.
- Cover your nose and mouth with anything you have on hand. (Dense-weave cotton material can act as a good filter. Try to breathe through the material.)
- Tap on a pipe or wall so that rescuers can hear where you are.
- If possible, use a whistle to signal rescuers.
- Shout only as a last resort. Shouting can cause a person to inhale dangerous amounts of dust.

Source: Department of Homeland Security, 2005, www.dhs.gov.

Preparedness Against Biological and Chemical Attacks and Accidents

Preparedness against biological and chemical attacks and accidents poses a distinct challenge due to the unique consequences that they inflict and the relatively limited experience of emergency management professionals in dealing with them. This unique challenge is being addressed by many local, state, federal, private, and nonprofit agencies throughout the United States. In fact, the majority of preparedness funding under the Department of Homeland Security targets these WMD hazards.

Specific Challenges for Biological/Chemical Terrorism Incident Management

Deliberate biological or chemical incidents will present critical challenges to both the intended targets and those in charge of managing the incident that results. These agents, as with all WMDs, present public health threats that are not typically seen in either day-to-day or even major incidents of natural or accidental man-made nature. As such, the methods by which citizens and response officials can prepare for these attacks have only just begun to emerge in the past few years. Chemical incidents do occur with regularity, but it is very rare for them to deliberately target a human population.

Both chemical and biological agents, when used as weapons, have a significant potential to overwhelm the capabilities of the public health infrastructure. There have been several attempts to design a comprehensive framework to prepare for and manage mass-casualty medical incidents. The specific response challenges that those defining new preparedness methods must take into account are listed here:

- The existence of a chemical or biological attack may be hard to verify, due to delayed consequences or symptoms.
- The incident may involve multiple jurisdictions, which may make it much more difficult to organize a coordinated response.
- It may be time consuming to identify and isolate the type and source of the chemical or biological agent present on site.

- The incident may have a pinpoint target where a specific crowd is targeted, or may be designed to impact a larger geographic area and even larger crowds, both of which will likely create large crowds of morbidities if not mortalities.
- If large numbers of the public are impacted by the incident, the demand for health care may quickly exceed local, or even regional, medical resources.
- The identification of the involved chemical(s) or biological agent(s) may consume the capacity of local medical laboratories making it mandatory to integrate use of neighboring laboratories.
- Resources of the medical system may be consumed by not only the victims but also by those who perceive themselves as possible victims who may not be real victims.
- The emergency management officials may have to make extremely difficult public policy decisions very quickly, where lives may have to be sacrificed to save other lives.
- It may be necessary to quarantine the impacted region to insulate the nonimpacted geographies from potential contamination.
- The medical units may have to triage arriving victims if the incoming demand dramatically exceeds the capacity of available resources.
- To decontaminate the impacted geographies and those who were contaminated by the release, necessary decontamination systems, equipment, and human resources may be necessary at multiple locations.
- The medical system may not only have to deal with the physical disease caused by the chemical or biological release but also with the mental impacts of the "mass paranoia" the incident may have triggered.

These are but a small subset of the potential challenges that must be met. Individual events will present individual response factors that may or may not be known beforehand. To address these issues, physical (equipment, tools, technology), financial, knowledge, and human resources are all necessary. More importantly, a comprehensive system to address these challenges is necessary, and the adequate utilization of such a system demands the provision of training and exercises to those who will be dependent on such a system in a time of crisis. See the sidebar titled "CDC's Strategic Plan for Preparedness and Response to Biological and Chemical Terrorism."

CDC's Strategic Plan for Preparedness and Response to Biological and Chemical Terrorism

The CDC has developed a plan, titled the "Strategic Plan for Preparedness and Response to Biological and Chemical Terrorism," that identifies preparedness and prevention, detection and surveillance, diagnosis and characterization of biological and chemical agents, response, and communication as the five focus areas for comprehensive mass casualty health incident management. Descriptions of each follow.

Preparedness and Prevention

Detection, diagnosis, and mitigation of illness and injury caused by biological and chemical terrorism are complex processes that involve numerous partners and activities. Meeting this challenge requires special emergency preparedness in all cities and states. CDC provides public health guidelines, support, and technical assistance to local and state public health agencies as they develop coordinated preparedness plans and response protocols. CDC also provides self-assessment tools for terrorism preparedness, including performance standards, attack simulations, and other exercises.

Detection and Surveillance

Early detection is essential for ensuring a prompt response to a biological or chemical attack, including the provision of prophylactic medicines, chemical antidotes, or vaccines. CDC is integrating surveillance for illness and injury resulting from biological and chemical terrorism into the U.S. disease surveillance systems, while developing new mechanisms for detecting, evaluating, and reporting suspicious events that might represent covert terrorist acts. As part of this effort, CDC and state and local health agencies form partnerships with frontline medical personnel in hospital emergency departments, hospital care facilities, poison control centers, and other offices to enhance detection and reporting of unexplained injuries and illnesses as part of routine surveillance mechanisms for biological and chemical terrorism.

Diagnosis and Characterization of Biological and Chemical Agents

The CDC and its partners created a multilevel laboratory response network (LRN). The LRN and its partners will maintain an integrated national and international network of laboratories that are fully equipped to respond quickly to acts of chemical or biological terrorism, emerging infectious diseases, and other public health threats and emergencies.

Response

A comprehensive public health response to a biological or chemical terrorist event involves epidemiologic investigation, medical treatment and prophylaxis for affected persons, and the initiation of disease prevention or environmental decontamination measures. CDC assists state and local health agencies in developing resources and expertise for investigating unusual events and unexplained illnesses. If requested by a state health agency, CDC will deploy response teams to investigate unexplained or suspicious illnesses or unusual etiologic agents and provide on-site consultation regarding medical management and disease control. To ensure the availability, procurement, and delivery of medical supplies, devices, and equipment that might be needed to respond to terrorist-caused illness or injury, CDC maintains a national pharmaceutical stockpile.

Communication Systems

U.S. preparedness to mitigate the public health consequences of biological and chemical terrorism depends on the coordinated activities of well-trained health care and public health personnel throughout the United States who have access to up-to-the minute emergency information. Effective communication with the public through the news media will also be essential to limit terrorists' ability to induce public panic and disrupt daily life.

Source: Centers for Disease Control and Prevention, "Biological and Chemical Terrorism: Strategic Plan for Preparedness and Response," 2005.

Comprehensive Medical and Health Incident Management System

The Medical and Health Incident Management System (MaHIM) designed by Joseph A. Barbera and Anthony G. Macintyre is one of the most recent and most comprehensive analytical tools designed to help communities develop their own medical mass-casualty incident management capacity. The system not only focuses on developing local capacities, but also proposes a framework that can be used to integrate interjurisdictional capacities, should the incident spread beyond local jurisdictional borders.

The goal of the framework is to define as a single system encompassing the medical and public health functions and processes required for adequate management of a mass-casualty incident. The system has been designed with an all-hazards approach where special consideration is given to bioterrorism.

The MaHIM system defines the goal of medical consequence management in a mass-casualty incident as follows: to maximally limit morbidity (injury or illness) and mortality (deaths) in the population exposed to a major hazard and to return the community to normalcy as soon as possible. The three primary medical objectives to attain this goal are as follows:

- *Reduce hazard exposure*: Avoid or minimize the hazard exposure to patients and the population after hazard "release."
- *Increase hazard resistance*: Maximize patient and population resistance to the hazard impact after exposure.
- *Promote/achieve healing from hazard effects*: Maximize the rate and degree of patient and population healing from the hazard impact.

To achieve these goals, the system utilizes principles of effective local and regional organization to provide a detailed description of necessary medical and health emergency operations, and the associated

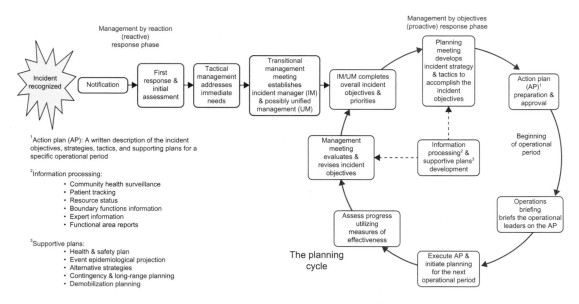

FIGURE 10–5 MaHIM management process. (Source: "Planning Cycle," U.S. Coast Guard Incident Management Handbook, U.S. Coast Guard COMDTPUB P3120, April 17, 2001)

subfunctions and processes. The system underlines the importance of responsibility and authority. It defines the operational requirements for surge capacity, and provides detailed explanations about support functions critical to system's operation. Figure 10–5 details the MaHIM management process.

MaHIM provides a new vision for the health and emergency medical service communities, and gives them an actionable tool with which they can now structure their preparedness and management efforts in a more systematic fashion. The system describes in detail all functional areas that should be included in a comprehensive, mass-casualty health incident management system. The system is currently being implemented in Arlington County, Virginia, as part of a pilot project. The project includes restructuring the county's entire emergency medical system. A more detailed functional description of the system can be downloaded from the following website: http://www.gwu.edu/~icdrm/publications/MaHIM%20Model%20Web%20Version%20FEB%2003.pdf (Barbera and Macintyre, 2002, 2003).

ANOTHER VOICE: WHY IS MITIGATION AND PREPAREDNESS THE ONLY SUSTAINABLE, COST-EFFECTIVE WAY OF DEALING WITH EMERGENCIES?

Pay Now or Later

Catastrophic disasters are associated with large losses of property and lives, where resources to cope with the disaster overwhelm local governments. Following such disasters, large amounts of capital in the form of disaster aid are necessary in order to put the physical infrastructure back to its original state. Even larger amounts — doubled, tripled, or sometimes quadrupled — are necessary to put the economic and social infrastructure back into a sustainable state. Therefore, local planners and policymakers should be extra careful when allowing settlements and the associated infrastructure systems in precarious zones such as active faults, coastal regions, flood zones, and nuclear power plants. These decisions should not only be based on scientific assessment of potential risks of failure (these are ideally embedded in building codes) but also "life cycle costs" of owning and operating infrastructure systems (LCCs are ideally factored into the "benefit-cost ratio" for capital allocation). LCCs should include allowances for scheduled and emergency maintenance for critical parts of the system, as well as economic allowances for failures.

Case in Point

In the immediate aftermath of Hurricane Katrina, the levees surrounding the city of New Orleans failed, causing the flooding of the entire city and incapacitating local response forces. The failure of the response is attributable, among other things, to the historic ill decision of settling in a very dangerous flood zone and continued expansion despite prior major flooding events, as well as the lack of funding that caused the poor maintenance and near-neglect of critical components of the levee structure which led to their compromise under extreme forces.

By Irmak Renda-Tanali, DSc, MSCE, Assistant Professor; Program Director, Homeland Security Management, Information and Technology Systems Department, Graduate School of Management and Technology, University of Maryland-University College.

Nuclear and Radiological Preparedness

The Nuclear Regulatory Commission (NRC) is the primary federal government agency in charge of regulating the commercial radiological operations within the United States. The NRC's mission is to regulate the nation's civilian use of by-product, source, and special nuclear materials to ensure adequate protection of public health and safety, to promote the common defense and security, and to protect the environment. The NRC's regulatory mission covers three main areas:

- Reactors: Commercial reactors for generating electric power and research and test reactors used for research, testing, and training
- Materials: Uses of nuclear materials in medical, industrial, and academic settings and facilities that produce nuclear fuel
- Waste: Transportation, storage, and disposal of nuclear materials and waste, and decommissioning of nuclear facilities from service

A key component of the mission of the NRC is to ensure adequate preparedness measures are in place to protect the health and safety of the public. These actions are taken to avoid or reduce radiation dose exposure and are sometimes referred to as *protective measures*.

The overall objective of NRC's Emergency Preparedness (EP) program is to ensure that nuclear power plant operators are capable of implementing adequate measures to protect public health and safety in the event of a radiological emergency. As a condition of their license, operators of these nuclear power plants must develop and maintain EP plans that meet comprehensive NRC EP requirements. Increased confidence in public protection is obtained through the combined inspection of the requirements of emergency preparedness and the evaluation of their implementation.

The NRC maintains oversight of the capability of nuclear power plant operators to protect the public by conducting thorough inspections. The NRC maintains four regional offices (Region I in King of Prussia, Pennsylvania; Region II in Atlanta, Georgia; Region III in Lisle, Illinois; and Region IV in Arlington, Texas) that implement the NRC's inspection program. In addition to these regionally based inspectors, the NRC places "resident inspectors" at each of the nation's operating nuclear plants to carry out the inspection program on a day-to-day basis.

The NRC assesses the capabilities of nuclear power plant operators to protect the public by requiring the performance of a full-scale exercise at least once every 2 years that includes the participation of government agencies. These exercises are performed in order to maintain the skills of the emergency responders and to identify and correct weaknesses. They are evaluated by NRC regional inspectors and FEMA regional evaluators. Between the times when these 2-year exercises are conducted, additional drills are conducted by the nuclear power plant operators that are evaluated by the resident inspectors (Nuclear Regulatory Commission, 2005).

Terrorism Preparedness and Mitigation: Community Issues

The terrorism threat knows no geographic, social, or economic boundaries. Every citizen and every community is potentially at risk. Although the DHS focuses on federal and state efforts to prepare for and combat terrorism, local communities are struggling to address the terrorism risk. The following sections explain several initiatives that have been launched to deal with community issues concerning the terrorist threat.

Corporation for National and Community Service

The mission of the Corporation for National and Community Service (CNCS), an independent federal agency under the White House, is to provide opportunities for Americans of all ages and backgrounds to engage in service that addresses the nation's educational, public safety, environmental, and other human needs to achieve direct and demonstrable results. In doing so, the corporation fosters civic responsibility, strengthens the ties that bind citizens together, and provides educational opportunities for those who make a substantial commitment to service.

CNCS provides opportunities for Americans to serve through three programs: Senior Corps, AmeriCorps, and Learn and Serve America. Members and volunteers serve with national and community nonprofit organizations, faith-based groups, schools, and local agencies to help meet community needs in education, the environment, public safety, homeland security, and other critical areas. The corporation is part of USA Freedom Corps, a White House initiative to foster a culture of citizenship, service, and responsibility and help all Americans answer the president's call to service.

Senior Corps taps the skills, talents, and experience of more than 500,000 Americans aged 55 years and older to meet a wide range of community challenges through three programs: RSVP, Foster Grandparents, and Senior Companions. RSVP volunteers conduct safety patrols for local police departments, participate in environmental projects, provide intensive educational services to children and adults, and respond to natural disasters, among other activities. Foster Grandparents serve one-on-one as tutors and mentors to young people with special needs. Senior Companions help homebound seniors and other adults maintain independence in their own homes.

Fifty thousand Americans are serving their communities 20 to 40 hours a week through AmeriCorps. Most of AmeriCorps' members are selected by and serve with local and national nonprofit organizations such as Habitat for Humanity, the American Red Cross, City Year, Teach for America, and Boys and Girls Clubs of America, as well as with a host of smaller community organizations, both secular and faith based. AmeriCorps operates in a decentralized manner that gives a significant amount of responsibility to states and local nonprofit groups. Roughly three-quarters of all AmeriCorps grant funding goes to governor-appointed state service commissions, which award grants to nonprofit groups in responding to local needs. Most of the remainder of the grant funding is distributed by the corporation directly to multistate and national organizations through a competitive grants process. AmeriCorps NCCC (National Civilian Community Corps) is a residential program for more than 1,200 members ages 18 to 24. Based on a military model, it sends members in teams of 10 to 14 to help nonprofit groups provide disaster relief, preserve the environment, build homes for low-income families, tutor children, and meet other challenges. Because members are trained in CPR, first aid, and mass care, and can be assigned to new duties on short notice, they are particularly well suited to meet the emerging homeland security needs of the nation.

Learn and Serve America provides grants to schools, colleges, and nonprofit groups to support efforts to engage students in community service linked to academic achievement and the development of civic skills. This type of learning, referred to as *service learning*, improves communities while preparing young people for a lifetime of responsible citizenship. In addition to providing grants, Learn and Serve America serves as a resource on service and service learning to teachers, faculty members, schools, and community groups.

CNCS is an important initiative for homeland security efforts at the local community level because it provides a significant portion of the total federal funding that goes to volunteer organizations and local communities that are trying to improve their homeland security capabilities.

On July 18, 2002, CNCS announced that it had acquired more than $10.3 million in grants. These grants supported 37,000 volunteers for homeland security in public safety, public health, and disaster mitigation and preparedness. The corporation announced on September 10, 2003, the renewal of 17 of the grants from the previous year totaling nearly $4.5 million for homeland security volunteer projects that were developed in the aftermath of the September 11 terrorist attacks.

In January 2004, CNCS announced the availability of $3.2 million in funding for organizations addressing homeland security concerns by engaging students in service learning activities in their schools and communities. The funding was made available through the Corporation's Learn and Serve America program, which provides grants to schools, colleges, and nonprofits to support programs that connect classroom learning with community service. The Homeland Security initiative aimed to engage young people aged 5 to 17 in planning for and responding to health, safety, and security concerns in their schools or communities, including natural disasters, school violence, medical emergencies, or terrorist acts. Examples of activities supported included engaging students in service learning projects to develop school crisis plans, distributing preparedness kits, conducting school safety audits and drills, providing health education, inventory and maintain emergency supplies, or providing language assistance to non-English-speaking populations.

In February 2004, CNCS announced the renewal of 13 AmeriCorps homeland security grants to support 362 AmeriCorps members serving in public safety, public health, and disaster relief and preparedness projects across the country. The grants totaled $3.5 million and supported AmeriCorps projects in 20 states. The grantees included 12 state or local groups and 1 national organization, the American Red Cross. The grants supported AmeriCorps members' efforts to recruit volunteers, develop disaster response plans, teach disaster preparedness to students, assist firefighting and police operations, train people in first aid and CPR, respond to national and local disasters, and develop partnerships with organizations involved in homeland security such as Citizen Corps councils and Neighborhood Watch Programs. (See sidebar titled "DHS Secretary Ridge Cites Neighborhood Security as Instrumental to Homeland Security.") Results from the 2003 activities sponsored by the grants included the following:

- AmeriCorps members serving in a program sponsored by the Florida Department of Elder Affairs have recruited over 600 disaster services volunteers who contributed more than 12,000 hours of service, distributed over 200,000 disaster services publications, and reached nearly 2,500 residents with presentations on safety.

- Serving with the Green River Area Development District in rural Kentucky, AmeriCorps members have utilized data from a Global Positioning System to map out information about fire stations, emergency shelters, HAZMAT storage facilities, medical facilities, and nursing homes.

- Just blocks from the World Trade Center site, Pace University AmeriCorps members have trained 250 people in English, Chinese, and Spanish in emergency preparedness techniques, created a resource list that consolidates all important emergency numbers, and built a "Downtown Needs" website that serves as a volunteer clearinghouse for 2,000 organizations in the downtown area.

- AmeriCorps members in the California Safe Corps have taught disaster preparedness classes to more than 1,000 community members, recruited more than 100 new volunteers who have provided over 250 hours of service, and assisted more than 200 victims of disasters.

- In Iowa, AmeriCorps members have made presentations on disaster preparedness at 400 schools across the state.

- In the summer of 2004, the devastation wrought by Hurricanes Charley and Frances in Florida prompted the CNCS to muster as much assistance as possible to the state. More than 600 national service volunteers have been deployed to provide both direct services and leverage the support of thousands of additional volunteers. The CNCS worked with state and federal disaster officials to deploy even more volunteers as needed.

AmeriCorps members and Senior Corps volunteers specially trained in disaster relief have responded to disasters in more than 30 states. The corporation has a long track record of working with FEMA and other relief agencies in helping run emergency shelters, assisting law enforcement, providing food and shelter, managing donations, and helping families and communities rebuild. Hundreds of national service volunteers have directly assisted victims of the September 11 terrorist attacks by providing family services, organizing blood drives, raising funds, and counseling victims' families (from http://www.nationalservice.org/news/factsheets/homeland.html and http://www.nationalservice.org/news/homeland.html).

CNCS volunteers proved to be especially useful and valuable in the aftermath of Hurricane Katrina. CNCS quickly activated its local volunteer base to join the response to the disaster, and also deployed many of its volunteers from other states to take part in the response and recovery operations. Response to Hurricane Katrina constituted the single largest nonmilitary volunteer disaster response in the history of the United States. Close to 600,000 volunteers took part in the response and recovery to Hurricane Katrina of which approximately 35,000 were participants of various CNCS programs. Volunteers with diverse skills and training supported many important activities such as management of evacuee shelter operations, food services, basic health-care services, informing disaster victims on available governmental and nongovernmental benefits, and general postincident counseling services. CNCS volunteers staffed the American Red Cross emergency call center in Fairfax, Virginia.

CNCS did not suspend its efforts in the hurricane-hit region after the response transformed into a long-term recovery operation. The organization worked with established partners including but not limited to FEMA, and the American Red Cross. Volunteers got involved with donation collection, and warehouse management activities. Alabama Emergency Management Agency's emergency phone answering system has been staffed by CNCS volunteers. The corporation funded volunteer-pilot-operated airlifts to transport patients out of the area, reunite families, and bring in medical supplies to the region. Trained and equipped members of American Radio Relay League, a CNCS partner, have supported emergency radio communications. In the later phases of the recovery effort volunteers collaborating with federal, state, and local response units; military units deployed to help with the recovery; and other nonprofit organizations and CNCS volunteers participated in debris removal, helped the elderly and the disabled, repaired damaged roofs, and staffed coordination offices. American Red Cross response vehicles such as mobile kitchens were also staffed by volunteers in many instances. CNCS encouraged the volunteering of college students during their winter and spring breaks, and created opportunities for their direct involvement in the hardest hit areas as volunteers. Those students participated in repair and reconstruction projects and enjoyed supporting local communities as they helped them recover from the devastation caused by Hurricane Katrina (CNCS, 2006, 2007a, 2007b).

The CNCS Homeland Security Grant Program was discontinued in 2006 after being funded at $10.3 million in FY 2003, at $9.88 million in FY 2004, and at $4.96 million in FY 2005, respectively. During that time frame, 17 grants were funded for a 3-year period and 12 grants were funded for a 2-year period (CNCS, 2005).

DHS Secretary Ridge Cites Neighborhood Security as Instrumental to Homeland Security

In Falcon Heights, Minnesota, a program that trains residents to respond to potential terrorist attacks is becoming a model for other cities and states. Falcon Heights Mayor Sue Gehrz, St. Paul Mayor Randy Kelly, and other officials were joined by Homeland Security Secretary Tom Ridge at a symposium in St. Paul exploring how Americans can protect their food supply, workplaces, and homes. "The potential destruction to life and property from man-made disasters is so large that communities can no longer assume" that agencies in neighboring communities will be available to help, Gehrz said. "That means more individuals need to be trained to assist their families and neighbors until help arrives," she said.

"The only way you can secure the homeland is to make sure the hometowns are secure," Ridge told about 350 people at the symposium. The nation has strengthened security in many ways since the terror attacks of 2001, yet it still needs a greater degree of readiness, he said. "We need to consolidate most of our computer systems and databases in one seamless operation, make it easier for police to communicate with each other, with the rest of federal government, right down to the state and locals," he said.

Since the September 11 attacks, the residents of Falcon Heights have worked together to plan a response to terror attacks, Gehrz said. They have created a community manual on their "intergenerational organizing model" and provided it to more than 70 Minnesota cities and counties. It has been used in Florida, South Carolina, and Washington, DC.

In Falcon Heights, which has a population of 5,600, a total of 65 "neighborhood liaisons" have collected the names, addresses, and phone numbers of people on their blocks, identifying who has medical training or other specialized skills or equipment that might be useful in a disaster, Gehrz said. A neighborhood commission worked with the Red Cross to provide free first-aid training for 62 residents. Police have trained 11 residents how to direct traffic during emergencies. Others will receive 21 hours of training in how to respond to emergencies. "Involving all ages helps reduce fear and protect civil rights," said Gehrz, who is trained as a psychologist. "One of the primary goals of terrorism is to make people feel isolated and vulnerable."

Source: "Falcon Heights Security Efforts Are Becoming a National Model," *Star Tribune*, June 20, 2003, p. 19A.

Citizen Corps

Following the tragic events that occurred on September 11, 2001, state and local government officials have increased opportunities for citizens to become an integral part of protecting the homeland and supporting local first responders. Officials agree that the formula for ensuring a more secure and safer homeland consists of preparedness, training, and citizen involvement in supporting first responders. In January 2002, President George W. Bush launched the USA Freedom Corps to "capture the spirit of service that has emerged throughout our communities following the terrorist attacks."

Citizen Corps, a vital component of USA Freedom Corps, was created to help coordinate volunteer activities that can make communities safer, stronger, and better prepared to respond to emergencies. It provides opportunities for people to participate in a range of measures to make their families, their homes, and their communities safer from the threats of crime, terrorism, and disasters of all kinds.

Citizen Corps is coordinated nationally by FEMA. In this capacity, FEMA works closely with other federal entities, state and local governments, first responders and emergency managers, the volunteer community, and the White House Office of the USA Freedom Corps. One of the initiatives supported by Citizen Corps is the Community Emergency Response Teams (CERT). The program trains citizens to be better prepared to respond to emergency situations in their communities. When emergencies happen, CERT members can give critical support to first responders, provide immediate assistance to victims, and organize spontaneous volunteers at a disaster site. CERT members can also help with nonemergency projects that help improve the safety of the community.

The CERT course is taught in the community by a trained team of first responders who have completed a CERT Train-the-Trainer course conducted by their state training office for emergency management, or FEMA's Emergency Management Institute (EMI), located in Emmitsburg, Maryland. CERT training includes disaster preparedness, disaster fire suppression, basic disaster medical operations, and light search and rescue operations. As of 2008, there were more than 2,800 CERT programs active in many states, counties, and communities nationwide. For more information on CERT, see the CERT web site at www.citizencorps.gov/programs/cert.shtm.

Another important Citizen Corps initiative is the Medical Reserve Corps (MRC) program, which coordinates the skills of practicing and retired physicians, nurses, and other health care professionals, as well as other citizens interested in health issues who are eager to volunteer to address their community's ongoing public health needs and to help their community during large-scale emergency situations.

Local community leaders develop their own MRC units and identify the duties of the MRC volunteers according to specific community needs. For example, MRC volunteers may deliver necessary public health services during a crisis, assist emergency response teams with patients, and provide care directly to those with less serious injuries and other health related issues. More information on the MRC program can be found at http://www.medicalreservecorps.gov.

The Neighborhood Watch Program (NWP) and Volunteers in Police Service (VIPS) programs are other Citizen Corps homeland security–related programs.

A relatively new partner program of the Citizen Corps initiative is the Fire Corps program. Launched in 2004, Fire Corps is a partnership between the International Association of Fire Chiefs' Volunteer and Combination Officers Section (IAFC/VCOS), the International Association of Fire Fighters (IAFF), the National Volunteer Fire Council (NVFC), and the U.S. Fire Administration (USFA). Its mission is to help career, volunteer, and combination fire departments supplement existing personnel resources by recruiting citizen advocates. In June 2005, the program signed up its first 250 fire departments in its "citizen advocates" program. The purpose of the program is to help fire departments expand existing programs — or assist in developing new ones — that recruit citizens who donate their time and talents to support the fire service in nonoperational roles. Within the first 4 years of its existence, Fire Corps has expanded its organization to many states. Currently, the organization has a division advocate for all 7 divisions across the United States, and 52 state advocates that represent 28 states. More information about Fire Corps can be found at http://firecorps.org (Fire Corps, 2008). The president's FY 2012 budget requested $9.8 million for the program (DHS, 2011b).

The SAFE Conference

The first annual conference on "The Community and Homeland Security," in cooperation with the SAFE project, took place in San Francisco on March 27 and 28, 2003. The aim of the conference was to bring together local leaders from several states, leaders responsible for shaping homeland security programs and activities in their communities, with representatives from federal, state, local, nonprofit, private, and international organizations working on homeland security-related issues. The conference allowed all these practitioners, participants, and representatives to voice their concerns and to share their experiences and gave them their first opportunity not only to work together to identify existing problems with homeland security at the local level but also to propose possible solutions to these problems.

Four principal areas of concern on the community level emerged from the discussions in the conference:

- Resources: Greater access to resources to fund homeland security programs and projects at the community level
- Information: Greater access to practical information about application, eligibility, recruitment, retention, and other concerns
- Programming: The need for innovative and effective programming ideas
- Customizing: The need to focus on diverse and "special needs" populations

To create more resources and to use available resources more effectively, the following ideas were developed in the conference:

- Block grants to communities are an efficient means for providing federal funding for community homeland security efforts.
- Communities should partner with the National Governor's Association, the United States Conference of Mayors, the League of Cities, and other professional associations seeking federal funding for community homeland security efforts.
- Creative funding ideas practiced in communities around the country need to be identified and widely disseminated among community homeland security officials.
- New partnerships need to be established with the country's business and philanthropic communities to leverage their resources for community homeland security efforts.

Suggestions for improving access to accurate and timely information regarding homeland security issues included the following:

- Establishing an information clearinghouse to catalog homeland security information sources
- Establishing a Web-based "chat room" for community officials to exchange ideas and best practices and to discuss current issues
- Establishing a "funding exchange" to share ideas on funding sources and creative funding ideas

- Partnering with the Department of Homeland Security and state homeland security operations to facilitate the flow of information on federal and state programs and funding opportunities to community officials.

In addition to the homeland security programming currently in place (e.g., CERT training, Medical RSVP), conference participants identified a need to design and implement programs that fully leveraged the capabilities of volunteers in the community. Several ideas were considered, including the following:

- The SAFE Project, designed to develop volunteer programs in support of community emergency management and homeland security operations
- The development of Community Emergency Networks (CENs), designed to facilitate communications between community residents and local homeland security officials before, during, and after a disaster or terrorism incident

Some of the ideas developed in the conference regarding the "special needs" populations were as follows:

- Reprogramming Community Development Block Grant (CDBG) funding targeted for "special needs" populations to include homeland security efforts
- Establishing "language and culture banks" in communities to facilitate communications and information flow between public safety and emergency officials and "special needs" populations
- Partnering with national associations and groups that represent the interests of special needs populations such as the elderly, veterans, minority populations, children, and the disabled
- Partnering with foundations and other philanthropic organizations, such as the Annie E. Casey Foundation, which focuses its efforts and funding in disadvantaged communities
- Partnering with local emergency management/homeland security and public health operations to help these groups identify and serve special needs populations in the community

The existence of voluntary activities for homeland security, such as the SAFE conference, is important because such activities bring together different stakeholders, provide an opportunity to share expertise and best practices, and create an environment in which public–private partnerships can be initiated and brainstorming can occur.

The primary concern of those in attendance was well stated by Carol Lopes (Berkeley, California), who said, "Though there has been a lot of progress, we are willfully unprepared. Community and neighborhood preparedness is the centerpiece of today's work. Our responsibility is to prepare a community before a disaster and assist after a disaster strikes. We must train a cadre of emergency prepared individuals who will interface well with first responders."

Said Chuck Supple (GO SERV): "We must engage citizens to address problems in their own communities to have the greatest possible impact in Community Homeland Security."

Said Valli Wasp (Austin, Texas): "Preparedness must be addressed locally. We need to take this to 'homes' — get rid of the 'land,' get rid of the 'security' — this is about people protecting their homes. If you want people to listen to you, you have to go to where they live."

Said Eileen Garry (U.S. Department of Justice): "Every good idea I have ever heard came from the local level."

One participant expressed concern that "making us fundraisers, in addition to our programmatic [tasks], really stretches municipalities' resources thin. The raw numbers of people required for fundraising exhausts programs." However, such fundraising actions are recognized as vital to any program's success, echoed by Doris Milldyke (Kansas) who said, "Money is the first goal, volunteers are the second." Ann Patton (Tulsa, Oklahoma) stated, "An information clearinghouse would be invaluable," while Doris Milldyke (Kansas) noted that information on VIPS, MRS, and other programs is "notoriously difficult to find," adding, "we need a golden key for information on getting grants."

Chuck Supple (California GO SERV) stated this position well in saying, "We've probably only thought of a 'minutia' of the areas where volunteers would be useful."

Ana-Marie Jones (Oakland, California) warned that "special needs communities are often isolated from services," adding that "[programs] must have a trusted leader who either speaks or has access to the languages of all representative groups — you need more than a 'Spanish press release.'" She suggested that participants "involve special needs communities before the disaster" to be effective.

Source: D. Coppola, G.D. Haddow, and J.A. Bullock, A Report on the First Annual Conference on "The Community and Homeland Security," March 2003, www.nccd-crc.org/new/chs_conference_1.pdf.

The American Red Cross

The American Red Cross (ARC) has always been one of the most important partners of the federal, state, and local governments in disaster preparedness and relief operations. Some of the daily community operations of the Red Cross chapters include senior services, caregivers' support, provision of hospital and nursing home volunteers, lifeline (an electronic personal emergency response service), transportation to medical/doctor's appointments and other essential trips, food pantry and hot lunch programs, homeless shelters and transitional housing services, school clubs and community service learning programs and projects, youth programs (violence and substance abuse prevention, peer education and mentoring, leadership development camps), food and rental assistance, language banks, and community information and referral.

From the first $10.3 million in federal grants provided to involve citizen volunteers in homeland security efforts in 2002, the ARC received $1,778,978, which was distributed by the national headquarters to many individual chapters. The recipient of the greatest portion of these funds was the Greater New York chapter, which received $500,000 of the funds for the recruitment, training, and mobilization of 5,000 new disaster volunteers equipped to respond to another terrorist attack on a local level. These volunteers work with Red Cross service delivery units in New York to train additional volunteers, exponentially increasing the city's force of disaster relief workers.

In 2002, another $371,978 was given to the ARC National Headquarters for a nationwide program aimed at increasing volunteers in communities most vulnerable to terrorist attacks. The grant supported a yearlong program with 30 Community Preparedness Corps (CPC) members working in 19 chapters. Corps members worked in chapters to ensure that all community members — totaling some 27 million — have a "family disaster response plan." They tailored plans for those with language barriers and disabilities and for children and the elderly. At the same time, CPC volunteers focused on minimizing intolerance across the country by teaching international humanitarian law and the principles of the International Red Cross Movement (humanity, independence, neutrality, impartiality, voluntary service, unity, and universality).

Corps members also recruited and trained an estimated 400 new volunteers and instructors who made the educational programs available to additional vulnerable communities. Ultimately, corps members working through Red Cross chapters will create a network of hundreds of skilled volunteers across the country.

Additional grants have since been awarded to Red Cross chapters nationwide. In California, funds have been dedicated to the implementation of homeland security measures in Los Angeles, San Francisco, and Sacramento. The Oregon Trail Chapter that was awarded a grant funding 400 new volunteers will perform 1,500 hours of service to disaster preparedness. On the East Coast, the Red Cross developed "Disaster Resistant Neighborhood" programs across eight wards of Washington, DC. Through the program these communities created disaster response plans. The southeast Pennsylvania chapter received a grant to create an alliance of more than 100 nonprofits in the Philadelphia area to form the Southeast Pennsylvania Voluntary Organization Active in Disaster (VOAD) to help citizens prevent, prepare for, and respond to disasters.

In 2003, the ARC participated in the TOPOFF 2 national training exercise. The Red Cross used this exercise to practice the screening of emergency shelter residents and supplies for radiation exposure, the logistical support when national stockpiles of medications were mobilized, and keeping the public informed as the national threat level reached the highest "red" alert. In the same year the Red Cross was actively involved with the development of the new NRP. The ARC was the only nongovernmental organization that was invited to the discussions.

Throughout 2004, the Red Cross taught 11 million Americans critical life-saving skills such as first aid, water safety, caregiving, CPR, and the use of automated external defibrillators (AEDs). In addition, the number of people attending presentations or demonstrations for Together We Prepare, community disaster education awareness, and the Masters of Disasters program climbed 6% to 3.9 million. Those programs aim to create safer families and communities.

Another 2004 initiative from the Red Cross involved expanding to diverse audiences with important preparedness and other information. To achieve this goal, the Red Cross expanded and detailed its Spanish-language website and first-aid and preparedness print materials. In cooperation with the CDC, the Red Cross initiated a multiyear project to develop and disseminate terrorism preparedness materials to the public.

In 2005, the year of several major hurricanes, some criticism emerged regarding the way the ARC handled its duties during those disasters. In the days leading to the landfall of Hurricane Katrina at the shores of Florida, the ARC was initially praised for its proactive approach in prestaging volunteers and mass care resources, but as the disaster unfolded and showed its destructive face in larger geographies, issues concerning the ARC response to the disaster became more apparent. At the center of the problem were issues between FEMA and the ARC regarding rules of engagement as partners under the new NRP. A Government Accountability Office (GAO) study that looked at the relationship of the two agencies during and after Katrina sheds light on some of the specific issues.

One major issue was the different interpretation of emergency support function 6 (ESF #6) responsibilities and process flow by FEMA and the ARC. The ARC and FEMA are the designated primary agencies for ESF #6 in charge of mass care, housing, and human services. The ARC is directly responsible for mass care. The NRP tasks an ESF #6 coordinator, a FEMA official with the oversight and coordination of all ESF #6 activities including mass care, which according to the ARC is not a perfect model since it designates the oversight of a core ARC competency to a non-ARC official. Therefore, during its response to Katrina, ARC in some instances bypassed the ESF #6 coordinator and tried to work with the FEMA Operations Section Chief. This resulted in tensions between the ARC and FEMA, and in many instances undermined a very much needed partnership between the two agencies.

Another issue that the ARC was criticized for was the frequently changing personnel at facilities that required ongoing working relationships with the staff of other agencies, primarily FEMA. Those short shifts also reduced the exposure of ARC representatives to the operational environment of the ESF #6. The primary explanation for this problem was the ARC's predisposition for involvement in disasters with much shorter life spans, and requiring shorter periods of continuous staffing — neither of which describe the needs of the Hurricane Katrina response where ESF #6 was active for more than 3 months. Also, since a significant portion of ARC personnel are volunteers, it is more difficult to engage those individuals in longer-term deployments than shorter ones.

In its response to GAO findings, the ARC underlined that it followed the guidance provided in the NRP as it worked with FEMA during Hurricane Katrina. Nevertheless, it is also mentioned that ARC and FEMA are in the process of developing policies and procedures to formalize their agreement on seemingly gray areas of responsibility and ESF #6 operations. Regarding the issues of frequent ARC personnel changes in ESF #6, ARC reports that it has improved the content of its ESF #6 training and hired 14 permanent employees to be trained in ESF #6 procedures and deployed at strategic locations in multiple states to coordinate with state emergency management agencies and officials (GAO, 2006; PBS, 2005; DHS, 2004).

Two other issues the ARC faced during its response to Hurricane Katrina were the fraudulent money transfers by some ARC subcontractors, and unacceptably long wait times on phone-based services. ARC provides cash payments to disaster victims to help them get through the first few days of a disaster until other means of relief become available. During Hurricane Katrina, ARC established call centers manned by subcontractors to register and provide cash payments to hurricane victims using the money wiring services of a private contractor. The procedure did not have adequate checks and protection against fraudulent money transfers; therefore a group of employees working for the subcontractor staffing the call center found loopholes to transfer money to themselves and their relatives who were not victims of the hurricane. None of those workers were actual ARC employees or volunteers. ARC has also been criticized by people trying to reach the call centers in that wait times were extremely long, and in many instances, hours. Some experts explain those management problems are the result of the unique financial structure of the ARC, which heavily relies on donations; donors generally want their money spent strictly on direct assistance of hurricane victims rather than fixing administrative or managerial problems. This may minimize budgets to fix problems related to functions such as operations, finance, and accounting (Washington Post, 2005).

DIGGING DEEPER: INFLUENZA PANDEMIC MITIGATION AND PREPAREDNESS.

An influenza pandemic is regarded as potentially the next large disaster that may threaten the entire globe and require the involvement of many nations and the international community for effective mitigation, prevention, preparedness, and response. Pandemic is the global outbreak of an infectious disease. The influenza pandemic is different from the seasonal flu in many ways. Among the differences are:

- Large or global geographic impact as opposed to local impacts of the seasonal flu
- Potential to quickly exhaust available resources of national health systems

- Potential to require medical supply and vaccine availability that is drastically different than what is required to deal with the seasonal flu to deal with a possible mandatory need to vaccinate masses of people within a very short time frame
- Long-lasting impact on the operations of the government, the general public, and the business sectors caused by drastic intervention measures, difficult to predict human response to those measures (such as risk perception and panic), suspended or delayed economic activity, and diminished confidence

Three influenza pandemics occurred during the 20th century:

- 1918: killed 675,000 in United States and around 50 million worldwide
- 1957: killed at least 70,000 in United States and 1 to 2 million worldwide
- 1968: killed about 34,000 in United States and 700,000 worldwide

The urgency for influenza pandemic mitigation and preparedness has increased in the past few years primarily due to two important medical incidents that at least partially shared the characteristics of an influenza pandemic or carried the potential to evolve into a serious global pandemic. These two incidents are SARS (severe acute respiratory syndrome) and avian influenza (bird flu). While some characteristics of the two diseases seem to be similar, essentially the root causes and the contagious behavior of those diseases are different. While both are potentially fatal respiratory infections that initiated in animals and then made the jump to humans with similar flu-like symptoms such as fever and difficulty breathing, there are two major differences. First, avian influenza is caused by a flu virus, whereas SARS has roots similar to the common cold. The second and more important difference is that SARS can be transmitted between humans, whereas in most cases of the avian flu, the transmission has occurred from a bird to a human.

SARS originated in southern China in late 2002. In February 2003, cases were reported in Hong Kong (China). In just a few days, cases were observed in Vietnam, Singapore, Canada, and Germany. Between November 2002 and July 2003, more than 8,000 cases of SARS were reported globally. Those cases caused 774 deaths in 26 countries — most of which were in the Western Pacific.

Avian influenza is bird disease caused by type "A" strains of the influenza virus. While most birds are vulnerable to the virus, many wild bird species carry the viruses with no apparent symptoms. Of all strains of avian influenza "A" viruses, only four are known to have caused human infections: H5N1, H7N3, H7N7, and H9N2. H5N1 causes the most dangerous and fatal infections for humans. From 2003 to 2008, 349 human cases of the avian flu from 14 countries were reported to the World Health Organization, of which 216 were fatal. Indonesia and Vietnam had the highest numbers of human avian influenza deaths, with 94 and 47 lives lost, respectively. While H5N1 is still primarily a virus that can transmit from an infected bird to a human, cases of human-to-human transmission have been confirmed in at least three incidents in Thailand, Indonesia, and Pakistan. In all of those instances, the transmission occurred through extended close contact (caretaker and infected person). Scientists are not too concerned about this type of transmission, since it is highly preventable, but the possibility of a mutation in the virus genetic code that makes the transmission among humans much easier and faster is of real concern to public health officials (see figure).

Because the entire world is at risk of influenza pandemic, every country is expected to enable resources for preparedness and response in case of a potential outbreak. The World Health Organization supports those efforts by making information, data, knowledge, expertise, research, and

(Continued)

DIGGING DEEPER: INFLUENZA PANDEMIC MITIGATION AND PREPAREDNESS. (CONTINUED)

Areas with confirmed cases of H5N1 Avian Influenza since 2003 (as of March 2011). Source: World Health Organization, 2011.

guidelines available to the international community. In 2005, the World Health Organization released the "Checklist for Influenza Pandemic Preparedness Planning." The goal of the checklist is to provide national planning authorities a list of required and desired tasks to be completed to achieve a minimum level of preparedness that would increase the chance of success in an actual influenza pandemic response. The checklist is intentionally kept generic to ensure applicability in many nations with varying levels of resources and technical expertise. The checklist includes the following seven items:

1. *Preparing for an emergency*: This step involves the completion of preplanning activities such as the creation of political and public awareness regarding an influenza pandemic, the establishment of an overall preparedness strategy, and the appropriation of a budget adequate to sustain preparedness activities and to pay for resources deemed essential in the preparedness strategy.
2. *Surveillance*: Surveillance is one of the most critical steps of pandemic preparedness, as early detection of an outbreak is key to minimize further spread of the disease and initiation of a timely response. Unique and complex predictive procedures may be necessary to detect an outbreak in a timely fashion, which should effectively monitor and analyze multiple parameters that may be early signals of an upcoming influenza pandemic. For example, constant monitoring

of daily cases that report to hospitals with flu-like symptoms may help in the creation of confidence intervals that designate normal conditions and abnormal conditions that may be associated with an uncommon demand for medical care related to a new flu outbreak.

3. *Case investigation and treatment*: This step ensures the creation of capability and resources to complete a first assessment of a virus when it shows signs of a known influenza strain. Adequate laboratory capability is mandatory. Established communication mechanisms with the World Trade Organization and other relevant organizations should occur to disseminate valuable new information in a timely fashion. Guidelines on clinical treatment of the new case should be established along with adequate training for first-response personnel.

4. *Preventing spread of the disease in the community*: Identification and initiation of postincident mitigation and prevention activities are crucial to stop dispersion of the disease to the general public, thus preventing an influenza pandemic outbreak. Some of the activities involved in this step are restrictions to mobility, setup of checkpoints, creation of rules for hospital admissions, creation of a communication system with the general public, and identification of priority rules in case vaccination becomes necessary with a limited supply of vaccine or other preventive medical supplies.

5. *Maintaining essential services*: Government organizations and other vital services should have internal organizational continuity plans to make sure that they can still provide the services the public expects from them even under the extreme operational conditions of an influenza pandemic outbreak. Government agencies in most nations have laws that require them to develop continuity plans, but those plans should be revised and improved based on the unique sets of challenges that may be posed as a direct consequence of the pandemic outbreak.

6. *Research and evaluation*: While countries dealing with an actual influenza pandemic outbreak are very likely to become stretched for resources, an actual outbreak is an important opportunity for research and data collection to improve existing strategies and to test control measures applied for their level of effectiveness. Therefore, nations should make research and evaluation part of their response strategy and establish relationships and partnerships with other nations to ensure that scientific exchange among research communities is not impaired by the circumstances of the ongoing incident.

7. *Implementation, testing, and revision of national plan*: Revision of the national plan for applicability and testing it to improve its use during an actual outbreak are necessary. Make sure to set clear goals and measures of effectiveness that make progress evaluation of the plan easier during actual plan activation.

In the United States, the Department of Health and Human Services (HHS) holds primary responsibility for the coordination of influenza pandemic preparedness, as determined by the Homeland Security Council document, "National Strategy for Pandemic Influenza." The strategy identifies the following three pillars for effective management of a potential influenza pandemic:

- *Preparedness and communications*: Understand roles and responsibilities of different government agencies for the purposes of a potential influenza pandemic outbreak. Establish communications mechanisms and chain of command for effective incident management and decision making.
- *Surveillance and detection*: Ensure continuous "situational awareness" for timely identification outbreaks to limit the spread and to protect the public.

(*Continued*)

DIGGING DEEPER: INFLUENZA PANDEMIC MITIGATION AND PREPAREDNESS. (CONTINUED)

- *Response and containment*: Develop the capacity to effectively respond to an outbreak and establish mechanisms to minimize the spread of an overall economic and societal impact of an outbreak in progress.

Sources: World Health Organization, "SARS," 2003; World Health Organization, "WHO Checklist for Influenza Pandemic Preparedness Planning," 2005; U.S. Department of Health and Human Services, "General Information on Pandemic and Avian Flu," 2008; WikiBirdFlu, "Relationship between Bird Flu and SARS," 2007; World Health Organization, "Cumulative Number of Confirmed Human Cases of Avian Influenza A/(H5N1) Reported to WHO," 2008; Reuters, "WHO Confirms Human-to-Human Bird-Flu Case," December 27, 2007; White House, "National Strategy for Pandemic Influenza," 2005.

The Role of the Private Sector in Mitigation and Preparedness Activities

The events of September 11 brought to light the importance of private-sector involvement in crisis, emergency, and disaster management. Since that time, an ever-expanding list of private entities has begun focusing on their needs in this area. This section discusses the essentials of private-sector business continuity planning and disaster management. Most of the components discussed next have been learned as a result of experience with natural disasters or man-made accidents; however, the September 11 attacks have proved that those important components of classical crisis management are also important for terrorism risk management:

Business impact analysis (BIA): The management-level analysis by which an organization assesses the quantitative (financial) and qualitative (nonfinancial) impacts, effects, and loss that might result if the organization were to suffer a business-interrupting event. Performing BIA as a preparedness measure is important because findings from BIA are used to make decisions concerning business continuity management strategy.

Crisis communications planning: Decision making about how crisis communications will be performed during an emergency is important because communication is a critical success factor for effective crisis management. Preventing rumors about your corporation as well as telling your story before someone else does it for you is only possible via a predefined communication policy.

Information technology (IT) and systems infrastructure redundancy planning: There are different techniques and approaches regarding the enforcement of systems redundancy. Each company is unique, with its own IT and system needs and processes; therefore, customized approaches have to be employed to build more reliable systems infrastructure (e.g., backup databases, software, hardware, and network redundancy).

Geographic location and backup sites: The selection of the geographic location of headquarters and offices and the distribution of key executives in those buildings are strategically important decisions with regard to minimizing potential losses (both human and physical) during a disaster. The availability of backup sites that allow employees to continue operations in case of physical loss of or damage to a primary facility is a key success factor, but, unfortunately, is usually difficult to justify in terms of cost and benefit.

Transportation planning: The transportation infrastructure is one of the most sensitive infrastructures to emergency and disaster situations. Overloaded transportation infrastructure during crisis is usually a reason for microdisasters in the midst of bigger ones. Therefore, realistic transportation planning is important for a successful response.

Crisis leadership: Research and experience have shown that during crisis situations, people (e.g., employees, staff, and customers) need someone to tell them what is going on and explain what is being done about it, even if the information this person communicates is obsolete or redundant. Strong leadership also helps people to regain self-esteem and motivates them to commit to the efforts to overcome the crisis.

Insurance: It is important for companies to have a feasible but protective insurance policy. Realistic risk assessments and modeling are necessary to establish this economic feasibility.

There surely are other components of private-sector risk mitigation and preparedness that are not mentioned in this text; however, these are the most important across the broad range of business types and sizes (Kayyem and Chang, 2002; Smith, 2002). See the sidebar titled "Private-Sector Homeland Security Checklist" for assistance provided by the DHS.

Private-Sector Homeland Security Checklist

The Department of Homeland Security released the following antiterror checklist for the private sector in its May 2003 Homeland Security Information Bulletin:

- Maintain situational awareness of world events and ongoing threats.
- Ensure all levels of personnel are notified via briefings, e-mail, voice mail, and signage of any changes in threat conditions and protective measures.
- Encourage personnel to be alert and immediately report any situation that may constitute a threat or suspicious activity.
- Encourage personnel to avoid routines, vary times and routes, preplan, and keep a low profile, especially during periods of high threat.
- Encourage personnel to take notice and report suspicious packages, devices, unattended briefcases, or other unusual materials immediately; inform them not to handle or attempt to move any such object.
- Encourage personnel to keep their family members and supervisors apprised of their whereabouts.
- Encourage personnel to know emergency exits and stairwells.
- Increase the number of visible security personnel wherever possible.
- Rearrange exterior vehicle barriers, traffic cones, and roadblocks to alter traffic patterns near facilities and cover by alert security forces.
- Institute/increase vehicle, foot, and roving security patrols varying in size, timing, and routes.
- Implement random security guard shift changes.
- Arrange for law enforcement vehicles to be parked randomly near entrances and exits.
- Review current contingency plans and, if not already in place, develop and implement procedures for receiving and acting on threat information; alert notification procedures; terrorist incident response procedures; evacuation procedures; bomb threat procedures; hostage and barricade procedures; chemical, biological, radiological, and nuclear (CBRN) procedures; consequence and crisis management procedures; accountability procedures; and media procedures.

- When the aforementioned plans and procedures have been implemented, conduct internal training exercises and invite local emergency responders (fire, rescue, medical, and bomb squads) to participate in joint exercises.
- Coordinate and establish partnerships with local authorities to develop intelligence and information-sharing relationships.
- Place personnel on standby for contingency planning.
- Limit the number of access points, and strictly enforce access control procedures.
- Approach all illegally parked vehicles in and around facilities, question drivers, and direct them to move immediately; if the owner cannot be identified, have vehicle towed by law enforcement.
- Consider installing telephone caller ID; record phone calls, if necessary.
- Increase perimeter lighting.
- Deploy visible security cameras and motion sensors.
- Remove vegetation in and around perimeters; maintain regularly.
- Institute a robust vehicle inspection program to include checking the undercarriage of vehicles, under the hood, and in the trunk. Provide vehicle inspection training to security personnel.
- Deploy explosive detection devices and explosive detection canine teams.
- Conduct vulnerability studies focusing on physical security, structural engineering, infrastructure engineering, and power, water, and air infiltration, if feasible.
- Initiate a system to enhance mail and package screening procedures (both announced and unannounced).
- Install special locking devices on manhole covers in and around facilities.
- Implement a countersurveillance detection program.

Source: Continuity Central, May 21, 2003.

Corporate Preparedness and Risk Management in the Sarbanes–Oxley Era

The Sarbanes–Oxley Act of 2002, written by Senator Paul Sarbanes (D-MD) and Representative Paul Oxley (R-OH), was created to protect investors by improving the accuracy and reliability of corporate disclosures. The act is in direct response to financial fraud discovered in the cases of both Enron and WorldCom. However, it was created to cover issues beyond fraud (establishing a public company accounting oversight board, auditor independence, corporate responsibility, and enhanced financial disclosure), and is now a driving force behind corporate business continuity planning. Although the phrase *business continuity planning* is not once mentioned in the language of the act, continuity professionals claim that Section 404 of the act implies that such measures must be taken for compliance. Section 404 of the act reads as follows:

SEC. 404. MANAGEMENT ASSESSMENT OF INTERNAL CONTROLS.

(a) RULES REQUIRED — The Commission shall prescribe rules requiring each annual report required by Section 13(a) or 15(d) of the Securities Exchange Act of 1934 (15 U.S.C. 78m or 78o(d)) to contain an internal control report, which shall

(1) state the responsibility of management for establishing and maintaining an adequate internal control structure and procedures for financial reporting; and

(2) contain an assessment, as of the end of the most recent fiscal year of the issuer, of the effectiveness of the internal control structure and procedures of the issuer for financial reporting.

(b) INTERNAL CONTROL EVALUATION AND REPORTING — With respect to the internal control assessment required by subsection (a), each registered public accounting firm that prepares or issues the audit report for the issuer shall attest to, and report on, the assessment made by the management of the issuer. An attestation made under this subsection shall be made in accordance with standards for attestation engagements issued or adopted by the Board. Any such attestation shall not be the subject of a separate engagement (Sarbanes–Oxley Act of 2002, http://thomas.loc.gov/cgi-bin/query/F?c107:6:./temp/~c107×5GHak:e143423).

Section 404 of the Sarbanes–Oxley Act requires companies to include an internal control report that states the responsibility of management for establishing and maintaining an adequate internal controls structure and procedures for financial reporting in their annual report. In addition, it requires management to ensure that the effectiveness of the internal control structure is assessed on an annual basis. The section also requires the external auditing entity to report on management's assessment of the effectiveness of the company's internal controls and procedures with respect to standards defined by the Public Company Accounting Oversight Board. Compliance with the act became effective in April 2005 for most companies.

Even though the section still focuses on financial record management and process control, in order to really ensure those things, it is almost a prerequisite for the company to ensure adequate protection and continuity of its entire core processes. This is where the "business continuity" aspect of the act becomes evident.

To protect the financial processes and records from misconduct or fraud, and to ensure data integrity and resilience, the first step is to identify the risks, threats, and vulnerabilities that may endanger those expectations defined by the act. This is possible through a comprehensive risk and vulnerability assessment followed by a BIA to identify the business consequences of possible adverse incidents. The BIA is usually considered as one of the main building blocks of business continuity planning, because its findings usually help the corporations identify and prioritize the risks it has to mitigate, and provide an understanding of recovery goals.

At present, it is too early to comment on whether there is full consensus between what the Sarbanes–Oxley Act demands from corporations and how the corporations interpret those expectations and what they are going to do about it. But it is true that business continuity concepts will adequately address some of the expectations of the act. Business continuity service providers seem to capitalize on this connection and enlarge the market for their services and products. The fact that the Sarbanes–Oxley Act places responsibility for compliance on top management makes it inevitable that these corporations will increase investments aimed at compliance. Business continuity is one of the answers.

Based on recent reports (2007), corporate spending on the Sarbanes–Oxley Act increased until 2005 and stabilized at about $6 billion a year. This includes all the money that corporations spend to comply with the requirements of the 2002 Act (Reuters, 2007b).

A recent business continuity planning-focused journal article has indicated that compliance may require more than basic business continuity planning. The article explained that the act will make senior management involvement in the planning process inevitable, and thus will require them to think about and find solutions beyond their organizations, while paying more attention to service-level agreements, continuity of vendors, and suppliers (Benvenuto, 2004; Berman, 2004; Williams, 2005).

DIGGING DEEPER: U.S. GOVERNMENT GUIDANCE ON PANDEMIC PREPAREDNESS PLANNING FOR BUSINESSES WITH OVERSEAS OPERATIONS.

Due to the global nature of a potential pandemic influenza outbreak, a panel of representative U.S. agencies (i.e., Department of State, Department of Health and Human Services, Department of Commerce, and Centers for Disease Control and Prevention) have established pandemic planning guidelines for U.S. businesses with overseas operations. A summary of the guidelines follows. The full document can be found at http://www.pandemicflu.gov/plan/workplaceplanning/businessesoverseas.pdf.

- Plan for Maintaining Business Continuity during and after a Pandemic
- Plan for the Impact of a Pandemic on the Lives and Welfare of Your Employees
- Establish Policies and Guidelines to Be Implemented during a Pandemic to Avoid Creating Policies "On Demand" in the Midst of a Pandemic
- Determine Resources Required to Fulfill Actions in Your Pandemic Plan
- Create an Emergency Communications System
- Work to Coordinate with External Organizations and Your Community
- Prepare for Postpandemic Scenarios

Source: U.S. Department of Health and Human Services, "Pandemic Preparedness Planning for US Businesses with Overseas Operations," 2007. See the companion website for the full text of this document.

Best Practices

The nature of crisis, emergency, and risk management is very complicated: No matter how much one may discuss the process in the theoretical sense, the complexity of the actual environment in which they must try to implement practical applications cannot be fully appreciated. The three case studies that follow document private-sector experience with disaster, individual mitigation and preparedness, and a governmental approach to mitigation and preparedness.

CASE STUDY 1: CANTOR FITZGERALD

For Joseph Noviello, September 11 began at 6:30 AM with a phone call confirming that an annual fishing trip with colleagues at the Cantor Fitzgerald bond trading firm was still on, despite some foul weather offshore. Minutes later, the most intense two days of his life would begin as the first plane hijacked by terrorists crashed into Cantor's building.

Watching on TV from his Manhattan apartment, Noviello had no way of knowing what lay in store. Clearly, this was a disaster of a proportion that neither he nor likely anyone in his position had dealt with before. Fortunately, he had a plan to follow.

That plan may have saved the company. No firm suffered a worse fate, in terms of lives lost on September 11, than Cantor Fitzgerald and its electronic marketplace unit, eSpeed. More than 700 employees of the two companies died in the destruction of the World Trade Center's north tower, where Cantor and eSpeed shared their headquarters and a vital computer center. Yet eSpeed was up and running when the bond market reopened at 8 AM on September 13, little more than 47 hours after the disaster.

"The difference for us was the planning we had in place," says Noviello, 36, who was promoted to eSpeed's chief information officer after the disaster. eSpeed's systems were built on a dual architecture that replicated all machines, connections, and functionality at the World Trade Center and at a Rochelle Park site, with a third facility in London.

eSpeed, which operates as a freestanding business and also serves as the trading engine for its parent company, lost 180 employees, including about half of its U.S.-based technology staff. But eSpeed had several important assets left. Most of the top technology executives had been out of the office, including Matt Claus, eSpeed's current CTO, and Noviello's right-hand man, who had been scheduled to go on the fishing trip.

The response atmosphere was tense, with people unsure as to what had happened to their friends or colleagues. "For days, every time a new face came in the door it was an emotional release," says Noviello. "There was a disaster-recovery contact list, but people were seeking to find each other not for work but to find out who was okay."

Beyond the technical questions were operational details such as advising staff on public transportation options to the suburban site, reestablishing shifts, and making sure there were counselors on duty. Conference calls every two hours kept track of milestones and objectives. "We were talking at 2 AM, at 4 AM," says Noviello. "Who is sleeping during something like this? Work is great therapy."

None of this effort would have succeeded without the duplicate architecture in Rochelle Park. Yet Cantor started moving into the facility only in February. From day one, Rochelle Park was seen as a concurrent system, not a disaster-recovery site.

All that redundancy would be stretched to the limit as eSpeed worked to overcome the technical hurdles before the opening of the bond market Thursday morning. Two of those hurdles were huge: the loss of eSpeed's private network connections and the destruction of the company's ability to handle fulfillment of trades.

The first problem was solved by allowing customers who had overseas offices connected to Cantor's London data center to reroute across their own networks to London. eSpeed worked with customers to reconfigure their servers to point to London and moved or expanded the permissions on customer accounts to connect to that site. For customers without overseas private networks, eSpeed worked to get them access over the Internet until the customers could get their high-speed connections hooked into the Rochelle Park facility.

To solve the second issue, help arrived in the form of one of eSpeed's competitors. ICI/ADP, another electronic trading company, offered to take care of eSpeed's clearing and settling of transactions through its own connection to banks. By Wednesday night, the eSpeed team had mapped its financial back-office system to ADP's system and had successfully sent test transactions to J.P. Morgan Chase & Co. and other banks. The cooperation of other companies, including vendors and fellow financial firms, turned out to be essential to Cantor/eSpeed's quick recovery.

The firm was weakened by the loss of so many people and the related shutdown of its voice-broker business. But it survived as a viable business. Thanks to planning, the company can keep operating, even if something should happen to Rochelle Park. Its data center in London will serve as the mirror site going forward.

And going forward, the company's systems should be even more resilient. "We are learning a lot of lessons as we are restoring the system," says Noviello, including how to automate more aspects of bringing systems back up. "And we are not restoring our bad habits" (Summarized from the original work of Cone and Gallagher, 2001).

CASE STUDY 2: HOME ALONE … EMERGENCY PLAN SAVES SISTERS

When the strongest tornado to hit Mississippi in more than 50 years tore through the small town of Smithville on April 27, 2011, 16-year old Audrey Herren and her younger sister Cassidy, 11, knew what to do, and it probably saved their lives. They went into emergency mode — covered themselves with blankets and huddled on the floor of an inside hallway — and emerged virtually unscathed from a home that had disintegrated around them.

April 27 started off on an ominous note as the town's siren was sounded several times during the morning to warn residents of the approaching severe weather system. As the potential threat to Smithville became more certain, the 600 students in the town's K-12 school complex were released early, at approximately 2 PM. Parents Jim and Carol Herren were at work at the time, but they had learned via broadcast warnings and access to radar images of the storm that Smithville was in the path of a possible tornado. They called their daughters and told them to exercise their emergency plan, which they had put to use during earlier severe thunderstorms as recently as the previous week.

The tornado reached Smithville at 3:44 PM., roaring through the middle of town with peak winds estimated at 205 miles per hour. Most buildings were flattened, including more than 150 homes, 14 businesses, and 2 churches. Seventeen people lost their lives, either during the tornado or later as a result of injuries.

When the Herrens reached Smithville about an hour after the tornado struck, their daughters were not at their home (or what was left of it) as they had been told to move away from the area because of possible gas leaks. They connected with the girls later. The Herren family was able to save a bit of clothing from their home, but none of their furnishings could be salvaged. Most importantly their daughters had survived the storm.

"Everybody in town has a tornado story," said Carol Herren, "but unfortunately, many didn't turn out as positive as ours." And although her family didn't have a safe room at the time of the tornado, she is glad they had an emergency plan and that the plan likely saved her daughters.

The Herren family had occupied their home along Mississippi Highway 25, the main road through Smithville, for about 13 years. They are now living in a rented home that is just outside the tornado's path of destruction. They plan to begin construction of safe room in a new home within the next few weeks that will specifically comply with the design criteria in FEMA 361, Design and Construction Guidance for Community Safe Rooms. They know several other neighbors who plan to do the same, and Jim Herren says he hopes that many others will decide to stay and rebuild in Smithville.

For additional information, contact the FEMA Safe Room Help Line at 866-222-3580 or at saferoom@dhs.gov. The help line provides information on where to go for assistance regarding hazard mitigation grants and other grant funding, project eligibility, and guidelines for safe room construction. FEMA's safe room website (http://www.fema.gov/plan/prevent/saferoom) is another source of information.

Source: FEMA, 2011, "FEMA Mitigation Best Practices Portfolio," http://www.fema.gov/mitigationbp/brief.do?mitssId = 8410

CASE STUDY 3: SAFE ROOM WITHSTANDS EF-4 TORNADO

Tuscaloosa County, Alabama

William Blakeney grew up in Tuscaloosa County and is well aware of the effects of disasters in the area. In an effort to prepare for disasters like the tornadoes in mid- and late April 2011, he built a safe room in his grandparents' home. Although they weren't home when the storms devastated the area, the only portion of their home left standing was the multipurpose safe room (see Figure 10–6).

Blakeney and his construction company had built a few safe rooms in the past, mainly in their family members' homes. While not built according to the design criteria of Federal Emergency Management Agency's publication FEMA 320, Taking Shelter from the Storm: Building a Safe Room For Your Home or Small Business, this safe room was able to withstand the strong winds of the EF-4 tornado that ravaged the area.

FEMA 320 includes construction plans and cost estimates for building individual safe rooms. A safe room, built according to the standards outlined in FEMA 320, in a home or small business provides "near-absolute protection" for its occupants.

"We were not familiar with FEMA specifications, but we had built a few safe rooms," said Blakeney. "I was actually at the office and used the safe room we had built there when the tornado came through."

FIGURE 10–6 Tuscaloosa, AL, June 12, 2011 — A FEMA mitigation specialist conducts an interview with local media prior to the Safer Alabama Summit at the Bryant Auditorium on the University of Alabama Campus. The summit provided information on how communities can best prepare for another catastrophic series of storms, and safe rooms will be on display to illustrate the building techniques required to withstand an F5 tornado. (Source: Photo by FEMA/Tim Burkitt)

(Continued)

CASE STUDY 3: SAFE ROOM WITHSTANDS EF-4 TORNADO (CONTINUED)

April's storms claimed over 40 lives in Tuscaloosa and left more than 2,000 residents homeless. The area experiences tornadoes early spring and late fall each year, but never as severe as those on April 2011.

"Tornadoes usually hit the southern or northern parts of the town," said Blakeney about the recent events. His family had lived in Tuscaloosa County for more than 71 years. "In my time, we've never seen one come through the area like that!" The home was recently renovated so his grandparents could move from the outskirts of the city and live closer to other relatives. In the additional wing, the master bedroom closet was the perfect location to reinforce as the safe room.

"They had a basement in their old home and that made them feel secure," said Blakeney. "Here, they had nothing." The major home renovation was completed just 2 weeks before the storm hit the city and destroyed the home. His grandparents had not completely moved into the house and Blakeney was still adding finishing touches to the home. Fortunately, no one was home when the tornado struck because the entire neighborhood was destroyed.

Safe rooms provide homeowners, like Blakeney's grandparents, relief during times where they have to quickly seek shelter. Should homeowners decide to build a safe room in their new or existing home, FEMA 320 provides examples of proper installation techniques and designs. Safe rooms built to FEMA 320 standards have saved the lives of people affected by events like the one that destroyed many areas of Alabama.

"We just think it is a great investment for the sense of security," Blakeney added. "We will be building more in the future using FEMA 320." Building safe rooms according to FEMA specifications helps ensure that they will be able to withstand high winds and provide the ultimate protection. Not building according to FEMA specifications is risky and increases the likelihood of the safe room not providing the needed protection.

For additional information, contact the FEMA Safe Room Help Line at 866-222-3580 or at saferoom@dhs.gov. The help line provides information on where to go for assistance regarding hazard mitigation grants and other grant funding, project eligibility, and guidelines for safe room construction. FEMA's safe room website (http://www.fema.gov/plan/prevent/saferoom) is another source of information.

Source: FEMA, 2011, "FEMA Mitigation Best Practices Portfolio," http://www.fema.gov/mitigationbp/bestPracticeDetail.do?mitssId = 8390

Exercises to Foster Preparedness

The Homeland Security Council (HSC), in partnership with DHS, and state and local homeland security agencies, has developed 15 all-hazards planning scenarios for use in national, federal, state, and local homeland security preparedness activities. These scenarios are designed to be the foundational structure for the development of national preparedness standards from which homeland security capabilities can be measured (Figure 10–7). For the earthquake scenario, see the sidebar titled "HSC Scenario 9."

FIGURE 10–7 Anniston, AL, January 21, 2011 — Health-care workers rush to decontaminate a simulated victim during an exercise at the Center for Domestic Preparedness, located in Anniston, Alabama. These students were attending the Hospital Emergency Response Training (HERT) for mass-casualty incidents course that places emergency response providers in a realistic mass-casualty training scenario. For more information on the CDP's more than 50 specialized programs and courses, please visit their website at: http://cdp.dhs.gov.

HSC Scenario 9: Major Earthquake

Executive Summary

- Casualties: 1,400 fatalities; 100,000 hospitalizations
- Infrastructure Damage: 150,000 buildings destroyed, 1 million buildings damaged
- Evacuations/Displaced Persons: 300,000 households
- Contamination: From hazardous materials, in some areas
- Economic Impact: Hundreds of billions
- Potential for Multiple Events: Yes, aftershocks
- Recovery Timeline: Months to years

Scenario Overview

General description: Earthquakes occur when the plates that form under the Earth's surface suddenly shift, and most earthquakes occur at the boundaries where the plates meet. A fault is a fracture in the Earth's crust along which two blocks of the crust have slipped with respect to each other. The magnitude of an earthquake, usually expressed by the Richter Scale, is a measure of the amplitude of the seismic waves. The intensity, as expressed by the Modified Mercalli Scale, is a subjective measure that describes how strong a shock was felt at a particular location.

The Richter Scale is logarithmic so that a recording of 7, for example, indicates a disturbance with ground motion 10 times as great as a recording of 6. A quake of magnitude 2 is the smallest quake normally felt by people. Earthquakes with a Richter value of 6 or more are commonly considered major; great earthquakes have magnitude of 8 or more. The Modified Mercalli (MM) Scale expresses the intensity of an earthquake's effects in a given locality in values ranging from I to XII. The most commonly used adaptation covers the range of intensity from the condition of "I — Not felt except by a very few under especially favorable conditions," to "XII — Damage total. Lines of sight and level are distorted. Objects thrown upward into the air."

In this scenario, a 7.2-magnitude earthquake occurs along a fault zone in a major metropolitan area (MMA) of a city. MM Scale VIII or greater intensity ground shaking extends throughout large sections of the metropolitan area, greatly impacting a six-county region with a population of approximately 10 million people. Subsurface faulting occurs along 45 miles of the fault zone, extending along a large portion of highly populated local jurisdictions, creating a large swath of destruction. Soil liquefaction occurs in some areas, creating quicksand-like conditions.

Timeline/event dynamics: While scientists have been predicting a moderate to catastrophic earthquake in the region sometime in the future, there were no specific indications that an earthquake was imminent in the days and weeks prior to this event.

Damage includes a large multistate area of several hundred square miles. Rapid horizontal movements associated with the earthquake shift homes off their foundations and cause some tall buildings to collapse or "pancake" as floors collapse down onto one another. Shaking is exaggerated in areas where the underlying sediment is weak or saturated with water. (Note: In the central and eastern United States, earthquake waves travel more efficiently than in the western United States. An earthquake of a given size in the central and eastern United States may cause damage over a much broader area than the same size earthquake in California.)

Several hours later, an aftershock of magnitude 8.0 occurs. Based on past events, additional aftershocks are possible. Sizable aftershocks (7.0 to 8.0 in magnitude) may occur for months after the original jolt.

Secondary hazards/events: As a result of the earthquake, hazardous contamination impacts of concern include natural gas compression stations and processing plants, oil refineries and major tank farms, and natural gas/crude oil pipelines. In addition, more than 2,000 spot fires occur and widespread debris results. Flooding may occur due to levee failures and breaks in water mains and sewage systems.

Transportation lines and nodes, power generation and distribution, communications lines, fuel storage and distribution, and various structures (ranging from dams to hospitals) may be damaged and will require damage assessment in order to continue operating. Reduced availability of services will be disruptive and costly.

Ground shaking from the earthquake has generated massive amounts of debris (more than 120 million tons) from collapsed structures. In addition, fuel pumps in several gas stations have sustained damage, leaking thousands of gallons of gasoline into the streets. There are numerous reports of toxic chemical fires, plumes with noxious fumes, and spills. Several other local waste treatment facilities have reported wastewater and sewage discharges. A large refining spill has contaminated the port facility and is spilling into the harbor. Significant concern for spilled hazardous materials from storage, overturned railcars, and chemical stockpiles make progress very slowly as triage is conducted.

Key implications: Approximately 1,400 fatalities occur as a direct result of the earthquake. More than 100,000 people are injured and continue to overwhelm area hospitals and medical facilities, most of which have sustained considerable damage. Approximately 18,000 of the injured require hospitalization. As many as 20,000 people are missing and may be trapped under collapsed buildings and underground commuter tunnels.

More than 1 million buildings were at least moderately damaged (40% of the buildings) and more than 150,000 buildings have been completely destroyed.

Service disruptions are numerous to households, businesses, and military facilities. Medical services are overwhelmed and functioning hospitals are limited. Fire and emergency medical services (EMS) stations and trucks were also damaged. Bridges and major highways are down or blocked and damaged runways have caused flight cancellations. There are widespread power outages and ruptures to underground fuel, oil, and natural gas lines. Water mains are broken. Wastewater primary receptors have broken, closing down systems and leaking raw sewage into the streets. As a result, public health is threatened.

More than 300,000 households have been displaced, and many businesses have lost employees and customers. The port has been adversely affected in its capacity to provide export/import and loading/unloading capabilities, and damage to vital parts of the communications infrastructure has resulted in limited communications capabilities.

The disruption to the nation's economy could be severe because the earthquake impacts major supply and transportation centers. Reconstruction, repairs, disposal, and replacement of lost infrastructure will cost billions of dollars. Replacement of lost private property and goods could also cost billions. An overall national economic downturn is probable in the wake of this event.

Mission Areas Activated

Prevention/deterrence/protection: After the earthquake occurs, actions should be taken to protect critical facilities from terrorist attacks and to maintain civil order.

Emergency assessment/diagnosis: Disaster assessments and aerial reconnaissance are necessary. Using real-time seismic data, FEMA runs an earthquake model to provide a preliminary "best guess" at the level of expected damage, subject to confirmation or modification through remote sensing and field assessments. Assessment teams must be deployed and remote sensing initiated.

Emergency management/response: Hazardous material spills must be managed. Emergency medical treatment, shelters, and food must be provided. A joint information center (JIC) is established, and search and rescue teams must be placed on alert, some of which should be activated and deployed. Public utilities and other basic-needs services must be repaired as quickly as possible, and damage assessments should be conducted.

Incident/hazard mitigation: Federal support will be required to coordinate the development of plans to execute mitigation efforts to lessen the effects of future disasters. Mitigation to minimize or avoid future impacts would largely be an issue for recovery and restoration.

Public protection: Structural engineers are inspecting critical building, bridge, freeway, waste facilities, etc., and inspection teams are deployed to inspect hundreds of homes for safe habitability.

Victim care: The massive number of injured and displaced persons requires a warning order for the activation of task forces for the delivery of mass care and health and medical services. Temporary housing strategies must be considered.

Investigation/apprehension: Not applicable.

Recovery/remediation: Hazardous materials will contaminate many areas, and decontamination and site restoration will be a major challenge.

Source: DHS and the Homeland Security Council.

Conclusion

Mitigation, prevention, and preparedness programs are vital to the safety and security of the nation. Since the onset of civilization, people have worked to limit their vulnerability to hazards once they recognized that those hazards existed. Since the attacks of September 11, the focus of mitigation has shifted primarily to mitigation, prevention, and preparedness for terrorist attacks, but the real threat has proven to be the traditional natural and man-made hazards that existed both before and after the attacks began. It is the responsibility of government, which rests most clearly on the Department of Homeland Security, to protect the nation from the consequences of disastrous events. For that reason, it is vital that the all-hazards approach to mitigation, prevention, and preparedness be maintained.

Key Terms

All-Hazards Planning: The disaster planning and preparedness philosophy that advocates for holistic preparedness and flexible disaster planning to ensure the response can be improvised to deal with the many unknowns of any disaster situation. In one sense, it is the opposite of "Scenario Planning."

Avian Influenza: An infection typically seen in birds, although in rare cases human transmission has been observed. Among four strains of the virus known to be infectious for humans, H5N1 is the most dangerous one. Avian influenza is also called "bird flu" in daily use.

Bird Flu: Please refer to Avian Influenza.

Business Continuity Planning (BCP): The process of identification and remediation of commercial and organizational impacts of disasters through planning and strategy. Business continuity planning typically involves strategizing for the continuity and protection of the human resource, critical business processes, information systems, infrastructure, and organizational reputation.

Business Impact Analysis (BIA): The management-level analysis by which an organization assesses the quantitative (financial) and qualitative (nonfinancial) impacts, effects, and loss that might result if the organization were to suffer a business-interrupting event. Performing BIA as a preparedness measure is important because findings from BIA are used to make decisions concerning business continuity management strategy.

Community Emergency Response Team (CERT): A community initiative of Citizen Corps to create disaster-resistant communities by training and disaster awareness. CERTs are composed of volunteers trained in basic disaster and medical response. As of 2008, there are more than 2,800 CERT programs all over the United States.

Crisis Management: A proactive management effort to avoid crisis, and the creation of strategy that minimizes adverse impacts of crisis to the organization when it could not be prevented. Effective crisis management requires a solid understanding of the organization, its strategy, liabilities, stakeholders, and legal framework combined with advanced communication, leadership, and decision-making skills to lead the organization through the crisis with minimizing potential loss.

Crisis: A critical turning point with impact to the future state of a given system. Although mostly signaling a deteriorating status of the system, if managed correctly, a crisis can be potentially beneficial. Example: Increased customer confidence to a company that has managed to survive a major crisis in the industry provides competitive advantage.

Disaster Recovery Planning (DRP): The planning effort that primarily deals with the continuity and timely recovery of physical and logical components of information systems infrastructure and applications. The first goal in DRP is to ensure a redundant infrastructure that provides for continuity of information technology (IT) systems that support critical business processes. The second goal is to develop a prioritized recovery strategy for systems and applications based on their criticalities for the organization in case of an inevitable system failure or a catastrophic incident.

Epidemic: An infection that affects the public in a larger proportion than day-to-day diseases and infections to the degree that resources of national medical care systems are exhausted or significantly constrained. Epidemics also typically have impacts on the social and economic infrastructures.

Emergency Support Function (ESF): A specific area of expertise deemed critical for a successful disaster operation as identified by the federal disaster response framework. The Federal Response Plan (12 ESFs), the National Response Plan (15 ESFs), and the new National Response Framework (15 ESFs) each identify the various ESFs as appendices. The ESFs in the National Response Framework follow: ESF #1 — Transportation, ESF #2 — Communications, ESF #3 — Public Works and Engineering, ESF #4 — Firefighting, ESF #5 — Emergency Management, ESF #6 — Mass Care, Housing, and Human Services, ESF #7 — Resource Support, ESF #8 — Public Health and Medical Services, ESF #9 — Search and Rescue, ESF #10 — Oil and Hazardous Materials Response, ESF #11 — Agriculture and Natural Resources, ESF #12 — Energy, ESF #13 — Public Safety and Security, ESF #14 — Long-Term Community Recovery, and ESF #15 — External Affairs.

Federal Response Plan (FRP): A signed agreement among 27 federal departments and agencies, including the American Red Cross, that provided a mechanism for coordinating the delivery of federal assistance and resources to augment efforts of state and local governments overwhelmed by a major disaster or emergency; replaced by the National Response Plan.

Hazard: A potential source of danger or unsafe environment.

Influenza: A contagious infection of the respiratory tract. Common symptoms include fever, muscular pain, general tiredness, and chills. Symptoms are typically felt stronger than those caused by the common cold.

Man-Made Disaster: Sometimes also called *technological disaster*. Man-made disasters have two common elements: (1) They are not primarily induced by a naturally occurring process. (2) In most instances, the cause of the disaster is human error or failure of systems designed by humans. Examples of man-made disasters include oil spills, radiological incidents, chemical releases, and transportation disasters.

Mitigation: A sustained effort taken to reduce or eliminate risk to people and property from hazards and their effects.

Natural Disaster: A disaster that is primarily induced by the destructive power of nature. Examples of natural disasters include hurricane, earthquake, tsunami, and snowstorm.

National Planning Scenarios (NPS): Fifteen disaster scenarios, each corresponding to one particular natural, technological, or terrorist hazard threats, which together or individually allow for a standard against which plans, capabilities, and policies may be exercised and otherwise tested or measured.

National Response Framework (NRF): Presents the guiding principles that enable all response partners to prepare for and provide a unified national response to disasters and emergencies— from the smallest incident to the largest emergency catastrophe; defines key principles, roles, and structures that organizes the way the nation responds; replaced the National Response Plan.

National Response Plan (NRP): A national-level plan which replaced the Federal Response Plan and which was created in keeping with the national Incident Management System model to align federal coordination structures, capabilities, and resources into a unified, all-discipline, and all-hazards approach to domestic incident management.

Pandemic: An epidemic that impacts a large region or has global impacts.

Postdisaster Mitigation: Mitigation activities typically performed in the aftermath of a disaster either to provide a safer environment for the ongoing response or recovery effort or to mitigate potential impacts of the next disaster based on immediate lessons learned from a current one.

Predisaster Mitigation: Mitigation activities engaged prior to the occurrence of the disaster to minimize its impact when it occurs.

Preparedness: A state of readiness to respond to a disaster, crisis, or any other type of emergency situation.

Prevention: Actions taken to avoid an incident or to intervene in an effort to stop an incident from occurring for the purpose of protecting lives and property.

Risk: According to Stan Kaplan, risk is comprised of three components: scenario, probability of scenario, and consequence of scenario.

Tabletop Exercise: A mock disaster game in which participants playing different roles such as decision maker, incident commander, or first responder typically gather around a table and discuss/decide their responses to the incident scenario presented by a moderator. The goal of a tabletop exercise is to simulate a disaster situation for the purposes of exposing the participant to the stressful decision-making conditions of a disaster. Tabletop exercises typically conclude with a debrief session where various parties discuss their respective roles, goals established, priorities, and challenges faced regarding the scenario played.

Terrorism: There are more than 100 definitions of terrorism in the literature. The United Nations defines terrorism as "an anxiety-inspiring method of repeated violent action, employed by (semi-) clandestine individual, group or state actors, for idiosyncratic, criminal or political reasons, whereby — in contrast to assassination — the direct targets of violence are not the main targets."

TOPOFF (abbreviation for "top officials"): TOPOFF is a congressionally mandated annual disaster preparedness and response exercise designed to improve the incident management/decision-making capability of the nation's top officials at every level of the government during an incident of national significance.

Review Questions

1. What are the initiatives that help local communities to mitigate/prepare against potential terrorist attacks? Why is community preparedness an important component of homeland security?

2. What mitigation/preparedness role does the private sector have in terms of homeland security? Do you believe that the private sector learned lessons from the 9/11 terrorist attacks?

3. Try to define terrorism mitigation using the common definition of mitigation in terms of the all-hazards approach. (Hint: Define risk as a combination of probability and consequence, and list all potential activities that can reduce both components of the potential terrorist event.)

4. What is the importance of international consensus and cooperation for terrorism mitigation/preparedness?

5. Take a quick look at the FEMA document, FEMA 426, Reference Manual to Mitigate Potential Terrorist Attacks against Buildings (available at www.fema.gov). What are the two most important factors to minimize damage caused by car bombs to buildings?

References

American Red Cross, 2003. Largest terrorism response drill in U.S. history begins, May 12. http://www.redcross.org/news/ds/terrorism/030512TOPOFF.html.

American Red Cross, 2008. Frequently asked questions. http://www.redcross.org/faq/0,1096,0_383_,00.html.

American Society of Civil Engineers, 2007. Dam Safety Act signed by president. https://www.aawre.org/pressroom/news/grwk/event_release.cfm?uid53912.

Association of State Dam Safety Officials, 2005. What is the National Dam Safety & Security Program and why should it continue? http://www.damsafety.org/media/Documents/Legislative%20Handouts/NDSPA%20Handout.pdf.

Barbera, J.A., Macintyre, A.G., 2002. Medical and Health Incident Management (MaHIM) System: A Comprehensive Functional System Description for Mass Casualty Medical and Health Incident Management. Institute for Crisis, Disaster, and Risk Management, The George Washington University, Washington, DC.

Barbera, J.A., Macintyre, A.G., 2003. *MaHIM*. Presentation at the ICDRM/SAIC Monthly Emergency Management Forum. George Washington University. Washington, DC, 2003.

Benvenuto, N., 2004. The relationship between business continuity and Sarbanes-Oxley. Protiviti KnowledgeLeader. http://www.protiviti.com/downloads/PRO/pro-us/articles/FeatureArticle_20040312.html.

Berman, A., 2004. Business continuity in a Sarbanes-Oxley world. Disaster Recovery Journal, Spring. http://www.drj.com/articles/spr04/1702-01.html.

Citizen Corps, 2003a. Citizen Corps councils. http://www.citizencorps.gov/councils/.

Citizen Corps, 2003b. Community emergency response team. http://www.citizencorps.gov/programs/cert.shtm.

Citizen Corps, 2003c. Medical reserve corps. http://www.citizencorps.gov/programs/medical.shtm.

CNN, 2008. Katrina timeline. http://www.cnn.com/SPECIALS/2005/katrina/interactive/timeline.katrina.large/frameset.exclude.html.

Cone, E., Gallagher, S., 2001. Cantor Fitzgerald — forty seven hours. www.baselinemag.com/print_article/0,3668,a517022,00.asp.

Congressional Research Service, 2007a. Aging infrastructure: Dam safety. www.fas.org/sgp/crs/homesec/RL33108.pdf.

Congressional Research Service, 2007b. FY2008 appropriations for state and local homeland security. http://www.fas.org/sgp/crs/homesec/RS22596.pdf.

Coppola, D.P., 2003a. A Report on the First Annual Conference on the Community and Homeland Security. Washington, DC: Haddow and Bullock, LLC (March).

Coppola, D.P., 2003b. Annotated Organizational Chart for the Department of Homeland Security. Bullock & Haddow, LLC, Washington, DC.

Corporation for National Community Service, 2005. Congressional budget justification for FY 2006. http://www.nationalservice.gov/pdf/2006_budget_justification.pdf.

Corporation for National Community Service, 2006. National service responds: The power of hope and help after Katrina. http://www.nationalservice.gov/pdf/katrina_report.pdf.

Corporation for National Community Service, 2007a. The power of help and hope after Katrina by the numbers: Volunteers in the Gulf. http://www.nationalservice.gov/pdf/katrina_volunteers_respond.pdf.

Corporation for National Community Service, 2007b. A resource guide for the strategic initiatives. http://www.nationalservice.org/pdf/07_0913_resourceguide_strategicplan.pdf.

Department of Homeland Security, 2004. National Response Plan Appendix ESF #6." Washington, DC. http://www.au.af.mil/au/awc/awcgate/nrp/esf06.pdf.

Department of Homeland Security, 2007a. Budget in brief 2008. http://www.dhs.gov/xlibrary/assets/budget_bib-fy2008.pdf.

Department of Homeland Security, 2007b. Overview: FY 2007 homeland security grant program. http://www.dhs.gov/xlibrary/assets/grants-2007-program-overview-010507.pdf.

Department of Homeland Security, 2007c. The National Response Framework. http://www.fema.gov/pdf/emergency/nrf/nrf-base.pdf.

Department of Homeland Security, 2007d. What's new in the NRF. http://www.in.gov/dhs/files/whatsnew.pdf.

Department of Homeland Security, 2008. Budget in brief 2009. http://www.dhs.gov/xlibrary/assets/budget_bib-fy2009.pdf.

Department of Homeland Security, 2011a. The National Response Framework. http://www.fema.gov/emergency/nrf/index.htm.

Department of Homeland Security, 2011b. Overview: FY 2011 Homeland Security Grant Program. http://www.fema.gov/pdf/government/grant/2011/fy11_hsgp_factsheet.pdf.

Emergency Management Australia, 2000. Emergency Risk Management: Applications Guide. Emergency Management Australia, Sydney.

European Commission, 2008. Threats to health — avian influenza. http://ec.europa.eu/health/ph_threats/com/Influenza/ai_human_en.htm.

Federal Emergency Management Agency, 2001. Multi-hazard mitigation planning. http://www.fema.gov/plan/mitplanning/index.shtm.

Federal Emergency Management Agency, 2003. Federal Emergency Management Agency 426: Reference Manual to Mitigate Potential Terrorist Attacks against Buildings. http://www.fema.gov/plan/prevent/rms/rmsp426.

Federal Emergency Management Agency, 2005. National Flood Insurance Program.

Federal Emergency Management Agency, 2005. Louisiana residents reminded floodplain development permit requirements still required for building repairs. FEMA Press Release. September 16. http://www.fema.gov/news/newsrelease.fema?id=18921.

Federal Emergency Management Agency, 2007a. Draft National Incident Management System. http://www.fema.gov/emergency/nims/.

Federal Emergency Management Agency, 2007b. Plan ahead for an earthquake. http://www.fema.gov/plan/prevent/earthquake/index.shtm.

Federal Emergency Management Agency, 2007c. About the National Dam Safety Program. http://www.fema.gov/plan/prevent/damfailure/ndsp.shtm.

Federal Emergency Management Agency, 2008a. FY 2007 Flood Mitigation Assistance (FMA) Program. http://www.fema.gov/government/grant/fma/fma2007.shtm.

Federal Emergency Management Agency, 2008b. FY 2007 repetitive flood claims grant recipients. http://www.fema.gov/government/grant/rfc/rfc_fy07_recipients.shtm.

Federal Emergency Management Agency, 2008c. FY 2008 Flood Mitigation Assistance (FMA) Program. http://www.fema.gov/government/grant/fma/fma2008.shtm.

Federal Emergency Management Agency, 2008d. Guidance for severe repetitive loss properties. www.fema.gov/pdf/nfip/manual200610/20srl.pdf.

Federal Emergency Management Agency, 2008e. Repetitive Flood Claims (RFC) Program (Fiscal Year 2007). http://www.fema.gov/government/grant/rfc/rfc_fy2007.shtm.

Federal Emergency Management Agency, 2008f. Repetitive Flood Claims (RFC) Program (Program Overview). http://www.fema.gov/government/grant/rfc/index.shtm.

Federal Emergency Management Agency, 2008g. Severe Repetitive Loss Program. http://www.fema.gov/government/grant/srl.

Federal Emergency Management Agency, 2010. Hazard Mitigation Assistance Unified Guidance, June 1. http://www.fema.gov/library/viewRecord.do?id=4225.

Federal Emergency Management Agency, 2011a. Federal Insurance and Mitigation Administration (FIMA). http://www.fema.gov/about/divisions/mitigation.shtm.

Federal Emergency Management Agency, 2011b. About the National Dam Safety Program. http://www.fema.gov/plan/prevent/damfailure/ndsp.shtm.

Federal Emergency Management Agency, 2011c. Hazard Mitigation Grant Program. http://www.fema.gov/government/grant/hmgp/index.shtm.

Federal Emergency Management Agency, 2011d. Hazard Mitigation Planning. http://www.fema.gov/plan/mitplanning/index.shtm#2.

Federal Emergency Management Agency, 2011e. Overview of Flood Map Modernization. http://www.fema.gov/plan/prevent/fhm/mm_main.shtm.

Federal Emergency Management Agency, 2011f. Pre-Disaster Mitigation Grant Program. http:// www.fema.gov/government/grant/pdm/index.shtm.

Federal Emergency Management Agency, 2011g. National Flood Insurance Program. http://www.fema.gov/plan/prevent/floodplain/index.shtm.

Federal Emergency Management Agency, 2011h. Severe Repetitive Loss Program. http://www.fema.gov/government/grant/srl/index.shtm.

Federal Emergency Management Agency, 2011i. Welcome to flood hazard mapping. http://www.fema.gov/plan/prevent/fhm/index.shtm.

Federal Emergency Management Agency, 2011j. Frequently Asked Questions Mitigation Grant Programs. http://www.fema.gov/government/grant/hmgp/

Federal Emergency Management Agency, 2011k. Louisiana Post-Katrina Recovery. http://www.fema.gov/hazard/hurricane/2005katrina/6year/iafm.shtm.

Fire Corps, 2008. Fire Corps National Advisory Committee Meets. http://firecorps.org/page/630/show_item/172/News.htm.

Frase Blunt M., 2003. Operation Topoff 2. http://www.aamc.org/newsroom/reporter/august03/bioterrorism.htm.

Government Accountability Office, 2000. Federal Emergency Management Agency Disaster Relief Fund. www.gao.gov/cgi-bin/getrpt?GAO/RCED-00-182.

Government Accountability Office, 2006. Hurricanes Katrina and Rita: Coordination between Federal Emergency Management Agency and the Red Cross Should Be Improved for the 2006 Hurricane Season. http://www.gao.gov/new.items/d06712.pdf.

Infoplease.com., 2008. Hurricane Katrina Timeline. http://www.infoplease.com/spot/hurricanekatrinatimeline.html.

Insurance Information Institute, 2008. National Flood Insurance Program. http://www.iii.org/media/facts/statsbyissue/flood/.

Kaplan, S., 1997. The words of risk analysis. Risk Analysis 17 (4), 408–409.

Kayyem, N.J., Chang, E.P., 2002. Beyond Business Continuity: The Role of the Private Sector in Preparedness Planning. Belfer Center for Science and International Affairs, John F. Kennedy School of Government, Harvard University, Cambridge, MA.

Kulling, P., 1998. The Terrorist Attack with Sarin in Tokyo. Socialstyresen, Stockholm.

National Commission on Terrorist Attacks upon the United States (9/11 Commission), 2004. What to Do? A Global Strategy. Chapter 12. Washington, DC.

National Earthquake Hazard Reduction Program, 2007. NEHRP 2007 Annual Report. http://www.nehrp.gov/pdf/2007NEHRPAnnualReport.pdf.

National Earthquake Hazard Reduction Program, 2008. NEHRP 2009 Program Budget. http://www.nehrp.gov/pdf/ppt_budget_fy09.pdf.

National Flood Insurance Program, 2008. Flood statistics. http://www.floodsmart.gov/floodsmart/pages/statistics.jsp.

Nuclear Regulatory Commission, 2005. Emergency preparedness and response. http://www.nrc.gov/about-nrc/emerg-preparedness/faq.html.

Public Broadcasting Service, 2005. American Red Cross troubles, December 14. http://www.pbs.org/newshour/bb/health/july-dec05/redcross_12-14.html.

Public Broadcasting Service, 2006. Fixing FEMA online news hour with Secretary M. Chertoff, February 13. http://www.pbs.org/newshour/bb/fedagencies/jan-june06/fema_2-13.html

Public Safety Canada, 2008. Is your family prepared? http://www.emergencypreparednessweek.ca.

Reuters, 2007a. WHO confirms human-to-human bird-flu case, December 27. http://www.reuters.com/article/scienceNews/idUSL2732429220071227.

Reuters, 2007b. Sarbanes-Oxley spending seen at $6 billion in 2007, February 22. http://www.reuters.com/article/fundsFundsNews/idUSN2217546720070222.

Smith, J.D., 2002. Business Continuity Management: Good Practice Guidelines. Business Continuity Institute, United Kingdom.

ThinkProgress.org., 2008. Katrina Timeline. http:// thinkprogress.org/katrina-timeline.

U.S. Department of Health and Human Services, 2007. Pandemic preparedness planning for US businesses with overseas operations. http://www.pandemicflu.gov/plan/ workplaceplanning/businessesoverseaspdf.pdf.

U.S. Department of Health and Human Services, 2008. General information on pandemic and avian flu. http:// www.pandemicflu.gov/general/index.html.

United Nations Development Programme, 1994. Vulnerability and Risk Assessment, 2nd ed. Cambridge Architectural Research Limited, Cambridge.

Washington Post, 2005. Fraud alleged at Red Cross call centers, December 27. http://www.washingtonpost.com/ wp-dyn/content/article/2005/12/26/AR2005122600654 .html.

White House, 2005. National strategy for pandemic influenza. http://www.whitehouse.gov/homeland/nspi.pdf.

WikiBirdFlu.org., 2007. Relationship between bird flu and SARS. http://www.wikibirdflu.org/page/Relationship1betwe en1Bird1Flu1and1SARS?t5anon.

Wikipedia, 2008. Hurricane Katrina. http://en.wikipedia .org/wiki/Hurricane_Katrina.

Williams, B., 2005. Sarbanes-Oxley: Another driver for business continuity management. http://www.disaster-resource.com/articles/03p_029.shtml.

World Health Organization, 2003. SARS. http://www.wpro .who.int/health_topics/sars/.

World Health Organization, 2005. WHO checklist for influenza pandemic preparedness planning. http://www .who.int/entity/csr/resources/publications/influenza/ FluCheck6web.pdf.

World Health Organization, 2008. Cumulative number of confirmed human cases of avian influenza A/(H5N1) reported to WHO. http://www.who.int/csr/disease/avian_ influenza/country/cases_table_2008_01_11/en/index.html.

Yale Center for Public Health Preparedness, 2006. Preparedness glossary. http://publichealth.yale.edu/ycphp/ Glossary.html.

11

Communications

What You Will Learn

- How risk communication efforts inform the public about what hazard risks they face and what they can do to prepare for or mitigate them
- How the federal government performs risk communication through the Ready.gov website and other efforts
- What role the news media has in informing the public about hazard risks
- How the federal government warns the public of terrorist risk through the National Terrorism Alert System (NTAS)
- The mission and assumptions that serve as the basis of crisis communications
- The growing role of social media and first informers in crisis communications
- How to build an effective disaster communications strategy

Introduction

Communicating messages to the general public is a critical yet underdeveloped aspect of effective emergency management. Such messages fall under three basic categories: risk communication, warning, and crisis communication. Risk communication involves alerting and educating the public to the risks they face and how they can best prepare for and mitigate these risks in order to reduce the impacts of future disaster events. Warning involves delivering notice of an actual impending threat with sufficient time to allow recipient individuals and communities to take shelter, evacuate, or take other mitigative action in advance of a disaster event. Crisis communication involves the provision of timely, useful, and accurate information to the public during the response and recovery phases of a disaster event.

The emergency management community as a whole has vast experience in practicing risk and warning communications. Preparedness programs have been an active part of emergency management in this country for decades, and public education programs conducted by the Federal Emergency Management Agency (FEMA), the American Red Cross, the Salvation Army, local fire departments, and other public- and private-sector agencies have disseminated millions of brochures and checklists describing the risks of future disaster events and the steps that individuals and communities can take to reduce and prepare for them. In recent years, these programs have embraced new technologies to disseminate this information, including video and, most significantly, the Internet. There is a wealth of knowledge supported by scientific research concerning effective means to communicate hazard risk messages for natural disaster and selected technological disaster risks.

The design and implementation of warning systems has similarly advanced in the past decades. From the Civil Defense sirens to the Emergency Broadcast Network to weather radios, warning systems alerting the public to sudden or impending disaster events have become more sophisticated and widely used. Broadcasting timely information that allows individuals to make appropriate shelter and evacuation decisions is at the core of the warning systems designed for natural hazards such as tornadoes and tsunamis. Watch and warning notices for floods and hurricanes provide individuals and community leaders with valuable information on the path and potential destructiveness of severe storms that could result in flooding events. The public media — television, radio, and most recently the Internet — are the mechanisms most often used by emergency officials to issue watch and warning notices.

The importance of communicating with the public during the response and recovery phases of a natural or technological disaster event has only recently been fully embraced by emergency officials. Too often in the past, little value was placed on communicating with the public during and after a disaster event, and emergency officials had little training and interest in this area. This changed in the 1990s as FEMA, under the direction of James Lee Witt, made a commitment and marshaled the resources to develop and implement an aggressive public affairs program designed to deliver timely and accurate messages to the public in a time of crisis. The messages focused on what measures government and private-sector officials were taking to help a community in responding to and recovering from a disaster event and the methods by which individuals and communities could apply for and receive federal, state, and local disaster relief. FEMA established a working partnership with the media to deliver these messages through press conferences, individual interviews, satellite feeds, radio actualities, and the Internet. One of their greatest accomplishments in this regard was the publication of *Recovery Times*, a newspaper supplement developed and maintained by FEMA to be distributed by local newspaper outlets in disaster-affected areas. Over time, this public affairs model created by FEMA has gained wider acceptance by state and local emergency officials.

The threat of terrorism has altered the playing field for emergency managers by introducing new hazards that are not fully understood, creating an altered risk perception among members of the public (who are concerned about terrorism victimization), and presenting new response and recovery (mostly cleanup) procedures and practices, new information uncertainties, new restrictions on the release of information to the public, and new demands for public information. Do the communications models developed in the past for communicating risk, warning, and crisis messages concerning natural and technological hazards apply to terrorism-related communications? Will the traditional delivery systems — television, Internet, radio, and print — adequately disseminate terrorism-related information? Will emergency and government officials find a balance between the need to provide timely and accurate information to the public and the need to conduct criminal investigations?

These are the types of questions that are addressed in this chapter, which includes sections on risk communication, warning, and crisis communication. A case study of the October 2002 sniper attacks in Washington, D.C., is also included in the chapter.

Risk Communication

The federal government, through the Department of Homeland Security (DHS), has initiated several programs to achieve a goal of community and individual resilience to the effects of terrorism and other disasters. One of the primary methods employed to achieve such preparedness is public education.

Public education has long been recognized as an effective method for decreasing the damaging potential of hazards and risks, and the media are often central in such projects (Mullis, 1998). Furthermore, the role of the media in previous risk-related public education endeavors dealing with natural and technological hazards and public health issues has been well documented. From teaching citizens to build tornado-resistant safe rooms to minimizing tsunami drowning and preventing teen pregnancy, public and private agencies have partnered with, cooperated with, or utilized the various players collectively referred to as the *mass media* to achieve the goal of reducing public risk.

Although the news media's reporting on risks has often been blamed for inciting a "culture of fear" (Glassner, 1999) in which people are afraid of a multitude of risks that have only a minute chance of ever occurring, the news media have also been integral in helping to create what could be considered the most risk-free era in recorded history (Walsh, 1996). However, no studies have been conducted to measure the efficacy of the media in informing and educating the public about terrorism and other "intentional" hazards.

The new focus on terrorism within the borders of the United States has brought to question the degree of risk faced by individual Americans. Although the topic has become a daily concern of all media outlets, the effect that this new attention has had on decreasing the vulnerability of the average citizen to that particular hazard is questionable. Citizens have indicated through polls that the threat of terrorist attacks on American soil is one of their primary concerns, and they have looked to their leaders for guidance on personal preparedness for such a threat. The federal government has recognized this concern and has sought to confront the preparedness issue through actions taken by DHS to address national vulnerabilities. DHS has also embarked on a public education campaign the likes of which have not been seen since the Civil Defense drills of the 1950s taught citizens to "duck and cover" during air raids (Waugh, 2000). The media have been involved in this effort from the beginning, and regardless of their goals, intentions, or the level to which they have actually partnered with the federal government in their actions, it is likely that the news media have never before played such a central role in risk communication.

With such a great quantity of headlines, stories, editorials, investigative reports, and briefings related to terrorism, it would seem that all citizens should be able to decode from the barrage of messages relayed by DHS the information they need to protect themselves. However, considering that never before have the media and government risk communicators focused on any one subject so intensely, established risk perception and communication models are largely ineffective. DHS and the emergency management community in general must ask the following questions now and before planning future activities:

How can risk communicators best make contact with the general public?
Can the news media serve as effective risk communicators for terrorism in the United States?
Do the established risk communications models apply to terrorism and other intentional hazards?

■ ■ Critical Thinking ■

Why are the news media considered such an important asset to emergency preparedness public education efforts? Are other sources more effective? Why or why not? Give examples to support your answer.

Emergency Management and Risk Communication in the United States

The most widely practiced form of emergency management in the United States, and the only form practiced by FEMA, is comprehensive emergency management (CEM). This four-phase cyclical system groups actions into the general categories of mitigation, preparedness, response, and recovery. For a given hazard there are generally pre-event actions (mitigation and preparedness) and post-event actions (response and recovery) performed. The response phase includes the immediate period of reaction after a disaster occurs (when critical emergency resources are required). Recovery includes the long-term rebuilding that begins after the emergency functions related to disaster response are no longer required. Mitigation is defined as any activity that prevents or reduces the impact of a disaster, and preparedness involves predisaster planning and training addressing the possibility of future disasters (Waugh, 2000). Like response, disaster preparedness is also always managed at the local level and is considered to be more of a local government responsibility than any of the other phases of CEM.

Preparedness generally consists of training the local first responders and educating the public about ways to prepare for specific hazards within specific communities. A hazard is an event or physical condition that has the potential to cause fatalities, injuries, property damage, infrastructure damage, agricultural loss, damage to the environment, interruption of business, or other types of harm or loss (FEMA, 1997). The risk associated with a hazard is identified as the probability (likelihood) of the hazard occurring, multiplied by the consequence of the hazard should it occur. For many hazard risks, public education is seen as the most effective means to reduce both the likelihood and consequence components significantly. Emergency management public education efforts utilize numerous resources, including in-school education, distribution of pamphlets and fact sheets, and inserts in phone books and utility mailings, among many others. However, it is the use of the various forms of the news media that has often been seen as the most effective means of public education.

The federal government took a more active role in community preparedness during the Clinton administration while FEMA was under the direction of James Lee Witt (a move taken by several governments throughout the world during the same period). Director Witt espoused the idea that the emergency response community must shed the view that the media were adversaries and work to form media partnerships in order to be more effective in public disaster preparedness education. Witt worked to institutionalize such tasks as creating media education materials and public service announcements, ensuring availability of "approved" hazard experts, providing training in emergency management terminology and actions for reporters and anchor people, and promoting more responsible reporting by the media. The success of these changes was measured through the increased resilience of communities to hazards in which such changes in individual behavior were known to be the primary means of reducing vulnerability (such as during tsunamis and tornadoes).

In the wake of the September 11, 2001, terrorist attacks and the anthrax mail attacks shortly thereafter, the "all-hazards" approach of the federal government focused its efforts on preparedness and mitigation (prevention) of future terrorist attacks (Figure 11–1). Although terrorism had been considered a high-risk hazard by the federal government for some time, it was not necessarily on the minds of the American public. After these events, however, terrorism became an obvious primary concern of both the government and its citizens. Terrorism was no longer seen as something that affected isolated locations known to be at high risk and was instead regarded as a hazard that could affect anyone at any place and any time, a hazard that could result in a mass casualty event (one that overwhelms the capacity of local health officials to respond).

Additionally, the possibility of terrorists employing weapons of mass destruction (WMD) — chemical, biological, radiological, explosive, or nuclear — became a reality.

On November 25, 2002, President Bush signed into law the Homeland Security Act of 2002, investing in the new DHS the mission of protecting the United States from further terrorist attacks, reducing the nation's vulnerability to terrorism, and minimizing the damage from potential terrorist attacks and natural disasters. DHS began working to organize the federal response to the consequences of disasters but concentrated its efforts on preparedness and response capabilities to combat terrorism (as is evident by changes in federal funding trends). DHS officials were still operating under the same constraints of the previous administration in terms of what they could do to increase preparedness at the community level. DHS repeatedly acknowledged that, even in the event that a terrorist attack be declared a national disaster, local communities would need to be prepared to be self-sufficient for a minimum of 48 hours. However, public demand for more federal action and information required DHS to address these public education needs.

FIGURE 11–1 Milwaukee, WI, September 29, 2010 — Carol Hector-Harris, a public information officer, is interviewed by Jeremy Rosenroth, a reporter for Fox 6 News. External Affairs personnel work with the press to keep the public informed. (Source: Photo by Ed Edahl/FEMA)

The Ready.gov campaign is DHS's primary effort to increase individual citizen preparedness at the community level. It is essentially a website, designed by the Ad Council, that offers citizens, businesses, and children with explicit directions detailing what they can do to prepare themselves and their families for all hazards, including terrorism. Initially, other efforts at informing the public, which are equal components in the larger public education effort, included the five-color–coded Homeland Security Alert System (HSAS) and more specific public announcements and alerts, such as the well-known "duct tape and plastic" incident (in which DHS Director Tom Ridge made a general appeal to people in the United States to buy those particular items to protect themselves from the effects of a possible WMD terrorist attack). In April 2011, DHS announced the implementation of the National Terrorism Advisory System (NTAS) that took the place of the HSAS.

Personal preparedness for disasters, as described by the Ready.gov website, includes three major components. They are "get a kit" (one that contains materials to ensure potable water, food, clean air, first aid, and special needs items), "make a plan" (in which individuals or families determine actions to be taken in the event of specific disasters), and "be informed" (generally by obtaining information about hazards and their associated personal mitigation and preparedness measures). To measure the effectiveness of a citizen's degree of terrorism–hazard preparedness, these three components must be used as performance measures. For the specific case of terrorism, "vigilance" (or actively looking for and reporting suspicious behavior that could be linked to terrorism) is included as a performance measure for personal terrorism preparedness (DHS, 2003).

Since late 2004, DHS has added two components to its Ready.gov site to expand on the specific groups that may benefit from the preparedness information they provide. The first group is the business community. The website instructs business owners and administrators on how to (1) plan to stay in business, (2) talk to your people, and (3) protect your investment. The second group is children.

Past Research Focusing on Risk Communication: The Power of the News Media

According to acclaimed risk communication experts Baruch Fischhoff, M. Granger Morgan, Ann Bostrom, and Cynthia Atman, risk communication is "communication intended to supply laypeople with the information they need to make informed, independent judgments about risks to health, safety, and the environment" (Morgan et al., 2002). Creating messages that satisfy these high ideals requires extensive time, experience, and planning, and is therefore more often successful in educating the public about old risks that are well understood than new risks such as terrorism. Although it would seem from a purist's point of view that anything short of the aforementioned definition would not suffice, some authors have defined risk communication to be the mere action of reporting on any existing or proposed hazard regardless of the story's ability to result in any increase in public awareness, knowledge, or preparedness (Willis, 1997).

The news media play a significant role in disaster and emergency management both before and after disasters occur. The media are well recognized for the invaluable service they have consistently performed during the initial critical moments of a disaster, when the emergency response efforts are mobilized. In these events, the media serve to transmit warning messages and alerts and give instructions on where to evacuate, where to seek medical care and shelter, and where to go for more specific information (Mileti, 1999). Jim Willis (1997) writes, "[T]here may be no other area of journalism [than risk communication] where the Fourth Estate has such an awesome responsibility." Furman (2002) contends that the media's ability to educate people during these times is, in many cases, more likely to save lives than many other components of emergency response, adding that "people will die if they don't get good information." The emergency response community has embraced the media for their capability in response, recognizing that they will be the primary, if not the only, means of informing large masses of potential victims (McCormick Tribune Foundation, 2002).

With regard to the preparedness phase of emergency management, the primary risk communication tasks that have been assumed by the media include raising citizen awareness to the presence of an existing or future hazard and providing information to those citizens regarding prevention or protection (Burkhart, 1991). The effectiveness of the media as a conduit of educational information has been studied extensively, most notably in the area of public health. A great number of these studies have shown a positive correlation between the use of the media and an increase in the promoted knowledge or behavior. Piotrow (1990) and a team of researchers working in Nigeria found that the promotion of family planning and clinic sites on local television played a significant role in the number of people utilizing those services. Westoff and Rodriguez (1995) found that there was a strong correlation between patients who reported that they had been exposed to family planning messages in the media and the use of contraceptives by those same patients.

Witzer (1997) writes that "exposure to electronic and print media is associated with later marriage and with greater knowledge and use of family planning among men and women in Sub-Saharan Africa." Jones, Beniger, and Westoff (1980) found that there was a strong correlation between mass media coverage of the adverse effects of the birth control pill and discontinuation rates among users. Similar results were found relating to sex education among young adults (Brown and Keller, 2000) and early initiation of breast-feeding (McDivitt et al., 1993). Nelken (1987) found in one study that more than 60% of Americans learn about cancer prevention from the media, whereas less than 20% do so from physicians.

With natural and technological hazards, the behavioral modifications and preparatory measures taken by recipients as a result of media risk communication also look promising. Mitigation specialists at FEMA claim that the media's role in community and citizen preparedness is critical if such efforts are to succeed (FEMA, 1998). Dennis Mileti (1999) found that personal preparedness was most likely to be undertaken by those people who are most attentive to the news media, but that other attributes are often necessary in conjunction with that attention. Media risk communication has been widely credited as an important supplemental component to official communication in public preparedness to hazards (Burkhart, 1991). Singer and Endreny (1993) contend that there are many factors determining how people view hazards (including personal experience and contact with other people), but with hazards that are extreme in consequence and rare in occurrence (such as terrorism) the media are the most influential source of information. Walsh (1996) found that several studies indicate that people use the media for obtaining information on hazards more than any other source.

The primary source of the news media's ability to effectively communicate and educate most likely lies in the institutionalized methods of attracting viewers and providing timely information that has been developed and refined over centuries. Burkhart (1991) writes, "[I]n the preparedness phase, the mass media are positioned between the actors who evaluate a threat and decide upon a message, and the media audience." Burkhart adds that it is the media's ability to influence perceived risk and the credibility of the source of information that gives them such power over public behavior. McCombs and Shaw's (1972) research, which found that audiences not only are alerted to important issues by the media, but also learn "how much importance to attach to an issue or topic from the emphasis the media place on it," supports Burkhart's convictions.

This positive view of the media as a successful risk communicator comes not without contention. There are many social scientists who feel that the media, for various reasons, are ineffective at informing the public about the risks they face. Winston (1985) feels that it is the "built-in, organizational, competitive, and institutional biases" that prevent the media from informing citizens about hazards. These biases are coupled with procedural standards that can also make effective communication of risk difficult. For instance, Singer and Endreny (1993) report that the media inform about "events rather than issues, about immediate consequences rather than long-term considerations, about harms rather than risks," and Wenham (1994) describes how the media "tell how bad things are, while [emergency management agencies] make things better." Burkhart (1991) feels that it is a deficiency of knowledge about hazards and disaster management among journalists that makes them unable to effectively communicate due to both a lack of understanding of the most basic concepts and their inability to act as a "surrogate for the layman, to absorb and transform technical information to a public that is often even less well-prepared to grasp technical information and concepts." Such criticisms are repeated by Singer and Endreny (1993). There are other, similar reasons identified by research efforts that sought to explain the media's risk communication deficiencies, including restrictions of time and space that prevent adequate knowledge transfer (Willis, 1997) and the media's insistence on taking control of the selection and presentation of message format that leads to a decrease in message effectiveness (Burkhart, 1991).

There is another subgroup of studies that find the news media to be largely ineffective as a risk communicator but assign less blame to them for such problems. Raphael (1986) turns the focus of the blame onto the public, stating that "citizens often display a magical belief in goodness and protection and a sense of generalized risk, which may explain why people pay less attention to preparedness information provided by the media outside of the context of an emergency." Jerry Hauer from the New York City Office of Emergency Management feels that it is the tendency of the emergency management community to exclude the media from training and drills due to the fear that the media will leak operational plans to terrorists and the fear that the media will cause mass public panic that has prevented them from being able to effectively inform the public (McCormick Tribune Foundation, 2002). This position is supported by Burkhart (1991), who states, "Media are often limited by the nature of the information they receive," and Bremer and Bremer (2002), who state, "Terrorism presents a major dilemma to political leaders in terms of how to get enough attention without bringing too much attention to the problem." Furman (2002) adds, "It is difficult to educate the American people because there's very little we can tell them to do …. You're faced with the problem of just how much you want to tell the American people, because, in the end, there's very little we can give them."

There is a third type of research that claims that while the news media are, in fact, ineffective at educating the public, they still play a vital role in risk communication. McCallum, Hammond, and Morris (1990) state that "regardless of reservations about their ability to play the role effectively, the media do carry considerable information about certain hazards and risks to most people." This view of the media as informer is fairly widespread. Willis (1997) states that while the media too often avoid contributing to the solution to the problems, they are effective at raising attention to issues and communicating degrees of urgency. Mullis (1998) further promotes this argument, stating that the media are effective at initiating preparedness activities. Burkhart (1991) found that while media warnings were too imprecise to be effective, they "were able to get people talking to other people about the danger mentioned in media warnings." Cohen (1963) succinctly characterized this phenomenon as follows: "The press may not be successful much of the time in telling its readers what to think, but it is stunningly successful in telling them what to think about."

■ ■ Critical Thinking ■

Do you feel that the media are effective risk communicators? Why or why not? If you do not believe that the media are effective risk communicators, then to which of the three schools of research regarding the effectiveness of news media risk communication listed above do you subscribe? (1) The news media are ineffective at informing the public of the risks they face because of media bias. (2) The news media are largely ineffective as risk communicators but the focus of blame falls on the public. (3) The media are ineffective at educating the public but still play a vital role in risk communication. Explain your answer.

Accuracy of Information

A second area that must be examined when considering the ability of the media to communicate risk is their capacity to do so in a way that imparts to the public an accurate perception of their personal risk of victimization. In what is probably one of the earliest descriptions of the media's power to influence public risk perception and, likewise, preparedness and mitigative behavior, Lippmann (1922) writes in his acclaimed *Public Opinion* that

> We shall assume that what each man does is based not on direct and certain knowledge, but on pictures made by himself or given to him. If his atlas tells him that the world is flat, he will not sail near what he believes to be the edge of our planet for fear of falling off.

Willis (1997) writes that because the media's depiction of public health- and safety-related issues has either an indirect or a direct effect on public behavior, the media's responsibility to be as accurate as possible in their presentation of such hazards is vital. In the case of terrorism, DHS has established a five-color–coded Homeland Security Alert System that is intended to inform the public about the current risk of a terrorist attack within the United States. At certain times, the risk is raised in specific locations, such as a city, a landmark, or a building. Although the media often refer to this system when it goes up or down in severity, they also provide exhaustive unrelated information that heavily influences public perception. It is this perception that people must use in judging their own risk and, likewise, preparing themselves appropriately. It is important for the media not to understate risks because people will otherwise not expend the time and money needed to adequately prepare themselves, but exaggerating the risk of a hazard can have drastic consequences, including stress-related health problems and financial and economic effects including business and tourism losses.

Thus far, research has found that the media tend to overstate the risk of the hazards on which they focus (which also tend to be those that are the least likely to occur), while they understate commonly occurring hazards (Singer and Endreny, 1993). Altheide (2002) found that almost 80% of Americans feel that they are subject to more risk than their parents were 20 years ago, when in fact evidence has shown that we have a "competitive advantage in terms of disease, accidents, nutrition, medical care, and life expectancy" and that the media's portrayal of risk is mainly to blame. One reason this occurs is that the media do not have the time or resources to ensure the accuracy of their reports beyond reasonable doubt. Willis (1997) found that while scientists use elaborate methods of ensuring the validity of their findings, journalists depend on secondary or tertiary sources that confirm or refute their primary source, all of whom may be incorrect in their assumptions. Warner (1989) feels the problem lies in the media's tendency to use vivid imagery in reporting risk, such as comparing the number of people who die as a result of smoking as equivalent to three fully seated jumbo jets crashing every day. Singer and Endreny (1993) claim that daily reporting of rare hazards, which tend to be more "newsworthy," makes these events subject to h availability heuristic. Walsh (1996) notes that over 2 million Americans canceled travel plans to Europe in 1986 because of fears of terrorism, when their actual risk would have been significantly reduced if they had lost 10 pounds and traveled to Europe as planned.

Related to this concern that the media do not give the public accurate perceptions of risks is the fear that the public will become emotionally afraid of risks rather than becoming aware of their dangers. This distinction is important because it determines the types of preparedness measures citizens take in response to the messages they receive and the rationality with which those actions are made. When people are presented with a risk, they are more likely to take preventive and preparatory measures if they are led to believe that the risk is a danger that can be managed rather than one that they should fear. Past research has found that increasing the levels of public fear can actually cause a decrease in public preparedness behavior (Mullis, 1998). Unfortunately, it may be that the nature of media culture promotes and even amplifies fear by attempting to draw viewers through entertainment and "framing." Walsh (1996) contends that the media pay attention only to issues and situations that frighten viewers, "filling coverage with opinions rather than facts or logical perspective." Furedi (1997) takes a slightly different but related alternative stance on the subject in stating that "the media's preoccupation with risk is a symptom of the problem and not its cause," as the media can only amplify fear that already exists.

Essential Components of Effective Risk Communication

Numerous components of effective risk communication have been identified as vital to the success of an effective campaign. Morgan and his colleagues (2002) conclude that effective risk communication requires authoritative and trustworthy sources. They add that if the acting communicators are perceived by the public as having a vested personal interest in the result of such preparedness, they may be skeptical about the communicators' intentions. Mileti (1999) contends that several characteristics must be considered in creating the messages, including the amount of material, speed of presentation, number of arguments, repetition, style, clarity, ordering, forcefulness, specificity, consistency, accuracy, and extremity of the position advocated. These characteristics are adjusted depending on whether the communicators intend to attract attention or enhance the acceptance of their message. Singer and Endreny (1993) claim that in order for a message to be considered comprehensive, it should contain an annual mortality associated with the hazard (if known), the "spatial extent" of the hazard, the time frame associated with the hazard, and the alternatives for mitigating the hazard.

Communicators must also ensure that their messages are understood by those whom they are trying to reach, which undoubtedly changes from community to community depending on the demographic makeup of each. Mileti (1999) writes, "Most hazard-awareness and education programs have assumed a homogeneous 'public,' and have done little to tailor information materials to different groups." He adds that hazard-awareness programs are more effective if they rely on multiple sources transmitting multiple messages through multiple outlets and that radio and television are best at maintaining hazard awareness, whereas printed materials tend to provide more specific instructions on what should be done.

These are obviously high standards when considering the strict time, length, and content guidelines within which journalists must work. Highlighting the difficulty of both creating and analyzing such endeavors and the need for such a study as this, Morgan and his colleagues (2002) write, "As practiced today, risk communication is often very earnest but also surprisingly ad hoc. Typically, one can find neither a clear analysis of what needs to be communicated nor solid evidence that messages have achieved their impact. Nor can one find tested procedures for ensuring the credibility of information."

Future Research to Improve News Media Risk Communication

The objectives of future research projects should be (1) to determine how effective the news media have been as a conduit of information to citizens as part of a larger terrorism-related public education campaign being conducted by DHS and (2) to develop a risk communications model by which media-provided public education pertaining to terrorism and other intentional hazards can be most effectively applied. Media reports in print, television, and radio formats should be examined for their content to (1) see if they meet the minimum information requirements established by risk communication experts, (2) determine if responsibility for preparedness is focused on the individual or the government, and (3) determine if an accurate portrayal of risk has been made. Surveys should be conducted with a random representative sample of American citizens to determine (1) the levels to which they have prepared for terrorism, (2) by what information they were motivated to do so, and (3) if their perception of risk reflects the level of risk portrayed by DHS and other federal sources. All collected and analyzed data should be used to determine which forms of risk communication are the most effective at creating a more informed, prepared citizenry and to generate a list of risk communications' "fundamental requirements" relating to the task of terrorism that builds on established risk communications models. From these models, strategic recommendations can be targeted to the various agencies and industries that regularly perform risk communication.

Existing Government Public Awareness Campaigns

Ready.gov, with its partners in the public, private, and volunteer sectors, is the government's official risk communication website, providing information to three primary groups (Figure 11–2): Americans (adult citizens), businesses, and children. Ready America, the original focus of the website, instructs the American public to perform three preparedness activities, namely:

> Get a Kit (see "Ready America Emergency Kit Recommended Contents" sidebar)
> Make a Plan (Figure 11–3)
> Be Informed (see "'Be Informed' Ready.gov Fact Sheets" sidebar)

This site also provides more specific emergency preparedness information for three special populations:

> Older Americans
> People with disabilities
> Pet owners

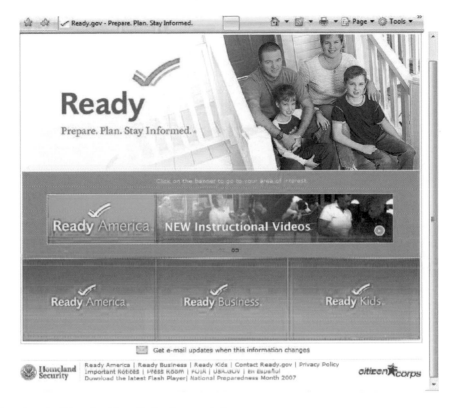

FIGURE 11–2 Department of Homeland Security Ready.gov website.

Ready Business was the second component developed in the DHS public education effort. Ready Business focuses on business continuity and crisis management concepts to help businesses prepare for and respond to disasters. Through this online instructional guide, businesses are instructed to take action in three primary subject areas.

Plan to Stay in Business: This includes the following actions:

Be informed (knowing what kinds of emergencies might affect the company)
Continuity planning (how to carefully assess how the company functions, both internally and externally)
Emergency planning (how to protect employees)
Emergency supplies (survival basics, including fresh water, food, clean air, and warmth)
Deciding to stay or go (basics for sheltering in place or evacuating)
Fire safety (fire is the most common source of business disasters)
Medical emergencies (information about first aid and CPR)
Influenza pandemic (basic information about how to get more information on pandemic planning)

Talk to Your People: This includes general advice on informing and educating employees in emergency management basics and response principles:

Involve coworkers (including all staff in the emergency planning process)
Practice the plan (planning and conducting emergency drills and exercises)

FIGURE 11–3 Ready America Family Plan cover page. (Source: Department of Homeland Security, "Ready America," 2008, http://www.ready.gov/america/_downloads/familyemergencyplan.pdf)

Promoting preparedness (encouraging employees to follow the Ready America advice)

Crisis communications plan (company planning on how to stay in contact with employees and customers in a disaster situation)

Employee health (addressing the special health needs of employees that arise in disasters)

Protect Your Investment: This instructs businesses in ways to ensure the safety of physical assets, including:

Insurance coverage
Planning for utility disruption
Securing facilities, buildings, and plants
Securing equipment
Protecting heating, ventilation, and air-conditioning systems
Ensuring cybersecurity

The third and final component of the Ready.gov website is Ready Kids. This web page is designed to help parents and teachers educate children in grades 4 and 5 about emergency preparedness, emergency response, and how to help their family to prepare for disasters. The site contains simple and illustrated step-by-step instructions about the kinds of things families can do to be better prepared, and the role that children can play in this effort (Figure 11–4). The website was developed in consultation with several established children- and emergency-focused organizations, including:

American Psychological Association
American Red Cross
National Association of Elementary School Principals
National Association of School Psychologists
National Center for Child Traumatic Stress
National PTA
U.S. Department of Education
U.S. Department of Health and Human Services

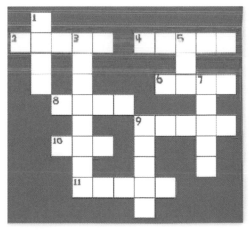

DEAR FAMILY,

Family Reproducible Worksheet

To prepare for emergencies, families can collect items that might be useful and put them in an emergency supply kit. Go to www.ready.gov and click on *Ready Kids* to find out how your family can prepare for unexpected situations. Then complete this crossword puzzle to give you an idea of what kinds of things should be part of your family's emergency supply kit.

CLUES

ACROSS:

2. _ _ _ _ _ light: A handy tool to have if the lights go out!

4. Every person needs one gallon of this per day!

6. This comfortable piece of furniture should not be part of a family's supply kit.

8. Furry family members that should be part of your preparedness plan.

9. Some people have a _ _ _ _ between meals if they are hungry.

10. You might find water, a flashlight, or a whistle in an emergency supply _ _ _.

11. Fun items that families can play together.

DOWN:

1. Families can create a communication _ _ _ _ so that they know where to meet and who to call during an emergency.

3. _ _ _ _ _ _ _ bag: Great for napping or keeping warm.

5. Every family member should carry a contact list with at least _ _ _ different phone numbers that will allow you to keep in touch during an emergency.

7. It's important to get the _ _ _ _ _ about different kinds of emergencies, so that you know what to expect.

9. Keep an extra pair of these in your supply kit to keep your feet dry!

FIGURE 11–4 Crossword puzzle from the Ready.gov Ready Kids website. (Source: Ready.gov, 2008)

Ready America Emergency Kit Recommended Contents

Water (1 gallon of water per person per day for at least 3 days, for drinking and sanitation)
Food (at least a 3-day supply of nonperishable food)
Battery-powered or hand-crank radio and a NOAA Weather Radio with tone alert and extra
   batteries for both
Flashlight and extra batteries
First aid kit
Whistle to signal for help
Dust mask to help filter contaminated air and plastic sheeting and duct tape to shelter-in-place
Moist towelettes, garbage bags, and plastic ties for personal sanitation
Wrench or pliers to turn off utilities
Can opener for food (if kit contains canned food)
Local maps

   Other items listed for consideration include:

Prescription medications and glasses
Infant formula and diapers
Pet food and extra water for your pet
Important family documents such as copies of insurance policies, identification, and bank account
   records in a waterproof, portable container
Cash or traveler's checks and change
Emergency reference material such as a first aid book or information from www.ready.gov
Sleeping bag or warm blanket for each person. Consider additional bedding if you live in a
   cold-weather climate.
Complete change of clothing including a long-sleeved shirt, long pants, and sturdy shoes.
   Consider additional clothing if you live in a cold-weather climate.
Household chlorine bleach and medicine dropper — When diluted nine parts water to one part
   bleach, bleach can be used as a disinfectant. Or in an emergency, you can use it to treat water
   by using 16 drops of regular household liquid bleach per gallon of water. Do not use scented,
   color-safe bleaches, or bleaches with added cleaners.
Fire extinguisher
Matches in a waterproof container
Feminine supplies and personal hygiene items
Mess kits, paper cups, plates and plastic utensils, and paper towels
Paper and pencil
Books, games, puzzles or other activities for children

Source: DHS, "Ready America," 2008, http://www.ready.gov/america/getakit/index.html.

"BE INFORMED" READY.GOV FACT SHEETS (EXAMPLES)

The Ready America website contains preparedness and response information for citizens in the following areas:

Biological threat
Blackouts
Chemical threat
Earthquakes
Explosions
Extreme heat
Fires
Floods
Hurricanes
Influenza pandemic
Landslide and debris flow (mudslide)
Nuclear threat
Radiation threat
Thunderstorms
Tornadoes
Tsunamis
Volcanoes
Wildfires
Winter storms and extreme cold

As with any emergency, local authorities may not be able to immediately provide information on what is happening and what you should do. However, you should watch TV, listen to the radio, or check the Internet often for official news and information as it becomes available.

Source: Department of Homeland Security, www.ready.gov.

The Ready.gov campaign is an ongoing multiyear project funded through the DHS budget, designed and administered by the Advertising Council (www.adcouncil.org), an organization with over 60 years of experience in developing public service announcements. The website itself is just one (albeit, the primary) component of a much larger preparedness campaign that includes television, radio, print, outdoor, and Internet advertisements that inform recipients on the importance of emergency preparedness and guide them to the website as a repository of information.

The Ready.gov website came under considerable criticism in 2006 by the Federation of American Scientists (FAS) for containing information that was reputed to be inaccurate and incomplete. FAS released an analysis of Ready.gov, identifying shortcomings and offering suggestions for improvement. FAS maintains that the Ready.gov website, which has been accessed by over 23 million individuals, contains numerous problems despite being updated in July 2006. The FAS posted a website, Really Ready (www.reallyready.org), that mirrors the government website — even containing identical illustrations, colors, and fonts — which offers risk information to the public on the same topics addressed by the Ready.gov website.

■ ■ Critical Thinking ■

Do you believe that the Ready.gov website offers useful information to the public? If so, do you believe that average Americans will access this information and use it to their benefit? Why or why not? Can you think of a more effective way to communicate risk to the general public?

Warning

On April 20, 2011, DHS Secretary Janet Napolitano announced the implementation of the NTAS. The NTAS took the place of the much-maligned color-coded Homeland Security Advisory System (HSAS) (Figure 11–5) that had been in place since 2002.

Since its inception, concerns had been raised about the level of information provided through the HSAS. These concerns were shared by both the general public and members of the first-responder community (e.g., police, fire, and emergency medical technicians), as well as local officials responsible for ensuring public safety. The Partnership for Public Warning (PPW) was formed in January 2002 as a partnership among the private sector, academia, and government entities at the local, state, and federal levels for the purpose of better coordinating disaster warning programs. PPW is a nonprofit entity with its

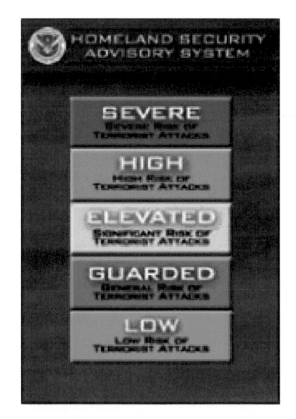

FIGURE 11–5 Homeland Security Advisory System (2002–2011).

stated mission to "promote and enhance efficient, effective, and integrated dissemination of public warnings and related information so as to save lives, reduce disaster losses and speed recovery" (PPW, 2008). In May 2003, PPW published "A National Strategy for Integrated Public Warning Policy and Capability," which examined the current status of public warning systems, practices, and issues across the United States. The report stated, "Working together in partnership, the stakeholders should assess current warning capability, carry out appropriate research and develop the following:

- A common terminology for natural and man-made disasters
- A standard message protocol
- National metrics and standards
- National backbone systems for securely collecting and disseminating warnings from all official sources
- Pilot projects to test concepts and approaches
- Training and event-simulation programs
- A national multimedia education and outreach program (Partnership for Public Warning, 2003)

In her announcement concerning the NTAS, Secretary Napolitano stated, "The terrorist threat facing our country has evolved significantly over the past ten years, and in today's environment — more than ever — we know that the best security strategy is one that counts on the American public as a key partner in securing our country." DHS released the document entitled "A Public Guide to the NTAS" as part of its effort to announce its establishment (DHS, 2011). Additional information concerning the NTAS released by DHS in April 2011 is presented in the sidebar "National Terrorism Advisory System (NTAS)."

National Terrorism Advisory System (NTAS)

Under NTAS, DHS will coordinate with other federal entities to issue detailed alerts to the public when the federal government receives information about a credible terrorist threat. NTAS alerts provide a concise summary of the potential threat including geographic region, mode of transportation, or critical infrastructure potentially affected by the threat, actions being taken to ensure public safety, as well as recommended steps that individuals, communities, businesses, and governments can take to help prevent, mitigate, or respond to a threat. NTAS Alerts will include a clear statement on the nature of the threat, which will be defined in one of two ways:

- "Elevated Threat": Warns of a credible terrorist threat against the United States
- "Imminent Threat": Warns of a credible, specific, and impending terrorist threat against the United States

Depending on the nature of the threat, alerts may be sent to law enforcement, distributed to affected areas of the private sector, or issued more broadly to the public through both official and social media channels — including a designated DHS webpage (www.dhs.gov/alerts), Facebook, and Twitter @NTASAlerts. NTAS alerts and posters will also be displayed in places such as transit hubs, airports, and government buildings.

NTAS threat alerts will be issued for a specific time period and will automatically expire. Alerts may be extended if new information becomes available or as a specific threat evolves.

Source: DHS, 2011, http://www.dhs.gov/ynews/releases/pr_1303296515462.shtm.

■ ■ ■

As part of the announcement of the NTAS, DHS released the following information presented in the sidebars "A Public Guide to the NTAS" and "Frequently Asked Questions of the NTAS." A sample NTAS alert is presented in Figure 11–6.

■ ■ ■

A Public Guide to the NTAS

The National Terrorism Advisory System

The National Terrorism Advisory System, or NTAS, replaces the color-coded Homeland Security Advisory System (HSAS). This new system will more effectively communicate information about terrorist threats by providing timely, detailed information to the public, government agencies, first responders, airports and other transportation hubs, and the private sector.

It recognizes that Americans all share responsibility for the nation's security, and should always be aware of the heightened risk of terrorist attack in the United States and what they should do.

NTAS Alerts

After reviewing the available information, the Secretary of Homeland Security will decide, in coordination with other Federal entities, whether an NTAS Alert should be issued.

NTAS Alerts will only be issued when credible information is available.

These alerts will include a clear statement that there is an imminent threat or elevated threat. Using available information, the alerts will provide a concise summary of the potential threat, information about actions being taken to ensure public safety, and recommended steps that individuals, communities, businesses, and governments can take to help prevent, mitigate, or respond to the threat.

The NTAS Alerts will be based on the nature of the threat: in some cases, alerts will be sent directly to law enforcement or affected areas of the private sector, while in others, alerts will be issued more broadly to the American people through both official and media channels.

NTAS Alerts contain a sunset provision indicating a specific date when the alert expires — there will not be a constant NTAS Alert or blanket warning that there is an overarching threat. If threat information changes for an alert, the Secretary of Homeland Security may announce an updated NTAS Alert. All changes, including the announcement that cancels an NTAS Alert, will be distributed the same way as the original alert.

The NTAS Alert — How can you help?

Each alert provides information to the public about the threat, including, if available, the geographic region, mode of transportation, or critical infrastructure potentially affected by the threat; protective actions being taken by authorities; and steps that individuals and communities can take to protect themselves and their families, and help prevent, mitigate or respond to the threat.

National Terrorism Advisory System
Alert
www.dhs.gov/alerts

DATE & TIME ISSUED: XXXX

SUMMARY
The Secretary of Homeland Security informs the public and relevant government and private sector partners about a potential or actual threat with this alert, indicating whether there is an "imminent" or "elevated" threat.

DURATION
An individual threat alert is issued for a specific time period and then automatically expires. It may be extended if new information becomes available or the threat evolves.

DETAILS
• This section provides more detail about the threat and what the public and sectors need to know.

• It may include specific information, if available, about the nature and credibility of the threat, including the critical infrastructure sector(s) or location(s) that may be affected.

• It includes as much information as can be released publicly about actions being taken or planned by authorities to ensure public safety, such as increased protective actions and what the public may expect to see.

AFFECTED AREAS
■ This section includes visual depictions (such as maps or other graphics) showing the affected location(s), sector(s), or other illustrative detail about the threat itself

HOW YOU CAN HELP
• This section provides information on ways the public can help authorities (e.g. camera phone pictures taken at the site of an explosion), and reinforces the importance of reporting suspicious activity.

• It may ask the public or certain sectors to be alert for a particular item, situation, person, activity or developing trend.

STAY PREPARED
• This section emphasizes the importance of the public planning and preparing for emergencies before they happen, including specific steps individuals, families and businesses can take to ready themselves and their communities.

• It provides additional preparedness information that may be relevant based on this threat.

STAY INFORMED
• This section notifies the public about where to get more information.

• It encourages citizens to stay informed about updates from local public safety and community leaders

• It includes a link to the DHS NTAS website http://www.dhs.gov/alerts and http://twitter.com/NTASAlerts

If You See Something, Say Something™. Report suspicious activity to local law enforcement or call 911.

The National Terrorism Advisory System provides Americans with alert information on homeland security threats. It is distributed by the Department of Homeland Security. More information is available at: **www.dhs.gov/alerts.** To receive mobile updates: **www.twitter.com/NTASAlerts**
If You See Something Say Something™ used with permission of the NY Metropolitan Transportation Authority.

FIGURE 11–6 A sample NTAS alert. Source: DHS, 2011, http://www.dhs.gov/xlibrary/assets/ntas/ntas-sample-alert.pdf

Citizens should report suspicious activity to their local law enforcement authorities. The "If You See Something, Say Something™" campaign across the United States encourages all citizens to be vigilant for indicators of potential terrorist activity, and to follow NTAS Alerts for information about threats in specific places or for individuals exhibiting certain types of suspicious activity. Visit www.dhs.gov/ifyouseesomethingsaysomething to learn more about the campaign.

Alert Announcements
NTAS Alerts will be issued through state, local, and tribal partners, the news media, and directly to the public via the following channels:

- Via the official DHS NTAS webpage — http://www.dhs.gov/files/programs/ntas.shtm
- Via email signup at — http://public.govdelivery.com/accounts/USDHS/subscriber/new?topic_id=USDHS_164
- Via social media
     Facebook — http://www.facebook.com/NTASAlerts
     Twitter — http://twitter.com/#!/NTASAlerts
- Via data feeds, web widgets, and graphics — http://dhs.gov/files/programs/ntas-developer-resources.shtm
     The public can also expect to see alerts in places, both public and private, such as transit hubs, airports and government buildings.

Source: DHS, 2011, "NTAS Guide: National Terrorism Advisory System Public Guide," http://www.dhs.gov/xlibrary/assets/ntas/ntas-public-guide.pdf

Crisis Communications

Communications has become an increasingly critical function in emergency management. The dissemination of timely and accurate information to the general public, elected and community officials, and the media plays a major role in the effective management of disaster response and recovery activities. Communicating preparedness, prevention, and mitigation information promotes actions that reduce the risk of future disasters. Communicating policies, goals, and priorities to staff, partners, and participants enhances support and promotes a more efficient disaster management operation.

Communications failures by government responders in Hurricane Katrina were noted in a report prepared by the U.S. House of Representatives that stated, "The lack of a government public communications strategy and media hype of violence exacerbated public concerns and further delayed relief." The House report also asked "why coordination and information sharing between local, state and federal governments was so dismal … Why situational awareness was so foggy, for so long … Why unsubstantiated rumors and uncritically repeated press reports — at times fueled by top officials — were able to delay, disrupt, and diminish the response" (Select Bipartisan Committee to Investigate the Preparation for and Response to Hurricane Katrina, 2006).

The purpose of this section is:

- To define the mission of an effective disaster communications strategy
- To examine communicating in the era of homeland security

- To examine the various forms of media that emergency managers have historically relied on and the new forms of media that are changing how disaster news and information is shared with the public
- To detail the seven elements that we believe will comprise an effective crisis communications capability in the future

Mission

The mission of an effective disaster communications strategy is to provide timely and accurate information to the public in all four phases of emergency management:

- *Mitigation*: To promote implementation of strategies, technologies, and actions that will reduce the loss of lives and property in future disasters
- *Preparedness*: To communicate preparedness messages that encourage and educate the public in anticipation of disaster events
- *Response*: To provide to the public notification, warning, evacuation, and situation reports on an ongoing disaster
- *Recovery*: To provide individuals and communities affected by a disaster with information on how to register for and receive disaster relief

The foundation of an effective communications strategy is built on five critical assumptions (see the sidebar entitled "Five Critical Assumptions for a Successful Communications Strategy"):

- Customer Focus
- Leadership Commitment
- Inclusion of Communications in Planning and Operations
- Good Information
- Media Partnership

Five Critical Assumptions for a Successful Communications Strategy

1. Customer Focus — Understand what information your customers and your partners need and build communications mechanisms that deliver this information in a timely and accurate fashion.
2. Leadership Commitment — The leader of the emergency/homeland security operations must be committed to effective communications and must participate fully in the communications process.
3. Inclusion of Communications in Planning and Operations — Communications specialists must be involved in all emergency/homeland security planning and operations to ensure that communicating timely and accurate information is considered when action decisions are being considered.
4. Timely and Accurate Information — Effective communications is based on the timely collection, analysis and dissemination of information from the impacted area in accordance with basic principles of effective communications such as transparency and truthfulness.

5. Media Partnership — The media (i.e., television, radio, Internet, newspapers, etc.) are the most effective means for communicating timely and accurate information to the public. A partnership with the media involves understanding the needs of the media and including trained staff who work directly with the media to get information to the public. And now that citizen journalists and new media technologies (cell phones, laptops, digital cameras) have become more vital and accepted sources of information and imaging from the front lines of a disaster, methods for incorporating these data and information must also be implemented.

Customer Focus

An essential element of any effective emergency management/homeland security system is a focus on customers and customer service. This philosophy should guide communications with the public and with all partners in emergency management. A customer service approach includes placing the needs and interests of individuals and communities first, being responsive and informative, and managing expectations.

The customers for emergency management/homeland security are diverse. They include internal customers, such as staff, other federal agencies, states, and other disaster partners. External customers include the general public, elected officials at all levels of government, community and business leaders, and the media. Each of these customers has specific information needs, and a good communications strategy considers and reflects their requirements.

Leadership Commitment

Good communications starts with a commitment by the leadership of the emergency management organization to sharing and disseminating information both internally and externally. One of the lessons learned from Hurricane Katrina is, "We need public officials to lead. Communicating confidence to citizens and delivering on promises are both critical in crises" (Kettl, 2005).

The leader of any disaster response and recovery effort must openly endorse and promote open lines of communications among the organization's staff, partners, and publics in order to effectively communicate (Figure 11–7). The leader must model this behavior in order to clearly illustrate that communications is a valued function of the organization (see the sidebar "Leadership Modeling Good Communications").

Leadership Modeling Good Communications

In the 1990s, FEMA Director James Lee Witt was a strong advocate for keeping FEMA staff informed of agency plans, priorities, and operations. Director Witt characterized a proactive approach in communicating with FEMA's constituents. His accessibility to the media was a significant departure from previous FEMA leadership. Director Witt exhibited his commitment to effective communications in many ways:

- He held weekly staff meetings with FEMA's senior managers and required that his senior managers hold regular staff meetings with their employees.
- He published an internal newsletter to employees entitled "Director's Weekly Update" that was distributed to all FEMA employees in hard copy and on the agency electronic bulletin board that updated employees on agency activities.

FIGURE 11–7 Milwaukee, WI, June 18, 2008 — Michael Morgan, Secretary of the Wisconsin Department of Administration, and Dolf Diemont, Federal Coordinating Officer for Disaster 1768, speak at the opening of a Disaster Recovery Center in Milwaukee. FEMA public affairs personnel work closely with the state in a disaster situation. (Source: Photo by Ed Edahl/FEMA)

- He made himself and his senior staff available to the media on a regular basis, especially during a disaster response, to answer questions and to provide information.
- During a disaster response, he held media briefings daily and sometimes two to three times a day.
- He would hold special meetings with victims and their families.
- He led the daily briefings among FEMA partners during a disaster response.
- He devoted considerable time to communicating with members of Congress, governors, mayors, and other elected officials during both disaster and non-disaster times, at times holding joint press briefings with these officials.
- He met four to five times per year with the State Emergency Management Directors, FEMA's principal emergency management partners.
- He gave speeches all over this country and around the world to promote better understanding of emergency management and disaster mitigation.

Inclusion of Communications in Planning and Operations

The most important part of leadership's commitment to communications is inclusion of communications in all planning and operations. This means that a communications specialist is included in the senior management team of any emergency management/homeland security organization and operation. It means that communications issues are considered in the decision-making processes and that a communications element is included in all organizational activities, plans, and operations.

In the past, communicating with external customers, and in many cases internal customers, was not valued or considered critical to a successful emergency management/homeland security operation. Technology has changed that equation. In today's world of 24-hour television and radio news and the Internet, the demand for information is never-ending, especially in an emergency response situation. Emergency managers must be able to communicate critical information in a timely manner to their staff, partners, the public, and the media.

To do so, the information needs of the various customers and how best to communicate with these customers must be considered at the same time that planning and operational decisions are being made. For example, a decision process on how to remove debris from a disaster area must include discussion of how to communicate information on the debris removal operation to community officials, the public, and the media.

Again the response to Hurricane Katrina clearly illustrates the downside of failing to include consideration of communications issues in conducting a response operation. The Lessons Learned report prepared by White House Homeland Security Advisor Francis Townsend noted, "The lack of communications and situational awareness had a debilitating effect on the Federal response. The Department of Homeland Security should develop an integrated public communications plan to better inform, guide, and reassure the American public before, during, and after a catastrophe. The Department of Homeland Security should enable this plan with operational capabilities to deploy coordinated public affairs teams during a crisis" (Townsend 2006).

Situational Awareness

Situational awareness is key to an effective disaster response. Knowledge of the number of people killed and injured, the level of damage at the disaster site, the condition of homes and community infrastructure, and current response efforts provides decision makers with the situational awareness needed to identify need and appropriately apply available resources. The collection, analysis, and dissemination of information from the disaster site are the basis for an effective communications operation in a disaster response.

This is also true during the disaster recovery phase especially early in the recovery phase when the demand for information from the public, and therefore the media, is at its highest. Developing effective communications strategies to promote community preparedness and/or mitigation programs requires detailed information about the nature of the risk that impacts the community and how the planned preparedness programs will help individuals and communities to be ready for the next disaster and the mitigation programs will reduce the impacts of future disasters.

A glaring lack of situational awareness was identified as a severe hindrance to the government response to Hurricane Katrina (see the sidebar "Situational Awareness and Media Stories").

Situational Awareness and Media Stories

Without sufficient working communications capability to get better situational awareness, the local, state, and federal officials directing the response in New Orleans had too little factual information to address — and, if need be, rebut — what the media were reporting. This allowed terrible situations — the evacuees' fear and anxiety in the Superdome and Convention Center — to continue longer than they should have and, as noted, delayed response efforts by, for example, causing the National Guard to wait to assemble enough force to deal with security problems at the Convention Center that turned out to be overstated.

Source: Select Bipartisan Committee to Investigate the Preparation for and Response to Hurricane Katrina, 2006, "A Failure of Initiative: Final Report of the Special Bipartisan Committee to Investigate the Preparation for and Response to Hurricane Katrina," Government Printing Office, February 15, 2006, http://www.gpoacess.gov/congress/index.hmtl.

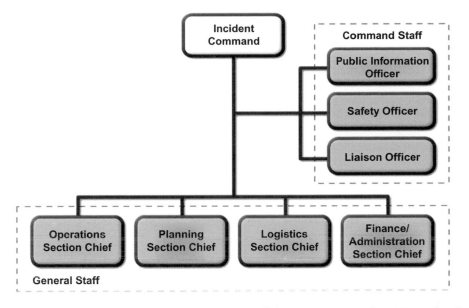

FIGURE 11–8 Incident Command System: Command Staff and General Staff. (Source: FEMA, December 2008, "National Incident Management System, http://www.fema.gov/pdf/emergency/nims/NIMS_core.pdf)

FEMA's National Incident Management System (NIMS) includes a section on Public Information in its Incident Command System (ICS) component. One of the three top command staff reporting to the Incident Commander in ICS is the Public Information Officer (see Figure 11–8).

FEMA's NIMS document states, "Public Information consists of the processes, procedures, and systems to communicate timely, accurate, and accessible information on the incident's cause, size, and current situation to the public, responders, and additional stakeholders (both directly affected and indirectly affected). Public information must be coordinated and integrated across jurisdictions and across agencies/organizations; among Federal, State, tribal, and local governments; and with the private sector and NGOs. Well developed public information, education strategies, and communications plans help to ensure that lifesaving measures, evacuation routes, threat and alert systems, and other public safety information is coordinated and communicated to numerous audiences in a timely, consistent manner. Public Information includes processes, procedures, and organizational structures required to gather, verify, coordinate, and disseminate information" (FEMA, 2007).

Media Partnership

The media plays a primary role in communicating with the public. No government emergency management/homeland security organization could ever hope to develop a communications network comparable to those networks already established and maintained by television, radio, newspapers, and online news outlets across the country. To effectively provide timely disaster information to the public, emergency managers must establish a partnership with their local media outlets.

The goal of a media partnership is to provide accurate and timely information to the public in both disaster and nondisaster situations. The partnership requires a commitment by both the emergency manager and the media to work together, and it requires a level of trust between both parties.

Traditionally, the relationship between emergency managers and the media has been strained. There is often a conflict between the need of the emergency manager to respond quickly and the need of the media to obtain information on the response so it can report it just as quickly. This conflict sometimes results in inaccurate reporting and tension between the emergency manager and the media. The loser in this conflict is always the public, which relies on the media for its information.

It is important for emergency/homeland security managers to understand the needs of the media and the value they bring to facilitating response operations. An effective media partnership provides the emergency/homeland security manager with a communications network to reach the public with vital information and provides the media with access to the disaster site, access to emergency/homeland security managers and their staff, and access to critical information for the public that informs and ensures the accuracy of their reporting.

Communications Infrastructure

FEMA built a substantial communications infrastructure to support its communications objectives. Resources were devoted to hiring and training staff with experience in working with the media and community and providing these employees with the tools they needed to be successful. FEMA built and maintained a television studio with satellite capabilities and an audio studio with radio broadcast capabilities. The agency also established an interactive website where radio actualities and print information could be posted instantaneously. FEMA hired still and video photographers who were dispatched to the field, filing their photos electronically each night. These photos were then made available to media outlets around the country via the Internet.

Local emergency managers developed similar capabilities on a smaller scale in communities around the country. A research project conducted by graduate students at George Washington University found that many jurisdictions in the Washington, D.C., metro area have built varying degrees of communications infrastructure such as communications plans, web and fax communication capabilities, and trained staff who served them well during recent natural and man-made events. A copy of the research project is presented in the sidebar "Communicating during Emergencies."

DIGGING DEEPER: COMMUNICATING DURING EMERGENCIES BY JANE A. BULLOCK, GEORGE D. HADDOW, AND RICHARD BELL

(Note: Research support for this paper was provided by Lauren Block, Tracy R. Bolo, Amina Chaudary, Brian D. Cogert, David DeCicco, Aspasia Papadopoulos, Robert Paxton, and Michael Stinziano.)

Introduction

Communicating with the public is one of the critical tasks facing emergency management agencies (EMAs). Reaching the widest possible audience with the most up-to-date, credible information can save lives and property, reduce public fears and anxiety, and maintain the public's trust in the integrity of government officials.

We recently conducted a survey of how EMA communicators had fared during a number of national disasters and terrorist attacks. Our concern about the adequacy of EMA communications planning has been heightened by a striking change in the intensity of media coverage. In describing their work with the press, our respondents used imagery very much like that which they applied to the emergency event itself. They found themselves swamped by a veritable "tidal wave" of reporters almost literally beating down their doors.

In this article, we review the findings of our survey and interviews and lay out the principal suggestions we received from a cross-section of EMAs on putting the personnel and infrastructure in place to execute robust, flexible communications plans.

Methodology

This article is based on responses to a questionnaire that we received from communicators involved in the following recent natural disasters or terrorist attack, including interviews in most cases with the principal spokesperson involved:

Tropical Storm Allison, Harris County Texas, Office of Emergency Management, Mayor's Office, June 5–10, 2001

The Hayman forest fire, Colorado, Public Affairs, U.S. Forest Service, Rocky Mountain Region, Summer 2000

Attack on the Pentagon, northern Virginia, Office of the Assistant Secretary of Public Affairs and Media Relations, U.S. Department of Defense, September 11, 2001

Attack on the Pentagon, northern Virginia, Capitol Police, September 11, 2001

Sniper attacks, Washington, DC, metro area, Media Services, Montgomery County Police Department, Fall 2002

Anthrax attack on Hart Senate Office Building, Washington, DC, October 2001

Anthrax attacks, Office of Communications, Division of Media Relations, Centers for Disease Control and Prevention, Fall 2001

F4 level tornado, La Plata, Maryland, Maryland Emergency Management Agency, April 28, 2002

Planning

Creating a communications plan on the fly during a crisis is an extremely daunting task. The absence of a plan virtually guarantees that communicators will not be able to reach the public as effectively as they would if they had a plan in place.

Producing a workable written plan is inherently an agency-by-agency process, contingent on available personnel, budget limitations, and so on. By soliciting critical review of the plan from all the affected participants — the public, the press, other government agencies — EMAs have the opportunity to produce the best possible plan under the circumstances.

Some of the EMAs with whom we talked had highly elaborate communications plans. But regardless of length, they all agreed that their plans made them more effective during emergencies. And the EMAs who had been through a trial by fire without a written communications plan were equally adamant about putting such a plan in place as soon as possible.

People

The most well-written communications plan is not worth much without a strong commitment from elected officials and department managers to put the infrastructure in place to carry out the plan.

The spokesperson's credibility is a key to his/her effectiveness at representing the government, reassuring the public, and keeping the media happy. In some jurisdictions, the highest ranking elected official or the head of the department managing the crisis will be the lead communicator, giving them a kind of automatic credibility at the onset of an event (like New York Mayor Rudy Giuliani after 9/11).

Given the increasing intensity of media coverage, the media spokesperson plays an increasingly important role in ensuring the overall effectiveness of an EMA. In order to maintain the spokesperson's credibility as a source with the media, the spokesperson needs to be "at the table" for all senior

(Continued)

management decisions. If reporters believe that a spokesperson is not fully integrated into the decision-making process, they will inevitably be more suspicious of the information they do receive.

By participating in decision making, the spokesperson can also play a vital internal role by making sure that decision makers have fully considered how their decisions may play out in the media, giving them a better chance of avoiding public relations blunders.

After the terrorist attack on the Pentagon on September 11, 2001, Arlington County officials significantly upgraded its top public communications official. The change was more than just a title change (from Assistant County Manager for Public Information to Director of Communications and Public Affairs). The county also raised the position's salary and provided that the new director would report directly to the county manager. The job description for this new position includes the development of "a comprehensive communications program that will provide a cohesive image, identity, and brand message both externally and internally by optimizing the use of existing electronic resources (Internet, intranet, and cable television) and nonelectronic sources (print media) as well as developing new communications venues."

If possible, one person should be the principal spokesperson (the single voice/single face model). Nothing is likely to be more confusing to the media or the public than dealing with a constantly changing array of talking heads. (There's a reason almost all the daily White House press briefings are handled by one person!)

Media Training

Learning to be a media spokesperson in the middle of a crisis is risky. There is no substitute for practical media training before a crisis arrives. In Harris County, Texas, the three authorized spokespeople had all been through a FEMA-approved 32-hour public information officer (PIO) course offered through the Texas Department of Public Safety's Office of Emergency Management. The Forest Service spokesperson during the 2002 Hayman forest fire had roughly 50 hours of formal media training. In addition, the agency's public affairs staff worked with him on "war game" crises, creating what he called "murder boards" to put him through the kind of tough questioning he would encounter in a real crisis. And the Capitol Police officer who handled the anthrax attack on the Senate Hart Building was a media trainer himself with over 160 hours of training.

Infrastructure

Building an Emergency Operations Center

Just as some jurisdictions had no written EM plan, some did not have an emergency operations center (EOC), although there was broad agreement that having a well-equipped EOC was the physical foundation for an effective communications effort.

For planning purposes, the EOC should have redundant communications capabilities, both internally and with the outside. No communications technology works every time. Land lines can fail; during the attack on the Pentagon, there were frequent problems with cell phones.

Without a well-equipped EOC, crisis managers face difficult hurdles staying on top of what is happening. After the September 11 attack on the Pentagon, local officials found that their EOC was ill equipped for the emergency management team to communicate with first responders or to receive accurate information from the scene. Phone lines were down, and the room was not equipped with radios or televisions. They were forced to delay press briefings until they could verify facts with first responders and people on-site.

EOCs should be designed with the media in mind. The Harris County, Texas, EOC has an on-site press room with telephone and computer access. EOCs can make life easier for television reporters by preparing video footage (called "B-roll") of scenes that reporters could use, like the interior of the emergency operations center. EOCs can also prepare fact sheets and other printed background materials on the major threats that the agency has identified.

Communicators can also provide the press with special support if necessary. During the Hayman forest fire, the Forest Service gave out personal protective equipment to reporters (hard hats, fire clothes, etc.).

Carving through the Jurisdictional Jungle

The communications plan provides a framework for mapping and, where possible, negotiating communications procedures about how to handle one of the most common problems of the EMA universe, overlapping jurisdictions. Such overlaps are inherent in the nature of almost every large-scale emergency event. A comprehensive plan must include not only local, state, and federal law enforcement and emergency management agencies but also the spectrum of veterinary and public health agencies (in light of the threat of the use of biological, chemical, or radiological weapons by terrorists).

In the aftermath of the anthrax attacks, the Centers for Disease Control and Prevention has published a useful analysis of the similarities and differences in public health and law enforcement investigations and the steep learning curves for both sets of agencies in their collaborations. ("Collaboration between Public Health and Law Enforcement: New Paradigms and Partnerships for Bioterrorism Planning and Response," by Jay C. Butler et al., http://www.cdc.gov/ncidod/EID/vol8no10/020400 .htm). The authors emphasize the importance of preexisting relationships between law enforcement and public health agencies and the need for practice exercises, and call for adding liaisons who are cross-trained in the public health aspects of communicable diseases and in law enforcement and criminal investigations.

Even without a written communications plan, an informal prior agreement can be helpful in reducing confusion. In the case of the anthrax attack on the Hart Senate Office Building, there was no written plan. But the Capitol Police Board and the House and Senate leadership had previously determined that the Capitol Police would be the designated agency to handle media inquiries after any terrorist or criminal incidents within the Capitol complex. Members of Congress — a group not known for being media-shy — conferred with the police spokesperson before holding their own press conferences, and the spokesperson attended these events, off camera, to provide guidance as needed.

In our study, several communicators highlighted the importance of maintaining clear channels of communications with all of the government agencies involved, regardless of which agency had been designated the lead communications agency. This cross-agency communication is essential for keeping everyone "on the same page" so that reporters do not get confusing or conflicting information from their contacts at other agencies. Up-to-date e-mail and fax lists are a relatively cheap way to distribute breaking information to other agencies in a timely way.

The Office of Emergency Management in Harris County used an Internet e-mail and pager software they developed to reach more than 140 media outlets in the region, 125 law-enforcement agencies, 54 fire departments, 29 cities, and selected individuals throughout the surrounding 41 counties. After tropical storm Allison, the office expanded the list of individuals requesting real-time information, adding more elected federal, state, and local officials and media outlets. (Copies of the Harris County plans can be downloaded from http://www.hcoem.org.)

(*Continued*)

Working with the Media

Building Prior Relationships

The media play an integral part in EMA outreach efforts to keep the public informed and up-to-date. But without preexisting relationships with reporters, it's not uncommon or unexpected that in the heat of the moment, EMAs might come to look upon the press in a crisis as adversaries engaged in a "feeding frenzy" for new facts.

Planning is essential to building relationships with the media, so that EMAs and the media understand each other's needs and operating styles and how to work together as much as possible as allies. Both EMAs and the press share a deep concern about protecting the health and welfare of the public. Far from being adversaries, reporters can be valuable allies, particularly in devising an effective communications plan in the first place.

Harris County's Office of Emergency Management had a policy of inviting reporters in twice a year to talk about how the agency could better meet the needs of the press. Such conversations are no guarantee, of course, against future disagreements. But such meetings do allow for EMAs and reporters to share each others' perspectives in a nonstressful environment, reducing the possibility of misunderstandings later on during crises. And such exchanges also allow EMAs to plan to meet the media's needs where possible. Another useful technique for improving media relations is to schedule meetings with the editorial boards of local media outlets.

Conserving Credibility with the Media

Credibility is a dynamic asset in a crisis; a spokesperson can lose credibility quickly if the media and the public come to believe they're being misinformed or underinformed. Every effort should be made to ensure that whatever information is released to the public is accurate and up-to-date. As one PIO told us, his goal was to be "the first and best source of information, especially if it's bad news."

Misinformation only compounds one of the other common communications problems during crisis, the rapid spread of unfounded rumors, the rebutting of which can take up valuable time. During the Capitol Hill anthrax attack, many Capitol Hill reporters — who were used to covering policy debates, not terrorist attacks — were anxious about their own medical conditions, having been in the "hot zone" at some point. Congressional staffers, their usual sources of information, were also anxious about their own health and provided information often based on rumor, outside their areas of legislative expertise. Reporters, frustrated with what seemed to them to be the slow release of information, would go with these rumor sources and end up being forced to backtrack later. Many of the communications managers in our survey said that combating such rumors was one of the most difficult tasks they faced during a crisis.

Limiting the amount of information that reaches the public poses a different kind of challenge. It is not uncommon for government or corporate managers to use the control of the release of information as a way of gaining or preserving bureaucratic power. But in a crisis, this withholding tendency can aggravate the public's anxieties. In Arlington County, Virginia, after the September 11 attack on the Pentagon, officials found that although they might not have any new, more specific information about what might happen next, citizens still wanted frequent updates and reassurances from their county government.

In a crisis management setting, withholding information may very well result in a loss of power and control. Our respondents agreed that one should lean in the direction of making more, rather than less, information available, consistent with law enforcement and public safety considerations.

In a full-blown media circus, even a vigorous attempt at openness may not be enough to halt a media feeding frenzy. One of the more striking examples of this press intensity came from the Montgomery County, Maryland, police during the Washington, DC, area sniper attacks in fall 2002. The department was already providing frequent media releases, one-on-one interviews, Web updates, and as many as four press briefings a day.

But reporters wanted more. Some went so far as to peer through a half-inch opening in the window shades at the operations center, stealing a look at text on a dry erase board. Within seconds, they were questioning Montgomery County police chief Charles Moss about the information they had gleaned, showing little concern about whether their questions might endanger public safety.

Keeping Alternative Media Channels Open

In addition to the traditional media (TV, radio, newspapers), EMAs have access to newer media like e-mail, websites, and local cable TV, which can be used to reach the public directly. Because these tools also do not reach as wide an audience as traditional mass media, they should be seen as adjuncts, not substitutes.

These unmediated channels can be very effective tools for providing the public with a great deal of information without tying up large numbers of EMA staff. However, if an EMA is using a website, it is essential that staff update the site on a frequent basis; stale information drives users away.

The agencies we surveyed reported a wide range of satisfaction in using new media tools. In some cases, results were disappointing because too few people were aware of the local cable TV channel or did not know the agency had a website. On the other hand, one agency reported over 1.6 million contacts on its website from press, first responders, and the public and regarded the website as a valuable component of its overall communications strategy.

Conclusion

Communicating during emergencies is necessarily fraught with uncertainty: The unexpected is most likely to happen. No emergency communications plan can fully encompass all of the scenarios that may arise. But the findings from our survey show that EMAs can take steps to create a robust communications plans, train spokespeople, and build the infrastructure that will allow EMAs to roll with the punches and maximize their effectiveness at getting their messages to the press, the public, and other government agencies.

Terrorism Application

As noted earlier, Mayor Giuliani was an effective communicator in the aftermath of the World Trade Center attacks. He quickly assumed the role of principal government spokesperson, providing information, solace, and comfort to victims and their families, fellow New Yorkers, the nation, and the world through a series of planned and unplanned media events and interviews over the course of the days and months after September 11. Giuliani has been praised for his candor, his sensitivity, and his availability during these efforts. He has set a standard by which public officials will be judged in future tragedies.

In Washington, D.C., a different communications scenario surfaced in the days and weeks after the first anthrax-contaminated letter was discovered in the office of the then U.S. Senate Majority Leader Tom Daschle in October 2001. A series of public officials and scientists issued often-conflicting information to the public as both the officials and the public struggled to understand the nature and the reach of the anthrax threat. The failure to communicate accurate and timely information reduced public confidence in the government response and increased the confusion and misinformation surrounding the events.

What factors made Mayor Giuliani's efforts successful and caused the situation in Washington to worsen? What type of information and infrastructure support did Giuliani have that may or may not have been available to the public officials in Washington? Was the commitment to inform the public different in New York City than it was in Washington, D.C.?

A study of the anthrax attacks, funded by the Century Foundation, concluded that "the timely flow of information from experts to the public via the mass media will be the nation's best protection against panic and potential disaster" (Thomas, 2003). To reach this goal, the media and public officials will need to change the way they work together and possibly establish new protocols for determining the methods by which sensitive information is collected and disseminated to the public. These issues must ultimately be balanced against the public's right to know. As the study found, the public is often smarter and better informed than both the media and public officials believe (Thomas, 2003).

A report entitled "What Should We Know? Whom Do We Tell? Leveraging Communications and Information to Counter Terrorism and Its Consequences" found that the dissemination of information before a terrorist incident is as critical, if not more so, as delivering timely and accurate information during and after a crisis (Chemical and Biological Arms Control Institute, 2002). Preincident planning and coordination and public education and awareness campaigns are critical elements in establishing clear lines of communications among responding agencies, significantly improving the opportunities to collect accurate information and make it available to the public through the mass media. Again, changes in current practices and relationships among responders and with the media must occur to meet the information needs before, during, and after future terrorist attacks (Chemical and Biological Arms Control Institute, 2002).

The Washington, D.C., sniper attacks provide valuable insight into the difficulties in communicating with the public during an ongoing crisis. The tension between the need to provide timely and complete information when such information was lacking and the need to avoid compromising an ongoing criminal investigation was clearly evident during this nearly month-long crisis. A case study of this event and its media coverage is presented at the end of this chapter.

Communicating in the Era of Homeland Security

Communicating with the public is an area that needs to be improved if the nation is going to have a truly effective homeland security system. From its inception, the DHS has shown little interest in communicating with the public, and when it has the results have not always been positive — the "duct tape and plastic" fiasco and past reports of former DHS Secretary Ridge questioning terror alert warnings serve as classic examples. DHS communications have improved during the Obama Administration, but DHS and its state and local partners still need to address three factors in order to further improve their communications with the American people.

First, there must be a commitment from the leadership, not only at DHS and its state and local partners, but also at all levels of government including the executive level to communicate timely and accurate information to the public. This is especially important in the response and recovery phases to a terrorist incident.

In a disaster scenario, the conventional wisdom that states information is power, and that hoarding information helps to retain such power, is almost categorically reversed. Withholding information during disaster events generally has an overall negative impact on the well-being of the public, and on the impression the public forms about involved authorities. In practice, sharing of information is what generates authority and power, when that information is useful and relates to the hazard at hand. A good example of this fact are the actions of former New York City Mayor Rudy Giuliani after the September 11 attacks. Giuliani went to great lengths to get accurate and timely information to the public in a time of crisis, and his efforts both inspired the public and greatly enhanced the effectiveness of the response and recovery efforts he guided.

Historically, DHS leadership and the political leadership have been reluctant to make this commitment to share information with the public. This is something that must change if they expect the American people to fully comprehend the homeland security threat and to become actively engaged in homeland security efforts. Few citizens have any idea of what actual terrorism risks they face, and fewer can actually relate those risks in any comparable fashion to the risks they face every day.

Second, homeland security officials at all levels must resolve the conflict between sharing information with the public in advance and in the aftermath of a terrorist incident that has value for intelligence or criminal prosecution purposes. This is directly linked to the commitment issue discussed in the previous paragraphs and has been repeatedly cited by homeland security officials as reasons for not sharing more specific information with the public.

Also at issue is the question of when to release relevant information to the public without compromising intelligence sources and/or ongoing criminal investigations. This is an issue that rarely if ever confronts emergency management officials dealing with natural and unintentional man made disasters. Therefore, there is little precedent or experience for current homeland security officials to work with in crafting a communications strategy that balances the competing need for the public to have timely and accurate information with the need to protect intelligence sources and ongoing criminal investigations. To date, the needs of the intelligence and justice communities have clearly been judged to outweigh those of the public — but at a cost.

Withholding information leaves the public vulnerable and suspicious of the government. Lucy Dalglish, executive director of the Reporters Committee for the Freedom of the Press, said her task, and the task of journalists, was to convince government officials that over the long run transparency can build trust and save lives: "The same information that a terrorist can use to do great damage can possibly give families information about which escape route to use to get away from a nuclear power plant. I think we're going to find that if we have a flu pandemic, the information that can be used to terrorize and scare people can also be used to save their lives. I think what we have to do is work very hard at convincing people that access to information is ultimately going to be our friend" (May, 2006).

The recent implementation by the Obama Administration of the national Terrorism Advisory System that replaced the much-maligned Homeland Security Advisory System (HSAS) is a critical first step in reestablishing trust with the public for the warning system. From this starting point, additional communications mechanisms can be developed to ensure that the public gets timely and accurate information both in advance of any terrorist incident and during the response and recovery phases in the aftermath of the next terrorist attack.

Third, more effort must be invested by federal departments and agencies to better understand the principal terrorist threats that our nation faces (i.e., biological, chemical, radiological, nuclear, and explosives), and to develop communications strategies that educate and inform the public about these threats with more useful information. The 2001 Washington, D.C., anthrax incident is a perfect example of uninformed or misinformed public officials sharing what is often conflicting and, in too many instances, wrong information with the public.

The nation's public officials must be better informed about these principal risks and be ready and capable of explaining complicated information to the public. As the anthrax incident made clear, this is not a luxury, but a necessity if the response to similar incidents in the future is to be successful.

Decades of research and a new generation of technologies now inform emergency managers as they provide information about hurricanes, tornadoes, earthquakes, and hazardous materials incidents to the public. A similar research effort must be undertaken for these five new terrorist risks and communications strategies that will ensure that homeland security officials at all levels are capable of clearly explaining to the public the hazards posed by these threats.

These communications strategies must consider how to communicate to the public when incomplete information is all that is available to homeland security officials. In the vast majority of cases, this partiality of information is probable. A public health crisis will not wait for all the data to be collected and analyzed, nor will the public. Homeland security officials must develop strategies for informing the public effectively, as the crisis develops, by forming effective messages that are able to explain to the public how what is being said is the most accurate information available based on the information that, likewise, is available — despite its incomplete nature. Clearly, this is not an easy task, but it is not impossible. The public will increasingly expect such communications efforts, so the sooner such a system is in place, the better the next incident will be managed.

Disaster Communications in a Changing Media World

Working with the media before, during, and after a disaster or terrorist event is a fact of life for an emergency management/homeland security official. The media remains the single most effective means for communicating timely and accurate information to the public. Historically, emergency managers have shied away from talking to the media especially during a disaster response. That day is over. As we noted earlier, emergency/homeland security officials involved in disaster response can no longer ignore the media. Developing a partnership with the media should now be standard operating procedure for any and all emergency management/homeland security operations in this country and around the world.

However, the media is constantly changing and emergency/homeland security managers must keep up with these changes to have an effective communications operation. Historically, traditional media such as radio, television, and newspapers delivered emergency messages to the public.

The radio has become over time an integral part of communicating warning messages to the public before the next tornado or hurricane strikes. In turn, radio has often been the sole source of information in the immediate aftermath of a massive disaster that cuts off electricity to the disaster area for days at a time because of the availability of transistor and crank radios that do not require electricity.

Television has become a big part of disasters in the past 50 years. The pictures and stories that are generated by disaster events are a natural fit for television. It was the size of the satellite photo of Hurricane Floyd on television coupled with evacuation warnings from local, state, and federal officials transmitted by television that prompted 3 million residents in Florida, Georgia, and South Carolina to evacuate their homes as the storm threatened the Eastern Seaboard. It is also television that graphically communicated the sorry events that occurred in New Orleans after Hurricane Katrina.

Over time, television has changed considerably. The three national networks and usually three to four local stations in any given community have given way to hundreds of channels available nationwide along with 24/7 news channels and the Weather Channel, and they are available across the country.

The rise of the Internet as a source for disaster and emergency-related information and news has been spectacular. A survey conducted in April 2008 by the Canadian Centre for Emergency Preparedness (CCEP) found that the Internet has passed newspapers on the list of emergency information sources used by the Canadian public. Television and radio are ranked 1 and 2 on this list, but it may not be long before the Internet grabs even more of the public's attention especially as older and low- to moderate-income individuals and families gain access to the Internet.

The media continues to change with the advent of "first informers," ordinary citizens armed with a cell phone who can take pictures and/or video at the disaster site and add commentary and post their

FIGURE 11–9 Nashville, TN, May 5, 2010 — Nashville resident and disaster survivor Amy Frogge uses social media to display pictures that document the flood and damage to her home in Davidson County. FEMA is responding to the severe storms and flooding that damaged or destroyed thousands of homes in May 2010 across Tennessee. (Source: Photo by David Fine/FEMA)

submissions on the Internet or provide them to CNN or MSNBC or other outlets (Figure 11–9). Some of the first photos and commentaries coming out of the Asian tsunami disaster in 2004 were filed by these "first informers" who were one there when the tsunami struck and survived to provide information and images of the damage and destruction.

The Evolution of New Media Use in Disasters

The magnitude and frequency of natural disasters are increasing. According to the Center for Research on the Epidemiology of Disasters, there were four times as many weather-related disasters in the last 20 years than in the previous 75 years. With this new "Age of Extreme Weather," has come the evolution and maturation of new media tools and technologies, a dramatic rise in the number of citizen journalists, and an almost annual increase in their contribution to the flow of new information during disasters. "Disasters have provided a unique trigger that have consolidated technological advances in concert with democratizing influences operating outside the traditional brokers of information and aid" (Laituri, 2008).

Even though the 1990s was a time of transformation in communications technology with the emergence of the World Wide Web, 24/7 cable television, and an array of digital tools — from affordable and widely available wireless mobile devices and high-resolution satellite maps — new media was not a factor in natural disaster coverage or recovery until 2001.

In the aftermath of the September 11, 2001, terrorist attacks, citizen-shot videos of the attacks on the Twin Towers dominated news coverage and Americans turned to the Internet for information. But the sharp spike in traffic froze and crashed websites. In many ways, 9/11 was the last disaster covered under the old model of crisis communications: Newspapers printed "Extra" editions, people turned to television for news and "the familiar anchors of the broadcast networks — Tom Brokaw, Peter Jennings, and Dan Rather — took on their avuncular roles of the past for a nation looking for comfort and reassurance" (May, 2006).

Every disaster since 9/11 has involved more citizen journalists and expanded the use and utility of the new media tools and technologies. In 2003, during China's SARS epidemic, people used text messaging to exchange information the government tried to suppress (Hattotuwa, 2007). Three major disasters within nine months — the Asian tsunami (2004), the London transit bombings (2005), and Hurricane Katrina (2005) — marked the coming of age of participatory media.

The December 26, 2004, Asian tsunami has been defined as "the turning point — a before-and-after moment for citizen journalism." Blogs, websites, and message boards provided news and aid — and in real time. One blog, "waveofdestruction.org" logged 682,366 unique visitors in four days (Cooper, 2007). Wikipedia — a group-created website that is editable by any user — became the site for basic information, particularly for hotlines that allowed people to search for missing loved ones and find housing, medical, and other assistance.

Minutes after four bombs rocked London's transportation system, a definitive webpage "July 7, 2005 London Bombings" was started with five sentences on Wikipedia. The page "received more than a thousand edits in its first four hours of existence as additional news came in." Users added links to traditional news sources, and information was posted about what public transportation was shut down, listing contacts to help track a missing person and offering directions to commuters trying to get home. "What was conceived as an open encyclopedia in 2001 [became] a general purpose tool for gathering and distributing information quickly ..." (Shirky, 2008).

A cell phone photo taken by a commuter in a smoked-clogged tunnel in the Tube became the iconic image of the disaster. Londoners pooled their digital photos on Flickr — a photo-sharing site and service that allows people to tag pictures with comments and labels. "The photos that showed up after the bombings weren't just amateur replacements for traditional photojournalism: people did more than provide evidence of the destruction and its aftermath. They photographed official notices ("All Underground services are suspended"), notes posted in schools ("Please do not inform children of the explosions"), messages of support from the rest of the world ("We love you London"), and within a day of the bombings, expressions of defiance addressed to the terrorists ("We are not afraid" and "You will fail"). Not only did Flickr host all of these images, but also they made them available for reuse, and bloggers writing about the bombings were able to use the Flickr images almost immediately, creating a kind of symbiotic relationship among various social tools" (Shirky, 2008). Police asked people to supply them with cell phone pictures or videos because they might contain clues about the terrorists (Shirky, 2008).

In September 2005, Hurricane Katrina, a category 3 hurricane, tore through New Orleans, Louisiana, Mobile, Alabama, and Gulfport, Mississippi. Over 1,500 people were killed and tens of thousands left homeless. Blogs became the primary information-providing tool used by both traditional media and citizen journalists. Staff reporters for New Orleans' daily newspaper, the *Times-Picayune*, created a blog that for a time became the front page of their news operation. It enabled members of the community isolated by flood waters and debris to show and tell each other what they were seeing (Gillmor, 2006).

Message boards provided critical information about shelter locations, family tracing, and missing persons. Internet expert Barbara Palser counted 60 separate online bulletin boards that were created to locate missing people within 2 weeks of the storm. "These sites included major portals such as Yahoo and Craigslist, an array of newspaper and television sites, websites hosted by government and relief organizations, and individual technologists, including a group of programmers who enlisted about 2,000 volunteers to create a database called the Katrina PeopleFinder Project." PeopleFinder was established "to create a consolidated database of missing people built outside the traditional, centralized institutions (i.e., FEMA, Red Cross)" (May, 2006). Google Earth and Google Map that provide and use online satellite imagery were used to illustrate damage assessments — particularly to the Gulf Coast and barrier islands (Laituri, 2008).

After the Java earthquake in 2006, mobile phones became mobile news services. Internews, an international media support group, worked with 180 Indonesian journalists to set up a text messaging service that helped local radio stations to report on the recovery (Hattotuwa, 2007). (See Case Study in New Media: Cyclone Nargis, Myanmar.)

CASE STUDY IN NEW MEDIA: CYCLONE NARGIS, MYANMAR

On May 2, 2008, Cyclone Nargis struck the Irrawaddy Delta region of Myanmar (Burma). The cyclone with winds of 120 mph made landfall at the mouth of the Irrawaddy River — a low-lying, densely populated region — and pushed a 12-foot wall of water 25 miles inland, killing at least 80,000 people, leaving as many as 2.5 million homeless.

Ten days later, on May 12, 2008, a 7.9 earthquake devastated China's Sichuan province, toppling buildings, collapsing schools, killing more than 69,000, injuring over 367,000, displacing between 5 and 11 million people.

Two disasters. One common link. They demonstrated that new technologies — the Internet, text messaging systems, camera phones, Google Map mash-ups — and citizen journalists, especially bloggers, have irrevocably altered the nature of disaster reporting and replaced the top-down flow of information from the government and the traditional media in times of crisis with a dynamic and democratic two-way exchange.

In Myanmar, where Internet and cell phone access is limited, the military government refused to allow aid workers or journalists to reach disaster areas and moved fast to restrict communications. Ironically, it was a local online news source, Burma News, that reported on the "guidelines" the junta had set for journalists' coverage, specifically prohibiting showing dead bodies or reporting about insufficient aid for victims (Burma News, 2008).

In spite of these restrictions, Burmese blogs and news sites were quick to react by posting eyewitness accounts of the disaster and mobilizing fundraising efforts.

According to BBC News, "People inside Burma have been giving their updates from the disaster zone. Burmese blogger Nyi Lynn Seck has a section of his blog devoted to daily updates from the Delta region. 'They are seeing dead bodies,' he writes. 'Nobody has cremated or buried these dead bodies.' He also carries a report of how one private donor in Bogalay was forced to give his donation to the local authorities rather than people in need" (BBC News, 2008).

The BBC also noted that the Mizzima news site, based in India and run by Burmese exiles, used long-standing personal networks to gather compelling accounts of loss and survival. Other exile Burmese news sites such as Yoma3 reported on the spread of disease among the cyclone victims in Bogalay. Stories of monks and local residents pulling together and co-coordinating local cleanups and sharing water could be found on the Democratic Voice of Burma and other sites such as The Irrawaddy. *The Rule of Lords* blog reported that people had been turned away from hospitals because of the lack of electricity and water.

In addition to the news gathering done by citizen journalists online (bloggers), other new media technologies helped tell the story of the Burmese disaster and recovery:

- Twitter — a short messaging service (SMS) — that uses cell phones and 140 character messages that are also posted online — emerged quickly as an important medium for coverage of the crisis. Aid agencies working in Burma including AmeriCares and the Salvation Army are also using Twitter to disseminate information and coordinate activities (Washkuch, May 20, 2008).
- YouTube hosted scores of videos recording the devastation and feeble response. User AfterNargisYgn uploaded a multi-part series of videos featuring images of the effects of the cyclone in Yangon, Myanmar's largest city, previously known as Rangoon. His series also documents the growing anger and desperation of the storm victims. Burma4u uploaded a video

(Continued)

of the aftermath in Latbutta, with Cyclone Nargis' victims crowded in refugee shelters, trying to sleep. Videos depicting dozens of people who died in the cyclone, which are banned by the junta, are also posted on YouTube (Rincon, May 16, 2008, YouTube).

- Google Earth and the Associated Press produced interactive maps that tracked the cyclone's passage through the county and illustrated the extent of the storm damage — especially the dramatic erosion of shoreline and degree of inundation.
- Global Voices Online and traditional media like the New York Times, BBC and CNN featured, linked to or aggregated coverage by bloggers and linked to videos and photos recorded by eyewitnesses.

In October 2007, wildfires in Southern California resulted in the loss of nearly 2,200 homes and over $1 billion in damages and marked a major step forward in the integration of mainstream media and citizen journalists. "Local media has been highlighting user-submitted photos and videos, and embedding new technology in their prime coverage. San Diego's public television station, KPBS, used Twitter to give its audience updates when its website went down, and the Twitter updates now have a prominent place on their home page" (Glaser, 2007).

San Diego TV station News 8 responded to the crisis by taking down its entire regular website and replacing it with a rolling news blog, linking to YouTube videos of its key reports, plus Google Maps showing the location of the fire (Stabe, 2007). Also on the site were links to practical information that viewers needed, including how to contact insurance companies, how to volunteer or donate to the relief efforts, evacuation information, and shelter locations. "It's an exemplary case study in how a local news operation can respond to a major rolling disaster story by using all the reporting tools available on the Internet" (Catone, 2007).

Local and national television stations asked for submissions from wildfire witnesses and victims. The NBC affiliate in San Diego received over 2,000 submissions of pictures and video related to the wildfires. CNN's I-Reports section reportedly received about the same number of fire-related submissions (Catone, 2007). The Google Map (Internet GIS) tool was used to develop maps of shelter locations and fire updates (Wagner, 2007).

Social media experts were able to track cell phone calls on the island of Haiti after the 2010 earthquake in order to track the spread of cholera. Thousands of Twitter messages from individuals in or near the site of the 2010 Japanese earthquake and tsunami provided the first messages, pictures, and videos of the massive destruction caused by these twin events. Individuals, voluntary groups, and government agencies used various social media sites to communicate recovery and reconstruction messages in Joplin, Missouri, in the aftermath of the 2011 tornadoes.

Clearly, a symbiotic relationship is emerging between citizen journalists and the mainstream news media. With every new major disaster, the mainstream media's use of Internet-facilitated reporting increases. Government, however, has been slow to appreciate the power or potential of the new media tools and Internet culture.

New Media: New World

When disasters happened in the past, we learned about them after the fact. No more. New technologies — laptops, cell phones, text messaging systems, digital cameras, the Internet — have changed the way news is gathered and distributed. These technologies have also profoundly altered the flow of information, undermining the traditional gatekeepers and replacing the centralized, top-down model used by the government and professional media with a more dynamic flow of information that empowered citizens and created ad hoc distributive information networks.

"… these technologies create new ways for citizens to be heard, governments to be held accountable and the State to answer to failures of governance. Ordinary citizens … are increasingly using technology, through devises such as mobile phones, to support powerful frameworks of transparency and accountability that citizens can use to hold decision makers responsible for the action, and indeed, inaction," Dan Gillmor and Sanjana Hattotuwa explained in their essay, "Citizen Journalism and Humanitarian Aid: Boon or Bust?" (Gillmor, 2007).

According to Gillmor, the days of news as a "lecture" — when traditional media told the audience what was news — are done. Now news is more of a conversation and the lines have blurred between producers and consumers: "The communications network itself will be a medium for everyone's voice, not just the few who can buy multimillion-dollar printing presses, launch satellites, or win the government's permission to squat on the public's airwaves… (Gillmor, 2006).

"The venerable profession of journalism finds itself at a rare moment in history where, for the first time, its hegemony as gatekeeper of the news is threatened by not just new technology and competitors but, potentially, by the audience it serves" (Bowman, 2003).

The once passive audience has become an active participant in the creation and dissemination of news, and the flow of information is no longer controlled by journalists and government agencies. The increasing participation and power of ordinary citizens in emergency communications are starting to have more observable consequences. The Aspen Institute report, *First Informers in the Disaster Zone: The Lessons of Katrina,* noted in its conclusion, "… there was a difference in how the online environment changed the media mix and altered the flow of information during and after the disaster …. At times the traditional flow of information from government to media to public reversed course   As one pair of new media experts put it, Katrina 'revealed extraordinary changes taking place within a society increasingly connected by digital networks, a society at the cusp of a new era in human history in which individuals possess an unprecedented capacity to access, share, create and apply information'" (May, 2006).

One participant in the Aspen Institutes assessment of lessons learned from Katrina was Jon Donley, the editor of NOLA.com — the *New Orleans Times-Picayune*'s online companion and the primary source of news when the daily could not print in the weeks following the hurricane. He explained that the new media had fostered a two-way flow of information, in contrast to the old paradigm in which information flows down from government and media to a passive audience. "I would really encourage everybody to think about this new media age that we're in, where the audience isn't playing that game anymore. We have had a revolution" (May, 2006).

In addition to forcing the traditional media to reconsider and redefine its role in disaster communications, the new participatory media enhanced the amount of information and number of sources and added to the problems endemic in disaster — the need to sort truth from rumor and the tension between media demanding transparency and accessibility and government officials changed with managing information during a disaster.

The information available to citizens at times of crises is often inadequate, incorrect, or dated. According to Gillmor and Hattotuwa, "Studies show that the problem lies not with the technologies (or lack thereof) but with the culture of information sharing. The access, dissemination and archiving of information is often controlled by government's agencies, institutions who have a parochial interest in controlling its flow — what gets out where, to whom, how and when" (Gillmor, 2007).

"If we waited for the government to release information during a disaster, it would be days before the public would know anything," complained to one participant in the Aspen Katrina assessment. Chet Lunner, acting director of state and local government coordination in DHS and a former national reporter for the Gannett News Service, spoke from the government's perspective in the Aspen session. He disagreed with a comment from CNN's David Borhman that the government instinct in a crisis was to hide. "They are not hiding. They are sort of defensive, in a crouch ... because [they] don't trust the media" (May, 2006).

Katrina, the Aspen report concludes, exacerbated the already burgeoning distrust between media and government. "As rival proxies for the public, the two institutions clashed openly during and after the storm .... The first failure was caused by lack of good situational awareness by federal officials themselves, who painted a rosy scenario that clashed with the pictures and reports from the scene from journalists. 'Don't you guys watch television? Don't you guys listen to the radio?' ABC's Ted Koppel famously asked Michael Brown, then FEMA director .... 'Federal, state, and local officials gave contradictory messages to the public, creating confusion and feeding the perception that government sources lacked credibility,' the White House report concluded" (May, 2006).

The emergence and proliferation of citizen media complicated the information mix and increased the tension between the government and traditional media.

"Information in the hands of citizens continues to instill fear and loathing in the minds of those who wish to manufacture public opinion to their benefit by the careful selection and publication of information ...," explained Sanjana Hattotuwa in "Who Is Afraid of Citizen Journalists?" (Hattotuwa, 2007).

Government official Chet Lunner explained his unease in the Aspen report: "I get concerned when I see the term 'citizen journalists' and 'blogs' lumped in with everything else as if that were journalism in the way that it is practiced by professionals. That is often the problem we have, which is that something that starts out as a blog does not necessarily meet the standards of most source-tested journalism that has been in practice for all these years .... We have enough trouble with things that do go through the [mainstream media] filter. The amount of time and energy and social unrest by readers and/or the people trying to practice in the field dealing with these things that are exaggerated rumors, etc., is a problem, particularly in the framework of these disaster times when people are depending upon or relying on that" (May, 2006).

"On the other hand," the editor of NOLA.com explained, "The very first reports [that] we had of life threatening flooding in New Orleans came from citizens typing it into cell phones. The very first news we had of clear levee breaks, of looting, of a shooting death, or a suicide in the Superdome — every one of those things we heard first from citizens who we were encouraging to have a two-way dialogue with us" (May, 2006).

Participatory journalism and the generation of news and information from "first informers" — citizens on the scene when disaster happens — are not trends that are going to go away. In fact, as noted previously, the 2008 disasters in Burma (see the sidebar "Case Study in New Media: Cyclone Nargis, Myanmar") and China may mark the coming of age of text messaging, blogging, and video sharing as tools that can bring faster coverage of a news event than traditional media.

The challenge now for traditional news sources and cautious governmental hierarchies is to plan for and maximize the use of an increased and accelerated flow of information, to seize the opportunity to share information and build community that online media creates.

In recent years, FEMA and DHS have embraced all forms of new media and begun to engage the public in new forms of communications. In a press release explaining FEMA's involvement in social media, the agency reported that, FEMA has been engaging in Web 2.0 tools and on social media sites nationwide as part of its mission to prepare the nation for disasters. FEMA's goals with social media are to provide timely and accurate information related to disaster preparedness response and recovery, provide the public with another avenue for insight into the agency's operations, and engage in what has already become a critical medium in today's world of communications. FEMA's social media ventures function as supplemental outreach, and as appropriate channels for unofficial input (FEMA, 2011). FEMA's and DHS's Internet and social media presence has grown considerably since 2009 (see the sidebar "Social Media at the Department of Homeland Security").

Social Media at the Department of Homeland Security

The Department of Homeland Security is using "Web 2.0," social media technologies and Web sites to provide information in more places and more ways. The following is a list of tools and sites that DHS (including its component agencies) uses to provide up-to-date information "straight from the source".

Web 2.0 and Communications on Department Sites

Online Subscription Services

- RSS and Atom feeds at the Department of Homeland Security: http://www.dhs.gov/xutil/feeds.shtm
- E-mail updates from the Department of Homeland Security: http://www.dhs.gov/xutil/gc_1193765609028.shtm

Media Galleries

- Department and component links to multimedia: http://www.dhs.gov/ynews/gallery/

Blogs

- The Blog @ Homeland Security, Department of Homeland Security: http://www.dhs.gov/journal/theblog/
- TSA Blog, Transportation Security Administration: http://www.tsa.gov/blog/
- Coast Guard Compass, U.S. Coast Guard: http://coastguard.dodlive.mil/
- Chief's Corner, U.S. Fire Administration: http://www.usfa.dhs.gov/about/chiefs corner/
- FEMA Blog, FEMA: http://blog.fema.gov/
- The Beacon, U.S. Citizenship and Immigration Services: http://blog.uscis.gov/
- The U.S. Coast Guard maintains additional blogs that are not on Department sites, which can be found at: http://www.dhs.gov/xabout/gc_1245941465213.shtm#1

Mobile Web Sites

- FEMA: http://m.fema.gov/
- TSA: http://www.tsa.gov/mobile
- ICE: http://m.ice.gov/

Podcasts

- U.S. Coast Guard: http://www.uscg.mil/top/podcast.asp

Widgets

- Federal Hurricane Response Widget, Department of Homeland Security: http://www.dhs.gov/files/programs/gc_1220128923561.shtm
- Emergency Preparedness and Response Widgets, FEMA: http://www.fema.gov/help/widgets/
- Wait Time Calculator, Transportation Security Administration: http://www.tsa.gov/travelers/waittime.shtm
- Most Wanted, Latest News, Detainee Locator, ICE: http://www.ice.gov/news/widgets/

Web 2.0 and Communications on Non-Government Sites

Blogspot

- Coast Guard All Hands, U.S. Coast Guard: http://coastguardallhands.blogspot.com/

Facebook

- Department of Homeland Security: http://www.facebook.com/homelandsecurity
- U.S. Department of Homeland Security Blue Campaign: http://www.facebook.com/home. php#!/bluecampaign
- FEMA: http://www.facebook.com/fema
- ICE: http://www.facebook.com/homelandsecurity#!/wwwICEgov
- U.S. Coast Guard: http://www.facebook.com/uscoastguard

Flickr

- U.S. Coast Guard, U.S. Coast Guard: http://www.flickr.com/photos/coast_guard/

iTunes

- Transportation Security Administration: itms:\--itunes.apple.com-WebObjects-MZStore.woa-wa-viewPodcast?id = 310038315

Ning

- Our Border, Department of Homeland Security: http://ourborder.ning.com/

Twitter

- DHSJournal, Department of Homeland Security: http://twitter.com/DHSJournal
- National Terrorism Advisory System (NTAS), Department of Homeland Security: http://twitter.com/#!/NTASAlerts
- Citizen Corps, FEMA: http://twitter.com/citizen_corps
- FEMA: http://twitter.com/fema
- Craig Fugate, FEMA: http://twitter.com/craigatfema
- FEMA Region 1: http://twitter.com/femaregion1
- FEMA Region 2: http://twitter.com/femaregion2
- FEMA Region 3: http://twitter.com/femaregion3
- FEMA Region 4: http://twitter.com/femaregion4
- FEMA Region 5: http://twitter.com/femaregion5
- FEMA Region 6: http://twitter.com/femaregion6
- FEMA Region 7: http://twitter.com/femaregion7
- FEMA Region 8: http://twitter.com/femaregion8
- FEMA Region 9: http://twitter.com/femaregion9
- FEMA Region 10: http://twitter.com/femaregion10
- FEMA LRO: http://twitter.com/femalro
- Ready.Gov: http://twitter.com/ReadydotGov
- Science and Technology Directorate: http://twitter.com/dhsscitech
- Transportation Security Administration: http://twitter.com/TSABlogTeam
- U.S. Citizenship and Immigration Services: http://twitter.com/uscis
- U.S. Coast Guard: http://twitter.com/uscoastguard
- CG Compass; U.S. Coast Guard: http://twitter.com/cgcompass
- iCommandant, U.S. Coast Guard: http://twitter.com/iCommandantUSCG
- U.S. Customs and Border Protection: http://www.twitter.com/customsborder
- U.S. Fire Administration, FEMA: http://www.twitter.com/usfire/
- U.S. Immigration and Customs Enforcement: http://www.twitter.com/wwwicegov

YouTube

- U.S. Department of Homeland Security: http://www.youtube.com/ushomelandsecurity
- FEMA: http://www.youtube.com/user/fema
- Transportation Security Administration: http://www.youtube.com/user/TSAHQpublicaffairs
- U.S. Coast Guard: http://www.youtube.com/uscgimagery
- U.S. Customs and Border Protection: http://www.youtube.com/customsborderprotect
- U.S. Immigration and Customs Enforcement: http://www.youtube.com/wwwicegov

DHS does not currently use Myspace, Picasa, Vimeo, or virtual worlds like Second Life.

Source: DHS, 2011. "Social Media at the Department of Homeland Security," http://www.dhs.gov/xabout/gc_1238684422624.shtm

Building an Effective Disaster Communications Capability in a Changing Media World

The world of emergency management/homeland security is changing rapidly. The onslaught of major catastrophic disasters around the world, the projected impact of global climate change, and the continuing threat of terrorism have forced the emergency management/homeland security community to reexamine all of its processes, including communications. Managing information before, during, and after a disaster or terrorist attack has changed significantly in recent years and emergency/homeland security operations at all levels — local, state, and national — must recognize and acknowledge this change and adapt accordingly.

As we have noted earlier in this chapter, the biggest change in disaster communications has come with the emergence of the "first informers" — citizen journalists — and their use of new, widely available online and digital technologies to gather and share information and images. No organization working in the emergency management/homeland security field — government, nongovernmental groups, voluntary agency, private sector — can ignore the role these "first informers" and their information networks will play in future disasters.

In the future, emergency management/homeland security organizations must establish partnerships with both the traditional media outlets and the new media in order to meet their primary communications mission of providing the public with timely and accurate information before, during, and after a disaster.

The purpose of this section is to detail the seven elements that we believe will comprise an effective disaster communications capability in the future. These seven elements include:

- A Communication Plan
- Information Coming In
- Information Going Out
- Messengers
- Staffing
- Training and Exercises
- Monitor, Update, and Adapt

A Communication Plan

Disaster communication plans can take several forms. Planning for communicating in disaster response focuses on collecting, analyzing, and disseminating timely and accurate information to the public. A disaster response communication plan will include protocols for collecting information from a variety of sources including citizen journalist, analyzing these data in order to identify resource needs and to match available resources to these needs, and then disseminating information concerning current conditions and actions to the public through both traditional and new media outlets. The plan will identify trusted messengers who will deliver disaster response information to the public. The plan will identify how disaster communications will be delivered to special needs and non-English-speaking populations.

The disaster response communications plan will include a roster of local, state, and national media outlets, reporters, and first informers. This roster will be contacted to solicit information and to disseminate information back out to the public. Finally, the plan should include protocols for monitoring the media, identifying new sources of information collection or dissemination, and evaluating the effectiveness of the disaster communications. This information would be used to update the plan.

A communications plan for the recovery phase will look very similar. The recovery phase plan must also include protocols for collecting, analyzing, and disseminating timely and accurate information. During the recovery phase, much of the information to be disseminated to the public will come from government and other relief agencies and focus on available resources to help individuals and communities to rebuild.

The communications plan must place a premium on delivering this information to the targeted audiences and must identify the appropriate communications mechanisms to communicate these messages. Information collection from the field from a wide variety of sources must be a priority in the communications plan for the recovery phase. Community relations staff, community leaders, and first informers are good sources of information on the progress of recovery activities and can provide valuable perspective of the mood of the individuals and communities impacted by the disaster. These sources are also effective in identifying communities, groups, and individuals who have been passed over by recovery programs. It is in the recovery phase that consensus is sought since crucial long-term decisions have to be made at the state and community levels.

Information Coming In

Information is the basis of effective disaster communications. In disaster response, receiving and processing regular information concerning conditions at a disaster site and what is being done by agencies responding to the disaster allows disaster communicators to provide timely and accurate information to the public. In collecting this information, no potential source should be ignored and all possible sources should be encouraged to forward relevant information. To be successful in this task, you should identify all potential sources of information and develop working relationships with these various sources *before* the next disaster strikes. You must also be prepared to identify and partner with new sources of information as they come on the scene in the aftermath of a disaster.

Potential disaster information sources include:

- Government damage assessment teams: Government disaster agencies at every level have staff responsible for assessing damages in the aftermath of a disaster. For a major disaster, a damage assessment team may include representatives from local, state, and federal response agencies. The information collected will include deaths, injuries, damage to homes, infrastructure, and the environment, and other critical data.
- First responders: These are among the first on the scene at any disaster, equipped with the necessary communications devices and trained to be observant.
- Voluntary agencies: These groups often have members or volunteers located in the disaster areas trained in damage assessment who can make first and ongoing assessments. For example, the Red Cross has extensive experience in reporting damage to homes and numbers of people evacuated and in shelters.

- Community leaders: Trusted leaders who have their own neighborhood network or work with community-based organizations with networks into the community can be a valuable source of on-the-ground information.
- First informers: Individuals in the disaster site with the wherewithal to collect information and images and to communicate that information and images by cell phone, handheld device, or laptop.
- New media: Blogs (weblogs), Google Earth, Google Map, Wikis (Wikipedia), SMS (text messaging postings — Twitter), Flickr, Picasa (photo survey sites), YouTube (video sharing sites).
- Online news sites: Aggregate of community news, information, and opinion.
- Traditional media: Television, radio, and newspaper reporters, editors, and news producers can be good sources of information especially if they have deployed news crews to the disaster area before or just after a disaster strikes.

Having identified the potential information sources in your area, you must reach out to these sources to develop a working partnership and to put in place whatever protocols and technologies are needed to accept information from these sources. It is important that all potential sources of information understand what types of information you need from any situation so that they are looking for the information you need to make decisions. Government response agencies and voluntary agencies practicing NIMS and ICS will know what information to collect. You must reach out to the nongovernmental, nontraditional information sources before the next disaster to let them know what information you need and how to communicate that information to you.

Ideas for developing these working partnerships with nongovernmental, nontraditional information sources include:

- Building neighborhood communications networks: Partner with community-based organizations, churches, and neighborhood associations to build neighborhood communications networks. Local residents can be trained in information collection, maybe as part of Community Emergency Response Team (CERT) training, and local community leaders can be entrusted to collect this information and forward it to emergency officials. These networks could also be used to send messages from emergency officials to neighborhood residents through trusted community leaders.
- Creating and distributing a disaster information protocol for first informers: List what information you will be seeking over the course of a disaster response and get this list out to the public. Make sure they know where to e-mail or post the information and images they collect.
- Establishing a point of contact within your organization for information sources: Designate staff that will work with information sources during a disaster and are accessible.
- Creating an electronic portal for information from the field: Wikis and weblogs (blogs) can accept and aggregate comments from users, set up a Twitter website that can be updated via text messages, and create a homepage on YouTube and Flickr.
- Including first informers and traditional and new media outlets in disaster response training and exercises: Incorporate these information sources into your disaster exercises to identify issues and gaps and to update plans accordingly. Media are not always included in exercises nor are first informers, but by including these groups in your exercises you make the exercise more authentic and you create an opportunity to identify difficult issues prior to facing them in the next disasters and you can make appropriate adjustments. It is also a chance to get to know each other.
- Meeting with traditional and new media types on a regular basis: Another way to create personal relationships with these critical partners in any disaster response.

- Including information sources in your after-action debrief: Their perspectives and experiences can be used to update plans and operations.

Many of these information sources can be identified as part of a hazard mitigation and preparedness campaign. Working relationships can be developed during these nondisaster periods that will facilitate information collection and flow in disaster response.

Information Going Out

If information coming in is the basis for disaster communication, then information going out is the goal. Timely and accurate information can save lives in disaster response and in hazard mitigation and preparedness programs. In getting information to the public, you must use all available communications mechanisms including:

- Traditional media: Television, radio, newspapers, and the Internet
- New media: Post new information on community websites, blogs, wikis, and bulletin boards; share timely photos and video online; and tell traditional media that online outlets are being updated routinely
- Neighborhood communications networks: Trusted community leaders who go door to door

Historically, emergency officials have disseminated disaster information to the traditional media by means of press conferences, briefings, tours of the disaster site, one-on-one interviews with disaster officials, press releases, situation reports, and postings on the Internet. Radio actualities, photographs, and videotape have also been provided to traditional media. In major disasters, emergency management agencies have used satellite uplinks and video and audio press conferences to reach traditional media outlets across large sections of the country.

Disseminating information through new media outlets is something new for emergency officials and will require patience and understanding of how these new media functions with their audiences. Most of this work can occur during nondisaster periods. This is the time to learn more about Wikipedia, Twitter, blogs, Flickr, Facebook, YouTube, and social networking sites, and to discover how you as an emergency manager can best use these new media to deliver preparedness and hazard mitigation messages as well as communicate with their target audiences in the disaster response and recovery phases.

Prior to the next disaster, you might consider:

- Starting a blog: Get your message out there about the risks your community faces: how to take action to reduce those risks and protect your family, home, and business; how to prepare for the next disaster; when to evacuate and how; what will happen when your organization responds; and how members of your community can become first informers.
- Creating a bulletin board: This could serve as a link to community leaders involved in hazard mitigation and preparedness programs in the neighborhoods and could be accessed by all community members before, during, and after a disaster.
- Establishing accounts and actively engaging in Twitter, Facebook, YouTube, and other active social media sites: This presents opportunities to engage in an ongoing dialogue with the public and has proved to be an effective means for communicating emergency messages and receiving real-time emergency information.
- Getting on Wikipedia: Load preparedness and hazard mitigation information and links for more information on the site. Understand that this site will grow with information added by readers.

- Starting a YouTube site: That features "How To" videos on how to disaster-proof your home, office, and business. Post videos that explain how to survive the next disaster (how much water and food to have on hand; where to go for information).
- Creating a Google Map: This is of the locations of designated shelters and evacuation routes.

When the next disaster strikes, consider:

- Regular updates on your blog: This allows you a direct link to members of your community. Include time in your schedule to get interactive and answer questions and inquiries.
- Regular updates on your bulletin board: Again another opportunity to talk directly to members of the community, to get interactive.
- Review and update Wikipedia: Place your information in the Wikipedia file on the disaster and keep it regularly updated. Update disaster aid and shelter information and links to missing persons sites and correct inaccurate information and confront rumors.
- Post on Twitter, Facebook, and other social media sites: Emergency messages and information from you to the public and collect information from reliable individual sources.
- Post on YouTube: Videos from informational briefings, from affected neighborhoods, and appeals for help.
- Update Google Map: To show locations of open shelters, hospitals.
- Display on Google Earth: Locations of affected areas.

Maintain and regularly update all of these sites during the recovery phase.

Messengers

The person who delivers the messages plays a critical role in disaster communications. The messenger(s) puts a human face on disaster response and this person(s) is critical to building confidence in the public that people will be helped and their community will recover. Public Information Officers (PIOs) regularly deliver information and messages to the media and the public. However, the primary face of the disaster response should be an elected or appointed official (i.e., mayor, governor, county administrator, city manager) or the director of the emergency management agency, or both. These individuals bring a measure of authority to their role as messenger and in the case of the emergency management director, someone who is in charge of response and recovery operations.

The public wants to hear from an authority figure and the media wants to know that the person they are talking to is the one making the decisions. Elected officials who served as successful messengers in recent disasters include California Governor Arnold Schwarzenegger during the 2007 southern California wildfires, New York City Mayor Rudy Giuliani during the September 11 attacks, Florida Governor Jeb Bush during the four hurricanes that struck Florida in 2004, and Oklahoma Governor Frank Keating during the 1995 Oklahoma City bombing. Successful emergency managers as messengers include former FEMA Director James Lee Witt and California Office of Emergency Services Director Dick Andrews in the 1994 Northridge Earthquake and Craig Fugate with the Florida Division of Emergency Management during recent hurricanes, tornadoes, and wildfires in Florida. Former FEMA Director Witt and Former President Clinton worked very well together in delivering messages concerning federal relief programs in numerous disasters in the 1990s.

Prior to the next disaster or terrorist attack, each emergency management/homeland security agency should determine whether an elected or appointed official will serve as the primary messenger alone or in tandem with the emergency agency director. It is best to work out in advance what types of information will be delivered by which messenger. Protocols for briefing books and situational updates should be developed. A determination should be made as to who will lead press briefings and news conferences, who will be available to the media for one-on-one interviews, and who will be involved in communicating with the new media outlets. Again, all of these activities can be shared by the elected/appointed official and the emergency agency director.

Emergency management/homeland security agencies should also designate appropriate senior managers who will be made available to both the traditional and new media to provide specific information on their activities and perspective. This is helpful in even the smallest disaster when persons with expertise in specific facets of the response can be very helpful in delivering disaster response information and messages.

Staffing

Not many emergency management/homeland security agencies have a single communications specialist much less a communications staff. Federal agencies such as FEMA, DHS, HHS, and others involved in disaster have extensive communications staff. Most state emergency management/homeland security operations have at least a communications director. The depth of staff support for communications varies widely. Emergency management/homeland security agencies in major cities in the United States often have communications directors and in some case extensive communications staff. Small- to mid-sized cities and communities are unlikely to have a communications director or staff.

The time has come for all organizations involved in emergency management/homeland security to establish an ongoing communications staff capability. For agencies in small- to mid-sized communities, this may require enlisting help from the local government's communications staff. One way to do this is to provide funding for a percentage of this individual's time each month. In this way, communications activities required during nondisaster periods could be acquired on a consistent basis. This will also allow for the local government communications staff and director to be better informed of the emergency management/homeland security agency's activities and be better prepared to work with the emergency/homeland security agency director during disaster response and recovery.

For large cities and federal and voluntary agencies with existing communications staff, it is now a matter of reordering priorities to meet the demands of working with the new media. Staff will be required to establish and maintain working relationships with new media outlets and to interact with the various blogs, bulletin boards, social networking sites, and other new media outlets that serve their community. At minimum, there should be one designated staff person on the communications staff who is responsible for the day-to-day interaction with new media. Additional staff should be made available in a major disaster to work with these groups.

The new media designated staff would also work with new media outlets in promoting hazard mitigation and preparedness campaigns in the community and serve as the staff support for the establishment and maintenance of neighborhood communications networks working with trusted leaders in the community.

Training and Exercises

An effective disaster communications operation requires well-trained messengers and staff and should be a vital part of all disaster exercises. Elected/appointed officials, agency directors, and public information officers should all receive formal media training in order to become comfortable working with the media to communicate disaster messages to the public. Media training teaches how to communicate a message effectively, helps to learn techniques for fielding difficult questions, and provides the opportunity to practice delivery outside the crucible of a crisis. If possible, media training should be provided to senior staff who may appear in the media.

Staff training should come in several forms including:

- Media relations: Learn how to work with traditional and new media including meeting deadlines, responding to inquiries, scheduling interviews, understanding what types of information each media outlet requires, and how a news operation works

- New media: Learn what a blog is, how social networking works, and how to establish and maintain a neighborhood communications network
- Marketing: Learn how to pitch a story idea for a preparedness program or hazard mitigation project to all forms of media, how to develop supporting materials for preparedness and hazard mitigation campaigns, and how to evaluate the effectiveness of such efforts

Communications operations must always be included in future disaster exercises. It is highly recommended that these exercises include reporters from traditional media outlets, representatives from the new media including bloggers, and online news sites. Working with new media and online news sites should be included in the exercise such as updating and correcting a Wikipedia site and posting information on a community bulletin board. Community leaders involved in neighborhood communications networks should also be included in the exercise.

Monitor, Update, and Adapt

Staff should be assigned to regularly monitor all media outlets. Summaries of news stories in the traditional media should be compiled regularly. Staff should routinely monitor new media outlets and provide regular summaries of news on these sites. This activity is especially important during a disaster response. Through monitoring, the media staff is capable of identifying problems and issues early in the process and can shape communications strategies to address these issues before they become big problems. This is also an opportunity to identify trends in how information flows through the media to the public and to identify areas for improvement of message development and delivery. Regular monitoring will identify rumors and misinformation and speed corrections.

The information collected as part of monitoring activities can be used to update communications plans, strategies, and tactics. This data can be used to determine how to allocate staff resources and to update training and exercise programs. Emergency management agencies must be constantly on the lookout for emerging communications technologies and opportunities.

Conclusion

The experience of emergency managers with natural disasters provides at minimum a guide to the development of effective terrorism-related communications strategies. However, there is much work to be done to adapt existing risk, warning, and crisis communications models to the new hazards, the new partners, and the new dynamic between response and recovery and criminal activity associated with the new terrorist threat. One thing will remain constant: Communication with the public about the terrorist threat must receive the same attention and resources that are now going to new technologies, new training programs, and new organizations. It has never been more important that public officials talk to the public, and it has never been more difficult than it is now. If this problem is not addressed properly, it can only compound in the worst way the terrible consequences of any terrorist incident.

CASE STUDY1: QPS MEDIA: SOCIAL MEDIA CASE STUDY

The QPS Media in Australia did an amazing job with social media during the flooding and cyclone events earlier this year. I was so impressed with their use of the medium that I documented their efforts in this presentation. They have just completed a case study of the experience and have compiled this report. Their major findings and lessons learned amplify some of the messages the #SMEM community

(*Continued*)

CASE STUDY1: QPS MEDIA: SOCIAL MEDIA CASE STUDY (CONTINUED)

here in the U.S. have been stating for a while and transcend national boundaries. Here are their 7 major lessons in quotation — I have added a few of my own insights as well:

1. **If you build it, they will come.** The number of "likes" on their Facebook page skyrocketed as the crisis worsened. "If you are not doing social media, do it now. If you wait until it is needed it will be too late."
2. **Social media is "social" — people expect interaction:** "Do not use social media solely to push out information. Use it to receive feedback and involve your online community."
3. **The need for speed is essential:** "Rethink clearance processes. Trust your staff to release information."
4. **Add a social media expert to your team.** "While there should be shared responsibility for uploading information and moderating social media sites, expert technical advice and trouble-shooting will be necessary from someone with an IT background."
5. **Ensure that information is accessible.** "A PDF is not the most accessible way to deliver information. Machine-readable information such as geocoding allows the information to be more accessible and usable for others."
6. **Do not treat social media as something special or separate from normal work processes.** "It should be integrated as standard practice."
7. **Use the sites that are available to everyone.** "Established social media sites are free and robust which can handle volumes of traffic much larger than agency websites."

The report also gives a great overview of the "why" of social media. These bullets are direct quotes from the report:

- It is immediate and allowed Police Media to proactively push out large volumes of information to large numbers of people ensuring there was no vacuum of official information;
- The QPS Facebook page became the trusted, authoritative hub for the dissemination of information and facts for the community and media;
- Large amounts of specific information could be directed straight to communities without them having to rely on mainstream media coverage to access relevant details;
- The QPS quickly killed rumor and misreporting before it became "fact" in the mainstream media, mainly through the #mythbuster hashtag;
- It provides access to immediate feedback and information from the public at scenes;
- The mainstream media embraced it and found it to be a valuable and immediate source of information;
- It provided situational awareness for QPS members in disaster-affected locations who otherwise had no means of communications.

Related articles

- During a crisis, will press releases be the thing of the past? (idisaster.wordpress.com)
- The fabulous case study of Queensland Police on Facebook (rossdawsonblog.com)

Source: idisaster 2.0, 2011, "QPS Media: Social Media Case Study, http://idisaster.wordpress.com/2011/07/29/qps-media-social-media-case-study/.

CASE STUDY 2: WASHINGTON, DC, SNIPER ATTACKS

Introduction

In America's post-9/11 era of terror awareness, the extreme actions of groups like Al-Qaeda are no longer necessary to spark detrimental anxiety-based social reactions. The two "snipers" who placed the nation's capital under a state of siege for 3 weeks with one rifle and a box of bullets confirmed this fact. Washington, DC's latest duct-tape and plastic "panic buying" spree, set off by the Department of Homeland Security's momentary "Terrorism Threat Index" increase, illustrates that the mere hint of a future event can now induce "irrational" behavior. Clearly, the emergency management community can no longer simply blame the media for such strong public sentiments.

Controlling public fear is a public safety task that falls squarely on the shoulders of local government, but like other terrorism preparedness and response functions, fear management must be supported by the federal government to be effective. There exists a rapidly growing need for agencies to adopt formal fear management capabilities staffed by appropriately trained, dedicated officials. In many cases of terrorism, fear is the greatest emergency that must be managed, and irresponsible or inadequate attempts to do so can actually increase the public's risk. Using the recent sniper crisis as an example, this case study will examine the roots of public fear and the often distorted reality of risk and will propose methods by which emergency management agencies can successfully manage fear should a terror-based event occur within their jurisdiction.

Background

The residents of the Washington, D.C., metropolitan area[1] were confronted with a dramatically heightened sense of personal vulnerability in the 12 1/2 months leading up to the sniper crisis. On September 11, 2001, during the worst terrorist attack to take place on American soil, the city became the target of two hijacked airplanes.[2] Less than 1 month later, several letters containing anthrax were mailed to federal government offices, resulting in the closing of several buildings,[3] a mass prophylaxis with the antibiotic Cipro, and the death of several Washington, D.C., postal workers. Ever-increasing security measures became impossible to avoid, with numerous streets surrounding federal buildings closed to the public, military vehicles with mounted machine guns positioned around the Pentagon, and all the while the media reporting that the emergency response capabilities of the Washington, D.C., government would be severely deficient should a mass casualty event occur in the near future (Ward, 2001).

It was easy to surmise that, to international and "homegrown" terrorists alike, Washington, DC, was a likely target. Reported levels of stress among area residents were much higher than those observed throughout the rest of the country, as indicated by several polls (Diaz and O'Rourke, 2002). By the time the sniper announced his presence on the morning of October 3, 2002, by killing four people, Washingtonians had already been pushed to the limits of their psychological stress tolerance.

---

[1] This includes the District of Columbia, Northern Virginia, and several counties in Maryland. The population of this region, according to the 2000 census, is 4,922,640 (FAIR, 2002b).

[2] While only one plane crashed into a building in the Washington, D.C., metropolitan area (the Pentagon), it is believed that the plane that crashed into a Pennsylvania field was heading for either the White House or the U.S. Capitol (Lochhead, 2002).

[3] As of late November 2002, the Brentwood Postal Facility, where the three postal workers who contracted anthrax worked, remained closed, with no planned reopening in the near future (Fernandez, 2002).

(Continued)

CASE STUDY 2: WASHINGTON, DC, SNIPER ATTACKS (CONTINUED)

Reactions and Actions

To study this case, we must first examine the reactions and actions of the authorities (the police department and other government officials), the media, and the public. These three groups were intimately linked by the virtual dearth of information that was available. The links can be simplified through the understanding that the authorities gathered and analyzed the information, the media broadcast the information, and the public received the information and acted upon it. The information flow diagram shown in Figure 11–10 depicts these links.

The following pages provide a broader understanding of each of these groups' actions in order to offer insight into why each may have acted as they did.

The Authorities

The individuals considered the "authorities" include the local, state, and federal government officials who were involved with the various aspects related to the response to the sniper crisis. Because this was primarily a law enforcement response to an event that involved only conventional weapons, the local police departments were the lead agencies involved.[4] These authorities were the sole source of credible information during the crisis.

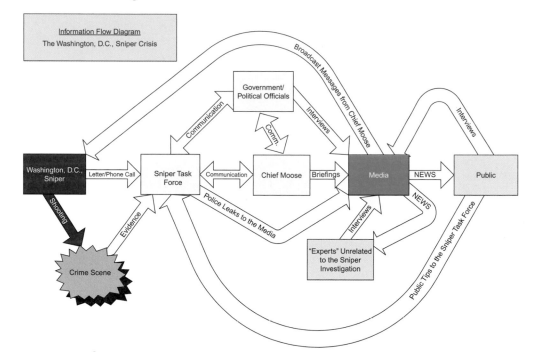

FIGURE 11–10 Information flow diagram during the Washington, D.C., sniper crisis.

---

[4] Presidential Decision Directive-39 (PDD39), signed by President Clinton in 1995, gives the Department of Justice, through the Federal Bureau of Investigation (FBI), lead agency authority in incidents where weapons of mass destruction are used or if the event is considered terrorism (Watson, 2000). The sniper crisis was never officially classified as such, so Chief Moose remained in command.

The Montgomery County Police Department (MCPD) was the first to become involved in the crisis on the morning of October 3, primarily because the majority of killings had taken place in Montgomery County, Maryland. Having authority in the affected jurisdiction, the MCPD put forth Chief Charles Moose as the official spokesperson for the media.[5] Although Chief Moose could provide only basic information concerning the characteristics of the victims and the locations of the shootings, he was immediately recognized as the leader in the crisis.[6] For the remainder of the crisis, the media (and likewise, the public) continued to look to Chief Moose for information and guidance. In fact, even though FBI agents ultimately arrested the suspects outside of Chief Moose's jurisdiction, it was Chief Moose who officially announced the arrest.

Chief Moose proclaimed that this was one of the greatest challenges he had ever faced (Stockwell, Ruane, and White, 2002). He had never been required to fulfill such an important public relations role. The crisis quickly escalated to an international scale, and Chief Moose became the one man the world turned to for information so desperately sought. Chief Moose faced a major problem in that he often did not have very much information to give, and when he did, he felt that giving anything specific would jeopardize the investigation.

Chief Moose provided very little information detailing the actual risk people faced. He would regularly assure the public that police were doing their best to keep people safe and that the bulk of police resources were focused on solving the case, but he could not tell people how concerned they should be about personal safety. On at least one occasion, he even stated that "we've not been able to assure anyone their safety in regards to this situation" (Ruane and Stockwell, 2002).

The Washington, D.C., Metropolitan Police Department (MPD) publicly issued a list of "Tips for Staying Safe." This list told residents to keep moving when outside, to walk in a rapid zigzag pattern, and to avoid brightly lit open spaces. It also stated, "Remember that a sniper with the right equipment can shoot accurately from about 500 yards, the equivalent of five football fields" (Hurdle, 2002). These tips did not give any indication to residents of what their actual risk from the sniper might be. Some residents followed the advice they were given in these messages, but it is arguable that the lack of Chief Moose's endorsement of the tips prevented them from being widely observed.

School administrators became major players in the response to the sniper threat. Several schools were closed in the Richmond, Virginia, area after a sniper letter proclaiming that children were not safe was found at a shooting scene. Schools in other areas of Virginia and Maryland were closed as well, though no specific threats were given to the administrators of those schools as in Richmond. These closings were said to have been the result of a fear of liability among school administrators (*Economist*, 2002) and were not based on solid evidence. While they claimed that "there was no other way to guarantee students' safety" (Gettleman, 2002), the fact remained that they did not want to be held responsible for making a decision to let school stay in session and then have a child shot in

---

[5] Initially, MCPD spokeswoman Captain Nancy Demme was issuing statements to the media, but Chief Moose assumed the public relations role upon further consideration of the severity of the crisis.

[6] Chief Moose, who holds a PhD in urban studies, was seen not only as a trustworthy leader but also as the lead decision maker. It was important that he addressed the media, considering all information passed through his hands — something a spokesperson of a lower rank could not claim. Moose was credited for his on-camera compassion, shedding tears on occasion, and uttering comments throughout the crisis that showed his "human" side. At one point, for instance, he urged parents to spend more time with their children (Sun and Ly, 2002).

(*Continued*)

their "jurisdiction" during such a high-profile crisis. In fact, none of the schools shut down during the sniper crisis were shut down after the September 11 terrorists attacks or after any other unsolved murders in the area (Reel, 2002). A further explanation could be heard in the words of Henrico County Public School Superintendent Mark Edwards, who stated, "The decision was not based on any specific threats, but on 'the volume of concern'" (Gettleman, 2002). Such statements strengthened arguments that these actions were based on a reaction to fear, not the risk itself. Of course, it is undeniable that there existed a genuine concern for the safety of the children in the motivation of these decisions, echoed by Montgomery County Superintendent Jerry West, who said, "We have always taken very seriously every day the level of threat to our children. We have always consistently done everything we can do to keep our children safe" (Schulte, 2002). The closing of schools became a focus of media attention and undoubtedly affected public opinion about personal safety.[7]

Politicians also become involved in the public reaction to the crisis, and in several cases used the events to further their own agendas. Kathleen Kennedy Townsend, in her gubernatorial campaign in Maryland, began attacking her opponent's opposition to a federal ban on assault weapons, stating that the gun control would be an answer to the voters' fears (Fineman, 2002). Connie Morella, campaigning for the House of Representatives, said, "I'm still knocking on doors, and when I do that, I think I'm a comfort to the people at home. I mean, if I'm out there doing that, people say, 'Hey, it must be all right'" (Barker, 2002).

There is finally the issue of unnamed authorities passing unreleased information to the media. It is important to stress both the detriment and opportunities presented by these insider "leaks." In numerous instances, the press learned of confidential information that was either never to be shared or not to be released immediately, and they broadcast that information, to the obvious dismay of Chief Moose. While on many occasions these leaks increased the tensions observed between the Sniper Task Force officials and the media, it cannot be overlooked that leaks were directly attributed to the capture of the two suspects.

The Media

The media was virtually the only bridge of information between the authorities and the public (see Figure 11–9). Media agencies gleaned information from a myriad of sources, but the only information broadcast that could be deemed "factual" or "credible" almost always came directly from Chief Moose. In addition, that which was leaked was usually confirmed or denied by Chief Moose. Media coverage, regarding air time, was almost total when the crisis began and immediately after each successive victim. Regular news shows became dominated by the case, and there were constant "special reports" with additional information that was considered "related" to the case.

Coverage of the sniper crisis spanned the globe, and early on there were as many international news agencies as national ones camped outside the Montgomery County Police Department. The number of articles seen in the national and international press surged with each successive shooting, peaking immediatcly after the capture of Muhammad and Malvo. The actual daily number of articles, taken from major national and international newspapers, is displayed in Figure 11–11.[8] The media had

---

[7] In a *Washington Post* poll, 82% of respondents said that they approved of the way their local schools were handling the situation (*Washington Post*, 2002b).
[8] Numbers attained by searching for the keyword "sniper," using the Lexis/Nexis "general news search" of 47 major newspapers from throughout the world.

a particularly strong influence in this crisis. Because the events were statistically so rare, and there were so few victims overall, there were startlingly few people outside of the immediate families and close friends of those victims who had any personal experience with "sniping" events.[9] In light of this fact, it is safe to say that members of the public received more than 99% of their information concerning the crisis from the media.[10] To put this statistic in perspective, it can be compared to the findings of an *Los Angeles Times* poll in which respondents claimed their "feelings about crime" were based 65% on what they read and saw in the media, and 21% on experience[11] (Walsh, 1996, p. 9).

The media agencies often looked to alternate sources of information to achieve a competitive edge over one another. It was not uncommon to see "serial killings" experts speaking on news talk shows or to see "geographic profiling" experts doing the same (most notably after Chief Moose announced that geographic profilers were being used in the case). None of these alternate sources could provide any factual information outside of what was already known by the public, as they were not directly connected to the investigation (see Figure 11–10).

As stated earlier, there existed an explicit tension between the media and Chief Moose. This rift was most visible on October 9, when Chief Moose lashed out at the press for publishing information pertaining to a message written on a tarot card found at the school where a 13 year-old boy was shot. In another instance that angered Chief Moose, CNN reported, hours before the information was

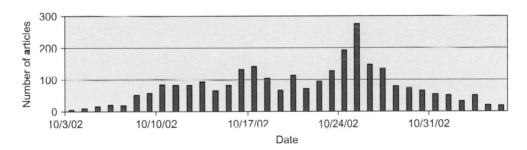

FIGURE 11–11 Number of articles related to the sniper crisis appearing in 47 major international newspapers.

[9] Many people were affected by the secondary effects of the sniper, such as long traffic jams caused by roadblocks or school closings. However, as the direct consequence of the sniper was death or injury caused by shooting, only a very small group was *directly* affected.

[10] Fear of crime, often cited as being overestimated by the public, is also mainly established through media coverage. In the 1990s, when the murder rate in the United States dropped by 20%, the murder coverage on network newscasts increased by 600%. As a result, 62% of Americans "believed crime was soaring, and described our society as 'truly desperate' about crime" (Jacobson, 2001).

[11] The findings of this poll have been reinforced by other studies on the subject. When Esther Madriz, a professor at Hunter College in New York City, interviewed women in New York City about their fears of crime they frequently responded with the phrase "I saw it in the news." The interviewees identified the news media as both the source of their fears and the reason they believed those fears were valid. Asked in a national poll why they believe the country has a serious crime problem, 76% of people cited stories they had seen in the media. Only 22% cited personal experience (Glassner, 1999, p. xxi).

(*Continued*)

officially released, that the 13th shooting victim had died (Shales, 2002). Chief Moose's public scolding of the media (the result of a combination of sustained high levels of stress and inexperience with such high-profile events), however, was limited after the initial statements made in relation to the tarot card.

A fact that must be noted for its uniqueness is that the media was obviously used by the police as a direct mode of communication with the sniper. Chief Moose would "speak" to the sniper using cryptic messages at regularly scheduled press conferences without giving the media any prior indication that he would be doing this. Chief Moose did acknowledge his recognition of this important role the media played, one they were more than willing to fulfill.

The Public

The general public includes, for the sake of this case study, the people of the Washington, D.C., and Richmond, Virginia, metropolitan areas. These people were the vulnerable group involved in the crisis — the sniper's targets. They were also the target of the media's and the authorities' information. The public was not only a target of these other players (including the sniper) but also a major source of information and action. The public demand for information fueled the media frenzy that occurred. Their fear of the sniper was the driving force in many of the decisions, rational or irrational, that were made by the authorities. Finally, the public was an integral component in the hunt for the sniper, and it was tips received from several members of the public that eventually led the police to Malvo and Muhammad.

Public action and reaction became the subject of many stories. This exhibited behavior became the focus of countless articles, detailing "newsworthy" actions that were performed in the name of safety.

Examples of such actions, followed by percentages of the affected population who admitted to performing them, derived from a *Washington Post* poll (if available), include the following:

Used different gas stations than one normally used (Morin and Deane, 2002) — 36%
Avoided stores/shopping centers close to highways (Morin and Deane, 2002) — 32%
Crouched down while pumping gas (Ropeik, 2002a)
Ran or weaved through parking lots (Walker, 2002)
Avoided outdoor activities (Irvin and Mattingly, 2002) — 44%
Kept constant movement in public places (Eccleston, 2002)
Stayed at home except when absolutely necessary (Johnson and Finer, 2002) — 13%
Drove when one would normally have taken Metro (*Washington Post*, 2002b) — 11%
Watched or listened to the news more than usual (*Washington Post*, 2002b) — 71%

Gas station attendants were witness to much of this fear because so many people believed that the stations were a preferred target location of the sniper. One attendant reported that "some people, when they get out of their cars, they are so scared that their hands shake, and they can't get their [credit] cards into the [gas pumps]" (Nakamura and Davis, 2002).

The public was a responsible recipient of this flood of information, and generally followed any behavioral advice they were given by the authorities. They learned the meaning of terms like "Code Blue" and "Code Red,"[12] how to identify .223-firing assault rifles, the meaning of ballistics tests and

---

[12] School security codes — Code Blue signifies that all outdoor activities are canceled and positive ID is required to enter the building, and Code Red signifies that students are locked in their classroom in case a threat actually exists within the building (Lambert, 2002).

what government agency conducts them, and how to identify box trucks, Chevy Astro vans, and ladder racks. The public was told to call in their tips to the FBI tip line, and by the time the sniper was caught, over 90,000 calls had been placed (Whitlock, 2002).

What the public did not do, however, was panic. As much as the media wrote stories detailing the "paralyzing fear" experienced by the average person, life did go on with civility. There were no events where people were pushing each other over to get inside the "safety" of a store, for example. The public was fearful but intelligent, receptive to advice, and obviously able to process information well enough to locate the sniper within 24 hours once they learned the car and license plate information.

So Why Was Everyone So Afraid?

In their article "Rating the Risks," Slovic, Fischhoff, and Lichtenstein (1979) begin as follows: "People respond to the hazards they perceive." The exhibited responses to the sniper at personal, local, regional, and even federal levels would indicate that sources influencing risk perception during the crisis existed at extreme levels. In this section, the sniper crisis will be compared to models developed in recent and historical research in order to better explain the peculiar public risk behavior observed. This examination will be structured according to the four "Risk Perception Fallibility" conclusions of Slovic, Fischhoff, and Lichtenstein found in their 1979 article "Rating the Risks."

Risk Perception Fallibility Conclusion 1: "Cognitive limitations, coupled with the anxieties generated by facing life as a gamble, cause uncertainty to be denied, risks to be distorted, and statements of fact to be believed with unwarranted confidence."

People tend to fear a risk less as they become better informed, with more specific details of the risk. However, the amount a person can discover about a risk will almost never be complete, as the actual likelihood or consequence most risks pose cannot be quantified in a way that addresses the specific threat faced by individuals (even well-known risks such as cancer or heart disease) (Ropeik, 2002c). The more uncertainty a risk poses, or, as Slovic, Fischhoff, and Lichtenstein state, "the more of a gamble something is," the more people will fear it. The sniper, who could strike anyone, anywhere, at any time, presented citizens in the Washington, D.C., metropolitan area with the ultimate in uncertainty.

In the face of uncertainty, people will consciously or subconsciously make personal judgments based on very imperfect information in order to establish some individual concept of the risk they face (Slovic, Fischhoff, and Lichtenstein, 1979). These judgments, based on uncertainties and imperfect information, often cause people to wrongly perceive their own risk, more often in a way that overstates reality. There could scarcely have been more uncertainty in regard to the public's knowledge of useful information in the sniper crisis. Members of the public were constantly told by the media that the police had very little to work with, because the sniper was leaving few clues at crime scenes (Patrick, 2002). People had no idea how great of a threat the sniper was in comparison to other public safety threats the police handled during routine action because these statistics were never released. Considering the amount of resources police dedicated, it would appear that the threat to public safety was greater than anything people in the area had ever faced, and considering the ineffectiveness of

(Continued)

the actions of the police in catching the sniper (such as the systems of roadblocks),[13] the public could assume only that the police were powerless to combat this "enormous" threat. Many other factors external to the investigation gave an impression of dire seriousness and great uncertainty as well. Every time a media "expert" would attempt to define the sniper's actions, stating that he would likely not strike in place X or at time Y, the sniper would strike in that place or at that time. The great number of white vans in circulation gave the impression that the sniper was everywhere.[14] The fact that schools were being closed, outdoor activities were regularly canceled, the government was talking of bringing in the National Guard, and the New York-based Guardian Angels were in the area pumping gas only strengthened the public's view that the risk was greater than it actually was. Frequent talk that the crisis may be the result of terrorism propagated the idea that the sniper might be just the first in a series of snipers that could become a regular part of life in America.[15] In a survey that asked citizens of the Washington, D.C., metropolitan area how concerned they were that they might personally become a victim of the sniper, 19% said a great deal and 31% said somewhat scared — a total of 50% (*Washington Post*, 2002b).

Risk Perception Fallibility Conclusion 2: "Perceived risk is influenced (and sometimes biased) by the imaginability and memorability of the hazard. People may, therefore, not have valid perceptions even for familiar risks."

People are more afraid of those things that they can imagine or that they can remember. These easily available risks, as they are called, tend to be overestimated regarding their likelihood of occurrence. Generally, people tend to fear what they hear about repetitively or constantly. This phenomenon is referred to as the *availability heuristic,* which states that people perceive an event to be likely or frequent if instances of the event are easy to imagine or recall. This is a perception bias that can be corrected when considering events that are, in fact, frequently observed, such as in the case of those who believe that automobile accidents are common because almost everyone they know has been involved in one. However, when a risk that is spectacular but not necessarily common receives constant media

---

[13] In one of the most comprehensive roadblock systems set up after the October 22 shooting (which occurred during the morning rush-hour traffic), one person was quoted in the *Washington Post* as saying that, after getting off the highway and onto the back roads, "I didn't see a single police car on the way in [to his job in College Park, Maryland]. If you're trying to stop someone, you'd have to have a tighter net, and that simply wasn't there. I was a novice trying to make my way through, and it was fairly easy" (Layton and Shaver, 2002).

[14] Mark Warr, a sociology professor at the University of Texas, Austin, writes, "People may experience fear merely in anticipation of possible threats or in reaction to environmental clues (e.g., darkness, graffiti) that imply danger" (Warr, 2000). To many people, the sight of ever-present white vans was a constant reminder that the sniper was still at large. To some, the sight of a white van was influential enough to elicit a physical response. A Connecticut business traveler, working in the area in a white Chevy van, stated, "I pull into a gas station, and people jump down. Little kids point and say, 'Look, the sniper'" (Snyder, 2002).

[15] During the sniper crisis, it was reported in several newspapers that an Al-Qaeda suspect in Belgium had admitted during interrogations that members of Al-Qaeda had been trained in the terrorist training camps to shoot targets from 50 to 250 meters. The suspect added that Al-Qaeda planned to use snipers to kill U.S. senators while they were golfing (Reid, 2002).

attention, such as high-school shootings did in the 1990s (particularly the Columbine attack),[16] people often wrongly assume that similar events are very likely to occur. In the case of the sniper, where coverage in newspapers and on television, radio, and the Internet was constant, receiving front-page placement every day from October 4 until the suspects were captured on October 24,[17] it would follow that people would likely assume their personal risk was greater than it actually was. Again, the omnipresence of white vans and white box trucks, both intimately associated with the sniper crisis through the police and the media, gave people a constant reminder of the sniper. Many of the decisions by government officials to close schools, restrict the movement of students, and cancel outdoor activities altered people's daily lives in such a way that they were made constantly aware of the crisis around them. In addition, seeing sniper victims on TV who were similar to themselves, doing things they regularly did, made it easy for people to imagine succumbing to the same fate.

In an October 13 *Washington Post* poll that asked participants if they felt most threatened by the sniper shootings, the anthrax letters, or the September 11 attacks, 44% responded the sniper shootings, 29% responded the September 11 attacks, and 13% responded the anthrax letters (*Washington Post*, 2002b). Slovic and his colleagues (1979) described how events that are "out of sight [are] effectively out of mind." It would follow that the opposite was true of the sniper: that which is always in sight is always on people's minds.

Risk Perception Fallibility Conclusion 3: "[Risk management] experts' risk perceptions correspond closely to statistical frequencies of death. Laypeople's risk perceptions [are] based in part on frequencies of death, but there [are] some striking discrepancies. It appears that for laypeople, the concept of risk includes qualitative aspects such as dread and the likelihood of a mishap being fatal. Laypeople's risk perceptions were also affected by catastrophic potential."

It can be difficult for people to completely understand the statistics they are given, and even more difficult for them to conceptualize how those statistics apply to them personally. Furthermore, these statistics tend to do little to affect the way people perceive the risks that are calculated. This is not to say that the average person lacks sufficient intelligence to process numbers; it is just that the numbers are not the sole source of influence on public risk perception. In ranking their risks, people tend to rely more on qualitative factors than on the quantitative likelihood of a hazard resulting in personal consequence (Slovic, Fischhoff, and Lichtenstein, 1979). People are generally more concerned with the consequences than the likelihoods of risks.

In consideration of the statistics provided to the public by the media, it is important to examine their quality and usefulness to the recipients. While it is clear that everyone knew the number of people killed by the sniper, few knew the actual number of people living in the affected area or the actual murder rate in "normal" years within that same area. Without complete information, the given statistics were meaningless and likely misleading. In fact, in the absence of complete information, people assumed that their chances of becoming a sniper victim were much greater than they really were. Economists have classified this tendency of people to overestimate unknown or unclear risks as "risk-ambiguity aversion" (*Economist*, 2002). However, even if the statistics were straightforward, it is

---

[16] In 1999, two students of Columbine High School in Littleton, Colorado, shot and killed 13 of their classmates. The extensive media coverage led to the public perception that school shootings were on the rise, when in fact the incidence of school shootings was actually falling that year (Kisken, 2001).

[17] As of November 15, the sniper case was still receiving daily front-page coverage in the *Washington Post*.

(*Continued*)

difficult for people to understand how those numbers affect them as individuals, even if they are risk "experts" (Jardine and Hrudey, 1997).

Slovic, Fischhoff, and Lichtenstein (1980), in their article "Facts and Fears: Understanding Perceived Risk," proposed that there are 18 risk characteristics that influence public risk perception. These qualitative measures have helped to explain what attributes of a risk cause public fear. According to their measures, the risk of being killed by the sniper ranks among the most feared risks, as it is dreaded, has consequences that are fatal, "affects me," is new, is not easily reduced, and is uncontrollable, among other reasons. The sniper risk, not surprisingly, falls close to terrorism and crime on the authors' ranking of risks' ability to elicit fear.

Risk Perception Fallibility Conclusion 4: "Disagreements about risk should not be expected to evaporate in the presence of 'evidence.' Definitive evidence, particularly about rare hazards, is difficult to obtain. Weaker information is likely to be interpreted in a way that reinforces existing beliefs."

The sniper announced his presence with a true mass-murder event.[18] The initial news reports described an ensuing crisis that left open the possibility that the murders may continue at an equally high rate of incidence (five killings in 16 hours). By the end of October 3, police had little to work with, and there was little hope that the sniper would be quickly captured. The public had been told from the very beginning that they were dealing with a killer who was a grave threat to public safety. Due to psychological factors described in the previous three risk perception fallibility conclusions, people were made to believe they were at high risk. This became the frame of reference in which the public was to define the sniper risk, and one that would now be very difficult to alter.

The crisis continued for 3 weeks. Many (often heavily editorialized) articles did try to enlighten people about their actual personal risk, some even giving detailed statistics that illustrated to the public that their vulnerability to the sniper was extremely low. Unfortunately, not only did these articles rarely (if ever) get front-page coverage, but also they were greatly outnumbered by articles telling people that their lives were in grave danger from the sniper. In the end, it was not the "long-shot" statistics or the articles that told people to remain calm that were believed but the fear-mongering and sensational articles given priority coverage by newspapers and news networks. This is not surprising, considering the findings of Slovic, Fischhoff, and Lichtenstein's research. They state that "people's beliefs change slowly and are extraordinarily persistent in the face of contrary evidence. New evidence appears reliable and informative if it is consistent with one's initial belief; contrary evidence is dismissed as unreliable, erroneous, or unrepresentative." They add that "convincing people that the catastrophe they fear is extremely unlikely is difficult under the best conditions. Any mishap could be seen as proof of high risk, whereas demonstrating safety would require a massive amount of evidence" (Slovic, Fischhoff, and Lichtenstein, 1979), evidence that is sometimes impossible to obtain in an accurate or timely manner.

This stoicism is compounded by the fact that once people make their initial judgments, they believe with overwhelming confidence that their beliefs are correct. This phenomenon, called the *overconfidence heuristic*, suggests that people often are unaware of how little they know about a risk and

---

[18] The sniper was, by definition, both a serial killer and a mass murderer. Serial killers are defined as people who kill several people over a period of days, weeks, or years, killing in cycles, shifting between active and "cooling off" periods, while mass murderers kill several people at one time, usually in one location, over a couple of hours without a "cooling off" period (Macalester College, 2002).

how much more information they need to make an informed decision. More often than not, people believe that they know much more about risks than they actually do. With regard to the sniper, having overconfidence in incorrect information was inevitable considering the nature of the media coverage. For instance, with "expert" profilers giving descriptions of the killer's "most likely" demographics as a lone young, white male, it is no surprise that everyone was caught off guard when the pair turned out to be two black males (Fears and Thomas-Lester, 2002). However, with no confirmed information provided about the suspects prior to their arrest, there logically should have been no surprise no matter what race/ethnicity or age he, she, or they were.

This phenomenon has been linked to media coverage of other spectacular events in the past, specifically in regard to the way in which people's rating of risks depends on the amount of media coverage a risk receives. For example, one study showed that the percentage of crimes covered by the media that involve perpetrators and victims of different races is of a greater proportion than occurs in reality. In other words, one is more likely to see a news story describing a white victim of a black attacker than a story depicting a black victim of a black attacker, even though the latter is more common. This inconsistency in coverage is seen as the main reason that Caucasians overestimate their likelihood of being a victim of interracial crime by a factor of 3 (Twomey, 2001). Paul Slovic wrote in his 1986 article "Informing and Educating the Public about Risk" that "strong beliefs are hard to modify" and "naïve views are easily manipulated by presentation format."

Often, it is only time that can change people's opinions about the risks they personally face. One major reason people are more scared of a new risk than an old risk is that they have not been able to gather enough information to alter their initial impression. After time has passed, and they realize that their expectations for victimization have not been realized for themselves or anybody that they know, they begin to question the validity of their views. Had the sniper not been caught, the general public would have gained a more accurate appreciation of how small their chance of becoming a victim was, much in the manner that people are no longer as concerned about the child abductions that seemed to plague the United States during 2001.[19] Fortunately, the sniper was caught before this hypothesis could be tested.

Reality: Statistics of the Crisis

"Of all the grim facts surrounding [the] Oklahoma City [bombing], perhaps the grimmest is the one nobody talks about: against the backdrop of everyday American tragedy, 167 deaths is not many …. In a typical year, guns kill 38,000 Americans and about that many die on our roads. These numbers routinely go up or down 2% or 3% — half a dozen Oklahoma bombings — without making the front page" (political commentator Robert Wright, *Time*, May 1995, cited in Walsh, 1996, p. 18).

In the 3 weeks during which the sniper terrorized more than 5 million people in the Washington, D.C., metropolitan area, shooting 13 people and killing 10, "routine" crime took place virtually unnoticed. In the District of Columbia alone, there were 239 assaults with a deadly weapon, 32 people shot,

---

[19] After a media frenzy followed a series of high-profile child abductions during the early summer of 2001, there was great apprehension reported among parents who began to fear for the safety of their children. Later reports showed that the majority of child abductions were due to child custody disputes and not performed by strangers. The frenzy quickly died down once public knowledge about these facts became more common (STATS, 2002).

(*Continued*)

and 22 people murdered (Barger, 2002). This accounts for just 10% of the total area where the sniper operated, so it can be assumed that there were far more of these "routine" murders than 22. However, not one of these crimes merited front-page coverage in the newspapers.

In the previous section, it was necessary to put aside statistics in order to understand public risk perception, but now the statistics alone must be analyzed to determine how the real risk people faced during those 3 fearful weeks from the sniper compared to the other risks they face in their daily lives without second thought. Richard Wilson of Harvard University writes in his article "Analyzing the Daily Risks of Life" that "to compare risks we must calculate them" (1979, p. 57). To calculate the statistical risk that the citizens of the Washington, D.C., metropolitan area faced, it is necessary to ascertain the population of the area where the sniper operated. These statistics will not be perfect by any means, as they cannot account for the ever-increasing zone in which the sniper operated (*Economist*, 2002). Additionally, although the sniper operated within a large geographic area, there was not an equal distribution of murders across the total area (Montgomery County was the location of seven of these murders, for example). However, these statistics will be more accurate in terms of personal risk (see description in notes 24 and 25), because the virtually random selection of victims who were performing a wide range of activities brings the population and personal risk almost to equality.

To achieve this rough estimate of personal risk, it would be possible to consider the number of victims, divided into the total population of the affected area, spread out over the period in which the sniper was operating. This would not be accurate in projecting future risk, however, because the operating environment changed for the sniper in the early morning of October 3. When the police were not aware of his presence, it was possible for the sniper to repeatedly attack within a short period of time. Shortly after initiation of the crisis, when the sniper's presence was officially recognized, his attacks required more time[20] (presumably for more detailed planning). It is therefore necessary to estimate how the murders would have progressed over the course of a year in the context of a postawareness scenario. In operating under this assumption, it can be said that the four murders that took place on the morning of October 3 would have likely been only one murder had the police been on alert for the sniper. In that case, the statistics to work with are as follows:

- Number of people shot (adjusted for postawareness): 10
- Number of people killed (adjusted for postawareness): 7
- Population, Washington, D.C., metropolitan area:[21] 4,922,152 (83.16% of total sniper-area population)
- Population, Richmond–Petersburg metropolitan area:[22] 996,512 (16.84% of total sniper-area population)
- Population, total affected area: 5,919,152
- Number of days the sniper operated (10/2/02–10/24/02):[23] 23

---

[20] In addition, the sniper attacks waned in frequency over time, but this factor will not be considered because the sampling period was too short to derive a long-term frequency (*Economist*, 2002).

[21] 2000 census information (FAIR, 2002a).

[22] 2000 census information (FAIR, 2002b).

[23] The murders that took place before this date were committed for the purposes of robbery or passion and are therefore not included in the analysis of population risk.

- Multiplier (for 365-day average): 15.870
- National murder rate: 5.5/100,000
- Washington, D.C., metropolitan area murder rate: 7.4/100,000
- Richmond–Petersburg metropolitan area murder rate: 11.1/100,000

Using these numbers, we may derive the following population risk factors for the people living in the area where the sniper operated:

- Chance of being shot by the sniper in the next 12 months:[24] 2.7/100,000 or 1/37,297
- Chance of being killed by the sniper in the next 12 months:[25] 1.9/100,000 or 1/53,325

Comparing these figures against the risks that people face in their daily lives with little or no concern will put the real risk from the sniper into statistical perspective. Table 11–1 lists the likelihood of death from various causes, listed in order of decreasing risk. According to these figures, a

Table 11–1 Likelihood of Death from Various Causes

Hazard	Annual Risk	Lifetime Risk
2000 murder rate, sniper area (weighted)[a]	1/12,870	1/167
2000 murder rate, national	1/18,182	1/236
Car accident[b]	1/18,752	1/244
Accidental fall	1/20,728	1/270
Accidental poisoning	1/22,388	1/292
Murdered with a gun	1/25,196	1/328
Shot by sniper	1/37,297	1/484
Hit by car while walking	1/45,117	1/588
Killed by sniper	1/53,325	1/693
Drowning (accidental)	1/77,308	1/1,008
Fire/smoke inhalation	1/81,487	1/1,062
Lightning	1/4,262,813	1/55,578

[a]The Washington, D.C., metropolitan area (WMA)/Richmond–Petersburg metropolitan area (RPMA) combined crime rate was found by taking the crime rate of the WMA (7.1/100,000) and multiplying it by the WMA percentage of total population area (83.16%), and then taking the RPMA crime rate (11.1/100,000) and multiplying it by the RPMA percentage of total population (16.84%), to give a combined crime rate of 7.77/100,000. The WMA and RPMA 2000 murder rate data are taken from *Crime in the United States, 2000* (FBI, 2001).
[b]See Memmott (2002b). All figures other than those associated with the sniper are attributed to this source.

[24] The number of people in the affected area (5,919,152) divided by the number of people shot during the sniper crisis (10, adjusted), times the year-adjustment multiplier (15.870).
[25] The number of people in the affected area (5,919,152) divided by the number of people killed during the sniper crisis (7, adjusted), times the year-adjustment multiplier (15.870).

(Continued)

person was more likely to be accidentally poisoned or to die in a car accident than to be shot and possibly killed by the sniper. As previously noted, the other risks have higher variance between individual and population risk, as more can be done on the personal level to mitigate them (such as wearing a seat belt or a life preserver), but the fact remains that for the average of all people these statistics are accurate.

Lessons Learned and Future Implications

Now that the sniper crisis has been compared to risk perception models and the population risk statistics have been calculated, we can ask the question, "Should the public have been so deeply fearful during the sniper crisis?" The answer, according to these established models, is yes, they definitely should have been, considering the information they received. However, according to the statistical data and risk comparison, they did not need to be so afraid, and there are ways in which the media, emergency responders, and other federal, state, and local government officials can limit this type of fear in the future.

1. Respond Separately to the Event and to the Fear

The authorities, namely, the police and the government officials, dedicated a vast amount of resources to the sniper investigation because of the high level of public fear and concern, not because of some recognized disproportionate threat to public safety.[26] Conversely, they did little, if anything, to treat the fear itself. When emergency management agencies respond in this way, they can actually amplify the level of anxiety by signaling to the public that their crippling fears are justified,[27] and move emergency management and police resources away from routine but necessary public safety work. These actions increase people's susceptibility to other health-related risks by preventing them from exercising and through the damaging physiological effects of fear-induced stress.[28] Variations of the statement, "People will never feel safe again until the sniper is caught," repeated in every newspaper, echoed the primary motivation behind this large-scale response.

In the future, police and government officials should treat the event and the fear of the event as two separate problems that need to be addressed separately. This is a need that has already been recognized in past crime and terrorism crises (Warr, 2000). There should be a separate function of emergency management — a "fear management team" consisting of members with backgrounds in sociology, psychology, emergency management, public education, and public relations, among others. This team would have several subfunctions, described below.

---

[26] This is not an uncommon action for authorities to take. For instance, the Environmental Protection Agency's Science Advisory Board discovered that "agency resources tend to be directed to problems 'perceived' to be the most serious rather than those that actually pose the greatest threat" (Walsh, 1996).

[27] Barry Glassner writes in *The Culture of Fear* that "the turnabout in [American] domestic public spending over the past quarter century, from child welfare and antipoverty programs to incarceration, did not … produce reductions in *fear* of crime. Increasing the number of cops and jails arguably has the opposite effect: It suggests that the crime problem is all the more out of control" (Glassner, 1999).

[28] James Walsh (1996), author of *True Odds: How Risk Affects Your Everyday Life*, writes, "When European terrorism reared up in 1986, 2 million Americans changed their travel plans. The reality, of course, was that most of these people could have done a lot more to enhance their life expectancies by losing 10 pounds and going to Europe as planned."

Measure levels of public fear: There are established ways in which fear can be measured in real-time status, including by conducting surveys, recognizing behavioral indicators (what people are doing to avoid what they fear — changes in routine, for example), and establishing recognition triggers for "transient public episodes of fear" (how a population is acting as a whole in response to fear — drops in the number of public transportation users, for example) (Warr, 2000). Emergency management can only respond to a high level of fear if they know it exists. Not all events will be as obvious as the sniper crisis.

Develop an informed, educational public relations message: As a part of regular emergency management operations, a trusted leader with decision-making power must be identified and put forth to communicate with the public through the media. The members of the fear management team would process information culled from their monitoring of public fear to create communications through the trusted official in a manner that adequately and accurately addresses public fear. They would develop mental models that give emergency responders a clear understanding of what exactly the public does and does not understand about the risk and what they believe emergency responders are doing and/or are able to do to ensure their security. They would work directly with the emergency response team to inform them about the exact information the public needs to correct or adjust their belief in order to more closely match reality. They would work with government officials as well, helping them to inform the public through reinforcement of the messages given by the emergency response spokesperson.

Address public fear directly: The fear management team would coordinate the services of mental health specialists in an effort to further reduce public fear to more "healthy" levels. These public health officials would address the public directly, through media outlets, or through community groups.[29] Because they would have information directly related to the crisis, they would be able to make accurate and informed communications through the media (unlike the uninformed "experts" that were prevalent during the sniper crisis who did not have access to secure information). The information would not be compromised by this team, because it would not be necessary to share the specifics — however, the public would recognize that the team members, as trusted public health officials, were making informed decisions and would more likely invest more faith in these opinions in adjusting their perceptions.

Assist local government/community authorities in decision making: Both local government and community groups must respond to crises, and their actions often directly affect the public. School superintendents need to know when it is appropriate to cancel school, and community groups need to know when public events must be postponed. Without direction from emergency response (the most "informed" source of information), they will not act with consistency and will likely send a mixed message to the public. In addition, the overreaction by one influential government or community leader can lead to secondary responses from other less organized or less informed groups.[30] This fear

---

[29] In Loudoun County, a community group formed after 9/11 to help people cope with the stress gave free public seminars on the sniper stress (Helderman and Goldenbach, 2002).
[30] Barry Glassner, author of *The Culture of Fear*, wrote, "Since the first sniper shooting October 2, a sort of domino effect has spurred decision-makers: School systems have decided, in conference calls with local law enforcement arranged through the Washington Council of Governments, to suspend all outdoor activities. Then day-care centers and youth soccer leagues have followed the lead of their public school systems, and the smaller community groups have fallen into line" (Reel, 2002).

(Continued)

management team would serve as an advisory board for government and community groups, ensuring that their leaders are able to make decisions based on the most complete and current information, and allowing the groups to work in consensus rather than as separate entities.

2. Increase Responsible Reporting by the Media

The media have a responsibility to ensure that during crisis events, public safety information reaches a wide audience in a timely and accurate manner, a duty they are recognizing and embracing more each year (Moore, 2002). However, most newspaper and television news employees have never received crisis communications training and, therefore, have no idea how to fulfill this role. The media operate as a business and are motivated primarily by ratings and viewer and reader numbers, which ensure steady income generation; the media cannot be expected to cease provisions of blanket coverage during extreme events such as the sniper crisis. The industry functions within a time-compressed environment in which editors often must develop stories using incorrect or incomplete information. Journalists will continue to proactively seek information on crises using their own means, and there will always be leaks made to the media by emergency management and public officials.

The media are adroit at using scare tactics and fear-mongering to harness public attention and often do little to calm nerves once that attention is obtained. These agencies must learn as an industry that they can contribute to public safety by providing accurate, responsible, and useful information while still maintaining these traditional "shock" methods to attract viewers, and thereby preserve a competitive edge without sacrificing integrity. For the media to participate in a crisis response constructively, they need to add to the glut of sensationalism a balance of rationality — a reality check for the public to process information and judge individual risk. If they broadcast a message that says, "Four of the victims were shot while pumping gas at local gas stations," for example, they need to qualify this statement by adding, "however, there have been approximately 10.5 million gas transactions made at over 1,000 gas stations in the affected area during the crisis so far" (Memmott, 2000b), in order to give adequate perspective to the original statement. Emergency management must recognize the media as willing participants in the process and provide them with this information that may not be readily available otherwise.

The media should recognize and act upon the public's tendency to anchor and adjust[31] in forming perceptions on risk. This cannot be denied. If a story informs citizens that "this is the greatest number of law enforcement officers ever dedicated to a criminal investigation in county history,"[32]

---

[31] The anchoring and adjustment heuristic states that people use a natural starting point as a first approximation in analyzing how a risk affects them. The initial anchoring point is then adjusted as more information is received (Slovic, Fischhoff, and Lichtenstein, 1979). (Anchors are generally set according to the first information a person receives about a risk.)

[32] In a CNN article titled "Sniper Probe 'Unprecedented' for Region," it was reported that "a conservative estimate would put at 1,000 the number of officers and experts from various federal, state, and local law enforcement officers assigned to the case, and the size of the investigation grows with each new development — and shooting — in the case" (Loughlin, 2002).

readers may incorrectly infer that their lives are at greater risk than ever before,[33] and all future information will be processed within this context. If they are later told in an article that is given proportional emphasis,[34] for instance, that, "although 10 people have been killed by the sniper in the past 3 weeks, there are an average of 38 people killed in traffic accidents alone during the same time period in the Washington, DC, metropolitan area" (Memmott, 2002b), they will be able to rank their personal risk more appropriately.

Media agencies must also avoid irresponsible reporting aimed at "creating" stories. Martha Moore of *USA Today* cites as an example of this phenomenon the many cases in which local news stations will make announcements, before a coming storm, for example, that "people should prepare by stocking up on batteries and water before the stores run out of these items." Following this statement, the news agency will post teams at local stores to report that people are crowding these local stores in order to get their hands on the few remaining batteries and bottles of water, causing successive waves of panic buying[35] (Moore, 2002). Similar situations occurred during the sniper crisis. The media would report that "gas stations are the preferred location of the sniper," and then run stories showing how people were not going to gas stations, which had the snowball effect of making consumers progressively more afraid to visit gas stations.

The media agencies are not villains. Quite to the contrary, they are a vital component to emergency management without which risk communication would be nearly impossible. Also, not all of today's media reporting is misinformed or irresponsible. There are many news agencies that employ reporters who are trained or knowledgeable in crisis communications and risk perception and who regularly practice the suggestions made above. For example, in a *USA Today* article titled "How to Cope? Keep Guard and Spirits Up," the author suggested that residents of the DC area "take a lesson from people in other nations who confront such fears every day: Get on with life — but be more alert than ever to dangers and more kind than ever to others" (Memmott, 2002a). The knowledge and experience of reporters like this must be shared across the industry. The journalist's goal is to provide

---

[33] Irresponsible reporting has not only caused undue stress on numerous occasions, but also hurt local economies as well. In the 1990s, the media widely reported on a crime wave against tourists in Florida, which resulted in 10 murders. Barry Glassner (1999), author of *The Culture of Fear*, writes that the event was labeled a crime wave only because the media chose to label it as such. "Objectively speaking, 10 murders out of 41 million visitors did not even constitute a ripple, much less a wave, especially considering that at least 97% of all victims of crime in Florida are Floridians. Although the Miami area had the highest crime rate in the nation during this period, it was not tourists who had most cause for worry. One study showed that British, German, and Canadian tourists who flock to Florida each year to avoid winter weather were more than 70 times more likely to be victimized at home." This type of reporting made many tourists think twice before traveling to Florida, and the tourism industry suffered as a result.

[34] Often, articles that proclaim bad news are given front-page coverage and are in great quantity while those reported good news are given secondary status and appear less frequently (Johnson, 2002).

[35] The phenomenon observed when people irrationally stock up on certain "survival" groceries they believe will be needed but unavailable after a disaster occurs.

(*Continued*)

the public with timely information; the extent to which that information is both accurate and effective depends largely on the level of cooperation provided by emergency management.

3. Establish Public Risk Perception and Risk Communication Training Standards for Emergency Management, Government Officials, and the Media

The federal government requires both emergency responders and public officials to complete training and prove competencies in performing many of the tasks associated with their job duties. While many first responders who communicate directly with the public are trained in public relations and communications, they are often not trained in crisis communications, risk perception, or risk communication. Their support teams, who provide the information on which their public response is based, are just as likely to lack adequate training in these areas. A statement from an ATF agent who described the extensive damage a .223 bullet fired from a rifle does to the human body and the MPD safety tip that reminded residents that a sniper could hit victims from 500 yards are examples of statements that neither provided useful information to the public nor controlled fear. If emergency responders and government officials are to effectively treat the fear associated with a crisis, they must be trained in methods that have proved successful in the past and develop a clear understanding of what drives human fear. Training in these studies will not become institutional unless the need is recognized throughout the emergency management sector. These training opportunities must also be made available to the media in order to ensure a comprehensive approach to fear management. If this training is conducted through a partnership between media and emergency management, interpersonal relationships will likely be created, thus further enhancing fear management.

If training in risk perception and risk communication became a requirement for emergency management public relations — related tasks, fear management would become a routine organizational function. The existence of a fear management team, as proposed above, would be better understood and utilized across all functions of emergency management agencies if management-level employees had a more comprehensive understanding of its purpose. Industry observance of this requirement would be more accepted if the federal or state government covered the costs for this training as they do for many other law enforcement and public safety programs.

Chief Moose did an outstanding job as a crisis manager and leader, but he did little to combat fear directly. Considering the lack of experience among emergency response officials with terrorism in the United States, it is unlikely that many of them would be prepared to take on such a difficult task as fear management. However, if the threat of terrorism is growing, as the FBI and the DHS claim it is, then the need for such training is obvious.

4. Seize the Opportunity during Periods of Increased Public Attention for Risk Education

Almost every person in the Washington, D.C., metropolitan area and likely the entire United States can say with confidence that they know what a .223 caliber bullet is and what it looks like, can identify Bushmaster as a brand of rifle, can tell approximately how far (in meters) a sniper can hit a target, can describe a box truck, and knows what a ladder rack on a Chevy Astro van looks like. When people are afraid, they pay attention and they learn. It cannot be overlooked that despite the number of police looking for the sniper, it was a truck driver who located the sniper after learning the make, model, and license plate number of the sniper's vehicle on the news.

People will listen to emergency response and government suggestions if the source of information is trusted and holds decision-making authority.[36] These rare mass-education opportunities must not be wasted. Emergency managers have a moral obligation under such circumstances to inform people of the real risks they face and tell them what they need to do to protect themselves from those risks. Telling people to weave while going through a parking lot during the sniper crisis is likely to make people think twice about going to the store, but it is unlikely that the information will save more than a few, if any, lives. Telling people that if they feel the need to drive long distances to purchase gas in order to feel safe, then they must also be sure to wear their seat belt because car accidents are a much more likely killer than the sniper, instantly contributes to a decrease in risk of thousands of people.

Modified Information Flow Diagram: The Road Ahead

On March 1, the emergency management functions of the federal government were officially transferred to the DHS. Secretary Tom Ridge has been given exactly 1 year to reorganize and improve the functions of 22 absorbed agencies in a way that more effectively prevents, prepares for, responds to, and recovers from future terrorist attacks (and natural and technological disasters). Concurrently, the states have been spending billions of their own dollars to prevent and prepare for terrorist attacks, primarily following the direction of the federal government. This opportunity to improve current emergency management systems must not pass by without a full examination of the vital importance of managing public fear.

The information flow diagram shown in Figure 11–12 is provided as a possible solution to managing fear at the local level. The diagram depicts how a fear management team would operate within the overall flow of crisis information and within the range of emergency management activities. Federally funded crisis communications training is displayed in order to indicate the likely recipients of this training. Although this design is simplified, it can be easily adapted to suit the needs of almost any local emergency response to a crisis that captures extensive public attention. Figure 11–12 does not directly address where the additional resources provided in federally declared disasters would apply or how the command structure would accommodate these resources, as it remains to be seen how the DHS reorganization will alter existing response systems.

Conclusion

Fear is irrational only if people have enough information about a hazard to perform a personal risk analysis, find that the likelihood of the hazard affecting them is smaller than or equal to risks they face on a daily basis with little or no thought, and are still afraid. When there are little or no means for people to gather information to make informed personal risk analyses, they tend to overestimate

---

[36] People tend to heed government suggestions, so they should be rational and helpful, and, most importantly, carefully thought out. During the anthrax crisis, when public fear was at epidemic levels, 36% of Americans were washing their hands after opening mail as the U.S. Postal Service had instructed them to do. In areas where people had actually contracted anthrax-related sicknesses, hand-washing incidence was higher — 45% in Washington, D.C., and 57% in Trenton, New Jersey — this from an attack that killed only 5 of over 400 million people. People were not acting irrationally, but listening to the advice they had been told by their government (Pelton, 2001). The government warned the public not to hoard the antibiotic Cipro, but the media reported they were stockpiling the drug to such an extreme as to cause pharmacy shortages. Surveys showed that only 4% of Americans had bought the antibiotic against the advice of the government.

(*Continued*)

CASE STUDY 2: WASHINGTON, DC, SNIPER ATTACKS (CONTINUED)

personal vulnerability because of incomplete and often incorrect information. Only information can combat fear, and only the government (in partnership with the media) can provide for that need.

On November 7, 2002, two people in New York City were hospitalized and confirmed to be infected with bubonic plague — the first cases in that city in more than 100 years. Bubonic plague is a disease that is historically one of the greatest killers of humankind, decimating over a third of the population of Europe during the Middle Ages. To the people of New York City, this disease was dreaded, new, fatal, globally catastrophic, involuntary, and notoriously hard to control. Why did fear not reign in New York when this information hit the newsstands? The answer lies in the way the information was first reported by Dr. Thomas Frieden, the health commissioner of New York City (a city that has in recent years experienced two major health crises — the first U.S. outbreak of West Nile virus and the anthrax letters in 2001). After announcing the two cases of the disease, Dr. Frieden made the following statement:

Bubonic plague does not spread from person to person. There is no risk to New Yorkers from the two individuals who are being evaluated for plague. Those patients became ill within 48 hours of arriving in New York City. Therefore, we are confident that their exposure occurred in New Mexico. More than half of the plague cases in the United States are in New Mexico. A wood rat and fleas from the rodent that were found on the couple's property in Santa Fe, New Mexico, tested positive in July for plague. Bubonic plague is a bacterial disease in rodents transmitted to humans through the bites of infected fleas (CNN, 2002).

The story barely lasted a week.

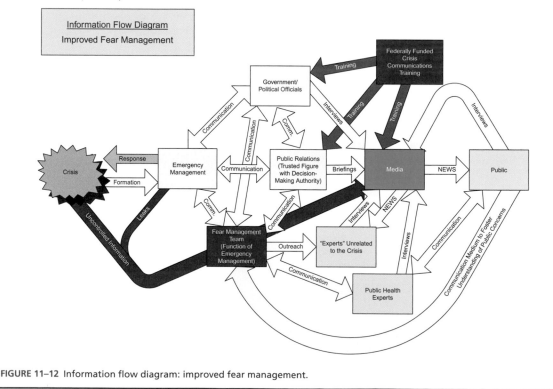

FIGURE 11–12 Information flow diagram: improved fear management.

Key Terms

Comprehensive Emergency Management: An emergency management philosophy that seeks to reduce risk and prevent injuries, damages, and fatalities by treating hazards before, during, and after an event has occurred. There are generally four accepted functions performed in comprehensive emergency management: mitigation, preparedness, response, and recovery.

Crisis Communication: The provision of timely, useful, and accurate information to the public during the response and recovery phases of a disaster event.

Mass Media: Channels of communication for popular consumption, which could include books, magazines, advertisements, newspapers, newsletters, radio, television, the Internet, cinema, theater, and videos, among many others.

National Terrorism Advisory System: A robust terrorism advisory system that provides timely information to the public about credible terrorist threats and replaced the former color-coded Homeland Security Advisory System (HSAS).

News Media: A subcomponent of the mass media focused on presenting current news to the public.

Ready.gov: A government-sponsored website developed by the Advertising Council to educate the public, businesses, and children about hazard risks in the United States.

Risk Communication: Any communication intended to supply laypeople with the information they need to make informed, independent judgments about risks to health, safety, and the environment (Morgan et al., 2002).

Warning: The delivery of notice of an actual impending threat with sufficient time to allow recipient individuals and communities to take shelter, evacuate, or take other mitigative action in advance of a disaster event.

Review Questions

1. Identify and discuss the four critical assumptions underlying the crisis communications efforts of the Federal Emergency Management Agency (FEMA) in the 1990s.
2. Discuss the role of the mass media in risk and crisis communications.
3. Review the content and communication delivery mechanisms used in the Department of Homeland Security's Ready.gov campaign. Do you feel this is useful information that could effectively prepare the public for a disaster?
4. How would you reengineer the Homeland Security Advisory System (HSAS)? How many alert levels would you include, what colors and titles would you associate with each alert level, and what preparedness messages designed for individuals and communities would you associate with each alert level?
5. In reviewing the case study of the Washington, D.C., sniper attacks, it is clear that Montgomery County Police Chief Charles Moose was the principal government spokesperson and appeared in front of the media daily. In many of his media appearances, Chief Moose had little information to share with the media and the public principally because of the sensitive nature of the ongoing criminal investigation to identify and apprehend the snipers. These media appearances were a unique opportunity for Chief Moose to deliver preparedness messages to the community. Identify those preparedness messages that Chief Moose did deliver to the community over the course of the sniper crisis and provide suggestions of additional preparedness messages he could have delivered.

References

Airline Industry Information (AII), 2002. BALPA issues advice to concerned crew traveling to Washington, DC (October 18).

Altheide, D.L., 2002. Creating Fear: News and the Construction of Crisis. Aldine de Gruyter, New York.

Anderson, P. 2002. Sniper suspect linked to tacoma shootings. Seattlepi.com (October 28). http://seattlepi .nwsource.com/local/93210_tacoma28ww.shtml.

Ansell, J., Wharton, F., 1992. Risk: Analysis, Assessment, and Management. John Wiley & Sons, Chichester, England.

Atwater, B.F., Marco, C.V., Bourgeois, J., Dudley, W.C., Hendley II, J.W., Stauffer, P.H., 1999. Surviving a Tsunami — Lessons Learned from Chile. USGS Information Services, Hawaii, and Japan. Washington, DC.

Barger, B., 2002. At the intersection of bravado and fear. The Washington Post, November 3, B2.

Barker, J., 2002. Montgomery seeks to ensure safety of voters. The Baltimore Sun, October 22, 1B.

BBC News, 2008, Burmese blog the cyclone (May 8). http://www.news.bbc.co.uk/2/hi/asia-pacific/7387313.stm.

Bowman, S., Willis, C., 2003. We Media: How Audiences are Shaping the Future of News and Information. The Media Center at the American Press Institute. http://www .hypergene.net/wemedia/download/we_media.pdf.

Bremer, A.L., Bremer, P., 2002. The terrorist threat. In: Ethiel, N. (Ed.), Terrorism: Informing the Public. McCormick Tribune Foundation, Chicago, pp. 14–39.

Brown, J.D., Keller, S.N., 2000. Can the mass media be healthy sex educators? Family Planning Perspectives 32 (5), 255–256.

Bullock, J., 2003. Several Interviews over a 2-Month Period with the Former FEMA Chief of Staff. Washington, DC.

Burkhart, F.N., 1991. Media, Emergency Warnings, and Citizen Response. Westview Press, Boulder, CO.

Burma News, 2008. Burmese journals face restriction on cyclone coverage (May 13). http://www.myamarnews .blogspot.com/2008/05/burmese-journals-face-restrictions-on.html.

Catone, J., 2007. Online citizen journalism now undeniably mainstream, readwriteweb. (October 26). http://www .readwriteweb.com/archives/online_citizen_journalism_ mainstream.php.

CBS News, 2002. A deadly journey? crimes and clues. http:// www.cbsnews.com/htdocs/maryland_ murders/frame-source.html, 540,400.

Centers for Disease Control and Prevention, 2002. Suicide in the United States. National Center for Injury Prevention and Control. www.cdc.gov/ncipc/factsheets/suifacts .htm.

Chemical and Biological Arms Control Institute, 2002. What Should We Know? Whom Should We Tell? Leveraging Communication and Information to Counter Terrorism and Its Consequences. Michael J. Powers, Project Director. Washington, DC, December.

Chronicle, H., 2002. Sniper's score: 5 shots, 5 dead. Houston Chronicle, October 4, A1.

Clines, F. 2002a. Widening fears, few clues as sixth death is tied to sniper. New York Times, October 5, p. A1.

Clines, F., 2002b. The hunt for a sniper. New York Times, October 15, p. A1.

CNN, 2002. Bubonic plague suspected in NYC visitors. CNN.com (November 7). http://www.cnn.com/2002/ health/11/07/ny.plague/index.html.

Cohen, B.C., 1963. The Press and Foreign Policy. Princeton University Press, Princeton, NJ.

Connor, T., Kennedy, H., 2002. Cops flood site of VA shooting. Daily News (New York) October 20, 3.

Cooper, G., 2007. Burma's bloggers show power of citizen journalism in a crises. Reuters Alert Net (October 3). http:// www.alertnet.org/db/blogs/30708/2007/09/3-134022-1 .htm.

Coppola, C. P., MD. Series of interviews. Dr. Coppola operated on the 13-year-old boy who was shot at the middle school in Bowie, Maryland, on October 7, 2002.

Coppola, D., 2002. Unpublished research on public risk perception in Mexico City, Mexico.

De Morales, L., 2002. Did on-the-spot coverage put lawmen on the spot? The Washington Post, October 24, C1.

Department of Homeland Security (DHS), 2003. Ready.gov website. Washington, DC: DHS. http://www.ready.gov.

Diaz, K., Rourke, L.O., 2002. D.C. area breathes easier, but not deeply. Star Tribune (Minneapolis), October 25, 20A.

Disaster Management Center, 1995. Disaster preparedness. The University of Wisconsin. http://www.dmc.engr.wisc.edu/courses/preparedness/BB04-intro.html.

Dishneau, D., 2002. Virginia shooting linked to sniper spree. The Toronto Star, October 6, A9.

Ebner, J., Herring, L., 2002. In disasters, panic is rare; altruism dominates. American Sociological Association (August 7). http://www.asanet.org/media/panic.html.

Eccleston, R., 2002. Killings have Washington terrorized. The Australian, October 14, 12.

Economist, 2002. The logic of irrational fear. The Economist October 19.

Enders, J., 2001. Measuring community awareness and preparedness for emergencies. Australian Journal of Emergency Management, Spring, 52–59.

Fears, D., Thomas-Lester, A., 2002. Blacks express shock at suspects' identity. The Washington Post, October 26, A17

Federal Bureau of Investigation, 2001. Crime in the United States, 2000. The Federal Bureau of Investigation (FBI) Uniform Crime Reports. Washington, DC: FBI (October 22).

Federal Emergency Management Agency (FEMA), 1997. Multi Hazard Identification and Assessment. FEMA, Washington, DC.

Federal Emergency Management Agency (FEMA), 1998. Making Your Community Disaster Resistant: Project Impact Media Partnership Guide. FEMA, Washington, DC.

Federation for American Immigration Reform, 2002a. PMSA. Washington, DC. http://www.fairus.org/html/msas/042dcwdc.htm.

Federation for American Immigration Reform, 2002b. Richmond-Petersburg metropolitan area. http://www.fairus.org/html/msas/042varip.htm.

FEMA, 2007. National Incident Management System: FEMA 501/Draft August 2007. FEMA, Washington, DC.

FEMA, 2011. Use of Social Media Tools at FEMA, http://www.fema.gov/news/newsrelease.fema?id=49302.

Fernandez, M., 2002. Brentwood postal plant fumigation postponed. The Washington Post, November 13, B3.

Ferrara, L., 2007. AP's "NowPublic" Initiative, Remarks at the Associated Press Managing Editors' Conference. Fast Forward to the Future (October 2). http://www.j-lab.org/apme07notesp5.shtml.

Fineman, H., 2002. The "anxiety election." National Affairs, October 21, 32.

Furedi, F., 1997. Culture of Fear. Risk-Taking and the Morality of Low Expectation. Cassell, London.

Furman, M., 2002. Good information saves lives. In: Ethiel, N. (Ed.), Terrorism. Informing the Public. McCormick Tribune Foundation, Chicago, pp. 54–57.

Gettleman, J., 2002. The hunt for a sniper: The scene. New York Times, October 21, A14.

Gillmor, D., 2006. We the Media: Grassroots Journalism by the People, for the People. O'Reilly Media Inc.

Gillmor, D., Hattotuwa, S., 2007. Citizen journalism and humanitarian aid: boon or bust? ICT for Peacebuilding. http://ict4peace.wordpress.com/2007/07/30/citizen-journalism-and-humanitarian-aid-bane-or-boon/.

Glaser, M., 2007. California Wildfire Coverage by Local Media, Blogs, Twitter, Maps and More. MediaShift (October 25). http://www.pbs.org/mediashift/2007/10/the listcalifornia_wildfire_co_1.html.

Glassner, B., 1999. The Culture of Fear. Basic Books, New York.

Global Voices Online, Myanmar cyclone 2008. http://www.globalvoicesonline.org/specialcoverage/myanmar-cyclone-2008/.

Government Executive Magazine, 2008. DHS says responders resistant to communications sharing. GovExec.com (April 2). http://www.govexec.com/story_page.cfm?articleid539677&sid560.

Government Printing Office, 2002. U.S. Code Title 28, Part II, Chapter 33, Section 540B. http://www.access.gpo.gov/uscode/uscmain.html.

Haddow, G., 2003. Several interviews over a 2-month period with the former FEMA deputy chief of staff. Washington, DC.

Hattotuwa, S., 2007. Who is afraid of citizen journalists? Communicating Disasters, TVA Asia Pacific and UNDP Regional Centre in Bangkok, 2007.

Helderman, R., Goldenbach, A., 2002. Autumn's diversions disrupted. The Washington Post, October 20, T3.

Higham, S., Kovaleski, S., 2002. Encounters with sniper suspects. The Washington Post, November 3, A1.

Hurdle, J., 2002. Holidaying in the line of fire. The Daily Telegraph (London), October 19, 4.

Instituto Ciudadano de Estudios Sobre la Inseguridad A.C., 2002. Primera encuesta nacional sobre inseguridad publica en las entidades federativas. Mexico City. May.

Irvin, C.W., Mattingly, D., 2002. Anxiety becomes part of daily routine. The Washington Post, October 17, T3.

Jacobson, L. 2001. Media — the perception of panic. McGill Tribune via U-Wire, November 14.

Jardine, C.G., Hrudey, S.E., 1997. Mixed messages in risk communication. Risk Analysis 17 (4), 489–498.

Johnson, D., Finer, J., 2002. Sniper casts shadow of fear over weekend. The Washington Post, October 13, C1.

Johnson, P., 2002a. Out in TV land, "local news is in bad shape." USA Today Online, November 11.

Johnson, P., Moore, M., 2002b. Media reports touch raw nerves in Washington. USA Today, October 10, 2A.

Jones, E.F., Beniger, J.R., Westoff, C.F., 1980. Pill and IUD discontinuation in the United States, 1970–1975: The influence of the media. Fam. Plann. Perspect. 12 (6), 293–300.

Kennedy, H., Mbugua, M., Pienciak, R., 2002. Cops hunt two targets. The Daily News (New York), October 24, 2.

Kettl, D.F., September 2005. The Worst Is Yet to Come: Lessons from September 11 to Hurricane Katrina. Fels Institute of Government, University of Pennsylvania.

Kisken, T., 2001. Climate of fear overblown, sociologist says. Ventura County Star, November 6, B1.

Kornblut, A., 2002. Elusive sniper joins DC's nightmares. The Boston Globe, October 20, A1.

Kovaleski, S., Ruane, M., 2002a. Hundreds of leads to a gunman. The Washington Post, October 7, A1.

Kovaleski, S., Ruane, M., 2002b. Boy, 13, shot by sniper at school. The Washington Post, October 8, A1.

Kovaleski, S., Williams, M., 2002c. Experts suggest motive is tied to crafts store. The Washington Post, October 16, A13.

Kurtz, H., 2002. The leak that sank the suspects. The Washington Post, October 25, C1.

Laituri, M., Kodrich, K., 2008. On Line Disaster Response Community: People as Sensors of High Magnitude Disasters Using Internet GIS. Sensors, Colorado State University. http://www.mdpi.org/sensors/papers/s8053037.pdf.

Lambert, R., 2002. The Washington sniper is not the only fear stalking the United States right now. The Times (London), October 18.

Layton, L., Shaver, K., 2002. Experts, travelers question efficacy of massive dragnets. The Washington Post, October 23, A17.

Lichtblau, E., van Natta, D., 2002. The hunt for a sniper. New York Times, October 25, A1.

Lippmann, W., 1922. Public Opinion. Free Press, New York.

Lochhead, C., 2002. One year later. San Francisco Chronicle, September 12, A17.

Loughlin, S., 2002. Sniper probe "unprecedented" for region. CNN Washington Bureau (October 24).

Macalester College, 2002. Serial Killers. http://www.macalester.edu/academics/psychology/whathap/ubnrp/serialkillers/serialkillers.html.

May, A.L., 2006. First Informers in the Disaster Zone: The Lessons of Katrina. The Aspen Institute.

McCallum, D.B., Hammond, S.L., Morris, L., 1990. Public Knowledge of Chemical Risks in Six Communities. Georgetown University Medical Center, Institute for Health Policy Analysis, Washington, DC.

McCombs, M., Shaw, D., 1972. The agenda-setting function of mass media. Public Opin. Q 36, 176–187.

McCormick Tribune Foundation, 2002. Terrorism: Informing the public. In: Ethiel, N. (Ed.), Cantigny Conference Series. McCormick Tribune Foundation, Chicago, pp. 173–193.

McDivitt, J.A., Zimicki, S., Hornik, R., Abulaban, A., 1993. The impact of the healthcom mass media campaign on timely initiation of breastfeeding in Jordan. Stud. Fam. Plann. 24 (5), 295–309.

Memmott, M., 2002a. How to cope? Keep guard and spirits up. USA Today, October 18, 6A.

Memmott, M., 2002b. Fear may be overwhelming, but so are the odds. USA Today, October 18, 6A.

METRO, 1998. Washington Metropolitan Area Transit Authority. National Transit Database. http://www.ntdprogram.com/NTD/Profiles.nsf/19981301Largest1Agencies/3030/$File/P3030.PDF.

Miga, A., 2002a. Sniper "witness" arrested. The Boston Herald, October 19, 3.

Miga, A., 2002b. Death penalty sought for sniper. The Boston Herald, October 26, 1.

Miga, A., Rothstein, K., 2002c. Zeroing in. The Boston Herald, October 24, 1.

Mileti, D.S., 1999. Disasters by Design. Joseph Henry Press, Washington, DC.

Miller, J., 2002. Who? how? when? what? where? In: Ethiel, N. (Ed.), Terrorism: Informing the Public. McCormick Tribune Foundation, Chicago, pp. 50–54.

Moore, M.T., 2002. Presentation at the NAS Natural Disasters Roundtable. National Academy of Sciences, Washington, DC. October 31.

Morello, C., Stockwell, J., 2002a. No attacks, no arrests, no shortage of anxiety. The Washington Post, October 14, A1.

Morello, C., White, J., 2002b. Eighth killing linked to sniper. The Washington Post, October 12, A1.

Morello, C., Davenport, C., Harris, H., 2002c. Pair seized in sniper attacks. The Washington Post, October 25, A1.

Morgan, M.G., Fischoff, B., Bostrom, A., Atman, C.J., 2002. Risk Communication: A Mental Models Approach. Cambridge University Press, Cambridge.

Morin, R., Deane, C., 2002. Half of area residents in fear, post poll finds. The Washington Post, October 24, A1.

Mullis, J.-P., 1998. Persuasive communication issues in disaster management. Aust. J. Emerg. Manage. (Autumn), 51–58.

Nakamura, D., Davis, P., 2002. Suddenly, D.C. gas looks cheap enough. The Washington Post, October 15, A7.

Naudet, J., Naudet, G., 2001. September 11 Documentary. CBS. Two-hour film shot during the September 11 World Trade Center attack response.

Nelken, D., 1987. Selling Science: How the Press Covers Science and Technology. W.H. Freeman, New York.

Nielsen, S., Lidstone, J., 1998. Public education and disaster management: Is there any guiding theory? Aust. J. Emerg. Manage. (Spring), 14–19.

Ottawa Citizen, 2002. Canadians told to avoid Washington. The Ottawa Citizen, October 13, A8.

Partnership for Public Warning (PPW), 2003. A national strategy for integrated dissemination of public policy and capability. http://www.partnershipforpublicwarning.org/ppw/docs/nationalstrategy.pdf.

Partnership for Public Warning (PPW), 2008. PPW mission. http://www.partnershipforpublicwarning.org/ppw/about.html#mission.

Patrick, A., 2002. Eight dead, but still no real clues. Sunday Age (Melbourne), October 13, 1.

Pelton, T., 2001. 36% of Americans wash up after handling mail. The Baltimore Sun, December 18, 8A.

Perspectives.org, 2002. Friend's apparent accidental shot lodges near brain. http://www.perspectivescs.org/guns/example2.htm.

Phillips, C., 2002. Malvo spent childhood looking for father figure. The Seattle Times, November 21, A1.

Pienciak, R., Kennedy, H., 2002. Sniper's ransom. The Daily News (New York), October 22, 3.

Piotrow, P.T., Rimon, J.G., Winnard, K., Kincaid, D.L., Huntington, D., Convisser, J., 1990. Mass media family planning promotion in three Nigerian cities. Stud. Fam. Plann. 21 (5), 265–274.

Raphael, B., 1986. When Disaster Strikes: How Individuals and Communities Cope with Catastrophes. Basic Books, New York.

Rashbaum, W., Flynn, K., 2002. Sniper hits a teacher at Stuyvesant town. New York Times, October 3, B1.

Reel, M., 2002. A region running scared? The Washington Post, October 19, A1.

Reid, T., 2002. Al Qaeda trained snipers for U.S. attacks. The Times (London), October 19, 21.

Rennie, D., 2002. Sniper stretches city's nerves to breaking point. The Daily Telegraph (London), October 22, 10.

Rincon, J., 2008. Myanmar: Citizen videos in Cyclone Nargis aftermath. Reuters Global News Blog (May 16). http:// www.blogs.reuters.com/global/tag/burma/.

Ropeik, D. 2002a. Fear factors in an age of terrorism. MSNBC Online (October 15).

Ropeik, D., 2002b. We should fear too much fear. Mil. J. Sentinel, October 23, 23A.

Ropeik, D. 2002c. Presentation on risk perception. The National Academy of Sciences Roundtable on Natural Disasters, October, p. 31.

Ruane, M., Stockwell, J., 2002. Montgomery bus driver fatally shot. The Washington Post, October 23, A1.

Schulte, B., 2002. Schools shaken by threat but won't shut down. The Washington Post, October 23, A1.

Select Bipartisan Committee to Investigate the Preparation for and Response to Hurricane Katrina, 2006. A failure of initiative: Final report of the special Bipartisan Committee to investigate the preparation for and response to Hurricane Katrina. Government Printing Office (February 15). http://www.gpoacess.gov/congress/index.hmtl.

Self Knowledge, 2002. Definition of fear. http://www .selfknowledge.com/35217.htm.

Shales, T., 2002. TV news feels its way in dark times. The Washington Post, October 23, C1.

Shirky, C., 2008. Here Comes Everybody: The Power of Organizing Without Organizations. The Penguin Press, New York, NY.

Shrader-Frechette, K.S., 1991. Risk and Rationality. University of California Press, Berkeley.

Singer, E., Endreny, P.M., 1993. Reporting on Risk: How the Mass Media Portray Accidents, Diseases, Disasters, and Other Hazards. Russell Sage Foundation, New York.

Slovic, P., 1986. Informing and educating the public about risk. Risk Analysis 6 (4), 403–415.

Slovic, P., Fischhoff, B., Lichtenstein, S., 1979. Rating the risks. Environment 21 (3), 14–20, 36–39.

Slovic, P., Fischhoff, B., Lichtenstein, S., 1980. Facts and fears: Understanding perceived risk. In: Schwing, R., Albers Jr., W.A. (Eds.), Societal Risk Assessment: How Safe Is Safe Enough? Plenum, New York, pp. 181–214.

Slovic, P., Fischhoff, B., Lichtenstein, S., 1996. Cognitive processes and societal risk taking. In: Carroll, J.S., Payne, J.W. (Eds.), Cognition and Social Behavior. Lawrence Erlbaum Associates, Potomac, MD, pp. 165–184.

Snyder, D., 2002. Fear is traveling the lanes of I-95. The Washington Post, October 21, A14.

Stabe, M., 2007. California wildfires: A round up. OJB Online Journalism Blog (October 25). http:// www .onlinejournalismblog.com/2007/10/25/california-wildfires-a-roundup/.

STATS, 2002. Abducting the headlines. http://www.stats .org/newsletters/0208/abduction.htm.

Stephen, A. 2002. America — Andrew Stephen reports on panic in Washington. New Statesman, Ltd (October 22).

Stockwell, J., Ruane, M., White, J., 2002. Man shot to death at Pr. William gas station. The Washington Post, October 10, A1.

Sun, L.H., Ly, P., 2002. Story "not about me," reserved Moose says. The Washington Post, October 28, A10.

The Australian, 2002. Sniper search goes airborne. The Australian, October 17, 8.

Thomas, P. 2003. The Anthrax Attacks. New York: The Century Foundation (June 1).

Timberg, C., Shear, M., 2002. Dragnet comes up empty again. The Washington Post, October 21, A1.

Townsend, F.F., 2006. The Federal Response to Hurricane Katrina Lessons Learned. The White House, February 2006.

Tresniowski, A., Podesta, J.S., Morehouse, M., Billups, A., 2002. Stalked by fear. People Magazine, October 28, 58.

Twomey, J., 2001. Media fuels fear about youth crime. The Baltimore Sun, May 13, 1C.

Vulliami, E., 2002. America stays indoors as sniper roams free. The Observer, October 13, 1.

Wagner, M., 2007. Google Maps and Twitter are essential resources for California fires. Information Week (October 24). http://www.informationweek.com/blog/main/archives/2007/10/google_maps_and.html.

Walker, W., 2002. Terror grips D.C. region. Toronto Star, October 23, A20.

Wallace, C. 2002. A new kind of killer? ABC News (October 15).

Walsh, J., 1996. True Odds: How Risk Affects Your Everyday Life. Merrill Publishing, Santa Monica, CA.

Ward, B., 2001. History's lessons lost in the turmoil. The Ottawa Citizen, September 18, A10.

Warner, K.E., 1989. The epidemiology of coffin nails. In: Moore, M. (Ed.), Health Risks and the Press: Coverage on Media Coverage of Risk Assessment and Health. The Media Institute, Washington, DC, pp. 73–88.

Warr, M., 2000. Fear of crime in the United States Avenues for research and policy. In: Duffee, D. (Ed.), Measurement and Analysis of Crime and Justice. National Institute of Justice, Rockville, MD, pp. 451 489.

Washington Post, 2002a. Crime and justice. The Washington Post, October 3, B2.

Washington Post, 2002b. Washington area sniper poll. The Washington Post, October 24.

Washkuch, F., 2008. Relief groups turn to Twitter amid crises. PR Week (May 20). http://www.prweekus.com/Relief-groups-turn-to-Twitter-amid-crises/article/110368/.

Watson, D., 2000. Statement of Mr. Dale Watson, Asst. Director, FBI Counterterrorism Division, before the Subcommittee on National Security. U.S. House of Representatives (March 22).

Watson, R., 2002. Suburbs in terror of the Beltway sniper after boy is shot. The Times (London), October, 8.

Waugh Jr., W.L., 2000. Living with Hazards, Dealing with Disasters: An Introduction to Emergency Management. M.E. Sharpe, New York.

Wenham, B., 1994. The media and disasters: Building a better understanding. In: Cate, Fred H. (Ed.), International Disaster Communications: Harnessing the Power of Communications to Avert Disasters and Save Lives. The Annenberg Washington Program., Washington, DC http://www.annenberg.northwestern.edu/pubs/disas/disas6.htm

Westoff, C.F., Rodriguez, G., 1995. The mass media and family planning in Kenya. Int. Fam. Plan. Perspect. 21 (1), 26–31, 36.

Whitlock, C. 2002. The sniper case: Out of 90,000 calls, just 3 broke it open. Post Gazette (Pittsburgh) (October 25). http://www.post gazette.com/nation/20021025probenat2p2.asp.

Wiggins, C., 2002. Warm waters attract people and sharks. The Standard (Baker County), March 27.

Willis, J., 1997. Reporting on Risks: The Practice and Ethics of Health and Safety Communication. Praeger, Westport, CT.

Wilson, R., 1979. Analyzing the daily risks of life. Technology Review 81 (4), 41–46.

Winston, J.A., 1985. Science and the media: The boundaries of truth. Health Aff. 6, 5–23

Witzer, M., 1997. In sub-Saharan Africa, levels of knowledge and use of contraceptives are linked to media exposure. Int. Fam. Plan. Perspect 23 (4), 183–184.

YouTube, http://www.youtube.com/user/AfterNargisYgn.

12
Science and Technology

What You Will Learn

- How homeland security research and development funding is distributed among various federal government agencies
- What research and development efforts are performed by the Department of Homeland Security, and by what offices that work is done
- Where in the federal government structure research and development are performed in the areas of weapons of mass destruction and information and infrastructure
- The names and functions of the various government research facilities
- The source and function of maritime homeland security research
- Where homeland security research and development efforts are occurring outside the Department of Homeland Security

Introduction

The Department of Homeland Security (DHS) announced at the time of its establishment that it "is committed to using cutting-edge technologies and scientific talent" to create a safer country. In this vein, the Science and Technology Directorate (S&T) was formed, which still exists today despite the many iterations of DHS organizational change. The S&T Directorate was tasked under the original development plans with assuming the research needs of the new department, and for organizing the scientific, engineering, and technological resources of the country in order to adapt their use to the newly recognized needs under the counterterrorism drive created by the September 11, 2001, terrorist attacks. Universities, the private sector, and federal laboratories have all become important DHS partners in this endeavor.

Tens of billions of dollars have already been spent by DHS and other agencies with related missions on developing and exploiting technologies for use in the fight against terrorism and, on occasion, for emergency management in general. As is true in all areas of research, not all of the technology developed has been successful, although many innovative and useful systems have resulted. These efforts come not without critics, and many people have expressed sentiments that the push toward increased use of technological solutions does not necessarily decrease vulnerabilities, but rather increases reliance on technologies that could fail. For this reason, there remains significant dissent over the actual overall value of technology as a homeland security tool.

Despite these controversies, it is undeniable that the way of life in the United States has changed as the result of a great investment in technology by the federal government. This chapter examines that investment and offers different views on its value.

Overview of Involved Agencies and Budgets

Although the DHS has the most prominent stake in homeland security–related research efforts, there are many other agencies that are involved in homeland security R&D efforts dispersed throughout the federal government. As DHS was gaining center-stage prominence in the homeland security effort and was emerging as a leading agency for these issues, many research and scientific programs were under way under the other agencies' management that preceded the Department's creation. The efforts of these organizations were almost immediately given new direction and resources to use in the fight against a more prominent terrorist hazard — a "shot in the arm," so to speak. Table 12–1 lists the agencies involved in the homeland security R&D field and their recent budgets.

The American Association for the Advancement of Science in its 2011 report of the Federal Government's FY 2012 budget noted, "Federal homeland security-related R&D would decline 0.8 percent to $5.9 billion in FY 2012. R&D in the Department of Homeland Security (DHS), for example, serves the three missions of administration of justice, general science, and transportation. The majority of the multi-agency portfolio remains outside the Department of Homeland Security (DHS), with the second largest part in NIH for its biodefense research portfolio. NIH's portfolio, mostly in the National Institute of Allergy and Infectious Diseases (NIAID), would total $1.9 billion in FY 2012 (up 3.1 percent). The largest agency contributor, DOD, with a decrease of 11.0 percent to $2.1 billion, would be the main reason for the decline in R&D investment in homeland security" (AAAS, 2011). Figures 12–1 and 12–2 show funding distribution by agencies and years.

Department of Homeland Security

Before the establishment of DHS, most R&D efforts dealing with issues relevant to homeland security were dispersed among a wide variety of agencies, and this situation remains. However, the clear trend since 2003 has been to make DHS a focus for such R&D, and as of 2008 over one-fifth of all R&D

Table 12–1 Federal Homeland Security R&D Appropriations ($ in millions)

Agency	FY 2002	FY 2003	FY 2004	FY 2005	FY 2006	FY 2007	FY 2008	FY 2009	FY 2010	FY 2011
Agriculture	175	155	40	161	105	45	129	97	85	88
Commerce	20	16	23	73	62	59	68	76	135	177
DOD	259	212	267	1,079	1,270	1,175	1,278	1,505	2,376	2,115
Energy	50	48	47	67	68	68	71	81	89	90
DHS	266	737	1,028	1,240	1,300	1,005	996	1,033	887	1,054
EPA	95	70	52	33	40	41	53	74	66	42
HHS	177	1,653	1,724	1,795	1,827	1,829	1,815	2,106	1,871	1,929
NASA	73	73	88	89	93	97	94	109	20	6
NSF	229	271	321	326	329	329	357	358	370	395
DOT	106	7	3	2	3	1	2	1	0	0
All others	0	0	32	42	41	42	40	36	47	4
Total	1,451	3,243	3,626	4,893	5,138	4,691	4,902	5,475	5,946	5,900

Source: Office of Management and Budget, Budget of the U.S. Government FY 2008, 2008, http://www.whitehouse.gov/omb/budget/fy2008/; American Association for the Advancement of Science (AAAS), 2011, AAAS XXXVI: Research and Development FY2012, http://www.aaas.org/spp/rd/rdreport2012/.

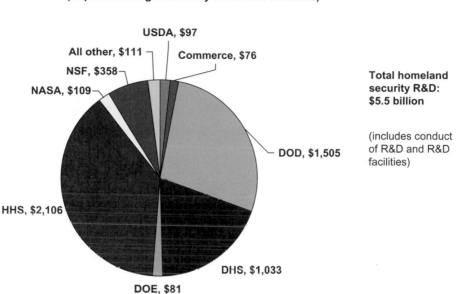

FY 2009 Federal Homeland Security R&D, by Agency
(requested budget authority in millions of dollars)

USDA, $97
All other, $111
Commerce, $76
NSF, $358
NASA, $109

Total homeland security R&D: $5.5 billion

(includes conduct of R&D and R&D facilities)

DOD, $1,505

HHS, $2,106

DHS, $1,033

DOE, $81

FIGURE 12–1 Distribution of the FY 2009 federal funds between agencies (in millions of dollars). (Source: AAAS, 2011, based on Office of Management and Budget data. Includes conduct of R&D and R&D facilities. March '08 REVISED © 2008 AAAS)

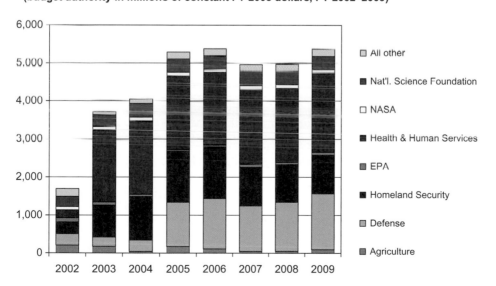

Federal Homeland Security R&D, by Agency
(budget authority in millions of constant FY 2008 dollars, FY 2002–2009)

☐ All other
■ Nat'l. Science Foundation
☐ NASA
■ Health & Human Services
▣ EPA
■ Homeland Security
☐ Defense
▣ Agriculture

FIGURE 12–2 Federal homeland security R&D budget authority by agency (in millions of dollars). (Source: AAAS, 2011. Based on Office of Management and Budget data. Includes conduct of R&D and R&D facilities. Note: DOD expanded its reporting of HS spending beginning in 2005. MARCH '08 REVISED © 2008 AAAS)

funding is managed by DHS (placing it second only after HHS). Inside DHS, the S&T Directorate has been established in order to coordinate and manage R&D efforts. For the first 3 years of the directorate's existence, R&D efforts were dispersed throughout the various directorates and independent agencies (e.g., the Coast Guard). However, as early as FY 2006, all R&D efforts were consolidated under S&T. A more detailed description of S&T and the research this directorate conducts follows.

DHS Science and Technology Directorate

The Science and Technology Directorate (S&T), led by an undersecretary of homeland security, is the primary R&D office within the Department of Homeland Security. Since November 12, 2009, S&T has been led by Dr. Tara O'Toole. In her testimony at two Congressional hearings held in March 2011, Dr. O'Toole outlined the current vision for S&T to achieve its mission to "strengthen America's security and resiliency by providing knowledge products and innovative technology solutions for the Homeland Security Enterprise." The following sidebar presents excerpts from Dr. O'Toole's testimony.

Excerpts from testimony of Dr. Tara O'Toole, Under Secretary for Science and Technology Directorate (S&T) before the House Committee on Science, Space, and Technology on March 15, 2011, and before the House Committee on Appropriations, Subcommittee on Homeland Security, "S&T Fiscal Year 2012 Budget Request" on March 30, 2011.

The mission of the S&T Directorate is to:

Strengthen America's security and resiliency by providing knowledge products and innovative technology solutions for the Homeland Security Enterprise.

Congress created S&T as part of the Homeland Security Act of 2002 to "conduct basic and applied research, development, demonstration, testing, and evaluation activities relevant to any or all elements of the Department." S&T also has a statutory responsibility to transfer useful technologies and information to state and local governments, the first responder community and the private sector.

During the past eight years, S&T has undergone many changes and continues to mature. Because DHS's mission is so broad, S&T's work must address a wide and varied range of programs. DHS is primarily an operational agency, and its components need analyses and technologies that provide near-term improvements in operational effectiveness; our staff serves as the technical core of the Department. Moreover, some of S&T's most important contributions are not technologies alone, but knowledge products — assessments of technical problems or feasible solutions; analyses of complex issues; objective tests of proposed technologies; and the creation of consensus standards which enable cost-effective progress across many fields.

S&T is the main source of scientific expertise and technological research and development for DHS, and it provides vital homeland security-related knowledge and technologies to the nation's first responders.

In the past eight years, S&T has undergone many changes and continues to evolve. Because the mission of the Department of Homeland Security is extraordinarily broad, S&T's work must address a wide and varied array of programs. These range from technical analyses, to the development of new technologies, to the adaptation of existing technologies in support of near-term operational needs.

The president's FY 2012 budget requests $1.2 billion for the DHS S&T Directorate. I fully recognize that in today's fiscal environment, S&T must be a responsible steward of taxpayers' dollars and must address critical technological challenges facing the Homeland Security Enterprise of today and tomorrow in an efficient and cost-effective manner. The budget request before you represents investments that are critical to the security of our nation.

Since I became Under Secretary in November 2009, the Directorate has established a process of ongoing review of our entire R&D portfolio to ensure that we are investing in technologies that will have significantly improved DHS's efforts to make America secure. We are working closely with Component leaders across the Department to identify and solve high-priority problems. One way we are doing this is through the establishment of an office dedicated to serving First Responder needs. This office is led by a former fire chief who reports directly to me.

We are also placing more emphasis on ensuring that our research and development projects transition to use in the field, and we have instituted new approaches to make sure we leverage R&D investments and technologies already developed or under way by other federal agencies, universities, and the private sector. We have also sought to be innovative in our business practices as well as in our scientific endeavors.

The Department of Homeland Security cannot fulfill its missions without the creation and effective use of technology. The complexity and breadth of available technologies relevant to DHS' purposes, the rapid pace of technological change, and the scale and varied environments within which DHS must operate make S&T's task extremely challenging. Through these initiatives, combined with the talent of S&T staff and the support of Congress, the S&T Directorate can meet these challenges to the benefit of the Department and the nation.

Source: Testimony of the Honorable Dr. Tara O'Toole, Under Secretary for Science and Technology Directorate, before the House Committee on Science, Space, and Technology, Release Date: March 15, 2011, http://www.dhs.gov/ynews/testimony/testimony_1300132944135.shtm; Under Secretary Tara O'Toole, Science and Technology Directorate, before the House Committee on Appropriations, Subcommittee on Homeland Security, S&T Fiscal Year 2012 Budget Request, Release Date: March 30, 2011, http://www.dhs.gov/ynews/testimony/testimony_1301519363336.shtm.

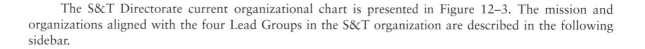

The S&T Directorate current organizational chart is presented in Figure 12–3. The mission and organizations aligned with the four Lead Groups in the S&T organization are described in the following sidebar.

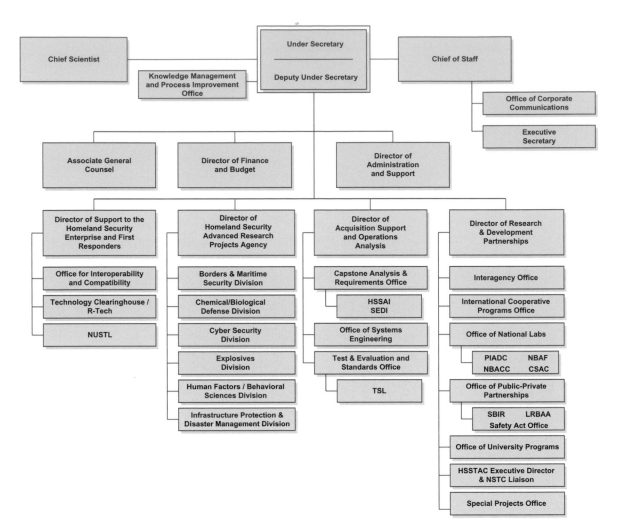

FIGURE 12–3 Science and Technology Directorate organizational chart. (Source: DHS, 2011)

DHS Science and Technology Directorate Lead Groups

- The Director of Support to the Homeland Security Enterprise and First Responders Group (FRG) identifies, validates, and facilitates the fulfillment of First Responder requirements through the use of existing and emerging technologies, knowledge products, and the acceleration of standards. This organization manages working groups, teams, and stakeholder outreach efforts to better understand the requirements of first responders. FRG manages the following offices:

Office of Interoperability and Compatibility

Technology Clearinghouse/R-Tech

National Urban Security Technology Laboratory (NUSTL)

- The Director of Homeland Security Advanced Research Projects Agency manages a portfolio of highly innovative programs that are transforming the future mission space for Homeland Security. HSARPA projects push scientific limits to address customer-identified needs. HSARPA manages the following technical divisions:

Borders & Maritime Security Division develops and transitions tools and technologies that improve the security of our nation's borders and waterways, without impeding the flow of commerce and travel.

Chemical/Biological Defense Division works to increase the nation's preparedness against chemical and biological threats through improved threat awareness, advanced surveillance and detection, and protective countermeasures.

Cyber Security Division

Explosives Division develops the technical capabilities to detect, interdict, and lessen the impacts of non-nuclear explosives used in terrorist attacks against mass transit, civil aviation, and critical infrastructure.

Human Factors/Behavioral Sciences Division develops the technical capabilities to detect, interdict, and lessen the impacts of non-nuclear explosives used in terrorist attacks against mass transit, civil aviation, and critical infrastructure.

Infrastructure Protection & Disaster Management Division focuses on identifying and mitigating the vulnerabilities of the 18 critical infrastructure and key assets that keep our society and economy functioning.

- The Director of Acquisition Support and Operations Analysis (ASOA) serves as a conduit for Department components seeking support on a range of technical and analytical requirements and document development throughout the acquisition life cycle. ASOA is made up of three primary components including:

Office of Systems Engineering (SYS)

Capstone Analysis & Requirements Office (CAR)

Test & Evaluation and Standards Office (TES)

- The Director of Research and Development Partnerships (RDP) conducts effective stakeholder outreach and engagement through close partnerships with eight Departments of science and technology groups. The RDP groups include:

Interagency Office

International Cooperative Programs Office

Office of National Laboratories

Plum Island Animal Disease Center (PIADC)

National Biodefense Analysis and Countermeasures Center (NBACC)

National Bio- and Agro-Defense Facility (NBAF)

Chemical Security Analysis Center (CSAC)

Office of Public–Private Partnerships

Small Business Innovative Research Office (SBIR)

Long Range Broad Agency Announcement Office (LRBAA)

SAFETY Act Office
Commercialization Office
Office of University Programs
Homeland Security Science and Technology Advisory Committee (HSSTAC)
Executive Director & National Science and Technology Council (NSTC) Liaison
Special Projects Office

Source: DHS, 2011, http://www.dhs.gov/xabout/structure/editorial_0530.shtm.

In her Congressional testimony before the House Committee on Appropriations, Subcommittee on Homeland Security on March 30, 2011, Dr. O'Toole stated that "S&T instituted an inclusive and comprehensive strategic planning process" that resulted in the development of five strategic goals for S&T. Dr. O'Toole also outlined planned S&T activities to "address all five mission areas described in the 2010 Quadrennial Homeland Security Review, and include both late-stage "applied" technology development efforts, and more fundamental research." The following sidebars "S&T Strategic Goals" and "Science and Technology Directorate Research, Development, and Innovation Activities" present Dr. O'Toole's detailed explanations of current S&T goals and activities.

S&T Strategic Goals

S&T Goal #1 — Rapidly develop and deliver knowledge, analyses, and innovative solutions that advance the mission of the Department.

- *Ongoing Review of the R&D Portfolio*
- *Becoming Best-in-Class at Technology Foraging, Outreach to Private Sector*

S&T Goal #2 — Leverage S&T's technical expertise to assist DHS Components' efforts to establish operational requirements, and to select and acquire needed technologies

- *Test and Evaluation*
- *Supporting Departmental Acquisition Requirements and Systems Engineering*

S&T Goal #3 — Strengthen the Homeland Security Enterprise and First Responders' capabilities to protect the homeland and respond to disasters

S&T Goal #4 — Conduct, catalyze, and survey scientific discoveries and inventions relevant to existing and emerging homeland security challenges

- *Supporting University Centers of Excellence*
- *Stewardship of Laboratory Infrastructure for Homeland Security*

S&T Goal #5 — Foster a culture of innovation and learning in S&T and across DHS that addresses mission needs with scientific, analytic, and technical rigor.

- *Build a Culture of Innovation and Learning*
  The full text of this document is available on the companion website.

Source: DHS, 2011, Under Secretary Tara O'Toole, Science and Technology Directorate, before the House Committee on Appropriations, Subcommittee on Homeland Security, S&T Fiscal Year 2012 Budget Request, http://www.dhs.gov/ynews/testimony/testimony_1301519363336.shtm.

Science and Technology Directorate Research, Development, and Innovation Activities

The S&T Directorate is supporting over 200 projects in its R&D portfolio. These projects address all five mission areas described in the 2010 Quadrennial Homeland Security Review, and include both late-stage "applied" technology development efforts, and more fundamental research. The purpose of these projects is motivated by mission needs and "capability gaps" identified by DHS components and first responder representatives. Some current projects are long-standing efforts (e.g. explosive detection efforts), while others are just getting under way (e.g., bulk currency detection).

The selection of projects described here is not comprehensive, but is meant to be representative of the range and variety of research responsibilities within the Directorate that are supported by the FY 2012 budget request. Many of these projects could warrant an extended briefing, which we would be happy to provide. In addition to the support to NBAF mentioned above, the FY 2012 budget request includes funding to support the following projects.

Mission 1: Preventing Terrorism and Enhancing Security

- Explosives Detection
- Preventing and Detecting a Chemical or Biological Terrorist Attack
- Preventing Agro-terrorism
- Infrastructure Protection

  Mission 2: Securing and Managing Our Borders
  Mission 3: Enforcing and Administering Our Immigration Laws

- Identity Verification

  Mission 4: Safeguarding and Securing Cyberspace

- Protecting Internet Usage
- Protecting the Internet Infrastructure
- Protecting the User

Mission 5: Ensuring Resilience to Disasters

- Critical Infrastructure Resilience
- Tools for the First Responder
- Resilience to Chemical, Biological, Radiological, and Nuclear (CBRN) Attacks

---

Source: DHS, 2011, Under Secretary Tara O'Toole, Science and Technology Directorate, before the House Committee on Appropriations, Subcommittee on Homeland Security, S&T Fiscal Year 2012 Budget Request, http://www.dhs.gov/ynews/testimony/testimony_1301519363336.shtm. See the companion website for the full text of this testimony.

S&T Budget

The amount of funding under the overall DHS budget dedicated to science and technology has steadily risen each year since the department's creation. This growth signifies the steadily increasing role that technology is taking on in modern emergency management, especially in the area of terrorism prevention and response. It is important to remember that these funds are only in addition to similar project funds being supplied by many other federal agencies, which together comprise a much larger homeland security–related R&D budget (see Tables 9–2 and 12–2).

In her Congressional budget testimony, Dr. O'Toole noted that as a result of the Quadrennial Homeland Security Review (QHSR) and the Bottom-Up Review (BUR) concluded in 2010, S&T had realigned its "existing projects into a budget structure that provides a framework that effectively supports our strategic goals and initiatives and aligns with the DHS BUR. This budget structure allows greater transparency into S&T R&D work while encouraging multi-disciplinary approaches to solve the diverse problems within the homeland security mission. This structure clearly aligns S&T funding to the functional missions that we are addressing" (DHS, 2011). See sidebar "S&T and Quadrennial Homeland Security Review (QHSR) and the Bottom Up Review (BUR)."

Table 12–2 Department of Homeland Security R&D (S&T Directorate) Budget ($ in millions)

FY 2004	FY 2005	FY 2006	FY 2007	FY 2008	FY 2009	FY 2010	FY 2011	FY 2012
$912,751	$1,115,450	$1,467,075	$846,916	$830,118	$932,587	$1,006,471	$1,006,471	$1,176,432 (requested)

S&T and Quadrennial Homeland Security Review (QHSR) and the Bottom Up Review (BUR)

BUR Review

Strengthen DHS ability to protect cyber networks. DHS is responsible for the protection of Federal networks (the .gov domain), excluding civilian national security systems. However, further efforts are needed to effectively fulfill this responsibility. To this end, DHS will increase its cybersecurity activities for Federal civilian networks (excluding civilian national security systems) to ensure that national cybersecurity requirements are met, as well as additional resources to develop the capabilities necessary to effectively implement those authorities in close collaboration with other departments and agencies. In order to keep pace with emerging threats and new technologies, DHS will also seek to use new models for developing, acquiring, and disseminating cybersecurity technology, including technology leasing arrangements, technical service agreements, and development of secondary markets for cybersecurity technology among State, local, tribal, and territorial governments. Finally, DHS' effort to "design-in" greater resilience for critical infrastructure to ensure national security requirements are met will include a cybersecurity focus.

BUR Review — Day in the Life of DHS
Science and Technology Directorate will:
- Lead 200 projects to provide solutions to protect us from chemical, biological, and explosive attacks, provide security for our borders and shores, protect key parts of our infrastructure, and mitigate the effects of natural disasters.
- Assess 22 technology companies for product applicability to first responder customers, develop standards for first responder technologies to ensure high quality transitions, and provide test and evaluation services for DHS.

QUAD Review
Goal 4.2: Promote Cybersecurity Knowledge and Innovation
Ensure that the Nation is prepared for the cyber threats and challenges of tomorrow. Cybersecurity is a dynamic field, and cyber threats and challenges evolve at breathtaking speed. Education, training, awareness, science, technology, and innovation must flourish in order to meet this challenge. While we must protect the Nation from cyber attacks that occur today, we must also prepare now to mitigate the most consequential cybersecurity risks that the United States and its people will face in 5, 10, and 20 years. We must make long-term investments that sustain a safe, secure, and reliable cyber environment, enable prosperity, further social and community uses of the Internet, and facilitate transactions and trade, while safeguarding privacy and civil liberties.

Objectives
Invest in innovative technologies, techniques, and procedures: Create and enhance science, technology, governance mechanisms, and other elements necessary to sustain a safe, secure, and resilient cyber environment. Cyberspace's inherent characteristics demand constant innovation in order to effectively counter threats. Small vulnerabilities can lead to severe challenges in securing the Nation's vast—and vastly critical information infrastructure. Relatively small investments in adversary attack capabilities can require disproportionately large investments in defense. Technology will assist us, and better ways of using technology and people will allow us to bring capabilities to bear more effectively. There must be continuous emphasis on cyber research, development, innovation, and interoperability, which drives advances in technologies, techniques, and procedures. As part of the homeland security enterprise, government should work creatively and collaboratively with the private sector to identify tailored solutions that both take into account the need.

Enhance Shared Awareness of Risks and Threats
Screen and verify identity: Establish a robust approach to identity verification that safeguards individual privacy and civil rights. Robust procedures to screen and verify identities are critical to helping accurately identify people and assess risk. Future systems will need to be increasingly secure,

efficient, easy to use, and flexible. Ongoing research into emerging technologies will help to expand screening and verification capabilities. At the same time, we must adhere to privacy standards and ensure that we fully respect individual rights and liberties. Information needed to achieve homeland security objectives must be collected and used consistent with applicable law and policy. Training, audits, and other oversight mechanisms are essential to ensuring information is used lawfully and appropriately.

Mature the Department of Homeland Security

Improve DHS's organizational and programmatic alignment and its management systems and processes. DHS must lead by example. Ensuring unity of effort across the homeland security enterprise requires unity of effort within the Department. Critical to unifying DHS is improved organizational alignment, particularly among DHS headquarters components, enhanced programmatic alignment to the homeland security missions, and more efficient and effective management processes, including strategic planning, performance management, and accounting structure. DHS must complete a thorough review of its own organizational structures and programmatic activities, align programs and budgets to homeland security missions, and strengthen its management processes. This work began during the QHSR process and continues through the Department's bottom-up review.

Foster Innovative Approaches and Solutions Through Leading-Edge Science and Technology

Ensure scientifically informed analysis and decisions are coupled to innovative and effective technological solutions. We must be able to address a highly dynamic, broad, and ever-changing spectrum of threats, vulnerabilities, and disaster scenarios and to design and implement cost-effective operational and technological solutions across a wide array of operational contexts, in a manner that protects American values. Although many of the security threats now confronting the United States are driven by the global diffusion of technology, science and technology can also provide new and more effective methods for preventing and mitigating these threats, as well as natural disasters. The Federal Government must have a robust research effort in homeland security that is grounded in sound science, and a rigorous and disciplined approach to technology development, acquisition, and deployment.

Objectives

Scientifically study threats and vulnerabilities: Pursue a rigorous scientific understanding of current and future threats to homeland security and the possible means to their prevention and mitigation. A comprehensive and vivid understanding of the probability and potential consequences of homeland security threats and hazards and the relative risk they pose forms the strategic foundation of the homeland security enterprise. Ongoing analyses of threats, vulnerabilities, and the efficacy of our countermeasures by both the public and private sectors will inform homeland security priorities and help ensure that investments and operations focus on the most urgent problems and the most effective means for addressing them.

Develop innovative approaches and effective solutions: Encourage and enable innovative approaches to critical homeland security challenges, fostering collaborative efforts involving government, academia, and the private sector. Achieving the goals of the core homeland security missions will require scientific research to discover new knowledge and methods that can be applied to homeland security challenges, and the creation of new technologies and new ways of thinking about problems and possible solutions. Technological feasibility, operational requirements, training needs, and financial sustainability must all be considered in developing and deploying new technologies. We must seek to foster a rich and wide-ranging capacity to identify and think through complex and unfamiliar problems and to formulate effective and inventive solutions spanning many difficult and varied operational contexts. We must engage a wide range of stakeholders in this endeavor, including government laboratories, universities, federally funded research and development centers, and the private sector.

Source: DHS, 2010, Quadrennial Homeland Security Review Report, http://www.dhs.gov/xlibrary/assets/qhsr_report.pdf; DHS, 2010, Bottom Up Review Report, http://www.dhs.gov/xlibrary/assets/bur_bottom_up_review.pdf.

The American Association for the Advancement of Science in its report on the S&T FY 2012 budget request notes, "R&D for DHS has been divided between the Science and Technology Directorate (S&T) and the Domestic Nuclear Detection Office (DNDO). However, as proposed in FY 2011, DHS again proposes moving DNDO's only R&D program, Transformational Research and Development, to be funded at $109 million, to S&T. The total FY 2012 budget request for S&T is $1.18 billion, a 16.9% increase from the FY 2010 funding level of just over 1.0 billion. S&T's Research, Development, and Innovation budget would increase 14.3% from $577 million in FY 2010 to $660 million in FY 2012. Laboratory Facilities would increase 84.1% from $150 million in FY 2010 to $277 million in FY 2012. University Programs would decrease by 25.9% from $49 million in FY 2010 to $37 million in FY 2012" (AAAS, 2011).

The following sidebar details the new budget structure for S&T that was presented by S&T Under Secretary O'Toole in her testimony to Congress.

Realignment of the S&T Budget Structure

Over the past year, S&T has been part of the unprecedented departmental effort to develop and implement the Quadrennial Homeland Security Review (QHSR) and the Bottom-Up Review (BUR), which established a strategic framework and programmatic structure for homeland security missions and goals. In addition to realigning S&T, we realigned our existing projects into a budget structure that provides a framework that effectively supports our strategic goals and initiatives and aligns with the DHS BUR. This budget structure allows greater transparency into S&T R&D work while encouraging multi-disciplinary approaches to solve the diverse problems within the homeland security mission. This structure clearly aligns S&T funding to the functional missions that we are addressing.

Research, Development and Innovation (RD&I)

RD&I provides state-of-the-art technology and/or solutions to meet the needs of the operational components of the Departments and the first responder community.

	FY10/FY11CR1	FY12
Research, Development & Innovation	$598.5	$659.9
RD&I APEX STORE	$0.0	$17.9
Border Security	$47.7	$43.0
Bioagent Threat Assessment	$59.5	$44.3
Bioagent Detection	$47.7	$50.4
Bioagent Attack Resiliency	$49.5	$50.0
Chemical Threat Assessment	$13.4	$10.0
Chemical Detection	$20.6	$16.7
Chemical Attack Resiliency	$23.9	$19.2
Explosives Threat Assessment	$14.6	$21.1
Explosives Detection	$106.2	$101.2
Explosives Attack Resiliency	$21.6	$13.0
Rad/Nuc Detection	$0.0	$98.7
Rad/Nuc Resiliency	$0.0	$10.3
Natural Disaster Threat Assessment	$0.0	$2.5
Natural Disaster Detection	$0.0	$1.1
Natural Disaster Resiliency	$60.0	$20.2
Information Sharing, Analysis, & Interoperability	$35.4	$23.7
First Responder Capability	$27.5	$25.7
Cyber Security	$41.7	$64.1
Hostile Behavior Predict and Detect	$22.7	$14.6
Identity Management	$6.3	$12.2

Acquisition and Operations Support

Provides expert assistance with transition, acquisition, and deployment of technologies, and information to DHS components and entities across the Homeland Security enterprise.

	FY10/FY11CR	FY12
Acquisition & Operations Support	$65.3	$54.2
Operations Research & Analysis	$13.1	$11.7
Standards	$22.2	$16.5
T&E	$8.5	$6.6
Safety Act	$8.9	$8.9
Technology Transition Support	$12.6	$10.4

Laboratory Facilities

The Office of National Laboratories has responsibility to ensure that required infrastructure laboratory facilities will support the ongoing Science and Technology mission of research and development activities.

	FY10/FY11CR	FY12
Laboratory Facilities	$150.2	$276.5
NBAF Design & Construction	$32.0	$150.0
Infrastructure Upgrades	$5.0	$18.2
Laboratory Operations	$83.2	$77.4
NBACC Operations	$30.0	$30.9

University Programs

Focuses on building the homeland security expertise within the academic community, creating strategic partnerships among universities and public agencies, and developing the next generation scientific workforce of homeland security experts.

	FY10/FY11CR	FY12
University Programs	$49.4	$36.6
Centers of Excellence	$39.4	$29.9
Education Programs	$6.1	$3.3
Minority Serving Institutions	$3.9	$3.3

Source: DHS, 2011, Under Secretary Tara O'Toole, Science and Technology Directorate, before the House Committee on Appropriations, Subcommittee on Homeland Security, S&T Fiscal Year 2012 Budget Request, http://www.dhs.gov/ynews/testimony/testimony_1301519363336.shtm.

ANOTHER VOICE: DEPARTMENT OF HOMELAND SECURITY, BY LYNN J. DANIELS AND GERALD L. EPSTEIN, AMERICAN ASSOCIATION FOR THE ADVANCEMENT OF SCIENCE.

Highlights

- The Department of Homeland Security (DHS) research and development portfolio would see a substantial increase in FY 2012, with respect to the fiscal year (FY) 2010 enacted budget, with a request of $1.05 billion, an increase of 18.8 percent or $167 million.
- The $109 million Transformational Research and Development (R&D) program would be transferred from the Domestic Nuclear Detection Office (DNDO) to the Science and Technology (S&T) Directorate, where it would become an eighth technical division (Radiological/Nuclear). (This transfer was originally proposed in the FY 2011 budget request, which Congress did not act upon.) Following the transfer, no R&D funding would remain in the DNDO.
- With this transfer, the Science and Technology Directorate's research and development funding would grow by 20.2 percent, an increase of $173 million. In addition to Transformational R&D, specific additions include an increase of $18 million for cybersecurity research as well

(Continued)

as $150 million for the construction of the National Bio- and Agro-Defense Facility (NBAF) in Manhattan, Kansas. Without the construction funds, however, the S&T Directorate budget for R&D would increase by only 2.7 percent.

- University programs funding would experience a 44 percent drop, from $65.6 million in FY 2010 to $36.6 million in FY 2012. The proposed cut would include the elimination of the National Transportation Security Center of Excellence and one or more Minority Serving Institution programs. The FY 2012 budget also would cut approximately $1.9 million from scholarship and fellowship funding.

DHS R&D in the FY 2012 Budget

Research and development remains a small but important part of the overall DHS budget, which would total $57.0 billion in 2012. Whereas the FY 2011 request for R&D funding requests represented a decrease from FY 2010 levels, the proposed DHS FY 2012 R&D budget of $1.05 billion would mark an increase of 18.8 percent or $167 million over the FY 2010 enacted budget.

The importance of science and technology for meeting a wide range of homeland security missions was highlighted by a National Academies landmark study *Making the Nation Safer,* initiated soon after the September 11 attacks (Committee on Science and Technology for Countering Terrorism, National Research Council, *Making the Nation Safer: The Role of Science and Technology in Countering Terrorism* (Washington, DC: The National Academies Press, 2002). This study was released on the same day in 2002 that legislation to create the Department of Homeland Security was introduced in Congress.

Whereas most of the new Department of Homeland Security consisted of agencies and offices moved from elsewhere in the federal government, the Science and Technology Directorate (S&T) was largely original, reflecting the fact that R&D specifically for the purpose of preventing, mitigating, or responding to terrorist attacks upon the United States had not been a major federal mission prior to the September 11 attacks. Although some technologies pursued by DHS are similar to those developed by the military, the needs and the users for homeland security technologies are sufficiently different that the new Department needed to perform its own research and development. Following the Quadrennial Homeland Security Review (QHSR), the S&T Directorate has been structurally reorganized into four Group Leads to emphasize cross-S&T communication and teamwork. The four Group Leads are: Homeland Security Advanced Research Projects Agency (HSARPA), Homeland Security Enterprise and First Responders, Acquisition Support and Operations Analysis (ASOA), and Research and Development Partnerships (RDP).

Mission-Oriented Programs. The HSARPA Office is divided into seven technical divisions that address critical homeland security needs. The budget document is organized differently, however: research and development projects have been aligned with six "thrust areas" rather than with the particular divisions in which those projects were placed in the FY 2010 budget. This reorganization makes direct comparisons to FY 2010 enacted levels difficult. The thrust areas are: Apex R&D, consisting of cross-cutting, multi-disciplinary research projects with short turn-around; Border Security; Chemical, Biological, Radiological, Nuclear, and Explosive Defense (CBRNE); Counter Terrorist; Cyber Security; and Disaster Resilience.

Radiological and nuclear countermeasures would continue to comprise the largest part of the DHS R&D portfolio in 2012, including both the DNDO and radiological and nuclear projects within the S&T Directorate. DNDO was carved out of the S&T Directorate in 2006 as a stand-alone entity; in FY 2011, its longer-term research mission — the $109 million Transformational Research and Development program — was to be transferred back to the S&T Directorate, where it would comprise a Radiological and Nuclear division. This transfer was not enacted by Congress and is proposed again in FY 2012, unchanged from when it was first proposed. Although the FY 2011 budget request showed some $158 million of R&D funding would remain in DNDO after the transfer, in the FY 2012 request some of the remaining applied research projects within DNDO — including work on radiation detector systems, systems engineering, and nuclear forensics — appear to have been redefined as non-R&D. Moreover, prior-year budgets have been adjusted to reflect this change.

Within the CBRNE thrust, chemical and biological countermeasures would receive $193.9 million, a decrease of $12.9 million or 6.2 percent from the FY 2010 Chemical and Biological division R&D portfolio. Programs in this thrust area are for the detection and threat assessment of biological and chemical agents, including the SAFECON and TRUST cargo screening technologies. The total also includes $69.3 million for bioagent and chemical attack resiliency within the Disaster Resilience thrust, including research for decontamination and community restoration.

The remaining component of the CBRNE thrust is Explosives, which would receive $133.1 million for FY 2012, an increase of $12.3 million or 10.2 percent over the FY 2010 Explosives division budget. This total includes $13.1 million for resiliency R&D with a focus on materials research to mitigate explosives damage to buildings.

Cybersecurity R&D would receive an increased focus in response to the President's *National Strategy to Secure Cyberspace* and the *Comprehensive National Cybersecurity Initiative* (CNCI). The former DHS Cybersecurity Office has been elevated to a division within HSARPA and would receive $64.1 million in FY 2012, an increase of $18 million. This would include funding for user identity and data privacy technology, secure protocols, and software assurance research.

The remaining thrust areas in order of decreasing size are Border Security, Counter Terrorist, and Apex research and development. Apex R&D currently funds a single project — Science & Technology Operational Research Enhancement (STORE) — that seeks to better integrate technologies with the United States Secret Service.

Cross-cutting Programs. The Science and Technology Directorate's R&D funding also supports a number of offices that cut across individual mission areas. The Homeland Security Enterprise and First Responder Group was created in order to respond to the needs of first responders with a focus on equipment standards and interoperability; this Group contains the Office for Interoperability and Compatibility. The Acquisition Support and Operations Analysis Group was created in order to leverage the S&T Directorate's technical capabilities to develop testable operational requirements for acquisitions; this Group now contains the Test and Evaluation and Standards Office. Neither the Transition nor Innovation Office have been retained under the restructuring; projects formerly within these offices have been realigned into their appropriate R&D thrust area.

The Test and Evaluation and Standards office oversees the Department's test and evaluation programs and also provides technical assistance to state, local, and federal first responders in acquiring safe, reliable, and effective equipment. The programs within the Standards thrust would receive $16.5 million in FY 2012; Testing and Evaluation would receive $6.64 million. The combined budget of these two thrusts would experience a 20.2 percent cut from the FY 2010 Test and Evaluation and Standards Office.

(Continued)

Technology Transition thrust projects facilitate the transfer of S&T solutions to other DHS components, industry, and other federal agencies. These programs would receive $10.4 million in FY 2012.

Laboratory Facilities and University Programs. The Research and Development Partnerships Group was created to facilitate outreach to the private sector and academia and it supports the Laboratory Facilities and University Programs budgets. Laboratory Facilities, budgeted at $276.5 million for FY 2012, would be funded at a level that exceeds all thrust areas except CBRNE. The FY 2012 budget request represents an increase of over $100 million, or 57 percent. However, $150 million of that amount represents funds for the construction of the National Bio- and Agro-Defense Facility (NBAF); without these funds, Laboratory Facilities would see a 28.2 percent budget cut.

The construction funding request for NBAF comes after the completion of a biosafety and biosecurity risk mitigation assessment for the facility in October 2010. The NBAF would replace the Plum Island Animal Disease Center (PIADC) and was originally to be financed using sales proceeds from the disposal of PIADC. However, sales estimates were considerably overestimated, and the FY 2012 budget requests direct appropriations of $150 million. Until NBAF is completed, however, Plum Island continues to be operational and receives funding through the Laboratory Facilities budget. The General Services Administration (GSA) is currently working with DHS to put this property on the market. Proceeds from the sale will then be made available for reimbursement through an offsetting account.

The remainder of Laboratory Facilities funding in FY 2012 would support the operation of DHS laboratories: the National Biodefense Assessments and Countermeasures Center (NBACC), for which construction was recently completed in Frederick, MD; the National Urban Security Technology Laboratory in New York City, which was transferred into DHS at the Department's onset from the Department of Energy; and the Transportation Security Laboratory in Atlantic City, New Jersey, which was transferred into DHS from the Federal Aviation Administration.

The DHS University Programs budget is proposed to be funded in FY 2012 at $36.6 million, $29 million or 44 percent less than its FY 2010 level. University Programs supports university-based Centers of Excellence (COE), which are multi-year university consortia to perform R&D on homeland security-related topics. Also funded in this line are efforts to promote research, education, and training at Minority Serving Institutions (MSI) in areas critical to homeland security. This line also funds fellowships to encourage U.S. students to pursue scientific and technical degrees. The proposed cut in University Programs funding would eliminate funding for the National Transportation Security Center of Excellence (NTSCOE). Currently there are twelve Centers, one of which is funded jointly with EPA.

The newest center was created in 2010 following a re-competition, focusing on risk and economic analysis of terrorist events. The proposed reduction in funding will also eliminate $1.9 million from the Scholarship and Fellowship program.

Historical Context

The DHS S&T Directorate was created in March 2003 with an R&D budget of $918 million for its first full year (Cindy Williams et al., "Department of Homeland Security Science and Technology Directorate: Developing Technology to Protect America," a Report of a Panel of the National Academy of Public Administration, June 2009, p. 5) but without a concise, overarching statutory mission. Subsequently, S&T ran into trouble with Congress early in its tenure. In the spring of 2005, Congressional dissatisfaction with S&T led Congress to take the nuclear detection mission away from the Directorate and give it to a newly-created Domestic Nuclear Detection Office. In June 2006, the Senate Appropriations Committee called the Directorate a "rudderless ship." In 2007, Congress slashed S&T's funding dramatically. The final 2007 appropriations bill rescinded $125 million in unspent R&D funds, cut most research programs, and required S&T to submit a five-year research plan with priorities, performance measures, and resource needs for each R&D area. This plan was submitted and most recently updated in August 2008. Following structural changes implemented by current Under Secretary for Science and Technology Tara O'Toole, congressional criticism of S&T has been muted. In March 2011, members of the House Subcommittee on Technology and Innovation expressed approval of the progress that S&T had made toward becoming a more mature and productive R&D organization, with concerns focusing more on actual research conducted by S&T rather than organizational or mission-related criticisms.

Following the slashing of S&T funding, the 2007 and 2008 R&D total budget requests were well below appropriations of previous years. However, DHS continued to work through a backlog of unspent funds; at the end of FY 2007, even after rescissions and budget cuts, the S&T Directorate still had nearly $300 million in unspent funds to carry over to FY 2008. So while DHS' appropriations history is uneven, the actual outflow of money is smoother as appropriations stretched out into outlays over several years. After two years of R&D funding increases in FY 2009 and 2010 followed by a 10.4 percent reduction in the FY 2011 continuing resolution, S&T R&D funding is proposed to see a substantial increase in FY 2012.

In FY 2008, the most recent year figures are available (National Science Board, *Science and Engineering Indicators 2010* (NSB 10-01), Appendix Table 4–20), DHS spent the plurality of its R&D funds in industrial firms (43.1 percent), with federal intramural laboratories receiving the second largest share (25.1 percent). Another 20.1 percent went to federally funded research and development centers (national laboratories, mostly DOE laboratories). Only 6.3 percent of DHS R&D was spent in universities and colleges in FY 2008.

Current Issues

Congressional appropriators continue to face the general challenge of how to allocate funding to DHS as compared to other agencies and what share of the DHS budget should be invested in R&D. Specifically, DHS continues to struggle with how to balance funding between basic and applied research as well as the relative funding given to academia, industry, and government laboratories. The S&T Directorate has been criticized for a focus on short-term customer-driven technologies rather than thinking towards longer-term research. This was addressed during confirmation hearings for current Under Secretary Tara O'Toole. She testified that "DHS' operational needs continue to demand significant investments in near-term technology development," adding that "the S&T enterprise would benefit from additional investments in fundamental scientific discovery."

Given the uncertainty in the nature of the terrorist threat facing the United States, the variety of modes of attack, and the imprecision with which R&D investments can translate to reduced risk or enhanced security, the task of developing a methodology for objectively determining R&D funding levels is formidable. The difficulty for Congress in determining funding priorities is worsened by a perceived lack of transparency and responsiveness on the part of DHS. It has been increasingly difficult to track budgetary trends as well as identify R&D priorities due to frequent restructuring within the S&T Directorate. The FY 2011 budget request allocated funds according to the divisions and offices within the S&T Directorate; however, the current year FY 2012 budget request realigns projects with research

(Continued)

ANOTHER VOICE: DEPARTMENT OF HOMELAND SECURITY, BY LYNN J. DANIELS AND GERALD L. EPSTEIN, AMERICAN ASSOCIATION FOR THE ADVANCEMENT OF SCIENCE (CONTINUED).

"thrust areas." Thus, while many programs included specific itemized budget requests in FY 2011, many of these same projects appear as non-itemized components of a larger thrust area in the FY 2012 budget request. Without the ability to track these budgetary trends, the strategy and research priorities of the S&T Directorate continue to be difficult to ascertain.

This lack of transparency has also led to difficulty with transitioning technologies to the private sector. Although progress has been made toward improving the technology transition process, the S&T Directorate has been criticized for a lack of timeliness in communicating with the private sector and a lack of clarity in its research priorities. Without a long-term strategic vision and improved outreach, the business community remains hesitant to invest in S&T technologies. The S&T Directorate has begun to address these issues by placing a strong focus on technology foraging — scanning the output of academia and industry for technologies that match DHS needs — and developing closer relationships with its customer base in the private sector. Further, in order to develop a more transparent, strategic R&D vision, the S&T Directorate has committed to an annual review of its R&D portfolio that includes the input of outside experts as well as DHS representatives.

A final concern with the S&T Directorate is the lack of a fully-integrated acquisitions process. Testimony from the Government Accountability Office (GAO) at a March 2011 House hearing criticized the S&T Directorate for acquisitions decisions that failed to adequately test technologies prior to purchase as well as the lack of a rapid acquisition process to meet emergency needs. During the recent restructuring of the S&T Directorate, the Acquisitions Support and Operations Analysis Group was created in order to provide a more coordinated testing, evaluation, standards, and acquisitions process.

Source: American Association for the Advancement of Science (AAAS), 2011, AAAS XXXVI: Research and Development FY2012, http://www.aaas.org/spp/rd/rdreport2012/12pch11.pdf.

The S&T Directorate is responsible for setting the national agenda and giving direction and setting priorities for R&D efforts in other departments and agencies, regardless of the funding source. S&T is unique among federal R&D agencies in that it has responsibility for the entire cycle of science and technology (i.e., from product research to bringing the product to the market and deploying it).

The S&T Directorate established the Homeland Security Advanced Research Project Agency (HSARPA). This agency, based on the existing model of the Defense Advanced Research Project Agency (DARPA) in the Department of Defense (DOD), distributes resources within the directorate, awards money for the extramural grants, develops and tests potential technologies, and accelerates or prototypes development of technologies for deployment. The directorate has also created a Homeland Security Advisory Committee consisting of 20 members appointed by the undersecretary representing first responders, citizen groups, researchers, engineers, and businesses to provide science and technology advice to the undersecretary. DHS has also created a new federally funded R&D center (FFRDC), the Homeland Security Institute, to act as a think tank for risk analyses, simulations of threat scenarios, analyses of possible countermeasures, and strategic plans for counterterrorism technology development. Table 12–1 presents the homeland security R&D budget for those departments and agencies currently involved in homeland security R&D. Various successes identified by DHS are listed in the sidebar "Science and Technology Directorate Accomplishments."

Science and Technology Directorate Accomplishments in FY 2010

- SAFETY Act
- Borders/Maritime Standards Program
- Explosives Standards
- System Assessment and Validation for Emergency Responders (SAVER) Program
- International Programs
- Container Security Device (CSD)
- Hybrid Composite Container
- Scholars and Fellows
- Laboratory Construction
- National Biodefense Analysis and Countermeasures Center (NBACC)
- Internet Measurements Techniques Project (formerly Internet Route Monitoring)
- Process Control Systems (PCS) Security Project
- Real-Time Data Processing and Visualization Project
- Compliance Assessment Project (CAP)
- Converged Interoperable Communications
- Air Cargo Project
- Automated Threat Recognition (ATR)
- Risk Prediction Project
- Validation of SPOT (Screening Passenger by Observation)
- Decision Support Tools Project
- Facility Restoration Demonstration Project
- Chemical Security Analysis Center (CSAC) Project
- Contractor-to-Federal Employee Conversions (DHS, 2011, FY 2012 Budget in Brief)

See the companion website for the full text of this document.

■ ■ Critical Thinking ■

In your opinion, is federal funding better spent on all-hazards first-responder preparedness, or on R&D efforts to find new emergency management solutions for terrorist hazards? Based on the FY 2012 funding levels for both of these activities (listed throughout this chapter), would the American public be better served by transferring funding from R&D to first-responder preparedness, or vice versa? Explain your answer.

R&D Efforts Focused on Weapons of Mass Destruction

The DHS website states, "The S&T Directorate will tap into scientific and technological capabilities to provide the means to detect and deter attacks using weapons of mass destruction. S&T will guide and organize research efforts to meet emerging and predicted needs and will work closely with universities, the private sector, and national and Federal laboratories." This effort can be subdivided into two fields: chemical and biological, and radiological and nuclear. In both fields, the Directorate's aim is to carry research to develop sensors to detect such weapons from production to employment. The different organizations within the federal sector that will support and serve the R&D efforts of S&T are detailed in the following section.

Chemical, Biological, Radiological and Nuclear Defense Information and Analysis Center

The Chemical, Biological, Radiological and Nuclear Defense Information Analysis Center (CBRNIAC), formerly known as the CBIAC, is a full-service DOD Information Analysis Center (IAC). The CBRNIAC is the authoritative resource for DOD Chemical, Biological, Radiological and Nuclear (CBRN) Defense and Homeland Security scientific and technical (S&T) information.

The CBRNIAC generates, acquires, processes, analyzes, and disseminates CBRN Defense Science and Technology Information (STI) in support of the Combatant Commanders, warfighters, the Reserve Components, the CBRN Defense Research, Development, and Acquisition community, and other federal, state, and local government agencies. The CBRNIAC assists these agencies in implementing high-priority research and development (R&D) initiatives by:

- Identifying and acquiring relevant data and information from all available sources and in all media
- Processing data and acquisitions into suitable storage and retrieval systems
- Identifying, developing, and applying available analytical tools and techniques for the interpretation and application of stored data and acquisitions
- Disseminating focused information, datasets, and technical analyses to managers, planners, scientists, engineers, and military field personnel for the performance of mission-related tasks
- Anticipating requirements for CBRN Defense STI
- Identifying and reaching out to emerging CBRN Defense organizations (Department of Defense, 2011, https://www.cbrniac.apgea.army.mil/About/Pages/default.aspx).

Defense Threat Reduction Agency

The Defense Threat Reduction Agency (DTRA, www.dtra.mil) safeguards national interests from weapons of mass destruction (WMDs) (chemical, biological, radiological, nuclear, and high explosives) by controlling and reducing the threat and providing quality tools and services for the war fighter. DTRA performs four essential functions to reach its mission: combat support, technology development, threat control, and threat reduction. Moreover, the agency's work covers a broad spectrum of activities:

- Shaping the international environment to prevent the spread of WMDs
- Responding to requirements to deter the use and reduce the impact of such weapons
- Preparing for the future as WMD threats emerge and evolve

  The activities concerning homeland security are as follows:

- DTRA draws on the disparate chemical and biological weapons defense expertise within the DOD to increase response capabilities.
- The Advanced Systems and Concepts Office (ASCO) stimulates, identifies, and executes high-impact seed projects to encourage new thinking, address technology gaps, and improve the operational capabilities of DTRA.

Department of State

The Department of State (www.state.gov) contributes to the counterterror effort related to WMDs through diplomatic and intelligence gathering efforts. The Department of State provides information and assessments of potential chemical and biological weapons sources throughout the world and analyzes what different countries and groups are doing to increase, decrease, or support WMD development and stockpiling.

Centers for Disease Control and Prevention

The Centers for Disease Control and Prevention (CDC, www.cdc.gov) is recognized as the lead federal agency for protecting the health and safety of people by providing credible information to enhance health decisions and promoting health through strong partnerships. CDC serves as the national focus for developing and applying disease prevention and control, environmental health, and health promotion and education activities designed to improve the health of the people of the United States, with the mission to promote health and quality of life by preventing and controlling disease, injury, and disability. CDC provides information about the effects and treatment for exposure to chem-bio weapons and has valuable expertise in its 12 centers, institutes, and offices. The most prominent and relevant of the 12 follow:

- The National Center for Chronic Disease Prevention and Health Promotion prevents premature death and disability from chronic diseases and promotes healthy personal behaviors.
- The National Center for Health Statistics provides statistical information that will guide actions and policies to improve the health of the American people.
- The National Center for HIV, STD, and TB Prevention provides national leadership in preventing and controlling human immunodeficiency virus infection, sexually transmitted diseases, and tuberculosis.
- The National Center for Infectious Diseases prevents illness, disability, and death caused by infectious diseases in the United States and around the world.
- The National Immunization Program prevents disease, disability, and death from vaccine-preventable diseases in children and adults.
- The Epidemiology Program Office strengthens the public health system by coordinating public health surveillance; providing support in scientific communications, statistics, and epidemiology; and training in surveillance, epidemiology, and prevention effectiveness.
- The Public Health Practice Program Office strengthens community practice of public health by creating an effective workforce, building information networks, conducting practice research, and ensuring laboratory quality.

Lawrence Livermore National Laboratory

The Lawrence Livermore National Laboratory (LLNL, www.llnl.gov) provides information about nuclear and radiological weapons. Its activities are explained more broadly in the R&D section.

U.S. Nuclear Regulatory Commission

The U.S. Nuclear Regulatory Commission (NRC, www.nrc.gov) is an independent agency established to regulate civilian use of nuclear materials. The NRC's mission is to regulate the nation's civilian use of by-product, source, and special nuclear materials to ensure adequate protection of public health and safety, to promote the common defense and security, and to protect the environment. The NRC's regulatory mission covers three main areas:

- *Reactors*: Commercial reactors for generating electric power and nonpower reactors used for research, testing, and training
- *Materials*: Uses of nuclear materials in medical, industrial, and academic settings and facilities that produce nuclear fuel
- *Waste*: Transportation, storage, and disposal of nuclear materials and waste, and decommissioning of nuclear facilities from service

The NRC carries out its mission by conducting several activities, but most of them are not directly related to the homeland security purpose. The commission performs them as part of its mission to regulate the normal use of radiological material, but many of its capabilities and resources can be used during a radiological or nuclear incident. The major contribution fields are commission direction setting and policymaking, radiation protection, establishment of a regulatory program, nuclear security and safeguards information on how to promote the common defense and security, public affairs, congressional affairs, state and tribal programs, and international programs.

Efforts Aimed at Information and Infrastructure

DHS has been given the primary responsibility for detecting and deterring attacks on the national information systems and critical infrastructures, and the S&T Directorate is developing a national R&D enterprise to support this mission. The three main issues concerning information and infrastructure are as follows: Internet security, telecommunication, and the security systems. The directorate coordinates and integrates several organizations to accomplish its mission, as discussed in the next sections.

SANS Institute

The SANS (Systems Administration, Audit, Network, Security) Institute (www.sans.org) is active in the fields of information security research, certification, and education, and provides a platform for professionals to share lessons learned, conduct research, and teach the information security community. Besides the various training programs and resources aimed at informing its members and the community, the centers described below are part of SANS.

- *Internet Storm Center*: This center was created to detect rising Internet threats. It uses advanced data correlation and visualization techniques to analyze data from a large number of firewalls and intrusion detection systems in over 60 countries. Experienced analysts constantly monitor the Storm Center data feeds, and search for trends and anomalies in order to identify potential threats. When a potential threat is detected, the team immediately begins an intensive investigation to gauge the threat's severity and impact. The Storm Center may request correlating data from an extensive network of security experts from across the globe, and possesses the in-house expertise to analyze captured attack tools quickly and thoroughly. Critical information is then disseminated to the public in the form of alerts and postings.
- *Center for Internet Security (CIS) and SCORE*: CIS formalizes the best practice recommendations once consensus between the SANS Institute and SCORE is reached and the practices are validated. The latter become minimum standard benchmarks for general use by the industry. Both organizations rely on and have very broad contact with the field experts.

CERT Coordination Center

The CERT Coordination Center (CERT/CC, www.cert.org) is located at the Software Engineering Institute (SEI), an FFRDC at Carnegie Mellon University in Pittsburgh, PA. SEI was charged by DARPA in 1988 to set up a center to coordinate communication among experts during security emergencies and to help prevent future incidents.

The CERT/CC is part of the larger SEI Networked Systems Survivability Program, whose primary goals are to ensure that appropriate technology and systems management practices are used to resist attacks on networked systems and to limit damage and ensure continuity of critical services in spite of successful attacks, accidents, or failures. The center's research areas are summarized below.

- *Vulnerability analysis and incident handling*: Analyze the state of Internet security and convey that information to the system administrators, network managers, and others in the Internet community. In these vulnerability and incident-handling activities, a higher priority is assigned to attacks and vulnerabilities that directly affect the Internet infrastructure (e.g., network service providers, Internet service providers, domain name servers, and routers).
- *Survivable enterprise management*: Help organizations protect and defend themselves. To this end, risk assessments that help enterprises identify and characterize critical information assets and then identify risks to those assets have been developed, and the enterprise can use the results of the assessment to develop or refine their overall strategy for securing their networked systems.
- *Education and training*: The center offers training courses to educate technical staff and managers of computer security-incident response teams as well as system administrators and other technical personnel within organizations to improve the security and survivability of each system. The center's staff also take part in developing curricula in information security and has compiled a guide, *The CERT® Guide to System and Network Security Practices*, published by Addison-Wesley.
- *Survivable network technology*: The center focuses on the technical basis for identifying and preventing security flaws and for preserving essential services if a system is penetrated and compromised. The center does research for new approaches to secure systems and analysis of how susceptible systems are to sophisticated attacks and find ways to improve the design of systems. Another focus is on modeling and simulation. The center has developed "Easel," a tool that is being used to study network responses to attacks and attack mitigation strategies. And finally, the center is also developing techniques that will enable the assessment and prediction of current and potential threats to the Internet. These techniques involve examining large sets of network data to identify unauthorized and potentially malicious activity.

National Communications System

Through the National Communications System (NCS, www.ncs.gov), DHS supports the telecommunications critical infrastructure and R&D of tools and technology to prevent disruption or compromise of these services. The NCS was established in 1963 as a "single unified communications system to serve the president, DOD, diplomatic and intelligence activities and civilian leaders." The NCS mandate included linking, improving, and extending the communications facilities and components of various federal agencies, focusing on interconnectivity and survivability. The NCS's national security and emergency preparedness (NS/EP) capabilities were broadened in 1984 when it began coordinating and planning NS/EP telecommunications to support crises and disasters.

With the U.S. Information Agency being absorbed into the U.S. State Department in October 2000, the NCS membership currently stands at 24 members. The NCS also participates in joint industry–government planning through its work with the President's National Security Telecommunications Advisory Committee (NSTAC), with the NSC's National Coordinating Center (NCC) for Telecommunications, and the NCC's subordinate Information Sharing and Analysis Center (NCC-ISAC).

The NCS comprises numerous programs and committees that represent the majority of the national efforts in the field of communication for national emergencies and crises. The President's National Security Telecommunications Advisory Committee (NSTAC) and the Office of the Manager NCS (OMNCS) have been given the tasks of providing access control, priority treatment, user authentication, and other survivability features supporting NS/EP telecommunications to the Advanced Intelligent Network (AIN).

The OMNCS staff resources are organized into four branches: Technology and Programs, Critical Infrastructure Protection (CIP) with the NCC, Plans and Resources, and Customer Service.

The OMNCS is responsible for:

- Providing the expertise for the planning, implementing, administering, and maintenance of approved NS/EP communications programs and NCS baseline activities
- Conducting technical studies, analyses, and assessments pertaining to the effectiveness of NS/EP communications programs and the effects of these programs on the Nation's critical infrastructures
- Consulting with the Committee of Principals (COP), the NCS Council of Representatives (COR), and the President's National Security Telecommunications Advisory Committee (NSTAC) on issues pertaining to NS/EP telecommunications
- Participating on federal councils and boards, such as the Government Sector Coordinating Council and the National Infrastructure Advisory Council (NIAC), that develop telecommunications policies, standards, national initiatives, and performing research on emerging technologies
- Monitoring international emergency telecommunications planning activities and offering assistance to international emergency planning groups
- Developing, planning, and implementing NCS strategic goals and objectives
- Assisting individual NCS member organizations in developing efficient cost-effective solutions to complex communication/information requirements and resolutions to organizational communication/information issues (DHS, 2011, www.ncs.gov)

The OMNCS has established an AIN Program to address the emerging technology and an associated AIN Program Office to plan, coordinate, and oversee the effort. Two very important examples of initiatives follow:

- The Alerting and Coordination Network (ACN) provides a stable emergency voice communications network connecting telecommunications service providers' Emergency Operations Centers (EOCs) and Network Operations Centers (NOCs) to support NS/EP telecommunications network restoration coordination, transmission of telecommunications requirements and priorities, and incident reporting when the Public Switched Telephone Network (PSTN) is inoperable, stressed, or congested. The ACN is operational 24 hours a day, 7 days a week, to support the NCC during normal and emergency operations.
- The Emergency Notification Service (ENS) is a full-time service established to notify critical government personnel during emergencies using multiple communication channels, including telephone, short message service (SMS), pager, and e-mail. Within minutes of receiving an activation order from an authorized representative of an organization, an automated process makes multiple attempts to reach intended recipients until they confirm delivery or until a predetermined number of attempts have been made. After 30 minutes, a report detailing confirmation of delivery is returned

to the originator of the notification. Messages can be recorded in advance or when the notification is initiated and can be sent as a general notification or a sensitive notification.

To initiate, coordinate, restore, and reconstitute NS/EP telecommunications services or facilities, the NCS continues to develop new capabilities and reevaluate or upgrade older ones. The NCS's current capabilities are given in the sidebar titled, "Service Programs of the National Communications System."

■ ■ ■

Service Programs of the National Communications System

GETS Program Information
The Government Emergency Telecommunications Service (GETS) is a White House-directed emergency phone service provided by the National Communications System (NCS) in the Office of Cybersecurity and Communications Division, National Protection and Programs Directorate, Department of Homeland Security. GETS supports Federal, State, local, and tribal government, industry, and non-governmental organization (NGO) personnel in performing their National Security and Emergency Preparedness (NS/EP) missions. GETS provides emergency access and priority processing in the local and long distance segments of the Public Switched Telephone Network (PSTN). It is intended to be used in an emergency or crisis situation when the PSTN is congested and the probability of completing a call over normal or other alternate telecommunication means has significantly decreased (DHS, 2011, http://gets.ncs.gov/program_info.html).

About the Telecommunications Service Priority (TSP)
On November 17, 1988, the Federal Communications Commission (FCC) issued a Report and Order (FCC 88-341) establishing the TSP Program ....

The TSP Program's goal is to ensure priority treatment for our nation's most important NS/EP telecommunications services. The TSP Program is the regulatory, administrative, and operational framework for the priority restoration and provisioning of any qualified NS/EP telecommunications service. NS/EP services are those services used to maintain a state of readiness or to respond to and manage any event or crisis (local, national, or international) that causes or could cause injury or harm to the population, damage to or loss of property, or degrades or threatens the NS/EP posture of the United States.

In addition, priority treatment may be authorized at the discretion of, and upon special arrangements by the NS/EP TSP Program users involved, to government or noncommon carrier services which are not connected to common carrier provided services, and portions of U.S. international services which are provided by foreign correspondents (DHS, 2011, http://tsp.ncs.gov/about_tsp.html).

Shares
The National Communications System (NCS), in its role of planning and preparing for national security and emergency preparedness (NS/EP), has undertaken a number of initiatives to provide communications to support all hazards situations. One of these initiatives, developed through the combined efforts of the 23 NCS member organizations, is the SHAred RESources (SHARES) High Frequency (HF) Radio Program.

The purpose of SHARES is to provide a single, interagency emergency message handling system by bringing together existing HF radio resources of Federal, state and industry organizations when normal communications are destroyed or unavailable for the transmission of national security and emergency preparedness information … (DHS, 2011, http://www.ncs.gov/shares/program_info.html).

Route Diversity

The Route Diversity Project helps local, state, and Federal agencies increase the availability of communications by employing diverse routing, defined as "communications routing between two points over more than one geographic or physical path, with no points in common." The project includes the tools and capabilities necessary to assist an agency with risk and infrastructure analyses. It also presents information on available communications technologies and services, including those evaluated by the NCS during "real-world" field trials.

See the companion website for a fuller description of these programs.

Source: DHS, 2011, http://www.ncs.gov/rdp/.

Wireless Priority Service (WPS)

During emergencies cellular networks can experience congestion due to increased call volumes and/or damage to network facilities, severely curtailing the ability of national security and emergency preparedness (NS/EP) personnel to make emergency calls. With an increasing number of NS/EP personnel relying on cell phones while performing their emergency duties, the NCS developed Wireless Priority Service to provide priority for emergency calls made from cellular telephones.

Key Federal, State, local, and tribal government, and critical infrastructure personnel are eligible for Wireless Priority Service. Typical users are responsible for the command and control functions critical to management of and response to national security and emergency situations. Wireless Priority Service is an easy-to-use, add-on feature subscribed on a per-cell phone basis; no special phones are required.

Wireless Priority Service is implemented as software enhancements to cellular networks, and is being deployed by cellular service providers in their coverage areas throughout the United States.

Wireless Priority Service (WPS) is a priority calling capability that greatly increases the probability of call completion during a national security and emergency preparedness (NS/EP) event while using their cellular phone. To make a WPS call, the user must first have the WPS feature added to their cellular service. Once established, the caller can dial 272 plus the destination telephone number to place an emergency wireless call.

WPS and its companion priority service, the Government Emergency Telecommunications Service (GETS), are requested through a secure on-line system. Before service can be requested, participating organizations must establish a Point of Contact (POC) account. The GETS/WPS POC serves as each organization's program administrator. Once an organization has an established POC, they can request GETS and WPS. The NCS recommends that each WPS user also have a GETS card ….

For assistance and information on all NCS Priority Telecommunications programs contact the Priority Telecommunications Service Center toll free at 866-627-2255 (DC metro area, please use 703-760-2255) or gwids@saic.com.

Source: DHS, 2011, http://wps.ncs.gov/program_info.html.

Laboratories and Research Facilities

The R&D function is the most important aspect of the S&T Directorate. It relies on several existing agency programs to accomplish this task, including DOD, Department of Energy (DOE), and U.S. Department of Agriculture (USDA) programs, among others. A significant portion of the funding attached to these programs comes from DOD's National Bioweapons Defense Analysis Center, responsible for nearly the entire biological countermeasures portfolio.

S&T's Office for National Laboratories coordinates DHS interactions with DOE national laboratories with expertise in homeland security. The office has the authority to establish a semi-independent DHS headquarters laboratory within existing federal laboratories, national laboratories, or FFRDC to supply scientific and technical knowledge to DHS and has done so with at least five national laboratories. In addition to Livermore, DHS has established four other laboratories-within-laboratories at the Los Alamos, Sandia, Pacific Northwest, and Oak Ridge National Laboratories. DHS will also establish one or more university-based centers for homeland security.

The national and federal laboratory system possesses significant expertise in the area of WMDs in addition to massive computing power. These laboratories include the following:

- *DOE National Nuclear Security Administration Laboratories*: Lawrence Livermore Laboratory, Los Alamos National Laboratory, and Sandia National Laboratory
- *DOE Office of Science Laboratories*: Argonne National Laboratory, Brookhaven National Laboratory (BNL), Oak Ridge National Laboratory, Pacific Northwest National Laboratory, and other DOE laboratories
- *Department of Homeland Security Laboratories*: Environmental Measurements Laboratory (EML) and Plum Island Animal Disease Center
- *Department of Health and Human Services Laboratories*: HHS operates several laboratories focused on wide-ranging health and disease prevention issues
- *U.S. Customs Laboratory and Scientific Services*: The U.S. Customs Laboratory and Scientific Services perform testing to determine the origin of agricultural and manufactured products.

This section starts with an overview of the facilities cited above and relevant programs and then discusses other R&D activities, such as the university-based center approach, and partnerships between DHS and other agencies.

Lawrence Livermore National Laboratory

The Homeland Security Organization at Lawrence Livermore National Laboratory (LLNL, www.llnl.gov) provides comprehensive solutions integrating threat, vulnerability, and trade-off analyses, advanced technologies, field-demonstrated prototypes, and operational capabilities to assist federal, state, local, and private entities in defending against catastrophic terrorism. The center is also dedicated to pursuing partnerships with universities and the private sector to fulfill its mission.

Los Alamos National Laboratory

Los Alamos National Laboratory (LANL, www.lanl.gov) is a DOE laboratory, managed by the University of California, and is one of the largest multidisciplinary institutions in the world. The Center for Homeland Security (CHS) was established in September 2002 to engage the laboratory's broad capabilities in the areas of counterterrorism and homeland security. It provides a single point of contact for all external organizations.

The organization's emphasis is on the key areas of nuclear and radiological science and technology, critical infrastructure protection, and chemical and biological science and technology. Current LANL projects with a key role in homeland security include the following:

- BASIS (the Biological Aerosol Sentry and Information System), a biological early warning system that was tested and installed at the 2002 Salt Lake City Winter Olympics.
- A novel nuclear detector, the Palm CZT Spectrometer, is also in development and deployment, providing real-time gamma and neutron detection and isotope identification in a handheld device.
- LANL has also been active in the anthrax bacterial DNA analysis and the computerized feature identification tool known as GENIE, for Genetic Image Exploitation.

Sandia National Laboratory

The Sandia National Laboratory (www.sandia.gov) has been active since 1949 in the development of science-based technologies that support national security. Through science and technology, people, infrastructure, and partnerships, Sandia's mission is to meet national needs in following six key areas:

- Nuclear weapons
- Nonproliferation
- Defense systems and assessments
- Homeland security
- Science, technology, and engineering
- Energy and infrastructure assurance

Argonne National Laboratory

Argonne National Laboratory (www.anl.gov) is one of the DOE's largest research centers. It is also the nation's first national laboratory, chartered in 1946. Argonne's research falls into four broad categories:

- *Basic science*: This program seeks solutions to a wide variety of scientific challenges. This includes experimental and theoretical work in materials science, physics, chemistry, biology, high-energy physics, and mathematics and computer science, including high-performance computing.
- *National security*: This program has increased in significance in recent years. This program uses Argonne capabilities developed over previous years for other purposes that help counter the terrorist threat. These capabilities include expertise in the nuclear fuel cycle, biology, chemistry, and systems analysis and modeling. This research is helping develop highly sensitive instruments and

technologies to detect chemical, biological, and radioactive threats and identify their sources. Other research is helping to detect and deter possible weapons proliferation or actual attacks.

- *Energy resources*: This program helps to insure that a reliable supply of efficient and clean energy exists in the future. The laboratory's scientists and engineers are working to develop advanced batteries and fuel cells, as well as advanced electric power generation and storage systems.
- *Environmental management*: This program includes work on managing and solving environmental problems and promoting environmental stewardship. Research includes alternative energy systems, environmental risk and economic impact assessments, hazardous waste site analysis and remediation planning, treatment to prepare spent nuclear fuel for disposal, and new technologies for decontaminating and decommissioning aging nuclear reactors.

Industrial technology development is an important activity in moving benefits of Argonne's publicly funded research to industry to help strengthen the nation's technology base.

Brookhaven National Laboratory

Established in 1947 on Long Island, New York, Brookhaven National Laboratory (BNL, www.bnl.gov) is a multiprogram national laboratory operated by Brookhaven Science Associates for the DOE. Six Nobel Prizes have been awarded for discoveries made at BNL. Brookhaven has a staff of approximately 3,000 scientists, engineers, technicians, and support people, and hosts more than 4,000 guest researchers annually. BNL's role for the DOE is to produce excellent science and advanced technology with the cooperation, support, and appropriate involvement of our scientific and local communities. The fundamental elements of BNL's role in support of the four DOE strategic missions follow:

- To conceive, design, construct, and operate complex, leading edge, user-oriented facilities in response to the needs of the DOE and the international community of users
- To carry out basic and applied research in long-term, high-risk programs at the frontier of science
- To develop advanced technologies that address national needs and to transfer them to other organizations and to the commercial sector
- To disseminate technical knowledge, educate new generations of scientists and engineers, maintain technical capabilities in the nation's workforce, and encourage scientific awareness in the general public

Major programs that are managed at the laboratory include the following:

- Nuclear and high-energy physics
- Physics and chemistry of materials
- Environmental and energy research
- Nonproliferation
- Neurosciences and medical imaging
- Structural biology

Oak Ridge National Laboratory

The Oak Ridge National Laboratory (ORNL, www.ornl.gov) is a multiprogramming science and technology laboratory managed for the DOE by UT-Battelle, LLC. Scientists and engineers at ORNL conduct basic and applied R&D to create scientific knowledge and technological solutions that strengthen the nation's leadership in key areas of science; increase the availability of clean, abundant energy; restore and protect the environment; and contribute to national security. In their national security mission, ORNL provides federal, state, and local government agencies and departments with technology and expertise to support their national and homeland security needs. This technology and expertise are also shared with the private sector.

Pacific Northwest National Laboratory

The Pacific Northwest National Laboratory (PNNL, www.pnl.gov) is a DOE laboratory that delivers breakthrough science and technology to meet selected environmental, energy, health, and national security objectives; strengthen the economy; and support the education of future scientists and engineers.

PNNL's mission in national security supports the U.S. government's objectives against the proliferation of nuclear, chemical, and biological WMDs and associated delivery systems. About one-third of PNNL's $600 million annual R&D budget reflects work in national security programs for the Departments of Energy, Defense, and most other federal agencies. The focus is on issues that concern the Air Force, Army, Defense Advanced Research Projects Agency, Defense Threat Reduction Agency, Navy, and nuclear nonproliferation.

Scientists and engineers at PNNL are finding ways to diagnose the life of the Army's Abrams tank, developing technologies that verify compliance with the Comprehensive Nuclear Test Ban Treaty, helping North Korea secure spent nuclear fuel in proper storage canisters, and training border enforcement officials from the United States and foreign countries.

Other Department of Energy Laboratories and Objectives

The DOE (www.energy.gov) also has other affiliated organizations in addition to the ones cited above that focus on various homeland security issues. The topics addressed in these facilities include:

- *Cybersecurity protection*: These programs are aimed at protecting the information and systems that the DOE depends on, which only increases in scope as it grows in dependence on newer technologies.
- *Managing operations security*: This program seeks to manage security operations for DOE facilities in the national capital area and to develop policies designed to protect national security and other critical assets entrusted to DOE.
- *Preventing the spread of WMDs*: DOE plays an integral part in nuclear nonproliferation, countering terrorism, and responding to incidents involving WMDs. The department does this by providing technology, analysis, and expertise developed through this program.

Environmental Measurements Laboratory

The Environmental Measurements Laboratory (EML, www.eml.st.dhs.gov), a government-owned, government-operated laboratory, is directly part of the S&T Directorate. The laboratory advances and applies the science and technology required for preventing, protecting against, and responding to radiological and nuclear events in the service of homeland and national security.

EML's current programs focus on issues associated with environmental radiation and radioactivity. Specifically, EML provides DHS with environmental radiation and radioactivity measurements in the laboratory or field, technology development and evaluation, personnel training, instrument calibration, performance testing, data management, and data quality assurance.

The two unique facilities of the lab follow:

- *Environmental chamber*: A 25-m^3 facility, the only one in the United States that can generate atmospheres with controlled aerosols and gases for calibration and testing of new instruments
- *Gamma spectrometry laboratory*: A fully equipped laboratory with high-efficiency, high-resolution gamma sensors

Plum Island Animal Disease Center

The Plum Island Animal Disease Center (PIADC, www.ars.usda.gov/plum/) became part of DHS on June 1, 2003. Although the center remains an important national asset in which scientists conduct basic and applied research and diagnostic activities to protect the health of livestock on farms across the nation from foreign disease agents, it was also tasked with a new mission to help DHS to protect the country from terrorist threats, including those directed against agriculture.

The USDA is responsible for research and diagnosis to protect the nation's animal industries and exports from catastrophic economic losses caused by foreign animal disease (FAD) agents accidentally or deliberately introduced into the United States. While continuing its mission, it works closely with DHS personnel to fight agroterrorism.

On September 11, 2005, the Department of Homeland Security announced that the Plum Island Animal Disease Center would be replaced by a new federal facility, the National Bio- and Agro-Defense Facility (NBAF). The NBAF will research high-consequence biological threats involving zoonotic (i.e., transmitted from animals to humans) and FADs. It will allow basic research; diagnostic development, testing, and validation; advanced countermeasure development; and training for high-consequence livestock diseases. The new facility is being designed to:

- Integrate those aspects of public and animal health research that have been determined to be central to national security
- Assess and research evolving bioterrorism threats over the next five decades
- Enable the Departments of Homeland Security and Agriculture (USDA) to fulfill their related homeland defense research, development, testing, and evaluation (RDT&E) responsibilities

Department of Health and Human Services Laboratories

The Department of Health and Human Services (www.hhs.gov) operates several laboratories focused on various health and disease prevention issues. The laboratories have extensive programs, and more details can be found later in this chapter.

U.S. Customs Laboratory and Scientific Services

DHS Customs and Border Protection Laboratories and Scientific Services (LSS) (www.cbp.gov/xp/cgov/import/operations_support/labs_scientific_svcs/) coordinates technical and scientific support with all CBP trade and border protection activities. The mission of the program is to provide rapid, quality scientific, forensic, and WMDs services to the CBP officials and other counterparts. One of the principal responsibilities of the CBP science officers is to manage the Customs Gauger/Laboratory Accreditation program. The program calls for the accreditation of commercial gaugers and laboratories so that their measurements and analytical results can be used by customs for entry and admissibility purposes. The staff edits and publishes the Customs Laboratory Bulletin, which, as a customs-scientific journal, is circulated internationally and provides a useful forum for technical exchange on subjects of general customs interest. U.S. Customs and Border Protection maintains the following laboratory facilities:

- *Springfield (VA) Laboratory*: The Springfield Laboratory is a centralized facility that provides scientific support to CBP headquarters and the laboratories listed below. This facility provides analytical services to CBP legal and regulatory functions and to CBP offices that require scientific support, and develops new analytical methods and evaluates new instrumentation. The activities of this facility vary in supporting CBP commercial and enforcement mission. The laboratory maintains the analytical uniformity among all CBP laboratories and maintains technical and scientific exchange with other federal enforcement agencies, technological branches of foreign customs agencies, and the military.

- *New York (NY) Laboratory*: The New York CBP services the greater New York City area including the New York Seaport, JFK Airport, the Port of Newark, and Perth Amboy. The laboratory provides scientific, forensic, and WMD services to CBP customers, including radiation detection, chemical WMD detection and identification, participation in the LSS national WMD strike team, and membership in the Food Emergency Response Network (FERN). This laboratory also trains DHS personnel on field radiation equipment.

- *Chicago (IL) Laboratory*: The Chicago Laboratory services all of the New England states, Illinois, Iowa, Nebraska, Wisconsin, Michigan, Kansas, Missouri, Indiana, part of Minnesota, and New York except the New York City Metro area. This facility provides technical advice and analytical services to CBP officers, U.S. Immigration and Customs Enforcement (ICE) agents, border patrol officers, and other entities on a wide range of issues. These services assist CBP officers in collecting revenue based on import duties and enforcing the law. The services provided to ICE agents and border patrol officers pertain primarily to law enforcement and forensics-related issues. The laboratory also provides training to its customers on interdiction, identification, and determination of WMDs.

- *Savannah (GA) Laboratory*: The Savannah Customs Laboratory serves ports from Philadelphia, PA, to Key West, FL. The facility conducts chemical and physical testing of all types of commodities, narcotics, and other controlled substances. The Savannah Laboratory operates two state-of-the art, custom-built mobile laboratories to meet the on-site testing needs of southeastern U.S. ports used for the detection of materials for WMD.

- *Southwest Regional Science Center (Houston, TX)*: The Southwest Regional Science Center provides technical and scientific services to all of the ports of entry and Border Patrol sectors in the following eight states: Alabama, Tennessee, Mississippi, Louisiana, Arkansas, Oklahoma, Texas, and New Mexico. This geographic area contains 80% of the border between the United States and Mexico. This facility provides technical and scientific services to manage, secure, and control the nation's border and to prevent terrorists and terrorist weapons from entering the United States. Services provided include forensic crime scene investigation, WMD interdiction, and trade enforcement. Forensic scientists provide support to law enforcement investigations with the analysis of latent prints, controlled substances, pharmaceuticals, audio and video enhancements, accident investigation, and expert witness testimony.

- *Los Angeles (CA) Laboratory*: The Los Angeles Laboratory services all of southern California, and southern Nevada, including Las Vegas, Arizona, and the California–Mexico border in these areas. The staff of chemists, textile analysts, and physical scientists is trained to assist in meeting the CBP mission in areas of trade, forensics, and WMDs. Among the laboratory's functions are forensic support such as evidence collection and analysis of trace, controlled substances and pharmaceuticals; technical support for chemical, biological, explosives, and radiation WMD issues;

and latent print processing at the crime scene or in the laboratory. The laboratory has mobile vans equipped with field instrumentation to analyze and identify certain unknown chemicals, textile construction and applications on textiles, controlled substances, explosives, and WMD chemical agents and radiation. The Los Angeles laboratory has vehicle-mounted and handheld detectors for rapid scan and identification of radiation sources from cargo containers.

- *San Francisco (CA) Laboratory*: The laboratory serves the northern two-thirds of California, as well as the states of Oregon, Washington, North Dakota, South Dakota, Minnesota, Alaska, Hawaii, Colorado, Utah, Nevada, Montana, and Idaho. Major ports located in this service area include San Francisco, Portland, Seattle, Blaine, Anchorage, Honolulu, and Denver. This facility provides technical advice, forensic, and other scientific services to the CBP officials and other agencies on a wide range of imported and exported commodities. The laboratory also provides supports in WMDs, explosives, hazardous materials, and crime scene investigation. Several staff members are qualified radiation isotope identification device (RIID) trainers, and continuously provide RIID operation trainings and CBP Radiation Detection Program and Response Protocol at the PNNL Radiation Academy (RADACAD) in Richland, Washington. The laboratory operates a small mobile unit that provides on-site examination and analyses of commercial shipments and training for local CBP officers, and crime scene investigation (fingerprint collection), and examination and analysis on any suspicious illicit radioactive materials entering this country.

- *San Juan (PR) Laboratory*: The San Juan Laboratory serves the ports of Puerto Rico and the U.S. Virgin Islands. This facility conducts chemical and physical testing of a wide variety of importations and forensic samples. Most of the facility's specialization has been in the area of controlled substances and other forensic samples. The San Juan Laboratory provides vital technical support and training to local and foreign law enforcement officials in areas such as WMD, radioactive material detection, crime scene management, and narcotics field test kits. The San Juan Laboratory mobile operations encompass active participation in WMD activities, forensic analysis, and crime scene management through all ports of Puerto Rico and the U.S. Virgin Islands.

Academic Research Institutions

Universities, their research centers, institutes, and qualified staff represent a very important portion of the scientific research in the United States. These facilities account for an estimated one-third of the total federal budget available for R&D activities. The S&T Directorate has already started to show its recognition of the importance of these institutions in the overall homeland security R&D effort through both awarding them R&D grants and funding Homeland Security Centers of Excellence on their campuses.

Homeland Security Centers of Excellence

The S&T Directorate, through its Office of University Programs, is furthering the homeland security mission by engaging the academic community to create learning and research environments in areas critical to homeland security. Through the Homeland Security Centers of Excellence program, DHS has invested in university-based partnerships to develop centers of multidisciplinary research where important fields of inquiry can be analyzed and best practices developed, debated, and shared. The department's Homeland Security Centers of Excellence (HS-Centers) bring together the nation's best experts and focus its most talented researchers on a variety of threats that include agricultural, chemical, biological, nuclear/radiological, explosive, and cyberterrorism as well as the behavioral aspects of terrorism. The current HS-Centers are listed in the "Homeland Security Centers of Excellence" sidebar. In FY 2012, $29.9 million in funding will be available for university programs.

■ ■ ■

Homeland Security Centers of Excellence

There are currently 12 Centers of Excellence across the country.

The Center for Risk and Economic Analysis of Terrorism Events (CREATE), led by the University of Southern California, develops advanced tools to evaluate the risks, costs, and consequences of terrorism.

The Center for Advancing Microbial Risk Assessment (CAMRA), led by Michigan State University and Drexel University established jointly with the U.S. Environmental Protection Agency, fills critical gaps in risk assessments for mitigating microbial hazards.

The Center of Excellence for Zoonotic and Animal Disease Defense (ZADD), led by Texas A&M University and Kansas State University, protects the nation's agricultural and public health sectors against high-consequence foreign animal and emerging and zoonotic disease threats.

The National Center for Food Protection and Defense (NCFPD), led by the University of Minnesota, defends the safety and security of the food system by conducting research to protect vulnerabilities in the nation's food supply chain.

The National Consortium for the Study of Terrorism and Responses to Terrorism (START), led by the University of Maryland, informs decisions on how to disrupt terrorists and terrorist groups through empirically grounded findings on the human element of the terrorist threat.

The National Center for the Study of Preparedness and Catastrophic Event Response (PACER), led by Johns Hopkins University, optimizes our nation's preparedness in the event of a high-consequence natural or man-made disaster.

The Center of Excellence for Awareness & Location of Explosives-Related Threats (ALERT), led by Northeastern University and the University of Rhode Island, will develop new means and methods to protect the nation from explosives-related threats.

The National Center for Border Security and Immigration (NCBSI), led by the University of Arizona in Tucson (research co-lead) and the University of Texas at El Paso (education co-lead), are developing technologies, tools, and advanced methods to balance immigration and commerce with effective border security.

The Center for Maritime, Island and Remotes and Extreme Environment Security (MIREES), led by the University of Hawaii and Stevens Institute of Technology, focuses on developing robust research and education programs addressing maritime domain awareness to safeguard populations and properties in geographical areas that present significant security challenges.

The Coastal Hazards Center of Excellence (CHC), led by the University of North Carolina at Chapel Hill and Jackson State University in Jackson, Miss., performs research and develops education programs to enhance the nation's ability to safeguard populations, properties, and economies from catastrophic natural disaster.

The National Transportation Security Center of Excellence (NTSCOE) was established in accordance with HR1, Implementing the Recommendations of the 9/11 Commission Act of 2007, in August 2007. The NTSCOE will develop new technologies, tools, and advanced methods to defend, protect, and increase the resilience of the nation's multimodal transportation. It comprises seven institutions:

- Connecticut Transportation Institute at the University of Connecticut
- Tougaloo College
- Texas Southern University

- National Transit Institute at Rutgers — the State University of New Jersey
- Homeland Security Management Institute at Long Island University
- Mack Blackwell National Rural Transportation Study Center at the University of Arkansas
- Mineta Transportation Institute at San José State University

The Center of Excellence in Command, Control and Interoperability (C2I), led by Purdue University (visualization sciences co-lead) and Rutgers University (data sciences co-lead), will create the scientific basis and enduring technologies needed to analyze massive amounts of information to detect security threats.

Source: DHS, 2011, http://www.dhs.gov/files/programs/editorial_0498.shtm.

Maritime Research

The scope of the S&T Directorate encompasses the pursuit of a full range of research into the use, preservation, and exploitation of the national waterways and oceans. The U.S. Coast Guard Research and Development Center is in charge of conducting research to support defense of this resource and of the homeland.

U.S. Coast Guard

The Research and Development (R&D) Center is the Coast Guard's (www.uscg.mil) sole facility performing research, development, test, and evaluation (RDT&E) in support of the Coast Guard's major missions of maritime mobility, maritime safety, maritime security, national defense, and protection of natural resources. The center has as its mission "to be the Coast Guard's pathfinder, anticipating and meeting future technological challenges, while partnering with others to shepherd the best ideas into implementable solutions."

The Coast Guard RDT&E program produces two types of products: the development of hardware, procedures, and systems that directly contribute to increasing the quality and productivity of the operations and the expansion of knowledge related to technical support of operating and regulatory programs.

R&D Efforts External to the Department of Homeland Security

The majority of homeland security R&D funding is provided to federal agencies other than the DHS.

Department of Health and Human Services

National Institutes of Health

The National Institutes of Health's (NIH, www.nih.gov) most relevant effort in homeland security R&D is in bioterrorism-related research. It has conducted work in the field for much longer than the existence of the DHS, but it emerged as a high-priority R&D agency after the 2001 anthrax mail situation. Budget allocations, which tend to be a reliable predictor of federal priorities, have clearly indicated that this dedication to bioterrorism detection and countermeasures remains. In the FY 2012 budget, NIH saw a minor increase in homeland security research funding of 3.1% from the previous year, up to $1.929 billion. NIH is clearly the leader within the federal government for homeland security R&D efforts for its biodefense research portfolio. The biodefense priorities of NIAID include, in addition to biodefense research, the development of medical countermeasures against radiological and nuclear threats, and medical counter-measures against chemical threats.

Centers for Disease Control and Prevention

The Centers for Disease Control and Prevention (CDC, www.cdc.gov) is another component of HHS that traditionally performed WMD terrorism R&D. However, with the opening of the Biodefense Advanced Research and Development Agency, CDC homeland security R&D funds have diminished. In fact, the majority of CDC terrorism activities, which are not R&D in nature, include the management of the Strategic National Stockpile (SNS) and funding for state and local responders to upgrade their abilities to prepare for and manage WMD events.

Biodefense Advanced Research and Development Agency

As part of its expanding effort to fund anthrax research and other R&D related to defenses against ter-rorist threats, the Office of the Secretary of Health and Human Services funded biodefense R&D in the Biodefense Advanced Research and Development Authority (BARDA, www.hhs.gov/aspr/barda/index .html). BARDA funds advanced R&D of new biodefense countermeasures as part of an HHS-wide effort to secure an adequate supply of such countermeasures for the SNS.

Department of Defense

The Department of Defense (DOD) has had a fluctuating budget for homeland security R&D since 2001. In FY 2012, DOD R&D funding decreased by 11%, to a total allocation of $2,115 billion. The vast majority of DOD R&D funding is provided through the Defense Advanced Research Projects Agency (DARPA), which works mainly on applications that serve the needs of the military (e.g., biological war-fare defense and the Chemical and Biological Defense Program). The outcome of this research, however, often has applications that can be applied by civilian first responders despite the military origin of the projects that generated them. The DOD Chemical and Biological Defense Program (CBDP) is another research-oriented agency that performs homeland security research activities.

Department of Agriculture

Even more so than DOD, the USDA has witnessed widely fluctuating R&D budgets since the September 11 terrorist attacks. Actual fiscal year funding amounts have varied from less than $50 million to over $170 million. Since 9/11, USDA has invested a considerable amount of research effort toward developing security mechanisms to protect dangerous pathogens, which could be used as terror weapons and are located in many laboratories dispersed throughout the United States. Increases in funding in FY 2006 and 2007 were dedi-cated to renovating facilities that performed animal research and diagnosis at the National Centers for Animal Health in Ames, Iowa. These efforts are aimed at protecting the U.S. food supply from acts of sabotage and terrorism — both of which could have potentially devastating effects on the U.S. economy. The FY 2012 fund-ing for USDA homeland security R&D efforts is $88 million, an increase of almost 4% over the previous year.

Environmental Protection Agency

The Environmental Protection Agency (EPA) has seen steady but small federal allocations of Homeland Security R&D funding since September 11. Since that year EPA research related to homeland security has been focused primarily on drinking water security research (which would involve EPA efforts to develop better surveillance and laboratory networks for drinking water supplies to counter potential terrorist threats) and decontamination research (to develop better technologies and methods for decontaminating terrorist attack sites). EPA also conducts threat and consequence assessments and tests potential biodefense and other decontamination technologies. Much of this work is conducted at EPA's National Homeland Security Research Center (NHSRC) in Cincinnati. NHSRC develops expertise and products that are used to prevent, prepare for, and recover from public health and environmental emergencies arising from terrorist threats and incidents. Research and development efforts focus on the following five primary areas:

- *Threat and consequence assessment*: Investigates human exposure to chemical, biological, and radiological contaminants to define dangerous levels of these contaminants and establish protective cleanup goals.
- *Decontamination and consequence management*: Focuses on decontamination of buildings and outdoor environments, as well as the safe disposal of contaminated materials.
- *Water infrastructure protection*: Protects the nation's drinking water sources and distribution systems and ensures the safety of wastewater collection, treatment, and disposal procedures.
- *Response capability enhancement*: Works directly with emergency responders and local governments to provide tools and information needed to make informed decisions in the event of an attack.
- *Technology testing and evaluation*: Evaluates technologies that show potential for use in homeland security applications. These evaluations are used by water utility operators, building owners, emergency responders, and others to make informed decisions when purchasing security technology.

National Institute of Standards and Technology

The Department of Commerce (DOC) is home to the National Institute of Standards and Technology (NIST), which funds R&D in cryptography and computer security and which provides scientific and technical support to DHS in these areas.

National Science Foundation

The National Science Foundation (NSF) funds research to combat bioterrorism in the areas of infectious diseases and microbial genome sequencing. These programs increased to $395 million in FY 2012.

Conclusion

Homeland security represents an entirely new spectrum of issues of R&D and technology and an opportunity to revitalize old issues under the homeland security umbrella. Establishing DHS and the S&T Directorate brought a new, major player into the federally supported R&D efforts. There was much discussion and disgruntlement within the research community concerning the lack of involvement of the NSF in the development of the homeland security R&D agenda. In fact, several people questioned the need for the S&T as opposed to just increasing the NSF's or NIST's portfolios.

With a spectrum of activity varying from research to development to deployment, and a span of subjects from bioterrorism to personal protective equipment, from communication tools to nonproliferation, and from detection devices to mass production of vaccines, the S&T Directorate has been given a monumental task. The directorate not only coordinates the R&D facilities of many organizations but also has the authority to set priorities in others. The university-based HS-Centers provide a level of funding

FIGURE 12–4 New York City, NY, September 29, 2001 — Lobby of hotel near the World Trade Center site. (Source: Photo by Andrea Booher/FEMA News Photo)

that has not been available for some time and provide one of the best funded opportunities for specific R&D to benefit emergency management.

Although the context of change leaves little room for conclusions, the extraordinary budget given to the S&T Directorate either in existing programs or in new ones will provide the emergency-management and first-responder communities new capabilities never before imagined. It is to be hoped that these technological "toys" do not give a false sense of confidence and overshadow the real requirements of building an improved capacity to mitigate, prepare for, respond to, and recover from the risks of terrorism (Figure 12–4).

The changes that can be implied with the establishment of the university-based centers should be watched closely. These centers comprise the most concrete platform for the partnership, or "integration," of academia, the private sector, and the federal government in support of homeland security. The establishment and progress of these centers must be followed carefully in order to discover the answer to two fundamental questions:

- How ready are these sectors to work together? That is, can the most basic goal of survival and safety of the homeland be a motivation strong enough to overcome the sectors' administrative and functional differences?

- Will real integration occur? The R&D field may be the place that shows whether integration at the large scale as proposed by the DHS is really possible or not. This field is probably the most appropriate one because research, development, and deployment are very close functions. But this task may be more difficult than it seems because it involves many different organizations, whose cooperation, successes, or failures can put the success of the entire organization at risk.

Key Terms

BioWatch: A program aimed at detecting the release of pathogens into the air, thereby providing warning to the government and public health community of a potential bioterror event. This is performed through the use of aerosol samplers mounted on preexisting EPA air-quality monitoring stations that collect air, passing it through filters. These filters are manually collected at regular, reportedly 24-hours, intervals and are analyzed for potential biological weapon pathogens using polymerase chain reaction (PCR) techniques. Although filters from the BioWatch program were initially shipped to and tested at a federal laboratory in California, state and local public health laboratories now perform the analyses.

MANPADS: A man-portable air defense system is a missile firing device, used to destroy aircraft, that is easily carried or transported by a person.

SAFECOM: A communications program of the DHS Office for Interoperability and Compatibility that, with its federal partners, provides research, development, testing and evaluation, guidance, tools, and templates on communications-related issues to local, tribal, state, and federal emergency response agencies.

Review Questions

1. Identify the four lead groups of research in the DHS Science and Technology Directorate and explain what each does to contribute to counterterrorism efforts.
2. Define in your own words why HSARPA was established, and explain its scope and objectives.
3. What are the Homeland Security Centers of Excellence, and what are the research and development goals of each?
4. What government laboratories are working to develop WMD countermeasures? What specific areas of research is each focused on?
5. What government laboratories are working to protect critical information and infrastructure from terrorist attack? What specific areas of research is each focused on?

References

American Association for the Advancement of Science (AAAS), 2011. AAAS XXXVI: Research and Development FY2012. http://www.aaas.org/spp/rd/rdreport2012/.

DHS, 2004. National Response Plan. http://www.scd.hawaii.gov/documents/nrp.pdf.

DHS, 2011, Under Secretary Tara O'Toole, Science and Technology Directorate, before the House Committee on Appropriations. Subcommittee on Homeland Security. S&T Fiscal Year 2012 Budget Request. http://www.dhs.gov/ynews/testimony/testimony_1301519363336.shtm.

Department of Homeland Security, 2003. Medical treatment of radiological casualties. http://www.appc1.va.gov/emshg/docs/Radiologic_Medical_Countermeasures_051403.pdf.

Office of Homeland Security, 2002. National strategy for homeland security. http://www.whitehouse.gov/homeland/book.

Telecommunications Service Priority, 2003. Welcome to the TSP website, National Coordination Center for Telecommunications (NCC), December 4. http://www.tsp.ncs.gov/.

13

The Future of Homeland Security

Introduction

This chapter is provided to identify and briefly explain several of the most pressing issues confronting the role of emergency management and disaster assistance programs in homeland security, both in general and specific to the Department of Homeland Security (DHS). Just as the Federal Emergency Management Agency (FEMA) has been the federal government leader in the national emergency management system since its 1979 inception, DHS has assumed a similar leadership role in the creation and management of a national system to ensure the security of the nation.

Even now, 10 years after the September 11 attacks, a measure of how effectively DHS can perform in this leadership position and exactly what role emergency management and disaster assistance functions will ultimately play within DHS and the national homeland security system have not been adequately developed. The massive failure of the federal government's response to Hurricane Katrina in August 2005 and the ongoing failure of the recovery efforts nearly 6 years later indicate very clearly that this single critical issue is yet to be resolved.

We believe that FEMA's history offers two important lessons for DHS as it progresses in its difficult mission. First, it is critical for DHS to take all the necessary steps to ensure that the nation's emergency management and disaster assistance capabilities, especially those at the federal government level, are not marginalized. Additionally, these emergency management agencies must be given the tools that enable them to effectively manage the new terrorist threat with which they are confronted. Second, terrorism, in all of its forms, must not become the singular risk driving DHS policy. In the absence of an all-hazards approach coupled with the growing risk caused by global climate change, the scene will surely be set for a repeat of the Hurricane Katrina fiasco.

The FEMA History Lesson

Prior to 1979, federal emergency management and disaster preparedness, response, and recovery programs and capabilities were scattered among numerous federal government agencies, including the White House. There was little, if any, coordination among these disparate parts. Communicating with the federal government during a disaster had become such a problem that the National Governor's Association petitioned then president Jimmy Carter to consolidate all federal programs into a single agency.

On April 1, 1979, President Carter signed the executive order that established the Federal Emergency Management Agency, moving federal disaster programs, agencies, and offices from across the federal government into a single executive branch agency. The director of FEMA was charged with integrating these diverse programs into one cohesive operation capable of delivering federal resources and assistance through a new concept called the *integrated emergency management system*. This system was centered on an all-hazards approach.

With the election of President Ronald Reagan in 1980, the focus of FEMA's policies and programs shifted dramatically from an all-hazards approach to a single focus on nuclear attack planning through its Office of National Preparedness. At the same time, agency leadership and personnel struggled to integrate its many diverse programs. This focuses on a single low-probability/high-impact event and the inability of the agency's many parts to function effectively as one led to the disastrous responses to Hurricane Hugo, the Loma Prieta earthquake, and Hurricane Andrew. There were numerous calls for the abolition of FEMA, including from several members of Congress.

President Bill Clinton, elected in 1992, appointed the first FEMA director who was an experienced emergency manager. Under James Lee Witt's leadership, FEMA once again adopted an all-hazards approach, became a customer-focused organization that worked closely with its state and local emergency management partners, and effectively responded to an unprecedented series of major disasters across the country. These included not only major natural disasters but also terrorist events such as the first World Trade Center bombing and the Oklahoma City bombing.

The new FEMA successfully launched a national community-based disaster mitigation initiative, Project Impact, and for the first time reached out to the nation's business community to partner in emergency management at the national and community levels.

By the time of the election of President George W. Bush in 2000, FEMA had gained the trust of the public, the media, its partners, and elected officials in all levels of government. FEMA functioned as a single agency as envisioned when it was created in 1979 and possessed one of the most favorable brand names in government.

Upon taking office in 2001, the Bush administration began to deconstruct FEMA. It was assumed that a program like Project Impact, which focused on individual and private sector responsibility, would thrive under a Republican administration. Instead it was eliminated (based on an argument that it was not effective), and funding for other natural disaster mitigation programs was dramatically reduced. However, the effect of Project Impact was given national media attention after an earthquake struck Seattle in February 2001 and the mayor of Seattle credited his city's participation in the Project Impact program for the minimal losses the city experienced as a result of that quake.

The emphasis on the national security functions of FEMA was highlighted when new FEMA Director Joe Allbaugh was reinstated to the Office of National Preparedness and all indications were that FEMA would once again focus on national security issues.

This process was accelerated after the September 11, 2001, terrorist attacks. FEMA became part of the new DHS, and the all-hazards approach, while acknowledged in speeches, was replaced by a single focus on terrorism. More importantly, the director of FEMA no longer reported directly to the president and was replaced in the president's cabinet by the DHS secretary. In the first major reorganization of DHS that began in July 2005, the FEMA of the 1990s was disassembled and its parts spread throughout the department.

In August 2005, Hurricane Katrina stuck the Gulf Coast and history repeated itself. DHS/FEMA was unable to provide the support needed by state and local officials for adequate response and hundreds of Americans died as a result. DHS/FEMA continues to fail to this day in the recovery phase as well. As this chapter is written in July 2011, FEMA's reputation has finally begun to improve following its response to the tornadoes in Tuscaloosa, AL, and Joplin, MO, in 2011, but for most of the public FEMA's reputation remains as sullied as it was in August 1992 after the botched response to Hurricane Andrew.

Despite DHS's current organizational restructuring, serious questions remain concerning FEMA's and the federal government's capabilities in responding to a catastrophic disaster, whether it be a hurricane, earthquake, flood, or another terrorist attack. The nation's emergency management system remains broken. How it will be repaired and returned to its former capability remains to be seen.

Lessons for Homeland Security from the FEMA Experience

The writer George Santayana once famously said, "Those who ignore history are doomed to repeat it." There are two critical lessons to be learned from the FEMA experience that provide some perspective on how the DHS may function in the future.

First and foremost, it will take time for DHS to become a functioning organization. DHS was cobbled together in much the same way that FEMA was bringing together an estimated 178,000 federal workers from 22 agencies and programs in a very short time period. It took FEMA nearly 15 years and several reorganizations to effectively coordinate and deliver the full resources of the federal government to support state and local governments in responding to major disasters. DHS is less than 10 years old and has already undertaken three major reorganizations. If FEMA's experience is any kind of indicator, it will be at least another 5 years before DHS will achieve full functionality.

Second, the single focus on a low-probability/high-impact event (i.e., a major terrorist attack similar to September 11) will undermine DHS's capabilities in responding to high-probability/low-impact events. A FEMA staffer once said that you don't plan for the maximum event probable; you plan for the maximum event possible. This is especially critical for FEMA's response and recovery and preparedness and mitigation programs. In terms of natural and traditional man-made disasters (hurricanes, earthquakes, hazardous materials incidents, etc.), these programs' capabilities have been marginalized. The 2005 hurricanes in Florida and the resulting congressional and media investigations of fraud and incompetence that characterized the federal response and the miserable performance in Hurricane Katrina are clear evidence of the negative impact this single focus can have in an all-hazards world.

Clearly, DHS has repeated the mistakes made by FEMA in the past and at this time seems intent on continuing on this path in the future. These mistakes will impact the department's functions as a whole but none more so that the traditional emergency management functions: mitigation, preparedness, response, and recovery

DHS's primary mission is to prevent a terrorist attack on American soil. The emergency management and disaster assistance functions centered in FEMA contribute little to this mission. However, should another terrorist event occur in the future, as everyone concedes that it will, these emergency management and disaster assistance functions will be critical in preparing our people, reducing the impact, and mounting an effective response and recovery that gets Americans back on their feet quickly. Marginalizing these capabilities as it pursues its primary mission is a mistake that FEMA made in the past and one that DHS cannot afford to repeat now and in the future.

The Future of Emergency Management in Homeland Security

Rebuilding the nation's emergency management system, especially the role of the federal government in this system, does not conflict with the primary mission of DHS. In fact, it is a critical element in the overall homeland security strategy. However, we feel several steps must be taken to rebuild and enhance the nation's emergency management system and to return the federal government to a leadership role in this area.

Reestablish FEMA as an Executive Branch Agency

In March 2004, former FEMA Director James Lee Witt, in testimony before a joint hearing of two House Government Reform subcommittees, strongly recommended that FEMA be removed from DHS and be reestablished as an executive branch agency that reports directly to the president. Witt stated, "FEMA, having lost its status as an independent agency, is being buried beneath a massive bureaucracy whose main and seemingly only focus is fighting terrorism while an all-hazards mission is getting lost in the shuffle" (Peckenpaugh, 2004).

Moving FEMA out of DHS and consolidating its traditional mitigation, preparedness, response, and recovery programs will ensure that the all-hazards approach will be reinstated and that FEMA and its state and local partners will once again focus on dealing with all manners of disaster events including terrorist attacks. Emergency management professionals will once again be in charge of preparing the public, reducing future impacts through hazard mitigation, and managing the resources of the federal government in support of state and local governments in responding to major disasters and fostering a speedy and effective recovery from these events.

This system worked very well in the 1990s when the United States had the most sophisticated and efficient emergency management system in the world. This system effectively responded to hundreds of major natural disasters across the country and successfully managed the federal response to the Oklahoma City bombing and the September 11 attacks in New York City and at the Pentagon. This system also produced comprehensive preparedness and training programs and the first national community-based hazard mitigation initiative.

The post-Katrina reorganization of DHS and FEMA has returned the preparedness, mitigation, response, and recovery programs to FEMA. But this reorganization did not provide the FEMA administrator direct access to the president of the United States. Only the president can vest the authority in the FEMA administrator that is needed for a successful federal response.

Reestablishing FEMA outside of DHS will not conflict with DHS's primary mission to prevent terrorist attacks on American soil and will enhance those critical elements in the homeland security system that will be called upon when the next event occurs.

Re-create the Federal Response Plan

The Federal Response Plan (FRP) successfully guided the federal government's response to over 350 presidentially declared disasters from Hurricane Andrew through the September 11 attacks. The FRP was an agreement signed by department and agency heads from 32 federal departments and agencies and the American Red Cross.

The FRP had three critical elements:

1. The president designated and empowered the director of FEMA to direct the actions of the 32 signatories to the plan.
2. Each signatory to the plan agreed to make specific resources available during a major disaster event.
3. Each signatory to the plan would be reimbursed for any resources expended at the direction and authorization of FEMA.

The bottom line is that when the president declared a major disaster event, the FRP ensured that the full resources of the federal government would be brought to bear in support of state and local government and directed by FEMA. No single agency was expected to carry the full federal responsibility and everyone knew that the director of FEMA was in charge.

The FRP was replaced first by the National Response Plan in 2004 and most recently by the National Response Framework in 2008. The FRP was developed through extensive planning and negotiations among emergency management specialists at FEMA and the other federal agencies over a five-year period. The National Response Plan was developed by DHS in less than a year with limited involvement from outside of DHS. The National Response Framework was developed by the DHS deputy secretary's office after an aborted attempt by the emergency management community to reform the National Response Plan.

The National Response Plan attempted to build on the FRP, but instead managed to confuse the roles of the individual departments and agencies and to marginalize the authority and the role of the FEMA Director in directing the federal response. The National Response Framework is just what its title indicates, a framework for how the nation as a whole will prepare for and respond to a major disaster. It is not a plan for managing the federal response to a major disaster and, similar to the National Response Plan, fails to designate what agency will direct the federal response.

A major step in rebuilding the nation's emergency management system and rebuilding the trust of the state and local emergency managers and the public must be re-creating the FRP with FEMA returned to the role of directing the plan. The FRP is a proven method for delivering federal resources in support of state and local efforts in a timely and cost-efficient manner.

Encourage Community-Based Homeland Security

Since September 11, 2001, the federal government has taken the lead in homeland security and the vast majority of policy and program initiatives have focused on federal capabilities and responsibilities. With the exception of the Citizen Corps program and Web based awareness campaigns such as Ready.gov, very little has been done to effectively involve the American public in homeland security activities.

The "Redefining Readiness" study conducted by the New York Academy of Medicine identified numerous problems with the assumptions of homeland security planners in developing smallpox and dirty bomb plans without input from the public. Involving the public in developing community-based homeland security plans is critical to the successful implementation of these plans.

This study and others have discovered that a large segment of the public is ready and willing to participate in these planning efforts and to be part of a community-based effort to deal with the new homeland security threats. Mechanisms for involving the public in this process are needed.

A good model for such a mechanism is Project Impact, the former FEMA initiative to develop disaster-resistant communities. At its height, more than 225 Project Impact communities were functioning across the country with support from FEMA. Each community had created a community partnership that involved all stakholders in the community, including the business sector, in identifying community risks, identifying what could be done to mitigate these risks, and developing and implementing a plan to take action to reduce the impacts of future disaster events in their community.

The Project Impact model is based on an all-hazards approach, and including the new risks from terrorism into this model would be simple. The city of Tulsa, Oklahoma, has done just that, successfully incorporating homeland security efforts into its Project Impact programs that were originally developed to address flood and tornado risks.

The bottom line is that the general public must be involved in the development and implementation of community homeland security plans, and DHS and its partners in state and local government should invest more resources in developing the planning processes needed to involve the public in the nation's homeland security system.

Improve Communications

Communicating with the public is another area that needs to be improved if the nation is going to have a truly effective homeland security system. To date, DHS has shown little interest in communicating with the public, and when it has, the results have not always been positive — the "duct tape and plastic" fiasco serves as a classic example. FEMA's failed communications in Hurricane Katrina is another. DHS and its state and local partners need to address three factors to improve its communications with the American people.

First, there must be a commitment from the leadership, not only at DHS and its state and local partners, but at all levels of government, including the executive level, to communicate timely and accurate information to the public. This is especially important in the response and recovery phases to a terrorist incident.

In a disaster scenario, the conventional wisdom that states information is power and hoarding information helps to retain such power is almost categorically reversed. Withholding information during disaster events generally has an overall negative effect on the well-being of the public and on the impression the public forms about involved authorities. In practice, sharing of information is what generates authority and power, when that information is useful and relates to the hazard at hand. Two shining examples of this fact are the actions of former FEMA Director James Lee Witt and former New York City Mayor Rudy Giuliani. Both leaders went to great lengths to provide accurate and timely information to the public in a time of crisis, and their efforts both inspired the public and greatly enhanced the effectiveness of the response and recovery efforts they guided.

To date, DHS leadership and the political leadership have been reluctant to make this commitment to share information with the public. This is something that must change if they expect the American people to fully comprehend the homeland security threat and to become actively engaged in homeland security efforts. Few citizens have an idea of what actual terrorism risks they face, and fewer can actually relate those risks in any comparable fashion to the risks they face every day without notice.

Second, homeland security officials at all levels must resolve the conflict between sharing information with the public in advance and in the aftermath of a terrorist incident that has value for intelligence or criminal prosecution purposes. This is directly linked to the commitment issue discussed in the previous paragraphs and has been repeatedly cited by homeland security officials as reasons for not sharing more specific information with the public.

This is a very difficult issue that DHS has tried to ignore in the past. The continued frustration among the public and state and local officials with the Homeland Security Advisory System (HSAS) was just one sign that this issue would not solve itself or just go away.

Also an issue is the question of when to release relevant information to the public without compromising intelligence sources and/or ongoing criminal investigations. This is an issue that rarely, if ever, confronts emergency management officials dealing with natural and unintentional man-made disasters. Therefore, there is little precedent or experience for current homeland security officials to work within crafting a communications strategy that balances the competing need for the public to have timely and accurate information with the need to protect intelligence sources and ongoing criminal investigations. To date, the needs of the intelligence and justice communities have clearly been judged to outweigh those of the public.

The implementation of the National Terrorism Alert System (NTAS) that replaced the much maligned HSAS will hopefully be a critical first step in reestablishing trust with the public for a terrorism warning system. From this starting point, if the commitment is there among the homeland security leadership, additional communications mechanisms can be developed to ensure that the public gets timely and accurate information both in advance of any terrorist incident and during the response and recovery phases in the aftermath of the next terrorist attack.

Third, more efforts must be invested by federal departments and agencies to better understand the principal terrorist threats that our nation faces (i.e., biological, chemical, radiological, nuclear, and explosives) and to develop communications strategies that educate and inform the public about these threats with more useful information. The 2001 Washington, DC, anthrax incident is a perfect example of uninformed or misinformed public officials sharing what is often conflicting and, in too many instances, wrong information with the public.

The nation's public officials must become better informed about these principal risks and be ready and capable of explaining complicated information to the public. As the anthrax incident made clear, this is not a luxury, but a necessity if the response to similar incidents in the future is to be successful.

Decades of research and a new generation of technologies now inform emergency managers as they provide information about hurricanes, tornadoes, earthquakes, and hazardous materials incidents to the public. A similar research effort must be undertaken for these five new terrorist risks and communications strategies that will ensure that homeland security officials at all levels are capable of clearly explaining to the public the hazards posed by these threats.

These communications strategies must consider how to communicate to the public when incomplete information is all that is available to homeland security officials. In the vast majority of cases, this partiality of information is probable. A public health crisis will not wait for all the data to be collected and analyzed, nor will the public. Homeland security officials must develop strategies for informing the public effectively, as the crisis develops, by forming effective messages that are able to explain to the public how what is being said is the most accurate information available based on the information that, likewise, is available — despite its incomplete nature. Clearly, this is not an easy task, but it is not impossible. The public will increasingly expect such communications efforts, so the sooner such a system is in place, the better the next incident will be managed.

Partner with the Business Sector

The DHS and numerous business groups, such as the Business Roundtable, U.S. Chamber of Commerce, ASIS International, acknowledge that an effective partnership between the government and business groups must be maintained as part of the nation's homeland security efforts. This is only logical considering that the nation's economic security depends in part on the success of the nation's national security policies. A number of steps have been taken in the recent years to enhance this partnership, but there remains more work to be done in aligning the full strengths of the public and private sector in the homeland security mission space.

President Barack Obama stressed the convergence of economic and national security policies in the May 2010 release of his National Security Strategy. The Quadrennial Homeland Security Review also noted this relationship by including the private sector as part of the defined group of stakeholders referred to as the "homeland security enterprise." During the pandemic of 2009, DHS, HHS, and DOC were lauded by businesses for holding numerous joint conference calls with industries of every size, providing access to the latest scientific data, coordinated messaging, and protective actions leaders could take to protect their employees. A number of private-sector elements within DHS are focused on improving the effectiveness of government coordination with the private sector as well as creating the opportunity for business to partner with government. But this is a two-way street and government cannot do so much; industry too must be prepared to share essential information and collaborate.

The DHS Private Sector Office created a private-sector resources catalog[1] to centralize all the services offered to the private sector in the homeland security space from across the department. A Loaned

---

[1] For details on numerous DHS programs involving the private sector see http://www.dhs.gov/privatesector.

Executive Program was created to allow experts from industry to serve in limited appointments within DHS to share their specific expertise. Recommendations for improving information sharing have been developed with industry leaders including the National Infrastructure Advisory Council and the Critical Infrastructure Partnership Advisory Council. The Office of Infrastructure's Protective Security Advisors (PSAs) work closely with owners and operators of critical infrastructure as well as the DHS Office of Intelligence & Analysis and state and local personnel at the fusion centers to constantly address the dynamic risk environment. The PSAs are consistently referenced by business and state and local government leaders as vital to their all-hazards response and risk management activities.

However, in the nearly 10 years since the attacks of September 11, 2001, more focus and commitment can be directed in ensuring the private sector is a ready and prepared partner for the next crisis. There has been some progress and cooperation, but there is no overall strategy in place to incorporate the business sector into the government's emergency management planning for homeland security.

This issue was clearly illustrated in the response to Hurricane Katrina. There are countless examples of efforts by members of the business community to provide resources and assistance to the victims of the hurricane only to be frustrated by uncooperative federal officials.

Numerous issues must be resolved before such a strategy can be designed and implemented. A significant issue that must be addressed is how the government will protect and use confidential information that it is asking or requiring the business community to provide. The business community, which has vast institutional knowledge about this privacy issue as well as countless other issues that have been presented in the homeland security approach, must be included in the planning process not only for terrorism response planning but also for natural disaster management. FEMA has taken steps in the right direction by placing Private Sector Liaisons in each FEMA region and has created a Private Sector Division within FEMA External Affairs to coordinate with the private sector more readily. FEMA also established a Private Sector Representative seat in the National Response Coordination Center to ensure the private-sector perspective was available and a constant part of FEMA response operations. Some businesses have begun sharing RSS and Geo-RSS feeds of their stories in an impacted area to speed coordination and recovery. According to FEMA, over 3,000 private-sector entities participated in the 2011 National Level Exercise simulating an earthquake along the New Madrid Seismic Zone. When combined with a more holistic strategy for private-sector capability alignment across the homeland security mission areas, these many initial actions could have significant longer term impact.

One possible avenue for establishing and nurturing an effective partnership with the business sector is to start at the community level. Issues such as what the government will do with confidential information are likely to be less critical at the community level, allowing for lessons to be learned in progressive steps. Additionally, there is an established history of public–private partnerships in emergency management at the community level, many of which started with FEMA's Project Impact program. To illustrate this point, the following message received by our team of authors from Kathleen Criss, emergency management coordinator for the University of Pittsburgh Medical Center, is provided:

> *I want to share with you the PA Region 13 program, which has been acknowledged as one of the first and is considered a national best practice for regional mutual aid by FEMA and several other organizations. Robert Full, Chief of Allegheny County Emergency Services and the nominated Chair of the PA Region 13 Counter-terrorism Task Force, has been actively working with the business community since 1999. A public/private partnership was established during the Year 2000 planning and continues today to address "all-hazards" and homeland security concerns.*

There is a formal plan in place to activate the Business Liaison role in the Allegheny County Emergency Operations Center during a crisis; this plan has been tested several times through actual disaster events and drills. We are currently working on IT solutions to improve emergency communications, alerting capabilities, and resource sharing at times of disaster. Members of the business community were also invited to attend hazard mitigation training courses with first responders, participate in workshops to improve security in chemical and other "critical infrastructure" organizations, and planning meetings to document the County's hazard mitigation plan for submission to the Commonwealth of Pennsylvania. We also participate regularly in annual disaster drills — from planning to the final after-action report and follow-up to correct deficiencies (Criss, 2005).

Criss indicated in her message that she has been working closely with officials at DHS to promote their efforts as a best practice to other areas of the country, and that

DHS does understand this problem and is trying to the best of its ability to work with these existing groups to improve its own programs, where possible. It is not a quick or easy process to implement. It takes trust and dedication from the public and private sectors to begin this relationship to allow the two sides to work together for the betterment of the community it serves.

FEMA will eventually deploy trainings from EMI that support the alignment of the private sector within the community preparedness paradigm, but it will fall to community, government, and industry leaders to ensure their personnel take the courses and implement the lessons and processes necessary for any training to be successful in action. There are other examples of public–private partnerships working in homeland security that are built on the attributes noted by Criss. We believe that this bottom-up approach to developing public–private partnerships may be the best avenue for homeland security officials at all levels to pursue.

ANOTHER VOICE: FOUR OPPORTUNITIES FOR FUTURE HOMELAND SECURITY LEADERS BY BRIDGER MCGAW.

The following four opportunities offer future homeland security leaders the ability to improve the effectiveness of homeland security policies and programs:

Opportunity #1: Evolve Emergency Management for the Cyber-Age
Whether it's the operation of interoperable radios, 911 networks, proliferation of smart phones, emergency operations centers, evacuation coordination, or electric grid resilience, cyber and information technology infrastructure are essential to the effective efforts of the emergency management and homeland security enterprise. The interdependencies between critical infrastructure and cyberspace only continue to increase, requiring more attention from public and private sector leaders. If emergency managers are to be effective in the cyber-age, they must rapidly acknowledge this new paradigm in deterring, preparing for, responding to, or recovering from a future crisis or terrorist event.

While cybersecurity rhetorically is included within the "all-hazards" framework, homeland security advisors, emergency managers, chief information officers, and chief information security officers

(Continued)

will have to work and train more closely and aggressively to make it a reality. Public and private sector decision makers should integrate cybersecurity measures into business continuity plans and incident response and recovery plans, and clearly lay out how their respective organizations will work together to respond to events during a cyber incident.

At the national level, the National Cyber Incident Response Plan is a step in the right direction, but State and local governments and critical infrastructure owners and operators must evaluate their preparations for addressing the cyber threat and the possibility for physical impacts. As more and more essential government and industry processes or services are placed in the cloud or managed online, the security of this information and resiliency of networks must be improved against a diverse number of potential attackers. One challenge that should become clear for decision makers is that the business case for closer collaboration between cyber and physical security officials is being made with every successful attack viewed in the news. Ensuring emergency management officials are part of that solution will be helpful.

Opportunity #2: Support Information Sharing and Intelligence Fusion Centers

The 9/11 Commission made it clear that removing barriers to information sharing would improve counterterrorism actions by government agencies. Leaders in the national security community must make this effort a long-lasting reality. Success of the information-sharing effort cannot be under-valued.

A tool that Federal, State, and local homeland security entities are embracing is the State and Major Urban Area Fusion Center.[1] The National Strategy for Information Sharing describes how the Fusion Center concept has rapidly evolved to "foster a culture that recognizes the importance of fusing 'all crimes' with national security implications and 'all-hazards' information (e.g., criminal investigations, terrorism, public health and safety, and emergency response) which often involves identifying criminal activity and other information that might be a precursor to a terrorist plot."[2] As each Fusion Center, managed by the state or local governments, grows and matures, homeland security leaders must coordinate collaboration among the fusion centers as well as use them to promote cross-culture interaction between law enforcement and other critical public health and safety communities to improve preparedness and protect individual rights. If ensuring private sector partnership with Emergency Operations Centers is essential to community response and recovery operations, consider information sharing and analysis with the private sector through the fusion centers to be an essential part of preventing future attacks. Collaboration across these cultures could create business efficiencies ensuring the longer term sustainability of the fusion center capability.

Opportunity #3: Integrate Journalists as "First Amendment Responders"

Effective emergency response always cites the use of the "traditional" and "new" media for providing the public with assurance and direction in a crisis. The provocative and emotional series of special programming around the 10 year anniversary of the Attacks of September 11th clearly show the

---

[1] For more information, see "Federal Efforts Are Helping to Alleviate Some Challenges Encountered by State and Local Fusion Centers," Government Accountability Office, October 2007, http://www.gao.gov/new.items/d0835 .pdf. See also "Federal Agencies Are Helping Fusion Centers Build and Sustain Capabilities and Protect Privacy, but Could Better Measure Results," September 2010, http://www.gao.gov/new.items/d10972.pdf.

[2] "The National Strategy for Information Sharing," October 2007, http://www.whitehouse.gov/nsc/infosharing/ index.html. Appendix 1.

vital role journalists can play in creating situational awareness during a crisis. More and more after-action reports in numerous exercises have stated how improved response plan implementation requires public communications plans and established, trusted, and working relationships with the media and better use of social media tools. Journalists can no longer play a reactive role in homeland security and need to be embraced as true partners in the homeland security enterprise in advance of the next crisis. Trying to control the media is no longer logistically viable because Web 2.0 technologies and mobile devices have allowed everyone to potentially be a citizen journalist. Enabling journalists to more knowledgeably perform their First Amendment responsibilities in crises will improve delivery of trusted, accurate, and timely information on what the public needs to know in order to protect their communities and families, as well as support government response operations. Perhaps even consider actual journalist play in emergency exercises instead of simulated media. More engagement with the press and smarter use of social media tools will only improve efforts to create the much discussed "culture of preparedness" in our communities that we need.

Opportunity #4: Invest in the Next Generation of Homeland Security Professionals

Ensuring the quality and effectiveness of the future homeland security workforce should be a national priority. Trained and knowledgeable experts are in high demand across the spectrum of critical homeland security capabilities in both the public and private sectors. Defining the capabilities and knowledge that future homeland security professionals should possess must be undertaken while the subject matter and department are still evolving.

Thankfully, some activities are under way. In May 2007, President Bush signed Executive Order 13434 for "National Security Professional Development" aiming "to promote the education, training, and experience of current and future professionals in national security positions in executive departments and agencies."[3] In December 2007, DHS unveiled an internal Homeland Security University System to help improve professional development within its own employee ranks, including a Homeland Security Academy built on a partnership with the Navy Postgraduate School Center for Homeland Defense and Security. There are also DHS Centers of Excellence and a "Scholarship for Service" Program that recruits students for vital cybersecurity jobs in Federal departments and agencies as repayment for the government's funding of their education. President Obama's National Security Strategy stresses the investment in education as a key driver of our national security policy.

Aligning these policy initiatives and envisioned outcomes with the academic community and existing scholarships and grants is under way but sustained support across government agencies will be needed. This will help create a stronger process for educating, recruiting, training, and retaining the qualified public service personnel necessary to implement homeland security programs in the long term. A clearer public service career path will help the "best and brightest" once again see opportunity in government service, improving the likelihood that not only a smaller government, but a more effective one is built. Internal coordination of these policy areas may also create opportunity to increase the role the U.S. Department of Education can play over the long term to ensure the preparedness and resiliency of our college and university campuses.

---

[3] For details of the Executive Order, see press release, May 2007, http://www.whitehouse.gov/news/releases/2007/05/20070517-6.html. For President Obama's National Security Strategy, May 2010, see http://www.whitehouse.gov.

(Continued)

ANOTHER VOICE: FOUR OPPORTUNITIES FOR FUTURE HOMELAND SECURITY LEADERS BY BRIDGER MCGAW (CONTINUED).

These four opportunities offer a place to focus attention where real progress can be achieved with long-lasting positive impact towards enhancing the resiliency of our nation.

Bridger McGaw is a graduate of Harvard College and the John F. Kennedy School of Government and was a homeland security policy and strategic communications consultant. He has held several positions as policy adviser, public affairs officer, and press secretary to senior leaders in the Department of Defense, White House, Capitol Hill, and state and local governments. McGaw served on the Century Foundation's 2006 Task Force on homeland security. The ideas and opinions of the writer are his own.

Conclusion

We believe that the FEMA experience from 1979 to the present may be a harbinger of the Department of Homeland Security's fate as it struggles in the coming decade to establish an integrated and effective national homeland security system. At a minimum, FEMA's experiences should serve as a cautionary tale for homeland security officials at the federal, state, and local levels of government.

The Hurricane Katrina experience should also serve as a warning to DHS that a coordinated federal response is critical during a major catastrophic event and that marginalizing the strong national emergency management system built on a partnership of federal, state, and local emergency operations in the 1990s was a terrible mistake.

Reestablishing FEMA as the leader of the nation's emergency management system, re-creating the FRP, supporting community-based homeland security efforts involving the general public, communicating timely and accurate information to the public, and establishing a strong and vital partnership with the business sector could ease DHS's growing pains and pave the way for the establishment of a comprehensive homeland security system in this country.

One final note on the FEMA experience: At the core of FEMA's success in the 1990s was its focus on the needs of its customers, the American people. FEMA policies and programs from that period were driven by the needs of disaster victims and by the needs of community residents who wanted to reduce the terrible impacts of future events. Since its inception in 2002, the DHS and its partners in the federal government have been focused almost exclusively on their own needs. Policies and programs have been designed and implemented that meet the needs of these governmental departments and agencies and that were not informed by the needs of the public, their supposed customers.

If the officials at DHS that work in homeland security at the state and local levels change one thing in the future, it is critical that they shift their focus from themselves to the public, and that they plan and implement policies and programs with the full involvement of the public and their partners. It worked very well for FEMA, so there is no reason why it should not do the same for DHS.

References

Criss, K., 2005. E-mail message to George Haddow, July 14.

Peckenpaugh, J., 2004. Regional Homeland Security Offices Will Be Small. GovExec.Com, March 24. http://www.govexec.com/story_page.cfm?articleid528072&printerfriendlyVers51&.

Index